RAVE

"Been thumbing through a new copy of the Adventure TravelGuide that is worth its weight in daydreams."

—*STANDARD*

"Now if a bored spouse or friend says 'Why don't we do something *different* this year?'—you can throw the book at them. It's the most complete guide to adventure trips we've ever seen."

—*TRAVEL HOLIDAY*

"The exhaustively researched Worldwide Adventure TravelGuide is a must for people who like adventure, the outdoors, or just plain good reading."

—*MASSASOIT REVIEW*

"Authoritative . . . The 1979 Worldwide Adventure TravelGuide covers much of the globe."

—*THE NEW YORK TIMES*

"If spring has roused your hibernating wanderlust, and dreams of travel persistently invade your thoughts, a glance through the Worldwide Adventure TravelGuide will put you well on your way to making some of those dreams reality."

—*KALAMAZOO GAZETTE*

"Here's a guide to some of the country's most enticing vacations . . . An exhaustive list of America's outdoor education groups."

—*CHICAGO TRIBUNE*

PRAISE FROM OUR READERS

"I expect my Adventure TravelGuide will be my best-read book for the coming years. You are offering a much-needed and tremendous service for us all!"

—*ALEX NESENJUK*
Plainsboro, New Jersey

"Your new publication is one of the finest sourcebooks on adventure travel available. The narrative style in which each trip is described should definitely prove to be an asset to all travel and trip operators fortunate enough to be included in your publication."

—*ROBERT W. DIETZ*
Grand Junction, Colorado

"The proliferation of exploratory expeditions and trips in all formats . . . has made this directory a necessity. It shows a high degree of proficiency."

—*IRVING W. ROBBINS, JR.*
Atherton, California

"I have just purchased your 1979 Worldwide Adventure TravelGuide. I am really impressed! You've put the most fantastic adventures in the world at my fingertips!"

—*SOPHIE GATOWSKI*
Calgary, Alberta

1980 WORLDWIDE

PUBLISHED BY THE

AMERICAN ADVENTURERS ASSOCIATION

To order additional copies of the 1980 Worldwide Adventure TravelGuide (or to place advance orders for the 1981 edition), contact:

AMERICAN ADVENTURERS ASSOCIATION
Suite 301, 444 NE Ravenna Blvd.
Seattle, WA 98115, USA

CONTENTS

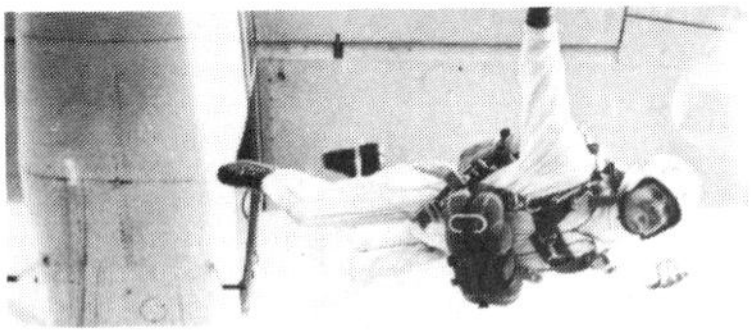

Note: The **(M)** at the end of many of the write-ups in this book indicates that those trip operators are members of the American Adventurers Association, as of July 1979. We encourage all trip operators, members and nonmembers alike, to send us their current brochures and to keep us up to date on new trip information.

1980 WORLDWIDE ADVENTURE TRAVELGUIDE

Bob Citron, *Publisher*
Barbara L. Sleeper, *Executive Editor*

Kristin Tregillus, *Managing Editor*
Kris Fulsaas, *Production Editor*
Constance Balint, *Consulting Editor*
Rick Hermann, *Production Assistant*
Nicholas H. Allison, *Writer*
Douglas Honig, *Copy Editor*
David Azose, Gordon Hardy, Dawn Heathers,
Lynn Knight, *Production Staff*
Carrie Seglin, *Photography Editor*
Carol Baker, *Photography Assistant*

Elizabeth Watson, *Art Director*
Margarite Hargrave, Jennifer Summers, *Graphic Artists*

Craig Sternagel, *Advertising Manager*
Deborah Mann, Steve Maris, Kim Salzwedel, *Advertising Staff*
Sandy Halladay, *Marketing Coordinator*

American Adventurers Association, Publishers of Adventure Travel Magazine

Bob Citron, *Founder and President*
Barbara L. Sleeper, *Vice President and Treasurer*
Ken Gouldthorpe, *Editor/Executive Publisher*
Greg Peters, *Business Manager*
Jay Stelzer, *Advertising Director*
Claudia Mirchel, *Executive Assistant*
Howard Baldwin, *Membership Services Coordinator*
Donn Cave, Eric Lindh, *Mailing*
Alison Wells, *Circulation Director*
Lyn Klein, *Assistant Circulation Director*
Maggie Riester, *Business Office*

Cover: Rafters power through the Five Falls section of the Chattooga River on the border between South Carolina and Georgia. Photograph by Rob Lesser.

The American Adventurers Association has compiled the information contained in this guidebook for its members. While extreme care has been taken in compiling and verifying the information, the association cannot be held responsible for errors or changes in trip description, itineraries, schedules, costs, etc.

International Standard Book Number 394-738-72-1
International Standard Serial Number 0148-2300
Library of Congress Number LC-78-24728

Distributed in the United States by Random House, Inc. and in Canada by Random House of Canada, Ltd. Printed in the USA. First Printing Jan. 1980: 25,000 copies.

Mt. Adams Wilderness Institute

About the American Adventurers Association

The American Adventurers Association was founded in 1976 to promote the participation of men and women in adventurous activities worldwide. More than 2,000 organizations around the world sponsor over 6,000 different adventure trips open to public participation. The adventure travel industry is booming—more than two million people go river rafting, ballooning, backpacking, scuba diving, bicycle touring and trekking each year. We knew there was a lack of readily available information on who was doing what, where, when and how. We also realized that there was no focal point, no international repository, no data center, where reliable information on adventure travel could be obtained.

In the past four years the association has become *the* worldwide clearinghouse for information on adventure trip opportunities open to the public. It has developed an international constituency of hundreds of organizations, businesses and institutions that organize adventure trips, training programs and seminars. The association has also established an adventure trip evaluation program to evaluate individual trips with regard to their cost, environmental impact and public appeal; trip operators are evaluated with regard to their expertise, reliability and responsibility shown to the participants and to the environment (for more information on our Trip Evaluation Service, see page 525).

Our most exciting achievements are our publications. *Adventure Travel Newsletter* is the most definitive source of adventure travel information. Award-winning *Adventure Travel* magazine has been described as "the most beautiful travel magazine ever published." And our annual *Worldwide Adventure TravelGuide* is a comprehensive and authoritative reference on adventure trip information.

The book that you are holding in your hands represents a full year of exhaustive work by a very dedicated team of people. We hope you enjoy using it, not only to titillate your fancies for adventure, but to actually plan, schedule and participate in *your own adventure.* This book is designed to help you make your travel dreams come true!

Bob Citron
Founder and President
American Adventurers Association
January 1980

How to Use the TravelGuide

The *TravelGuide* is divided into four major sections—Land, Air, Water and Underwater. Each section is further divided into activities offered within that medium. For instance, under Air Adventures you will find Ballooning, Soaring, Flying, Hang Gliding, Parasailing and Parachuting.

In turn, each activity is divided into major geographic regions. All seven continents are used for these divisions, as well as marine areas such as the Caribbean, Pacific, Atlantic and Indian oceans, and the cultural region of the Middle East. These areas are then further broken down into individual countries. In the case of North America, Mexico, Canada and the United States are treated as major geographic regions, which are subdivided into states or provinces.

At the end of most activities with the *TravelGuide* is a Resource addendum which names clubs, associations, rental agencies and consultants involved in each activity, so you can write to them for further information. There are also two useful indexes to the *TravelGuide.* One lists the type of trip by geographical area (e.g., Nepal, river rafting) and the other lists the trips by the operators who run them. An appendix lists the organizational members of the American Adventurers Association as of July 1979.

In most cases, the trips described represent just a partial listing of the trips offered by each operator. For additional information on any particular trip, or for a complete list of current trips, write to them directly. If you are a member of the American Adventurers Association, we can also provide you with more details. We hope this *TravelGuide* assists you in participating in some of the world's most exciting adventures. □

Land Adventures

MOUNTAINEERING

From Alexander the Great's conquest of a mountain fortress in Persia in the first century B.C. to Hillary's ascent of Mt. Everest with Tenzing Norgay in 1953, mountains have symbolized man's aspirations and ambitions. They have been barriers to military expansion, exploration, communication and trade, but they have also been objects of veneration as citadels of the gods. Every summer thousands of Japanese make a pilgrimage to climb Fujiyama, which they hold sacred.

Yet mountaineering doesn't attract the millions of people that other outdoor sports do. Climbers must have great physical endurance, good judgment and an ability to overcome such psychological barriers as vertigo and fear of injury. Mountaineering is intense, testing one's courage, strength and stamina in high-risk situations. It is as much a group activity as it is a solo effort. Each member is supported by the team; the team's success depends on the individual.

There are many skills involved in mountaineering: balance and coordination, belaying, rappelling, an ability to find proper hand- and footholds and specialized techniques on rock, snow and ice. You can learn these skills in a variety of places around the globe from Hong Kong and New Zealand to the Swiss Alps and the Shawungunks in Virginia. Courses and climbs are offered in just about every mountain range of the world, for all levels of interest and skill, and for all ages. Once you have mastered the basic skills and gained some climbing experience, you can join commercial trips which will take you to the rock faces and ridges of the Andes, Rockies, Himalayas or the Caucasus.

Mountaineering is a challenging sport and can be dangerous. Bad weather, falling rocks, avalanches, ice falls, crevasses and snow cornices have threatened the lives of even the most experienced climbers. Yet the physical and spiritual satisfaction a climber gains through personal effort and contact with nature's beautiful and unpredictable elements makes the risks worthwhile. The joys and challenges of mountaineering await you wherever there is a rock face, ice slope or pinnacle to climb. □

Climbers from the North Cascades Alpine School hike a switchback trail down Table Mountain, across the valley from 10,778-foot Mt. Baker. (North Cascades Alpine School)

MOUNTAINEERING

AFRICA

Kenya

Mt. Kenya Ascent: Mountaineers proficient in roped technical climbing are offered guide service to the summit of 17,058-foot Mt. Kenya. Although the exact schedule of each ascent is worked out separately, at least 6 days are recommended for the trip to allow time for acclimatization. The climb departs from Nairobi. Also offered in the area are instruction in rock climbing at Lukenya, a crag located 30 miles east of Nairobi, and advanced instruction in mountaineering. **Cost:** $371 to $583 for Mt. Kenya climb, depending on size of party, includes transportation from Nairobi, food, some equipment, guide; other rates on request. **When:** Year-round. **Contact:** Tropical Ice (Mountain Guides), P.O. Box 57341, Nairobi, Kenya; phone 743463.

Tanzania

Kilimanjaro Climb: After arriving in Marangu a group begins a 5-day trek to the summit. On the first day of the 75-mile trip, participants hike through rain forest to the Mandara hut, which lies close to the Maundo Crater at 9,000 feet. From here, the 3-day ascent of Mt. Kilimanjaro continues on gentle-slope paths in open moorland to the Horombo hut at 12,000 feet. Participants pass through the entire spectrum of climatic zones from tropical to arctic en route to Kibo Hut. On the third day the group starts for the summit on steep, fairly heavy screes and rock crops up to Gillman's Point on the crater rim. Then it's 45 minutes along the rim up to Uhuru Peak, the highest point on the mountain. The group traverses part of the inner crater, where sulphurous gases escape fumaroles around the ash pit cone. A descent is then made to Marangu where trip members enjoy a hearty meal. **Cost:** $180 includes meals, guides; equipment rentals available. **When:** On request. **Contact:** Tanzania Tourist Corp., P.O. Box 2485, Dar Es Salaam, Tanzania.

ASIA

Hong Kong

Hong Kong Climbing: A non-profit mountaineering association offers a 30-day course in mountaincraft training for adults. Instruction on selection, care and improvisation of equipment, plus an introduction to environmental education are also part of the course. Instruction, which includes 10 lecture sessions, takes place outside Hong Kong on weekends. **Cost:** $450 includes roundtrip transportation from Hong Kong, equipment. **When:** Year-round except August. **Contact:** Hong Kong Mountaineering Association, P.O. Box 20519, Hennessy Rd. P.O., Hong Kong.

Nepal

Rowaling and Teshi Lapcha: Participants climb steep snow slopes to reach a 19,100-foot pass on a strenuous mountaineering trek lasting 26 days. The trip begins with a bus ride from Kathmandu to Bara Besi. From here the group hikes along fertile hillsides to the Rowaling River and continues through dense forests via a trail that passes through a waterfall. After crossing the river, mountaineers ascend to the village of Bedding at the tree line and climb along the edge of an ice fall and up snow slopes to reach Teshi Lapcha pass; the night is spent camped by a mountain wall near the summit. The descent leads through the Khumbu region to Namche Bazar. A side trip is made to the Thyangboche Monastery before the group flies back to Kathmandu. Participants should be in excellent condition and have previous experience using an ice ax and crampons. **Cost:** $1,600 from Kathmandu includes food, equipment, porters, guides. **When:** November. **Contact:** Fantasy Ridge, P.O. Box 2106, Estes Park, CO 80517, USA; phone (303)586-5391.

Soviet Union

Pamir and Caucasus Climbing: A 31-day program in the Soviet Union provides the opportunity to hike or climb in either the Pamir or Caucasus mountains. The trips operate out of various base camps. In the Pamirs climbers can attempt 23,400-foot Lenin, 24,583-foot Communism and others on the ridges of Peter the Great and Academy of Sciences. In the Caucasus, closer to Europe, ascents can be made on a number of peaks over 16,000 feet, and non-climbers can spend 7 to 10 days walking the area's ridges. Mountaineering experience and good physical condition are necessary. Special instruction in high-altitude climbing is available. **Cost:** $880 to $1,540, depending on schedule and location, includes transportation from Moscow, food, accommodations, guides. **When:** July. **Contact:** REI Adventure Travel, Inc., 1525 11th Ave., Seattle, WA 98122, USA; phone (206)322-7800. *(M)*

ATLANTIC

Iceland

Climbing the Land of Ice: Instruction in basic glacier mountaineering

A 26-day mountaineering journey through New Zealand is offered by North Cascades Alpine School, with excursions to the Hooker Valley and cloud-capped Mt. Cook for experienced climbers. (North Cascades Alpine School)

highlights a 3-week trip through Iceland, known as the "land of fire and ice." The party, which is composed of novice as well as experienced climbers, meets in Reykjavik and sets out backpacking into the countryside, investigating many unusual geological formations and meeting local residents. On the Snaefellsjokull participants learn to use ice axes, crampons and ropes as they travel across the massive glacier's fields of ice. Many inland streams are also explored. Group members spend most nights camping, with occasional stays in hotels. **Cost:** $880 includes transportation, 2 meals a day, accommodations, group equipment, instruction, guide. **When:** June. **Contact:** Adventure Unique Inc., 19 Washington St., Santa Clara, CA 95050, USA; phone (408)446-2347. ***(M)***

AUSTRALASIA

New Zealand

Mountain Climbing in the Central Alps: Guides take groups of up to 4 persons across the 7,000-foot Copland Pass for 1½ days starting from Mt. Cook and traveling through the Copland Valley, or for 3½ days from Mt. Cook to Fox Glacier. Trip members may use aircraft for their return or retain the guide for return via Graham Saddle. A separate 8-day Graham Saddle alpine crossing is also offered. During 2 or 3 days climbers learn basic snow and icecraft techniques, and ascend Tasman, Rudolf and Franz Josef glaciers. **Cost:** $30 for 1½ days, $70 for 3½ days, $140 for 8 days. **When:** November to March. **Contact:** Alpine Guides (Mt. Cook) Ltd., Mt. Cook National Park, P.O. Box 20,

Mt. Cook, New Zealand; phone Mt. Cook 834.

Wide-Range Wanderings: Travelers participate in a wide variety of outdoor activities on a 26-day journey that explores several areas of New Zealand. Group members backpack on the Routeburn Track, climb in the Southern Alps, hike through coastal forests and on glaciers and snorkel in the South Pacific. Visits are made to investigate the spherical boulders at Moeraki, the Shag Point penguins, the volcanoes of Tongariro National Park, geothermal activity at Rotorua and a cave with a roof covered by glowworms. The journey begins in Christchurch and ends at Auckland. Accommodations are in hotels, huts and in tent camps. **Cost:** $1,678 includes roundtrip airfare from Los Angeles, food, accommodations, activities, equipment, guide. **When:** February. **Contact:** North Cascades Alpine School, 1212 24th G, Bellingham, WA 98225, USA; phone (206)671-1505. ***(M)***

CANADA

Ranging the Northern Rockies: Mountaineers take about 37 days to backpack and climb in the Rockies of Wyoming, Montana and Canada. Beginning in Grand Teton National Park, participants hike to several mountain lakes as they become acquainted with high altitudes. Group members then hike through the Gallatin Range in Montana, a region where the elevation averages over 8,000 feet. The hike ends in the Spanish Peaks Primitive Area, a fairly remote part of the Montana Rockies. The next stop is Banff National Park in Alberta where a summit climb is made close to the Valley of the Seven Peaks. Mt. Robson is the fourth climbing site visited; it is the tallest mountain in the Canadian Rockies, and its glaciers feed hundreds of lakes and streams. The final trek is made through the Bugaboos of British Columbia; much technical rock and ice climbing may be expected as the group travels through the region. **Cost:** $1,395 includes roundtrip land transportation from Poughkeepsie, guide/instructor, food, cooking equipment, tents, technical equipment. **When:** July to August. **Contact:** Wilderness Bound, Ltd., RD 1, Box 365, Highland, NY 12528, USA; phone (914)691-2377.

Alberta

Leadership Training in the Columbia Icefields: A 1-week training trip enables the intermediate climber to improve on a variety of mountaineering skills. The first few days are spent at the clubhouse in Canmore, and all rock climbing takes place from this location. The remaining days are based at Hilda Creek Youth Hostel close to the Columbia

Icefield and concentrate on snow and ice climbing techniques. Participants are expected to have prior knowledge of rock, snow and ice climbing. A ratio of 1 guide for each 10 participants allows for individualized instruction. All chores are shared. **Cost:** $125. **When:** July. **Contact:** The Alpine Club of Canada, P.O. Box 1026, Banff, AB Canada T0L 0C0; phone (403)762-4481.

Schools on Rock and Ice: In the Canadian Rockies participants receive instruction in rock climbing techniques ranging in difficulty from getting into a climbing harness to accomplishing difficult moves in chimneys and jam cracks. The courses last 1 or 2 days, with the 1-day courses divided into 3 levels depending on the individual student's experience and ability. During 2-day rock climbing instruction in the Banff area, students go through a basic beginner's course on the first day, then climb one of the surrounding peaks, such as Mt. Edith. For the 2-day snow and ice schools, group members should have some prior climbing experience. **Cost:** $18 to $35 for 1 day, $45 to $75 for 2 days includes instruction. **When:** June to September. **Contact:** Banff Alpine Guides, P.O. Box 1025, Banff, AB Canada T0L 0C0; phone (403)762-4277.

Alpine Junior Mountain Camps: A 10-day introduction to the Canadian Rocky Mountains is offered for children ages 8 to 12. Set in the valley of an extensive glacier system 30 miles south of Banff, the camp is surrounded by peaks, ponds and lakes. The campers undertake easy climbs and alpine hikes, explore a glacier, attend a basic rock climbing school and spend a few days camping in the wild. Environmental awareness is stressed by discussing basic geology and alpine flora and fauna in the area. Group sizes are from 6 to 9 persons so that leaders can provide individualized attention. Subgroups composed of campers of similar ability may be formed for specific activities. Participants are encouraged to bring musical instruments to enjoy around the evening campfires. **Cost:** $250 includes meals, instruction, lodging. **When:** July. **Contact:** High Horizons, P.O. Box 1166, Banff, AB Canada T0L 0C0; phone (403)762-2868.

Canadian Rockies Mountain Programs: Three different week-long programs for adults cover backpacking, beginning mountaineering and intermediate/advanced mountaineering in the mountains outside of Banff. Starting at Sunshine Village, an alpine backpacking journey proceeds to Mt. Assiniboine, Marvel and Spray Lakes, continues up the Spray River, and crosses over a high meadow to reach Burstall Lakes. From a base camp in the Burstall Lakes area, beginning mountaineering is taught according to individual ability. Included is instruction in compass orientation, pace setting, trip planning, botany and basic survival knowledge. In addition to rock and ice climbing instruction, the week includes climbs of some of the local peaks. The intermediate/advanced group climbs several of the classic routes on such peaks as Eisenhower, Louis Mountain, Edith, Rundle and

Tower of Babel. There is a maximum of 3 participants with each guide on these outings. **Cost:** $250 to $300 includes instruction, guides, meals (food extra in advanced/intermediate climbing). **When:** July, August. **Contact:** High Horizons, P.O. Box 1166, Banff, AB Canada T0L 0C0; phone (403)762-2868.

British Columbia

Canadian Climbing Camp: A graduated series of mountaineering schools offers instruction in snow, ice and rock climbing in British Columbia. Base camps, located in the mountains near an alpine lake, are established for each level of ability. From the base, over a dozen peaks can be reached on routes of varying difficulty. Longer routes are offered for intermediate climbers, and more severe routes are planned for advanced climbers. Groups are kept small so students receive individual attention. Climbs are selected to be challenging, yet within the ability of the participants. Special sessions can be arranged, such as advanced glacier travel, crevasse rescue and high-angle ice courses. An exploratory climbing expedition beginning with a rugged 10- to 15-mile hike with and without trails, may involve load relaying. The group may attempt first ascents of peaks over 10,000 feet. **Cost:** $185 to $270 for 8-day climbing camps, $25 to $50 a day for special sessions includes guides and instruction. **When:** May to October. **Contact:** Northern

Under the watchful eye of experienced mountaineers from Northern Lights Alpine Recreation, climbers attempt peaks and glaciers in the Bugaboos of British Columbia. (Arnor Larson/Northern Lights Alpine Recreation)

Lights Alpine Recreation, Box 399, Invermere, BC Canada V0A 1K0; phone (604)342-6042.

Winter Climbing on Waddington: Mt. Waddington, the highest peak in the Coast Mountains of British Columbia at 13,147 feet, was once called Mystery Mountain for its remoteness. A 29-day introduction to mountaineering offers participants a chance to camp on Mt. Waddington's Tiedemann Glacier and possibly make a summit attempt. The party gathers at a lodge in Strathcona Provincial Park, on the northern part of Vancouver Island, for a week of preparation and training before being airlifted onto the glacier to establish base camp. At this point the expedition leaders make a decision whether or not to attempt the summit based on the weather. If not, participants spend time rock climbing on Mt. Tiedemann and exploring many smaller peaks and glaciers nearby. After 3 weeks on the mountain the party returns to Strathcona Park by air. **Cost:** $800 includes air transportation to and from the mountain, food, most equipment, instruction, guide. **When:** September. **Contact:** Strathcona Park Lodge, Outdoor Education Society, Box 2160, Campbell River, BC Canada V9W 5C9; phone Campbell River radiophone operator.

EUROPE

England

Climbing Crags and Walking Fells: Six participants join 2 or 3 guides on a 35-day trip climbing and hiking through England, Scotland and Wales. The group flies from New York to London to begin sightseeing and rock climbing. Climbing sites include Almscliffe, a gritstone crag in Yorkshire, the Isle of Skye in the Inner Hebrides, the Carn Dearg Buttress at Ben Nevis and Tremadoc. At Wasdale Head the group makes a technical rock climb up Napes Needle, and climbers who are able climb the Centurian route on the Carn Dearg Buttress, one of Britain's most challenging big wall climbs. Also on the itinerary are Stonehenge, Liverpool,

Edinburgh and London. Some backpacking and climbing experience is preferred but not required for making the trip; the age for participants is 15 to 21. **Cost:** $1,830 includes airfare from New York. **When:** July. **Contact:** North Country Mountaineering, Inc., P.O. Box 951, Hanover, NH 03755, USA; phone (603)643-3299. ***(M)***

Sea Cliff Climbing: Groups of 6 to 10 mountaineers receive 14 days of climbing instruction on the sea cliffs of southwest Britain and Wales. After meeting in London, participants drive to West Penwith in Cornwall from where they receive training at Chairladder, Devon, Snowdonia and Anglesey. Experienced instructors accompany groups, with a ratio of 1 instructor for every 2 students. Accommodations include inns and huts. **Cost:** $1,080 includes accommodations, some meals. **When:** April. **Contact:** Palisade School of Mountaineering, P.O. Box 694, Bishop, CA 93514, USA; phone (714)935-4330. ***(M)***

France

Alps Adventure: Two famous climbing regions in the French and Swiss Alps are visited on a 35-day trip which includes a training period in Britain. High school-age participants meet in London and drive to the Lake District and Snowdonia for intensive training and practice in climbing techniques. Proceeding to Chamonix, the group has access to Mont Blanc and all the Chamonix Aiguilles as well as the chance to meet other mountaineers. The next and final base is Zermatt; here climbers may attempt the Monte Rosa, Weisshorn, Rimpfischhorn and Dom, and at the trip's climax, the Matterhorn. Some prior hiking and rock climbing experience is desirable but not necessary for this strenuous trip. **Cost:** $1,375 from London includes transportation, equipment, food, instruction. **When:** July. **Contact:** Crossroads International, Hillsboro, NH 03244, USA; phone (603)478-5251. ***(M)***

Scotland

Scotch on the Rocks: Advanced rock and ice climbers can experience some of Scotland's most challenging and scenic alpine routes on a winter trip. Short practice climbs begin the journey, allowing participants to assess their skills and set goals for the trip. The several classic routes are climbed on Ben

Nevis, including Point-5, Zero and Minus One gullies. For the trip's conclusion, the party travels to the Cairngorms to test their skill on the ice routes there. Participants have ample opportunities to meet with local Scots and to experience the region's hospitality. Travel arrangements and details such as trip length and itinerary are available on request. Food, lodging and transportation are provided in the trip cost. **Cost:** On request. **When:** Winter; by arrangement. **Contact:** Alpine Guides, Ltd. School of Climbing, 2206 N. Alder, Tacoma, WA 98406, USA.

Switzerland

Alpine Climbing School: Courses for beginning, intermediate and advanced climbers are offered in the Alps. Instruction in rock and ice climbing is given by a staff of climbers experienced in both Alpine and Himalayan mountain environments. Over 100 climbing routes in the area near Leysin offer ample opportunity for instruction at all levels of climbing capability. The standard introductory class lasts 6 days, as does the intermediate course, which includes climbs in the Mont Blanc area or the Swiss Valaisian Alps. Advanced courses are by arrangement. Lodging is at a mountain club for international travelers, with bunk accommodations and communal dining. Instruction is in English. **Cost:** $440 for introductory, $472 for intermediate course. **When:** June to September. **Contact:** International School of Mountaineering, Club Vagabond, 1854 Leysin, Switzerland; phone (025)34-13-21; or 308 E. 18th St. New York, NY 10003, USA; phone (212)982-2198. ***(M)***

The Classics: A 2-week trip in Europe provides mountaineers the chance to climb in the 3 classic regions of the Alps: Chamonix, nestled at the foot of Mont Blanc; Grindelwald, near the Eiger, Monch and Jungfrau; and Zermatt, by the towering Matterhorn. The trip's itinerary is flexible to accommodate weather conditions and individual preferences, but at least one ascent of a big peak is guaranteed in each area. Those with no previous climbing experience should take a basic climbing course before embarking on the trip. The tour starts in Zurich. **Cost:** $975. **When:** August. **Contact:** Liberty Bell Alpine Tours, Mazama, WA

The Matterhorn is one of the classic peaks in the Alps that may be climbed during a 2-week Liberty Bell Alpine Tours trip. (Keith Gunnar)

98833, USA; phone (509)996-2250. ***(M)***

Wales

Welsh Climbing: An outdoor activities center in the north of Wales provides instruction in rock climbing to students at various skill levels. Basic classes, lasting 1 or 2 weeks, and intermediate classes, lasting a week, provide flexibly paced instruction at a ratio of 1 instructor to 2 students. The basic course is designed for those with little or no climbing experience; the intermediate course teaches more advanced skills including double rope, multiple rappels and self-rescue. The minimum age for the basic course is 17, but a special course is offered for 15- and 16-year-olds. Evening lectures supplement the day's climbing in all courses. **Cost:** $132 for 1-week basic or intermediate, $118 for young people's basic, $240 for 2-week basic includes food, accommodations, equipment, instruction. **When:** March to October. **Contact:** Plas Y Brenin, Capel Curig, Betws y Coed, Great Britain; phone (06904)280.

MEXICO

Puebla

Mountain Ascents: Seven- and 14-day trips are available for beginning and intermediate climbers who wish to climb 3 Mexican peaks—Orizaba, Ixtaccihuatl and Popocatepetl. The program includes technical instruction in snow and ice climbing. The peaks are ascended by moderate routes, with most encampments in huts. Before each climb participants stay in towns at 7,000 and 8,000 feet for acclimatization where they may visit the ruins of Aztec, Olmec and Toltec civilizations. For advanced climbers, more demanding routes are available on Orizaba and Ixtaccihuatl after conditioning sessions on Popocatepetl. Each climbing group has 6 to 10 members and 2 instructors. **Cost:** $290 per week includes transportation within Mexico, accommodations, food, equipment, instructor-guides. **When:** November to March. **Contact:** North Cascades Alpine School, 1212 24th G, Bellingham, WA 98225, USA; phone (206)671-1505. ***(M)***

Climbing in the Land of the Aztecs: Reaching the summits of 2 of the highest peaks in North America is the goal of a group of 13 guided by 2 experienced mountaineers. The 8-day trip begins with sightseeing in and around Mexico City, including visits to the Aztec pyramids of Teotihuacan. Then the expedition proceeds to Tlamacas Lodge at the base of 17,887-foot Popocatepetl. Climbers begin the ascent early the next morning so that the climb can be done in 1 day without having to carry heavy gear. Participants need to know such climbing techniques as self-arrest, cramponing and rope handling. Returning to Mexico City, participants board jeeps for a short drive on the high, semi-arid tableland approach to 18,800-foot Orizaba. The Piedra Grande Hut houses climbers before and after the climb to its summit. **Cost:** $460 from Mexico City includes meals, equipment, guides, accommodations, transportation. **When:** November, January. **Contact:** REI Adventure Travel, 1525 11th Ave., Seattle, WA 98122, USA; phone (206)322-7800. ***(M)***

Two Peaks: A group of up to 15 climbers assembles in Mexico City to make summit assaults on 2 peaks: Popocatepetl and Pico de Orizaba. Popocatepetl, at 17,887 feet, is the second-highest mountain in Mexico and is located only a day's drive from Mexico City. Following the ascent the party returns to Mexico City to regroup for the Pico de Orizaba climb. At 18,800 feet the peak is the third-highest in the western hemisphere and the climbing is more challenging than on Popocatepetl. Costs for all transportation within Mexico and food and lodging in Mexico City are pooled; climbers are responsible for their own meals while on the climbs. **Cost:** On request. **When:** Winter. **Contact:** Rainier Mountaineering, 201 St. Helens, Tacoma, WA 98402, USA; phone (206)627-6242, summer 569-2227.

Volcanic Ascents: Climbers ascend the adjacent volcanoes of Popocatepetl and Ixtaccihuatl on an 8-day trip. The trip begins and ends in Mexico City, with the new Popo Hut serving as base camp for the ascents. Both mountains may be climbed with or without a high camp, depending on weather conditions and the participants' strengths and preferences. Ample time is allowed for rest and acclimatization during the ascents. While the climbs involve technical mountaineering skills and require excellent physical condition, participants need not be experienced climbers. **Cost:** $450 includes transportation in Mexico, accommodations, most food, tents, technical gear. **When:** November, December. **Contact:** The Wilderness Institute, 333 Fairfax, Denver, CO 80220, USA; phone (303)393-0400.

MIDDLE EAST

Oman

Off to Oman: The unusual mountain scenery of Oman, little explored by Western travelers, is the setting for a 21-day hiking and mountaineering trip. Until 1975 the southern Jabal Akhdar region was the scene of political insurgency, and thus out of reach to most travelers. The expedition travels from the capital city of Muscat by dhow to Sur, in the south, before embarking by jeep across the Wahibah sands to the south end of the Jabal. The party then walks into the Jabal for 8 days climaxed by an ascent of the highest peak, 9,863-foot Jabal Sham. All participants in the small group are expected to contribute to the cooking, setting up and carrying chores. **Cost:** $2,280 includes roundtrip transportation from London, food, equipment, guides. **When:** November. **Contact:** High Adventure, Alan Seeger Ltd., 1 Salterns Wy., Lilliput, Poole, Dorset BH12 8JR, Great Britain; phone 0202 708471. *(M)*

SOUTH AMERICA

Bolivia

En la Cordillera: A small group of fairly experienced climbers makes 3 ascents in the Cordillera Real on a 22-day trip. Since the peaks are all within a day's travel from La Paz, layover days are scheduled there between the climbs, with some time allowed for exploring the city's Spanish history. In the mountains, enjoyment and nontechnical climbing are emphasized; but since some of the area's peaks rise over 21,000 feet, participants need to have some experience in glacier travel and in climbing with ax, rope and screws. They also need to be Sierra Club members. **Cost:** On request.

When: July. **Contact:** Sierra Club Outing Dept., Trip #600, 530 Bush St., San Francisco, CA 94108, USA; phone (415)981-8634. ***(M)***

Peru

Cordillera Blanca Expeditions: Participants travel through the Cordillera Blanca on 2 trips lasting 9 and 15 days. Members of one expedition meet at Huaraz and begin hiking at Cachipampa, following a trail that leads up the Quebrada Santa Cruz. After crossing Union Pass into the forests of Huaripampa, hikers descend the Quebrada Llanganuco. Along the hike the group passes near 5 mountains all over 19,500 feet high. The second trip follows the same route in reverse, but includes options for climbing Nevado Pisco (18,764 feet) and Parish (17,963 feet). Guided hikes are scheduled for non-climbers while veteran mountaineers with some glacier climbing experience may attempt the higher peaks. **Cost:** $495 for first trip, $790 for second trip includes food, guide, accommodations. **When:** May to September. **Contact:** Andean Outfitters, P.O. Box 7007, Angels Camp, CA 95222, USA; phone (209)736-4830. ***(M)***

Southern Heights: Dramatic contrasts in both culture and landscape are encountered on a 23-day trip in Peru and Bolivia offering special options for non-climbers and intermediate and expert climbers. After touring Lima and Cuzco, trip members visit ancient ruins, hike the Inca Trail to Machu Picchu, boat on Lake Titicaca, explore the altiplano of Bolivia, trek through the Cordillera Real, and either ascend several spectacular peaks or hike through the Napo jungle in the Amazon

Viewed on the approach route to base camp, 19,968-foot Potosi is one of the major goals in the North Cascades Alpine School's 23-day expedition to Peru and Bolivia. (North Cascades Alpine School)

Basin. Cultures encountered vary from modern and urban to primitive Indian, and environments vary from dense, tropical forests and windswept altiplano to icy alpine regions. Some nights are spent camping and some in hotels. Good physical condition is a prerequisite for all participants, climbers and non-climbers alike. **Cost:** $1,294 includes roundtrip airfare from Miami or Los Angeles, transportation, food, accommodations, fees, equipment, guides. **When:** May, June. **Contact:** North Cascades Alpine School, 1212 24th G, Bellingham, WA 98225, USA; phone (206)671-1505. *(M)*

High and Low in Peru: A 17-day trip to Peru offers 2 alternatives for the first 10 days, either climbing or river rafting, and then finishes with a week of cultural investigation around Lima. Rafters run the Huallaga, offering alternating calm and whitewater through the jungles of central Peru. Climbers first visit Lake Titicaca or another highland location for acclimatization and then travel to the volcanic peaks of Chichani and Misti, both around 19,000 feet; they receive climbing instruction and attempt an ascent of one or both of the peaks. In the final week, participants visit archaeological sites, small villages, beaches and various attractions in Lima. Previous climbing or rafting experience is not necessary, but good physical condition is. **Cost:** $1,495 includes roundtrip airfare from Miami, food, accommodations, transportation, instruction. **When:** December to February, April, September. **Contact:** Outdoor Leadership Training Seminars, 2220 Birch St., Denver, CO 80207, USA; phone (303)333-7831. *(M)*

Andean Peaks and Pre-history: Several objectives are set for a 19-day trip into the Andes which begins with a flight from Miami to Lima. Although the trip focuses on a climb via non-technical routes up Chachani and Misti, participants also spend time visiting selected archaeological sites and gaining an understanding of Peruvian culture by meeting the country's inhabitants. From Lima, the group flies to Ayacucho in the central highlands for exploration of the Indian market and also to begin acclimatization. Cuzco is visited, and an optional side trip to Machu Picchu is offered. Participants fly to Arequipa where the approach to the mountains is planned and organized; base camp is established below Nevado Chachani, a 19,921-foot peak. While established at the camp, participants take part in climbing workshops and practice climbing skills and rope handling on the lower slopes. The attempts on Chachani and Misti are optional; those choosing not to climb are offered other activities such as lower-elevation trekking, photography and exploration. Return is made to Arequipa for rest and touring, then group members fly back to Lima where 3 days are spent before the return flight to Miami. **Cost:** $1,697 includes transportation from Miami, hotel and tent lodging, group equipment, meals, guides. **When:** September, February. **Contact:** Travel Exploration, P.O. Box 17641, Denver, CO 80217, USA. ***(M)***

UNITED STATES

Western Mountaineering: A 35-day course includes hiking and climbing all across North America for youths 14½ to 21. En route to the west coast, the group stops at Clifton Gorge, Ohio and the Black Hills of South Dakota for rock climbing instruction. Instruction continues in the Olympics at a base camp at Mt. Lacrosse. Courses include snow climbing, glacial travel and glacial ascents, glissading, crevasse and snowbridge crossing, crampon use and ice ax self-arrest. After training in the Olympics, the group tackles Mt. Rainier, the second-highest glaciated massif in the continental United States. Descending from the mountain environment, the group enters British Columbia to hike the entire West Coast Trail, which offers spectacular mountain and ocean scenery. Previous backpacking and mountaineering experience is recommended. Four guides accompany the group of 10. **Cost:** $1,395. **When:** July, August. **Contact:** North Country Mountaineering, Inc., Box 951, Hanover, NH 03755, USA; phone (603)643-3299. ***(M)***

Alaska

Ice Cap Mountaineering: Outfitting and transportation are available to river rafters and mountaineers within the Stikine River area of Alaska, near Kate's Needle. The Stikine Ice Cap region contains many remote peaks, a number of which are as yet unclimbed. Access to and from the area is by aircraft or, when available, river boat. Outfitting is also offered for self-guided river trips down the Stikine in 12-foot canoes or inflatable rafts. **Cost:** $200 a person roundtrip from Wrangell by air, about $140 by river boat; $475 for river trip. **When:** By arrangement. **Contact:** Alaska Wilderness Expeditions, Inc., P.O. Box 7814, Ketchikan, AK 99901, USA.

To the Top of McKinley: Expedition members spend at least 30 days making their way to the summit of Mt. McKinley on a route known as "The Long Walk." After a train ride from Talkeetna to McKinley Park, climbers begin the journey going over the Dutch Hills to Kahiltna Glacier and passing the jagged peaks of "Little Switzerland" and Kahiltna Pass. The route continues on to Windy Corner, the West Buttress and Denali Pass be-

Owning a Rollei says something about you.

You leave the beaten path to others while you go to great lengths to get the photographs you want. Rollei owners are like that—active people who make photography an important part of their lifestyle. Some have owned other SLRs, some are new to photography, but all are serious about taking good pictures.

Good pictures—even great pictures—come easy with the Rolleiflex SL35E. Compact and easy to handle, the SL35E lets you make one simple lens setting, focus on your subject and shoot.

You'll get good results the first time you use your SL35E in the automatic mode. Then, as you become more experienced, you can use this Rollei manually for full control of lighting and for special effects such as multiple exposure.

The Rolleiflex SL35E comes with a superb 50mm f/1.8 Zeiss-designed Planar lens.* For added versatility, you can choose from an assortment of Rollei interchangeable lenses and other useful accessories.

Outstanding German design, the Rollei tradition of quality and a reasonable price make the SL35E one of today's great camera values.

See it at your photo dealer's soon, or write for a free brochure to: Rollei of America, P.O. Box 1010, Littleton, Colorado 80160. In Canada, Rollei Canada Ltd., Downsview, Ontario.

* Made by Rollei under license from Carl Zeiss, Oberkochen, West Germany.

Rollei

High camp on a 30-day Hondo Rast expedition in the Chugach Mountains of Alaska consists of a line of dome tents dug into an exposed snow ridge. (Hondo Rast & Co.)

fore winding its way to the south peak of Mt. McKinley. The group descends by Denali's north side through Muldrow Glacier and McGonagall Pass, and fords McKinley River. The trip ends with a train journey back to Talkeetna. Much of the trip is on snow and ice. Participants should be proficient in the use of ice ax and crampons, and should be in excellent physical and mental condition. A physician's certificate is required. The goal of the climb is to reach the summit, and participants should be ready for a concentrated effort with a positive attitude. **Cost:** $1,680 includes roundtrip transportation from Talkeetna, food, general expedition gear, leadership. **When:** May. **Contact:** Genet Expeditions, Talkeetna, AK 99676, USA; phone (907)733-2306.

Glacier Expedition: A 30-day expedition explores the ice and snow of the Chugach Mountains outside Anchorage. The expedition begins on the exposed, dense ice at the snout of the Matanuska Glacier. Here participants receive instruction in climbing techniques, the use of crampons, ice axes and hammers, probing and wanding, crevasse rescue and self-rescue systems. The trip proceeds through the Chugach Mountains where participants use crampons, ropes, axes and snowshoes according to the terrain. Trip members must be 17 years of age or older but need no prior knowledge of climbing. **Cost:** $795 from Anchorage. **When:** June to July. **Contact:** Hondo Rast and Co., P.O. Box 231, Hamilton, MT 59840, USA; phone (406)363-3440.

(M)

Sanford Seminar/Climb: Mt. Sanford at 16,185 feet is an extinct volcano and part of the proposed Wrangell-St. Elias National Park. A 16-day snow and ice climbing trip here provides strong backpackers with a good introduction to expedition techniques. The trip includes an intensive 3-day seminar at base camp and a 6-day guided ascent of Mt. Sanford to practice newly acquired climbing skills. The trip begins with a day of sightseeing in Anchorage, a drive to Glenallen the next day and then a bush flight to the mountain base where a camp is set up for the seminar and ascent. After the climb the party walks for a day through tundra and evergreen forest to the Copper River and then takes a 30-mile float trip down the river, returning to Anchorage by road. **Cost:** $1,050. **When:** June. **Contact:** Mountain Travel Inc., 1398 Solano Ave., Albany, CA 94706, USA; phone (415)527-8100. ***(M)***

Mt. Sanford Ski Mountaineering: A major glacier system in eastern Alaska provides relatively easy access to a 16,185-foot peak with an excellent view of 4 surrounding mountain ranges. Participants on a 10- to 14-day trip depart from Anchorage, travel by road to Gulkana, continuing by plane to the base of Mt. Sanford, an extinct volcano. The mountain offers a 10,000-foot ski descent in powder snow, and the run is good even in summer. Group members should be at least intermediate-level skiers and have mountain skis, climbing skins and mountaineering bindings. On a cross-country tundra hike from the airstrip to the glacier, participants have close-up views of sheep, caribou and other wildlife. **Cost:** $750 includes community camping equipment, guides. **When:** June. **Contact:** Mountain Trip, Rt. 2, Box 526, Kasilof, AK 99610, USA.

California

Bay Area Rock Climbing: A 2-day class in rock climbing takes place in the San Francisco Bay area. This is a beginners' class. Instruction is given in the use of chocks, nuts and natural runners that preserve the rock; techniques covered are belaying, rappelling and climbing on vertical and overhanging rock. Emphasis is placed on such nonphysical aspects of climbing as awareness and judgment. Each day's class meets in San Rafael in the morning and returns in late afternoon. **Cost:** $35 includes transportation to and from San Rafael, equipment, instruction. **When:** April to October. **Contact:** Mountain People School, 157 Oak Spring Dr., San Anselmo, CA 94960, USA; phone (415)457-3664.

Rock Climbing in the Eastern Sierra: A 5-day climbing program challenges beginning and advanced climbers alike. By car-camping participants are able to spend time at several different climbing sites and experience a wider variety of rock faces. Students learn a spectrum of rock climbing techniques including use of basic holds and body movement. In addition, participants are introduced to the proper use of modern safety equipment including knots, belaying, anchors, rope management, rappelling, prussiking and self-rescue. Technical rock ascents are the priority for advanced students who learn progressively more difficult methods of climbing in arduous and exposed conditions. Limited to no more than 3 students for each instructor, the program enables individuals to progress at their own pace. **Cost:** $395 includes food, gear. **When:** May. **Contact:** Palisade School of Mountaineering, P.O. Box 694, Bishop, CA 93514, USA; phone (714)935-4330. ***(M)***

Sierra Avalanche Seminars: A 4-day program, based in the Sierra Nevadas, teaches participants to recognize avalanche conditions and terrain, and to know when and how to travel safely and when not to travel. Eighty percent of the instruction takes place in the field, alternating with illustrated lectures. Weather phenomena, terrain and vegetation, and snowpack structure are observed and related to various degrees of avalanche hazard. Throughout the seminar, instructors emphasize route-finding and the evaluation of avalanche hazards. At the end of the seminar students should have an understanding of the different types of avalanches and their causes, how to avoid them, and what to do if rescue is required. Participants must be in good physical condition and able to ski up and downhill on changeable terrain in varying snow conditions. Students provide their own food, lodging, and equipment. Seminars are limited to 6 students. **Cost:** $125. **When:** February, March. **Contact:** Sierra Avalanche Seminars, P.O. Box 8, Norden, CA 95724, USA; phone (916)426-3037.

Colorado

Climbing in Boulder: Courses in all aspects of rock and ice climbing are offered in the foothills of the Rockies for climbers at any level of experience. Knot tying, rope handling, safety procedures, rappelling, belaying and the use of chocks, caribiners and slings are taught in a basic 2-day course for the serious beginner. In the final lesson, students climb a route requiring the utilization of a full range of techniques. An advanced 12-hour course concentrates on artificial or free climbing. The final multi-pitch free climb is preceded by practice in direct aid climbing, racking the hardware, seconding with jumars, climbing and resting in slings, placing chocks for aid, climbing in etriers, pack hauling and climbing overhangs and roofs using specialized equipment. An ice climbing course covering modern techniques is also available. Classes are limited to 3 students, and can accommodate individual needs. **Cost:** $40 to $140 includes equipment. **When:** Year-round for rock climbing, December to March for ice climbing. **Contact:** The Bob Culp Climbing School, 1335 Broadway, Boulder, CO 80302, USA; phone (303)442-8355.

Rock Climbing and Mountaineering Course: Beginning with a 3-day orientation expedition into the mountains to learn navigation, mountain campcraft and emergency medical aid, participants receive intensive instruction in mountaineering and rock climbing for a total of 23 days. The 6-day introduction to rock climbing begins on easy pitch slabs and progresses to multi-pitch climbs on 600-foot rock faces. Fourteen days are then spent in the mountains of Colorado climbing several 14,000-foot peaks. Snow and ice climbing, belaying on snow, glissading, self-arrest and the construction of emergency snow shelters are among the subjects taught. Students have numerous opportunities to make decisions in the planning of mountain expeditions and should be capable of leading technical rock climbs at the end of the course. Academic credit is available. **Cost:** $575 from Crested Butte includes transportation, meals, guides, instruction, accommodations, equipment. **When:** June to August. **Contact:** Challenge/Discovery, The Wilderness Center, Box 229, Crested

Butte, CO 81224, USA; phone (303)349-5432.

School of Hard Rocks: Lumpy Ridge, an extensive rock formation in Rocky Mountain National Park, is the site of 3 daylong courses in rock climbing. The beginning course covers knots, anchoring, belaying, rappelling and some climbing techniques, with the emphasis on gaining confidence. The next course reviews these basics and then moves on to free climbing techniques, culminating in the ascent of a 400-foot face requiring 2 rappels on the way down. Following this course, students should gain some field experience before taking the advanced course, which covers prussiking from a loose rope and advanced chock placement before an ascent of Twin Owls, a challenging face. **Cost:** On request. **When:** Year-round. **Contact:** Fantasy Ridge, P.O. Box 2106, Estes Park, CO 80517, USA; phone (303)586-5391.

Wet Mountain Climbing: Bear Basin Ranch, located atop the Wet Mountains of Colorado, serves as a base for rock climbing courses in the Sangre de Cristo Mountains. Courses run in 3- and 5-day sessions with basic, intermediate and advanced instruction available. Instruction is tailored to the individual. Each course stresses safe, state-of-the-art techniques with an emphasis on achieving a high level of free climbing ability through on-the-rock practice and multi-pitch guided climbs. Mountaineering courses emphasize mixed snow and rock climbing during the summer and ski mountaineering during the winter. Each course includes a technical climb on one of Colorado's 14,000-foot peaks. **Cost:** $90 and $150 for rock climbing courses, $150 and $200 for mountaineering courses includes food, group equipment, instruction. **When:** April to November for rock climbing; year-round for mountaineering. **Contact:** International Alpine School, Eldorado Springs, CO 80025, USA; phone (303)494-4904.

Idaho

Rockface Seminars: Participants engage in 1-, 2- and 6-day seminars in the Sawtooth Mountains covering various mountaineering skills. Rock I is a basic course designed for the rank amateur; techniques such as belaying, rope handling and rappelling are discussed and practiced. Rock II is a more advanced course in which skills such as slab, face and crack climbing are explored. Both courses are 1-day ventures. The 2-day projects involve participants in alpine snow and ice climbing; techniques for anchoring, knots, glissading, self-arrest, belaying and rappelling are practiced. The course is designed for mountaineers who wish to augment their skills. Climbers who elect to take the 6-day seminar learn basic skills as well as more advanced techniques including route selection, trip planning, bivouacking and group organization. A summit climb concludes the seminar. **Cost:** $18 for Rock I, $20 for Rock II, $35 for Alpine, $125 for 6-day seminar. **When:** June to August, or by arrangement. **Contact:** Sawtooth Mountaineering, 5200 Fairview Ave., Boise, ID 83704, USA; phone (208)376-3731.

With prices beginning at $150, 3- to 5-day International Alpine School courses combine snow and rock climbing practice in the Sangre de Cristo Mountains of Colorado. (E.M. Watson)

Iowa

Basic Rock Climbing Course: Intensive instruction in the essentials of rock climbing is provided in a 7-day course in Devil's Lake State Park. Skilled mountaineers teach climbers the fundamental principles of the sport: balance climbing, friction, jam and opposition techniques, belays and practice falls, suspension traverse and other skills. Evening lectures are held to discuss such topics as route selection, weather and equipment. No prior experience is necessary, but participants should be in good shape. **Cost:** $100. **When:** May, June. **Contact:** Iowa Mountaineers, 30 Prospect Pl., P.O. Box 163, Iowa City, IA 52240, USA; phone (319)337-7163.

New Hampshire

Rock Enroll: Complete instruction in mountaineering and rock climbing is offered by a climbing school. Students at any level of expertise can be accommodated through standard basic and advanced courses, daily classes, private lessons, custom group classes and short expeditions. The basic rock climbing course takes 4 days, which can be split into 2 weekends, and teaches knots, equipment use, belaying, rappelling, the use of chocks and multi-pitch faces. The instruction is tailored to each student's pace, and the in-the-field portions of the course are designed by the instructor accordingly. The 3-day advanced rock climbing course builds on the skills learned earlier; aid climbing and more difficult, sustained routes are covered. Also offered is instruction in winter camping, ice climbing and expedition planning, and courses designed specifically for instructors. **Cost:** From $75 for rock climbing course; from $25 for daily classes; additional rates on request. **When:** Year-round. **Contact:** International Mountain Climbing School Inc., Main St., Box 494, North Conway,

NH 03860, USA; phone (603)356-5287.

Franconia Ice Climbing: Novice and experienced climbers can participate in ice climbing seminars lasting from 3 to 5 days. During a 3-day course beginners learn proper use of ice axes, ice climbing hammers, crampons, ice screws and snow pickets. Novices practice belaying, rappelling and self-arrests on a number of ascents including Willey's Slide, Franconia Slide and the Flume Route on Mt. Willard. The dangers of hypothermia are discussed in evening lectures. In another 3-day class for advanced climbers, students learn special maneuvers including the Lowe Brothers' Monkey Hang and the Double Hummingbird front-pointing technique. Climbers then have the chance to test their new skills on major guided ascents in the White Mountain Range. In a 5-day seminar, intermediate and advanced techniques are taught to participants with some previous ice climbing experience. At the conclusion, all students should be able to complete guided ascents. Participants should provide their own sleeping bags and daypacks. **Cost:** $205 to $385 includes accommodations, meals, guides, instruction, equipment. **When:** January through March. **Contact:** North Country Mountaineering, Inc., P.O. Box 951, Hanover, NH 03755, USA; phone (603)643-3299. ***(M)***

New York

Northeastern Sampler: Rock climbing, kayaking and backpacking are covered during a 15-day trip for adventurers aged 14 to 19 beginning and ending in Poughkeepsie. The trip's first leg is in the Shawangunk Mountains, rising from the Hudson Valley floor and offering good rock climbing terrain; rope handling, basic climbing moves and rappelling are covered. The group then travels to the Adirondacks for several days of backpacking and an ascent of 5,300-foot Mt. Marcy. Then, in the final stage of the journey, participants head to Connecticut for kayaking on the Housatonic River, which meanders through woods and farmlands before it picks up speed to the south and begins to form rapids. Instruction is offered in basic kayak techniques including the Eskimo roll, and students have a chance to test their skills for several days on various parts of the river before returning to Poughkeepsie. **Cost:** $450 includes transportation from Poughkeepsie, food, equipment, instruction. **When:** June to August. **Contact:** Wilderness Bound, Ltd., RD 1, Box 365, Highland, NY 12528, USA; phone (914)691-2377.

North Carolina

Weekend Rock Climbing Clinic: Two days of intensive field instruction in rock climbing are conducted, with no more than 3 students to an instructor. Participants travel from Bryson City to a 300-foot rock face at Devil's Courthouse, on the Blue Ridge Parkway near Balsam Gap. Here they receive instruction in knots, signals, rope handling and basic rock climbing techniques. Each clinic begins with dinner on Friday followed by an orientation session and then 2 days on the rock. Private instruction is also offered for those unable to make the scheduled clinics. **Cost:** $75 includes equipment, meals, instruction. **When:** April to October. **Contact:** Nantahala Outdoor Center, Star Rt., Box 68, Bryson City, NC 28713, USA; phone (704)488-2175. *(M)*

Oregon

Northwest Climbing Seminars: Ice climbing, rock climbing, mountain medicine and rescue, and advanced mountaineering are taught in outdoor seminars usually lasting 3 to 5 days. There are 2 ice climbing courses: one teaches basic skills for the novice entering the sport, and the other covers more advanced techniques, concluding with a north face ascent of Mt. Hood. The rock climbing seminars are likewise divided into a basic course, held on volcanic formations in central Oregon, and an advanced seminar, held on granite in central Washington. The mountain medicine and rescue seminar is designed to evaluate and treat the critically injured, control of hemorrhage, splinting, frostbite and cold injury. It ends with a climb of Mt. Hood. A 12-day alpine mountaineering seminar is also planned; at the close of the seminar members ascend a difficult ice route in the Cascades. **Cost:** $240 to $750. **When:** June to August. **Contact:** Lute Jerstad Adventures, P.O. Box 19527, Portland, OR 97219, USA; phone (503)244-4364. *(M)*

Virginia

On the Rocks: Rock climbing instruction for all levels of skill is offered in Great Falls Park near Vienna. A basic rock climbing course provides a half-day of instruction and introduction to climbing equipment in a "hands on" session. The use of hand- and footholds, correct belay technique, moderate rappels and safety are covered. The intermediate and advanced courses are continuations of the basic course, covering more advanced techniques such as jamming and chimney climbing, overhangs and face climbing. Another course presents the concept of aid climbing as a method of handling pitches of extreme free climbing difficulty. Private instruction allows the student to choose specific areas of interest. Guided trips offer a challenging climbing experience for intermediate and advanced climbers in the Shawangunks. **Cost:** $20 for each course. **When:** Year-round.

Contact: Geneva Spur Ltd., 1109 Lakewood Dr., Vienna, VA 22180, USA; phone (703)281-3316. *(M)*

Washington

Cascade Climbing Courses: Climbers of every degree of skill may take part in basic, advanced and wall climbing in the heart of the North Cascades. Five days are spent in both basic and advanced courses; subjects include rock climbing and mountain safety in the basic course, and snow, ice and rock ascents in the advanced program. For those with extensive mountaineering experience, wall school is available; this involves a 2-day climb up the east face of Liberty Bell Mountain. Bivouacking along the face in hammocks is part of the venture. **Cost:** $190 for basic, $200 for wall school, $220 for advanced. **When:** June to September. **Contact:** Liberty Bell Alpine Tours, Mazama, WA 98833, USA; phone (509)996-2250. *(M)*

Wilderness Mountaineering Courses: Students on 8- and 12-day mountaineering expeditions climb 12,326-foot Mt. Adams, the second highest peak in the Pacific Northwest. Courses begin with food and gear preparations at a ranch in the mountain's shadow, and culminate with a roped ascent to the ice-clad summit. With two instructors, the small group of adult-age participants backpack into the heart of a heavily glaciated and wildly volcanic mountain wilderness. Here they attain proficiency in the classic and modern techniques of snow, rock and ice climbing as well as a keen appreciation for the mountain's natural history. Instruction is intense and individualized for such skills as belaying, cramponing, rappelling, glissading, uses of the ice ax, anchor placement, crevasse rescue, navigation, route finding, etc. Base camps en route provide days for practice climbs on nearby rock cliffs, icefalls and glaciers. Every degree of difficulty is present to challenge the climbers, who need no previous experience to attend. The summit climb is made via Mazama Glacier and an 8,300-foot high camp. **Cost:** $350 for 8 days, $450 for 12 days includes transportation from Portland, food, climbing and camping gear. **When:** June to August. **Contact:** Mt. Adams Wilderness Institute, Flying L Ranch, Glenwood, WA 96819, USA; phone (509)364-3511 or 364-3488. *(M)*

Cascade Alpine Mountaineering and Rock Climbing: The high country of North Cascades National Park is the setting for 4- to 6-day courses in basic alpine mountaineering and rock climbing. The 4-day basic rock program covers equipment, knots, free climbing techniques, placing, protection, belaying and rappelling, with practicum on 5th class routes. The 6-day alpine mountaineering course involves largely off-trail travel in a highly glaciated area. Fundamental mountaineering skills taught include selection of equipment, use of ice ax and crampons, belaying techniques, rappelling, crevasse rescue, first aid, survival techniques, avalanche prediction and map and compass reading. The advanced rock programs include a seminar of demonstration and practice in an easily accessible area and a practicum of multi-pitch climbs. A maximum of 2 students per instructor is allowed in a 4-day advanced rock program. Difficult crack, chimney and face climbing problems are dealt with in the seminar, and the uses of specialized equipment, chocks and the Yosemite method of big wall climbing precede advanced climbs of major routes. Students may take only the seminars if desired. **Cost:** $130 for 4 days of basic rock, $200 for 4 days of advanced rock, and $160 for 6 days of alpine mountaineering includes instruction, guide fees, technical equipment. **When:** May to October. **Contact:** North

A climber employs a chimneying maneuver to inch up through hard ice in a North Cascades ice fall. (Harry Olsen/North Cascades Alpine School)

Cascades Alpine School, 1212 24th G, Bellingham, WA 98225, USA; phone (206)671-1505. *(M)*

Trying Traverses: Three high alpine traverses are offered in the North Cascades, all requiring mountaineering skills but varying in difficulty. Mountaineers spend 8 days on the Ptarmigan Traverse, in North Cascades National Park and Glacier Peak Wilderness Area, following a route along glaciers and rock ridges through spectacular country; the easier version makes a few moderate climbs, while the more advanced party ascends as many peaks as possible and encounters some challenging routes. Lasting 9 days, another trip follows the almost virgin Pyramid-Inspiration Glacier Traverse in a rugged trailless area of North Cascades National Park. The traverse itself requires a wide array of mountaineering and wilderness travel skills, and again as many of the region's difficult ascents are made as possible. For all trips participants must either complete prerequisite courses or demonstrate equivalent proficiency. **Cost:** $170 for Ptarmigan route, $250 for advanced Ptarmigan route, $310 for Pyramid route includes food, group equipment, guide. **When:** On request. **Contact:** North Cascades Alpine School, 1212 24th G, Bellingham, WA 98225, USA; phone (206)671-1505. *(M)*

The High Cascades: Mountaineering instruction at all levels of expertise is offered during week-long sessions in the Cascade Mountains. The area, stretching from Snoqualmie Pass to the Canadian border, presents a wide variety of climbing situations, from the smooth granite towers of Enchantment Plateau to glacier-draped volcanoes and ice-carved pinnacles of the Pickett Range. Basic courses cover equipment, glacier and rock climbing, rope-handling and route finding on peaks including Stuart, Liberty Bell, Monte Cristo and Baker. Advanced courses focus on technical climbing, expedition training and high-angle rock climbing. **Cost:** On request. **When:** On request. **Contact:** REI Adventure Travel, 1525 11th Ave., Seattle, WA 98122, USA; phone (206)322-7800. *(M)*

Rainier's Summit: A day-long snow climbing school serves as the introduction and prerequisite for an overnight climb of 14,410-foot Mt. Rainier. The snow climbing school, held daily during the climbing season, teaches most of the basic techniques: rope travel, knots, self and team arrest, and cramponing. After completing the course, participants should be eligible to make the summit climb. This is an excellent introductory climb and is held frequently throughout the summer. Some equipment may be rented at the Paradise Guide House, where the climb begins. Transportation is available from Seattle. **Cost:** $25 for snow climbing school, $75 for summit climb, includes instruction, food, group equipment, guide. **When:** May to October. **Contact:** Rainier Mountaineering, 201 St. Helens, Tacoma, WA 98402, USA; phone (206)627-6242, summer 569-2227.

Wyoming

Rock Climbing Instruction:

Three-day rock climbing sessions teach climbers of varied skill levels basic climbing techniques and the use and protection of equipment. Grand Teton National Park provides a scenic learning environment for the programs. Basic courses cover fundamentals on moderate-angle rock, use of rope for protection in belaying and anchoring, and rappelling. The intermediate course covers high-angle climbing and more extensive rappelling, and the advanced course is oriented to special techniques for difficult climbs. **Cost:** $20 for basic course, $25 for intermediate, $35 for advanced. **When:** June to September. **Contact:** Exum Mountain Guide Service and School of American Mountaineering, Moose, WY 83012, USA.

Climbing Camps and Classes: A variety of climbing instruction programs is available in the rugged terrain of the Grand Tetons and Wyoming Rockies. Participants in 8-day climber camps stay overnight in mountaineering tents and study either basic, intermediate or technical ice climbing or mountain photography. Special camps for fathers and sons, women only or entire families may be arranged. A sequence of day-long classes limited to 4 students covers beginning to advanced mountaineering skills, with an ascent of a 600-foot wall serving as the finale for advanced students. A day-long snow school teaches the navigation of steep snow passes in the mountains. A guide service for expeditions of climbers' own choosing is also

available. **Cost:** $365 to $465 for camp, $22 to $40 for classes, $48 to $58 a person for guide service. **When:** Year-round. **Contact:** Jackson Hole Mountain Guides, Teton Village, WY 83025, USA; phone (307)733-4979.

Gannett Peak Winter Ascent: Harsh weather conditions make an 11-day climb of Wyoming's highest mountain, 13,804-foot Gannett Peak, an ideal training ground for advanced winter skiing and technical mountaineering. The climb, an expedition training series for Mt. McKinley, is taxing but not technically difficult. Climbers should be in strong physical condition, be intermediate alpine or nordic skiers, and have some experience with climbing, camping and rope handling. **Cost:** $315 includes equipment, most meals, accommodations. **When:** December. **Contact:** Skinner Brothers Mountaineering, Box B, Pinedale, WY 82941, USA; phone (307)367-2270. ***(M)***

Beartooth Climbing: During either 1- or 2-week trips in Montana's Beartooth Range, participants learn the fundamentals of rock and ice mountaineering. The courses take place at a camp located well away from the popular climbing centers of the region, and class sizes are limited to 3 climbers per instructor; learning proceeds at an individual pace. Both the 7- and 14-day courses culminate in an actual ascent

Mountaineering techniques can be practiced without scaling peaks; this student rappels down a high-angle face on Grand Teton in Wyoming. (North Country Mountaineering, Inc.)

during which students must plan a route, set up a bivouac, make judgments about the weather and deal with potential hazards such as avalanches and rock falls. In addition, a 4-day course is offered at the same alpine camp that focuses only on rock climbing. Subjects covered include belaying, fixing anchors, protection and safety. All the courses emphasize not only the technical skills required but also aspects of mental attitude and alpine philosophy. **Cost:** $460 for 1 week, $850 for 2 weeks, $275 for 4-day rock course includes food, accommodations, equipment, instruction. **When:** July to September. **Contact:** Yellowstone Wilderness Guides, Box 446, Red Lodge, MT 59068, USA; phone (406)446-2636.

RESOURCES

Clubs and Associations

Alpine Club of Canada
Box 1026
Banff, AB Canada T0L 0C0

Alpine Club of Peru
Las Begonias 630
Lima 27, Peru

American Alpine Club
113 E. 90th St.
New York, NY 10028, USA
Phone (212)722-1628

British Mountaineering Council
Crawford House, Precinct Ctr.
Manchester U., Booth St. E.
Manchester M13 9RZ, Great Britain

Czechoslovak Alpine Club
Na Porici 12
Prague 1, Czechoslovakia

Federation Francaise de la Montagne
7 rue la Boetie
Paris 8e, France

Federation of Mountaineering Clubs
7 Sorbonne, Ardilea Estate
Dublin 14, Ireland

German Alpine Association
Praterinsel
Munich 22, Germany

Hong Kong Mountaineering Association
P.O. Box 20519
Hennessey Rd. Post Office, Hong Kong

Iowa Mountaineers
30 Prospect Pl., P.O.Box 163
Iowa City, IA 52240, USA
Phone (319)337-7163

Italian Alpine Club
Via Ugo Foscolo 3
Milan, Italy

Mazamas
909 NW 19th
Portland, OR 97209, USA
Phone (503)227-2345

Mountain Club of East Africa
P.O. Box 66
Moshi, Tanzania

Mountain Rescue Society
P.O. Box 67
Seattle, WA 98111, USA

Northwest Mountaineering Club
10922 88th Ave.
Edmonton, AB Canada

Norwegian Alpine Club
c/o Wilhelmsen
Roald Amundsensgt. 5
Oslo, Norway

Spanish Mountaineering Federation
Barquillo 19
Madrid 4, Spain

Swiss Alpine Club
Swiss Center, 1 New Coventry St.
London W1, Great Britain

Yugoslav Alpine Club
Postni Predal
Ljubljana, Yugoslavia

SKIING

Cross-country skiing is one of the fastest-growing winter sports in the world, and there's little wonder why. Relatively inexpensive, ideal for people of all ages and available wherever there is adequate snow cover—be it your backyard or a distant slope—cross-country skiing has freed the winter housebound and provided access to some of the most beautiful winter wilderness areas around the world.

Developed during the past 100 years in Norway as an essential means of winter transportation, it has spread as a sport in the last 20 years. Trail systems and cross-country lodges have sprung up across the United States; instruction is offered all over. A few hours of practice and pointers enable most people to pole off into a winter wonderland. More refined skiing techniques are taught on organized trips in some of the most scenic spots in the world.

Professional guides will lead you over the slopes of Kashmir, above the Arctic Circle in Greenland, on ski routes in the Peruvian Andes and on trails through the Canadian Rockies. If downhill skiing is more your speed, you can race the slopes of Vail or fly by helicopter to the high mountains of the Ohau Range in New Zealand to ski down a 10,000-foot slope. Helicopter skiing can also be done in the Cariboo and Monashee mountains of Alberta.

You can practice close to home, or take several weeks to brush up on cross-country and downhill techniques with instructors who also teach winter camping and survival skills. Whatever your choice, the challenges of skiing and the access it provides to pristine wilderness areas can't be beat. □

A ski tour can assume many moods, varying with the terrain, weather and pace; these two skiers enjoy a self-guided trip in Washington's Mt. Rainier National Park. (Keith Gunnar)

SKIING

ASIA

India

Skiing in Kashmir: Based at Gulmarg, a village on the slopes above the Vale of Kashmir, participants on a 14-day trip encounter a wide range of snow conditions and grades of difficulty as they ski the surrounding area. Hanging glaciers and the peaks of the Pir Panjal Range form a backdrop for skiers at the lower elevations where pine forests and snow-covered meadows are part of the terrain. Instruction in both downhill skiing and cross-country touring is offered, and more adventurous journeys through the sparsely populated region can be arranged for experienced skiers. **Cost:** $1,497 to $1,864 includes roundtrip airfare from Australia or New Zealand, hotel accommodations, most meals. **When:** January. **Contact:** Ausventure, P.O. Box 54, Mosman, N.S.W. 2088, Australia; phone 960-1677.

ATLANTIC

Greenland

Ski Touring with Dogsled Escort: A 10-day cross-country skiing trip above the Arctic Circle begins in Holsteinsborg with a 10-mile training tour before setting out across the open country. Averaging about 20 miles a day, participants ski across plains and frozen lakes, through valleys, and up steep snowbanks in alpine areas. Supplies are carried on dogsleds which

One way to reach remote skiing areas is by small plane. Groups of 6 to 8 can be flown in by a Mt. Cook Airlines fleet to the Tasman Glacier for a full day of skiing. (Air New Zealand)

accompany the expedition. Skiers, who camp in 4-person tents, should be prepared for temperatures as low as -5°F. The trip ends in Sondre Stromfjord with time set aside for relaxation. Group size is limited to 12 participants, who should bring ski touring equipment and sleeping bags. **Cost:** $627 includes food, transportation from Holsteinsborg, guides, tents. **When:** March, April. **Contact:** Preben Schleimann, Box 9, DK-3911 Holsteinsborg, Greenland.

AUSTRALASIA

Australia

Winter Activities: A variety of alpine activities is available to winter sports enthusiasts in New South Wales. Ski touring, snow camping and winter survival skills are among the offerings on trips lasting from 1 to 5 days. Beginning skiers can take a weekend course near Sawpit Lake that covers cross-country techniques, equipment and safety procedures. Students spend the night either at an established campsite, in snow tents or in snow caves and igloos built as part of the course. Experienced skiers can join overnight trips into either the Cascades or the Main Range, honing their skills under the leadership of an instructor. Sunday ski trips for families, equipment rental, a custom guiding and instruction service and a January trip to ski the Himalayas in Kashmir are also available. **Cost:** From $13 for day trips to $138 for 5-day course; other rates on request. **When:** June to September. **Contact:** Wilderness Expeditions, Berridale, N.S.W. 2628, Australia.

New Zealand

High Mountain Helicopter Skiing: Jet helicopters transport skiers to the high mountains of the Ohau Range bordering Mt. Cook National Park. Guided groups of 6 to 8 ski down slopes of 9,900 vertical feet for a full day. Groups ski different runs according to their ability, though everyone should be intermediate to expert in skill. It is more important to be able to turn with confidence in untracked snow than to manage perfect parallels. Standard downhill skis and boots are used, although shorter ski lengths are recommended. The guide skis with a pack of emergency and survival equipment and briefs the party on mountain safety, helicopter procedure and the use of avalanche transceivers. **Cost:** $85 a day includes helicopter, guides, use of avalanche transceivers, lunch. **When:** September to October. **Contact:** Alpine Guides (Mt. Cook) Ltd., Mt. Cook National Park, P.O. Box 20, Mt. Cook, New Zealand; phone Mt. Cook 834.

CANADA

Alberta

Ski Mountaineering Camps: A variety of week-long ski camps in western Canada is provided for both ski mountaineering and cross-country skiing. These include helicoptering into and skiing out from the Slocan Chief cabin in the Kokanee area, suitable for ski mountaineering or cross-country; an advanced ski camp in the northern Purcells; skiing to and from the Skoki area, primarily for cross-country; and a New Year's trip into

Eremite/Tonquin for both types of skiing. The trips' accommodations vary from prepared meals and beds to shared chores on lower-budget trips. Ski trips to Oregon's Mt. Hood and to France, with the possibility of skiing the Haute Route are also available for experienced ski mountaineers. **Cost:** On request. **When:** December to April. **Contact:** The Alpine Club of Canada, P.O. Box 1026, Banff, AB Canada T0L 0C0; phone (403)762-4481.

Advanced Skiing Instruction: Special instruction is given to the advanced skier who wishes to prepare for a week of helicopter skiing outside Banff. A private instructor skis with the student during an entire day to ensure an intensive educational session and to act as a guide to the best locations with the fewest skiers. Deep snow instruction is also offered and helps the student decide whether he or she is qualified for the type of skiing available by helicopter. **Cost:** $78 to $100 a day, depending on season. **When:** December to May. **Contact:** Canadian Mountain Holidays Ltd., P.O. Box 1660, Banff, AB Canada T0L 0C0; phone (403)762-4531. *(M)*

Touring in the Canadian Rockies: Cross-country skiers and ski touring enthusiasts have the opportunity to explore the countryside while spending a week at a remote cabin in the Canadian Rockies. Participants gather in Banff, drive to a drop-off point and ski in on the trips, some of which are suited to alpine skiing and some to cross-country. One of several available cabins is used, at either Little Yoho, Robson, Eremite, Hooker, Mummery or Bow Emerald; the selection is made according to season. Custom guided trips may also be arranged, and equipment rental is available. **Cost:** $280 to $390 for skiing weeks, depending on location, includes food, accommodations, transportation to and from the trailhead, guide. **When:** February to April. **Contact:** Canadian Mountain Holidays Ltd., P.O. Box 1660, Banff, AB Canada T0L 0C0; phone (403)762-4531. *(M)*

Deep Powder Skiing: Skiers who have maneuvered on the steeper slopes at Aspen, St. Moritz, Whistler and places of like terrain may join a week-long helicopter skiing experience in the Cariboo and Monashee mountain ranges. Skiers meet at the town of Blue River, 1,800 feet above sea level, and board a helicopter for one of numerous landing sites located at elevations between 8,000 and 9,000 feet or Mt. Cheadle at 10,500 feet. Divided only by the narrow valley of the Thompson River and the Yellowhead Highway, the 2 ranges are located in a snow belt where reliable powder and packed skiing conditions await participants. Ski runs vary in steepness and length, ranging from a gentle glacier run to a 5,300-foot vertical drop. Runs sometimes begin in deep soft powder and end in an area of trees, making it necessary to cross some creeks to get to the helicopter pickup point. Instruction is available for skiers with little experience in deep powder snow. English, German, French and some Italian are spoken by guides. **Cost:** $1,065 includes a week of helicopter transport, meals, accommodations. **When:**

Accessible through a number of trip operators, the Canadian Rockies offer a wide variety of first-rate skiing terrain, appropriate for ski mountaineering, heli-skiing and alpine and cross-country skiing. (Keith Gunnar)

January to April. **Contact:** Cariboo Helicopter Skiing Ltd., Box 1824, Banff, AB Canada T0L 0C0; phone (403)762-4171.

Skiing in the Canadian Rockies: Mt. Assiniboine, the "Matterhorn of Canada," is the setting for a variety of both downhill and cross-country skiing trips. Participants arrive from the Banff area by helicopter. Lodging is provided at an isolated chalet situated in the meadows at 6,800 feet on the shore of Magog Lake. Another trip is provided at the alpine retreat of Skoki located in the Slate Mountains, also part of the Canadian Rockies and opposite Mt. Temple's 4,000-foot north wall. Skiers of all interests and abilities can be accommodated on both ski tours. **Cost:** $375 for 1 week. **When:** Winter months. **Contact:** Royal Gorge Nordic Ski Resort, P.O. Box 178, Soda Springs, CA 95728, USA; phone (916)426-3793.

British Columbia

Cross-Country Skiing at Whistler Mountain: Weekend, midweek or daily instruction programs in cross-country ski touring are available to guests of the Whistler Hostel. Students begin with an introduction to ski equipment, control on skis and snow conditions given near the hostel. Participants may then proceed deeper into the snow-clad valleys and ridges of the mountain terrain; in addition, they may travel to remote, open snow fields by helicopter for a week-long skiing experience through miles of

wilderness. **Cost:** $90 to $300 includes instruction, food, accommodations, helicopter transportation. **When:** January to March. **Contact:** Canadian Hostelling Association, Pacific Region, 10-1557 W. Broadway, Vancouver, BC Canada V6J 1W6; phone (604)736-2674.

Coastal Mountains: The Dickson Range in the eastern part of the Coastal Mountains receives plenty of snow from moist Pacific air masses, but its proximity to the interior keeps the snow dry. These favorable skiing conditions are experienced on 2 trips leaving from Vancouver: an 8-day trip which features skiing from a cabin deep in the mountains, and a more strenuous 10-day trip covering 80 miles to the glaciers near upper Warner Creek. On the 8-day outing skiers make day trips with excellent meadow skiing and spend 3 nights away from the cabin. Participants on the 10-day trip follow extensive 8,000-foot ridges, make ski ascents of Mts. Sheba and Lizard and also find good meadow skiing. All skiers return by train from Lillooet. **Cost:** $285 for either trip includes transportation from Vancouver, food, guide. **When:** March. **Contact:** ECOsummer, Box 191, Heriot Bay, BC Canada V0P 1N0.

Advanced Glacier Skiing: A small group skis the high mountain glaciers near Invermere for a week. A hike of approximately 6 miles brings skiers to a base camp where

Trips from 2 to 7 days can be taken in the Canadian Rockies on skiing trips with Northern Lights Alpine Recreation. (Arnor Larson)

they may enjoy skiing on glaciers with vertical descents of up to 3,500 feet over 4 miles. After the downhill runs, skiers may engage in such activities as climbing practice, hiking, photography or resting and relaxing. All uphill transportation is by foot, so participants should be in good physical condition. Some instruction is necessary for this type of skiing, and skiers are taught skills such as knots, prussiking, self-arrest, crevasse rescue and roped skiing. The trip is open to intermediate or better skiers who have had some camping and hiking experience. **Cost:** $200 a week. **When:** May, June. **Contact:** Northern Lights Alpine Recreation, Box 399, Invermere, BC Canada V0A 1K0; phone (604)342-6042.

Guided Touring in the Rockies: Kootenay National Park, the Purcell Range and other areas of the southern Canadian Rockies are the location of ski touring experiences of 2 to 7 days. Accompanied by a guide and instructor, skiers tour the entire day, eating lunch on the trail and returning for the evening to home-cooked meals at a mountain lodge. Skiing in a small group, participants can receive instruction at any time during the trip, or a whole day may be set aside for instruction. The levels of physical and technical difficulty can be arranged to accommodate all group members, and participants may make use of the guide service as they wish. Skiers travel on unmarked trails that are well known to the guide. Participants can also spend time soaking in the nearby pools of Fairmont and Radium hot springs. **Cost:** $60 a day depending on length of stay includes meals, guide, instruction, lodging. **When:** December to March. **Contact:** Northern Lights Alpine Recreation, Box 399, Invermere, BC Canada V0A 1K0; phone (604)342-6042.

Purcell Range Ski Touring: Forty miles wide and 150 miles long, the Purcell Range is a large tract of wilderness that includes the 325,000-acre Purcell Wilderness Conservancy, St. Mary's Alpine Park and the famous Bugaboos. On skiing trips in the range participants may see moose, elk, mountain goats, caribou, lynx, wolverines and snowshoe hares as well as winter birds. Log cabins heated by wood stoves are provided for overnight stays. From the cabins group members take day tours into nearby alpine basins and valleys where summits of the surrounding peaks attain heights of 8,500 to 10,000 feet. The day trips provide choices ranging from skiing in gentle terrain to deep powder runs on steeper slopes. Daily outings are tailored to individual ability. Options are also available for overnight trips to high mountain huts. **Cost:** $35 a day from Kimberley includes accommodations, food, guides. **When:** December to March. **Contact:** Ptarmigan Tours, 255 Wallinger, Kimberley, BC Canada V1A 1Z2; phone (604)427-3510.

Chilcotin Cross-Country: Log cabins with wood-burning stoves and kerosene lamps provide accommodations for groups of 2 to 6 people during ski trips in and around the Chilcotin Valley. There are several packed and marked trails for novice and intermediate skiers, and miles of virgin snow on the logging roads. The average snow depth is 2 to 3 feet. Guides are available for a variety of trips, and participants are expected to bring all their own equipment. The road into the area is all-weather gravel, covering 60 miles to the ski area from Williams Lake. **Cost:** On request. **When:** Winter months. **Contact:** TH Guest Ranch, Hanceville, BC Canada V0L 1K0; phone (604)394-4263.

A Visit to Valhalla: The village of New Denver, in east central British Columbia, is the starting point for ski trips in the Valley of the Valhallas lasting anywhere from 1 to 4 or more days. A dormitory-style center in town and an alpine cabin in the back country enable skiers to make either day trips or extended sojourns. Guides familiar with the area have their own itineraries or will design one to match the skier's interests. The inn features international cooking and an informal atmosphere. Ski equipment may be rented and helicopter flights can be arranged for glacier skiing. **Cost:** $45 a day for 1 or 2 days, $40 a day for 3 or more days includes 3 meals a day, accommodations, guide service, snowcat transportation to the back country. **When:** November to May. **Contact:** Valhalla Mountain Touring, Box 284, New Denver, BC Canada V0G 1S0; phone (604)358-7714.

Ontario

Weekend on Skis: Participants are invited to spend 2 days touring the Madawaska area, 70 miles northwest of Toronto. The skiing excursions, which begin in the Madawaska Kanu Camp, are for those who feel comfortable on skis and desire a true wilderness environment to traverse. Led by an experienced guide, groups travel all over the trails of Renfrew County in central Ontario. Accommodations are provided in the rustic hostels of the Kanu Camp. **Cost:** $75 includes lodging, meals, guide. **When:** January, February. **Contact:** Algonquin Waterways Wilderness Trips, 271 Danforth Ave., Toronto, ON Canada M4K 1N2; phone (416)469-1727.

EUROPE

Finland

Lapland Ski Trek: Cross-country skiers explore the Saariselka fell area of Finland on an 8-day trip. After the trip from Helsinki to Ivalo, by train and bus or by plane, participants spend 4 days traveling about 12 miles a day, staying overnight in modest huts. Most of the area is treeless and the slopes are generally of moderate difficulty. Participants should be in good physical condition and willing to share the cooking. **Cost:** $450 by air from Helsinki; $362 by bus and train. **When:** February to April. **Contact:** Globaltravel Ltd., Yrjonkatu 8A, 00120 Helsinki 12, Finland; phone 171 202.

Norway

Skiing the Norse Way: Norway provides many schools and touring routes for winter ski enthusiasts. The climate of the country is varied, from the sunny south coast up to the northernmost province beyond the Arctic Circle, with most terrain suitable for day and night skiing.

Skiers outfitted with small day packs break trail across a meadow in the Cascades; some trip operators also take skiers on longer trips involving instruction in overnight camping techniques. (Keith Gunnar)

The main concentration of ski centers is in the mountain ranges along the 2 principal railroads between Oslo and Bergen and between Oslo and Trondheim. Several other ski centers are located in the province of Telemark. Many towns and villages provide floodlighting for evening runs on ski trails. Instruction is available in the art of ski waxing, as well as ski maneuvering and safety procedures. Norwegian ski schools operate throughout the country at sites that include Beitostolen, Geilo, Oslo, Rauland, Rjukan, Tretten, Tyin, Vinstra and Voss. **Cost:** On request. **When:** Winter months. **Contact:** Norwegian and Swedish National Tourist Offices, 75 Rockefeller Plaza, New York, NY 10019, USA; phone (212)582-2802.

Scandinavian Touring Trails: Advanced and beginning skiers can join a 15-day cross-country ski trip to Norway. After a brief stay in Oslo, skiers hop a train to Lillehammer for 5 days of gliding along hundreds of miles of maintained trails. Skiers can remain in the hotel area for low-level ski paths or take a bus to high mountain trails, including the one on Nordseter-Sjusjoen that offers adventurers 12½ miles of downhill skiing via a restored medieval farm village. The next 5 days find participants skiing above timberline and staying at an alpine hotel. Returning to Oslo, skiers can explore the city or ski the hundreds of miles of greenbelt surrounding it. At the Holmenkollen Festival, an international event, the group sees the finest nordic skiers compete and all have a chance to enter Holmenkollmarsjen, a family-style cross-country race with a huge smorgasbord lunch at the halfway point. Skiers observe the giant ski jump competition along with 70,000 other spectators before returning to Seattle. **Cost:** $1,130 from Seattle includes accommodations, guide, most meals, transportation. **When:** February. **Contact:** REI Adventure Travel, Inc., 1525 11th Ave., Seattle, WA 98122, USA; phone (206)322-7800. *(M)*

Nordseter Ski Touring: Two weeks are spent skiing remote areas of Norway in late winter. The first skiing is done in the area of Lillehammer, on the great municipal ski track system and in the nearby mountains of Nordseter. The trip then moves on to Rondane National Park, where skiers travel from hut to hut, trying out new trails and watching for wildlife, including the frequently sighted wild reindeer. **Cost:** $1,150 includes food, transportation within Norway, accommodations. **When:** March. **Contact:** Royal Gorge Nordic Ski Resort, P.O. Box 178, Soda Springs, CA 95728, USA; phone (916)426-3793.

Viking Ski Trips: Both the experienced skier and the novice take part in a 2-week trip in Norway. Two members of a Norwegian hiking club guide a small group of skiers on daily excursions and overnight tours. Skiers can learn Norwegian touring techniques from the guides as well. Club huts or lodges provide base camp for the touring party in at least 3 areas—Finse, Hardangervidda on the Oslo-Bergen railroad, Gjendesheim in the Jotunheimen mountains and Rondvassbu in the rolling Rondane National Park. The trip is led by a guide from the United States and leader approval is required for participation. **Cost:** On request. **When:** March. **Contact:** Sierra Club Outing Dept., 530 Bush St., San Francisco, CA 94108, USA; phone (415)981-8634. *(M)*

Nordic Skiing: Cross-country skiers tour idyllic mountain terrain on a 16-day trip which begins with a few days of sightseeing in Oslo. The group then travels by train to Lillehammer for 8 days of skiing in the area. After a day of rest, skiers may compete in the famous 33-mile Birkebeiner'n Ski Marathon from Lillehammer to Rena. Participants then proceed to Geilo in the Bergen Mountains for a few more days of skiing. A day's visit to Bergen concludes the trip. Accommodations while ski touring are in fully equipped mountain huts scattered a day's skiing apart. **Cost:** On request. **When:** March. **Contact:** Travel Exploration, P.O. Box 17641, Denver, CO 80217, USA. *(M)*

Switzerland

Ski Mountaineering from Galenstock: Participants take a 7-day course in European ski touring. From the foot of the Galenstock, groups climb a peak in the Furka area, just east of the famous Jungfrau range. After a day of instruction and practice, groups return to their hut, where slide shows and lectures are used to teach snowcraft, avalanche safety, navigation, weather and first aid. Three levels of touring are available: easy touring, including visits to Winterhorn, Kleines Buelenhorn, Kleines Furkahorn, Tiefenstock and Stotzigen Firsten; intermediate touring, with a more intensive treatment of the above; and high-alpine tours, which include further instruction in glacier knowledge, crevasse rescue, rope work and uses of crampons and ax. **Cost:** $352. **When:** January to April. **Contact:** Alpine Sportschule Gotthard, 6490 Andermatt, Switzerland; phone (044) 6 77 33.

Traversing the Alps: An 18-day trip takes a small group of skiers along the Haute Route, a famous ski touring route through the Alps. Stretching more than 80 miles past great alpine peaks from Saas Fee to Chamonix, the route crosses 11 glaciers and makes ascents and descents totaling over 65,000 feet. Lodging immediately before and after the trip is in hotels; while on the trail, skiers stay in mountain huts and lodges. The trip is led by an English-speaking Swiss guide. **Cost:** $975 includes local transportation, group equipment, food, accommodations, guide. **When:** April. **Contact:** Liberty Bell Alpine Tours, Mazama, WA 98833, USA; phone (509)996-2250. *(M)*

SOUTH AMERICA

Argentina

Andean Ski Touring: A 3-week trip to the eastern slope of the Argentine Andes provides an opportunity for ski touring during the middle of the northern hemisphere summer. Group members fly from California to San Carlos de Bariloche, a small city about 500 miles south of Santiago, Chile. Skiing can be done either on the new municipal track system or in the surrounding Nahuel Huapi National Park, about the size of Yellowstone. The trip is suitable for all levels of cross-country skiers. **Cost:** $1,775 includes transportation from Los Angeles or New York, food, accommodations, guide. **When:** July. **Contact:** Royal Gorge Nordic Ski Resort, P.O. Box 178, Soda Springs, CA 95728, USA; phone (916)426-3793.

Chile

Summer Skiing: Located at an altitude of 10,000 feet, Portillo offers a variety of natural ski slopes. A 2-week program begins in Santiago, followed by a week of skiing in Portillo and finally 6 days in Lima. In the mountains it snows considerably between June and September, and in September and October the fields are covered with powder and hard snow. A hard base of 18 feet and 2 to 4 inches of powder cap await skiers. **Cost:** On request. **When:** June to October. **Contact:** Traveling Taj, Inc., 420 Lexington Ave., Suite 2609, New York, NY 10017, USA; phone (212)687-3717.

UNITED STATES

Alaska

Kenai Heliskiing: From a base of operations at Girdwood, 40 miles southeast of Anchorage, skiers can

Instruction in skiing is usually conducted in small classes, like this women's seminar in the Sierra Nevada Range. (Woman's Way Ski Seminars)

fly to either the Kenai or Chugach mountains for helicopter skiing. The week-long trips include slopes in excess of 4,000 vertical feet and between 80,000 and 100,000 vertical feet of skiing. Good snow is encountered about 75 percent of the time. Other custom trips can be arranged to the Talkeetna Mountains north of Anchorage, the Alaska Range and the foothills of Mt. McKinley. Summer river expeditions to Alaskan wilderness areas are also available. **Cost:** $1,500 for week-long package includes transportation from Anchorage, 2 meals a day, hotel accommodations, skiing, guides. Other rates on request. **When:** Winter. **Contact:** Far North Ski Guides, Inc., 401 E. Northern Lights Blvd., Suite 203, Anchorage, AK 99504, USA; phone (907)279-2314.

Arctic Skiing: Two different ski touring trips out of Bettles are offered in Alaska's remote Brooks Range, one in the Gates of the Arctic area and the other in the Arrigetch Peaks. The first begins with a flight to a base camp on the North Fork of the Koyukuk River, making day trips to Gates of the Arctic and Mt. Doonerak. After a few days skiers travel up Ernie Creek, accompanied by dogsleds, to the Arctic Divide. Time is allowed for frequent side trips, explorations and summit ascents if desired. Finally, after reaching Ernie Pass, skiers follow the Anaktuvuk River back to Anaktuvuk Pass, returning to Bettles by air. Participants in the Arrigetch trip are flown to a base camp site near Arrigetch Valley and from that base make exploration trips with day packs. The area is rich with remnants of glacier activity. Return to Bettles is by air. **Cost:** $400 for Gates of the Arctic trip; $450 for Arrigetch trip includes transportation to and from Bettles, food, equipment, guide. **When:**

March, April. **Contact:** Sourdough Outfitters, Bettles, AK 99726, USA; phone (907)692-5252. *(M)*

Touring the Nizina Valley: A ski touring trip through the Nizina River Valley is assisted by a dog team which hauls the equipment. The 10-day trip covers about 40 miles, a pace which allows time for in-depth exploration of the countryside. Emphasis is placed on observation and interpretation of trail signs, plant identification, watching for wildlife, studying geological formations and awareness of human impact on the area. Bands of sheep and goats are commonly seen on the lower south slopes, and a careful stalk often yields good photos. The party, which is limited to 5 participants and 2 guides, flies into and out of the area from either Glenallen or Anchorage. **Cost:** $750 includes food, sled service, group equipment, guide. **When:** March. **Contact:** Wrangell Mt. St. Elias Outfitters, Dan Creek, via Glenallen, AK 99588, USA. *(M)*

Arizona

Cross-Country Skiing near Flagstaff: Participants may travel over 500 square miles of remote terrain south of Flagstaff. Setting a personal itinerary, skiers wander along 50 miles of marked and maintained ski trails, and through aspen meadows with mountain views. The 7,200-foot basin of Mormon Lake gives travelers solitude in a pristine wilderness. Accommodations in motels or log cabins can be found in the town of Mormon Lake. Rental equipment and group instruction are available. Moonlight trips are also offered. **Cost:** $8 a day for rental equipment, $10 to $24 for lodging. **When:** December to February. **Contact:** Mormon Lake Ski Touring Center, Mormon Lake, AZ 86001, USA; phone (602)354-2240.

California

Skiing El Dorado: Beginning, intermediate and advanced cross-country courses are offered in the El Dorado National Forest area, along with opportunities for guided trips. A 2-hour beginning class is designed to give an understanding of basic equipment and techniques, while a 2-hour intermediate class works on techniques of kicking, gliding and poling as well as individual problems. Fast speeds are required in the advanced class for skiers who want to refine their abilities, attack difficult terrain, race efficiently and save energy. Rental equipment is available. **Cost:** $8 for lessons, $12 for guided tours. **When:** Winter months. **Contact:** Kirkwood Ski Touring Center, P.O. Box 77, Kirkwood, CA 95646, USA; phone (209)258-8864.

Western Ski Touring: Using Tamarack Lodge as a base of operation, cross-country skiers spend 1, 2 or more days taking advantage of a variety of touring activities. Instruction is offered for the neophyte, and guided tours are available for nature lovers. For the hardy, classes and 3-day expeditions in snow camping and wilderness survival teach snow cave construction and route finding. Trails are maintained and patrolled and are suitable for all levels of ability. Children's and adults' skis, wax and non-wax, are available for rent. Reservations for all instruction, guided touring and rental are necessary. **Cost:** $7 to $20 a day for touring instruction; $10 for guided day tours; $20 to $50 for winter survival instruction. **When:** November to May. **Contact:** Mammoth Ski Touring Center, P.O. Box 102, Mammoth Lakes, CA 93546, USA; phone (714)934-6955.

Sierra Ski Mountaineering School: Mountaineers spend a week in the upper Rock Creek Canyon area of the Sierra Nevadas. Students in the group learn wilderness skiing, climbing techniques, mountain safety, equipment, how to read changes in snow and weather conditions, route selection and snow camping. Participants must be familiar with skiing over varied terrain and in many different types of snow. Little Lakes Valley and the surrounding mountains are explored, along with the upper Rock Creek area. **Cost:** $395. **When:** February, March. **Contact:** Palisade School of Mountaineering, P.O. Box 694, Bishop, CA 93514, USA; phone (714)935-4330. *(M)*

Sierra Sky and Ski: Snow lovers set their own itinerary for a combination helicopter and skiing tour of the Toiyabe National Forest area north of Bridgeport. Set in the heart of California's snow country, between Tahoe and Mammoth ski areas, Toiyabe presents skiers with some of the deepest snow in North America; each year some 37 feet of dry powder fall on Toiyabe's eastern faces. Guides with extensive ski instruction and safety patrol experience lead participants through safe yet challenging areas of the national forest. Helicopters transport skiers to otherwise inaccessible slopes, where they may take runs averaging 2 to 3 miles. Slopes are chosen with each skier's ability in mind. Accommodations may be found in the town of Bridgeport. **Cost:** $165 a day. **When:** November to June. **Contact:** Sierra Guide Service, P.O. Box 697, Bridgeport, CA 93517, USA; phone (714)932-7778.

Skiing High Plateaus: A 6-day trip traverses the rolling terrain above timberline on the Bighorn and Kern plateaus. Passing through scenic foxtail pine forests, skiers reach the plateaus and find themselves in view of Mt. Whitney, surrounded by the jagged Kaweah Range and the Great Western Divide. The route then crosses Siberia Pass to a prime skiing area near Whitney's base, where a layover day provides the opportunity to ski without a pack. Group size is limited to 6 people, who should have some nordic skiing experience. **Cost:** $200 includes transportation from Mammoth Lakes, food, equipment, guide. **When:** April. **Contact:** Sierra Ski Touring, P.O. Box C-9, Mammoth Lakes, CA 93546, USA; phone (714)934-4495.

The Sierra Snows: A variety of trips and courses is offered in the Sierra Nevada Range to cross-country skiers. Daylong courses for beginners involve few uphill stretches as students learn the telemark position, step turns, the stem christie and parallel turns. Individual lessons (with rental or owned equipment) can be arranged on a custom basis. A basic winter camping course teaches avalanche safety, route finding and wilderness survival skills during an overnight trip. More concentrated clinics are also offered in winter survival and avalanche safety. Longer trips include a 5-day trans-Sierra traverse and custom designed outings. **Cost:** $12 for lesson with rental, $45 for overnight course; other rates on request. **When:** Winter. **Contact:** Sonora Mountaineering, 171 N. Washington St., Sonora, CA 95370, USA; phone (209)532-5621.

Skiing among the Sequoias: Yosemite National Park is the setting for a variety of 2- to 4-day ski touring camps. Departing from the mountain school at Yosemite, students may take a 3- to 5-mile ski run to a winter lodge nestled among sequoias. Participants may need to carry the skis part of the way as the snow is very sparse in places. For skiers and non-skiers alike, an overnight experience designed to teach and offer practice in the basics of winter camping and survival is also available. Students build various types of snow shelters, including mound houses, snow caves and igloos. For more competent skiers, high intermediate-level trips are also available. Participants ski up to 9 miles at 7,500 feet with 20- to 25-pound backpacks to Glacier Point on the rim of Yosemite Valley or to a ski hut at Ostrander Lake. Participants travel for 2 or 3 days during the trips, with daily jaunts ranging from 6 to 8 miles on an unplowed road. **Cost:** $50 to $75 includes dinner, breakfast. **When:** By arrangement. **Contact:** Yosemite Mountaineering, Yosemite National Park, CA 95389, USA; phone (209)372-4611, ext 244.

Colorado

Castle Creek Cross-Country: The historic ghost town of Ashcroft is the site of a variety of cross-country skiing experiences including guide service and instruction. With more than 20 miles of groomed trails, skiers can spend a half-day, a day, an overnight or a longer period of time in either a program of instruction or simply exploring. Beginners spend a half-day learning basic exercises on prepared tracks, eventually journeying into the heart of the valley. Instruction on trails of

Learning to cross-country ski can be a simple matter of getting into the mountains with a knowledgeable friend, or taking advantage of organized lessons. (Christian Kallen)

greater length gives intermediate skiers more challenge during a day-long tour. The high country tour is ideal for those who have thoroughly mastered prepared trails and are looking for fresh snow and the unexpected. After warming up on valley runs, cross-country enthusiasts travel to more challenging terrain. The overnight tour provides participants with dinner cooked over a wood stove and accommodations in a cabin at the end of the valley. Weather and snow conditions permitting, tours can be arranged for a minimum of 6 persons to the Toklat Chalet, a private mountain hut near timberline at the gateway to Pearl Pass. The guide service can plot ski tours in Hayden, Star or Cooper bowls or guide skiers to Crested Butte. Private lessons are also available. Free transportation is provided to and from Aspen. **Cost:** $11 to $35 depending on program includes transportation from Aspen; $4 for daily trail fee; $20 an hour for private lessons for 1 or 2 people. **When:** Winter months. **Contact:** Ashcroft Ski Touring Unlimited, P.O. Box 1572, Aspen, CO 91611, USA; phone (303)925-1971.

Collegiate Skiing and Mountaineering Course: A 21-day course provides experience in cross-country skiing, ice climbing, igloo building and snow cave digging. Training is also given in winter first aid and avalanche forecasting. Since groups are formed by skill level and non-skiers receive special attention, the training is particular-

On day or overnight high country tours offered by Ashcroft Ski Touring, participants who have mastered touring on prepared trails can forge new routes of their own across open terrain in the Rockies. (Carol Baker)

ly valuable to complete novices. The course is given at a mountain center west of Leadville in the Collegiate Range. Travel is entirely on skis and packs are heavy. Following the training phase, participants make an alpine expedition, a solo and a marathon on skis. A shorter 10-day course is similar in content, providing a condensed version for people with limited time. **Cost:** $625 includes equipment, meals, instruction. **When:** January to April. **Contact:** Colorado Outward Bound School, 945 Pennsylvania Ave., Denver, CO 80203, USA; phone (303)837-0880.

Tennessee Pass Winter Survival: Eighty hours of instruction are offered during an 8-day cross-country skiing and winter survival camp on Tennessee Pass northwest of Leadville, Colorado. Taught by 4 experienced instructors, participants learn cold weather survival techniques such as building survival shelters, detecting avalanche slopes and conditions, treating hypothermia and route finding. Clothing, equipment, pacing and rhythmic breathing, and expedition behavior are also discussed. Instruction in cross-country skiing is enhanced by the fine alpine skiing conditions in the heart of the Collegiate Range. Special tents and equipment allow for comfortable living regardless of temperature on the 10,500-foot Tennessee Pass. A certificate of training is issued to each person completing the course. University credit is available. **Cost:** $178. **When:** January. **Contact:** Iowa Mountaineers, 30 Prospect Pl., P.O. Box 163, Iowa City, IA 52240, USA; phone (319)337-7163.

Lodging in the San Juans: A lodge deep in the San Juan Mountains near the mining town of Silverton serves as a base for cross-country skiing trips. Stays of any length can be arranged. The rustic lodge, wood-heated and kerosene-lit, supplies dormitory-style accommodations, community meals and customized instruction and guide service; equipment can be rented as well. Skiers leave their cars about a mile from the lodge and ski or snowshoe in along a route which novices can handle. Once at the lodge participants can choose from a variety of day trips or lessons, or can explore the region on their own. Discounts are available for large groups. **Cost:** $25 a day includes food, accommodations, instruction. **When:** November to April. **Contact:** St. Paul Cross-Country Ski Lodge, Box 463, Silverton, CO 81433, USA.

Skiing at Vail: Skiers may avail themselves of 163 miles of skiing terrain in White River National Forest for a wide range of ski touring. Beginning, intermediate and advanced classes teach such subjects as backcountry skiing, powder skiing, racing and downhill techniques. Tours range in difficulty from an easy glide through the golf course to a challenging run down a mountain slope. All-day classes start with a lesson in the morning and move to an afternoon tour, which ranges from short and easy for the beginner to long and arduous for the advanced. Lessons and touring may also be taken separately. Lessons are given at a ski school near Golden Peak. **Cost:** $10 for half-day classes or touring, $13 for 1 day. **When:** Winter. **Contact:** Ski School at Vail, P.O. Box 819, Vail, CO 81657, USA; phone (303)476-3239.

Idaho

Sawtooth Ski Touring: Galena Lodge offers skiers over 37 miles of trails through the Sawtooth National Recreation Area. Marked trails, prepared and unprepared tracks, trail maps and information are all available. In addition, guided day tours, moonlight tours, overnights, historical and powder terrain tours are offered. Tours may be on or off trails; the length and location of any tour depends on the ability and stamina of the group. Participants may also receive instruction in basic ski touring, advanced touring, free-style powder skiing, telemark technique and backpack skiing. Accommodations are at the lodge, and rentals are available. **Cost:** $20 for day tours, $8 for moonlight tours, $40 for overnight expeditions; $15 for private, $10 for group tour. **When:** December to March. **Contact:** Galena Lodge Touring Center, Ketchum, ID 83340, USA; phone (208)726-4010.

Sawtooth Ski Huts: Ski tours designed to fill the needs of skiers from beginner to expert are offered in the Sawtooth Mountains. A series of ski huts is located in an isolated wilderness where no motorized vehicles are allowed. The huts are from 5 to 11 miles apart. Planned tours are geared to the abilities of individual skiers and to the time they wish to spend at each hut. The terrain is varied to provide each skier with the type of touring he or she likes best, from flat meadows to 1,500-foot powder bowls. Each hut is warm and roomy, offering comfortable bunks and wood stoves. **Cost:** On request. **When:** Winter. **Contact:** Leonard Expeditions, P.O. Box 98, Stanley, ID 83278, USA; phone (208)774-3656.

Maine

Eastern Upland Trails: Cross-country skiing enthusiasts follow trails that lead over and around rolling hills to secluded mountain ponds and streams in western Maine. Over 30 miles of ski touring trails wind through the area, with difficult hillside routes available for more experienced skiers. Trails originate at a ski barn and are well marked and graded according to levels of ability. Lunches are available, and accommodations can be arranged in nearby log cabins. **Cost:** $6 a day for rental equipment, $2 for trail fees, $3 for guided tours. **When:** Winter months. **Contact:** Deer Farm Touring Center, Kingfield, ME 04947, USA; phone (207)265-2241.

Fly-in Ski Tour Expedition: Participants explore the famed Allagash Wilderness Region on a 10-day wilderness ski trip. After meeting in Greenville, members of the expedition ski 15 miles to a camp for a few days of orientation. Then the group is flown into the Allagash region and spends the next 5 days skiing from Churchill Pond to Chesuncook Lake, approximately 60 miles. Gear is transported in small backpacks and by sled. Travel is primarily by ski, although snowshoes may be used as conditions warrant. The group covers about 10 miles each day, crossing frozen lakes and streams. Camp is set up well before dark to allow for meal preparation and a bit of exploration. There is abundant wildlife to observe such as moose, martens and eagles. The trip is open to all intermediate skiers over 18 who are in good physical condition. Participants must provide their own clothing, sleeping bags and most of their own ski equipment, although rentals are available. **Cost:** $475 includes transportation, meals, guides, special instruction, some equipment. **When:** January, February. **Contact:** Overland Rolls, 1 Center St., Brunswick, ME 04011, USA; phone (207)725-5119. ***(M)***

Skiing Sunday River: The Sunday River ski area north of Portland, Maine offers individuals and family groups 25 miles of marked and maintained ski touring trails. Individualized instruction is available to skiers at all proficiency levels; equipment and accommodations can also be rented. At night, participants can ski by the light of kerosene lamps on the area's trails. Downhill skiing is also available on the slopes of Mt. Abram, 12 miles to the south. **Cost:** $4 to $10 includes lessons. **When:** Winter months. **Contact:** Sunday River Ski Touring Center, RFD 2, Bethel, ME 04217, USA; phone (207)824-2410.

Winter Wanderings: Four winter expeditions explore the wild areas of the northeast, with an emphasis on self-reliance and environmental concern. The shortest is a 4-day trip leaving from Boston which skis the Gulf Hagus region of Maine, spending nights in remote lodges. A 6-day trip for those involved in outdoor education and related fields offers skiing and camping in Maine and includes intensive training in navigation, leadership skills, first aid, winter ecology and similar subjects. A skiing and climbing trip teaches snow and ice climbing, geology, snow condition evaluation and other skills during a 7-day trip in the White Cap-Baker Mountain area. Participants on a 10-day expedition spend 3 days at a base camp preparing for the ski trip into the remote Allagash River area. On all trips some previous experience is helpful. **Cost:** From $185 for 4 days to $475 for 10 days includes transportation, group equipment, food, guides. **When:** January to March. **Contact:** Treeline Associates, 56 Boston St., Middleton, MA 01949, USA; phone (617)774-6536.

Massachusetts

Down on the Farm: A converted farm set on 700 acres of rolling terrain in the Berkshire Hills offers ski touring all winter. Beginners and experts can ski 25 miles of groomed trails for a small usage fee. Courses for the novice, expert or instructor are run on a regular basis. A dormitory-style lodge accommodates as many as 30 skiers, and small, wood-heated cabins are situated through the countryside for overnight trips. Among the other facilities are a complete rental and sales center and a restaurant; snowmobiles are forbidden. **Cost:** $3 a day for trail use; $20 a night for lodging includes 2 meals; other rates on request. **When:** Winter. **Contact:** Cummington Farm Ski Touring Center, South Rd., Cummington, MA 01026, USA; phone (413)634-2111.

Minnesota

North Star Ski Trips: Members of the North Star Ski Touring Club may join a wide array of weekend cross-country ski trips originating at various points in Minnesota. The events include clinics and trips to nearby states as well. A racing and touring clinic at the Environmental Learning Center near Isabella includes accommodations at dorms, food and a well-marked trail system. In addition, members may ski through Tierney's Woods during a day-long ski trip. At Bemidji participants may ski at both Buena Vista and Bemidji state parks. All 50 trips are scheduled for the winter season. North Star Club membership is required. **Cost:** On request. **When:** Winter months. **Contact:** North Star Ski Touring Club, P.O. Box 15144, Commerce Sta., Minneapolis, MN 55415, USA.

Montana

Skiers in the Sky: The area around Big Sky offers 35 miles of ski trails, with equipment rental and instruction available nearby. Passing through deep pine forests and alpine meadows, the trails range from a short beginners' trail to a 10-mile championship course. Wildlife is commonly sighted, and accommodations from resorts to campsites are found throughout the area. **Cost:** On request. **When:** Winter. **Contact:** Big Sky of Montana, P.O. Box 1, Big Sky, MT 59716, USA; phone (406)995-4211.

Skiing the High Country: A small, informal lodge/outfitter located 7,000 feet up the side of Cable Mountain offers 2- to 5-day ski touring trips through the surrounding alpine terrain. The recommended format is for a group of friends to organize the trip, but the outfitter can also try to match up individuals of similar ability if desired. The group size is limited to 6, which allows for intense, individual instruction in camp location and pitching, reading avalanche danger, route finding and skiing techniques. It is a fairly strenuous trip, and there is almost always some avalanche danger. The trip may be combined with a stay in guest cabins at the lodge, which are remnants of a turn-of-the-century gold-mining community. Instruction is offered there in all facets of winter mountain travel, from ski mechanics to the physics of snow. **Cost:** $20 a day for individuals in groups, $50 a day for private guide service includes food, some equipment, guide. **When:** Winter months. **Contact:** High Powder Mountaineering, Southern Cross, Anaconda, MT 59711, USA; phone (406)563-7630.

Ski Smorgasbord: A variety of options for the cross-country skier are offered out of a ranch near Big Sky. Bordering the Spanish Peaks Primitive Area, the ranch is the nucleus of a network of groomed and ungroomed trails ranging in length from 3½ to 8 miles. Daily guided trips into Yellowstone National Park and overnight trips to a nearby cabin are also offered. Rentals and self-guided trip outfitting are among the other services available. **Cost:** On request. **When:** Winter. **Contact:** Lone Mountain Ranch, Box 145, Big Sky, MT 59716, USA; phone (406)995-4644.

A cross-country ski race can be run by skiers at widely differing levels. Many of the participants are more interested in enjoying the terrain than in finishing quickly. (Keith Gunnar)

New Hampshire

Winter Skills for Women: A 10-day course teaches winter camping and ski mountaineering to women 30 and older. The course seeks to provide a sense of personal accomplishment and self-knowledge in addition to introducing participants to survival skills. Skills taught include camping in sub-zero temperatures, snowshoeing, ski mountaineering, fire building, and map and compass navigation. A canoeing course is also scheduled for May. **Cost:** $450 includes equipment, instruction; financial aid is available. **When:** February. **Contact:** Dartmouth Outward Bound Center, Box 50, Hanover, NH 03755, USA.

Skiing in the East: Teenaged ski novices and more seasoned enthusiasts spend 2 to 4 days on cross-country ski tours in the White Mountains of New Hampshire, or choose weekend jaunts to major downhill ski areas such as Burke Mountain or the Stowe Ski Area in Vermont. On cross-country trips participants learn the rudiments of ski techniques and winter camping while traveling on wilderness trails and spending nights either in warm backcountry huts or in tents. On the downhill skiing trips group members get in 2 full days of skiing, staying overnight Saturday at a ski dorm and arriving back in Boston on Sunday evening. No experience is required for the downhill weekends, but for the cross-country trips group members should have 2 days of previous summer camping experience. Lessons and equipment rentals are available at all the downhill ski areas. **Cost:** $40 to $75 includes guides, some meals, pre-trip accommodations for out-of-town participants, transportation from Boston. **When:** January to March. **Contact:** N & N Enterprises, Inc., Box 438, Allston, MA 02134, USA; phone (617)783-3568.

Waterville Valley Touring: A ski touring center in New Hampshire's Waterville Valley offers lodging and instruction as well as a trail network for cross-country skiers. The trail system, over 35 miles long, has portions graded from easy to difficult, with most routes making a loop so skiers rarely retrace their tracks. All trails are groomed and patrolled, with untracked skiing in the White Mountain National Forest. The trails wind through a variety of settings such as open fields, old logging sites and thick woods. Various services besides use of the trails are offered; included are skiing instruction, rentals, retail shop, lodging packages and, occasionally, workshop-type outings with the U.S. Cross-Country Ski Team. **Cost:** $3 a day for trail use, rentals from $8 a day for boots, skis and poles. **When:** Winter months. **Contact:** Waterville Valley Ski Areas, Box SV, Waterville Valley, NH 03223, USA; phone (603)236-8311.

New York

Nature Study Ski Tours: While skiing for 5 days in the northern Adirondack Mountains, participants gain an increased understanding of the natural world. Led by 2 guides, participants learn about the flora and fauna in the area, the history of the forest, and the calls of wintering birds, as well as wilderness skills. Beginning and experienced skiers find excellent skiing conditions on miles of snow-covered paths, old forest roads, open meadows and thickly iced lakes. Participants explore the nearby 18,000-acre St. Regis Canoe Area, a part of the Adirondack Forest Preserve. Skiers may silently come upon many kinds of wildlife including deer, bobcats, bears, foxes, coyotes, otters, minks, fisher and pine martens, beavers, and many of the 25 to 30 species of birds that winter in the Adirondacks. Fireside evening programs feature distinguished Adirondack writers, photographers, ecologists, conservationists or historians discussing subjects such as geology and conservation. Toward the end of the week there is an optional ski and snowshoe climb of 2,800-foot St. Regis Mountain. Equipment rental and instruction are available. **Cost:** $325 includes roundtrip transportation from Saranac Lake, guides, instruction, equipment use, meals, accommodations. **When:** December to March. **Contact:** Adirondack Ski Tours, Box 934, Saranac Lake, NY 12983, USA; phone (518)891-1080.

Cross-Country Skiing in the Adirondacks: Several hundred acres of cross-country skiing and hiking terrain are available to people who stay at a quiet farmhouse nestled in the heart of the Adirondack Mountains near the Olympic Village of Lake Placid in upstate New York. Certified instruction is available and for the more adventurous or experienced there is an extensive trail system and miles of untracked wilderness. "Bark Eater" is both the English translation of the Indian word "adirondack" and the name of the lodge. Accommodations are especially suited to families and small groups. Home-cooked meals, some done on an old wood stove, are served to skiers, and evenings are spent sitting around the fireplace or out skiing or walking in the moonlight. Mt. Marcy, Mt. Van Hoevenberg and Whiteface Mountain are a few of the peaks that people see in the area. **Cost:** $8 to $12 a day for trips, $195 a week (double occupancy) includes most meals, accommodations, trail use. **When:** Year-round. **Contact:** Bark Eater Lodge, Alstead Mill Rd., Keene, NY 12942, USA; phone (518)576-2221.

Ohio

Cross-Country East and Midwest: Cross-country beginners or enthusiasts can take lessons and tours at the Brecksville Reservation of the Cleveland Metroparks in Ohio, or travel to New York for a weekend of skiing in Allegheny State Park. The terrain at the Ohio ski center is gently rolling, and instruction is given at all levels. Group lesson rates are available upon request. Beginners can also learn to cross-country ski in the Allegheny State Park where lessons are conducted by 2 expert instructors. During the weekend trip, participants cover miles of trails winding through the hills and stay overnight in cabins. **Cost:** $6 to $8 daily for lessons in Ohio; $65 for Allegheny trip includes food, ski rentals, transportation, accommodations, lessons; deductions available if participants provide their own food, skis, or transportation. **When:** February for Allegheny trip. **Contact:** Wilderness Trails, 728 Prospect Ave., Cleveland, OH 44115, USA; phone (216)696-5222.

A 35-mile-long trail system winding through open fields, woods and old logging sites can be skied from a touring center in New Hampshire's Waterville Valley. (Waterville Valley Ski Touring Center)

Oregon

Ski Lessons for Women: Women can learn cross-country skiing via a series of lessons and cross-country trips designed for and by women. A 3-lesson package combines classroom instruction in Portland with skiing sessions on Mt. Hood. Skiers may also enjoy weekend cross-country trips on Mt. Hood. **Cost:** $35 for the 3-lesson series; $35 to $60 for weekend trips includes camping equipment, food, lodging. **When:** January to April. **Contact:** Keep Listening, Box 446, Sandy, OR 97055, USA; phone (503)622-3895 or (503)287-0380.

Winter Touring: Cross-country ski trips of 1 to 4 days travel through the winter landscapes of southern Oregon. The trips take place either in the vicinity of Crater Lake or around Sky Lakes. The trips may be tailored to any level of skier: fast-moving trips that cover a good deal of ground are offered for experienced skiers, and for beginners the trips may include instruction and appropriate pacing. Skiers may either camp out or stay overnight in lodges. **Cost:** $150 for 4-day trip includes equipment, food, transportation, guide. **When:** Winter months. **Contact:** Rogue River Outfitters, 8890 Rogue River Hwy., Grants Pass, OR 97526, USA; phone (503)582-1672. *(M)*

Utah

Winter Skiing Expedition: Guides instruct participants in a variety of wilderness skills on outings of varying lengths through the scenery around the High Uintas Range, the Kaibab Plateau overlooking Grand Canyon, the 10,000-foot Markagunt Plateau at Cedar Breaks and the Aquarius Plateau with vistas across Kaiparowits and into Colorado. Participants ski while sleds pulled by dogs carry equipment. Large white-walled miner's tents warmed by wood-burning stoves are used during the 2-day to 2-week outings. Groups are kept to a maximum of 10 people. **Cost:** On request. **When:** On request. **Contact:** Gypsy Wind Expeditions, 16601 Estralita Dr., Sonora, CA 95370, USA.

Vermont

Inn to Inn Ski Touring: Accompanied by guides, cross-country skiers cover 35 miles while traveling to 4 country inns in northern Vermont. Skiers meet at Long Run Lodge in Lincoln to begin the journey. Luggage is transported by jitney to the next night's lodging while skiers traverse the spine of the Green Mountains. For the second night ski tourers stay at the classic Chipman House in the mountain valley town of Ripton. From the Middlebury Snow Bowl in Ripton the trail winds around the west face of Worth Mountain until it descends to the Sucker Brook Trail. A long downhill run brings participants to the Blueberry Hill Farm to spend the night. On the next day skiers circle Hogback Mountain, then descend west into rolling terrain and hemlock forests to follow a long gradual downhill to the final evening's stay at Churchill House Inn. The skiers eat country foods from around the world while staying in the farmhouses and inns. Participants should be intermediate or better in touring skills. **Cost:** $192 from Lincoln includes transportation, luggage jitney, meals, accommodations, guide. **When:**

Five Oregon mountain adventures

including year-round skiing

Whatever your favorite mountain sport, Oregon has a peak or three to match.

The parent range of Mt. Hood, Mt. Jefferson and the Three Sisters, the Cascades divide Oregon from north to south. The Siskiyous in southeast Oregon include Mt. Ashland, a downhiller's paradise. Noted for cool, pine woods and quiet meadows, the Blue Mountains stretch across east central Oregon. An extension of the Blue Mountains, Elkhorn Ridge includes Anthony Lakes Resort, known locally as "Little Switzerland." In Oregon's northeast corner, the rugged Wallowas hide some 60 fish - filled lakes. And in southeast Oregon, the dramatic Steens Mountains abound with wildlife.

DOWNHILL SKIING

Mt. Hood offers North America's only year-round skiing. Short lift lines and uncrowded slopes are also available at 12 other resorts including Mt. Bachelor, Anthony Lakes Resort, Mt. Ashland, Multorpor Ski Bowl, Hoodoo Bowl and Spout Springs.

CLIMBING

From rock climbing to challenging ice climbing in the Cascades and Wallowas, Oregon's mountains accommodate every type of climber.

CROSS COUNTRY SKIING

No state surpasses Oregon's cross country skiing opportunities ranging from magnificent alpine wilderness touring to groomed trails.

BACKPACKING

Ideal territory ranges from moist, lush valleys to drier pine country and spectacular alpine wilderness.

SNOWMOBILING

The Blue and Wallowa Mountains are especially well suited with little underbrush and wide open areas.

EASY ACCESS

Eight regularly scheduled airlines serve Portland. Connecting service is available to Eugene and Medford, making it easy to reach the state's popular mountains any time of the year.

FREE TRAVEL GUIDE

. . . For more information, send for a free Oregon Master Travel Guide. Write: Travel Information Section / Room 7048 / Dept. of Transportation / Salem, OR 97310.

Winter months. **Contact:** Blueberry Hill, Goshen, VT 05733, USA; phone (802)247-6735.

New England Ski Touring: Cross-country skiers have access to 22 miles of trails in the Green Mountains while staying at a 19th-century inn. On day trips participants ski by ponds and through meadows on trails marked for the novice, intermediate and expert skier. Winter wildlife is abundant in the area and skiers occasionally see coyotes. Guide services, instruction and rental equipment are available at the inn, which is located along the Vermont Ski Touring Trail. **Cost:** $8 a day includes ski equipment. **When:** January to March. **Contact:** Churchill House Inn, RFD #3, Rt. 73E, Brandon, VT 05733, USA; phone (802)247-3300.

Ski Tips: Participants learn basic ski techniques in a weekend of skiing. Short trips over flat fields and gentle bumps follow each session of instruction. Small hills and trails provide more advanced terrain as competence increases. Students learn how to fall, slide, step turn and snowplow, as well as how to handle a variety of short tours. A special series of instruction is scheduled for those 50 years of age or older. Accommodations are provided at a farmhouse lodge in Gassetts near Chester. **Cost:** $98 for weekends, $239 for full weeks. **When:** January to March. **Contact:** Hike-Skitour Vermont, RFD 1, Chester, VT 05143, USA; phone (802)875-3631 or 875-3613. *(M)*

Cross-Country Skiing in New England: Complete facilities are provided for the cross-country skier on a variety of guided and self-guided trips near a mountain lodge in New England. The trail system spreads across 100 acres around Kent Lake and the surrounding hills, offering a variety of terrain for all levels of ability. Rental or new equipment is available, along with an instruction program that teaches the beginner basic techniques in 1 or 2 days, or helps polish the style of the advanced skier. Fifteen miles of groomed trails and many mapped woodland trails are available, as well as nighttime guided trips. **Cost:** $115 for 5 days includes accommodations, breakfast and dinner. **When:** Winter; guided tours by arrangement. **Contact:** Mountain Meadows Ski Touring Center, Killington, VT 05751, USA; phone (802)775-1010. *(M)*

Washington

Methow Valley Tour: Skiers lodge at a mountain hut, inns and motels on a 5-day cross-country tour through the Methow Valley in the North Cascades. Luggage is carried from inn to inn by car while members ski a high route with small day packs. On the first day the group skis to a hut overlooking the entire valley; after spending the night there, participants set off downhill into Winthrop, a town with an aura of the Old West. The next 2 days are spent at a lodge where group members can enjoy 30 miles of maintained trails and a hot pool. Skiers traverse the Methow Trail on the final day, winding through forests, meadows and open hillsides on the way back into Twisp, the trip's starting point. **Cost:** $225 includes lodging, meals, guide. **When:** December to April. **Contact:** Liberty Bell Alpine Tours, Mazama, WA 98833, USA; phone (509)996-2250. *(M)*

Cascade Cross-Country: Cross-country ski touring and lessons are offered in the Cascade Mountains east of Seattle. One package, designed to raise the beginner to an advanced intermediate status, consists of dry-land equipment sessions plus lessons held on 3 consecutive weeks. Prospective participants are welcome to try out cross-country skiing on Sundays before committing themselves to lessons. Night skiing by moonlight and special midweek and weekend packages are also available. **Cost:** $28 for 3-lesson package, $10 for Sunday tryouts, $60 for full weekend, $38 for midweek. **When:** December to February. **Contact:** Mountainholm Touring Center, Easton, WA 98925, USA; phone (509)656-2346.

Wisconsin

Skiing on Blackhawk Ridge: On bluffs overlooking the Wisconsin River Valley, skiers may traverse 13 miles of trails on primary paths and 25 miles of interconnecting side trails along the 650-acre Blackhawk Ridge. A 2-mile trail, meandering over the tops of the bluffs, is excellent for beginners while a 3-mile trail, illuminated for night touring, covers a steeper route. A 7½-mile loop crosses even more varied terrain, providing challenges for the experienced skier. On the demanding trails, the difficult areas can be bypassed by beginners. The trails lead through stands of oak, hickory, maple, elm and pine. Snowshoeing is also available. **Cost:** $2 to $3 for trail use. **When:** Winter months. **Contact:** Blackhawk Ridge, P.O. Box 92, Sauk City, WI 53583, USA; phone (608)643-3775.

On Wisconsin: A weekend cross-country skiing program is offered in the Nicolet National Forest of northern Wisconsin, near the town of Eagle River. Located in a rugged, hilly area, the program includes instruction as well as guided cross-country tours of the forest and its many lakes. The program begins with dinner at the lodge on Friday night and ends Sunday afternoon. Skating, moonlight skiing, sauna, swimming, video tape instruction review and various skiing clinics are all part of the program. Fifty kilometers of trails thread through the forest, and guests may try their skill at off-trail skiing, too. Special

Mountainholm Touring Center offers ski touring lessons and trips in the Cascades, beginning at $28 for a 3-lesson package. (Keith Gunnar)

rates for midweek skiing are also available. **Cost:** $75 includes trail use, lodging, food; children's and group rates are available. **When:** December to March. **Contact:** Eagle River Nordic Ski Center, P.O. Box 936, Eagle River, WI 54521, USA; phone (715)479-7285 or 479-7122.

Ski Touring the Green Lake Trails: Marked routes used exclusively for ski touring are categorized for beginners, intermediates and experts. Plenty of level land accentuated by gentle slopes typifies the beginning trails, while intermediate trails offer stands of pine, oak, maple and cherry on terrain with some short advanced slopes. "Expert" trails include parts of other trails plus challenging steep sections along the Green Lake shoreline. The area around the ski center itself is noted for its scenic woods, nature trails, stone fences, old estate farms, tall towers and panoramic views of the lake. **Cost:** $3 includes use of trails, ski lodge, warming shelter, medical insurance. **When:** Winter. **Contact:** Green Lake Chamber of Commerce, Box 78-W, Green Lake, WI 54941, USA; phone (414)294-3231.

Wyoming

Skiing Old Faithful: A winter lodge at Old Faithful is the base for ski trips through Yellowstone National Park on a 9-day outing suitable for beginners. After meeting in Provo, Utah, participants share the cost of a van ride to Jackson, where they spend 3 nights at a lodge on the shore of Jackson Lake while skiing the area by day. Following a snowmobile trip to Old Faithful, the group stays at the lodge for 3 nights to explore the park on skis. Participants ski to frozen lakes and geyser basins and enjoy dramatic views of the silent, snowbound landscape. Bison, elk and moose are some of the winter wildlife likely to be seen. **Cost:** $185 includes accommodations, transportation from Jackson to Old Faithful, trail lunches, guide; other meals, transportation extra. **When:** Winter. **Contact:** Earthtrek Expeditions & Travel, 1540 E. Edinger, Suite D, Santa Ana, CA 92705, USA; phone (714)547-5864. ***(M)***

Jackson Hole Heli-Skiing: An experienced mountain pilot takes groups of 7 skiers to a variety of isolated runs surrounding the Jackson Hole Valley. Alpine skiers board a helicopter in Teton Village or Jackson for a ride up to peaks in the backcountry of the Wyoming Rockies. Participants ski routes never before taken and have access to more than 500 square miles of terrain in 4 mountain ranges. Extended backcountry ski tours can be arranged. All guides are trained in first aid and avalanche detection. **Cost:** $35 for initial ride, $15 for additional runs. **When:** January to May. **Contact:** High Mountains Helicopter Skiing, Box 2217, Jackson, WY 83001, USA; phone (307)733-3274. ***(M)***

Yellowstone Park Ski Touring: A number of trails are available during the Yellowstone off-season for those wishing to explore the park's terrain. A guest ranch with log cabin facilities is the base from which skiers set out cross-country. The North Fork trail begins at the ranch and follows the north fork of the Gallatin River into the Spanish Peaks Primitive Area. Views on the way in are spectacular, and there are moose, coyotes, pine martens, snowshoe hares and mountain sheep. Another trail, the Upper Geyser Basin, starts at Old Faithful and winds through a geothermal area with close views of elk and bison. It is a 5-mile trip with cutoffs available for those who want a shorter trip. The Lone Star Geyser Trail also begins at Old Faithful and climbs 500 feet to Lone Star Geyser, which erupts approximately every 3 hours. The trail goes through densely wooded hillsides and is steep in places. The loop is 9 miles and is suitable for intermediate and advanced skiers. **Cost:** $243 to $374 depending on occupancy includes cabin accommodations, meals, transportation to trail heads. **When:** Winter months. **Contact:** Lone Mountain Guest Ranch, Box 145,

Big Sky, MT 59716, USA; phone (406)995-4644.

Winter in the Park: The isolation, silence and wildlife of Yellowstone National Park in winter can be experienced on a 5-day trip. A "snow coach" transports participants 20 miles into the park, where they don skis and packs to travel about 1½ miles to a meadow where base camp is established. From this base a number of activities are pursued: instruction in ski touring, winter camping and related skills; observation of the area's bison, elk and moose herds, which move down into the geyser basins during the winter; extended ski touring through the remote countryside; and investigation of the park's geological and geothermal features. On the trip's last day another snow coach ride takes skiers to Old Faithful and the Visitor's Center where a final night is spent indoors. **Cost:** $265 includes food, equipment, instruction, transportation, guide. **When:** January. **Contact:** MARV, Box 125, Spencer, IA 51301, USA; phone (712)262-5630.

Teton Touring: A variety of half- and full-day guided ski tours gives cross-country enthusiasts the opportunity to sample some of the gentle terrain in Jackson Hole country. Leaving from Teton Village, the most basic tours begin with brief instruction in equipment care and waxing, then introduce group members to flatland, uphill and downhill touring techniques on routes through Grand Teton National Park. For more advanced cross-country skiers, 8- to 12-mile tours cover more challenging terrain; the emphasis is on downhill turning techniques in a variety of snow conditions using the telemark, parallel and step turns. The naturalist ski instructors share their knowledge of the winter environment and how it relates to the area's flora and fauna. **Cost:** $12 to $20 includes equipment, lunch on full-day tours. **When:** Winter months. **Contact:** Powderhound Ski Tours, Box 286, Wilson, WY 83014, USA; phone (307)733-2208.

Yellowstone Ski Touring: Guides offer a mixture of tours and instruction lasting a week to skiers with the skills of advanced novice or above. The trip from Bozeman, Montana to Yellowstone begins with a bus ride to West Yellowstone. From there participants travel by snow coach to the Old Faithful Snow Lodge. Based at the lodge, skiers take a series of tours into the surrounding area. Upper Geyser Basin, Cascades of the Fire Hole and Fountain Paint Pot are on the itinerary as skiers glide out to see the extensive geothermal activity and abundant wildlife. Sometimes the touring party is accompanied by local elk. Skiers find that Yellowstone in winter provides a sharp contrast to the people-filled national park in the summertime. **Cost:** $295 from Bozeman includes transportation, guides, accommodations, meals. **When:** January. **Contact:** Royal Gorge Nordic Ski Resort, P.O. Box 178, Soda Springs, CA 95728, USA; phone (916)426-3793.

Touring the Tetons: Ski touring trips of varying lengths begin at Jackson Hole and go either to the

Bridger-Teton National Forest or the Gros Ventre Mountain Range. Day-long and 5-day trips are scheduled. The trips are designed for either advanced or relatively inexperienced skiers; a certified guide provides instruction at various ability levels. Beneath 10,000-foot peaks, participants traverse snow-covered forests and ski near rivers covered with ice. Wildlife is frequently seen in the region, including moose, elk, deer and mountain goats. The ski trips are not on a fixed schedule; the outfitter takes any group of 3 or more at their convenience. Other services include climbing instruction and backcountry outfitting during the warmer months. **Cost:** $20 to $185 depending on length of trip includes camping equipment, meals, guide. **When:** December to April. **Contact:** Wilderness Expeditions, Box 1533, Jackson, WY 83001, USA; phone (307)733-3595.

Geyser Touring: Cross-country ski enthusiasts spend from 5 to 7 days touring the countryside and wilderness of Yellowstone National Park. Beginning in West Yellowstone, Montana, participants drive to Old Faithful Geyser, don their skis and tour the local basin area, including Grotto Geyser, Castle Geyser and Old Faithful itself. The next day is spent wandering in the areas of Biscuit Basin, Sapphire Pool, Morning Glory Pool, Hillside Springs, Mystic Falls and the Little Firehole River. The third day opens with a trip to Mallard Lake and continues to favorite animal haunts. The next day skiers head out to Lone Star Geyser Basin and the surrounding area. Participants visit Midway Geyser Basin on the fifth day and for those on the 7-day trip, day 6 provides an extended tour to Madison Plateau, Summit Lake and Hot Springs. The seventh day involves an exploration of the Black Sand Geyser area. **Cost:** $275 for 5 days; $350 for 7 days includes instruction, guides, lunches, lodging, transportation. **When:** December to February. **Contact:** The Wilderness Institute, 333 Fairfax, Denver, CO 80220, USA; phone (303)393-0400.

RESOURCES

Clubs and Associations

Adirondack Mountain Club
172 Ridge St.
Glenfalls, NY 12801, USA
Phone (518)793-7737

Club Washington
411 N. Washington St., Suite 302
Alexandria, VA 22314, USA
Phone (703)836-2000

Green Mountain Club
Box 94
Rutland, VA 05701, USA
Phone (802)223-3463

National Hiking and Ski Touring Assn.
P.O. Box 7421
Colorado Springs, CO 80933, USA

Ski Club of Great Britain
118 Eaton Sq.
London SW1W 9AF, Great Britain

Ski Touring Council
West Hill Rd.
Troy, VT 05868, USA
Phone (802)744-2472

United States Ski Touring Association
1726 Champa St., Suite 300
Denver, CO 80202, USA
Phone (303)825-9183

SNOWSHOEING

Snowshoes may well be the world's oldest form of winter travel. They originated several thousand years ago in northern Asia and crossed the Bering Strait with the prehistoric nomads. Shaped out of branches with tough bark and leather strips, the broad, flat footgear became the principal means of travel for North American Indians and early settlers. Snowshoes are even more widely used today, having evolved into a variety of styles made of wood and plastic for the avid winter walker.

When you strap on a pair of snowshoes, deep powder snow, drifts and steep winter trails suddenly become avenues for winter exploration. Snowshoes, fitted according to your pack load and stride, enable you to walk on snow cover by distributing your weight over a larger surface area. There are two basic designs—a short, rounded "bearpaw" style and a long, narrow shoe with a tail. Terrain, depth of snow and maneuverability determine the shape and construction of the shoe.

Snowshoes can be a versatile means of travel. The addition of crampons makes it possible to climb steep snow faces and cross icy passes. Using long, narrow shoes and a bent-knee, shuffling gait, racers have covered a mile in 5 minutes, 100 yards in 12 seconds.

If you don't want to go quite so fast, a number of snowshoeing trips and courses are offered during the winter in some of the most scenic areas of North America. Equipped with a pair of snowshoes, you can explore the pristine winter wilderness of the Colorado Rockies, the Boundary Waters Canoe Area of Minnesota or the Green Mountains of Vermont. Whether you want to go fishing, backpacking, or mountain climbing in the winter, there has never been a better way to walk on snow. □

Trips of 1 day to 2 weeks, costing as little as $12 for equipment and instruction, take snowshoers through winter environments often hard to reach by any other means. (Keith Gunnar)

SNOWSHOEING

CANADA

British Columbia

Mountain Touring from a Remote Cabin: For 1 or 2 weeks, the Kootenays in southeastern British Columbia provide participants with an opportunity to ski tour through alpine bowls, wooded trails and meadows leading to secluded mountain lakes. Participants make home base in a small log cabin near the timberline 13 miles from the nearest dwelling. Skiers with mountain skis, considerable skiing experience and some mountaineering experience can take a more difficult alpine route to the "Hermitage." Skiers take 3 days to reach the cabin and camp en route, crossing 2 passes and an extensive area of alpine country. Whether taking the high alpine route or the standard route, skiers with the necessary equipment and experience can undertake a series of ascents giving an introduction to ski and winter mountaineering. The trip can also be made on snowshoes. **Cost:** $200 a week includes guide, lodging, instruction; food, equipment, transportation extra. **When:** December to April. **Contact:** Northern Lights Alpine Recreation, Box 399, Invermere, BC Canada V0A 1K0; phone (604)342-6042.

Winter Snow Travel: A 2-day program on snow travel and winter survival techniques is held on Vancouver Island. Instruction includes winter camping and emergency shelter building, route selection, winter first aid, care and use of equipment, and avalanche safety. A winter tour on skis or snowshoes is followed by an overnight camp where theory is put into practice. Also offered is a 2-day program in winter nature interpretation. On snowshoe or ski day trips, participants observe wintering swans and elk and learn to recognize animal tracks and the early signs of spring. **Cost:** $55. **When:** February. **Contact:** Strathcona Park Lodge Outdoor Education Society, Box 2160, Campbell River, BC Canada V9W 5C9; phone Campbell radiophone operator, ask for Strathcona Lodge.

Snowshoes provide the means for backpackers to try their survival skills in winter conditions. (Kristin Tregillus)

Ontario

Winter Sports Lodge: A remote lodge above North Bay offers accommodations and guide service for snowshoers and cross-country skiers. Abandoned logging trails take skiers over hilly and level terrain, around lakes and through forests. Participants stay in wood-heated cabins. Situated at the mouth of the Red Squirrel River on the northern end of Lake Timagami, the lodge is surrounded by many miles of trails. Ski trips can be arranged on a daily basis. In late March the camp caters especially to families. **Cost:** On request. **When:** January to March. **Contact:** Wanapitei, 7 Engleburn Pl., Peterborough, ON Canada K9H 1C4; phone (705)743-3774; summer, Camp Wanapitei, Timagami, ON Canada P0H 2H0; phone Timagami Island 1-R-13 (New Liskeard). *(M)*

UNITED STATES

California

Snowshoeing and Winter Survival Class: Two days in the Sierra Nevadas provide an opportunity to learn the basics of winter survival and camping. Leaving by bus from San Rafael early on a Saturday, students cover theoretical and preparatory aspects en route and then snowshoe in to camp. While striking camp, students learn the basics of camping and snow cave construction. On Sunday morning, participants take a snowshoe walk, then break camp and head back out. **Cost:** $45 covers transportation, camp equipment, snowshoes, food, guide. **When:** Most winter weekends. **Contact:** Mountain People School, 157 Oak Spring Dr., San Anselmo, CA 94960, USA; phone (415)457-3664.

Colorado

Wilderness Snowshoeing: Both novice and experienced snowshoe enthusiasts broaden their knowledge of winter environments and snowshoeing techniques in separate 5-day courses offered near Vail, Colorado. Both courses are based in a cabin on land adjacent to the Holy Cross Wilderness Study Area. In the novice course, students tour each day through forests of lodgepole pine and return at night to the cabin for meals, discussions and sleep. The advanced course also begins at the cabin, but on the second day the group leaves for an extended tour of the vicinity, camping in tents along the way. The exact itinerary is left open so that travel may be adjusted to the participants' abilities. Additional winter mountain travel courses are scheduled when enough people are interested. **Cost:** $275 a course includes snowshoes and winter camping equipment, meals, instructors, cabin accommodations. **When:** December to April. **Contact:** University of the Wilderness, P.O. Box 1687, Evergreen, CO 80439, USA; phone (303)674-9724. *(M)*

Minnesota

Winter Travel Camp: A 3-day weekend at a winter base camp north of Ely provides opportunities for snowshoeing, dogsledding and ski touring. Instruction in any form of winter travel is available at the camp, situated near the Boundary Waters Canoe Area. Weather is

Snowshoes don't necessarily have to be bigger than you are to get you where you want to go. (Johann Mountain Guides)

usually mild. Sleeping bag accommodations are provided in heated arctic tents and tepees, and activities include moonlight skiing and listening to wolf calls. **Cost:** $90 includes meals, accommodations, equipment, instruction. **When:** March. **Contact:** Lynx Track Winter Travel, 5375 Eureka Rd., Excelsior, MN 55331, USA; phone (612)474-5190.

Winter Skills along the Gunflint: The howling of wolves can be heard by participants on a 1-week cross-country ski and snowshoe trip through the winter stillness of northern Minnesota, about 3 miles below the Canadian border. Transportation is arranged from Roseville to a cabin camp along the Gunflint Trail, within a mile of the Boundary Waters Canoe Area. Activities include a variety of guided and overnight trips. Participants may also choose to remain at the base camp to take photographs, sketch and make short excursions. No experience is necessary; informal instruction is offered in the basics of snowshoeing, skiing and winter living. The minimum age for participants is 15. **Cost:** $190 includes meals, cabins, some equipment, guide. **When:** February. **Contact:** Sierra Club Outing Dept., 530 Bush St., San Francisco, CA 94108, USA; phone (415) 981-8634. ***(M)***

New York

Winter Sports Medley: A variety of

winter sports activities is offered outside Pulaski in northeastern Oswego County. Instruction is given in snowshoe orienteering and ski touring for beginners. Activities include winter wildlife snowshoe tours with varying degrees of difficulty. Extensive use is made of state forest and wildlife management land in the area. Tours include night trips, stream fording and unmarked forest skiing. Lodging and instruction are provided at a nature center. **Cost:** On request. **When:** Winter months. **Contact:** Greater Pulaski Chamber of Commerce, P.O. Box 136, Pulaski, NY 13142, USA.

Oregon

Wilderness Snowshoeing for Women: Opportunities are available for women to join single-day snowshoeing trips in the Mt. Hood National Forest. Led by experienced female guides, the group receives basic instruction in snowshoeing and winter survival skills before exploring the wilderness area to see how plant and animal life adapt to the cold. With the freedom afforded by snowshoes, participants can travel off the trails into the deeper reaches of the forest where animals and their tracks are readily found. The most commonly sighted are deer, rabbits, marmots and birds such as ravens and jays. The trips are designed to teach women outdoor skills in a supportive, noncompetitive group. Safety and minimal impact on the wilderness are emphasized. Trips are limited to 10 participants. **Cost:** $12 includes instruction, snowshoes, leader. **When:** January. **Contact:** Keep Listening, Box 446, Sandy, OR 97055, USA; phone (503)622-3895 or (503)287-0380.

Vermont

Green Mountain Ski and Snowshoe: More than 55 miles of snowshoeing and mountaineering trails are open around and within the Green Mountain National Forest. Beginning at an elevation of over 2,000 feet, well marked and patrolled trails are suitable for skiers and mountaineers of all levels of skill. Guided tours and overnight expeditions are offered, as well as night skiing tours. Rental equipment and instruction are available in the immediate area as are meals and accommodations at a local inn. **Cost:** Free trail use. **When:** November to March. **Contact:** Mountain Top Inn, Box SC, Chittenden, VT 05753, USA; phone (802)483-2311.

Wyoming

Winter Photography in Yellowstone: Five days in Yellowstone National Park and Jackson, Wyoming are spent photographing a variety of winter scenery. Among the photogenic phenomena to be found are "ghost" trees covered with frozen steam as well as a variety of wildlife that includes bison, elk, deer, bighorn sheep and coyotes. Nights are spent at the Old Faithful Snow Lodge situated in the park. A professional photographer accompanies the group during the day, providing expert instruction. **Cost:** $185 to $233 depending upon accommodations. **When:** February. **Contact:** Wilderness Adventure, 904 Mt. Holyoke Pl., Swarthmore, PA 19081, USA; phone (215)543-4639.

DOGSLEDDING

"Gee!" yells the driver, and the sled veers to the right. "Haw!" and the sled angles left. Controlled entirely by voice, a team of 7 huskies pulls a dogsled across the frozen tundra of the Yukon. Eskimos have used dogsleds for centuries to transport hunting parties and to travel between remote Arctic villages. Even with the introduction of snowmobiles and aircraft, dog teams and sleds are still used in Alaska, the Canadian Northwest, Greenland, Finland and the northern United States.

You, too, can experience the frozen wonderland of the Eskimo, the Finnish Lapps and the early Arctic explorers whose very existence depended on a reliable team of dogs. You can explore Mt. McKinley National Park on week-long dogsledding trips, ride a reindeer-drawn sleigh through northern Lapland for 5 days or sled in Minnesota's Nemadji State Forest for a weekend. Departing from Denmark, Great Britain or New York, you can learn winter camping and survival skills and the proper handling of dog teams on 3-day to 2-week dogsledding trips in Greenland.

Dogsledding also means racing. Modern racing sleds made out of ash with aluminum runners weigh only 30 pounds. Specially bred and trained Samoyeds, malamutes and huskies pull the sleds in a "gang hitch." With a good match of dog team and musher, sleds can travel at speeds of over 20 miles an hour. The most famous race is the annual 1,000-mile Iditarod Trail Race from Anchorage to Nome; a 2-week dogsledding trip in March covers 100 miles of this trail.

Whether you bundle up in furs and practice dogsled runs in Greenland, mush through the frozen Yukon Territory near Lake Atlin or visit Eskimo villages on the Seward Peninsula, a team of trained dogs—or reindeer—will pull you into a winter experience of bright sun, vast snowfields and sub-zero camping. □

Speed competition, like this race in Switzerland's Upper Engadine Valley, is one facet of dogsledding. But sled dogs have been an important means of transport and communication for centuries in some regions. (Swiss National Tourist Office)

DOGSLEDDING

ATLANTIC

Greenland

Polar Sledding: A 10-day trip transports participants from New York to Holsteinsborg, trains them in the handling of dog teams, provides a 3-day circular run in the surrounding polar terrain and then flies them back to New York. Though the trip involves some strenuous activities and challenging conditions, all training and equipment are supplied. After arriving in Greenland, the party stays 3 nights at a hotel in Holsteinsborg where individuals are fitted in furs, learn about dog teams and attempt short practice runs with sleds. The fourth night may find participants camping outdoors, depending on how fast the group has learned skills and acclimatized. Following the preliminary training, participants begin the 3-day expedition by dogsled. After the return to Holsteinsborg, an evening is spent at a Greenlandic feast where participants may join in some local dancing. Return to New York is by air. **Cost:** On request. **When:** February to April. **Contact:** Danish National Tourist Office, 75 Rockefeller Plaza, New York, NY 10019, USA; phone (212)582-2802.

Spring Travel in the Arctic: An exploratory overnight camp and some short day trips on frozen fjords introduce participants to the art of dogsledding and arctic living. Based on Greenland's east coast, trip members spend 18 days on 2 to 3 sledding expeditions lasting several days each. Sledders traverse steep-sided fjords and travel through mountainous areas to the settlements of Angmagssalik and Kungmiut. Also included in the itinerary is a boat trip to offshore pack ice to spot polar bears. **Cost:** $3,019 includes roundtrip airfare from London, meals, lodging. **When:** March, April. **Contact:** Explore Beyond Ltd., 167 Earls Court Rd., London SW5, Great Britain; or Adventure Center, 5540 College Ave., Oakland, CA 94618, USA; phone (415)654-1879.

Northern Lights Expedition: Hardy travelers journey for 14 days along the west coast of Greenland. Starting from New York, participants fly to Denmark, then to the expedition base of Jakobshavn via a helicopter ride from Sondre Stromfjord. After 2 or 3 days at the Hvide Falk Hotel the group sets out by dogsled, traveling north. The itinerary is governed by weather conditions, but one goal of the trip is the Jakobshavn Glacier, an extraordinary ice floe that moves at 3 feet an hour and discharges millions of tons of ice into the sea daily. Participants spend most of their time on the sleds but are expected to help the Eskimo drivers on steep inclines whenever necessary. On day 14 the group returns to Jakobshavn for another couple of nights before retracing its flights back to Sondre Stromfjord, Copenhagen and New York. Participants in good condition should enjoy the challenges and rigorous activities involved in dogsledding wintry terrains. **Cost:** $2,450 plus airfare. **When:** March. **Contact:** Hanns Ebensten Travel

Inc., 55 W. 42nd St., New York, NY 10036, USA; phone (212)354-6634.

Go with the Floe: The ice and snow of southeastern Greenland are explored via dogsled on a 15-day trip. Participants fly from New York via Reykjavik to Angmagssalik, which serves as a base for 2 days of short sled trips and equipment familiarization. They then set out across the sea ice of the great fjords and frozen lakes to Tiniteqilaq and Quernertuarssuit; return to Angmagssalik is made on the fourth day. Each participant has his or her own sled, dog team and driver. In deep snow or on hills riders need to disembark and walk, so good physical condition is important. Except on the 4 days of sledding, accommodations are in hotels. **Cost:** $3,193 to $3,293, depending on date, includes transportation from New York, food, accommodations, equipment, guides. **When:** March, April. **Contact:** Lindblad Travel, Inc., 8 Wright St., Westport, CT 06880, USA; phone (203)226-8531 or tollfree (800)243-5657. *(M)*

Sledding on Greenland's West Coast: Travelers arrive by air at Sondre Stromfjord from Copenhagen and can choose 1- to 3-day dogsled trips along the island's rugged west coast. A short trip, guided by a native sled driver, takes participants along Greenland's longest road—a 9-mile journey. The road hugs the contours of the fjord, but goes essentially nowhere. A longer dogsled trip lasts 3 days and leads travelers across lakes, fjords and low mountains to Holsteinsborg, Greenland's second-largest town. At night group members stay in tents along the

Participants on a 10-day trip offered by the Danish National Tourist Office learn the rudiments of dogsledding in Holsteinsborg before embarking on an expedition across an uninhabited region of Greenland. (Danish Tourist Board)

trail. Once in Holsteinsborg the dogs get a rest and sledders take a 45-minute helicopter ride back to Sondre Stromfjord where they can catch flights to Copenhagen. **Cost:** $60 a day includes a team of huskies and a driver. **When:** Winter until approximately April. **Contact:** SAS Ski Desk, 1120 Fourth Ave., Seattle, WA 98101, USA; phone (206)682-5250.

CANADA

British Columbia

North to Alaska: For 8 days a small group lives and travels like early Alaskan prospectors and trappers. They begin at Whitehorse in the Yukon Territory and drive 110 miles to Lake Atlin where the retired early-day lake steamer *Tarahne* is beached and many vintage buildings are still in use. Participants reach the base camp at Antler Bay by ski plane. The next day participants learn about dogsledding and familiarize themselves with equipment. After practicing on short runs, the group makes a 15-mile trek to Llewellyn Glacier, part of the 1,500-square-mile Juneau Icefield, where some survival techniques are taught. On returning to Antler Bay individuals unhitch and feed their team before enjoying dinner in the log cabin. Then participants choose their own itinerary before returning to Atlin on an overnight sledding trek which al-

Dogsleds pull supplies across northern Canada's snow-covered flatlands on an 8-day Special InteresTours trip to Lake Atlin. (Keith Gunnar) lows everyone to experience the feeling of long-distance travel. On arrival, the Atlin Inn provides travelers with modern conveniences. The trip ends with an exploration of the ghost town of Discovery and a drive back to Whitehorse. **Cost:** $940. **When:** April. **Contact:** Special InteresTours, P.O. Box 37, Medina, WA 98039, USA; phone (206)455-1960.

EUROPE

Finland

Reindeer Trek: A 5-day trip begins in a northern stretch of Lapland fells. Equipment checks are run in Enontekio before the next day's departure for an uninhabited region beyond the timberline. One reindeer-drawn sleigh is provided for each participant. Lapps prepare the meals as well as instruct participants on the care of their reindeer. On the third day trekkers reach an ice-covered lake where they can try their hands at guiding reindeer over the ice. The final 2 days are spent relaxing at lodge accommodations. During the trip overnighting is done at modestly equipped wilderness cabins. **Cost:** $600 from Helsinki. **When:** March. **Contact:** Globaltravel Ltd., Yrjonkatu 8A, 00120 Helsinki 12, Finland; phone 171 202.

Reindeer Run-down: Travelers spend 4 days north of the Arctic Circle exploring the Lapp region of Finland by snow-scooter, ski and reindeer sled. The reindeer safari starts in Lulea in northern Sweden, about an hour from Stockholm by air, and includes activities such as reindeer sledding on frozen lakes, dinner and an overnight stay in a Lapp hut, and a ceremony where group members are presented with reindeer "driver's licenses" by their Lapp hosts. Hotels along the way offer group members a chance to relax with a sauna or swim in a heated pool. **Cost:** On request. **When:** Until the end of April. **Contact:** SAS Ski Desk, 1120 Fourth Ave., Seattle, WA 98101, USA; phone (206)682-5250.

UNITED STATES

Alaska

Mushing in McKinley: Individually planned dogsledding trips lasting up to several days explore Mt. McKinley National Park, which contains over 3,000 square miles of icy sawtooth mountains, rolling tundra and deep valleys. While a guide drives a dog team over the trails, participants traverse the area on skis and snowshoes, working with the musher when help is needed. Under optimum conditions in the below-zero temperatures, dog teams pull their loads of several hundred pounds for 30 miles or more a day; people as well as huskies require stamina and coordination to maintain the pace. Children are allowed to participate on the 1- and 2-day trips when they are accompanied by an adult. On a more remote trip to Lake Kantishna, group members fly into the area and ski back, supported by a dog team. Winter camping experience is suggested for those considering the journey. Participants supply their own food and personal gear. **Cost:** $100 a day includes cabins or heated tents, dog teams, guide. **When:** November to April. **Contact:** Denali Dog Tours and Wilderness Freighters, Box 1, McKinley Park, AK 99755, USA; phone (907)683-2266.

Arctic Dog Team Trek: A 100-mile segment of the Iditarod Trail, which stretches over 1,000 miles from Anchorage to Nome, is traversed during a 2-week dogsledding trip. Participants meet in Anchorage before flying to Nome, where the journey begins. For part of the trip, participants travel on cross-country skis and snowshoes. Supplies are transported by 2 dog teams, led by experienced drivers. The route crosses the Norton Sound ice pack, the taiga and tundra, ending at White Mountain where participants are flown back to Nome by ski plane. Participants, who occasionally help with dog mushing, spend the nights in trappers' cabins, tents and igloos built with the help of Eskimo guides. Wildlife in the area includes wolves, reindeer, walruses and seals. Due to temperatures as low as -20°F, participants should be in top shape and familiar with winter camping conditions. **Cost:** $1,200 includes food, accommodations, equipment, transportation, guide. **When:** March. **Contact:** Mountain Travel Inc., 1398 Solano Ave., Albany, CA 94706, USA; phone (415)527-8100. ***(M)***

Dogsledding the Iditarod Trail: Traveling as the Eskimos have for centuries, participants set off from Anchorage on dogsledding treks in the Alaskan wilderness. On trips of varying lengths group members learn from experienced mountaineers the arts of subsistence living and arctic survival. The route along the Iditarod Trail is illuminated by the aurora borealis. Trips are planned with the resources and skills of participants in mind. **Cost:** On request. **When:** January to March. **Contact:** Otis B. Driftwood Adventures Unlimited, 8701 Kathleen, Anchorage, AK 99502, USA.

Lynx Track Winter Travel takes dogsledders on trails and old logging roads through the Nemadji State Forest in Minnesota on weekend trips in February. (Lynx Track Winter Travel)

Seward Sledding: Dogsledding trips of varying lengths can be arranged on the Seward Peninsula of northwestern Alaska. Participants visit Eskimo villages, hot springs and other remote sites on the tundra or in the tree country.

The trips provide excellent opportunities for wildlife observation and photography, as well as for meeting natives of the Bering Sea coast. Travel by sled may also be combined with cross-country ski trips. All trips depart from Nome or White Mountain and are tailored to the desires of participants. **Cost:** About $100 a day per person. **When:** December to May. **Contact:** Peninsula Kennels & Exploration, Box 839, Nome, AK 99762, USA; phone (907)443-2176.

Arctic Dogsledding: A 10-day dogsledding trip travels near the Arctic Circle in wintertime. Beginning at the village of Anaktuvuk Pass in the Brooks Range, participants travel up the Anaktuvuk River. At its head, the route crosses the Arctic Divide at Ernie Pass and then follows Ernie Creek to its confluence with the North Fork Koyukuk. A base camp is set up from which trips are made into the surrounding area on skis, snowshoes and dogsleds to destinations such as the Gates of the Arctic, Hanging Glacier Mountain and Mt. Doonerak, the highest peak in the central Brooks Range. Wildlife in the area includes caribou, moose, foxes and wolves. Temperatures can get down to -25°F, so participants should be in good physical condition for the trip. There is a maximum of 2 clients for each guide and dog team. Sledders return to Bettles by ski plane. **Cost:** $995 includes roundtrip transportation from Bettles, food, equipment, guide. **When:** March. **Contact:** Sourdough Outfitters, Bettles, AK 99726, USA; phone (907)692-5252.

(M)

Minnesota

Winter Weekend Trip: A weekend trip in the Nemadji State Forest offers cross-country skiing, dogsledding and winter camping. The 3-day trip explores a wild and isolated section of the state about 150 miles north of the Twin Cities, a region of mixed hardwoods and pines. Many trails and old logging roads provide excellent dogsledding and cross-country skiing. A cabin is used for base camp, and heated arctic trail tents are provided for camping. Winter wildlife is plentiful in this beautiful and undisturbed environment. Members of the group are limited to 10 people, and should have basic cross-country skiing experience. **Cost:** $90. **When:** February. **Contact:** Lynx Track Winter Travel, 5375 Eureka Rd., Excelsior, MN 55331, USA; phone (612)474-5190.

RESOURCES

Clubs and Associations

International Sled Dog
Racing Association
Box 144
Ontario, NY 14519, USA

North Star Dog Sled Club
750 Stillwater St.
White Bear Lake, MN 55110, USA

Northern Pacific Sports
and Recreation
P.O. Box 2317
Renton, WA 98055, USA

Scott Polar Research Institute
Cambridge CB2 1ER, Great Britain

TREKKING

Few types of travel offer as many personal rewards or as much physical involvement with new cultures and environments as does trekking. Treks differ from backpacking trips in that native porters, acclimated to high altitudes and local foods, carry most of your gear. Cooks prepare all of your meals. This enables you to travel great distances for prolonged periods of time, as you hike to the tops of mountains, puff over alpine passes and explore ancient ruins otherwise accessible to only the most hardy.

Treks range from just a few days to a month or longer. A rugged 33-day trek in Tibet crosses several Himalayan passes and spends 24 days in complete isolation from the outside world. In Kenya you can join a 3-week trip by foot and camel across the Northern Frontier District, passing by the Ndoto Mountains and Lake Turkana. You might see wild boars, lynx, vultures and golden eagles on a 2-week trek through the Pindos Mountains of Greece. Or you can ride elephant-back through a jungle camp during a 4-week trek in Nepal.

You should be in good physical condition, know in advance how your body will respond to high altitudes and be prepared to get dirty and tired by the end of each day. At times even a small day pack and water bottle will weigh heavily across your shoulders as you trek to thin oxygen zones in the Himalayas or the Andes. You'll get dusty and sunburned, hot during the day and cold at night; you may sleep on a bedroll and wake at dawn to find your tent covered with ice crystals. Cold alpine streams or Inca fountains may provide your only opportunity to wash up during a 2-week trip.

Camaraderie is an important part of a trek, as the sharing of spectacular scenery, cultural encounters—and blisters—forge new friendships on any trail. You might find yourself hiking with a German alpine team, led by Peruvian guides with Huayruro porters, passing French and Swiss hikers along the way. At night, sing-ins around the campfire become an international fiesta of German, English, Spanish and Quechuan songs. After trekking in the footsteps of the Incas along their finely engineered stone paths or visiting the near-vertical world of the Hunza in Pakistan, you will return feeling as if you have been in another world. □

The rigors of high altitudes and extended foot travel make it necessary for most trekkers to rely on the assistance of native porters to help carry gear. (Keith Gunnar)

TREKKING

AFRICA

Kenya

Northern Frontier Trek: A small expedition of 8 to 12 people travels light as it treks across the Northern Frontier District for 3 weeks. Departing from Lake Baringo, the group takes a short jeep ride to the edge of the high country and proceeds by foot and camel past the Maralal Game Park and along the edge of the Ndoto Mountains. Mt. Nyiru is climbed before the final leg of the trek crosses the lava rock south of Lake Turkana. Expedition members share camp chores and function as a team. **Cost:** $1,860 includes roundtrip airfare from London, group equipment, food. **When:** May. **Contact:** High Adventure, Alan Seeger Ltd., 1 Salterns Wy., Lilliput, Poole, Dorset BH12 8JR, Great Britain; phone 0202 708471. *(M)*

Tanzania

To the Top of Kilimanjaro: Trekkers on a 12-day trip to Tanzania gain over 15,000 feet in elevation during an ascent of 19,340-foot Mt. Kilimanjaro. Participants take 5 days to make the nontechnical climb, moving slowly to acclimatize to the altitude. Accommodations are in comfortable huts along the way and porters carry all food and supplies. Lodging before and after the climb is at a hotel at the base of the peak, where wildlife safaris into the surrounding area may be arranged. No previous climbing experience is necessary, but trekkers should be in good physical condition. **Cost:** $1,750 includes transportation from the U.S., accommodations, meals at the huts. **When:** September. **Contact:** The Wilderness Institute, 333 Fairfax, Denver, CO 80220, USA; phone (303)393-0400.

ASIA

India

Kashmir Climbing and Trekking: On a hike through Himalayan valleys, travelers of all levels of experience explore peaks and hidden settlements. Depending on the location, duration and difficulty of the trip, group members may embark on journeys lasting anywhere from 6 to 30 days or more. In the lush, green Kashmir and barren Ladakh regions of India, there are several expeditionary climbs available to peaks reaching 23,000 feet. While departure points and durations vary according to group goals, treks in Kashmir Province include climbs to Kolhoi, Hormuch, Bobang and Parcha Kangri. Travelers explore and study the Buddhist monasteries of Leh, the capital of Ladakh. Climbs are also made to the Kishtwar Himalayas, typified

A 3-week High Adventure trek in northern Kenya takes hikers along the edge of the Ndoto Mountains and Lake Turkana. (High Adventure/Alan Seeger Ltd.)

by fluted ice ridges and steep rock faces. A trip to the site of the Hindu sacristy of Nanda Devi at 25,645 feet in the Gharwal Himalayas is also possible. In winter, skiing trips may also be arranged. **Cost:** $135 to $190 a day by arrangement. **When:** By arrangement; climbing from June to September. **Contact:** Adventure Tours, Hotel Shaheen, 4-Gupkar Rd., Srinagar 190001, Kashmir, India; phone 5248.

Going Tibet: An extremely rugged 33-day trek explores the remote wilderness areas of western Tibet, crossing several high passes and spending 24 days completely isolated from the outside world. Beginning in the Kulu-Manali area, trip members drive across the Rothang Pass to the village of Darcha, where the trek begins. They climb gradually to the Shingo Pass and cross the Punjab Himalaya into the moonscape of Ladakh. After passing through the hamlets of the Tsarap, Lingti and Zaskar valleys, the party enters the wilderness of the Zaskar Range and finally reaches Stok, home of Ladakh's former rulers and a center of Tantric Buddhist art. A few days are spent exploring Stok and the Indus Valley before trekkers proceed to Srinagar and the trip's end. Participants must be in superb condition to handle the trip's difficult routes on paths known only by the local shepherd/guides. **Cost:** $1,950 includes transportation, porters, food, group equipment, guides. **When:** July. **Contact:** Himalaya, 3023 Franklin St., San Francisco, CA 94123, USA; phone (415)441-2933. ***(M)***

Trans-Himalaya Trek: In the lush Vale of Kashmir, adventurers begin a 30-day journey of strenuous climbing across 3 high mountain passes, the highest being about 17,000 feet, and 3 major mountain chains. Rural Kashmir villages and Gujar nomads are found in the Warwan Valley after a crossing of the Pir Panjal Range. The Bhatkal Pass through the Great Himalayan Range leads into the drier but still fertile Suru Valley, peopled by the Baltis, Muslims of the Shia sect. Nunkun Base Camp is reached and with it views of 23,410-foot Nunkun, highest peak in the Himalayas between Nanda Devi and Nanga Parbat. The first Buddhist gompa is reached in Ladakh, often called "Little Tibet." The final range, Zaskar, is crossed by the 17,000-foot Kanji La Pass. There the trekking ends and participants continue by jeep to Leh, the capital of Ladakh. The trip ends with a return to Kashmir by road and a rest of 2 days in houseboats on Dal Lake. **Cost:** $1,775 includes accommodations, meals, guides, transportation from Kashmir. **When:** August, September. **Contact:** Mountain Travel Inc., 1398 Solano Ave., Albany, CA 94706, USA; phone (415)527-8100. *(M)*

Trekking in Lahoul: Travelers on a 26-day trip climb 4 mountain passes as they circumscribe the region of Lahoul near the Tibetan border. Flights leaving from New York take group members to New Delhi, then on to Kulu, a small Hindu village. From Kulu the expedition motors over the 13,500-foot Rohtang Pass on a road that has changed little since the days when it was a major Tibetan trade route. Taking to the trail, near Patseo, trekkers quickly approach the highest point along the route, 16,000-foot Baralacha Pass, then descend to the Chandra River. After hiking through Batal and reaching 14,000-foot Hamta Pass, participants make a short trek back to Manali in the Kulu region. With the actual trek behind them, trip members make side trips to Chandigarh, the Sariska Game Sanctuary south of New Delhi, and the Bharatpur Ghana Bird Sanctuary. The trip ends in New Delhi, where travelers catch a plane back to New York. **Cost:** $2,109 from New York includes airfare, all meals, accommodations, guides. **When:** August. **Contact:** REI Adventure Travel, 1525 11th Ave., Seattle, WA 98122, USA; phone (206)322-7800. *(M)*

Journey to Darjeeling: Nine days of trekking take participants through Raman and Sandakphu with a stay of several nights in Darjeeling. Cut into the mountainside, the village of Darjeeling is surrounded by tea gardens and fern-covered hills and affords views of peaks such as Kangchenjunga, Everest and Makalu. Visits are made en route to Buddhist shrines, monasteries and small villages. If Sikkim is opened to travelers, as it may be, a side trek is made to ancient Pamiyonche monastery and the base of Mt. Kabru, Kokhtang and Rathong. **Cost:** On request. **When:** March to

May, September to December. **Contact:** SITA World Travel, Pvt. Ltd., F-12 Connaught Pl., New Delhi, India 110001; phone 43103 or 45183.

Visit to a Small Kingdom: A group of about 15 spends 29 days exploring India and Sikkim. Several days are spent investigating Darjeeling and its environs before the 2-week visit to the state of Sikkim, a former mountain kingdom little changed for hundreds of years and relatively untouched by Westerners. Here visitors can see life as it has been lived in the Himalayas for centuries. Those wishing a shorter trip can leave after 3 weeks, before the trip makes a final week-long excursion up onto the ridge of Sandakphu and Phalut. This trek offers one of the world's great mountain vistas, a 200-mile view encompassing the entire Himalayan range from Everest to Sikkim and Bhutan. Participants must be Sierra Club members. **Cost:** On request. **When:** April. **Contact:** Sierra Club Outing Dept., Trip #565, 530 Bush St., San Francisco, CA 94108, USA; phone (415)981-8634. ***(M)***

From Paradise to Shangri-La: A group of trekkers travels from Kashmir, the "earthly paradise" of the Moghul Emperors, to Ladakh's capital of Leh, used as a model for Hilton's *Shangri-La*, on a 21-day trip involving some overland travel. After a flight from London to Delhi and a day's sightseeing there, trekkers fly to Srinagar, Kashmir for a night on Dal Lake on a houseboat. Then they drive to Pahlgam for a night's stay and set out on a week-long trek to Sanko. The route takes them up through pine forest, past glaciers and through meadows to bleak Bhutkal Pass, at 16,200 feet the gateway into Ladakh. The trek ends at Sanko; after a night there, trekkers make the 2-day drive to Leh. While staying at a yurt encampment outside town, they explore Leh's palace, monasteries and bazaar before returning by car to Srinagar. The return flight to London concludes the trip. **Cost:** $1,750 includes transportation from London, food except in Delhi, accommodations, equipment, porters, guides. **When:** July. **Contact:** Venturing, 49 Conduit St., London W1R 9FB, Great Britain; phone 01-439-6919.

Himalayan Hike: The area of Lahoul has recently been opened to travelers, who may now approach it by crossing a high mountain pass. Participants leave the forested hillsides of Kulu and enter a Buddhist culture much different from that on the other side of the pass. Travelers hike into the hills to visit monasteries, called gompas, and look down upon the flat-roofed houses of the villages below. Plentiful wild roses and other flowers

A trip offered by Himalaya ventures high into the mountains of Dolpo, a seldom-visited region of Nepal. The 32-day trek costs $1,650. (Keith Gunnar)

provide opportunities for photography. Trip members determine the trek's duration and itinerary. **Cost:** On request. **When:** June to October. **Contact:** West Himalayan Holidays, 49 Conduit St., London W1R 9FB, Great Britain; phone 01-439-4448.

Kashmir Valley Treks: A 16-day trek in the Himalayas passes through low and high terrain, from Kishtwar to Lahinwan, with camping along the picturesque river valleys of Jammu and Kashmir. The trek begins at Palmar and follows a bridle path over the Tilmil Pass. Hiking varies from zigzagging through fields and thick forests to negotiating "nullahs" or rivulets across the path. Stops are made at tea shops in the afternoons. The highlight of the trip is the route from Inshan over the Margin Pass at 12,500 feet, which means getting up at 4 a.m. to avoid the bad afternoon weather at the top. The trail is only tracks in the snow made by shepherds and their flocks. Upon arrival in Lahinwan, participants travel by coach to Srinagar via Daksum. **Cost:** $270 includes meals, accommodations, local transportation. **When:** May, September. **Contact:** Youth Hostels Association of India, 5 Nyaya Marg, Chanakyapuri, New Delhi 110021, India.

Nepal

Himalayas Trek: A group of 16 trekkers explores the Solu-Khumbu district of northeastern Nepal on a month-long journey. The trip begins with a flight from Kathmandu to Jiri, some 60 aerial miles east of the capital. From this point the trail crosses four low mountain passes in elevation from 9,000 to 12,000 feet before reaching the Dudh Kosi River in the Khumbu district. The route follows the river to Namche Bazar, once the biggest trading area between the Khumbu region and Tibet. Participants continue to the magnificent Gokyo Valley, nestled under the large peak of Cho Oyu, which is an easy scramble of about 18,000 feet. Although this is basically a hiking trip, it is strenuous due to the high altitude and many miles covered. **Cost:** $1,125 from Kathmandu. **When:** November. **Contact:** The Alpine Club of Canada, P.O. Box 1026, Banff, AB

Canada T0L 0C0; phone (403)762-4481.

Trekking to Dolpo and Phoksumdo Lake: A 32-day trek takes a small party to the fringes of the rarely visited land of Dolpo. Walking east from Jumla, participants hike up to Kagmara-la, a pass at 16,780 feet affording views of Ringmo, in the land of the Bon-Po religion that pre-dates Buddhism. Climbing past a thunderous waterfall, they pitch camp near Phoksumdo Lake. From here, several days are spent hiking in the area to observe the unique Himalayan wildlife and weathered Bon gompas that dot the region. The party then returns to Jumla via Rohagaon, Tibrikot and 2 fairly low passes. **Cost:** $1,650 from Jumla includes food, group equipment, porters, guide. **When:** October. **Contact:** Himalaya, 3023 Franklin St., San Francisco, CA 94123, USA; phone (415)441-2933. *(M)*

Gorkha Trek: A 31-day trip combines hiking through the Himalayas, rafting a whitewater river and observing wildlife near a jungle camp. After flying from New York, participants bus from Kathmandu to Pokhara to begin 15 days of hiking. Trekkers walk eastward across flower-lined ridges in the Annapurna Range to reach the town of Gorkha. Upon the hike's end the group transfers to rubber rafts for a 3-day trip down the Trisuli River. Three more days are spent at Tiger Tops jungle camp, where participants travel by native canoe and elephant-back to view wildlife. At the trip's end stops are made in India to visit the abandoned city of Fatapur Sikri, the Taj Mahal and the Chandella Temples, with their erotic carvings. Anyone physically fit and used to camping can handle the trek as the trails are in good condition, though often rough and very steep. **Cost:** $2,625 includes roundtrip airfare from New York, food, camping equipment, guides, porters. **When:** February. **Contact:** Himalayan Trekking Service, 5730 Rising Sun Ave., Philadelphia, PA 19120, USA; phone (215)342-8394.

To Everest Base Camp: Treks of 20 and 25 days from Kathmandu provide clear and close views of the world's highest mountain, known to the Nepalese as Chomolungma, Mother Goddess of the Earth. Participants walk up and down through winding terraced hillsides during the first part of the trek. Altitudes increase as trekkers pass Namche Bazar at 11,400 feet, Lobujya at 16,000 feet and Gorak Shep at 17,000 feet. Once at the base camp near the Khumbu Glacier members may climb the slopes of Kala Patar, visit Gokyo, a summer yak herders' village, or cross the South Chola Pass which has views of Everest, Makalu, Cho Oyu and the peaks that stretch into Tibet. The expedition returns to Kathmandu by charter flight from Lukla. **Cost:** $1,300 to $1,830 from Kathmandu includes transportation, food, equipment, guides. **When:** March, April, October, December. **Contact:** Mountain Travel Inc., 1398 Solano Ave., Albany, CA 94706, USA; phone (415)527-8100. *(M)*

Annapurna Trek: Travelers ride elephants, visit with villagers and trek at altitudes up to 10,000 feet during a 23-day expedition to study the cultural and natural features of Nepal. The trip begins with a flight from the United States to Kathmandu via Delhi. Highlights include an 11-day trek to explore the Annapurna region of central Nepal, with porters carrying the gear; a 3-day raft trip on the Trisuli River; and a 3-day visit to Royal Chitawan National Park to view wildlife. Trekkers have opportunities to visit religious shrines, cultural centers and bazaars in the Kathmandu Valley, as well as to study geology and plants in a Himalayan setting. Accommodations are mostly in tent camps, with a few nights spent in lodges and hotels. The trip ends with a return flight from Delhi. **Cost:** $1,490 from Kathmandu includes land transportation, accommodations, meals (except in Kathmandu), guide. **When:** March, October. **Contact:** Nature Expeditions International, 599 College Ave., Palo Alto, CA 94306, USA; phone (415)328-6572. *(M)*

In the Footsteps of Hillary and Tenzing: Two Nepal trekking itineraries beginning in Kathmandu trace the standard Everest Base Camp route from Lamosangu, a small village on the Tibetan border. For the first 2 weeks of both the 32- and 45-day itineraries, trekkers stay below 10,000 feet, crossing major ridges on the way east to the Dudh Kosi River valley which drains the Everest region. Turning north through Sherpa villages, group members climb to the yak pasture of Lobujyg at 16,000 feet; those who are acclimatizing well may climb to the summit of Kala Patar at 18,200 feet. Return is then made to Lukla, followed by a flight to Kathmandu for those on the shorter trek. Participants on the 45-day trip retrace the route from Thyangboche through Namche Bazar, Phakding and Puiyan, and continue east at Kharte. After climbing passes and visiting Rai villages in the Hongu Valley, trekkers follow the trail south through tropical countryside to Khare and the flight back to Kathmandu. **Cost:** $1,222 for 32 days, $1,703 for 45 days from Kathmandu includes accommodations

Trekkers traverse 2 major glaciers in Pakistan—Biafo and Hispar—during a 41-day trek and climb offered by Mountain Travel. The trek follows a route near some of the world's highest peaks. (Jack Turner/Mountain Travel Inc.)

in hotels or tent camps, sleeping bags, most meals. **When:** October to April. **Contact:** REI Adventure Travel, Inc., 1525 11th Ave., Seattle, WA 98122, USA; phone (206)322-7800. *(M)*

Helmu, Gosainkund and Langtang Treks: Trekkers may spend anywhere from 7 to 20 days exploring the Helmu Valley and its environs. Seven- to 10-day treks explore the area of Helmu, an alpine valley of pastures and forests dotted with Sherpa villages and Buddhist temples. A slightly longer trip, lasting from 12 to 14 days, first visits the Helmu Valley and then proceeds over a high pass into the remote Gosainkund Valley, which is dotted with small glacial lakes. Trekkers who wish a more extended trip then continue for another 5 days or so into Langtang, a national park, where villagers lead an austere life among yak pastures under the shadow of Langtang Himal and Langtang Lirung. Return is via either the Trisuli Valley or the more difficult Ganga La route. Other treks all through Nepal are also offered. Participants camp out while on the treks. **Cost:** On request. **When:** September to June. **Contact:** The Sherpa Cooperative, GPO Box 1338, Kamal Pokhari, Kathmandu, Nepal; phone 13887; or Exodus Expeditions, 167 Earls Court Rd., London SW5 9RF, Great Britain; phone 01-373-7895; or Adventure Center, 5540 College Ave., Oakland, CA 94618, USA; phone (415)654-1879. *(M)*

The Relics of Lake Rara: Situated 250 miles west of Kathmandu, Lake

Rara is Nepal's largest lake, with unplumbed depths believed to reach 1,800 feet. A 22-day trip from London explores the lake region on foot. Trekkers examine relics of the Malla kings, who ruled the area in the 12th century, as well as the area's fauna, which includes bears, cats, wolves, deer and diverse bird life. En route from Delhi to Kathmandu, a stop is made at Dudwa National Park and a nearby tiger sanctuary. The trip is exploratory, so participants should be prepared for the unexpected. **Cost:** $1,490 from London includes transportation, food, accommodations, equipment, guide. **When:** October, March. **Contact:** Sherpa Expeditions, 3 Bedford Rd., Chiswick, London W4, Great Britain; phone 01-994-7668; or Durbar Marg, P.O. Box 1519, Kathmandu, Nepal; phone 12422. *(M)*

Pakistan

To Hunza and Baltistan: During a month-long trek participants visit on foot the lands of Baltistan, virtually unchanged since medieval times, and Hunza, the nearly vertical world that inspired Hilton's fictional Shangri-La. Trip members meet in Skardu and travel by jeep to Khapalu, on the Shyok River, where goatskin rafts ferry them to the trailhead. In 10 days they reach Khorkundus, in a glacial basin beneath the high ice walls of Baltoro Kangri at 23,990 feet. After a brief visit, the group traverses the Sherpikang Glacier and the rolling, grass-tufted Plains of Deosai; descends through the Astor Valley to the Indus River and on to the bustling market town of Gilgit; and finally reaches Hunza, where terraced gardens and orchards house inhabitants of legendary longevity. Time and conditions permitting, trekkers drive into the Khunjerab Range on China's border to see some rare wildlife before the return trek. **Cost:** $2,380 from Skardu includes food, porters, transportation, group equipment, guide. **When:** September. **Contact:** Himalaya, 3023 Franklin St., San Francisco, CA 94123, USA; phone (415)441-2933. *(M)*

Through Hispar and Biafo: A long, difficult and unusual trip provides a small party of trekkers/mountaineers the opportunity to see a region of Pakistan described only in superlatives by the few who have experienced it. Lasting 41 days, the trip begins and ends in

New York and involves trekking from near Skardu to near Gilgit; the trip is run in reverse as well. Trekkers fly to Skardu via Rawalpindi and after a few days travel by jeep to Basha to begin walking. A week's trek takes them to Snow Lake, set in extraordinarily spectacular scenery at 16,000 feet in the Biafo Glacier region; 6 days are spent exploring the area. Then another week's walk over the Hispar Glacier and a short jeep ride takes the group to Hunza, where a day is spent before the drive to Gilgit. After several days here the party flies or drives to Rawalpindi and returns to New York. Excellent physical condition, strong basic rock climbing experience, general mountain knowledge and good humor are necessary for this exploratory expedition. **Cost:** $4,778 from New York includes transportation, food, group equipment, porters, guide. **When:** June. **Contact:** Mountain Travel Inc., 1398 Solano Ave., Albany, CA 94706, USA; phone (415)527-8100. *(M)*

Philippines

Luzon Trek: Participants on a 3-week trip explore for 15 days the mountains and jungles of Luzon, the largest of the Philippine Islands. A guide has just returned from an extensive exploration of the region and has located routes of interest in 3 principal parts of the island. One route travels through the northern part of Luzon, which is essentially made up of 2 parallel mountain ranges separated by a long valley. Departing from Legaspi in the south, another route climbs to Mayon, a volcanic peak; 2 days are spent on the climb, with gear transported by mules. The third area explored is Mt. Apo and the surrounding country. Participants ascend the peak and visit the region of Cotabato, where the Philippine government discovered a "lost" tribe of aboriginal inhabitants in 1971. Participants use the trip's final week to relax on any of numerous beaches in the Philippines. **Cost:** $1,339. **When:** June to August. **Contact:** Terres d'Aventure, 5, rue St. Victor, 75005 Paris, France; phone 033 63 51.

EUROPE

Greece

The Peaks of the Pindos: One of Europe's last wilderness areas, the Pindos Mountains stretch 150 miles from the Gulf of Corinth to Albania. Participants on a 15-day mountain trek begin the trip with a flight from Luton to Corfu and take a ferry/coach ride to Iaonnina, where the hiking begins. The route runs along grassy ridges among limestone peaks which range from 6,000 to 8,000 feet. Stops are made at numerous points of interest, including Perama, a recently discovered cave complex of over 150,000 square feet; Vikos Gorge, a deep and spectacular canyon near Papingo; Meteora, where monasteries perch atop massive vertical cliffs; and Dodoni, site of the ancient Oracle of Zeus. The region still contains a large wildlife population, including wolves, wild boars, brown bears, lynx, Egyptian and griffin vultures and golden eagles. The rough itinerary, which allows time to explore and relax, ends with a drive and flight from

Parga back to Luton. Nights are spent in hotels, local inns and campsites, and the trip is limited to 15 participants. **Cost:** $440 to $460, depending on date, includes transportation from Luton, accommodations, equipment, some meals, guide. **When:** May, June. **Contact:** Sherpa Expeditions, 3 Bedford Rd., Chiswick, London W4, Great Britain; phone 01-994-7668; or Durbar Marg, P.O. Box 1519, Kathmandu, Nepal; phone 12422. *(M)*

SOUTH AMERICA

Bolivia

Along the Andes and Altiplano: Trekking excursions of 7 to 15 days extend from lowland river basins to Andean passes in the western part of Bolivia. On the week-long trek participants depart from La Paz, hike to the base of Mt. Illimani, traverse a 16,000-foot mountain pass and visit both subtropical and altiplano villages before returning to the city. Starting near the town of Palca on the Altiplano, the 8-day journey follows the old Inca Road to Coroico in the Valley of the Yungas; members visit Tomonoco and canoe down the Beni River. On a 10-day trip that visits a largely unexplored archaeological zone, participants trek to the ancient Inca fortress of Iskanwaya. Group members on the 15-day trek leave from the altiplano town of Ancoma, the site of an abandoned Spanish colonial gold mine. On foot and by canoe the group descends the eastern slopes of the Andes to Rurrenabaque, then continues downriver for a visit to the Lake of the Caimanes. **Cost:** $280 for 7 days, $320 for 8 days, $400 for 10 days, $600 for 15 days. **When:** On request. **Contact:** Safari Travels, Edificio Libertad, Pasaje Peatonal No. 8, La Paz, Bolivia.

Peru

Inca Trailing: A 2-week trip allows time for exploring Lima and Cuzco before hiking the famous Inca Trail. The route follows the Urubamba River to the ruins at Llactapata, where camp is made. The next few days involve some strenuous hiking as trip members cross 3 high passes and visit Wayllabamba, Runkuraqay and Puyopatamarca, all in spectacular alpine settings. A day is spent at Machu Picchu and its environs, before a train ride back to Cuzco and the return flight to Lima. **Cost:** $590 from Lima includes transportation, food, equipment, guide. **When:** May to September. **Contact:** Andean Odyssey Tours, 2141 14th St., Suite 1, Boulder, CO 80302, USA. *(M)*

Inca Trails: The famous stone-paved Inca Trail is traversed from Llactapata to Machu Picchu on a 6-day trip departing from Cuzco. Travelers join a longer trip in progress, meeting early in the morning for a train ride and short hike to Llactapata. The next 5 nights are spent camping along the trail after 4 to 6 hours of leisurely hiking each day. Porters carry the gear and professionals set up camp and cook. Ample time is allotted for exploring the ruins, which include Wayllabamba, Runkuraqay, Puyopatamarca and Luyuchapampa. The trek reaches Machu Picchu on the fifth day, leaving almost a full day to explore the Inca city. A train returns trekkers to Cuzco. **Cost:** $395 from Cuzco includes food, accommodations, transportation, equipment, guides. **When:** May to October. **Contact:** Andean Outfitters, P.O. Box 7007, Angels Camp, CA 95222, USA; phone (209)736-4830. *(M)*

Six Inca Walks: A selection of hikes through Peru's Inca country lasts from 3 to 20 days. The departure points vary; many trips leave from Cuzco, others from smaller towns. Most Inca ruins are connected by a network of trails, including the famous and partly paved Inca Trail, and it is along these that the trips are routed. Two 5- to 8-day trips departing from Chillka or Cuzco visit Machu Picchu; another to the Vilcabamba highlands may last anywhere from 5 to 20 days and involves some mountain hiking; a hike among the glaciers and lakes of 20,000-foot Cordillera Vilcanota departs Cuzco and lasts from 5 to 7 days. Two other hikes set out for the mountain ruins of Waxra Pucara and Chinchero. Porters carry most gear on the longer hikes. **Cost:** On request. **When:** On request. **Contact:** Explorandes, Nicolas de Pierola 662, Lima, Peru; phone 238933. *(M)*

Exploring Inca Ruins: A trek of 19 days through the Cordillera Vilcabamba and down into the Upper Amazon Basin is part of a month-long exploration of Inca ruins. After spending 3 days visiting the ancient Inca capital of Cuzco, participants begin hiking at Mollepeta en route

South American Wilderness Adventures offers a 28-day trek in the Cordillera Blanca. The trip is designed for experienced hikers who supply their own gear and help with chores along the way. (Keith Gunnar)

to the 19,951-foot peak of Salcantay. After reaching the pampa north of the Apurimac River, trekkers follow the pampa west, passing the remote Inca site of Choquequirqo. The trail descends by an old Inca road to a camp near Vitcas, site of the last Inca capital. Descending through high jungle to the city of Vilcabamba, participants reach the recently discovered Espiritu Pampa. For several days the journey proceeds into the selva, the tropical rain forest of the Upper Amazon. Finally the group catches a train to Machu Picchu and spends 2 nights at the famous Inca ruins. **Cost:** $1,725 from Cuzco includes meals, accommodations, guides, transportation. **When:** July. **Contact:** Mountain Travel Inc., 1398 Solano Ave., Albany, CA 94706, USA; phone (415)527-8100. ***(M)***

Running the Inca Trail: A unique 16-day journey in the Andes culminates with a run of the centuries-old Inca Trail which connects the Urubamba Valley to the white stone ruins of Machu Picchu, the "Lost City of the Incas." The trip begins with daily hikes and runs, allowing group members to condition themselves. The key element in the Incas' superb ability to communicate messages quickly throughout their empire was their impressive system of roads and trails and the relay-running messengers called *chasquis*. Following in the footsteps of the *chasquis*, group members run the 35-mile trail in stages, with pack animals carrying the equipment. Participants camp at night near Inca ruins, explore Machu Picchu and spend time in Cuzco, the ancient capital of the Incas. The trip is led by an experienced running coach. The group is limited to 15 participants who are selected on the basis of physical condition and running experience. **Cost:** $990 plus airfare includes all meals, accommodations, group equipment, guides, land transportation. **When:** June. **Contact:** South American Wilderness Adventures, 1760 Solano Ave., Berkeley, CA 94707, USA; phone (415)524-5111.

Trekking with the Incas: Two trips that visit remote Inca ruins also feature trekking high in the Andes: a 28-day trip treks through the Cordillera Blanca, and a 25-day budget trip walks the Cordillera Vilcabamba. The first trip begins with a flight from Miami to Huaraz, for acclimatization and visits to local ruins. Then begins a 12-day trek from Quebrada Honda to Quebrada Santa Cruz that crosses 2 passes over 15,000 feet and affords views of Peru's highest peaks. Gear is carried by burros, but the walk is fairly strenuous. Finally a week is spent exploring the Urubamba Valley, including the Inca city of Machu Picchu. The second trip convenes in Cuzco for acclimatization, organizing the sharing of equipment and visiting local ruins. The party then moves to Lucma to begin the 10-day trek to Santa Tereza, near Machu Picchu, which encounters many spectacular alpine views. Participants should be strong hikers who can provide their own gear, as this low-cost trip involves sharing equipment and chores; 20 pounds per person are carried by burros. Visits are made to several ruins, including Vitcos, the last Incan capital. **Cost:** $1,995 for 28-day trip includes transportation, food, equipment, pack animals, guide; cost for 25-day trip on request. **When:** June. **Contact:** South American Wilderness Adventures, 1760 Solano Ave., Berkeley, CA 94707, USA; phone (415)524-5111.

Cordillera Blanca Traverse: Hikers cross a portion of the craggy, remote Cordillera Blanca during a fairly strenuous 10-day trek. The expedition begins and ends in the town of Huaraz. Trekkers have a

spectacular view of 22,220-foot Huascaran during a bus trip to the trailhead at Yrakcorral. For the next 9 days, the party hikes up and down steep switchbacks, along narrow ridges and over high passes, including Punta Union Pass at 16,072 feet. Along the way participants explore the pre-Inca ruins at Utcupampa, and photograph a number of alpine vistas. On the tenth day the party walks into the town of Caraz, where they catch a bus back to Huaraz. **Cost:** On request. **When:** On request. **Contact:** Trekking & Andes, P.O. Box 3074, Lima 100, Peru; phone 462775. *(M)*

WORLD

Around the World in 35 Days: Trekkers visit 6 scenic, alpine environments scattered all over the globe on a 35-day trip involving some hiking or, if desired, climbing. After flying from New York to London, trip members proceed to Snowdonia, in Wales, for hikes and visits with the many British climbers that frequent the area. After a week the party flies on to Chamonix to hike and climb in the heart of the French Alps, perhaps the world's most concentrated alpine center. After 4 days participants fly to Erzurum, Turkey and drive to Mt. Ararat to hike and meet local residents for 4 more days. The next stop is Kashmir, India for houseboat stays and views of mountain scenery; a stop at Agra precedes the flight to Kathmandu, Nepal for 4 days of hiking and more scenic views. Finally several days are spent in Hong Kong and its environs, and a 3-day visit to Canton, China is made before the return flight to New York. **Cost:** $4,630 to $5,030, depending on number in party, includes transportation from New York, some meals, accommodations, guides. **When:** May, September. **Contact:** Mountain Travel Inc., 1398 Solano Ave., Albany, CA 94706, USA; phone (415)527-8100. *(M)*

RESOURCES

Clubs and Associations

The Sherpa Cooperative
GPO Box 1338
Kamal Pokhari, Kathmandu, Nepal
Phone 13887

South American Explorer's Club
Casilla 3714
Lima 1, Peru

WILDLIFE SAFARIS

On a wildlife safari you experience the habitat as well as the animal. You feel the heat, taste the dust, get wet in a downpour. The territorial calls of birds, primates, even hippos, make you feel an intruder. Watching the predator-prey battles, the courtship and the foraging for food makes you appreciate the relative comfort of your own existence. Wildlife trips offered in Africa, Asia, the Americas and Europe bring you close to the world's most common as well as unusual animals.

On a week-long camping safari in Botswana, you can observe the vast game herds of the Savuti Channel and the water birds, hippos, and antelopes at the Okavango Swamp. Staff scientists from the Serengeti Research Institute lead 18-day trips to Olduvai Gorge, Ngorongoro Crater, Lake Manyara and Serengeti that study animal behavior and the discoveries of ape-like humans made by Lewis and Mary Leakey. Other African safaris visit the best wildlife areas of Kenya, travel by bush vehicle through Senegal and explore Zambia by dugout canoe, bush plane and overlanding vehicles.

Whether you are eager to see a particular endangered species in the wild, observe the wildlife of specific geographical areas or learn photography skills from specialists, there are safaris to match every interest and budget. In Nepal you can ride elephantback through Chitwan National Park to see rhinos, crocodiles, tigers and leopards, or you can visit any of 5 wildlife reserves in the Soviet Union. Australia has numerous trips to view such exotic wildlife as brumbies, dingoes, goannas and wallabies.

No two wildlife safaris are the same—each is a unique interplay of animals and people. Whether you catch a glimpse of a large predator stalking its prey, hear the night calls of jackals or witness the strong bond between a marsupial mother and her young, a wildlife safari gives you a close-up view of the natural world. Such a trip reminds us of our place in the animal kingdom and provides new perspectives on life in a "civilized" world. □

Lying in the shade of tall grass in one of Africa's many game reserves, a lion rests during the hottest part of the day on the savanna. (Rick Citron)

WILDLIFE SAFARIS

AFRICA

Africa by Air: Five different 16-day safaris in East Africa offer a variety of ways to view wildlife and experience the African bush. On an in-depth ecological safari, participants talk to game wardens and wildlife experts and learn tracking skills from a professional guide. A bush plane is used during another trip in Kenya to visit places difficult to reach by car, such as the Nguruman highlands overlooking Lake Natron. On a camping safari, participants visit Mt. Kilimanjaro in Tanzania and several major game reserves, sleeping in tents every night. Also offered are 2 trips with lodge accommodations, one to Ngorongoro Crater, Victoria Falls and other points in Tanzania and Zambia, and the other to game reserves and national parks elsewhere in East Africa. **Cost:** $942 to $2,250, depending on trip; details on request. **When:** Year-round. **Contact:** Abercrombie & Kent International, Inc., 1000 Oak Brook Rd., Oak Brook, IL 60521, USA; phone (312)654-2211.

Botswana

Southern Africa on Foot: Trips to Okavango and Botswana commence from Johannesburg. Five and 7 days of travel and exploration are arranged at Okavango. After arriving at Maun airport in Botswana, participants travel to Savuti Channel where a check-in is made at a tented camp. A full day of exploration at Savuti Channel, home of vast herds of big game, provides photographers with a variety of wildlife subjects. By way of Sand Ridge and the Mababe Depression, safari members arrive at Santawani and a lodge on the third day. A foot safari led by a licensed

Visitors to South Africa's Kruger National Park have the opportunity to view elephants in a habitat free of both natural predators and ivory poachers. (SATOUR)

government guide lends more insight into the area's natural inhabitants. Hippos and lechwe antelope are often highly visible along the edges of the Okavango Swamp. An early-morning drive through the Moremi Wildlife Reserve and a return drive to Santawani bring the 5-day journey to a close. On the 7-day trip, much of the same territory is explored with more time spent in the Santawani area. **Cost:** $355 all-inclusive from Johannesburg. **When:** Year-round. **Contact:** Afro Ventures, P.O. Box 10848, Johannesburg 2000, South Africa.

(M)

The Big Five: Travelers see the "Big 5"—lions, leopards, rhinos, buffalo and elephants—by hiking, overlanding in vehicles, paddling dugout canoes and flying in bush planes during a 23-day wildlife safari. Beginning and ending in Los Angeles, the trip is led by a biologist and the director of the Los Angeles Zoo. A flight via New York and London takes the party to Lusaka and Victoria Falls, where 2 days are spent before visiting Savuti. Here participants sleep in a tented camp and drive through the veldt to view game. The next stop is the Okavango Delta, a lush habitat hosting a huge variety of water birds and larger game, where vehicles and canoes take travelers close to buffalo and hippos. In the Kafue Valley expedition members view lions, leopards and rhinos while based at a remote lodge. The group then proceeds to the Luangwa Valley where a combination of low bush flights and walking safaris provide views of Africa's greatest concentration of elephants. The return flight to Los Angeles is via Chibembe, Lusaka, London and New York. Participants should be in good health and prepared for some rustic accommodations during the trip. Academic credit is available. **Cost:** $3,520 includes transportation from Los Angeles, food, accommodations, guides. **When:** July. **Contact:** UCLA Extension, Biological Sciences, P.O. Box 24902, Los Angeles, CA 90024, USA; phone (213)825-7093.

Kenya

East African Wildlife Safari: A 21-day opportunity to observe and photograph a variety of African animals and birds is offered to a group of 10 to 18 people. Members visit 8 major national parks and game-viewing areas including Masai Mara, Amboseli, Aberdare National Forest, Tsavo East and Tsavo West, Lake Nakuru National Park, the Samburu-Isiolo area and Kenya's Marine National Park. Other major points of interest include Masai manyattas and tribal dancing, Lake Naivasha, Mzima Springs, Treetops Lodge, historic Mombasa and coral reefs in the Indian Ocean. Mt. Kenya is circled and the group stays at the foot of Mt. Kilimanjaro. Nights are spent in game lodges and under canvas in camps with standard beds and showers. Minibuses with photographic hatches and some 4-wheel drive vehicles are used for transportation. **Cost:** $2,010 includes land cost from Nairobi, meals, lodging, guides, equipment, expedition leader. **When:** July. **Contact:** Adventures International, 4421 Albert St., Oakland, CA 94619, USA; phone (415)531-6564. ***(M)***

Your Own Game: Flexible, individually planned wildlife safaris for small groups are offered out of Nakuru to all parts of Kenya. Two popular areas to visit are the Masai Mara Game Reserve, where travelers camp by the Mara River and watch game every morning and afternoon, and Lakipia, site of another tented camp in north central Kenya. The general outline of a trip can be tailored to special interests in photography, birds, research or certain regions of the country; participants can also arrange visits to Kenya's tea plantations, tribal villages, working ranches and the like. Groups can be as small as 2 people. **Cost:** About $130 a day includes food, accommodations, transportation, activities, guide. **When:** Year-round. **Contact:** Baringo Ltd., P.O. Box 1375, Nakuru, Kenya.

Parks and Plains: Visits to 4 of Kenya's national parks and game reserves highlight an 11-day photo safari. After a day in Nairobi, the group drives south to Masai Amboseli Game Reserve in the foothills of Mt. Kilimanjaro; the reserve is noted for its rhino population, but elephants, buffaloes, zebras, giraffes and cheetahs may also be seen. Each day the group moves to a new wildlife region, visiting Tsavo National Park and Taita Hills. An airplane then transports the group to the Masai Mara Game Reserve, best known for its predators and concentration of plains animals. A flight back to Nairobi concludes the trip. **Cost:** $662 to $839, depending on number in party, includes meals, accommodations, guide, transportation from Nairobi. **When:** On request. **Contact:** Bestway Tours and Safaris Ltd., Woolworths Bldg., Box 44325, Nairobi, Kenya; phone 331261, 331262, 22297.

Personalized East African Safaris: Parties of up to 4 people design their own itinerary and are driven by an experienced naturalist/guide to game parks and other points of interest in Kenya. Accommoda-

A traveler plays an ancient African game with Samburu tribespeople during a 24-day NEI walking safari through Kenya's parks and wildlife reserves. (Nature Expeditions International)

tions are at lodges or camps in the national parks, and generally 3 or 4 days are spent in each location. Between parks, travelers stay in a house overlooking Lake Naivasha for bird watching, fishing and boating. **Cost:** $75 to $197 a day includes food, transportation, accommodations, guide. **When:** Year-round. **Contact:** Fisherman's Camp, P.O. Box 79, Naivasha, Kenya; phone 5Y2.

Four for the Game: A variety of remote areas are visited in Africa during a 32-day journey to observe the continent's rare and endangered wildlife. The entire trip visits 4 main areas: Madagascar, where the accommodations are primitive and strenuous walking is involved, but whose rewards include a large number of endemic species; the game parks of Kenya; the Seychelles, with generally good weather and spectacular bird colonies; and Tanzania's Selous Game Reserve, boasting the world's largest population of elephants. Kenya and the Seychelles can be visited on a 19-day portion of the trip; 24 days allows time to include Tanzania. **Cost:** $4,300 for 32 days, $3,450 for 24 days, $2,900 for 19 days includes

On Nakutravel safaris that depart from Nairobi, participants have an opportunity to view reticulated giraffes at Samburu. (Keith Gunnar)

transportation, food, accommodations, fees, guides. **When:** July. **Contact:** Forum Travel International, 2437 Durant, No. 208, Berkeley, CA 94704, USA; phone (415)843-8294.

Nairobian Eye: A 3-week trip to Kenya's wildlife reserves, national parks and ranches provides an excellent opportunity to learn nature photography. Most of the trip is spent in the Rift Valley, where participants explore by Land Rover during the day and sleep in tents at night. Led by a professional photographer, trip members receive instruction in wildlife photography while shooting lions, leopards, wildebeest, zebras, elephants, buffalo and rhinos. An optional hike on Mt. Kenya to Point Lenana at 16,355 feet is also offered. **Cost:** $2,450 includes roundtrip airfare from New York, food, accommodations, transportation, guide. **When:** August. **Contact:** Globe Treks, 410 Fifth Ave., Suite 10, Hendersonville, NC 28739, USA; phone (704)692-4294.

Wildlife Safari: Three 3-week trips are offered in East Africa, one exploring both Tanzania and Kenya, another including the Seychelle Islands and another exploring Kenya alone. The emphasis is on natural history, wildlife observation and photography. Roads and game trails are traveled by microbus and Land Rover. The itinerary is planned to take maximum advantage of daylight for photographing and observing the diversity of big-game species, colorful birds, and butterflies and other insects. Stops are also made to study tropical plants and unusual geological features. Among the game reserves visited are Masai Mara, Serengeti, Ngorongoro Crater and Samburu. Lake Naivasha is explored for its immense variety of birds including the sacred ibis, goliath heron and crowned crane. **Cost:** $1,800 to $2,500 from New York. **When:** August. **Contact:** Holbrook Travel, Inc., 3520 NW 13th St., Gainesville, FL 32601, USA; phone (904)377-7111.

Samburu Safaris: Wildlife trips out of Nairobi, from 1 day to several days long, take participants into various areas of Kenya. Day trips can be made to the Bomas of Kenya, Nairobi National Park, the Rift Valley or Lake Nakuru National Park. Other trips, ranging from 1 to 4 nights in length, are offered to the Aberdare Range, Masai Amboseli Game Reserve, Tsavo National Park, Samburu, Mt. Kenya and Nanyuki. Wildlife is plentiful on all trips, with the Samburu visit offering a chance to see rare reticulated giraffes, Grevy zebras and gerenuks. Overnight accommodations are provided at jungle lodges. **Cost:** $7 to $300 depending on length of trip includes food, transportation, guide, accommodations. **When:** Year-round. **Contact:** Nakutravel Ltd., Kearline Tours, Town House, Corner of Kaundra/Wavers Sts., P.O. Box 41564, Nairobi, Kenya; phone 332299 or 20363.

East African Natural History: Professional naturalists and other scientists guide adventurers on camping expeditions of 17 and 24 days through Kenya's parks, wildlife reserves and wilderness areas. Participants have the opportunity to study the natural and human history of Kenya and observe a variety of game animals. On the 17-day trips participants travel by 4-wheel drive vehicles and on foot to observe and photograph the wildlife and environments found in Meru and Tsavo national parks and Masai Amboseli Game Reserve, the Rift Valley lakes, Wamba and the Masai Mara Game Reserve. The 24-day trip in July emphasizes the northern frontier. A professional wildlife photographer accompanies the group in January. Travelers who would like to do more hiking can join a mountain walking safari of 24 days, beginning with a 4-day game viewing trek in the Chyulu Range. Participants then explore the isolated Matthews Range, visiting the Samburu Game Reserve en route. Ascending Mt. Kenya to a height of 13,000 feet, adventurers study the flora and fauna along the way. **Cost:** $1,790 for 17 days, $1,690 for 24 days includes guides, meals, equipment, ground transportation. **When:** January, June, August, September. **Contact:** Nature Expeditions International, 599 College Ave., Palo Alto, CA 94306, USA; phone (415)328-6572. ***(M)***

Wildlife Watch: An overnight plane flight from New York City begins a journey to Africa's eastern game reserves. For 23 days travelers observe and photograph a variety of wildlife. The trip begins in Nairobi. From there participants drive to the Samburu Game Reserve where the bird life includes immense flocks of tufted and vulturine guinea fowls, and the mammals include reticulated giraffes, Grevy zebras and Beisa oryx. The trip proceeds to a game viewing lodge on the slopes of Mt. Kenya. The lodge is adjacent to the traditional route used by elephants migrating to the Aberdare Range, and is located high above a water hole and salt lick. Other parts of the trip include Serengeti National Park where it is possible to see game in abundances reminiscent of the 1800s; Lake Nakuru with more than 400 species of birds; Tsavo National Park's variety of animal life; and the coastal city of Mombasa, chief port of Kenya. A farewell dinner in Nairobi and a flight back to New York via Brussels ends the journey. **Cost:** $2,713 includes roundtrip airfare from New York. **When:** January, April, July. **Contact:** Questers Tours and Travels, Inc., 257 Park Ave. S., New York, NY 10010, USA; phone (212)673-3120.

Rift Valley and Masai Mara: Participants launch an 8-day overlanding trip in Kenya with a drive from Nairobi north to Nyeri and the mountain lodge in the Mt. Kenya forest, where game lodges are set high on stilts above salt licks and water holes. The group crosses the equator on the second day, driving past Mt. Kenya to the Timau Escarpment, opening onto a land of scrub and semi-desert, sparsely populated by nomads. Two leisurely days are spent at the Samburu Game Reserve, home of the reticulated giraffe, Grevy zebra and the long-necked gerenuk. At the Naro Moru River Lodge, trip members may relax at the foot of Mt. Kenya, go horseback riding or fish. Descending into the Rift Valley to Lake Nakuru, the motorcoach drives across ranching farmlands via Nyahururu Falls. Lake Nakuru National Park is an ornithologist's paradise, renowned for its large numbers of flamingos. The morning of the sixth day is reserved to enjoy the variety of bird species, for water sports or an excursion to Crescent Island. The trip concludes with a day in the Masai Mara Game Reserve, where the black-maned lion is a principal attraction. Participants then return to Nairobi. **Cost:** $526 includes accommodations, meals, transportation. **When:** Year-round. **Contact:** United Touring Co., P.O. Box 42196, Nairobi, Kenya; phone 331960, ext. 266. ***(M)***

New York to Nairobi: On a 16-day trip departing from New York, travelers visit wildlife areas and national parks in East Africa while staying at lodges. Group members fly to Nairobi and spend the first 4 days exploring Tsavo National Park, Mzima Springs and Amboseli Game Park. Two days are spent in Mombasa on the Indian Ocean, one of the oldest cities on the continent. Returning to Nairobi, the group proceeds into the highlands of Kenya, to a lodge where wildlife can be viewed at night. Continuing north to the arid Samburu Game Reserve, participants stay in a lodge on the banks of the Uaso

Nyiro. The group spends a final 2 days in the Mt. Kenya area before flying back to New York via Brussels. **Cost:** $1,479 includes round-trip airfare from New York, accommodations, meals (except in Brussels), guide, entrance fees to parks. **When:** Year-round. **Contact:** World Adventure Safaris, Inc., 175 N. Marginal Rd., Ft. Lee, NJ 07024, USA; phone (201)461-6131.

Malawi

Spotting the Leopards: Group members observe leopards, lions, kudus, impalas, hartebeests and other wildlife on a 22-day game safari in Zambia and Malawi. After flying to Lusaka from New York or Toronto, participants travel by Land Rover and minibus to view game in a variety of wilderness settings, including Kafue National Park, South Luangwa National Park and Lengwe Game Reserve. Three-day visits are made to both Victoria Falls and Lake Malawi, and travelers are treated to scenic panoramas of forests, valleys, waterfalls and Mt. Mulanje while driving through the countryside. Accommodations are in hotels and lodges. **Cost:** $1,800 from Lusaka includes meals, accommodations, transportation in Africa. **When:** Year-round. **Contact:** Zambia Airways, 1 Rockefeller Plaza, New York, NY 10020, USA; phone (212)582-6637. *(M)*

Senegal

West African Wandering: Dakar, once part of the slave route along the west coast of Africa, is the first stop during a 15-day journey through parts of Senegal and Gambia. After flying from New York to Dakar, participants travel to the Niokolo-Koba Reserve, a 2-million-acre wildlife sanctuary near the borders of Guinea and Mali; while on safari through the reserve, trip members can view large game such as buffalo, hippos and elephants from the safe vantage of overland bush vehicles. Participants then return to the coast for short tours of Nianing and Joal-Fadiout before moving on to Gambia, where the first visits include Mandingo villages on the north bank of the Gambia River. Four days are spent in Gambia, with a 1-day optional stay in a village within the Diola/Mandingo area of Senegal. Participants return to Dakar for the return flight to New York. **Cost:** $1,460 to $1,700 includes roundtrip airfare from New York, accommodations, some meals. **When:** Year-round. **Contact:** East African Travel Consultants Inc., 33 Bloor St. E., Suite 206, Toronto, ON Canada M4W 3H1; phone (416)967-0067.

Tanzania

Animal Behavior in the Serengeti: Staff scientists from the Serengeti Research Institute lead an 18-day safari that studies animal behavior in Tanzania's parks and wildlife areas. Participants spend a day in London before flying to Arusha to begin the safari. Traveling by 4-wheel drive vehicle, the expedition visits Arusha and Tarangire national parks, Ngorongoro Crater and Olduvai Gorge. The group then spends 3 days observing and photographing wildlife in Serengeti National Park, an immense preserve that is home to wildebeest, gazelles, zebras, lions, cheetahs and leopards. Additional stops are made in the Ngorongoro Forest and Lake Manyara National Park before the return flight from Arusha to London. Accommodations are in first-class hotels and lodges, and the occasional nature walks are not rigorous. **Cost:** $1,490 includes transportation from Arusha, accommodations, all meals in Africa, guide service. **When:** February, July, August, October. **Contact:** Nature Expeditions International, 599 College Ave., Palo Alto, CA 94306, USA; phone (415)328-6572. ***(M)***

East Africa Exploration: Participants leave from London on a month-long journey through Zambia and Tanzania. An immense variety of culture, wildlife and history is explored en route. Participants engage in such activities as riding in jeeps to view game, witnessing tribal dances, living in the bush and relaxing in resort-style lodges. Among the places visited are the Selous Game Reserve, the largest game sanctuary in the world; the Rift Valley and Dodoma, the future capital city of Tanzania; Ngorongoro Crater with its abundant wildlife; and Lake Manyara National Park with its large bird population. **Cost:** $1,450 from London. **When:** Year-round. **Contact:** Semjon Lass Associates, Action Tours, Box 1000, Lowell, MA 01854, USA; phone (617)459-2104; or Talisman Travel Service, 3440 Geary Blvd., San Francisco, CA 94118, USA; phone (415)668-2956. ***(M)***

Zambia

Game Viewing in Africa: Central and East Africa provide the setting for a 29-day trip to observe wildlife.

In Luangwa Valley National Park, a greater kudu bull guards his harem. Zambia Airways offers 16- and 23-day safaris through game areas of both Zambia and Botswana. (Zambia Airways)

After arriving in Lusaka group members fly to Livingstone and then spend several days at Chunga Camp in Kafue National Park. Game viewing by Land Rover and on foot is spectacular here as well as at the Ntemwa/Moshi Camp. The final game viewing stop in Zambia takes place at Luangwa Valley National Park where guides lead the group through the bush over 6 to 8 miles of trails between campsites. The trails are not strenuous but are geared for people of all ages. The safari proceeds to Kenya for a night at the Ark to watch the wildlife attracted by the lodge's water hole and salt lick. Then the group departs for a 9-day camping excursion into the interior to view additional East African wildlife. Accommodations throughout the trip are in hotels, lodges and tents. Participants may join the trip for either the Zambia or Kenya portions if they so desire. **Cost:** $2,695 includes roundtrip airfare from London, transportation in Africa, accommodations, most meals, guides. **When:** June to November. **Contact:** Semjon Lass Associates, Action Tours, Box 1000, Lowell, MA 01854, USA; phone (617)459-2104; or Talisman Travel Service, 3440 Geary Blvd., San Francisco, CA 94118, USA; phone (415)668-2956. *(M)*

Chibembe Camp: Travelers are invited to stay at a new safari camp located in the South Luangwa Valley National Park. Accommodations at the camp include wooden chalets with beds and plumbing. Although located in the bush, the camp offers conveniences such as electricity, piped water, refrigeration and a swimming pool. The area surrounding the camp is full of wildlife, and every day experienced guides take participants on morning and afternoon motorized viewing excursions. Luangwa Valley National Park is a vast area inhabited by buffalo, elephants, zebras, and many different types of antelope. For bird watchers, over 370 different species in the region have been recorded. **Cost:** On request. **When:** May to November. **Contact:** Wilderness Trails Ltd., Cairo Rd., P.O. Box 3876, Lusaka, Zambia; phone 73027; or Zambia Airways, 1 Rockefeller Plaza, New York, NY 10020, USA; phone (212)582-6637.

Zambia Backcountry: Well-equipped safari expeditions take adventurers into the African wilderness on 16- and 23-day itineraries. Leaving from New York, participants arrive in Lusaka via London and are taken to a lakefront chalet at a new safari camp in Kafue National Park. Several days are spent viewing wildlife before participants move on to a camp hugging the bank of the Luangwa River, directly opposite the South Luangwa Valley National Park. On foot and by open Land Rover, group members spend several days in the valley exploring and photographing. Excursions into the neighboring republic of Botswana are also taken on the longer safari. A highlight of the Botswana trip is the Kalahari Desert. Although the Kalahari is arid, it is well vegetated by many species of trees, bush and grass. The 7 days in the Kalahari are a tented expedition with no fixed camp sites. All backcountry accommodations are in safari-style camps with conveniences such as beds and refrigerators. **Cost:** $1,489 for 16 days, $2,089 for 23 days, $2,399 for Zambia/Botswana includes hotel accommodations, most meals, guides, all land transportation and safari equipment. **When:** January to November for Zambia trips, March, May, July, September for Zambia/Botswana. **Contact:** Zambia Airways, 1 Rockefeller Plaza, New York, NY 10020, USA; phone (212)582-6637. *(M)*

ASIA

Faces of the Indian Subcontinent: Travelers visit cultural and religious landmarks as well as several wildlife reserves on a 25-day trip through India, Sri Lanka and Nepal. The trip begins in Bombay and ends in Delhi. Nature areas visited include the Gir Wildlife Sanctuary, last home of the Asiatic lion; Yala Game Park, with its elephants, chitals, sambars, wild boars, buffaloes and bears; the coast off Hikkaduwa, where a trip in a glass-bottom boat provides views of coral formations; the gem pits of Ratnapura; the Snake Park and Guindy Deer Park near Madras, where black bucks and chinkaras can be seen; Tiger Tops Jungle Lodge, in the Himalayan rain forest; and Bharatpur Bird Sanctuary, near Agra. Along the way,stops are made at spectacular temples and shrines, the alpine city of Kathmandu and the Taj Mahal. Accommodations are in hotels and game lodges; travel is by air and car. **Cost:** On request. **When:** Year-round. **Contact:** Dynamic Tours, Saha & Rai Travels (Pty) Ltd., 9-A Connaught Pl., Middle Circle, New Delhi 110001, India; phone 344569.

Nepal

Jungle Booking: Game viewing, bird watching, hikes, whitewater rafting and other activities are offered out of a remote jungle lodge in the Chitwan Valley, about 75 miles southwest of Kathmandu. The lodge facilities include several game-viewing blinds and a tented camp on an island in the Narayani River. After flying from Kathmandu, participants are transported by elephantback or Land Rover to the wildlife retreat or, alternatively, they may take a 2-, 3- or 4-day raft trip from Kathmandu down the Trisuli and Narayani rivers to the lodge's tented camp. Guided walks of any length are offered through the jungle, which contains over 300 species of birds as well as rhinos, several species of deer, crocodiles, tigers and leopards. **Cost:** On request. **When:** September to June. **Contact:** Tiger Tops Jungle Lodge, Durbar Marg, P.O. Box 242, Kathmandu, Nepal; phone 12706.

Soviet Union

Soviet Wildlife: The remote back country of the U.S.S.R. is accessible to travelers on 7- to 12-day trips. Each outing visits one of 5 wildlife reserves where participants stay in lodges, cabins or tents and can see a variety of indigenous animals. The North Ossetia Wildlife Reserve, encompassing the foothills and peaks of the Caucasus Range, is visited on a 10-day trip. A 12-day sojourn visits remote Lake Baikal, north of Irkutsk in Siberia, where Siberian roe deer, moose, musk deer, wolves, foxes and other animals can be seen. A week at Lake Seliger, 5 hours north of Moscow, offers chances to see brown bears, wild boars, wood grouse and assorted waterfowl. At Krasny Les, just north of the Black Sea, participants spend a week watching wildlife which includes European roe deer. Finally, 2 reserves in the Rostov State Forest Wildlife Reserve can be visited for 7 and 10 days. All trips include 2 days' sightseeing in Moscow. **Cost:** $575 to $1,132, depending on length of trip and location, includes most meals, accommodations, activities, transportation within wildlife areas, guide. **When:** June to October. **Contact:** Klineburger Worldwide Travel, 1519 12th Ave., Seattle, WA 98122, USA; phone (206)329-1600. *(M)*

Wild Places: Three wildlife photography trips visit remote areas of the Soviet Union for periods ranging from 4 to 7 days, in combination with 2 days' sightseeing in Moscow. All trips originate in London. An 8-day trip spends 4 nights at the Krasnodar State Forest in south Russia, in the flood plain of the Kuban River. The dense forest is inhabited by great European deer and roe deer. A trip to North Ossetian State Forest, on the northern ridges of the Caucasus Mountains, lasts 11 days and spends 7 of them at the reserve, where brown bears, wild boars, roe deer and Dagestanian wild goats live. In addition, the Mityakino Reserve, on a plain north of Rostove-on-Don, is visited for 6 days during an 11-day trip which also features a day in Rostov.

Wildlife in the reserve includes elk, roe deer and wild boars. Lodging on all trips is in hotels and forest lodges. **Cost:** $1,270 for Krasnodar trip, $1,540 for Ossetian trip, $1,242 for Mityakino trip includes transportation from London, food, accommodations, guide. **When:** June to August. **Contact:** Luce Travel, 17 Richmond Hill, Richmond, Surrey TW 10, Great Britain; phone 01-549-1872.

Sri Lanka

Photo Safari to Ceylon: Sri Lanka is the location of an 8-day nature trip for photographers. The island, which is 270 miles long and 80 miles wide, is home to 109 species of mammals and 380 species of birds. Participants view elephants, leopards, wild boars, samburs, crocodiles, monitor lizards and pythons. Bird sanctuaries shelter flamingos, pelicans, spoon bills, blue coots, kingfishers, bee eaters and many varieties of stork. Upon arrival at Colombo, participants leave for Wilpattu National Park 110 miles to the north. From there an overnight stay at Polonnaruwa is scheduled. By the fourth day participants leave for Inginiyagala, bordering the Gal Oya National Park, largest of the game sanctuaries in the country. Group members explore by boat the vast Senanayake Samudra, which flows through miles of petrified forest where bird and animal life abound. The group travels through the Kumana Bird Sanctuary, a lake surrounded by scrub jungle and teeming with birds; the next stop is the Yala sanctuary where elephants, wild boars and peacocks live. Driving down the southern coast, participants return to Colombo and end the journey. **Cost:** $220. **When:** Year-round. **Contact:** Walkers Tours & Travels Ltd., P.O. Box 1048, 11 York St., Colombo 1, Sri Lanka; phone 22553. ***(M)***

AUSTRALASIA

Australia

Wilderness Trip Down Under: Traveling by coach to points of interest in Darwin, a 1-day trip takes travelers into the bush for wildlife observation. Wilderness areas visited include the magnetic anthills of McMinns Lagoon, the Marakai Plains, western Arnhem Land and the huge Cathedral Anthills. Frequently sighted wildlife include wallabies, wild pigs, buffalo, a wide variety of birds, and occasionally dingoes, donkeys and goannas. A barbecue lunch is served at midday, and some instruction in native culture is offered. **Cost:** $20 ($10 for children under 15) includes transportation, food, guides. **When:** Daily year-round. **Contact:** Marakai Safari Tours, P.O. Box 38956, Winnellie, NT 5789, Australia; phone Darwin 88 1177.

Wildlife Observation: Traveling for 1 day by a specially equipped coach through the Marakai Plains wildlife area in northern Australia, participants visit Fogg Dam and the adjacent protected area. Commonly observed wildlife includes buffalo herds, brumbies, Timor ponies, dingoes, wild pigs and a wide variety of water birds. An Australian bush barbecue is served en route. **Cost:** $21. **When:** Year-round. **Contact:** Matilda Tours,

Hanns Ebensten offers a 6-day trip to the ice pack north of the Iles de la Madeleine, where participants can walk within feet of young fur seals. (Hanns Ebensten Travel, Inc.)

P.O. Box 5266, Darwin, NT 5794, Australia; phone 81-8055 or 81-8008.

CANADA

British Columbia

Camping in Remote Canada: A 12-day trip visits Mt. Edziza Park, an area penetrated by only a few hunters and prospectors. Participants fly from Eddontenajon Lake into the park and stay at a base camp there, making expeditions of varying lengths into the surrounding area. The trip is especially tailored for photographers and naturalists. Wildlife is abundant on both the mountain and surrounding alpine plateau. Hikers may see grizzly bears, timber wolves, moose, caribou, stone and Dall sheep, mountain goats, nesting gyrfalcons and many small animals. **Cost:** $840 includes transportation to and from Smithers' airport, hotel accommodation at Eddontenajon, camping equipment, food, guide. **When:** July, August. **Contact:** Black Tusk Touring and Guide Service Ltd., 3064 St. Kildas Ave., North Vancouver, BC Canada V7L 2A9; phone (604)985-9223.

Manitoba

Nanooks of the North: In late October of each year, hundreds of polar bears, called "nanooks" by the Eskimos, migrate to the shore of Hudson Bay and await the winter ice. A 5-day trip from Winnipeg to the town of Churchill takes 12 participants by land and helicopter to observe the 1,000-pound carnivores. Native guides and experienced group leaders explain the ecology and behavior of the polar bear and take participants close to the animals. Each trip member makes at least 2 'copter flights in addition to forays by land vehicle. The trip concludes with a flight back to Winnipeg. Included are natural history lectures and tips on sub-Arctic photography techniques. Accommodations are at an inn. **Cost:** $1,750 to $1,870, depending on lodging arrangements, includes transportation from Winnipeg, food, accommodations, guides. **When:** October. **Contact:**

Hanns Ebensten Travel Inc., 55 W. 42nd St., New York, NY 10036, USA; phone (212)354-6634.

Quebec

The Ice Pack Seals: Every year tens of thousands of seals end their southern migration on the Gulf of St. Lawrence ice pack, where they give birth to and nurse their offspring. A 6-day trip which flies from Montreal provides a rare chance to walk among and photograph this spectacle. Participants spend 4 days at Havre aux Maisons, in the Iles de la Madeleine, fly by helicopter out to the ice pack and walk among the seals, who are unafraid of humans since hunting is forbidden there. Amid the spectacular sub-Arctic scenery, the only sounds are the cries of the seals and the creak of the constantly moving ice pack. The group also visits points of cultural interest and meets local inhabitants near Havre aux Maisons before flying back to Montreal. Participants receive technical notes on photography prior to the trip. Lodgings are in a hotel. **Cost:** $1,085 to $1,095, depending on type of lodging, includes transportation from Montreal, food except in Montreal, accommodations, some equipment, guides. **When:** March. **Contact:** Hanns Ebensten Travel Inc., 55 W. 42nd St., New York, NY 10036, USA; phone (212)354-6634.

UNITED STATES

Alaska

Wildlife under the Midnight Sun: An 11-day trip explores back country in the Kachemak Bay area under the extended sunlight of the summer solstice. Trip members make forays to view wildlife from tent camps and lodges accessible only by boat or float plane. Flying from Seattle, participants spend a night in Anchorage before heading across Kachemak Bay by motorboat to spend 3 days at a lodge on China Poot Bay. Here they watch marine life and sea birds along the beach, hike through dense forest to reach glacial moraines and travel by kayak to search for octopi or dig for mollusks. The group then flies to a tent camp beside Chenik Lagoon, in an area featuring a large concentration of brown bears. After observing and photographing the bears for 2 days, the party proceeds to another tent camp by a mile-long lake among spruce forests surrounded by snow-capped peaks. A final highlight of the trip is a helicopter flight over the Doroshin and Wosnesenski glaciers before return flights back to Anchorage and Seattle. **Cost:** $2,545 to $2,585, depending on type of accommodations, includes transportation from Seattle, food except in Anchorage, accommodations, guides. **When:** June. **Contact:** Hanns Ebensten Travel, Inc., 55 W. 42nd St., New York, NY 10036, USA; phone (212)354-6634.

Idaho

Camera Safaris: Personalized trips to observe wildlife in their natural habitats are available in the Idaho Primitive Area. The home base for all trips is at the Salmon River Lodge, located in a mountainous gorge on the Salmon River and accessible only by boat. Photographers may take once-in-a-lifetime photographs of elk, bears, deer, mountain goats, bighorn sheep and cougars. The animals roam free in the area, where there are no roads or cars and the nearest town is 47 miles away. Individually planned trips include float trips, jetboat rides and horseback trips into the wilderness area. All equipment except sleeping bags is provided for camping trips.The months of March, April and early May are ideal for those wanting pictures of animals. Other seasons offer other sights but it is only in early spring that the herds, previously driven from higher altitudes by winter blizzards, remain concentrated in the lower, warmer areas near the lodge and the river. **Cost:** $40 a day from Salmon includes meals, lodging, guide services, horses, equipment. **When:** By arrangement from February to December. **Contact:** Salmon River Lodge, P.O. Box 58, Salmon, ID 83467, USA; phone (208)756-2646.

Wyoming

The Elk Highway: Every fall large numbers of elk pass through Yellowstone National Park on their way south, a spectacle few ever witness. During a hiking trip that lasts 7 or 8 days, a group of backpackers watches the elk as they migrate. Throughout the trip, as they pass through the scenic high country and wooded valleys, participants learn about the natural history and ecology of the Yellowstone region from guides familiar with the area. Weather conditions and the location of the elk herds determine each trip's exact itinerary; transportation arrangements can be made from local airports to the trips' staging area. **Cost:** $315 for 7 days, $350 for 8 days includes transportation, food, group equipment, guide. **When:** October. **Contact:** Yellowstone Wilderness Guides, Box 446, Red Lodge, MT 59068, USA; phone (406)446-2636.

RESOURCES

Clubs and Associations

India Tourist Office
30 Rockefeller Plaza
New York, NY 10020, USA
Phone (212) 586-4901

Outward Bound Trust
34 Broadway
London SW1H 0BQ, Great Britain

Rover Company Public Relations Dept.
The Rover Company, Solihill
Worcestershire, Great Britian

WEXAS
45 Brompton Rd.
Knightsbridge, London SW3 1DE
Great Britain

Zambia National Tourist Bureau
150 E. 58th St.
New York, NY 10022, USA
Phone (212)758-9450

Vehicle Rental

Highways, Ltd.
Kilidini Rd., P.O. Box 84787
Mombasa, Kenya

NATURE TRIPS

In 1804, Meriwether Lewis and William Clark departed on the first overland expedition to the Pacific coast. Accompanied by 40 people skilled in botany, zoology, celestial navigation and Indian sign language, they returned 2 years later with detailed maps and information on tribal cultures, plant and animal life and the geography of North America. Charles Darwin set sail in 1831 on a 5-year voyage that would revolutionize scientific and religious thinking. Studying the wildlife of the Galapagos Islands, the geology of Patagonia and the natives of the South Pacific, he returned home with the theory of natural selection to explain evolution.

Exploration, nature observation and physical exertion all lead to new discoveries about our world. Nature trips that are offered worldwide provide opportunities to learn about diverse habitats, see rare animal life, climb strange geological formations, mingle with new cultures and learn about the ecology of unusual environments. Traveling by raft, helicopter, sailboat, Land Rover and plane, the trips investigate everything from insects and stars to archaeological sites and arctic flowers.

The spring months could find you bird watching in the tropical jungles of Liberia and the Cameroon. In summer you could join a month-long trip with a naturalist to learn about geysers, koala bears and aboriginal cultures in Australia and New Zealand. Early fall could mean your departure on a 9-day trip by raft and helicopter over the spectacular glaciers, valleys and peaks of Canada's Cariboo Mountains. Rather than hibernate in the winter, you could watch hawks and bald eagles in Texas or observe wildlife on the Galapagos and Falkland islands.

Specialists will take you into isolated wilderness areas, help you catch a glimpse of endangered species and learn about the world's most fascinating cultures. Whether your goal is to gain a better appreciation of nature, meet new people with similar interests or just leave the pressures of home far behind, a nature trip will do all this and more. □

On nature trips, city-bound adventurers get the chance to see works of nature which dwarf those of people. Here a hiker contemplates spectacular Sipapu Bridge, one of Utah's natural bridges. (Keith Gunnar)

NATURE TRIPS

AFRICA

Liberia

Birds of West Africa: Led by an expert on the region's avifauna, a 27-day bird watching trip explores Liberia and Cameroon. Visiting some of Africa's best birding areas, participants spend most of the time in the field or traveling. The trip concentrates on the Upper Guinean zone jungles around Mt. Nimba and the lower jungle zones around Mt. Cameroon, although a few other habitats are visited such as the savanna area of northern Cameroon. An abbreviated version of the trip can be arranged, as can special activities en route which do not interfere with the main itinerary. **Cost:** $3,195 includes roundtrip airfare from Miami, food, transportation, accommodations, guide. **When:** April. **Contact:** Bird Bonanzas, Inc., 12550 Biscayne Blvd., Suite 501, N. Miami, FL 33181, USA; phone (305)895-0606.

ASIA

India

Asian Lepidoptera Study: Two nature trips, one lasting 8 days and the other 12, focus on observing the colorful and varied butterflies of India. The 8-day trip, originating in Calcutta, flies to Bagdogra and drives to Darjeeling, where 4 days are spent observing butterflies among the region's tea gardens, evergreens and alpine meadows burgeoning with plant life. A morning excursion to Tiger Hill provides a spectacular view of the sunrise over Everest. After a drive to Kalimpong there are 2½ more days of butterfly viewing before the return trip via Bagdogra to Calcutta. The other trip, lasting 12 days, originates in Delhi and begins with a flight to Srinagar and an overnight in a houseboat on Dal Lake. A drive to Gulmarg begins a sweep of several butterfly-rich regions, including Pahalgam and Sonemarg. At mid-trip a stopover is made at Srinagar before concluding the trip in Delhi. Accommodations on both trips are in hotels. **Cost:** On request. **When:** Year-round. **Contact:** Dynamic Tours, Saha & Rai Travels (Pty) Ltd., 9-A Connaught Pl., Middle Circle, New Delhi 110001, India; phone 344569.

Himalayan Nature Tour: A month-long journey into the Himalayas visits many fine bird and game sanctuaries. After a day in Bombay, participants fly to Nagpur and drive to Kanha National Park for 3 days of wildlife viewing. The group then flies to Delhi and drives to Keoladeo Ghana, one of the world's best bird sanctuaries. At Meghauli, participants observe Asian wildlife from elephantback in the Tiger Tops Jungle Park, then continue to the Kaziranga and Manas game sanctuaries and the Bhutan Forest Lodge. Other stopovers include the Taj Majal at Agra and Kathmandu. Accommodations are in hotels and ample time is provided for sightseeing and exploring. **Cost:** $3,485 to $3,575 includes transportation from New York, accommodations, guides, most meals. **When:** January to

March, October to December. **Contact:** Lindblad Travel, Inc., 8 Wright St., Westport, CT 06880, USA; phone (203)226-8531 or tollfree (800)243-5657. *(M)*

Malaysia

Kinabalu Nature Trip: Two-day to 3-week trips in Sabah, Sarawak and other Malaysian states explore a variety of tropical environments. Participants may visit coral reefs, an orangutan sanctuary, tropical forests from sea level to 6,000 feet and several national parks. In the state of Sabah participants can climb Mt. Kinabalu at 13,431 feet in a 2-day climb from the Kinabalu National Park headquarters at 5,800 feet, and on Peninsular Malaysia travelers tour Taman Negara National Park. From May to August the leatherback turtle, the largest living species of marine turtle, comes ashore on the east coast of the Malaysian peninsula to lay its eggs, and a 5-day trip in this area allows observation of this event as well as visits to local villages for a look at native culture. Special itineraries may be arranged for individuals and groups of less than 20. Transportation is largely by bus, and accommodations are in hotels. **Cost:** On request. **When:** Year-round. **Contact:** Malaysian Tours and Safaris Sdn. Bhd., 42-B, Jalan Sultan Ismail, Kuala Lumpur, Malaysia.

Nepal

Birds in the Bush: Participants prepare in Kathmandu for a trek of 24 days in India and Nepal. Land Rovers are used to transport trip members to a camp above the village of Betrawati. From there, the trek begins along the Trisuli Gorge to the high pastures and forests of the Gatlag Valley where, at 9,000 to 10,000 feet, mynahs, bulbuls, little forktails and spotted mumias are some of the bird species seen. Fourteen days are spent in this area, allowing ample time for individual bird watching itineraries. The wildflowers are also enticing and include wild roses, primula, rhododendrons, gentians, anemones, irises and bushes of white syringa. The last stop before the return to Kathmandu is a visit to the Ghana Bird Sanctuary at Bharatpur near Agra, known for its ibis, storks and herons. **Cost:** $1,500 includes roundtrip airfare from London. **When:** March, April. **Contact:** Thomas Cook Ltd., P.O. Box 36, Thorpe Wood, Peterborough PE3

6SB, Great Britain; phone Peterborough (0733)632000.

Sri Lanka

Indian Ocean Birding: An 8-day trip takes bird watchers to an area where there are over 380 species of indigenous birds and other migrant varieties. Within the 25,000 square miles of Sri Lanka, many bird sanctuaries are located, especially in the Dry Zone, an area less populated than the north. The trip begins with a tour of Colombo before heading south for the Kalametiya Bird Sanctuary, which features flamingos, spoonbills, painted storks and garganeys. The Yala National Game Sanctuary is the next stop, the home of elephants, samburs, jungle fowl and leopards. En route to Lahugala to see the Ceylon swamp elephant, bird watchers may spot kingfishers, mynahs, bee eaters and parrots. The best bird sanctuary is located in Kumana, where viewing is excellent in March, June and July, with opportunities to see spotted-bill pelicans, black-necked storks and plovers. The last 2 days are spent on a coast-to-coast drive through the central hills back to Colombo, where an afternoon can be spent at the zoological gardens and walk-in aviary. **Cost:** $220 includes transportation from Colombo, meals, lodging. **When:** Year-round. **Contact:** Walkers Tours and Travels Ltd., P.O. Box 1048, Colombo, Sri Lanka; phone 28575.*(M)*

ATLANTIC

Iceland

Birds in the Land of Ice: A 10-day trip investigates the aviary and geological rarities of Iceland. After meeting in Reykjavik, participants fly to Akureyri and bus to Storutjarnir, where they spend 4 days exploring the Myvatn area. Myvatn is a fertile lake set in a virtual moonscape and is home to over 100,000

On bird watching trips in Sri Lanka, participants can view relics like this enormous 2,500-year-old stone statue. (Ceylon Tourist Board)

waterfowl during the summer months, including 15 species of ducks. Other area features include hot springs and weird lava formations, and a visit is made to Dettifoss, Europe's largest waterfall. Then participants stay for several days at Selfoss, in the southwest, to observe various rare and common birds. Finally, a day is spent sightseeing in Reykjavik. An 8-day version of the same trip is also offered. **Cost:** $730 to $900 for 10 days, $500 to $620 for 8 days, depending on type of accommodations, includes food, transportation, accommodations, guide. **When:** June, July. **Contact:** Caledonian Wildlife Services, 2 Kingsmill Gardens, Inverness IV2 3LU, Great Britain; phone (0463)38257 or 33130.

Wildlife and Geological Trek: After arriving in Reykjavik, travelers proceed to Laugarvatn on the start of a 16-day journey. From Laugarvatn they drive to Thingvellir, the ancient cliff-rimmed site where Iceland's democracy was first developed more than 1,100 years ago. The southern coast route is taken to Skogar and Kirkjubaejarklaustur before the group arrives at Skaftafell National Park. Established in 1967 with the assistance of the World Wildlife Fund, this area is surrounded on three sides by Vatnajokull, Europe's largest glacier. Its plants and animals exist in conditions similar to those of the Ice Age. The Myvatn district offers a variety of natural beauty including many islands and rich flora. The district also contains strange rock formations of volcanic origin, and the bird population consists of 15 species of ducks. Travelers proceed to Husavik, a village on the north coast, and then to Akureyri, northern Iceland's largest town. The puffin colonies of Snaefellsnessysla are seen by boat. The return to Reykjavik takes passengers over Surtsey, the island formed in 1963 by underwater volcanic eruptions. **Cost:** $1,942 includes roundtrip airfare from New York. **When:** June to August. **Contact:** Questers Tours and Travels, Inc., 257 Park Ave. S., New York, NY 10010, USA; phone (212)673-3120.

AUSTRALASIA

Parks and People: A 30-day expedition studies the wildlife, plants, geology and people of Australia and New Zealand in a variety of natural environments. The trip begins in Auckland and ends in Sydney. Visits are made to Hauraki Gulf Maritime Park, the home of many rare birds; Rotorua, with its geysers, mud pools and hot springs; Fiordland National Park, known for its magnificent scenery; and Kinglake National Park, containing kangaroos, wallabies, and koala bears. Participants explore the major cities of Christchurch, Brisbane and Melbourne, and learn about the lifestyle on a sheep ranch and the culture of New Zealand's Maori people and Australia's aborigines. The group also travels by helicopter to Heron Island for a 2-day study of the Great Barrier Reef. Accommodations during the expedition are in hotels. **Cost:** $1,890 includes transportation in Australia and New Zealand, accommodations, most meals, guide. **When:** March, July, November.

Contact: Nature Expeditions International, 599 College Ave., Palo Alto, CA 94306, USA; phone (415)328-6572. *(M)*

Australia

Pan-Australian Birding: Birders experience the diverse climates and landscapes scattered across Australia on a month-long bird watching trip which travels to a new area almost every day. Beginning and ending in Los Angeles, the trip heads out from Sydney to visit birding spots that include Lamington National Park, where tame birds venture close to the lodge; the tidal flats of Cairns, which hosts nearly every type of Palearctic shorebird; the tropical rain forest of Lake Barrine; semi-arid Alice Springs, with its birds of prey; the marshlands and monsoon forests south of Darwin; the temperate environs of Perth; and the salt fields of Adelaide. Besides hundreds of species of birds, participants are likely to see such interesting mammals as the duck-billed platypus. Lodging is in hotels and wilderness lodges. **Cost:** $3,695 includes transportation from Los Angeles, food, accommodations, guide. **When:** October. **Contact:** Bird Bonanzas, Inc., 12550 Biscayne Blvd., Suite 501, N. Miami, FL 33181, USA; phone (305)895-0606.

Down Under In-Depth: During a 19-day trip that leaves from New York, participants interested in natural history visit remote rural and wilderness areas of Australia. After flying to Sydney, travelers meet with a naturalist and are given a brief introduction to the wildlife in the outback and the far north of the continent. Travel from Sydney is both over land and by air, depending on road conditions. During the early portion of the trip, group members visit Kinchega National Park, enjoy a day of bird watching at the wildfowl rookery on Menindee Lake, and fly to Mootwingee, an ancient, abandoned aborigine camp where rock paintings and carvings are still visible. Deep in the country's desert outback, travelers familiarize themselves with the area's ecology, climb to the summit of Ayers Rock and visit the caves and water holes at its base. Moving north to Cairns, a more tropical region of the country, group members are able to view a number of bird species, including shore birds. In order to study marine life systems, participants spend a day and night on a remote coral atoll off the coast. Travelers then return to Brisbane and can either fly back to New York or extend their tour down under with an additional 10 days in New Zealand. **Cost:** $2,579 includes roundtrip airfare from New York, hotel accommodations, camping equipment, guides, 10-day New Zealand option. **When:** September, October. **Contact:** Holbrook Travel, Inc., 3520 NW 13th St., Gainesville, FL 32601, USA; phone (904)377-7111.

CANADA

Alberta

Heli-Hiking in the Cariboos: Three days of riding in helicopters among spectacular mountain terrain are featured on a 9-day trip. The trip begins in Calgary, with a motorcoach ride to Banff for a 2-night stopover. Rafting the Bow River and hiking are available at the resort. Participants then continue along the Banff-Jasper Highway to Lake Louise for 1 night before going on to Jasper Park Lodge for 2 days of golf, tennis and other outdoor sports. The next day they fly by helicopter to a lodge in the Cariboos for 3 days of wilderness exploration by chopper. Group members touch down on peaks, glaciers and in valleys for short walks and panoramic views of the remote Cariboo area. The trip ends with a night in Edmonton, Alberta before flying home. **Cost:** $815 from Calgary includes transportation, accommodations, food, guides. **When:** June to September. **Contact:** Tauck Tours, 11 Wilton Rd., Westport, CT 06880, USA; phone (203)226-6911.

British Columbia

Symphony Lake Base Camp: Setting up a camp on the shores of a glacial lake at an altitude of 4,500 feet in the Coast Range, participants spend 7 days exploring the surrounding area on a series of day hikes. After traveling from Vancouver to the small coastal village of Bella Coola, group members head into the mountains via float plane. Canoes are kept on the lake to explore the shoreline and to provide easy access from the base camp to hiking areas surrounding the lake. Each day's activities are flexible; participants are free to stay at camp or accompany the guide on

A 3-week International Zoological Expeditions trip investigates the indigenous wildlife of Central America. Here a Tomandua anteater displays its prehensile tail. (International Zoological Expeditions)

hikes that explore the vicinity's glaciers, streams, alpine meadows, glacial moraines and snow fields. Meals featuring fish and fresh vegetables are prepared by the guide. **Cost:** $710 includes all transportation, canoes, meals, camping equipment, guide. **When:** July to September. **Contact:** Canadian Wilderness Experiences Ltd., Box 46304, Sta. G, Vancouver, BC Canada V6R 4G6; phone (604)325-9118. ***(M)***

Wilderness Exploring in the Klondike: Certified guides lead nature enthusiasts into areas of the Yukon Territory and British Columbia on an 8-day trip. Meeting at Whitehorse in the Yukon, participants begin the expedition with a ride to Bennett, British Columbia on the narrow-gauge Whitepass and Yukon Railway. After investigating the gold rush town and observing remnants of the Klondike era, participants return to Carcross by train and board a van for a ride to Atlin, a tiny town on the shores of Lake Atlin. From there they take a 20-foot freighter canoe across the lake, British Columbia's largest, and then shoot down the rapids of a river to Tagish Lake where camp is set up. Glacier-spawned streams from the Coast Range feed the lakes, which are suitable for fishing. Horsepacking trips into the mountains are then available which take photographers and naturalists above the timberline to observe moose, caribou, Dall sheep, mountain goats and bears. Transportation is provided back to Whitehorse. **Cost:** $675 from Whitehorse includes accommodations, camping equipment, meals, guides, horses; special rates for children are available. **When:** June to August. **Contact:** Taku Outfitters, Ltd., Box 30, Klahanie Dr., RR2, Powell River, BC Canada V8A 4Z3; phone (604)483-9238. *(M)*

Northwest Territories

Naturalists' Retreat: A lodge on Bathurst Inlet accommodates those on recreational or professional trips to the far north. Stays of any length can be arranged. The site offers access to nearby waterfalls, unusual geological formations, offshore islands and a variety of wildlife haunts. A charter flight from Yellowknife takes participants to the lodge, which has personnel and equipment to assist guests. Local wildlife includes caribous, Arctic wolves, barren-ground grizzly bears, musk oxen, golden eagles and peregrine falcons. During summertime, the tundra boasts an abundance of wildflowers. **Cost:** On request. **When:** Mid-June to mid-August. **Contact:** Bathurst Inlet Lodge, P.O. Box 820, Yellowknife, NT Canada X0E 1H0; phone (403)873-2595. *(M)*

Arctic Circler: Frobisher Bay is located just below the Arctic Circle but above the treeline in the permafrost region. Guides are available for 1-day trips through the area, where one can walk along the tundra and view delicate arctic flowers, moss and lichen. In the village, group members can purchase soapstone and ivory carvings, embroidered hats and mitts, parkas, wall hangings and fresh-frozen arctic char. The trip takes place in the middle of the night, the normal period of seasonal twilight. Warm clothing such as turtlenecks, ski jackets, gloves, hats and sturdy shoes is recommended. Photographers should bring fast film or flash. **Cost:** $199 includes roundtrip airfare from Montreal, Toronto or Ottawa, food, guides. **When:** June, July. **Contact:** Consolidated Tours Ltd., 550 Sherbrooke St. W., #480, Montreal, PQ Canada H3A 1B9; phone (514)849-1259. *(M)*

CENTRAL AMERICA

Central American Zoology: Starting from Belize City, participants travel for 3 weeks through Belize, Guatemala and parts of Mexico where a variety of marine and jungle wildlife is observed. At the beginning of the trip, group members pass through a lush tropical rain forest on the way to Dangriga, where time is taken for a swim in a giant natural well. Traveling overland on jungle trails, group members end up in the villages of the Kekchi-Mayan Indians where the rich flora and fauna of the Maya Mountains are studied; a side trip visits the underground river in St. Herman's Cave. Near the Sibun River, time is spent traversing the mountainous Pine Ridge country to a high waterfall in a hidden valley, then to the caverns of the Rio Frio. The expedition crosses into Guatemala, stopping at Lake Peten Itza and the ruins and wildlife sanctuary of Tikal where trip members have an opportunity to climb and explore the pyramids of the largest Mayan city. Participants visit Bacalar's freshwater lagoons before proceeding to Tulum, where more Mayan architecture may be viewed. The trip ends with a sightseeing jaunt to the island of Cozumel off the Yucatan Peninsula. Accommodations on the trip vary from resort inns to tent camps, and transportation consists of a combination of boats, ferries and overland vehicles. **Cost:** $789 includes roundtrip transportation from Belize, accommodations, meals, guides, equipment. **When:** April, May, July. **Contact:** International Zoological Expeditions, 210 Washington St., Sherborn, MA 01770, USA; phone (617)655-1461.

Belize

Island Exploring: A resort in Belize's Ambergris Caye is the base for a variety of island experiences including shell collecting on nearby beaches, observing tropical birds in the jungle and searching for lobsters in season among rocks along the shore. With the use of snorkeling gear, non-divers may explore an ocean reef by boat to observe many species of tropical fish in the clear waters. For those interested in botany, a large variety of exotic plants and trees is evident in the jungle. **Cost:** On request. **When:** Year-round. **Contact:** Casa Solana, Rt. 1, Box 40, Palacios, TX 77465, USA; phone (512)972-3314. ***(M)***

EUROPE

England

Stoke Bruerne Walking Tour: Those who prefer quiet countryside can enjoy self-guided walking tours of Great Britain's historical canal system. Hikers start in the Northampton town of Wolverton and walk 8 miles along the Stoke Bruerne canal towpath. Along the way they pass 15 bridges, 1 tunnel and many aqueducts; the first is the Great Ouse Aqueduct, a cast-iron trough set on stone pillars. Just beyond lie the Cosgrove Locks and the old Stratford and Buckingham Branch Canal. Walkers pass these and other sights as well as farms, inns and, in the town of Stoke Bruerne itself, the Waterway Museum. The museum is housed in an old stone mill. Boat rides along the canal are available in Stoke Bruerne. **Cost:** Free. **When:** Year-round. **Contact:** Great Trips, Box 5199, Grand Central Sta., New York, NY 10017, USA.

Greece

Bird Life and Cultural Trip: Two trips, either to Argolis or Crete, take in fall foliage, historical sites and bird life. Based in Tolos, the first trip lasts 9 days with side trips made to Mycenae, Tiryns, Argos, Navplion and Mistras. The second is a week-long visit to Agios Nikolaos on Crete, with numerous side trips available as well. Both trips allow leisure time for exploration and are led by scholars familiar with the area. A wide variety of birds inhabits the area, **Cost:** $400 for Argolis trip, $380 for Crete covers accommodations, meals, activities, guide. **When:** October, November. **Contact:** Peregrine Holidays, Town and Gown Travel, 40/41 S. Parade, Summertown, Oxford OX2 7JP, Great Britain; phone 511341.

Hungary

Hungarian Habitats: During a 16-day bird watching trip through Hungary, participants visit a variety of avian habitats. The group flies from London to Budapest and makes an expedition to the Buda and Visegrad Hills to view a representative selection of central European birds. From Eger the group explores the beech and oak forests of the Bukk Mountains and spends several days in the Hortobagy region, where numerous bird species inhabit the steppes, marshes and forests. Participants investigate the Tisza Valley, a major migration route, and a day each is spent in the Saser Reserve, the Gemenc Reserve, Lake Balaton's Kisbalaton region and the Dinnyes marshes. The trip is led by a trained ornithologist who assists in identifying and recording the avian species observed by the group. Participants travel by coach and spend nights in hotels. **Cost:** $794 includes transportation from London, food, accommodations, guide. **When:** May. **Contact:** Ornitholidays, 1/3 Victoria Dr., Bognor Regis, Sussex PO21 2PW, Great Britain; phone 21230.

Portugal

Penedageres Birding: Portugal hosts many of Europe's most interesting birds, and the relatively low prices and friendly people there make it an attractive place for bird enthusiasts. A 2-week trip explores a number of different areas of the country. After beginning in Lisbon with a brief look at that city, trip members proceed north to Penedageres National Park for several days of birding, and then drive to Elvas on the Spanish border to look for great and little bustards and black-shouldered kites. The party then encounters an extremely wide array of bird life as it works its way south through olive groves and cork oak forests, eventually arriving at the Algarve. The trip is led by a professional naturalist. **Cost:** $1,650 includes transportation from Boston, food, accommodations, activities, guide. **When:** June. **Contact:** Massachusetts Audubon Society, Lincoln, MA 01773, USA.

Scotland

Shetland Nature Walk: Hikes of 2 weeks in the Shetland Islands provide participants with opportunities to explore a variety of cultural and natural interests. After arriving at Lerwick, capital of the Shetlands, the group drives to Sumburgh Head and Jarlshof, scene of human habitation from the second millenium B.C. Crossing to the island of Mousal brings the group to a defensive tower built by the Picts over 2,000 years ago. The third day of the trip is spent walking the sheep-cropped sward (there are no roads) on the island of Noss, where striking cliffs are home to colonies of guillemots, razorbills, shags, kittiwakes, gulls and gannets. From Inverness, Land Rovers embark to the Isle of Skye where participants can explore Loch Ness, Urquart Castle and the imposing mountain scenery of Glen Clunie and Glen Shiel. Further sights on the trip include Kyle, Ardvasar, Broadford, Elgol and the Inner Hebrides. **Cost:** $167 a week. **When:** March to October. **Contact:** Aigas Field Centre, Highland Wildlife Enterprises, Aigas House, Beauly, Inverness-shire 1V4 7AD, Great Britain; phone (046371)2443.

Highlands Wildlife Trip: Parties of 8, accompanied by a naturalist guide, make day trips into the Scottish Highlands to observe wildlife from a home base at Inverness. Exact itineraries and schedules vary depending on the time of year and weather, but visits usually last 6 days, from Sunday through Saturday. A wide variety of terrains—from farmlands and gardens to hills and valleys—and wildlife, including various mammals and over 150 species of birds, are seen during the day trips. Schedules alternate from week to week so 2-week stays can be arranged. **Cost:** $192 includes

As characteristic storm clouds build overhead, two hikers investigate the tidal life on the Isle of Skye off the coast of Scotland. (Margarite Hargrave)

double-occupancy accommodations, food, transportation, guides, binoculars. **When:** April to November. **Contact:** Caledonian Wildlife Services, 2 Kingsmills Gardens, Inverness IV2 3LU, Great Britain; phone (0463)38257 or 33130.

MEXICO

Birding Western Mexico: An 8-day trip around Mazatlan provides birding enthusiasts with the opportunity to see a number of rare and colorful birds in several different regions. Participants meet in Mazatlan for an initial day of birding in the immediate area, which contains hundreds of waterbirds. Then 3 days are spent at a mountain hotel for bird watching in the brushy slopes and nearby canyons, including Barranca Liebre with its tufted jay. The next 4 nights are spent in the jungle around the town of San Blas looking for the San Blas jay, collared forest-falcons, bar-vented wrens and Mexican caciquea. On the last evening before leaving the jungle, participants take a boat ride to watch hundreds of jungle waterbirds, including rufous-necked wood-rails and potoos. On the way back to Mazatlan, a stop is made at Novilleros where bird watchers should catch a glimpse of the rose-breasted thrush-tanager in the area's coastal thorn forest. **Cost:** $630 includes local transportation, food, accommodations, activities, guide. **When:** March. **Contact:** Merlin Birding Tours, P.O. Box 19687, Houston, TX 77024, USA; phone (713)461-2589.

Baja California

Baja Whale Watching: During 7- and 8-day trips to the winter calving and mating grounds of the gray whale at San Ignacio Lagoon, participants sight mature whales and young calves. Some whales approach near enough to the Zodiac boats for group members to touch them. Departing from San Diego, participants fly to Guerrero Negro, then drive through Vizcaino Desert to the oasis village of San Ignacio. The next 3 days are spent at a tented base camp at San Ignacio Lagoon for whale watching and

En route between islands, participants on an 18-day Sea Trek Hawaii trip explore the volcanoes, rain forests and coral reefs of the islands. (Sea Trek Hawaii)

exploration of the lagoon by small boat. Participants may choose from a variety of fly-in or drive-in options for the trips. Hotel accommodations are provided on some nights. **Cost:** $389 to $689 includes some meals, transportation, accommodations, guide. **When:** January to March. **Contact:** Baja's Frontier Tours, 4635 N. Jersey, San Diego, CA 92116, USA; phone (714)299-1360.

Discovering the Sea Life of Baja: A week-long natural history voyage to the islands and lagoons off Baja California offers participants a rare chance to see killer and gray whales, elephant seals, sea lions and other aquatic life in their natural habitats. Members of the expedition, led by several noted scientists, meet in San Diego and live on board the *Qualifier 150*. Desert flora, tide pools, shelling beaches and hikes of varying degrees of difficulty are highlights of the trip. Meals are served onboard the boat. **Cost:** $695 includes a $50 tax-deductible contribution to the Museum of Comparative Zoology, which makes participants members of the Friends of the MCZ. **When:** January, February. **Contact:** Museum of Comparative Zoology, The Agassiz Museum, Harvard University, Cambridge, MA 02138, USA; phone (617)495-2463. ***(M)***

Oaxaca

Yucatan Exploration: Members of a 14-day archaeological, cultural and nature trek fly south to Oaxaca in central Mexico. Trip members explore Monte Alban, the site of an ancient Zapotec city and Mixtec burial ground. In San Cristobal de las Casas participants take a field trip to Lagunas de Montebello National Park with its forest trails and many colorful birds and orchids. The journey continues by plane to Bonampak's Mayan murals where an excursion is made to Yaxchilan, a Mayan ceremonial center largely buried under earthen mounds that have now been cleared of trees and shrubs. In Yucatan, 4 days are spent exploring the magnificent Mayan ruins at Uxmal and Chichen Itza. The trip ends in Merida. **Cost:** $1,166 includes transportation, accommodations, meals. **When:** March, October, December. **Contact:** Questers Tours and Travel, Inc., 257 Park Ave. S., New York, NY 10010, USA; phone (212)673-3120.

Tamaulipas

In the Clouds: The northernmost cloud forest in the Americas is the setting for a relatively unstructured week of nature walks and study. Operated by Texas Southmost College, a ranch at 3,700 feet in the Gomez Farias region 265 miles southwest of Brownsville hosts a group of about 16 travelers who are free to spend their days walking with guides, exploring on their own or pursuing specific studies. Frequent overnight thundershowers usually leave mild, dry days for outdoor activities. Eight of Mexico's 12 major vegetation zones can be seen within a few miles of the ranch, and at least 40 species of birds not found in the U.S. inhabit the area. Talks on the human and natural history of the area are offered each evening. Accommodations are in dormitory-style cabins, and meals are American style. **Cost:** $200 includes food, accommodations, instruction, activities. **When:** August. **Contact:** Rancho del Cielo Tours, 4926 Strass Dr., Austin, TX 78731, USA; phone (512)451-1669.

PACIFIC

Hawaii

Hilo, Maui, and Kauai: A 10-day trip to the Hawaiian Islands offers a chance to study the area's natural history and marine biology. The first 3 days are spent on Hilo, exploring active volcanic areas, bubbling lava lakes, craters, Hawaiian bird life, rain forests and other tropical vegetation. For the next 4 days participants stay on Maui, visiting 10,023-foot Haleakala, looking for silversword and other unusual plants and observing humpback whales from boats in the Alenuihaha Channel. The final 4 days are spent on Kauai, where participants visit ancient temples, Wailua River State Park, a bird sanctuary and Kokee and Waimea Canyon state parks. A marine biologist familiar with the area leads the trip. **Cost:** $790 includes accommodations, land transportation, guide. **When:** January, March, August. **Contact:** Nature Expeditions International, 599 College Ave., Palo Alto, CA 94306, USA; phone (415)328-6572. ***(M)***

Three Islands: Traveling overland in vans and between islands by sailboat and plane, participants on an 18-day trip visit the islands of Hawaii, Maui and Lanai. After arrival at the Kailua-Kona airport on the Big Island, group members spend the next 8 days hiking and exploring the island's massive volcanoes as well as Waipio Valley, the Waimea Plateau and Wahaula

Heiau, an ancient stone temple. Nights are spent in campgrounds, including one that is located on the slopes of Mauna Loa. Participants then fly to Maui to begin a 13-mile hike down and across the crater floor of Haleakala Volcano. A week is spent on Maui before participants set sail from the old whaling port of Lahaina and cross the Auau Channel to Hulopoe on the island of Lanai for 3 days of snorkeling and hiking. Group members then sail back to Lahaina on Maui to conclude the trip. An abbreviated, 11-day version of the trip is also available. **Cost:** $667 for 18 days, $460 for 11 days includes meals, lodging, local transportation, guides/instructors. **When:** January to August. **Contact:** Sea Trek Hawaii, Inc., 47-696-1 Hui Kelu St., Kaneohe, HI 96744, USA; phone (808)239-8669.

Flora and Fauna Adventure: Travelers depart from London for a 13-day trip emphasizing the plant and animal life of Hawaii. During a stopover in San Francisco, participants can observe the sea otters at Monterey, the redwoods on the north side of the Golden Gate Bridge and many shore birds at the Point Reyes Bird Observatory. The Hawaiian portion of the trip starts in Honolulu on Oahu where the main attraction is the coral gardens of Hanauma Bay. Participants proceed to the island of Hawaii where 3 days are spent investigating the volcanic areas of 13,796-foot Mauna Kea and 13,680-foot Mauna Loa, with chances to observe a wide selection of endemic birds, including the wild nene. Later a visit is made to the Kanaha Pond Waterfowl Refuge on Maui. After Maui the group proceeds to Kauai, the garden isle, where people can walk along the Alakai Swamp Trail in the Kokee Forest, a remote and unspoiled area. In the Hanalei National Wildlife Refuge are ducks, stilts, and the red-footed booby colony at Kilauea and the Waimea Canyon. The trip is led by a professor of the University of Hawaii. **Cost:** $1,488. **When:** May. **Contact:** Twickenham Travel Ltd., 2 Chester Row, London SW1W 9JH, Great Britain; phone 01-730-2297.

SOUTH AMERICA

Goin' South: Participants on a 33-day journey to the far reaches of South America fly from Miami via Buenos Aires to Comodoro Rivadavia and then on to the Falkland Islands to explore the area's landscape, wildlife and human history. Proceeding on to Ushuaia on the Tierra del Fuego archipelago, participants spend several days hiking in the fjords, mountain and beech forest regions of Lapataia National Park. There is also a visit to a local ranch. Leaving Argentina, the expedition flies to Quito where several days are spent exploring the Ecuadorian highlands. Group members spend a final 2 weeks exploring the Galapagos Islands by sailboat, observing the archipelago's unusual animal and plant life. **Cost:** $2,980 includes airfare from Miami, accommodations, food, transportation, equipment, guides. **When:** January, February. **Contact:** Mountain Travel Inc., 1398 Solano Ave., Albany, CA 94706, USA; phone (415)527-8100. *(M)*

Wildlife Odyssey: A 30-day trip to several areas of South America begins with a 10-day visit to the Falkland Islands where participants observe colonies of rockhopper, Magellanic, gentoo, macaroni and king penguins in the most extensive penguin rookeries outside of Antarctica. Group members then fly to Tierra del Fuego, the southernmost tip of the continent in Argentina, for several days of hiking and bird watching at Lapataia National Park. After a few days in the highlands of Ecuador, participants fly to the Galapagos Islands. The last week is spent cruising from island to island while observing and photographing animal and bird life. Local naturalists accompany the group during the journey. **Cost:** $2,800 includes roundtrip airfare from Miami. **When:** January. **Contact:** South American Wilderness Adventures, 1760 Solano Ave., Berkeley, CA 94707, USA; phone (415)524-5111. *(M)*

Argentina

South American Nature Hikes: After a flight from Miami or Los Angeles participants spend 28 days hiking, camping and taking nature walks in the Lakes District of Chile and a similar area in Argentina. A day of sightseeing in Santiago precedes a flight to Valdivia where the hiking and camping begin. Forests, lakes, rivers and glacier-covered volcanoes are explored during several days in the Lakes District. At the end of the trail hikers board a ferry and cross montane lakes into Argentina. Ascents of the volcanoes and granite spires near San Carlos de Bariloche provide options for group members hiking through countryside that is very much like the Chilean lake region. Buenos Aires is the departure point for return flights to the United States. Those who have additional time can extend the journey for 1 week to hike and camp on Easter Island. **Cost:** $1,700. **When:** November. **Contact:** Andean Outfitters, P.O. Box 7007, Angels Camp, CA 95222, USA; phone (209)736-4830. *(M)*

Patagonia Nature Trip: A 24-day trip takes travelers to remote areas of South America to study natural history, geology and wildlife. Flying from the United States, participants stop at Santiago before traveling by air to Easter Island for a 4-day investigation of archaeological sites. Then trip members fly to Puerto Montt in the Chilean lake region for a mountain crossing into Argentina. A day of travel in this mountainous country ends with a cruise to Bariloche followed by a flight to Ushuaia, Tierra del Fuego. After 2 days in the area, travelers fly to Calafate in the heart of Patagonia. Visits are made to Upsala and the huge Perito Moreno glaciers. A visit to Valdez Peninsula, with its sea lions, sea elephants and penguins, precedes the return home via Buenos Aires. Accommodations are in modest lodges and inns in the countryside. **Cost:** $2,495 includes meals, accommodations, land transportation, guide. **When:** October to March. **Contact:** Society Expeditions, P.O. Box 5088, University Sta., Seattle, WA 98105, USA; phone (206)324-9400. *(M)*

Colombia

Double Bill: Two successive birding trips can be taken individually or together. The first trip lasts 16 days and visits 3 areas of Colombia in which up to 550 species have been observed. Participants visit Santa Marta, with a wide variety of lowland habitats as well as Colombia's highest mountains. The tropical Pacific lowlands near Buenaventura and the area in the Andes

The peaks and icebergs of Patagonia dwarf the m.s. World Explorer *as it cruises the area during a 24-day trip.* (Society Expeditions)

around Cali and Popayan complete the itinerary. The second trip, which begins immediately after the first one ends, consists of 12 days on the Amazon and offers the possibility of seeing a number of spectacular jungle birds including Harpy's eagles, umbrellabirds and bare-necked fruitcrows. Both trips are led by an expert naturalist, and participants should expect to spend most of the time birding or traveling. Abbreviated versions of the trips may be arranged. **Cost:** $1,295 for Colombia trip, $1,595 for Amazon trip, $2,490 together includes transportation from Miami, food, accommodations, guide. **When:** August. **Contact:** Bird Bonanzas, Inc., 12550 Biscayne Blvd., Suite 501, N. Miami, FL 33181, USA; phone (305)895-0606.

Jungle Birding: A 9-day expedition uses a fishing camp in the Cordillera Central as a base for watching tropical birds in the surrounding jungle. Flying from Miami, the group arrives in Bogota and proceeds by bus and boat to a fishing camp on the shores of Lake La Raya, in the northern part of the Cordillera Central. Participants make daily excursions to the nearby rivers, swamps and jungle-covered mountains, with opportunities for watching macaws, quetzals, chachalacas, trogons, manakins and hundreds of other tropical species. Accommodations at the camp are in hotels. The trip concludes with a return journey to Bogota and flight to Miami. **Cost:** $997 includes roundtrip transportation from Miami, accommodations, meals, guide. **When:** September, January. **Contact:** Holbrook Travel, Inc., 3520 NW 13th St., Gainesville, FL 32601, USA; phone (904)377-7111.

Ecuador

Archipelago Adventure: A trip to the Galapagos Islands begins with a night flight from Miami to Quito, the capital of Ecuador. During the next few days of the 15-day trip, participants explore a variety of locations. They visit the Museum of Colonial Art and the Indian market at Otavalo and then drive south through Ecuador's central valley. A descent from the Andes to the coastal plain is made by narrow-gauge railway through villages and valleys, down precipitous mountain slopes, and across gorges and rivers. After the descent, a 582-mile voyage begins on the motor vessel *Buccaneer* to the Galapagos Islands. Dockings are made during the next few days to investigate several islands. One of the islands, Espanola, is an uplifted block of submarine lava which is the sole nesting place of the waved albatross and is where colonies of sea lions, marine iguanas and Sally Lightfoot crabs are in evidence. Isabela, the largest island in the archipelago, is composed of 6 volcanoes, 5 of which are active. Point Espinosa on Fernandina Island gives participants a chance to observe sea lions, land and marine iguanas, Galapagos penguins, flightless cormorants and Galapagos hawks. Baltra is the last stop before a flight back to Quito and then Miami. **Cost:** $1,704 includes roundtrip airfare from Miami. **When:** February, April, July, October. **Contact:** Questers Tours and Travel, Inc., 257 Park Ave. S., New York, NY 10010, USA; phone (212)673-3120.

French Guiana

Jungle Butterflies: Nearly 1,000 species of butterflies highlight a trip to the rich and varied jungles of Trinidad and French Guiana. The 10-day journey begins with a visit to the Wright Nature Center in Trinidad where hundreds of birds, reptiles and insects can be seen without even leaving the lodge. After a night in Cayenne, French Guiana, participants boat to the Iles de Salut to spend 3 days exploring the former penal colony immortalized in *Papillon* and the island, now characterized by dense flora and fauna. The group then travels to a lodge deep in the jungle near the Comte River. Led by Indian guides, trip members spend several days exploring the area by dugout and on foot, paying special attention to the area's large number of butterflies. After a canoe and bus trip back to Cayenne, the trip ends with a night in Martinique. **Cost:** $965 includes transportation from Trinidad to Martinique, food, accommodations, guides. **When:** August, October. **Contact:** Hanns Ebensten Travel Inc., 55 W. 42nd St., New York, NY 10036, USA; phone (212)354-6634.

Suriname

Guianan Rain Forest Birding: A trip into the forests of Suriname (formerly Dutch Guiana) is designed for the serious bird watcher. Portions of the journey are rugged, with a great deal of difficult trail walking and an overnight stay in a jungle camp at the base of Voltzberg Mountain. In the past, groups have also encountered heavy rains. Participants should make every effort to search out the rare species indigenous to the area. Some of the birds encountered may be capped herons, white bellbirds, cayenne jays and over 25 species of raptors. Three days are spent at the Brownsburg Nature Park and 5 days at the Raleigh Falls-Voltzberg Nature Reserve. Several open savanna forests and coastal marsh areas are visited but the majority of the time is spent in undisturbed rain forest. **Cost:** $1,351 includes roundtrip airfare from New York. **When:** March. **Contact:** Wonder Bird Tours, 500 Fifth Ave., New York, NY 10036, USA; phone (212)840-5950.

Venezuela

Birds of Latin America: An 18-day exploration of the natural history of Venezuela focuses on the numerous species of birds which can be seen. From Caracas the expedition travels by bus to wildlife areas such as Guatopo National Park, where participants explore evergreen rain forests and view some of the 400 species of birds living there. The trip continues through river valleys, deserts and farm country. At the Chichiriviche salt flats vast numbers of herons, egrets, ibis and other shore birds can be seen. After crossing a 13,000-foot pass high in the Andes, the group travels to La Azulita Road and University Forest areas to search for quetzals, toucans, woodcreepers, warblers and tanagers. The expedition continues to Henri Pittier National Park which contains 500 species of birds. In the lowlands at Camaguan participants view raptors, tree ducks and storks, as well as wildlife such as spectacled alligators. The trip is led by an associate professor of biology. **Cost:** $1,454 includes transportation from New York, guide, hotel accommodations, meals. **When:** January. **Contact:** Aventura Natural History Tours and Travel, 508 N. Sierra Dr., Beverly Hills, CA 90210, USA; phone (213)276-6081.

UNITED STATES

Alaska

In the Valley of 10,000 Smokes: Participants spend 2 nights in a remote lodge on the shores of Naknek Lake on a trip departing from Anchorage. A commercial flight connects to a bush flight in King Salmon that arrives at the lodge at Katmai National Monument in time for an afternoon of exploration. The entire area was formed by a large volcanic eruption in 1912 which left a spectacular array of cliffs, gorges and flat moonscape. During the full day there participants can take an all-day trip to the Valley of 10,000 Smokes, where hundreds of openings once spouted steam. The forested areas around the valley are rich in wildlife. A visit to a nearby Eskimo village on the third day and the return flight to Anchorage conclude the trip. **Cost:** $291 for adults, $243 for children includes transportation from Anchorage, accommodations. **When:** June to September. **Contact:** Alaska Tour & Marketing Services, Inc., Suite 312, Park Place Bldg., Sixth & University St., Seattle, WA 98101, USA; phone (206)624-8551 or tollfree (800)426-0600.

Mt. McKinley Adventures: A wilderness retreat located in the center of the recently expanded Mt. McKinley National Park offers activities such as hiking, canoeing, panning for gold and observing wildlife. Trips to and from McKinley Park Rail Depot are made each Monday and Friday. Wilderness workshops with field discussions and evening seminars are offered around a fireplace in the lodge. The camp is located 2 miles from Wonder Lake and includes 55 acres of tundra and spruce woods above Moose Creek. Facilities include cabins for 2 to 7 persons with wood stoves and cold running water. Family-style meals are served in a central dining room. Vacation packages of 3, 4 or 7 days are available. **Cost:** $90 per night all-inclusive, $595 for full week includes all transportation within McKinley Park, lodging, all meals, guided trips, evening programs, use of recreational equipment. **When:** June to September. **Contact:** Camp Denali, Box 67A, McKinley Park, AK 99755, USA; phone (907)683-2290, winter (907)683-2302.

Alaska Wilderness Camping: Individual or group camping is provided in the remote areas of the Kenai Peninsula, an area first settled in the 1890s by homesteaders and now left to its first inhabitants—black bears, moose, mountain goats, eagles and other wildlife. From Homer campers are flown into a lakeside lodge where guided and unguided hikes are planned. Depending upon the arrangements of each particular trip, members may pack in their own food and equipment or may be provided with all camping necessities. Trips are available into nearby ice caves and to mountain meadows above the timberline. **Cost:** $30 a day includes camp facilities; $50 includes guide service; food and camp gear provided upon arrangement. **When:** June to October. **Contact:** Kachemak Bay Wilderness Lodge, China Poot Bay, Homer, AK 99603, USA; phone (907)235-8910. ***(M)***

Arizona

Sonoran Desert Studies: Up to 60 participants and 6 qualified scientists and educators meet for 5 days of field studies in the Sonoran Desert. The institute, located 25 miles north of Tucson at the foot of the Catalina Mountains, is the base for daily sessions which include 3 field trips; afternoon study periods with optional workshops in environmental education, nature photography and water conservation; and a variety of evening programs. The course seeks to clarify the relationships between the plants, animals and physical characteristics of the desert, with an emphasis on how earth and life forms relate rather than on classification or identification. Participants are required to furnish their own camping gear, though all food is provid-

A specimen is pulled up for study at the large nature center at Land Between the Lakes, Kentucky, where many interpretive programs are offered. (TVA-Land Between the Lakes)

ed by an experienced chef. **Cost:** On request. **When:** May. **Contact:** Audubon Institute of Desert Ecology-AT, 1642 N. Westridge Ave., Tucson, AZ 85705, USA; phone (602)743-7862.

California

Mountain Field Studies: Participants on a 6-week backpacking field biology course in the Sierra Nevadas hike through mountainous terrain to the region's lakes and meadows. Hikers study wildlife communities and gain a better understanding of the wilderness during 3 interrelated courses taught by experienced naturalists; all of the courses stress self-reliance and learning by doing. Participants must be capable of hiking with backpacks for extended periods. **Cost:** $445 includes tuition, application fee, meals. **When:** April to June. **Contact:** Wilderness Studies, University of California Extension, Santa Cruz, CA 95064, USA; phone (408)429-2822.

Colorado

Mountain Conservation: During week-long programs in the Rocky, Adirondack or Blue Ridge mountains, participants study wilderness skills and conservation. Camping or lodge accommodations are available. Each mountain area offers individualized activities including the Blue Ridge Summit's Crafts Fair sponsored by the Southern Highlands Handicrafts Guild. Participants may fish, hike, backpack, swim or go horseback riding as part of each program. College credit is available. **Cost:** $204 to $315, depending on accommodations, includes tuition, meals, accommodations, instruction. **When:** June to August. **Contact:** Conservation Summit, National Wildlife Federation, 1412 16th St. NW, Washington, DC 20036, USA; phone (703)790-4363.

Rocky Mountain Research: The Rocky Mountains of northern Colorado provide the setting for 9 courses, each lasting 5 days, which study various aspects of the mountain environment. After orientation at the headquarters of Rocky Mountain National Park, students roam through the Rocky Mountain ecosystems at elevations up to 14,000 feet. Courses include studies of bird ecology, mountain ecosystems and geology and management of natural resources. All courses include extensive field work supplemented by lectures and discussions led by geology and biology professors from universities in Colorado. One course in early June emphasizes drawing as a means to record impressions of the natural environment. The series of courses ends in early August with 5 days of practice in color photography for students who wish to study landscape, close-up, flash and wildlife photography. Students may take as many of the courses as they wish; the prices are graduated so that taking a number of courses costs proportionally less than taking one. Students make their own lodging or camping arrangements, and provide their own meals and transportation. **Cost:** $60 for tuition for 1 course. **When:** June to August. **Contact:** Rocky Mountain Nature Association, Inc., Rocky Mountain National Park, Estes Park, CO 80517, USA.

Georgia

Sea Islands Photography Workshop: The teeming flora and fauna of several islands off the coast of Georgia are subjects for a 1-week nature photography course. The course emphasizes environmental color photography, macro work, specialized equipment and wet-weather shooting. The group camps on an isolated private island, venturing out by boat to several other islands. Aside from a wide variety of marine life, participants may photograph the inhabitants of freshwater ponds, tidal creeks and mudflats, which include deer, alligators, shore birds and nesting osprey. Advanced photographic skills are not required, but participants must bring their own equipment and film. Swimming ability is also required, and camping experience is helpful. **Cost:** $305 includes camping equipment, food, boat transportation. **When:** June. **Contact:** Wilderness Southeast, Rt. 3, Box 619 AA, Savannah, GA 31406, USA; phone (912)355-8008. *(M)*

Kentucky

Southern Nature Studies: Participants join in a variety of nature-related activities in the Kentucky countryside at a nature center staffed by ornithologists, wildlife biologists and naturalists. A youth station is operated year-round and accommodates kindergarten to university-level resident groups. Interpretive centers, educational and living history farms and field trips are available at no cost. One- to 3-day winter programs include the history of the area's rivers at Paris Landing State Park, bird migration studies, eagle searches and nature walks. A high point of the winter season is a weekend trek through the Land Between The Lakes during which participants study the golden eagle. Slides and lectures are usually combined with the outdoor activities. **Cost:** On request. **When:** Year-round. **Contact:** TVA-

Land Between The Lakes, P.O. Box 79G, Golden Pond, KY 42231, USA; phone (502)924-5602.

Montana

Bitterroot Camping: Wilderness living classes which include instruction in mountain horsemanship, map reading, first aid, trail maintenance, plant and wildlife identification and campfire cooking are offered to small groups during the summer season. People 14 years of age or older comprise the classes of 12 people or less. All classes meet near Victor, Montana, which is located 34 miles south of Missoula. Upon completion of classes, certificates of merit are awarded. **Cost:** $675 includes riding gear, tents, meals, instruction. **When:** June to August. **Contact:** Bob Crick High Country Outfitters, Rt. 1, Box 99A, Victor, MT 59875, USA; phone (406)642-3233.

Tennessee

Wildflower Photography: Amateur photographers make 6 excursions from Gatlinburg on a 3-day exploration of the Great Smoky Mountains during the late spring wildflower season. A guide instructs participants on the basics of camera equipment as well as techniques and aesthetics of color transparency flower photography. Before turning the photographers loose to take pictures of flowers, the guide locates and describes some of the more than 250 kinds of plants blooming in the area. All the nature walks are roundtrip, except for one on the Appalachian Trail where special transportation arrangements are made. Participants should arrange their own transportation to Gatlinburg and supply their own camera equipment. Lodging is available at a number of nearby motels. **Cost:** $60 includes guide. **When:** May. **Contact:** Wilderness Adventure, 904 Mt. Holyoke Pl., Swarthmore, PA 19081, USA; phone (215)543-4639.

Texas

Texas Wildlife: Half- and full-day birding trips in the Rockport area take travelers on an 80-mile loop through some of the richest hawk

A dash of water from a cool mountain stream refreshes this walker on a nature trip in the Necklace Valley of Washington's North Cascades. (E.M. Watson)

country in North America. Groups may observe over 100 hawks of 10 species, the successful nesting and fledging of young bald eagles, and varieties of prairie chickens and wintering geese. Other bird life in the area includes turkey vultures, sandhill cranes, white-tailed kites and woodpeckers. For beginning bird watchers, guided trips in the Arkansas Wildlife Refuge and the Rockport waterfront, one of the richest saltwater marshes on the coast, are also offered. All trips originate at the Sea Gun Marina in Rockport. **Cost:** On request. **When:** January to March. **Contact:** Victor Emanuel Nature Tours, Inc., P.O. Box 4429, Austin, TX 78765, USA; phone (512)454-0576. *(M)*

Washington

Alpine Explorations: A series of alpine walks and hikes and a mountain river float trip explore the flora, fauna and geology of the North Cascades National Park. Based at the Snowline Inn at the foot of Mt. Baker in the town of Glacier, alpine exploration programs are offered 4 times during the summer. On each trip participants travel in small groups accompanied by a staff biologist and mountain guide. Basic mountaineering, technical snow and ice climbing and technical rock climbing courses are available. The Cascade Mountains provide an array of alpine terrain including deep glaciated canyons, over 300 glaciers, hundreds of jagged peaks, mountain lakes and streams. Plant communities examined vary from rain forests in the west, to alpine tundra, to pine forests in the east. **Cost:** $86 to $130 depending on accommodations. **When:** July, August. **Contact:** North Cascades Alpine School, 1212 24th G, Bellingham, WA 98225, USA; phone (206)671-1505. *(M)*

RESOURCES

Clubs and Associations

Appalachian Trail Conference
Box 236
Harpers Ferry, WV 25425, USA
Phone (304)535-6331

Austin Natural Science Assn.
Natural Science Ctr.
401 Deep Eddy Ave.
Austin, TX 78703, USA

Federation of Western Outdoor Clubs
3340 Mayfield Ave.
San Bernardino, CA 92405, USA

Field Studies Council
9 Devereux Ct.
Strand, London WC2, Great Britain

National Audubon Society
950 Third Ave.
New York, NY 19022, USA
Phone (212)832-3200

Nature Conservancy
Attingham Park, Shrewsbury
Shropshire, Great Britain

Rocky Mountain Nature Assn.
Estes Park, CO 80517, USA

Sierra Club
1050 Mills Tower, 220 Bush St.
San Francisco, CA 94104, USA
Phone (415)981-8634

Wilderness Society
1901 Pennsylvania Ave. NW
Washington, DC 20006, USA
Phone (202)293-2732

CARAVANNING

The campfire casts long shadows on the trees around you, sounds of crickets and frogs fill the air, your horses munch steadily on their evening meal, freed of their harnesses and the wagon that is your temporary home.The nomadic way of life has been followed by many different peoples for a variety of reasons—the gypsies of Europe and Asia lived in their carts because they were without a homeland, the tinkers and medicine hawkers were better able to sell their wares by wandering the countryside, the American pioneers spent months of rugged travel in covered wagons in search of new homesteads in the West. Hardships such as inclement weather, difficult routes and terrain, fluctuating supplies of food and water, and crowded living space were compensated for by a relatively free, roaming life style full of adventure and the unknown.

If the wandering life appeals to you, or if you feel you were born in the wrong century, it's not too late to experience the life of a nomad on wheels. You can rent a gypsy-style wagon for a week to explore the villages and countryside of England, or you can roll across pastoral France in a horse-drawn caravan. Young people ages 12 to 16 can tour Greece with a wooden-wheeled farm cart for 10 weeks while exploring ancient ruins and meeting other people along the way. Horse caravans can also be rented for meandering along the country roads of Ireland. For those interested in reliving the era of the Wild West, it is possible to follow the rutted trails west on week-long caravanning trips in "prairie schooners"—ships of the American plains.

So pick up the reins, grab a pioneer dress or buckskin shirt, throw your belongings in a gypsy cart or covered wagon, and climb aboard a 4-wheeled time machine into the past. Whether you caravan across North America or Europe, whether your wagon is pulled by a team of 4 or by a single hefty pony, whether you traverse barren plains or village lanes, you'll learn to appreciate the challenges and rewards of wagon travel—and you may find that the pioneering and nomadic spirit is still alive, waiting to be discovered on your next adventure. □

Families can travel pioneer-style on a trip offered by Wagons Ho over 55 miles of the historic Smoky Hills Trail in Kansas. (Wagons Ho)

CARAVANNING

EUROPE

Denmark

Wagon Trek: Travelers spend time getting to know the countryside during 1-week trips in covered wagons. Participants drive the wagon, harness and unharness the horse, make camp and put the horse out to feed every night. The wagons are equipped with 2 to 4 berths, sleeping bags, kitchen equipment, cool-box and gas rings. At the start of the trip, instruction is given in map reading and handling and care of the horse and wagon. Wagon train trips are arranged in several places. On the island of Funen, participants explore the West Funen countryside, along the coasts, woods and villages, where one can stock up on provisions and visit churches, manor houses, castles and inns. Several routes with fixed camping sites are also offered on the island of Langeland. **Cost:** $200 to $360 for Funen trip, $253 to $388 for Langeland trip, depending on season. **When:** Year-round. **Contact:** Danish National Tourist Office, 75 Rockefeller Plaza, New York, NY 10019, USA; phone (212)582-2802.

England

Rural Wagoneering: A gypsy-style covered wagon acts as both the home and the horse-drawn transportation vehicle for 4 adults traveling the area of south Norfolk and north Suffolk. Overnight sites are located deep in the countryside and provide running water and grazing for the horses. Many picturesque villages and sites may be visited including the ancient abbey at Wymondham, East Harling with its 14th-century towered church and New Buckenham with its large village green fringed with cottages. Travelers also pass through miles of unspoiled rural area containing wildflowers, birds and regional attractions such as Knettishall Heath with its brick- and flint-decorated bridge. **Cost:** $160 to $250 a week depending on month. **When:** April to October. **Contact:** Breckland Holidays, Mill Farm, Deopham, Wymondham, Norfolk NR18 9DQ, Great Britain; phone Hingham (095 385)380.

France

Countryside Caravan: Travelers in horse-drawn wagons roll through the varied countryside of France on routes of their own choosing on trips of 2 days to several weeks. Caravans can be rented in centers in Brittany in the northwest corner of the country, in Limousin and Perigord in south central France and in Normandy, outside of Paris. The wooden wagons, which are built by local residents, sleep 4 adults and are equipped with modest kitchen facilities, 2 sleeping compartments which can be divided by a partition, water and feed containers for the horse. Prior to departure, participants are briefed on the care and feeding of the horse, suggested routes and farmhouses where travelers are welcome to stay overnight or take a shower. The horses are generally gentle, intelligent creatures and draw the wagons a total of 7 to 9 miles a day. **Cost:** $146 for 2 days,

$296 to $415 a week, depending on the region and the time of year. **When:** March to November. **Contact:** Hobby Voyage, 8 rue de Milan, 75009 Paris, France.

Gypsy Caravan in Provence: Riding in a horse-drawn gypsy wagon through the Provence region of southern France gives travelers a week-long break from modern life. The vehicle is an authentic gypsy wagon restored in the style of the 1920s, with corner closets, dressers, wall cupboards and a full bed inside. Each wagon can sleep four comfortably. Leaving from the village of Entraigues-sur-Sorgue 9 miles north of Avignon, the caravan takes one of several routes: either through the plain of Carpentras to the vineyards of Cotes-du-Rhone at the foot of the mountains, or through the valley of Le Luberon toward the Mediterranean. Travel can be either by individual wagon or by group caravan, and food is purchased in villages along the way. **Cost:** $250 to $1,400 depending on duration and season. **When:** Year-round. **Contact:** Joel and Christine Moyne, Domaine de Saint-Sauveur, 84320 Entraigues-sur-Sorgue, France; phone (90)83-16-26.

Greece

Youth Odyssey: Leading 2 horses, each harnessed to a wooden-wheeled farm cart, 10 young people aged 12 to 16 journey through rural Greece for 10 weeks. The group covers 12 to 30 miles a day through sometimes arduous conditions, pausing to explore ruins and socialize with farmers along the way. The young people gain confidence by learning camping and survival skills and through shared decision-making during the trip. Hour-long Greek lessons are provided daily, and students earn credits with their home schools through individual projects such as studies of Greek culture or geology. The trip is led by a young American couple fluent in Greek who have run similar trips for 7 years. **Cost:** $1,775 includes roundtrip transportation from New York to Athens, food, group equipment, insurance. **When:** February to April. **Contact:** Grassroots Educational Expeditions, Freedom, ME 04941, USA; phone (207)342-5422.

Ireland

Countryside Caravan: For unhurried travel on roads free from heavy motor traffic, horse caravans may be rented from many bases in Ireland. Travel averages about 9 miles a day, with the slow pace allowing for appreciation of the countryside and time to meet and chat with people along the way. The caravan itself provides simple, clean and compact accommodations with adequate cooking facilities and berths for 4 people. A short period of instruction on harnessing and horse care is given before launching out on routes chosen for variety and suitable overnight stopping places. Evenings may be spent at a farm or local pub where water and grazing are available for the horse and where riders may prepare a meal and relax with local inhabitants. **Cost:** On request. **When:** By arrangement. **Contact:** Cork Caravan Company Ltd., Rathmacullig West, Farmers Cross, Cork, Ireland; phone (021)961611 or 961612.

UNITED STATES

Arizona

The Honeymooners: Three-day covered wagon trips travel the Honeymoon Trail, once the principal route into Arizona from the north; its name comes from the many Mormon couples who used to travel on it to Utah for their weddings. One of the most spectacular of the pioneer routes, the trail crosses Paiute Indian land from Fort Kanab across the state line to Pipe Springs, Arizona. Giant vermilion cliffs and colorful stratified valleys highlight the scenery. Pioneer dress is recommended but not required. Evenings are spent listening to singers and storytellers. Some individual rides are offered, and participants may help guide the wagons. **Cost:** $225 includes transportation from Kanab, food, accommodations, gear. **When:** June to August. **Contact:** Honeymoon Trail, Inc., Moccasin, AZ 86022, USA; phone (602)643-5584.

Kansas

On the Wagon: Traveling by wagon train along the grass-covered ruts of the Smoky Hill Trail, participants re-create pioneer days on a 3-day trip in western Kansas. Eight to 12 covered wagons are pulled by teams of horses and mules on the 55-mile trip, and passengers may choose to walk or ride a saddle horse alongside the caravan. Evenings are spent around the campfire listening to music provided by trip members and stories of drivers and local farmers. In an attempt to make the journey as authentic as possible, wagons circle up at night, traditional meals are served and pioneer dress is available. Luggage is transported by modern means to campsites each evening and participants' vehicles are moved to the end of the trail by the operator. **Cost:** $267 to $387 includes meals, sleeping gear. **When:** June to August. **Contact:** Wagons Ho, P.O. Box 1879, Quinter, KS 67752, USA; phone (913)754-3347. ***(M)***

North Dakota

Spiritwood Trail by Wagon Train: A week-long trip originating in Jamestown attempts to re-create the Western pioneer traveling lifestyle for groups of up to 150 persons. Members of the caravan travel in canvas-topped wagons pulled by draft horses and mules along a 100-year-old trail through historic hills and prairies. Participants leave behind all reminders of modern conveniences; coolers, radios, suitcases and modern dress are forbidden on the trip. The wagon train is led by trained guides, and members of the wagon train party share in all the necessary daily chores such as chopping wood, carrying water, cleaning latrines and building fires. Due to the rigorousness of the routine during the trip, participants should be physically and mentally prepared for some hardships. Once the work of traveling through unpredictable North Dakota climates and of keeping horses and camp in order is done, members of the caravan take time to enjoy fireside stories, crafts and historic re-enactments. Throughout the trip, which covers an average of 3 to 4 miles an hour, the wagon train stops at marked and un-

Groups of young people adopt a gypsy lifestyle during a 10-week Grassroots Expeditions journey through rural Greece, learning local customs and language along the way. (Grassroots Educational Expeditions)

marked historical sites along the way. **Cost:** $110 plus $15 horsefeed fee; $60 for children 12 years and under. **When:** June. **Contact:** Fort Seward Wagon Train, P.O. Box 244, Jamestown, ND 58401, USA.

Wyoming

Sailing the Prairie: A group treks by "prairie schooners," or traditional covered wagons, on 5-day trips through the Targhee National Forest, located between Teton and Yellowstone national parks. After meeting in Jackson Hole, the party heads out onto back roads, with some horses available for riding alongside the wagons. Daily horseback trips into the surrounding countryside provide visits to more remote sites. The caravan pitches a new campsite each night, with 2 of them on the shores of high mountain lakes where loons, trumpeter swans, moose, elk and deer can be seen. Evening activities around the campfire include singing, square dancing and storytelling. On the fifth day the trip returns to Jackson Hole. **Cost:** $225 includes meals, accommodations, transportation, equipment, guide. **When:** June to August. **Contact:** Bar-T-5 Outfitters, Box 2140, Jackson, WY 83001, USA; phone (307)733-5386.

Wagon Train Trip: The Teton National Forest is the setting for a re-creation of pioneer wagon trains, with trips ranging in length from 2 to 6 days. The trips begin and end in Jackson and travel through the surrounding area. Besides riding in the wagon train, activities include hiking into forested areas, making horseback trips into the high country, observing and photographing wildlife, and studying flora and fauna. Evening activities are geared to the creation of a pioneer atmosphere, with singing, storytelling and group campfire cooking. **Cost:** $100 to $250 depending on length of trip includes meals, camping equipment, car shuttle. **When:** May to September. **Contact:** L.D. Frome, Outfitter, RFD, Afton, WY 83110, USA; phone (307)886-5240.

PACK TRIPS

Just outside your tent, a camel snorts and awakens you to the fact that you are on a 2-week trip across the Sahara by camelback. In Spain, a sure-footed Andalucian horse carries you from village to village through the Sierra Nevada Range. Llamas pack your gear during a week-long hiking trip into the Merced River valley of California. You mount a long-legged mule at the edge of the Grand Canyon and begin a steep descent to Indian Springs.

Horsepacking is more than a lazy man's way of exploring the wilderness. It is an adventure in cooperation between man and animal, a chance to live and work with packstock that make it possible to visit remote areas too difficult to reach by foot or overland vehicle. Mules and zebroids help carry your gear to the snowline of Mt. Kenya in East Africa. Camels transport you through the bushland of Australia. Trail horses take you to inaccessible areas of Canyonlands National Park in Utah.

Pack trips can last a day or 2 weeks and cost between $25 and $3,000. There are trips planned for every riding ability and interest. Sixty different riding centers throughout Wales offer horseback rides by the hour, half-day or week. Novice riders are welcome on horsepacking trips through the central Alaska range. Young people can join a month-long horsepacking trip across the Colorado Rockies. Trips designed for more experienced riders give participants the responsibility for saddling, bridling, grooming, feeding and watering their mounts. Whether you've dreamed about joining a canyonlands packtrain, riding the colorful high country of the West or crossing the Saharan sands, doing so on the back of a native mount will add a new dimension to the scenery, wildlife and people you encounter on your next adventure. □

Participants on a day-long ride through the Wyoming wilderness get a good view of the Grand Tetons rising majestically in the distance.

PACK TRIPS

AFRICA

Camel Caravan: A camel trek through Mali highlights a 2-week visit to West Africa. Meeting in Dakar in Senegal, the group flies to Bamako in Mali, where final preparations for the caravan are made. Participants then fly to Timbuktu where they learn the techniques, routines and traditions of travel by camel, including how to talk to camels and set up camp. Basic information is provided about the local culture and language. The camel caravan leaves Timbuktu, traveling in the morning and late afternoon with midday stops for lunch and siestas. The trip offers a chance to see the beauty of the desert and experience nomadic life. Nights are spent in tents and hotels. **Cost:** $2,095 includes double-occupancy accommodations, transportation, equipment, some meals. **When:** Year-round. **Contact:** East African Travel Consultants Inc., 33 Bloor St. E., Suite 206, Toronto, ON Canada M4W 3H1; phone (416)967-0067. *(M)*

Algeria

Hoggar Mountain Caravan: Travelers with a liking for desert climates and rugged travel spend 19 days caravanning on foot and camel through the Hoggar Mountains. Members of the native Tuareg tribe are camel drivers and cooks on the journey, and the trip leader is a French mountaineer who has adopted the nomadic Tuareg way of life. There is little water along the way and meals are simple, combining Tuareg-influenced dishes with occasional samplings of French cuisine. **Cost:** $1,515. **When:** November, December. **Contact:** Sierra Club Outing Dept., 530 Bush St., San Francisco, CA 94108, USA; phone (415)981-8634. *(M)*

Kenya

Camel Train Safari: A 4-day camel and walking safari in the Northern Frontier District of Kenya travels in special areas where motor vehicles are prohibited. Departing from Nairobi, safari members fly to the camel base camp at Colcheccio Ranch before embarking on the safari. A train of camels carries the equipment while trekkers either walk or ride. The trek provides many opportunities for bird watching, fishing and photography. Many large mammals may be seen, including elephants, lions, leopards, rhinos, giraffes, greater kudus, zebras and gazelles. After 2 days of camping on the trail, trekkers return to Colcheccio and fly back to Nairobi. **Cost:** $738 to $904 from Nairobi includes transportation, guides, camping equipment, meals. **When:** On request. **Contact:** Abercrombie & Kent International Inc., 1000 Oak Brook Rd., Oak Brook, IL 60521, USA; phone (312)654-2211.

Up Mt. Kenya on Horseback: Participants spend 4 days riding on horseback to the snowline of Mt. Kenya. Beginning in Nanyuki, trip members are driven to the starting point of the ride, where provisions and equipment are loaded onto mules and zebroids—horse-zebra hybrids. From a base camp at 14,000 feet, the group rides to a point near the peak for an hour's climb to the Lenana summit. The last day of the ride is spent in the Hinde Valley before the return to Nanyuki. Inexperienced riders and children are welcome. **Cost:** $128 to $234 a person depending on the size of the party includes guides, equipment, food. **When:** Year-round. **Contact:** Amber May Safaris, P.O. Box 2, Nanyuki, Kenya; phone Nanyuki 2193.

Morocco

Atlas Mountain Trek: Group members hike to over 12,000 feet in the High Atlas Mountains during a trekking expedition of 14 days. After flying from London to Marrakech, participants travel to the Atlas foothills to begin a short warm-up trek to Asni from Imlil. Trekkers then set off into the remote areas of the High Atlas range, following gorges and mountain crests along the desert edge of the range. Whenever possible, mules carry the gear, but travelers should be prepared to carry the equipment at times. The group camps out or spends the night in mountain huts or villages. Having experienced some rugged terrain and conditions, trekkers return to Imlil. Base camp is set up at 9,000 feet before the group climbs Toubkal, the highest mountain in Morocco. The itinerary is flexible, and the group may climb other mountains if time permits before returning to Marrakech and London. **Cost:** $543 includes transportation from London, food, mules, accommodations, guide. **When:** March to June, August to October. **Contact:** WEXAS International, 45 Brompton Rd., Knightsbridge, London SW3 1DE, Great Britain; phone 01-589-0500. ***(M)***

Niger

Through the Sahara on Camelback: Travelers explore Niger's southern Sahara on camel, by foot and by overland vehicle for 2 weeks. Flying from Paris, the group arrives in Agadez and drives to the village of Talat where a camel train and guides are waiting. Far from being a desert wasteland, the area is alive with people, animals, forests and gardens, and provides many comfortable camping sites. After passing through several villages, travelers ascend the Bagzane Mountains partly on foot. Caravan trails lead to isolated villages of the Kel Oui and to the volcano of Taghes Izzeguerit. Back on camels, travelers approach the dunes of Tenere via the canyon of Ighalabelane. Trekkers rest for a day at the palm-covered oasis of Timia where jeeps replace camels as transportation for the return journey to Agadez. A plane ride to Niamey provides the travelers with views of Zinder, Maradi and Tahona before connecting with a return flight to Paris. **Cost:** $1,450 from Paris includes transportation, meals, accommodations, camel train, guide. **When:** January, March. **Contact:** Terres d'Aventure, 5 rue St. Victor, 75005, Paris, France; phone 033-63-51.

Senegal

Trekking with the Tuaregs: Timbuktu, at the southern edge of the

Sahara, is the starting point of many caravans, some of them consisting of several hundred camels bound for the great salt mines of Taoudenni. The central activity during a 15-day journey to Mali involves 6 days of caravanning with Tuareg guides in the southern Sahara region. Travelers depart from New York, fly to Dakar, Bamako, then Timbuktu, an Islamic center that was founded around 1100 A.D. Two days are spent in Timbuktu preparing for the caravan and becoming acquainted with traditions of the area as well as the techniques of travel on camelback; participants learn how to quickly raise a tent made of camel hides, how to arrange a sleeping place, and how to speak a few basic words and phrases in Tamachek, the language of the Tuaregs. On caravan, group members travel northwest to Lake Faguibine, then turn south toward Goundam, passing through country inhabited by jackals, warthogs, gazelles and ostriches. After about 200 miles on camelback, participants leave the caravan and fly from Goundam back to Bamako and Dakar, then depart for New York. **Cost:** $2,950 from New York includes transportation, most meals, accommodations, camping equipment, guides, camels. **When:** Year-round. **Contact:** East African Travel Consultants Inc., 33 Bloor St. E., Suite 206, Toronto, ON Canada M4W 3H1. *(M)*

ASIA

India

Through the Desert on a Camel: A 10-day trip through India's deserts is highlighted by 5 days of camel trekking in the Great Indian Desert. The desert is dotted with settlements, occasional monuments and scenic oases. An emphasis is placed on meeting local inhabitants and sharing in their daily lives. After the camel portion of the trip, the party drives through other desert areas, visiting the legendary cities of Bikaner, Jaisalmer and Jodhpur. **Cost:** On request. **When:** On request. **Contact:** Dynamic Tours, Saha & Rai Travels (Pty) Ltd., 9-A Connaught Pl., Middle Circle, New Delhi 110001, India; phone 344569.

AUSTRALASIA

Australia

Kangaroo Island Camel Safaris: Travel by camel through bushland allows close approaches to animals in the Ravine de Casoars wildlife reserve on Kangaroo Island, off the southern coast of Australia. A day trip follows tracks among huge sugar gum trees and then travels along 600-foot cliffs which provide panoramic views of coastal scenery. Travelers on a 3-day safari ride along the De Molle River to its mouth proceed through the bush at the edge of Cape Torrens Conservation Park and then follow the cliff route used by the 1-day trip. Another 3-day trip covers 35 miles by varying routes to visit coastal caves and fairy penguin rookeries. Participants camp out overnight during the 3-day safaris and stay in cabins before and after the trips. Group size is limited to 6, and camels specifically trained for safaris are used. **Cost:** $25 for day trip; $100 for 3-day trip includes accom-

Horsepacking routes often cross rivers without bridges; guides make it easy by picking shallow fords with slow-moving water. (West Virginia Chamber of Commerce)

modations, most meals, guide. **When:** November to April. **Contact:** Transcontinental Safaris, The Ravine Wildlife Reserve, P.M.B. 251 Kingscote, Kangaroo Island, South Australia 5223, Australia; phone The Shackle 6. *(M)*

New Zealand

Horsepacking on North Island: A trek to the Maori territory of the Tuhoe tribe takes hikers around North Island's Urewera country, including 5 days in Urewera National Park. Accompanied by packstock, the group begins the trip at Mataatua Marae in Ruatahuna between Rotorua and Wairoa, following the Whakatane River through native forest abounding in wildlife and bird life. Following a circular route along the valley floor, hikers camp at Hanamahihi after crossing the river at Tarakena Rapids. The group may proceed to Ohaua Marae near an old Maori meetinghouse, Marumaru and Waikarewhenua, depending on the length of the trip. The history and natural beauty of the area lend themselves to activities such as photography, fishing, swimming, nature study or horse trekking. Weekend, 3- and 7-day variations are also available. Hikers need only provide and carry their personal effects. **Cost:** $39 to $145, with children's rates. **When:** November to April. **Contact:** Te Rehuwai Safaris Ltd., P.O. Box 2111, Rotorua, New Zealand; phone 89-063.

CANADA

Alberta

Hoofing the Skyline Trail: The alpine flowers and abundant wildlife of the Jasper National Park region are of interest to horsepacking visitors as they ride the Skyline Trail. Jaunts of 3, 6 and 14 days beginning at Jasper or the Sunwapta River travel through the high mountain country by way of the Little and Big Shovel passes. Overnight stops are made at wilderness cabins or tent houses. Previous riding experience is not required. **Cost:** $60 per day includes guide, horse, equipment, meals, accommodation. **When:** July to August. **Contact:** Skyline Trail Rides Ltd., Box 207, Jasper, AB Canada T0E 1E0.

New Trails, Old Passes: Participants spend 5 days riding through the Canadian Rockies wilderness near Banff. After setting up a base camp near the Upper Spray River, riders set out each day to explore new trails and old passes through uninhabited valleys and craggy peaks. Travelers stay in traditional teepees and eat meals prepared by the camp chef. Cowboy guides attend to the horses. Riding experience is not essential, and participants are matched with animals to suit their own skill and temperament. **Cost:** $325 includes round-trip bus transportation from Banff, horse and saddle, meals, accommodations, membership fee. **When:** July, August. **Contact:** Trail Riders of the Canadian Rockies, P.O. Box 6742, Sta. D, Calgary, AB Canada T2P 2E6; phone (403)287-1746.

Riding in the Rockies: Participants mount well-mannered horses to ride for 6 days in the Alberta foothills or in the Cascade Valley and Lower Flints Park area of Banff National Park. Meals are prepared by camp cooks, and the small group sleeps in tents at camps along the trail. On the spring trip a small group drives from Banff to Lake Minnewanka to board a sightseeing boat for Devil's Gap at the end of the lake. There participants meet guides and horses for a 9-mile ride to Devil's Head Ranch located east of the Devil's Head and Aylmer mountains. Camping in tents at the ranch riders make forays during the day on horse. In summer, riders use 2 main camps in Banff National Park as bases for 6 days of riding. On these trips riders are transported by bus to the trail-head corral at Mt. Norquay. From here the group heads out in a northerly direction across Elk Lake Pass to the first camp at Stoney Creek. In the Cascade River Valley the trip members have a chance to ford the river and see bighorn sheep, mountain goats, elk and moose. After a ride to Dormer Pass, riders move on to the Flints Park Camp and a day ride to Sawback Lake. Returning to Stoney Creek Camp, the group leisurely makes its way back to the trailhead corral. **Cost:** $275 to $330 depending on date of departure includes transportation from Banff, guides, meals, equipment, horses. **When:** April to September. **Contact:** Warner and MacKenzie Guiding and Outfitting, Box 448, Banff, AB Canada T0L 0C0; phone (403)762-4255.

British Columbia

Remote Trail Riding: One- and 2-week horsepacking trips cross the virgin forests of British Columbia, moving between established forest camps. The trips begin and end at a ranch at Chilko Lake, about 180 miles north of Vancouver, an area accessible only by air or 4-wheel drive vehicle. After a day acquainting themselves with the horses participants strike out onto trails through remote and wild mountain terrain, staking temporary camps as they go. The route runs through heavily timbered country, over mountain streams, and past snowfields and glaciers. Every 4 days a permanent tent camp, offering showers and amenities, is made home base for a few days of day hiking, fishing, photography or relaxing. Finally, the last night of the trip is spent back at Chilko Lake. **Cost:** $350 for 7 days; $700 for 14 days includes food, accommodations, horses, equipment, guide. **When:** June to September. **Contact:** Chilko Lake Wilderness Ranch Ltd., P.O. Box 4750, Williams Lake, BC Canada V2G 2V7; phone (604)-Chilko Lake Wilderness Ranch.

EUROPE

France

Vosges Retreat: The mountainous Vosges region of Alsace-Lorraine provides participants with a relaxing experience on horseback for 3, 6 or 10 days. Groups of 4 riders travel through the lush, variegated countryside of eastern France, stopping at hostelries and restaurants for meals and accommodations. All trips are guided by experienced horsemen, and no day includes more than 20 miles of travel. The area traversed is rural and quiet. **Cost:** $290 for 10 days, $97 for 3 days includes meals, accommodations. **When:** July to September. **Contact:** Societe Hippique d'Epinal, Ravin d'Olima, 8800 Chantraine Epinal, France.

Spain

In the Steps of Spanish Smugglers: The horse trails of Andalucia, once frequented mainly by smugglers, are explored on a 2-week horsepacking trip. After meeting in Seville, riders travel by car to San Jose de Valle for a day of familiarization with the horses before setting out into the hills. For the next 10 days, the group rides through rolling countryside, hilly areas and Atlantic beaches. Among the stops are Cape Trafalgar, where Nelson defeated the Armada; the prehistoric caves near Zahara de los Atunes; Bolonia, with its Roman ruins; and Sierra de la Plata, with a broad view of North Africa. Accommodations are in hotels. There is free time throughout for exploring, short side trips, swimming and other activities, before the return to Seville. **Cost:** $850 includes transportation from Seville, food, accommodations, horses, guide. **When:** May, June, September, October. **Contact:** Antonio Figueiredo, 13 Macdougal Alley, New York, NY 10011, USA.

Horseback through the Spanish Nevadas: Andalucian horses, known for sure-footedness, strength, courage and kind temperament, are ridden through the Sierra Nevadas on a 15-day trip. While on the trek riders are responsible for looking after the horses, including tasks such as feeding, watering, grooming and tacking up. The group departs London for Malaga by plane, then drives to Orgiva to

Riders and their Andalucian mounts stop for a rest on a rocky slope in the Spanish Sierra Nevada. WEXAS offers a 15-day horsepacking trip through the region for $730. (Diane Hucks)

meet the horses and guides. A briefing the following morning is followed by an afternoon ride along the Guadalfeo River. Then participants head out to ride from village to village, stopping each night in local inns known as posadas, where they dine on Andalucian home cooking. In the summer months riders climb gradually from the Mediterranean lowlands, eventually crossing the snowline at over 10,000 feet and reaching the highest peaks of the Sierra Nevada. In spring and autumn, when the highest mountains are deep in snow, mounted travelers follow the Valle de Lecrin on a route which explores a lower and warmer area. Both trips include 2 rest days in which members of the group can make excursions to Granada and the coast. **Cost:** $730 from London includes transportation, accommodations, meals, guide. **When:** March to October. **Contact:** WEXAS International, 45 Brompton Rd., Knightsbridge, London SW3 1DE, Great Britain; phone 01-589-0500.

(M)

Switzerland

Valais Canton by Mule: The countryside and mule paths of the Canton of Valais serve as unpaved highways for a week-long journey through mountainous terrain. Originally used to keep villages in touch with each other, the mule trails provide travelers an opportunity to meet residents of remote areas. Departing from Haute Nendaz or Grimentz, riders proceed over hilly country through meadows and larch forests to Beysonnaz for lunch and on to a view of the Rhone Valley at the day's end. The trip continues to the Pyramids of Euseigne, a rock formation caused by wind erosion; Rechy Valley with its abundant wildlife; and the mountain village of Vercorin. Participants generally walk 5 to 8 hours each day, with 2 people sharing each mule; luggage is transported by jeep. Accommodations are at local inns. **Cost:** $165 includes roundtrip rail transportation from Sion, meals, accommodations. **When:** May to October. **Contact:** Welcome Swiss Tours, 7 Ave. Benjamin-Constant, 1003 Lausanne, Switzerland; phone (021) 20 68 21.

Wales

Equestrian Experiences: Sixty riding centers throughout the Welsh countryside provide travelers with the opportunity to enjoy a variety of riding and trekking experiences. Some rides lead high into the hills while others follow easier routes. Most centers offer casual riding by the hour, half-day and day as well as week-long holidays that include accommodations. Riders at all levels of skill are equally welcome: experts can improve their competence and beginners can learn basic techniques. Specialized clothing is not required, though a list of recommended items is available. **Cost:** On request. **When:** Year-round. **Contact:** Wales Tourist Board, Llandaff, Cardiff CF5 2YZ, Great Britain; phone 022-27281.

Welsh Pony Trek: A week-long riding trip takes place in a remote area of Wales and is based at a youth hostel. Participants are met at the Abergavenny train station and transported to Capel-y-ffin hostel, a modernized farmhouse in the isolated Lanthony Valley. After a day of getting acquainted with the horses and making a short ride, members spend the week on progressively longer rides into the ridges and valleys of the area; participants return to the hostel each night. One day off in the middle of the week lets the horses rest while trip members travel by car for a night's stay at a nearby hostel. Participants must be 16 or older and weigh under 200 pounds. The week is suitable both for novices wishing to receive basic riding instruction, and for experienced riders wishing to have some free time for exploring. **Cost:** $120 includes transportation during the trip, accommodations, food, horses, instructor/guide. **When:** April to October. **Contact:** YHA Adventure Holidays, Trevelyan House, St. Albans, Herts., Great Britain; phone St. Albans 55215.

MEXICO

Chihuahua

Copper Canyon Trail Ride: Horseback riding through Copper Canyon in the mountains of Chihuahua highlights an 11-day trip that departs from El Paso, Texas. The trip begins with sightseeing in Chihuahua City. Then participants ride the trail at Creel, in the heart of the Sierra Madre Occidental, and at La Estancia, a hunting lodge in the mountainous area near Cuauhtemoc. Riders also follow the old Pershing Trail through Casas

Grandes, with its Mormon colony and prehistoric Indian ruins. When not on horseback, participants travel through the countryside by van. **Cost:** $520 from El Paso. **When:** July. **Contact:** International Training Programs, The University of Oklahoma, 1700 Asp, Norman, OK 73073, USA; phone (405)325-1941.

Adventure on the Border: An international horsepack trip takes riders from Lajitas, Texas to the arid regions of northern Mexico for 4 days. On the first day, participants ride to Nuevo Lajitas, a Mexican community on Arroyo San Carlos, where camp is set up in a cottonwood grove. On the second day, the group visits the Presidio Viejo and rides on to the village of San Carlos, an oasis in the desert. The route continues up San Carlos Canyon on the third day and ends with a ride back to Texas, stopping at a Mexican ranch for lunch. Riders must be at least 15 years old. **Cost:** $200 includes equipment, accommodations, food, guide. **When:** October to April. **Contact:** Lajitas Trading Post, P.O. Box 48, Terlingua, TX 79852, USA; phone (915)364-2234.

SOUTH AMERICA

Peru

Hiking the Cordillera Blanca: The remote and spectacular Cordillera Blanca is explored on a 16-day trip out of Lima. Traveling by bus via Huaraz to Quebrada Llanganuco, participants meet their pack animals there and head into the back country. In the next 2 weeks they cross several passes over 15,000 feet and encounter a number of panoramic mountain views. Remote canyons house Inca and pre-Inca ruins, and tiny towns cling to mountainsides; much of the trip is spent in completely untouched areas. The group finally arrives in the town of Caraz to catch a bus back to Lima via Huaraz. **Cost:** $695 from Lima includes food, equipment, transportation, guides. **When:** May to September. **Contact:** Andean Odyssey Tours, 2141 14th S., Suite 1, Boulder, CO 80302, USA. ***(M)***

UNITED STATES

Alaska

Nenana Horsepacking Trips: Central Alaska is the area where a guide service takes families and individuals through wilderness high country. The week-long trip follows a route from Brushkana Creek on the Denali Highway to Nenana Glacier at the headwaters of the Nenana River, and back. After one day at a remote lodge on Brushkana Creek, the group sets off for 5 days of packing in the vicinity of Mt. McKinley National Park. Dall sheep, moose, caribou

Riders explore Arizona's lower Sonoran life zone, where giant saguaro cacti are found, on a 5-day trip offered by American Wilderness Alliance. (Arizona Office of Tourism)

and grizzly bears are common, and there are opportunities for fishing en route. **Cost:** $595 includes meals, lodging, camping equipment, guide. **When:** July, August. **Contact:** Alaskan Adventure, P.O. Box 18, Hope, AK 99605, USA. *(M)*

Central Range on Horseback: Relatively unstructured horsepacking trips into the central Alaska Range last at least 7 days but longer trips can be arranged. After being flown or driven to Central or Fielding Lake, participants explore open tundra and aspen, birch and spruce forests. Participants need not be experienced riders, but should be in good shape. **Cost:** $1,050 includes tack, equipment, food, guides. **When:** June to September. **Contact:** Lee R. Spears, Outfitter, Goldstream Rd., SR Box 20237, Fairbanks, AK 99701, USA; phone (907)479-3351.

Arizona

Ups and Downs of the Santa Catalinas: Riders travel on horseback through landscapes ranging from deserts to southwestern mountains on a 5-day pack trip leaving from a ranch near Tucson and heading toward the Santa Catalinas, the southernmost portion of the Rocky Mountains. As group members ride, they travel through several distinct ecosystems: the lower Sonoran life zone where the trip begins, and the Montane and Canadian ecosystems at the higher elevations. The country is much as it was in Arizona's pioneer days, and riders are likely to see remnants of earlier inhabitants. One part of the trail intercepts the old stagecoach line into Tucson, and the group follows it up to about 6,000 feet and through the Carleau Gap. Most of the country the group traverses is in the Coronado National Forest and is part of the Canada Del Oro watershed. The trip is meant to strike a balance between comfort and the appeal of traveling in pioneer fashion through characteristically western landscapes; daily stints on horseback are limited to 3 or 4 hours. **Cost:** $1,000 includes horses, equipment, meals, lodging on the nights before and after the trip. **When:** September. **Contact:** American Wilderness Alliance, 4260 E. Evans, Denver, CO 80222, USA; phone (303)758-5018.

Horsepacking in the Superstitions: A 6-day horsepacking and camping trip explores many of the remains of the mixture of Spanish and Indian culture in the Superstition Mountains. Beginning in Apache Junction, the group spends the first day riding to Reevis Camp at about 5,000 feet, which serves as base camp for the next day's ride to the Spanish walled ruins. The trip continues with a descent through Rogers Canyon into the desert to camp near the little-known Salado Indian cliff dwellings, which date from the 13th century. After a layover day here, participants ride past ancient Indian pictographs to White Rock Springs to spend a day in sight of Weaver's Needle. A side trip is made to Peralta Camp, site of an Indian massacre of Spaniards, and on the last day the trip returns to Apache Junction. **Cost:** $50 to $55 a day includes food, horses, equipment, guide. **When:** March, April, May. **Contact:** American Wilderness Experience, P.O. Box 1486A, Boulder, CO 80306, USA; phone (303)449-0056.

(M)

California

I Remember Llama: The llama, used as a beast of burden in South America, has been eclipsed by horses and mules in this country. However, a variety of llama pack trips is offered in the Sierra Nevada range. Most of the trips are short, lasting from a weekend up to 7 days. Routes and conditions vary from a level trail along the Yuba River's south fork to mountainous terrain in the King Range, a secluded and spectacular area west of Garberville. Other trips explore the Merced River valley in the Yosemite area, the eastern Sierra high country near Bishop, Pt. Reyes National Seashore and Lassen Volcanic National Park. Generally, participants meet at the trailhead, where the llamas are loaded. Schedules and routes are very flexible, and chores are shared throughout the trip. **Cost:** $43 to $210 includes food, group equipment, llamas, guides. **When:** March to October. **Contact:** Mother Lode Llamas, 4935 Slate Creek Rd., Placerville, CA 95667, USA; phone (916)622-2566.

Horseback in the High Sierras: A variety of horsepacking trips lasting from 5 to 7 days is offered in the High Sierras. Participants may either hike or ride, with the pace on some trips specially geared for hikers. The trips include a 5-day expedition into the Minarets Wilderness area; a 6-day trip to Fish Creek and the John Muir Wilderness; a 6-day trip through Silver and Mono passes to Rock Creek; a 7-day trip up the upper Kern River to Sequoia National Park; and a 5-day trip to McGee Canyon. Also offered are a 2-day traditional-style horse drive from Mammoth to Owens Valley and custom pack trip outfitting. **Cost:** $165 to $295, depending on length of trip and mode of transport, includes food, equipment, guide. **When:** June to October. **Contact:** Red's Meadow Pack Stations, P.O. Box 395, Mammoth Lakes, CA 93546, USA; phone (714)934-2345 or 873-3928.

Sierra Nevadas Pack Trip: Participants may choose from among a wide variety of horsepacking trips into the Sierra Nevadas leaving from Bishop. A pack train takes travelers to one of 5 wilderness areas and returns later to pack them back out; the length of stay is up to trip members and does not affect packing costs. Or loads may be carried in to a specified area while parties hike or ride in to meet it. Another option is an extended pack trip on which the packer, stock and possibly a cook accompany participants throughout the trip. Day rides on saddle horses are also available. **Cost:** $50 to $140, depending on size of party and destination, for pack train trip; $102 a day for extended pack trip includes packer, stock, cook; $12 a day for saddle horses. **When:** Year-round except winter. **Contact:** Rock Creek Pack Station, Box 248, Bishop, CA 93514, USA; phone (714)935-4493, winter (714)872-8331.

On Trinity Trails: Hundreds of miles of riding trails are available in the Trinity Alps Primitive Area. A selection of fully or partially guided trips allows a maximum of travel flexibility. On one such trip participants and their gear are taken by horseback and pack animal to a campsite on a lake or stream. During the stay individuals may explore the surrounding wilderness at their leisure, and the guide returns on a pre-determined day. On other trips the guide remains with the party and escorts them through a variety of terrain including high alpine lakes, broad meadows, primeval forests and rugged sawtooth ridges. **Cost:** On request. **When:**

On request. **Contact:** Trinity Pack Trains, P.O. Box 277, Trinity, CA 96091, USA; phone (916)266-3305.

Colorado

Maroon Bells Riding: Groups of up to 17 riders gather at Aspen for 10-day trips high in the mountains to Maroon Bells-Snowmass. Trails reach elevations as high as 12,500 feet, providing panoramic views of surrounding peaks. Riders pass by deep spruce forests and wildflower patches as well as snow-fed streams and lakes that are home to a variety of trout. Trip members camp out in 2-person tents and carry no more than 30 pounds of gear on the trail. **Cost:** $490 from Aspen includes group equipment, food, horses. **When:** July, August. **Contact:** AFA Trail Riders of the Wilderness, 1319 18th St. NW, Washington, DC 20036, USA; phone (202)467-5810.

Crossing the Divide: The San Juan Mountains with their 14,000-foot peaks are the site of 6- and 12-day horsepacking trips starting at Pine River Campground and twice crossing the Continental Divide. One of these crossings is at Sawtooth Pass. Camps are pitched at Ribbon Falls and Johnson Creek, and when the rivers and creeks are full, alpine river running is included in scheduled activities. A glacial basin called Columbine Pass also affords spelunkers and rockhounds an opportunity for exploration. **Cost:** $50 to $55 a day includes

AFA Trail Riders of the Wilderness offer 10-day horsepacking trips through Colorado's Maroon Bells-Snowmass region. (Keith Gunnar)

food, equipment. **When:** June to September. **Contact:** American Wilderness Experience, P.O. Box 1486A, Boulder, CO 80306, USA; phone (303)449-0056. ***(M)***

Rocky Mountains Horsemanship Camp: Led by 4 counselors, 20 young people spend a month on a horsepack trip across the Colorado Rockies. After meeting in Denver, the group drives to a base ranch in the foothills of the Rockies, where a few days are spent on basic training in horsemanship and wilderness camping skills. Each camper is provided with a horse, and under the direction of an experienced wrangler, youngsters learn how to care for and feed them. While cross-country and trail riding through remote parts of Colorado National Forest for about 20 days, the group encounters timbered slopes, rocky gulches and mountain meadows. After gaining some experience riders return to the base for the last few days to practice riding skills and compete in gymkhana events. **Cost:** $750 includes meals, accommodations, guides, group camping equipment, horses and tack. **When:** June to July for boys; July to August for girls. **Contact:** C Bar T Trail Ranch, Box 158, Idledale, CO 80453, USA; phone (303)674-5149.

Overlooking the Great Divide: Trips into the Weminuche Wilderness Area and the Rio Grande National Forest give participants a chance to see a variety of small animal and plant life, as well as elk, deer and bighorn sheep. The 9-day trips begin from a lodge near South Fork where riders travel into the high country, climbing as high as 13,000 feet on horseback. One trip goes into an area known as La Garita, Spanish for "the overlook," which sits astride the Continental Divide. The other traverses the San Juan Mountains in the Weminuche region, one of Colorado's largest wilderness areas. During the trip participants cross the Continental Divide several times. A special Weminuche trip is offered which begins at Wolf Creek Pass, continues along the Skyline Trail of the San Juans and ends at the headwaters of the Rio Grande above Creede. **Cost:** $495 for Weminuche and Rio Grande trips, $995 for headwaters of Rio Grande trip includes camping equipment, horses, food, guides. **When:** June to August. **Contact:** Cottonwood Cove Lodge, Wagon Wheel Gap, CO 81154, USA; phone (303)658-2242.

Horsepacking in the Southwest: Horsepacking for 5 or 7 days in Arizona and Colorado leads participants over Weminuche Wilderness trails to Geronimo's Cave and the Angel Cliff Dwellings. Besides enjoying the diverse terrain, trip members ride through aspen and spruce thickets and may fish the emerald lakes. **Cost:** $275 to $310 includes meals, horses, accommodations, equipment, guide. **When:** March to September. **Contact:** Crader's Wilderness Safaris, 28481 State Hwy. 160, Durango, CO 81301, USA; phone (303)247-2533; winter, P.O. Box 742, Apache Junction, AZ 85220, USA; phone (602)986-0751 or 969-7361.

Rio Grande Horsepacking: Participants can either ride or hike and pack their gear on horses during week-long trips in Colorado's Rio Grande National Forest and surrounding wilderness areas. Trips are tailored to individualized interests. **Cost:** $40 to $50 a day. **When:** By arrangement. **Contact:** Wilderness Adventures, Inc., P.O. Box 82, South Fork, CO 81154, USA; phone (303)873-5331.

Idaho

Horsepacking and Rafting along the Salmon: A 7-day adventure in the Chamberlain Basin area offers a range of wilderness activities for individuals and families. The week begins with a 1-hour flight from Boise over Salmon Breaks Canyon, the nation's second deepest, to the basin where participants are transported to the Stonebraker Ranch. After fishing, relaxing and getting acquainted with their trail horses, the group heads toward the Salmon River on horseback. The ride continues downstream along Chamberlain Creek for about 4 hours to a campsite at Jenkins Crossing. At noon on the third day, the group boards rafts for a float down the Salmon River, through Salmon Falls and past Barth Hot Springs to the mouth of Bargamin Creek. Two more days of rafting follow before arrival at the Mackay Bar lodge, where the variety of activities available includes trail rides, backpacking, jet-boating, swimming and kayaking. The return to Boise is by charter aircraft. **Cost:** $700 includes meals, transportation, camping equipment except sleeping bag. **When:** July to September. **Contact:** Mackay Bar, 3190 Airport Wy., Boise, ID 83705, USA; phone (208)344-1881. ***(M)***

Custom Sawtooth Trips: The Sawtooth Wilderness has over 180 alpine lakes nestled among high peaks, 42 of which stand more than 10,000 feet high. A variety of pack trip options is available into the area from a headquarters between Alturas and Redfish lakes. The most economical trip uses packstock and a guide only to take a party in and out, so participants may pitch camp and hike or ride for as long as they wish. Fully guided trips are also available, with all gear, food and planning handled by professionals. The stock and packer may also be hired for trips which change camp every night or two. The Sawtooth area is fairly remote, and snowfields are found year-round on the shady side of tall peaks. Opportunities abound for wildlife observation, fishing and hiking. **Cost:** $15 a day; $40 a day for all-inclusive trip includes meals, camping gear, guide, horses; $75 for an overnight trip. **When:** May to September. **Contact:** Mystic Saddle Ranch, Box 461-AT, Mountain Home, ID 83647, USA; phone (208)587-5091; June to November: Box AT, Stanley, ID 83340, USA; phone (208)774-3591.

The Bitterroots by Horseback: Participants need bring only their personal effects on completely outfitted horsepack trips of 6 days in the central Idaho wilderness. Adventurers saddle up for rides into the Selway-Bitterroot Wilderness, Salmon River Wilderness, Bighorn Crags or the Continental Divide area in the Bitterroot Mountain Range. The small group of riders covers a variety of terrain once frequented by Nez Perce Indians, including steep canyons, high alpine meadows and hundreds of miles of rarely used trails through pine and fir forest and snow-capped granite peaks. Clear lakes and streams provide opportunities for swimming, fishing and relaxing. Riders travel deep within the Salmon River wilderness to reach Salmon Falls, one of the base camps, or journey to Selway Falls on Fog Mountain. Experienced guides lead all horsepack trips. **Cost:** $50 a day includes equipment, horses, guides, meals. **When:** July to September. **Contact:** Primitive Area Float Trips, Inc., P.O. Box 585, Salmon, ID 83467, USA; phone (208)756-2319.

Montana

Riding in the Bitterroot Backcountry: Surrounded by the peaks of the Bitterroot Mountains, which straddle the borders of Montana and Idaho, a group of 6 riders makes a trail through the colorful high country. The 6-day trip provides time for guided trail riding, camping, fishing, photographing and other activities, chosen by the group. The trip originates at a ranch located in the Bitterroot Valley on the edge of the Selway-Bitterroot Wilderness, the largest designated wilderness area in the nation. **Cost:** $375 includes equipment, food, transportation. **When:** June to August. **Contact:** Bob Crick High Country Outfitters, Rt. 1, Box 99A, Victor, MT 59875, USA; phone (406)642-3233. ***(M)***

Pack It In: A guest ranch in the foothills offers pack trips into the Spanish Peaks area and Yellowstone National Park. Arranged on a custom basis and usually taken in conjunction with a stay at the ranch, trips of any length can be organized. Awareness of fragile mountain ecology is emphasized by the guide, who sets up camp and cooks. Possible activities on the trip include photography, wildlife observation, bird watching, hiking, swimming and fishing. **Cost:** On request. **When:** Summer. **Contact:** Lone Mountain Ranch, Box 145, Big Sky, MT 59716, USA; phone (406)995-4644.

Hiking and Horsepacking: Seven-day walking trips and 10-day horsepacking trips are offered in the western Montana wilderness. A wide variety of trail rides and backpacking and walking trips with

Smoke rises from a breakfast fire as horsepackers begin breaking camp and preparing for the day's ride in the Pecos Wilderness of New Mexico. (Dode Hershey)

packstock is available. To minimize the environmental impact the number of participants is limited to 8 on horseback and 10 on hiking trips. Wildlife observation is done along the way amid spectacular natural scenery. The outings attempt to recreate the methods of early pioneer travel, combining traditional horsepacking techniques with campfire cookouts. All participants must be in good physical condition. **Cost:** $380 for 7-day hikes, $750 for 10-day horseback trips. **When:** July, August. **Contact:** Wildlife Outfitters, Rt. 1, Box 99B, Victor, MT 59875, USA; phone (406)642-3262. *(M)*

New Mexico

Pecos Horsepacking: Two horsepacking options are offered, one with only light riding in the Pecos, and one with more strenuous riding in Yellowstone. The trip to New Mexico's Pecos Wilderness lasts 6 days, with an average of 7 miles of riding each day. The trip to Yellowstone National Park in Wyoming covers about 15 miles a day for 7 days. Both trips offer ample opportunities for the amateur photographer, naturalist and fisher to observe wildlife. The ride through Yellowstone, the nation's oldest national park, traverses grassy meadowlands and mountain trails, some as high as 10,000 feet. Riding mainly through mountains and valleys, the Pecos trip is an appropriate trip for inexperienced riders. **Cost:** $390 for Pecos trip, $435 for Yellowstone trip, includes food, camping equipment, horses, guide. **When:** June to October. **Contact:** Dode Hershey, Box 1901, Santa Fe, NM 87501, USA; phone (505)471-6431.

North Carolina

Smoky Mountain Trails: A large ranch located at 5,000 feet in the Great Smoky Mountains provides a variety of horsepacking trips from a half-day to 10 days. Fifteen hundred acres in size, the ranch borders the Great Smoky Mountains National Park, so a wide selection of isolated terrain is within easy riding distance. The network of trails through the ranch and the park is lined with wildflowers, and the elevation offers moderately warm, bright days and clear, cool nights. Other activities available to ranch guests include swimming, hiking, tennis and fishing. Trips lasting a week to 10 days may be arranged in advance. **Cost:** On request. **When:** By arrangement. **Contact:** Cataloochee Ranch, Rt. 1, Box 500, Maggie Valley, NC 28751, USA; phone (704)926-1401.

Utah

High Plateau Horsepacking: Each season, 2 horsepacking trips are run into the high desert country of the San Rafael Swell and the Maze and Grand Gulch of Canyonlands National Park. In the San Rafael Swell, a 5-day trip ventures to the area on the north end of the Swell along the San Rafael River. Another 5-day trip heads south into the area surrounding Muddy Creek. Other trips take horsepackers to the Maze, west of the confluence of the Green and Colorado rivers, one of the most austere regions of the Colorado Plateau. Participants may also choose to visit the Grand Gulch Primitive Area, a northern drainage of the San Juan River, which features one of the most extensive sites of the Anasazi culture outside Mesa Verde National Park. **Cost:** On request. **When:** By arrangement. **Contact:** Hondoo Rivers and Trails, P.O. Box 377, Ferron, UT 84523, USA; phone (801)384-2961.

Canyonlands Packing: Canyonlands National Park is the site of a variety of 6- and 7-day horsepack trips to explore Indian ruins, eroded rock formations and abandoned camps of the Old West. The 7-day trips take participants through the park, past such natural wonders as Wedding Ring Arch, Fish Eye and Angel Arch. The 6-day journeys pass through the Maze and the Butch Cassidy/Sundance Kid area.Walking trips with packstock are also available. **Cost:** $300 to $420 includes meals, equipment, guide. **When:** June to August. **Contact:** Horsehead Pack Trips, P.O. Box 68, Monticello, UT 84535, USA; phone (801)587-2929.

Outlaw Trail Ride: Far away from the noise and pollution of jeep roads, trail horses take riders on a 7-day trip to areas of Canyonlands National Park. After arrival in Hanksville, horses and riders set out on the trail, which stretches from Utah to Mexico and was once used by outlaws. Covering only a few miles each day, participants encounter such places as Robbers Roost Canyon, Dirty Devil River and Horseshoe Canyon. Trip members continue across the Spur to Big Spring country and into Horseshoe Canyon, then return to Green River where they may spend a layover day before joining an optional 6-day raft trip. **Cost:** $590, $985 with raft trip. **When:** May, August, September. **Contact:** Outlaw Trails Inc., P.O. Box 336, Green River, UT 84525, USA; phone (801)564-3477. ***(M)***

Cascade Corrals' outdoor kitchen in the Cascade Mountains provides meals for participants on their Washington horsepacking trips, which cost as little as $65. (Cascade Corrals)

Washington

Horsepacking in the Northwest: A variety of trips is available in the North Cascades area, either riding or hiking with pack horses. The trips range in length from 3 to 9 days, and itineraries include North Cascades National Park, Glacier Peak Wilderness, Sawtooth Ridge and the Summit Trail. Custom trips can be put together, with September particularly reserved for this. Also offered is a 2-week class in mountain travel with horses, covering horse handling, tracking, shoeing and saddling, camp cooking, axmanship and guiding. **Cost:** $65 to $330 for trips, $500 for horsepacking school includes food, transportation from Chelan, horses, equipment, guide. **When:** May to October. **Contact:** Cascade Corrals, Stehekin, WA 98852, USA; phone (509)663-1822. *(M)*

Packing into the North Cascades: Summer horsepacking trips into the North Cascade Range utilize 2 large, semipermanent base camps in the wilderness. The trips, of flexible length, begin and end at a ranch located 18 miles from Winthrop. From there participants are packed into the woods to pursue a variety of activities, including photography, day hikes, wildlife observation, collecting alpine wildflowers and fishing. Some nights are spent at temporary, pitched camps and some at the 2 base camps, one at Hidden Lakes and one on Sheep Mountain. Previous riding experience is not necessary. **Cost:** On request. **When:** June to August. **Contact:** Claude Miller, Winthrop, WA 98862, USA; phone (509)996-2350.

West Virginia

Seldom Seen Ride: Riders combine horsepacking with a short float trip to cover 80 miles of West Virginia, from Cold Run Valley to the Potomac River, in a week-long trip. The route passes along the Cacapon

Ridge, past Bear Den Rocks and into a portion of the Seldom Seen Valley near the Virginia border. The group then fords the Cacapon River and travels along Sideling Hill Mountain, camping at the Ingleside Farm. Riders then transfer to rafts for a day of floating on the Cacapon and relaxing at camp. The final leg of the trip begins with a ride down the old railroad bed to Paw Paw on the way to Greenridge Mountain. **Cost:** $290 includes food, horses, equipment, guide. **When:** June to August. **Contact:** Coolfont Re+Creation, Inc., Berkeley Springs, WV 25411, USA.

Wyoming

Riding in the Mountains: The rugged Wyoming Mountain Range is the setting for a week-long horsepacking trip. Under the sponsorship of the American Forestry Association, the participants travel from Pinedale into the mountains to ride trails climbing to altitudes of about 10,000 feet. The party of up to 14 riders passes through alpine meadows and near high peaks in the northeast corner of the Bridger National Forest, which is adjacent to the Teton National Forest. Three different camps are established at elevations under 8,500 feet, with the layover time used for day rides to Lookout Mountain, Telephone Pass and McCain Meadows. Opportunities abound for the photographer, naturalist and fishing enthusiast. Participants encounter temperatures ranging from near freezing to the mid-seventies. **Cost:** $380 includes food, horses, camping equipment, transportation from Pinedale, guide. **When:** July. **Contact:** AFA Trail Riders of the Wilderness, 1319 18th St. NW, Washington, DC 20036, USA; phone (202)467-5810.

Shoshone National Forest Horse Ranch: Guests at a ranch 9 miles east of Yellowstone National Park participate in a variety of activities during a week's stay. Aside from horseback riding and an overnight pack trip, guests visit historical

A rider learns to properly fit cinches and straps to his packhorse. (West Virginia Department of Commerce)

A string of packhorses loaded with provisions and camping equipment moves slowly through a mountain meadow in Yellowstone National Park. (Wyoming Travel Commission)

attractions and raft the Shoshone River. **Cost:** $220 a week; $200 for 3 or more; half-price for children under 6. **When:** June to August. **Contact:** Crossed Sabres Ranch, Wapiti, WY 82450, USA; phone (307)587-3750.

Summer Pack Trips: A trip geared to appeal to backpackers and riders alike takes horsepackers into the Teton Wilderness for 7 days. The trip includes layovers of 1 or more days at each campsite so everyone has plenty of time to enjoy the wilderness and engage in individual activities. The outfitter can also plan a route and itinerary to suit any group's particular interests and riding ability. Destinations of custom-designed trips include the Washakie Wilderness, Yellowstone National Park and the Gros Ventre Wilderness. Gentle mountain horses are assigned to each guest, and enough packstock accompanies the trip to insure fresh meats and vegetables rather than dehydrated foods. **Cost:** $50 a day for riders; $40 a day for hikers. **When:** July for scheduled trip; summer trips by arrangement. **Contact:** L.D. Frome, Outfitter, RFD, Afton, WY 83110, USA; phone (307)886-5240.

Gros Ventre Horsepacking: The Gros Ventre Range is the site of 5-, 7- and 10-day horsepacking trips for small groups of no more than 6 people. Participants spend the first and last night of each trip at the ranch in the Hoback River basin. Camping near streams, waterfalls or beaver ponds, riders encounter wildlife including antelope, deer, elk, moose, beavers, sandhill cranes, eagles and hawks. All trips wander through the Wyoming Range or the Gros Ventre Mountains. On a trip in August the group rides along the Upper Hoback River, then climbs up into acres of alpine meadows filled with wildflowers in full bloom. The terrain keeps changing from the open and rolling hills on the back side of Hoback Peak to narrow and wooded sections over the passes to marshy meadows following the creeks. Through fir, pine, sage and willow thickets participants return to the ranch for the conclusion of the trip. **Cost:** $319 for 5 days, $431 for 7 days, $594 for 10 days includes accommodations, meals, guides, equipment, horses. **When:** June to October. **Contact:** Game Hill Ranch, Bondurant, WY 82922, USA; phone (307)733-2015 or 733-4120.

Yellowstone Packing: A week of horsepacking in Yellowstone National Park features a small group of 4 or less and a flexible itinerary. Leaving from Cooke City, Montana, riders travel through the northeastern area of the park and exercise one of several options: a base camp trip, in which day rides and overnights are taken out of a single, established camp; moving trips, during which every day or every other day are spent riding, with camp pitched anew each night; or fishing trips. All riding is done at a walk, regardless of the riders' experience, and a day's riding is about 4 hours. The guide prepares meals. **Cost:** $600 includes transportation, food, horses and equipment, guide, pickup service from Bozeman or Billings. **When:** June to September. **Contact:** Ralph Miller's Wilderness Pack Trips, Cooke City, MO 59020, USA.

RESOURCES

Clubs and Associations

American Guides Association
Box B
Woodland, CA 95695, USA
Phone (916)662-6824

American Horse Council
1700 K St. NW
Washington, DC 20006, USA
Phone (202)296-4031

Colorado Dude and Guest Ranch Assn.
Box 6440, Cherry Creek Sta.
Denver, CO 80206, USA
Phone (303)674-4906

Eastern Professional Outfitters Assn.
P.O. Box 252
Hot Springs, NC 28743, USA

Idaho Outfitters and Guides Assn.
P.O. Box 95
Boise, ID 83701, USA
Phone (208)376-5680

Ontario Trail Riders Association
2240 Kingston Rd.
Scarborough, ON Canada M1N 1T9

The Wilderness Society
1901 Pennsylvania Ave. NW
Washington, DC 20036, USA
Phone (202)467-5810

Wyoming Outfitters Association
Box A1
Jackson, WY 83001, USA

Riders may take 5-, 7- or 10-day Game Hill Ranch horsepacking trips through Wyoming's Gros Ventre Mountains wilderness. (Game Hill Ranch)

CATTLE DRIVING

Cowboys both real and mythical have figured prominently in American folklore for the past 150 years. The legend of the cowboy got its start in the 1820s when settlers first came across the Spanish and Mexican ranches in Texas. They quickly learned the methods of the *vaqueros* who rustled cattle on horseback using ropes, spurs and branding irons. During the era of the open range between 1866 to 1890, cowboys became national folk heroes. Over 5 million cattle were herded from Texas to Abilene and Dodge City, Kansas on the famous Chisholm Trail.

If you've watched westerns on television or imagined yourself in the saddle while reading a dime novel, you can live out your cowboy fantasies on hundreds of working ranches in the United States and Canada. Riding the range with modern cowboys, you can join a cattle drive, throw dogies and brand calves or herd horses on a fall roundup. You can sit back and soak up the atmosphere at a bustling ranch or pitch in to help mend fences, feed livestock or brush down mounts. While men once dominated the cowboy society of the past, women are now welcome to participate in all ranch activities.

Many ranches also provide access to nearby wilderness areas. Hiking, swimming and horseback riding are available to guests at a ranch in British Columbia. You can search for Indian arrowheads, explore abandoned settlements and look for dinosaur bones while staying at a spread in Colorado. In winter, cross-country skiing and sleigh rides are offered at a few ranches that put up guests year-round.

Every ranch provides a unique experience. You might stay in a rustic log cabin, share a bunkhouse with other tenderfoot wranglers or camp under the stars. Wherever you go, the aroma of bacon and coffee, the smell of sweating horses, the dusty trail filled with bawling cattle and the rhythmic creak of your saddle as you ride the open range will take you back a hundred years—to the days of the Wild West. □

Cattle ranching is still practiced in many areas of western Canada and the United States; dudes can lend a hand on spreads from Arizona to Alberta. (Arizona Office of Tourism)

CATTLE DRIVING

CANADA

Alberta

Stock Farm Stay: A working stock farm in east-central Alberta invites vacationers for stays either to participate in the daily chores or to travel in the area. The farm is located about 160 miles east of Edmonton in the middle of an extensive and well-established farming area; participants may drive cattle, ride horses, help tend grain, visit other farms in the area or make a trip to nearby Dilberry Provincial Park. Winter visits provide opportunities for cross-country skiing and ice skating. Family activities on the farm are also open to guests. **Cost:** $15 a day for adults, half-price for children under 6 includes room and board in the main house or a furnished guest house; $2 a day for camping privileges. **When:** Year-round. **Contact:** Poplar Bluff Stock Farm, RR 1, Chauvin, AB Canada T0B 0V0.

British Columbia

Summer Roundup: Families can enjoy summer stays at a 5,000-acre working ranch on the eastern slopes of the Canadian Rockies near Dawson Creek. Visitors not arriving by car can take a bus to the town of Chetwynd, where they are met by ranch hands. There are more than 100 head of horses, and participants are encouraged to help with roundups and various ranch chores. Accommodation is provided in log cabins, with home-cooked meals served in a nearby lodge

Displays of skill and daring, rodeos provide opportunities for cowboys and ranchers to practice techniques used on the range. (Arizona Office of Tourism)

building. The ranch sponsors a special program for boys between 10 and 16 years of age; for 10 days during the summer they stay at the ranch and learn riding skills, packing, camping, wilderness survival and general wilderness lore. **Cost:** $200 for boys camp includes accommodations in house-tents, all meals; $250 a person for family cabins includes accommodations and meals for 1 week. **When:** Summer months. **Contact:** Pruckl Ranch, Box 88, Chetwynd, BC Canada V0C 1J0.

Open Ranching: Participants gather at a historic cattle ranch in the Clinton Valley about 2½ miles northeast of the town of Clinton. At the working ranch, participants join in several outdoor activities including horseback riding, swimming and hiking. Guests are provided with a horse and tack suited to their ability and experience. A new trail ride occurs daily, led by experienced wranglers through meadows and open cattle ranges. Horseback games such as gymkhana barrel racing and boot racing are among the activities scheduled. **Cost:** $75 to $140 depending on length of stay includes meals, accommodations, guides, horses, equipment. **When:** May to June, September to November. **Contact:** Three Bar J Ranch, P.O. Box 189, Clinton, BC Canada V0K 1K0; phone (604)459-2254.

UNITED STATES

California

Horse Drive and Trail Ride: For 4 days participants help herd mules and horses from a winter range in Owens Valley to summer headquarters at Rock Creek Pack Station in the High Sierras north of Bishop. Those joining the drive do not have to be expert riders, but should have had some time in the saddle. The group begins early in the morning, rides during the cooler part of the day and makes camp in the early afternoon. A cook and camp crew travels ahead of the group to set up camp. Tents are provided but participants may sleep in the open if they choose. Riders are given a horse to match their riding abilities and various mounts are available. **Cost:** $145. **When:** June. **Contact:** Rock Creek Pack Station, Box 248, Bishop, CA 93514, USA; phone (714)935-4493, summer 872-8331.

Colorado

Roundup Welcome: Tenderfoot wranglers are invited to spend time at the Canyon Ranch at the mouth of Dry Creek Canyon. The canyon, long used by the Ute Indians as a wintering area, is replete with abandoned settlements, arrowheads, tools and crockery, not to mention dinosaur bones and old mines. At the ranch there is plenty of horseback riding, and participants may assist in the cattle driving as ranch hands move the livestock from pasture to pasture. Accommodations include a bunkhouse and a log guest house, both heated for the chilly summer nights, and meals are served in the dining hall. **Cost:** $125 a week includes horseback rides, accommodations, jeep trips, meals. **When:** On request. **Contact:** Canyon Ranch, Rt. 1, P.O. Box 61A, Olathe,

CO 81425, USA; phone (303)323-5288.

Working Vacation: Travelers interested in the ways of a working ranch are invited to stay at the S Bar S Ranch near Steamboat Springs. On a daily or weekly basis participants stay in private cabins, in an old homestead log cabin or in a community bunkhouse. Each cabin has electricity, gas heat, a cooking range, utensils and hot water. Activities at the ranch include fishing and floating on the Elk River, hay rides, camping trips, pack trips and cook outs. Winter brings sleigh rides, skiing and snowmobiling. Because the ranch is a working one, guests may involve themselves in such chores as branding, mending fences, feeding livestock, haying, throwing dogies and driving cattle. **Cost:** From $70 a week, from $4 to $8 a day. **When:** Year-round. **Contact:** S Bar S Ranch, Steamboat Springs, CO 80477, USA; phone (303)879-0788.

Rocky Mountain Ranching: Up to 100 people can be accommodated at a working cattle and horse ranch near Rocky Mountain National Park. While staying in cabins, the lodge or a barn, guests take part in cattle drives, rodeos, hay rides, fishing trips, square dances, hikes and trail rides. Handled by capable cowboy wranglers, the riding horses are well cared for and dependable. Greenhorns can ride the trails to Echo Park, Inspiration Point, the Old Canyon and the Big Dam on half- and full-day trips. Forest land is being kept as a refuge for wildlife and participants may hike there, in the mountains and along the Big Thompson River that flows past the main lodge. An overnight pack trip involves a 3-hour ride from the ranch to a remote campsite used for rounding up the cattle. Child care and activities especially designed for children are available. **Cost:** On request. **When:** Year-round. **Contact:** Sylvan Dale Ranch, 2939 N. County Rd. 31 D, Loveland, CO 80537, USA; phone (303)667-3915.

Idaho

Ranching in Challis National Forest: A working cattle ranch nestled in a valley of the Salmon River Mountains, part of the Challis National Forest, provides all ranching experiences as well as goldpanning in local streams. Visitors use cabins while at the ranch, once the prime stop for the mule teams bringing supplies and equipment to the Lost Packer Mine. Guests may visit the local sawmill or climb to Pinyon Peak to view the Montana and Wyoming landscapes in the distance. **Cost:** $240 to $550 depending on party size, accommodations, length of stay. **When:** June to September. **Contact:** Diamond D Ranch, Inc., Clayton, ID 83227, USA; phone (208)879-2372; winter, P.O. Box 36005, Grosse Pointe Woods, MI 48236, USA; phone (313)821-4975.

Up on Timber Ridge: A working stock ranch adjacent to Coeur d'Alene National Forest, in Idaho's panhandle, offers guests a wide array of recreational activities. Besides helping with daily chores at the ranch, participants can ride horses through the high country; cruise any of the 12 nearby lakes in a 24-foot pontoon boat or in small rafts and kayaks; make overnight pack trips into the surrounding area; attend community festivals; go cross-country skiing in the winter; and swim in either of the 2 major rivers nearby. All activities are optional. Accommodations are either in small log cabins or teepees. **Cost:** On request. **When:** Year-round. **Contact:** Timber Ridge Ranch, P.O. Box 83, Harrison, ID 83833, USA; phone (208)689-3422.

Montana

Dude's Delight: Would-be ranchers stay at a working ranch in the heart of Montana's cattle country. Because the ranch is an operating concern, participants help, if they wish, in the chores which include branding, roundups, animal husbandry and more. Accommodations are provided in 2-, 3- and 4-room cabins; meals are provided in the central dining lodge. A new recreation building with ping pong and a pool serves as a family gathering place. Other activities include swimming, pack riding, excursions into the mountains and fishing. Everyone may go horseback riding, and horses and saddles are included. **Cost:** $190 to $235 a week. **When:** March to October. **Contact:** Sixty-three Ranch, Livingstone, MT 59047, USA; phone (406)222-0570.

New Mexico

Home on the Ranch: A 4,200-acre working ranch at an altitude of 8,200 feet in the Sangre de Cristo Mountains is home to riders on sojourns lasting as long as participants wish. Nestled in a green valley adjacent to the Pecos Wilderness, the ranch is within easy hiking and riding distance of mountains reaching up to 12,000 feet. Participants may take part in daily ranch activities such as working cattle and haying; gentle horses are provided for children to ride. No specific activities are planned, but guests at the ranch are free to ride, climb, go bird watching and camp overnight. Accommodations are in private cabins suitable for individuals or families, and meals are served in the ranch house. Aided by frequent rain showers, summer temperatures are cool, and due to the altitude there are no mosquitoes or snakes. **Cost:** $50 a person per day includes accommodations, meals, riding, transportation to and from air, rail and bus terminals. **When:** June to September. **Contact:** Gascon Ranch, Rociada, NM 87742, USA; phone (505)425-7038.

Age is no barrier to helping with some ranch work, as these young dudes learn on a ranch in Washington. (J. Sam Smith)

Oregon

Ranching on the Rogue: Nestled in the Rogue River Valley in southern Oregon is a working ranch where guests can participate in the functioning of the ranch or relax and be lazy. On 300 acres of meadows and timber, participants find good riding trails, excellent horses, nature paths, a stocked pond, photography opportunities, hay rides, hoedowns and pony races. During the week many different activities are planned such as a cattle roundup, a 5-hour ride to Jump-Off-Joe Creek with fishing and swimming on the way, and a raft trip down the Rogue to Indian Mary Campground. Dudes stay in a cottage or bunkhouse, and children's activities are supervised. During the snow ski season, transportation to the slopes is provided. **Cost:** $26 to $32 a day; $170 to $192 for 6 days depending on age and season includes transportation from Grants Pass, meals, accommodations, horses, river trips. **When:** Year-round. **Contact:** Paradise Guest Ranch, 7000 Monument Dr., Grants Pass, OR 97526, USA; phone (503)479-4333.

Wyoming

Western Experience: A working horse and cattle ranch is available to riders and non-riders alike. The ranch is bordered on 3 sides by mountains and is 15 miles southwest of Cody. Guests are provided with horses and may take riding instructions. Miles of trails are traveled through the mountains and valleys nearby on overnight pack trips. For non-riders, foot trails and trout ponds are available. Guests may participate in the ranch work including driving horses out to pasture and back each day. Float trips down the Shoshone River are also available, as well as trips to the Cody Rodeo. **Cost:** $28 to $35 a day for adults; $23 to $30 for children under 17. **When:** May to August. **Contact:** Hidden Valley Ranch, P.O. Box 3650, Southfork Rd., Cody, WY 82414, USA; phone (307)587-5090.

Cattle Ranch Visit: A working cattle ranch in Wyoming's Sweetwater

Valley provides week-long visits for adventurers. Participants travel from Casper to the ranch at the base of the Ferris Mountains and start right in helping the cowhands with chores. Overnight pack trips are made into the surrounding high country and float trips, either on quiet water or rapids, are run down the Platte River. Swimming in Alcova Lake, riding and hiking are only a few of the possibilities open during the week of unscheduled activities. **Cost:** $350 includes food, accommodations, transportation to and from Casper, activities, most equipment. **When:** May to September. **Contact:** Special InteresTours, P.O. Box 37, Medina, WA 98039, USA; phone (206)455-1960.

Working a Cattle Ranch: Participants may join in the operation and stay as long as they like at a cattle ranch located in Wyoming and Montana. At the ranch home guests are lodged in a trailer house or camper, but most of the time they stay at one of the cow camps, tending the herds. Sleeping in tents and cooking over campfires, participants join ranch hands in chores that vary according to the time of year: spring branding, summer fence mending, fall gathering from the summer pastures. Riders are followed by a 4-wheel drive pickup, and saddle-sore riders may take a break, although they may ride every day if they wish. The ranch is near the Pryor Mountain Wild Horse Range, and riders may have a chance to see the wild horses running. **Cost:** $200 a week. **When:** April through October. **Contact:** TX Ranch, P.O. Box 453, Lovell, WY 82431, USA; phone (406)484-2583. *(M)*

Whistle Creek Ranching: All ages of horse and cattle lovers take self-scheduled vacations at a working ranch outside of Cody. Situated between the Rocky, Big Horn and Pryor mountains near Yellowstone National Park, the ranch offers participants the opportunity to work and play the western way. Diversions include branding cattle, roundups, swimming, fishing and general ranch work. Accommodations are in a log cabin or in any one of many guest rooms. Each guest is matched with a horse to suit his or her skill and temperament. Pack trips into the mountains are also available. **Cost:** $160 to $200 a week includes meals. **When:** March to October. **Contact:** Whistle Creek Ranch, P.O. Box 752, Lovell, WY 82431, USA; phone (307)548-2478.

BACKPACKING

There is no better way to find out how simple life can be than to put your essentials into a backpack and carry your "home" on your shoulders into the wilderness. Backpacking is economical, provides access to countless trails and new terrain and is ideal for the whole family. All types of packs, clothing, equipment and freeze-dried foods make it possible to backpack into the wilds close to home or into remote areas throughout the world.

Using an external-frame rucksack, an internal-frame pack or a packboard you can tote your bedroll and kitchen through the highlands of Sri Lanka, along the 32-mile Milford Track in New Zealand or into the White Mountains of Crete. In the United States you can hike the 2,000-mile Appalachian Trail, as Grandma Gatewood did at 68 in tennis shoes, or hike and camp along any number of other trails that are marked and maintained for public use.

Whether you want to rough it for a weekend or a month, hike solo or with a group, there are trips available for hikers of all interests and ages. You can explore the Grand Canyon on an 8-day journey in Arizona, hike through Yellowstone National Park in Wyoming and the Beartooth Primitive Area of Montana, or stay in country inns as you hike a 60-mile section of Vermont's Long Trail. Many outfitters provide all necessary gear and equipment, even food; others offer instruction in map and compass use, campcraft, and hiking and camping skills during the trip.

The ability to walk great distances without getting tired takes some training, but enhances other activities such as wildlife photography and bird watching. Backpacking is good physical training for all other endurance sports and is often combined with other outdoor activities during some trips. You can go river rafting on a combination hiking-rafting trip to New Guinea, explore archaeological sites while on the trail in Guatemala or observe wildlife on a nontechnical climb of Mt. Kenya.

Backpacking is an inexpensive way to vacation, live in the woods or seal yourself off from all communication with the outside world. In a world made increasingly more "comfortable" by civilization, it's nice to know that you can still drink from an alpine stream, camp in the snow, or sit on a peak in Africa having used your own feet to get there. □

Cresting a ridge is always a favorite moment for backpackers. Framed by the mid-afternoon sun, this hiker tops a rise near Sloan Peak, Washington. (Keith Gunnar)

BACKPACKING

AFRICA

Kenya

Walking to Point Lenana: Although Mt. Kenya's summit is accessible only via technical routes, hikers can reach Point Lenana, 1,000 feet below the 17,058-foot summit. A leisurely 5-day hiking trip originates in Nairobi; participants proceed by car to base camp on the mountain's northwestern slopes, spending the first afternoon exploring untracked forest nearby in hopes of seeing buffalo, bushbucks, waterbucks and other rare animals. Three days are then spent hiking up the north side of the mountain through Liki North and Mackinder valleys via a route that affords spectacular views. At Point Lenana hikers spend some time exploring the equatorial glaciers before returning down the mountain and to Nairobi on the fifth day. **Cost:** $180 to $453, depending on size of party, includes transportation from Nairobi, food, equipment, guide. **When:** On request. **Contact:** Tropical Ice (Mountain Guides), P.O. Box 57341, Nairobi, Kenya; phone 743463.

Lesotho

Hiking the Malutis: Trip members stay in a base lodge near the Madibamotso River during a 17-day visit in the now independent kingdom formerly known as Basutoland. Located deep in the Maluti Mountains, the lodge provides easy access to varied walks through valleys, over rolling hills, along ridges and up to summits. Participants may descend to the river's banks for swimming, and a wide variety of bird life may be observed. Accommodations are in 2-bed chalets, with a comfortable lounge and dining room nearby. **Cost:** $1,120 includes roundtrip transportation from London, accommodations, some meals. **When:** October. **Contact:** Waymark Holidays, 295 Lillie Rd., London SW6 7LL, Great Britain; phone 01-385-5015.

Tanzania

Kilimanjaro via Wales: Three days of hiking and rock climbing in the north of Wales precede an ascent of Mt. Kilimanjaro, Africa's highest peak. Backpackers begin the 17-day trip with a flight from New York to London and proceed by land to Pen-y-Pass in Snowdonia National Park. After 3 days here, participants fly on to Moshi, departure point for the climb of Kilimanjaro. Nights during the ascent are spent in modern climbing huts so as to allow backpackers to acclimatize to the elevation. After the descent from Kilimanjaro, a visit is made to the Arusha Game Park before the return flight to New York. **Cost:** $795 land cost includes meals, accommodations, guides, porters. **When:** January. **Contact:** Alpine Ventures, 83 Academy Rd., North Andover, MA 01845, USA; phone (617)687-3421.

ASIA

Japan

The Japanese Alps: A month in Japan Alps National Park allows a small group of backpackers to explore the area's crimson-colored ridges and mountain trails. This area, among Japan's highest country, contains peaks over 9,800 feet and offers spectacular scenery accessible to non-climbers. Members must provide their own camping gear and are joined on the alpine hikes by members of Japanese mountain clubs. The trip also includes visits to several small country towns and areas of cultural interest. Participants must be members of the Sierra Club. **Cost:** On request. **When:** September. **Contact:** Sierra Club Outing Dept., Trip #675, 530 Bush St., San Francisco, CA 94108, USA; phone (415)981-8634. *(M)*

Soviet Union

Caucasus Climbing: An ascent of Mt. Elbrus, at 18,500 feet the highest peak in Europe, highlights a 22-day climbing and hiking trip to the Caucasus Mountains. Participants fly to Moscow for 3 days of sightseeing before proceeding into the mountains. After some preliminary training and acclimatization, the group ascends Elbrus, which does not require technical skills but may be difficult due to elevation and possible high winds. A separate technical climb may be made if there is interest in the group. Participants must be Sierra Club members. **Cost:** On request. **When:** July. **Contact:** Sierra Club Outing Dept., Trip #595, 530 Bush St., San Francisco, CA 94108, USA; phone (415)981-8634. *(M)*

Sri Lanka

Highlands of Sri Lanka: Hikers explore Sri Lanka on a 7-day trek in higher elevations where temperatures range from 60° to 70°F. Participants stay overnight at guest houses, and the hiking sites are reached by car journeys of 30 to 100 miles. Expedition members climb 8,820-foot Mt. Pidurutalagala, neither a strenuous nor a hazardous climb, though the mountain is Sri Lanka's highest. At the summit of 7,353-foot Adam's Peak, or Sripada ("holy footprint"), participants may speculate concerning somewhat contradictory explanations for a footprintlike impression, and see a spectacular sunrise. On Horton Plains, a 7,000-foot plateau covered with pale green grass, dark forests, rhododendrons, orchids and clear pools, expedition members visit World's End, a precipitous drop-off of 2,000 feet. **Cost:** $220 from Colombo. **When:** Year-round. **Con-**

With Manaslu and Peak 29 towering behind them, a group of hikers pitches camp in a Himalayan meadow. Although trekking with porters is more common here, conditioned backpackers can explore Nepal too. (Keith Gunnar)

tact: Walker's Tours & Travels Ltd., P.O. Box 1048, 11 York St., Colombo 1, Sri Lanka; phone 22553.

ATLANTIC

Faroe Islands

Land and Sea of the Faroes: The Faroes, an 18-island archipelago between Shetland and Iceland, are the setting for a 20-day hiking and nature viewing trip. The region features over 250 varieties of birds, a well-preserved native culture and a wild, beautiful terrain. After flying from London via Glasgow and Reykjavik, participants land at Torshavn and drive to Streymnes, on the east coast of Streymoy, for 5 days of short hikes into the surrounding area. Drives are made to Saksun, Tjornuvik and Vestmanna. Then a bus and boat trip takes travelers to Mikladalur, on Kalsoy, for 5 more days of hiking before they return to Torshavn. From this last base backpackers take several more days for day trips to Sandoy and the local area. Accommodations are in hotels and huts. Participants may stop for a visit in Iceland on the return flight. **Cost:** $790 includes transportation from London, most meals, accommodations, guide. **When:** June, July. **Contact:** WEXAS International, 45 Brompton Rd., Knightsbridge, London SW3 1DE, Great Britain; phone 01-589-0500. *(M)*

Greenland

Greenland in Summer: Southwest Greenland is green and blooming in summertime, and this ancient area of rock, tundra, meadows, great highland ranges and deep fjords is explored during a hiking trip. Occasionally taking a boat or helicopter across the waterways, hikers sleep in tents on most nights and sometimes stay with local residents in their homes. Most days are spent hiking through remote, isolated areas. Included on the schedule is a trek across a glacier and an exploration of Erik's Fjord; additional details, including trip duration, are available on request. Participants must be Sierra Club members. **Cost:** On request. **When:** August. **Contact:** Sierra Club Outing Dept., Trip #650, 530 Bush St., San Francisco, CA 94108, USA; phone (415)981-8634. *(M)*

Iceland

On Foot in Iceland: Groups of 10 to 15 hike past Reykjavik through farmlands and past fjords into the harsh terrain of mountains, deserts and icecaps. Accommodations are provided in huts or tents and vary according to the length of each trip. Trip members take part in carrying loads sometimes up to 44 pounds, cooking meals and helping with other camp chores. Treks hours or weeks long can be made, some in the Torfajokull region where hikers visit Eldgja, reputedly the largest volcanic fissure in the world, or Fljotsdalur with its icecaps, glacial rivers and views of Markarfljot gorge. Parties walk day after day, occasionally the entire length of the trip, without meeting any other people. Mountain buses are used to carry hikers to remote starting areas. Full motor safaris are also offered. **Cost:** $168 to $800. **When:** June to September. **Contact:** Dick Phillips, Whitehall House, Nenthead, Alston, Cumbria CA9 3PS, Great Britain.

AUSTRALASIA

Australia

Out in the Outback: Several outdoor trips, some involving instruction and others more recreational, are offered in remote areas of Australia. Teenagers can spend a week at a camp in the lower Snowy River valley learning and practicing outdoor skills such as bush walking, canoeing, rock climbing and orienteering. A 6-day trip takes a group of hikers through 30 miles of alpine meadows in the Jagungal Wilderness. A more leisurely hike lasts 4 days and traverses the Pilot Wilderness from Dead Horse Gap, an area particularly rich in cockatoos, parrots and emus. Another 4-day hike, this one through the towering Main Range, includes visits to a number of alpine lakes and some nontechnical climbing. Other offerings include a combination rafting and hiking trip in New Guinea. **Cost:** $110 to $170 includes food, equipment, instruction, guide. **When:** December, January. **Contact:** Wilderness Expeditions, Berridale, N.S.W. 2628, Australia.

New Zealand

New Zealand Spring: A 3-week hiking trip in New Zealand is divided between the Southern Alps, Fiordland and the Queenstown area. The Alps are an immense glacial range dotted with lakes and stretching over 150 miles, the highest point being Mt. Cook at 12,346 feet. Hikers walk over the Copeland Pass and on the Tasman Glacier, the largest non-polar glacier in the world. Proceeding to remote Fiordland National Park, 3 million acres in size, the party walks the famous Milford Track, a 5-day, 32-mile hike through dense forests, open bush, mountain streams and along lake shores. The final stop is Queenstown, where side trips are made to Lake Wakatipu and the

Shotover River. Numerous optional activities, including rafting, backpacking and sightseeing, are also offered. **Cost:** $2,500 includes roundtrip airfare from the U.S., food, accommodations, equipment, transportation, guide. **When:** November. **Contact:** Globe Treks, 410 Fifth Ave., Suite 10, Hendersonville, NC 28739, USA; phone (704)693-0724.

Hiking in the Southern Alps: A 25-mile hike along the Routeburn Track on the South Island takes travelers through spectacular Fiordland and Mt. Aspiring national parks. The 4-day guided trip departs from Queenstown and explores the lakes, gorges and forests of this untouched region. Nights are spent in small mountain lodges. **Cost:** $120 for adults, $112 for children under 15. **When:** November to April. **Contact:** Routeburn Walk Ltd., P.O. Box 271, Queenstown, New Zealand; phone 100.

Two-Island Trip: Backpackers come to know the fascinating array of landforms on New Zealand during a 20-day trip. After a flight from Los Angeles to Auckland, participants spend a few days exploring the natural phenomena of North Island, including the geysers and mud pits at Rotorua and the glowworm caves at Waitomo. Taking a ferry to South Island, the group splits into 2 parts according to the interests of members. A hiking group walks the Milford Track and then the Routeburn Track for 10 days, while a climbing group spends the same time crossing glaciers and making peak ascents in the area of Tasman Glacier and Mt. Cook. The 2 groups rendezvous in Auckland for a flight to Fiji, where a few days are spent swimming, sailing and sunning on the beach before a return flight to the States. **Cost:** On request. **When:** November. **Contact:** Travel Exploration, P.O. Box 17641, Denver, CO 80217, USA. ***(M)***

Back and Forth on the Oamaru: A portion of the Oamaru River, which forms the border between

Backpackers rest beside a lake in New Zealand's Southern Alps. A number of outfitters offer hiking trips in the region, ranging in length from 4 days to 3 weeks. (National Publicity Studios)

Kaimanawa and Kaweka state forest parks, is hiked in 2 directions on a 5-day trip. After meeting in Ohakune, located between Auckland and Wellington, participants fly by helicopter to the Ngaruroro River and make a 2-hour trek to the first of 2 established base camps. After a night there, they hike about 5 miles up the Oamaru to Camp 2, where 2 nights are spent. The beech forest region hosts a variety of bird and animal life, including the elusive sika deer. A full day at Camp 2 may be spent hiking up the Kaipo, a scenic tributary of the Oamaru, or exploring the region around camp. Backpackers spend most of the next day walking back to Camp 1, where they have a few free hours the following morning before returning to Ohakune by copter and car. Accommodations are in tents at established camps. **Cost:** $157 for adults, $137 for children includes transportation from Ohakune, food, camping accommodations and equipment, guide. **When:** January, February. **Contact:** Venturetreks Ltd., P.O. Box 3839, Auckland, New Zealand; phone 799 855. *(M)*

CANADA

Alberta

Backpacking in Banff National Park: Beginning at the western boundary of the park, a 44-mile hike follows the Continental Divide through the forests and alpine meadows of the Canadian Rockies. Hikers travel 4 to 8 miles a day with professional guides who discuss the flora and fauna as well as cook, set up and break camp. A stay at 11,870-foot Mt. Assiniboine, the glacier-capped "Matterhorn of the Rockies," is planned. Opportunities are provided to see and photograph wildlife such as deer, elk, moose, bears, mountain goats, and small animals and birds. The hike is limited to 12 backpackers and lasts 7 days, starting and ending at Sunshine Lodge in the park. **Cost:** $235, all-inclusive. **When:** July. **Contact:** Aurora Borealis Expeditions, 132 Eileen Circle, Burnsville, MN 55337, USA. *(M)*

Along the Great Divide: A group of 12 strong hikers walks the southern section of the Great Divide Trail on a physically demanding 9-day trip. Participants meet in Banff and proceed by bus to the trailhead near Jasper, where they set out along the rugged high country trail. Over the next 8 days they cross high passes, encounter numerous changes of altitude and frequently cover long distances between campsites. Food preparation and campsite chores are community projects. Participants need to be in excellent condition for this trip due to the high altitudes and ruggedness of the trail. Inexpensive chalet accommodations are available before and after the trip. **Cost:** $130 includes food, group equipment, guide. **When:** August. **Contact:** Willard Kinzie, 135 Shanty Bay Rd., Barrie, ON Canada L4M 1E1.

British Columbia

West Coasting: The West Coast Trail follows a precarious route along 45 miles of Vancouver Island's west coast, overlooking a shoreline that has claimed 60 ships since 1854. Departing from Victoria, backpackers spend 8 days walking and camping along the trail. After a van ride to Port Renfrew, hikers begin a fairly strenuous walk full of changes in altitude. Along the way participants stop to examine Indian ruins, beachcomb on stretches of sandy beach, clamber up rock ledges and investigate the lush rain forest vegetation. After 6 days the group arrives in Bamfield, where they catch a ferry to Port Alberni and return by van to Victoria. Participants should be in good physical condition and need to supply their own individual gear, including sleeping bag. **Cost:** $135 includes transportation from Victoria, food, group equipment, guide. **When:** July, August. **Contact:** Canadian Hostelling Association, Pacific Region, 3425 W. Broadway, Vancouver, BC Canada V6R 2B4; phone (604)736-2674.

Custom Alpine Hiking: Guide service is available for summer hiking and backpacking trips in the Canadian Rockies. Hiking is over a wide variety of terrain, from well-groomed park trails to rugged cross-country trips through remote areas. Wildlife is plentiful and trips may focus on photography, mine exploration, wildflower identification or other activities. **Cost:** $125 to $175 for 8 days. **When:** June to October. **Contact:** Northern Lights Alpine Recreation, Box 399, Invermere, BC Canada V0A 1K0; phone (604)342-6042.

Cape Scott Hike: Participants spend about 4 days of an 8-day trip exploring the northwest end of Vancouver Island. Cape Scott lies on the westernmost tip, part of a provincial park area containing 40 miles of ocean front and 14 miles of beaches. Access to the park is by a muddy logging road 30 miles from Port Hardy on the east coast of the island. Camping is done on the beaches where participants observe the native wildlife and investigate the natural terrain. Some signs of humans are seen, including the remains of 19th-century log dwellings constructed by Danish settlers. Traveling eastward along the isolated coast, trip members explore sea caves and glaciated rock shelves. Bears, raccoons, deer, seals, sea lions and other animals are abundant. As the group leaves the ocean front, they pass through dense underbrush to the Nahwitti Plateau, a land of miniature trees, muddy bogs and Roosevelt elk. A logging road is used for the return to Port Hardy. **Cost:** $215. **When:** August, September. **Contact:** Western Outdoor Adventures Ltd., 16115 32nd Ave., White Rock, BC Canada V4B 4Z5; phone (604)531-3969.

Manitoba

Weekend Backpacking: The Winnipeg office of the Canadian Hostelling Association offers weekend hiking trips in the province of 100, 000 lakes. There are many wilderness parks, including Riding Mountain National Park, in which hikers can enjoy the Canadian outdoors. Trips are also available for canoeing and skiing, often offered in conjunction with the Manitoba Naturalist Society. One such trip is a 5-day canoeing trip in northwestern Ontario. In Manitoba the CHA offers a whale watching trip in August at Churchill, an inland port

Custom backpacking trips in British Columbia offered by Northern Lights Alpine Recreation take hikers on groomed park trails or up remote rockslides like this one. (Arnor Larson/Northern Lights Alpine Recreation)

where participants can watch whales and their offspring. Backpacking trips are planned each week for the upcoming weekend. **Cost:** On request. **When:** May through October. **Contact:** Canadian Hostelling Association, Manitoba Region, 698 Broadway, Winnipeg, MB Canada R3G 0X1; phone (204)772-7740.

Northwest Territories

Backpacking on Baffin Island: Exploring the remote Arctic by snowmobile, sled and on foot, hikers spend 2 weeks camping the Cumberland Peninsula on Baffin Island. After a flight to the tiny settlement of Broughton Island on the east coast, participants travel by snowmobile and sled across the frozen sea ice to Auyuittuq National Park. The goal of the trip is to traverse the Pangnirtung Pass to a camp at the head of North Pangnirtung Fjord, a distance of 60 miles. From there, hikers spend 3 days exploring the glaciers and peaks around Mt. Asgard. After a 2-day ascent to the head of the main Pangnirtung Fjord, a 1-hour trip by Eskimo canoe takes participants to the settlement of Pangnirtung to end the trip. **Cost:** $725. **When:** July. **Contact:** Canatrek Mountain Expeditions, P.O. Box 1138, Banff, AB Canada T0L 0C0; phone (403)762-3143.

CENTRAL AMERICA

Costa Rica

Up Chirripo and through Corcovado: Twelve days in Costa Rica's back country allows a group of travelers to make a nontechnical ascent of 12,606-foot Mt. Chirripo and hike through wild Corcovado National Park. Beginning and ending in San Jose, the trip starts with a drive along the Inter-American Highway through Costa Rica's remote southern Pacific coast. After a day's horseback ride, participants make the fairly strenuous climb to Chirripo's summit, exploring small glacial lakes en route. A bus ride and short plane flight take the party to Corcovado National Park for a 4-night stay. The park boasts 13 distinct life zones hosting some 285 species of bird and 135 species of mammal, including one of the world's greatest concentrations of jaguars; many of the animals are rare and endangered. Between 7 and 11 miles of walking are done each day, terminating at a beach where a plane shuttle and bus ride take participants back to San Jose. Some sightseeing there is included. **Cost:** On request. **When:** On request. **Contact:** Costa Rica Expeditions, Apartado 43, Turrialba, Costa Rica; phone 56-03-95; or P.O. Box 4112, Woodside, CA 94062, USA.

Guatemala

Highland Passage: Backpackers learn about the landscape, wildlife and culture of Guatemala on 14- and 22-day journeys. Trips begin with a 2-day exploration of Tikal, the ceremonial center of the Mayans. Travelers then fly to the Central Highlands to spend 5 days hiking and exploring the marketplaces around Lake Atitlan. Participants may climb such volcanoes as Acatenango and San Pedro on steep hikes involving no technical climbing or they may remain at lower altitudes to explore Indian villages and historical sites. The journey culminates with a visit to San Francisco El Alto, after which travelers return by bus to Guatemala City. **Cost:** $750 for 14 days includes land transportation in Guatemala, food, cooking gear, guides, hotel and tent accommodations. **When:** February, March. **Contact:** High Country Passage, P.O. Box 879, LaPorte, CO 80535, USA; phone (303)667-6360.

Backpacking in Central America: Participants use the local means of transportation, bus and foot, to explore Guatemala on a 9-day backpacking trip from Guatemala City. The flexible itinerary includes a visit to Antigua and passes through Quezaltenango and Huehuetenango. Hikers spend 5 to 6 days in rural Guatemala, visiting markets, shops, churches and homes. A high point of the trip is a hike to the summit of Volcan de Tajumulco (13,845 feet), an 8-hour climb which requires no special equipment. Along the way backpackers both stay in hotels and camp outdoors. The trip is scheduled to allow interested parties to join a 3-day climb of Popocatepetl in Mexico a week later. **Cost:** On request. **When:** On request. **Contact:** Johann Mountain Guides, P.O. Box 2334, Lincoln City, OR 97367, USA; phone (503)996-3232. *(M)*

EUROPE

Austria

High Hikes: A Salzburg-based trip explores the Austrian high country on foot for 15 days. Hikers take a bus from Salzburg to the lake district between Wolfgangsee and Mondsee for several days' walking, taking in some spectacular views of the whole area. After a free day in Salzburg, the party travels to Wersenweng, a small mountain village, where the nearby ice caves are visited before several days of hiking around Tennengebirge. After touring nearby towns and castles the trip finishes with 4 days of walking in the Hohe Tauern before participants return to Salzburg. Most nights are spent in small inns or mountain huts. **Cost:** $685 from Salzburg includes food, transportation, guide. **When:** July. **Contact:** Irmgard Wimberger, 796 NW Culbertson Dr., Seattle, WA 98177, USA; phone (206)365-1202.

Czechoslovakia

Czech Points: A 3-week walking trip explores several mountain ranges in Czechoslovakia. Beginning in Vienna, the group travels to the High Tatras, Slovak Ore, Kremnica and Giant mountains for generally easy hiking. Some time is spent in the scenic Obri Dul, a valley designated as a nature preserve. Accommodations are in alpine huts and hostels, with occasional village stays along the way. The trip terminates in Prague with a few days allowed for sightseeing. Participants must be Sierra Club members. **Cost:** On request. **When:** August. **Contact:** Sierra Club Outing Dept., Trip #635, 530 Bush St., San Francisco, CA 94108, USA; phone (415)981-8634. *(M)*

England

Hiking the South West Way: A 2-week backpacking trip takes participants through a 100-mile section of coastal scenery. The trek covers the area from the fishing village of St. Ives to the yachting harbor of St. Mawes in the Fal estuary, all part of the walking trail known as the South West Way. A variety of terrain is traversed, some of it challenging, though no more than 10 miles are covered in any one day. During the season of the trip, the cliffs are empty and the beaches nearly deserted. The cliffs and sands are rich in flora as well as wildlife that has been driven from the inland pastures by intensive modern agriculture. The villages along the route provide travelers with an understanding of local tradition, and in the evening participants may visit the local pubs and meet some of the village inhabitants. Hikers carry only day packs;

other gear is transported by Land Rover to the night's stopping place. Accommodations are usually in lodges, pubs, hotels or cottages. **Cost:** $575. **When:** May. **Contact:** Backpack Man, 11 Church St., Moulton, Northampton NN1 5DQ, Great Britain; phone 0604 48559.

France

Exploring Mediterranean Mountains and Shores: Participants on a 14-day trip spend 1 week each at the mountains and seashore of the island of Corsica. The group gathers at the mountain village of Evisa, which spreads along a ridge high over the area's deep valleys and gorges, and undertakes day trips to the surrounding peaks. From the central mountain region of Corsica, participants board a bus and travel to the town of Porto. Travelers stay in a hotel above the town and can take day trips to the seaside. Walks may be taken along rocky headlands and on inland hills covered with scented maquis, or among the rock formations of Les Calanches perched high above the sea between Piana and Porto. **Cost:** $500 includes accommodations, roundtrip transportation from London, most meals. **When:** May and September. **Contact:** Waymark Holidays, 295 Lillie Rd., London SW6 7LL, Great Britain; phone 01-385-5015.

Germany

A Walk through the Black Forest: A hiking trip explores the ancient Schwarzwald, or Black Forest. Beginning at Baden-Baden, a small group of hikers walks into the forest on its northern edge and then follows the Westweg, or Western Trail, for about 150 miles south. During stops at Freudenstadt, Titisee and Freiburg, hikers observe the region's farming, conservation and reforestation methods which have preserved the area for centuries. Participants must be Sierra Club members. Details, including trip duration, are available on request. **Cost:** On request. **When:** August. **Contact:** Sierra Club Outing Dept., Trip #645, 530 Bush St., San Francisco, CA 94108, USA; phone (415)981-8634. ***(M)***

Greece

Hiking the Mediterranean Countryside: Participants camp in meadows and on beaches during a month-long journey through Greece and Crete. Beginning in Athens, the group of 10 is transported by ferry to Crete for a week of hiking, dancing and beachcombing. A stop at the seldom-visited northeast coast of Evvoia precedes a 3-day hike to the summit of Mt. Olympus at 9,629 feet. **Cost:** $2,309 includes roundtrip transportation from New York, guide, meals, accommodations. **When:** April. **Contact:** Mountain Travel, Inc., 1398 Solano Ave., Albany, CA 94706, USA; phone (415)527-8100. ***(M)***

Cretan Walking: The history of the Mediterranean island of Crete stretches back 4,000 years to the Minoan culture. A small group of hikers explores this history in 2 weeks of walking through the island's barren mountains and along its sandy beaches. Places visited include the Gorge of Samaria, the White Mountains, Mt. Ida and the ruins at Knossos. Participants must be Sierra Club members. **Cost:** On request. **When:** June. **Contact:** Sierra Club Outing Dept., Trip #575, 530 Bush St., San Francisco, CA 94108, USA; phone (415)981-8634. *(M)*

Hike on a Grecian Range: With limestone peaks reaching up to 8,000 feet, the Pindos Mountains stretch 150 miles from the Gulf of Corinth to the Albanian border. For 15 days participants hike on a network of trails which connect the isolated villages of the Pindos range, sometimes camping out and sometimes staying at inns or mountain huts. Backpackers depart from Ioannina and along the way visit Vikos Gorge, the mountain town of Metsovon and the unusual rock formations at Meteora. Leaving the mountains at Agnanta, hikers head for the coast via Dodona, site of the oracle of Zeus, and end their hike at the beaches of Parga. **Cost:** $530 to $575, depending on date of departure, includes roundtrip airfare from England to Corfu, transportation within Greece, camping equipment, guide, most accommodations and meals. **When:** June, July, September. **Contact:** WEXAS International, 45 Brompton Rd., Knightsbridge, London SW3 1DE, Great Britain; phone 01-589-0500. *(M)*

Ireland

Shoreline and Highland Amble: A 15-day trek through Ireland's hill country and coastal areas includes visits to historic towns, centuries-old castles and islands where Gaelic is still spoken by the inhabitants. Participants fly from London to Dublin to begin the trip; easy day walks are followed each evening by meals and accommodations in hotels or farmhouses and country homes. From Galway, group members fly to the Aran Islands, one of the last enclaves of the ancient Gaelic language. A ferry ride back to the mainland is followed by exploration of the mountains, lakes and villages of Connemara. Participants attend a medieval banquet at Knappogue Castle in County Clare to round off one of the days. The walk is led by experienced Irish mountaineers. **Cost:** $680 includes transportation from London, meals, accommodations, guides. **When:** August. **Contact:** Thomas Cook Ltd., P.O. Box 36, Thorpe Wood, Peterborough PE3 6SB, Great Britain; phone Peterborough (0733)632000.

Italy

Pure Dolomite: The village of Selva, perched at 5,200 feet in the Italian Dolomite Range, is the base for a series of alpine walks on a 17-day trip; some climbing can be done as well. After flying from

Seattle and spending 2 nights in London and 1 in Venice, the party reaches Selva and begins hiking. The walks vary from moderate to strenuous, often using chairlifts or cable cars to reach high slopes and almost always covering some rough terrain. Hikes are made to the 10,000-foot summits of Boe and Pisciadu, and those wishing to do more climbing can hire local guides. An open-ended return air ticket allows participants to stay in the area after the organized trip ends. Lodging is in mountain huts and inns. **Cost:** $1,600 includes transportation from Seattle, accommodations, food, guide. **When:** August. **Contact:** Maggie Cornell, 4 Skagit Key, Bellevue, WA 98006, USA; phone (206)746-4929.

Norway

Norwegian Ups and Downs: Backpackers explore the peaks and fjords of 2 southern Norwegian mountain ranges on a 13-day hiking trip beginning in Oslo. After a train and bus ride to Aurlandsdalen Valley, the party walks down its length to the Sognefjorden, Norway's deepest fjord. Hikers cross the waterway on a small boat and climb past thundering Vetti Waterfall, cross over Mt. Fannarakin and traverse the Smorstabbre Glacier to Leirvassbu. Then the group hikes to Spiterstulen, the starting point for hiking and climbing excursions in the Svelnos Glacier region; one probable ascent is Mt. Galdhopiggen. After 3 days in the area, the group travels by bus and train back to Oslo. Accommodations throughout the trip are in mountain huts, lodges and hotels. **Cost:** $725 includes transportation from Oslo, food, accommodations, group equipment, guide. **When:** June to September. **Contact:** Peaks & Fjords, P.O. Box 9575, Egertorget, Oslo 1, Norway; phone 02-22 61 60. *(M)*

The Northern Back Country: A 22-day trip makes hikes in the Lofoten Islands, Swedish Lapland, the Lyngen Alps and North Cape. Beginning with a boat trip from Oslo to Varoy, backpackers spend a week in the Lofotens hiking, observing bird rookeries and ascending a peak. Then a steamer and train trip takes participants to Swedish Lapland, where they hike from hut to hut for 5 days, traveling from a mountain lodge to Abisko; frequent contact is made along the way with the area's original residents, the Lapps. After some additional hiking, the party flies to Mageroya and hikes to North Cape, Europe's northernmost point. Finally 2 days are spent hiking and sightseeing at Tromso before the return to Oslo. Each group can have the trip tailored to its own interests, giving emphasis to easier hiking, bird life, more climbing or other features. **Cost:** $1,235 to $1,385, depending on number in party, includes food, accommodations, transportation from Oslo, group equipment, guide. **When:** On request. **Contact:** Peaks & Fjords, P.O. Box 9575, Egertorget, Oslo 1, Norway; phone 02-22 61 60. *(M)*

Scotland

Scottish Walking Tours: Hikers explore the Scottish countryside on week-long expeditions with accommodations in hostels along the

The comforts of a home-cooked meal can be produced in the most unlikely places on backpacking trips, as these day hikers demonstrate. (Christian Kallen)

way. A trip in the western highlands takes participants through the Arrochar Alps to Loch Lomond with more hiking through the Mamore Forest to Glen Nevis and Fort William. Another tour focuses on the Trossachs region in central Scotland, hiking by Loch Venacher, Bens Ledi, Venue and Lomond to Loch Lomond. On a third hike participants explore mountainous terrain to the north, traveling through the hill pass of Lairig Ghru and seeing the mountains of Cairngorm, Ben Macdhui and Cairn Toul. Hikers must be at least 14 years old. **Cost:** $76 to $86 includes meals, accommodations, transportation, guide services. **When:** July, August. **Contact:** Scottish Youth Hostels Association, 7 Glebe Cresc., Stirling FK8 2JA, Great Britain; phone Stirling 2821.

Sweden

Sarek Trek: Sarek National Park is the largest wild area in Europe and also is representative of many European mountain regions in climate and topography. A trip lasting about 15 days explores the park and combines stays in European hostels and huts with rustic camping in tents. Overall the hiking follows valley contours and is not especially strenuous, but more challenging side hikes can be made. Participants must be Sierra Club members. **Cost:** On request. **When:** July. **Contact:** Sierra Club Outing Dept.,

In summer, when the deep snows have melted and backpackers can hike to increasingly higher altitudes, it is still common to find large snowfields on the trail. (Keith Gunnar)

Trip #625, 530 Bush St., San Francisco, CA 94108, USA; phone (415)981-8634. ***(M)***

Trekking the Royal Trail: A 16-day journey starts at Abisko in northern Lapland with participants hiking south as far as Lake Ladtjolaure. While at Abisko, a guided walk up Mt. Njuolia reveals a splendid array of plant life to observe. Once trekkers leave this area, a number of huts provide shelter and cooking facilities. Hikers may have some ice and snow to contend with at Marmotstugan Pass before the descent to Vistasstugan. Spectacular scenery is the rule along the way and the trip occurs at the height of the Lapland summer. Although the Lapps themselves are moving into communities now, many of them still herd reindeer and can be seen en route. After an overnight at Kebnekaise mountain center, trip members ascend Kebnekaise, the highest mountain in Sweden. The trek continues to Lake Ladtjolaure where participants take a spectacular flight by small sea plane over the entire route of the trek back to Abisko. Hikers carry packs of 25 to

35 pounds and should be in good condition. **Cost:** $670 includes roundtrip airfare from London. **When:** July. **Contact:** Thomas Cook Ltd., P.O. Box 36, Thorpe Wood, Peterborough PE3 6SB, Great Britain; phone Peterborough (0733) 632000.

Switzerland

Alpine Ramble: With the help of short hops by train and bus, backpackers may hike for 6 weeks from Zurich, Switzerland to Munich, Germany via Austria. Routes take hikers through the valley of Mont Blanc, along the base of the Eiger, Monch, Jungfrau and Matterhorn to St. Moritz and across the Zillertaler Alpen chain in Austria. The hiking trip ends in Munich with a train ride to Luxembourg City before the flight home. **Cost:** $1,230 includes roundtrip transportation from New York. **When:** July. **Contact:** American Youth Hostels, National Campus, Delaplane, VA 22025, USA; phone (703)592-3271.

Hiking a Swiss Canton: During a 17-day trip originating in Geneva, alpinists walk along hiking trails and mountain paths through the canton of Valais past the celebrated peaks of the Matterhorn, Zermatt and Sass-Fee. After traveling by train to Zermatt, group members begin with a training walk to the hamlets of Ried, Findeln and Riffelalp before embarking on a series of day hikes. The hikes, which depart from the villages of Zermatt and Sass-Fee, often cover 6 to 15 miles and extend over a period of 5 to 8 hours. From the lush meadows of Stafelalp to a lake which lies at the foot of the Matterhorn, the path ascends steeply to a hut situated at almost 11,000 feet. Hikers also ascend Trift Gorge en route to the highest alpine peak reached by the Mettlehorn hiking trail. During the 8-hour climb hikers cross a snow field, scramble to the summit and make a vertical ascent of 6,000 feet. A second guide leads less strenuous walks each day. **Cost:** $925 from Geneva includes accommodations, meals. **When:** June to September. **Contact:** Swissair Tour Dept., Bldg. #15, JFK International Airport, Jamaica, NY 11430, USA; phone tollfree (800)221-4750, ext. 4415.

Eager for the Eiger: Participants hike among the classic peaks of the French and Swiss Alps on a 16-day trip. Four days each are spent near the snow-covered summits of Mont Blanc, the Matterhorn, and the Eiger and the Jungfrau. Accommodations are in campgrounds or in huts, which allows hikers the freedom to either take day hikes or make overnight backpacking excursions. Mountaineers may take advantage of a climbing package option which offers technical climbs with guides and huts for overnight stays. The trip concludes with a day of sightseeing in Zurich, followed by a night in a hotel. **Cost:** $528 includes land transportation, accommodations, breakfast in hotel; $1,025 additional for climbing option. **When:** June, August. **Contact:** Travel Exploration, P.O. Box 17641, Denver, CO 80217, USA. *(M)*

Alp Hiking: A group of hikers explores the Swiss Alps for a week along remote trails that rarely intersect roadways. After meeting at

Sion, participants ride a bus to Vercorin, the hike's starting point at 4,400 feet. The next 5 days are spent traipsing through the wild Rechy Valley; Nax, overlooking the Rhone Valley; the forests around Mase and Eison; Euseigne, site of the erosion-molded Pyramids of Euseigne; the pastoral area around Heremence; and Haute-Nendaz, where hikers share a farewell dinner and return to Sion. Larger luggage is carried in a jeep along the hiking route, and nights are spent in small hotels and inns. Participants should be in good physical condition, as they spend 4 to 7 hours hiking each day. **Cost:** $305 includes roundtrip transportation from Sion, food, accommodations, equipment, guide. **When:** May to October. **Contact:** Welcome Swiss Tours, 7, Ave. Benjamin-Constant, 1003 Lausanne, Switzerland; phone (021)20-68-21.

MEXICO

Baja California

Baja Back Country: A nontechnical climb of Picacho del Diablo, at 10,000 feet the highest peak in Baja California, highlights a 9-day hiking trip through the peninsula. Departing from San Diego by van, the party drives to the road's end in San Pedro Martir National Park, where they strike out into the mountains with map and compass. Traversing an area similar to the southern Sierra Nevada range, backpackers make a circuit through high meadows to Picacho del Diablo, spectacularly set behind the deep, narrow Canon del Diablo. The ascent of about 4,000 feet from the canyon floor is made in a day and, weather permitting, the party bivouacs at the summit to watch the sunset and sunrise. The group exits along the canyon floor, passing through a variety of life zones. Guides provide instruction in map and compass use, campcraft and mountaineering during the trip. **Cost:** $250 includes roundtrip transportation from San Diego, food, group equipment, guide. **When:** April. **Contact:** Boojum, Box 99670, San Diego, CA 92109, USA; phone (714)481-5811.

Chiapas

Jungle Journey to Mayan Ruins: On a 10-day trip in the Lacandon Jungle, participants trek to ancient Mayan ruins. A bush plane takes group members from San Cristobal de las Casas, Chiapas to a trailhead at the ruins of Bonampak. In local villages, trekkers visit with Lacandon Indians, the last direct descendants of the Mayans. The sculpture and art at the ruins of Palenque are also viewed. Participants hike along rivers through the tropical forests of mahogany, red cedar, chicle and breadnut trees where bands of spider and howler monkeys feed. The bird life of the area includes parrots, toucans, scarlet macaws and the rare quetzal. Opportunities for photography, swimming and fishing are plentiful. **Cost:** $360 includes accommodations, meals, guides, local transportation. **When:** March. **Contact:** Sacred Monkey Expeditions, Box 363, Jerome, AZ 86331, USA; phone (602)634-5711. ***(M)***

Chihuahua

Barranca del Cobre Backpacking:

Hawaii Bound's 24-day adventure includes instruction in survival techniques and rope work. Suspended high over the Pacific, this participant readies for a rappel. (Hawaii Bound)

Four- and 5-day hikes take backpackers into the canyonlands of the Sierra Madre of northern Mexico. Trips begin in the mountain town of Creel and cross high open pine forests to the 7,000-foot-deep Barranca del Cobre, the deepest canyon in North America. Participants descend through differing zones of vegetation, stopping to explore Indian cave dwellings and visiting with the Tarahumara Indians. Part of the travel is on the Chihuahua el Pacifico railroad. Accommodations are in hotels the first and last nights of the trip. **Cost:** On request. **When:** May, November. **Contact:** Dos Gringos Mexican Adventures, 108 NE 53rd St., Seattle, WA 98105, USA.

PACIFIC

French Polynesia

Island Hiking: A 16-day trip includes a 3-day traverse of the island of Tahiti, explorations along ancient trails on the islands of Moorea, Huahine and Raiatea, and 2 days of snorkeling in the clear waters of Bora-Bora. On inland walks participants encounter ancient ceremonial platforms and archaeological ruins of Tahitian and Polynesian cultures. Tropical fruits abound on coastal and inland trails. The island people are generally warm and hospitable, particularly in the out-of-the-way villages where participants stay when not camping out. Opportunities to participate in evenings of informal singing and Tahitian dancing are available. The emphasis is on cultural experience. **Cost:** On request. **When:** May, June, August to October. **Contact:** Walkabout International, 386 60th St., Oakland, CA 94618, USA; phone (415)652-7825.

Hawaii

All Around Hawaii: Summer trips lasting 24 days are offered to persons 12 and older. Exploring Hawaii's oceans and mountains, participants learn to function completely alone or with the group. Several features of the island of Hawaii are explored, from the 13,000-foot summit of Mauna Loa to the tropical rain forests and the powerful Pacific. While backpacking on lava or navigating an outrigger canoe, participants learn by doing. Following a few days of physical conditioning, expert instruction is provided on topics such as first aid, search and rescue techniques, routefinding, and environmental awareness. Food and equipment are furnished. **Cost:** $896. **When:** May to August. **Contact:** Hawaii Bound, 825 Keeaumoku St., Rm. 220, Kailua, HI 96814, USA; phone (808)946-6502.

Island Hiking and Camping: Members of a 2-week trip hike and explore the unspoiled regions of Maui and Hawaii. Day-hike routes wind past volcano craters, the warm Pacific Ocean and an old whaling village. Trip members generally camp at grassy parks, delving into less accessible areas on two exploratory overnight hikes. Except on the overnight hikes, a bus provides transportation and a means for equipment storage and shuttling. A visit to Mauna Loa and Kilauea Crater, the only currently active volcanoes in the islands, and a stop at the black sand beach of Kalapana are scheduled. On Maui the group hikes to Haleakala National Park, from where the giant Haleakala Crater can be viewed. An optional 3-day extension for hiking and exploration on Kauai is also possible. **Cost:** $1,159 includes airfare from San Francisco. **When:** May, October. **Contact:** Mountain Travel Inc., 1398 Solano Ave., Albany, CA 94706, USA; phone (415)527-8100. ***(M)***

SOUTH AMERICA

Argentina

Exploring Patagonia: A 25-day trip to the southernmost end of South America begins in Tierra del Fuego with 3 days of hiking in and around Ushuaia and Lapataia National Park. Participants then fly north across the Strait of Magellan to Glacier National Park, site of the Fitz-Roy and La Torre massifs, where a week is spent backpacking in this region of glacier-encrusted peaks and thick forests. Visits are made to Lake Argentina and a boat is taken to view fjords and glaciers at the western end of the lake. Group members spend the final week hiking in Chile's Paine Towers National Park. **Cost:** $2,500 includes airfare from Miami. **When:** February. **Contact:** South American Wilderness Adventures, 1760 Solano Ave., Berkeley, CA 94707, USA; phone (415)524-5111. ***(M)***

Bolivia

Hiking and Climbing Inca Regions: The salty inland sea of Lake Titicaca, the bleak Altiplano and the summit of Nevado Huayna Potosi at 19,924 feet highlight 1- to 3-week hiking trips to Inca lands. Transportation on each trek is by boat, by bus and on foot. The pre-Inca ruins and colonial town of Tiwanacu afford trip members the opportunity of viewing the gateway, shattered terraces and roofless walls of a vanished civilization. With porters and guides available, climbers ascend to high camp and then continue to the summit the next day. Another hike brings group members to the Camino de Oro, a road built by Incas to carry gold from mines at Tipuani. Due to the rigor of some of the activities, climbers are expected to be experienced and self-reliant. Trips begin and end in La Paz. **Cost:** $395 to $1,350 includes transportation from La Paz, some meals, gear. **When:** May to September. **Contact:** Andean Outfitters, P.O. Box 7007, Angels Camp, CA 95222, USA; phone (209)736-4830. ***(M)***

Andean Adventure: A 3-week trip in the Andes Mountains combines climbing and backpacking, with 1 week devoted to an ascent of Nevado Aquia. During the first week, participants hike through Santa Cruz Valley, passing blue alpine lakes. The route swings behind towering Huandoy and comes down Quebrado Yanganuco beneath snow-capped Andes peaks. At the beginning of the second week, the group flies to Lima, then to the ancient Inca capital of Cuzco. Visits are made to Sacsayhuaman, the markets of Pisac and Chincheros, and to the ruins of Machu Picchu. Participants head for La Paz, Bolivia for the final week, crossing Lake Titicaca aboard a hovercraft. In Bolivia, group members can spend time climbing in the mountains, or trekking into a tropical valley with a side trip to the ruins of Tiahuanaca. During the trip, participants stay at small inns or pitch tent camps. **Cost:** $1,350 includes roundtrip airfare from Miami, guides. **When:** July. **Con-**

tact: Raven Rocks Mountain Institute, Ltd., Box G, Ligonier, PA 15758, USA; phone (412)238-5190.

Ecuador

Alpine Ecuador: Ecuador, which straddles the equator, is split from north to south by 2 mountain ranges, or cordilleras, with numerous ridges crossing from one to the other and creating a series of valley basins. A 2-week trip explores this mountain country through backpacking and climbing. Participants visit Quito, hike or climb on 20,561-foot Chimborazo, trek to the district capital of Riobamba for a local fair, bathe in the hot springs at Banos, hike or climb several other peaks, and make the spectacular rail journey from Quito to Guayaquil, on the Pacific coast. A 5-day trip up the Napo River to investigate the culture, flora and fauna of the tropical rain forest and an 8-day cruise to the Galapagos Islands are also available. **Cost:** $897 for 2-week trip includes roundtrip airfare from Miami, transportation, accommodations, food, guides; $195 to $305 for Napo River trip; $460 for Galapagos extension. **When:** May, August, February. **Contact:** North Cascades Alpine School, 1212 24th G, Bellingham, WA 98225, USA; phone (206)671-1505. *(M)*

Peru

Hiking in the Andes: Participants on a 17-day expedition may choose between high-altitude climbing, backcountry treks and visits to Lima and Cuzco. Sightseeing includes rural areas of the Peruvian Andes as well as museums and Inca ruins, including Machu Picchu. The expedition departs from and returns to Asheville, North Carolina. **Cost:** $1,425 from Asheville includes all expenses. **When:** August. **Contact:** Globe Treks, 410 Fifth Ave., Suite 10, Hendersonville, NC 28739, USA; phone (704)693-0724.

High-Altitude Hiking: Backpackers explore the mountainous terrain of the Cordillera Blanca high in the Andes Mountains. On one hiking program participants backpack beneath the snow-capped peaks of Huandoy and Huascaran, camping out along the shores of Lake Llanganuco at 13,100 feet. Ascents of relatively easy nearby peaks, such as Yanapaccha at 17,900 feet, may be made. Another option is a 14-day trek beginning in the mountains and descending via

A favorite time of day for backpackers comes when packs are taken off and camp is set up, especially when a pristine alpine lake or stream is nearby. (Idaho Division of Tourism)

little-used routes to the town of Tingo Maria on the banks of the Huallaga River. Along the way backpackers travel through the Portachuelo Pass at 15,100 feet and cross the Maranon River. **Cost:** On request. **When:** On request. **Contact:** Transcontinental S.A., Adventure Travel Dept., Jr. Ocona 180, Of. 406, Lima, Peru; phone 273901. *(M)*

UNITED STATES

Backpacking along the Appalachian Trail: Self-organized trips are possible anywhere along the 2,000-mile Appalachian Trail. Extending from Mt. Katahdin in northern Maine to the end of the Blue Ridge Mountains in Springer Mountain, Georgia, the trail is the longest continuous marked trail in the world designed for foot travel only. Fourteen states share the trail, which winds through 8 national forests, 2 national parks and 2 national recreation areas. Closed and open shelters are located about 8 miles apart along most of the trail and are available to hikers on a first come, first served basis. Exploration of side trails, photography or close observation of flora or geology is possible for the more leisurely hiker. **Cost:** Free. **When:** Year-round. **Contact:** The Appalachian Trail Conference Inc., P.O. Box 236, Harpers Ferry, WV 25425, USA; phone (304)535-6331.

National Parks Backpacking: High school-age youths travel across the country on 32- and 41-day backpacking trips which feature hikes through several national parks. The group travels by van from Boston, stopping occasionally to rent bikes, canoes or horses for an afternoon. The 32-day trip includes moderately paced hikes in Rocky Mountain, Grand Canyon and Yosemite national parks; the longer trip stops at these 3 parks plus Yellowstone and Jasper national parks. Participants share responsibility for food buying, cooking and camp chores. Trips end in San Francisco, and backpackers have the option of taking an additional 5 days to ride back to Boston by van with the group leaders. **Cost:** $1,275 for 32 days, $1,425 for 41 days includes transportation, food, leaders, pack, all camping equipment. **When:** July. **Contact:** Student Hosteling Program of New England, Inc., Maple Hill, Rochester, VT 05767, USA; phone (802)767-3297.

Alaska

Northern Continental Divide Hike: Hikers make their own arrangements to fly to Bettles, Alaska, where they meet a float plane that takes them to Chandler Lake for a 5-day hike. The hike crosses the Continental Divide at its northernmost point and travels through a valley to Anaktuvuk Pass, an old Eskimo village. The moderately paced hike travels through an area that is home to herds of caribou, wolves and foxes. Participants are flown back to Bettles from Anaktuvuk Pass. **Cost:** $500. **When:** August. **Contact:** Alaska Wilderness Treks, Inc., P.O. Box C, Eagle River, AK 99577, USA; phone (907)694-9400.

Kenai-Harding Icefield Adventure: Ten days of backpacking on the Kenai Peninsula allow time for detailed exploration of the region's highly varied terrain, flora and fauna. Jutting into the Pacific from south-central Alaska, the peninsula contains almost every major type of terrain found in the rest of the state, from spruce and birch forest to alpine tundra, from grassy slopes to jagged peaks, and from wooded valleys to a great icefield. The trip meets at Soldotna, a short flight from Anchorage, and travels to Tustumena Lake where the hike begins. Participants encounter a diversity of wildlife and birds, spawning salmon in season, and in clear weather a view of Mt. McKinley, 200 miles away. The party consists of between 5 and 10 people; minimum age is 18. **Cost:** $425 includes transportation from Soldotna, food, most equipment, guide. **When:** Summer. **Contact:** Kenai Guide Service, Kasilof, AK 99610, USA; phone (907)262-5496.

Backpacking the Chilkoot Trail: Following the route of the Alaskan Klondikers of 1898, a 5-day backpacking trip leaves from Skagway and cuts through Chilkoot Pass to Lake Bennett in British Columbia. The route follows a trail about 30 miles long and climbs to approximately 3,500 feet above sea level. From Lake Bennett group members float Marsh and Tagish lakes to the Yukon River, once a thriving waterway to the Dawson gold fields. Forgotten trappers' cabins, abandoned paddle wheelers and ghost settlements dot the shorelines, and bears and moose roam the area. The midnight sun illuminates the skies until August, and the spectacular displays of the northern lights can also be seen. **Cost:** $220 from Skagway includes lodging, transportation, trail equipment. **When:** June to August. **Contact:** Klondike Safaris, P.O. Box 1898, Skagway, AK 99840, USA.

Aleutian Backpacking: Hikes lasting from 5 to 15 days are available in Katmai National Monument in the Aleutian Islands Mountain Range. While traversing about 10 miles each day, participants carry packs weighing between 40 and 50 pounds. Backpackers encounter a variety of vegetation and wildlife including moose, caribou, wolves and peregrine falcons. **Cost:** $55 per day includes meals, tent, guide.

A 5-day Klondike Safaris trip beginning in Skagway, Alaska takes backpackers along an 1890s gold rush route. (Keith Gunnar)

Despite the harsh weather and terrain of the northern Canadian Rockies and Alaska, the North's spectacular beauty is accessible to properly equipped hikers. (Tauck Tours)

When: June to August. **Contact:** Otis B. Driftwood Adventures Unlimited, 8701 Kathleen, Anchorage, AK 99502, USA.

Brooks Range Backpacking: Two different backpacking trips, each lasting 8 days, are offered out of Bettles into Alaska's remote Brooks Range. Members on the first trip are flown to Walker Lake to hike through the highest peaks in the central and western mountains including 8,510-foot Mt. Igikpak. Frequently sighted wildlife includes peregrine falcons, eagles, caribou, Dall sheep, grizzly bears, wolverines and wolves. The trip ends in the Noatak drainage, where participants may arrange to join the Noatak River raft trip. The second trip begins with a flight to a lake near the Alatna River and the mouth of Arrigetch Creek for hiking in the Arrigetch Peaks area. A base camp may be set up for day hikes in the mountains and this trip may be combined with a float trip down the Alatna River. **Cost:** $500 for Noatak trip, $550 for Arrigetch trip, includes transportation to and from Bettles, food, equipment, guide. **When:** July, August. **Contact:** Sourdough Outfitters, Bettles, AK 99726, USA; phone (907)692-5252.

(M)

Exploring the Talkeetna Mountains: Hikers backpack over seldom-used trails originally constructed by miners and prospectors in the Talkeetna Mountains, a system of peaks northeast of Anchorage. For 7 days participants take a route through the southeastern Talkeetna Mountains, ascending the Chickaloon-Nelchina Trail up Boulder Creek to Chitina Pass. From the pass the group hikes down Chitina and Caribou creeks, then turns south to cross the divide en route to Hicks Lake. Participants set up camp at several spots along the way and take day trips into the surrounding mountains and valleys. **Cost:** $390 includes guides, group camping equipment. **When:** June to August. **Contact:** Wildernorth, Inc., Mile 102, Glenn Hwy., SRC Box 92E, Palmer, AK 99645, USA. ***(M)***

Arctic Exploration: From Juneau, travelers begin a 23-day exploration of Alaska's water and wilderness. Whales, seals and smaller sealife can be seen while participants canoe the salt waters around Admiralty Island on the west coast of the Alaskan Panhandle. Protection from the open sea is provided by a chain of islands. Admiralty Island itself hosts 80 percent of the eagle population of the world, as well as brown bears, loons, ducks and trout. After 8 days on or near the island, a bush pilot takes the group north to the Brooks Range, which runs east to west and lies entirely within the Arctic Circle. For 10 days, backpackers experience one of America's last virgin wilderness areas during the onset of fall. The mountain wanderings lead to the Eskimo village of Anaktuvuk where another bush plane awaits to transport travelers to Fairbanks for the end of the journey. **Cost:** $1,450 includes transportation from Juneau, guide, meals, accommodations, group equipment. **When:** August. **Contact:** Wind Over Mountain, Taunton Lake Dr., Newton, CT 06470, USA; phone (212)532-8350 or (203)426-9739.

Wrangell Backpacking: Three different hiking trips follow routes through the Wrangell Mountains high country. One trip goes between the Nizina Glacier and the White River, another passes through the Chitistone Mountain high country and a third proceeds for 15 days from the Nizina Glacier to the old mining town of McCarthy. Emphasis is placed on nature interpretation and observation of plants, wildlife, geologic formations and human impact on the environment. Each trip is limited to a group of 5 with 2 guides. Access is by light aircraft only. **Cost:** $75 a day includes food, cooking gear. **When:** June to August. **Contact:** Wrangell Mt. St. Elias Outfitters, Dan Creek, via Glenallen, AK 99588, USA. ***(M)***

Arizona

Southwest Explorations: One-day hikes, overnight trips, and longer camping expeditions lasting up to a week are available to points all over Arizona, departing from Tempe. Designed for easy hiking, possible ventures include camping in the Grand Canyon, an 8-mile backpack in the Havasupai Indian Reservation, and a day trip to Skull Valley in the heart of Arizona mining, ranching and forest harvesting country. The Vulture Gold Mine offers opportunities for rock hunting. Volcanic lava beds and ancient cliff dwellings highlight the trail from Ft. Verde State Park to Wupatki National Monument. **Cost:** $19 to $100 per person, assuming a 10-person minimum, covers food, equipment, transportation. **When:** Year-round. **Contact:** Excalibur Corp., Suite 102, 2212 S. Priest Rd., Tempe, AZ 85282, USA; phone (602)968-7811.

Grand Canyon Guided Hikes: Two 5-day trips for experienced hikers in good condition take participants along the Bass Trail and the Thunder River Trail. The Bass Trail hike begins at the North Rim of the canyon and proceeds over 30 miles of rugged terrain to Shinumo and the Colorado River. The trek involves some difficult hiking at the Redwall limestone stratum. The Thunder River Trail is a hike of medium difficulty running for 26 miles from the North Rim to Thunder Falls, where water gushes out of a cave to form Thunder River. Unlike the Bass Trail route, there is no water along the way. Both hikes

require a minimum of 2 participants; the maximum group size is 7. **Cost:** $200 to $350, depending on the number of participants, includes transportation to and from Flagstaff, guide, food, equipment rental. **When:** June to September. **Contact:** Grand Canyon Trail Guides, Box 2997, Flagstaff, AZ 86003, USA; phone (602)526-0924. *(M)*

Plateau Hikes: A variety of ecological and historical hikes takes backpackers to the Colorado Plateau area of northern Arizona. Two- to 14-day trips explore the graceful formations and vivid colors of the 130,000-square-mile plateau, a region of sedimentary rock 60 million years old. Led by experienced guides and naturalists, hikers learn about the area's history, biology, archaeology and geology as they pass through the varied terrain. The tours range from less than 3 miles to over 25 miles; some shorter trips are taken by river raft. Of the 13 hikes available, most are weekend trips. **Cost:** $30 to $700 includes food, transportation, guides, cooking gear. **When:** Year-round. **Contact:** Grand Canyon Youth Expeditions, RR4, Box 755, Flagstaff, AZ 86001, USA; phone (602)774-8176.

California

Mountain Skills Week: An isolated trailhead in the Sierra Nevadas is the point of origin for a 7-day wilderness skills trip. The first day is devoted to orientation as groups become familiar with equipment and itinerary. A few days are then spent learning camp craft, outdoor cooking, map reading, navigation, first aid and survival techniques. The group stays off trails whenever possible in order to learn to negotiate fallen timber, boulder fields and snow. Skills are tested as the exposure to tough hiking and problem solving increases with each day. On the last day, participants are introduced to rock climbing. **Cost:** $140 includes food, group equipment, transportation to and from the trailhead. **When:** June to September. **Contact:** Mountain People School, 157 Oak Spring Dr., San Anselmo, CA 94960, USA; phone (415)457-3664. *(M)*

Yosemite Mountain Women: A 3-day hiking and camping trip in Yosemite National Park imparts outdoor skills to women in a noncompetitive atmosphere. The trip's exact route is determined by seasonal conditions, but it begins and ends in Tuolumne Meadows, with some time probably spent on the Cathedral Lakes Trail. Along with practical instruction in the art of minimum-impact camping, the group receives instruction in Sierra Nevada geology, botany, insects, wildlife and ecological relationships. About 20 total miles are covered, and elevations to 10,000 feet are reached. **Cost:** $35 includes food, group equipment, guide. **When:** July. **Contact:** Yosemite Natural History Association, P.O. Box 545, Yosemite National Park, CA 95389, USA; phone (209)372-4532.

Colorado

Southwest Colorado Wilderness Exploration: An experienced guide native to the area takes groups on a variety of 6-day trips to the wilderness regions of southwest Colorado. Itineraries include the San Juan Mountains, the rugged Sangre de Cristo Mountains, or the mountain-lined terrain of the Great Sand Dunes. The guide provides instruction in outdoor survival skills such as making a fire without matches, improvising shelters, trapping and preparing and cooking edible plants. Each journey is conducted according to the abilities of the group. Shorter and longer trips can be arranged, and discounts on equipment are available if participants provide their own. **Cost:** $40 to $45 a day. **When:** June to September. **Contact:** American Wilderness Experience, P.O. Box 1486A, Boulder, CO 80306, USA; phone (303)449-0056. ***(M)***

High Country High School: Backpacking trips for high school students take place in the scenic high country of the Colorado Rockies. Between 4 and 8 miles are covered each day as hikers participate in a mobile seminar on outdoor life, learning subjects such as basic mountaineering, map and compass use, outdoor survival, first aid and edible plants. Previous experience is not necessary, as the instruction is tailored to individual levels. Combination backpacking and river rafting trips can also be arranged with instruction included. Each outing is custom-designed, and arrangements can be made for either individuals or larger groups. **Cost:** On request. **When:** Summer. **Contact:** Colorado Outdoor Educators, P.O. Box 18119, Denver, CO 80218, USA; phone (303)837-1411.

Easy Upland Climbing: Three-week trips into the Colorado Rockies depart from Denver, taking participants by car from the city to the trailhead. The first day in the mountains is primarily for warm-up, with daily hikes increasing in length as the trip progresses. Hikers cover 6 to 14 miles a day and make elevation gains of between 2,000 and 5,000 feet. There is no technical climbing during the daily hikes, but group members may attempt scrambling up some of the region's more challenging peaks, which rise to 14,000 feet and higher. Most of the hiking is in the vicinity of Rocky Mountain National Park, Leadville, Buena Vista, Fairplay and Aspen. All cooking and most camping equipment is provided. **Cost:** $575 includes group equipment, transportation, guides; $100 food kitty. **When:** July, August. **Contact:** Colorado Rocky Mountain Hiking, Box 376, North Conway, NH 03860, USA; phone (603)356-3594. *(M)*

Walking the Western Wilderness: A trip of 7 days is offered to those interested in exploring the Colorado wilderness. Backpackers travel through territory little changed in the 100 years since the earliest explorers traversed the area. The numerous streams and headwaters of 10 rivers wind their way through forested canyons thick with nearly black stands of spruce. The mountainsides contain aspen, and trip members may observe beavers in their natural pond habitats. Accompanying campers are guides knowledgeable in the flora and fauna of the region. **Cost:** $210. **When:** June. **Contact:** Three Eagles Expeditions, Inc., P.O. Box 2606, Jackson, WY 83001, USA; phone (307)733-4673.

Wilderness Watchdogs: Backpackers on 5-day trips scout endangered wilderness areas to provide information for environmental protection organizations. Groups limited to 10 participants review boundaries, study resource conflicts and note special features of roadless areas in Colorado. Areas surveyed on past trips include Rattlesnake Canyon, an area of red-rock canyons with natural bridges and arches; the South San Juans, a timbered wintering ground for elk; the Uncompahgre Primitive Area, containing 14,000-foot peaks towering above alpine meadows and forests; and the Wheeler-Wason region, containing the unusual rock formations of the Wheeler Geologic Area. Suitable for beginning backpackers, the trips are run in conjunction with the Colorado Open Space Council, a volunteer environmental advocacy group. **Cost:** $200 includes meals, all camping equipment, study leader, roundtrip transportation between rendezvous town and trailhead. **When:** Summer. **Contact:** Trailhead Ventures, P.O. Box CC, Buena Vista, CO 81211, USA; phone (303)395-8001. *(M)*

Five in the Rockies Highlands: Colorado's wilderness areas provide settings for 4 backpacking excursions designed for both families and individual hikers. Other five-day outings are available in the Buffalo Peaks area, which offers a profusion of blooming wildflowers and several species of birds; the Williams Fork peaks in a heavily forested roadless area southwest of Rocky Mountain National Park; and in the Holy Cross Wilderness, where participants can wander on game trails across alpine tundra, study a living rock glacier or poke around in mines deserted for 50

Backpackers on 5-day scouting trips offered by Trailhead Ventures study Colorado wilderness areas for environmental protection organizations. (Trailhead Ventures)

years. A 7-day trip explores the Conejos roadless area; group members hike in a region where alpine wildflower meadows meet subalpine forests and where elk, bighorn sheep, mule deer, black bears and coyotes are often sighted. **Cost:** $208 to $285 includes food, cooking equipment and community camping gear, guides. **When:** June to August. **Contact:** University of the Wilderness, P.O. Box 1687, Evergreen, CO 80439, USA; phone (303)674-9724. ***(M)***

Georgia

Appalachian Adventure: A 7-day camping trip combines backpacking in the southern Appalachian Mountains and rafting on the

Chattooga River. Starting in Clayton, Georgia, hikers begin the trip with a warm-up hike to Ellicot's Rock Wilderness. Moving camp each night, the hikers proceed to Three Forks Gorge, a more difficult hike. Participants may spend their free time taking exploratory hikes. Programs in ecology, survival, first aid and orienteering emphasize responsible camping. After some whitewater rafting instruction, participants spend 2 days on the Chattooga River. Camping is primitive, with no facilities other than a spring or stream. **Cost:** $190 includes all meals, equipment. **When:** June. **Contact:** Wilderness Southeast, Rt. 3, Box 619, Savannah, GA 31406, USA; phone (912)355-8008.
(M)

Appalachian Leadership Program: Several opportunities are available for seasoned backpackers to learn outdoor leadership skills, covering safety, emotional and interpersonal growth, human relations and communications. Participants spend from 5 to 14 days traveling through the southern Appalachian Mountains in groups of no more than 10 people. A leadership course for outdoor instructors is also available, providing an opportunity to refine outdoor and instructional skills. Backpackers in the winter leadership seminar spend 5 days in extreme weather conditions at altitudes above 6,000 feet in the Mt. Mitchell area. A 2-day seminar in

Wolfcreek Wilderness offers 2- to 14-day outdoor leadership courses in the southern Appalachians covering rescue, survival and interpersonal skills. (Wolfcreek Wilderness)

medical aid is also offered. Academic credit is available for some of the courses. **Cost:** $60 to $300 includes food, accommodations, equipment, transportation. **When:** November, December, May, July, August. **Contact:** Wolfcreek Wilderness, P.O. Box 596, Blairsville, GA 30512, USA; phone (404)745-6460.

Idaho

Crag Walking: Hiking trips in Idaho's Big Horn Crags last anywhere from 5 to 10 or more days and offer the chance to see a beautiful and little-traveled portion of the Idaho Primitive Area under the leadership of an experienced guide. After hiking up a long ridge from Panther Creek participants walk between high alpine lakes set under dramatic granite spires and crags, possibly seeing bighorn sheep, goats and other wildlife; they can then either walk out or hike down to the Middle Fork of the Salmon River and take a bush flight out. Trip highlights include fresh fruits and vegetables at meals, trout fishing in mountain lakes and a hiking pace tailored to each group's desires. **Cost:** $300 for 5 days includes transportation from Salmon, food, most equipment, guide; other rates on request. **When:** Summer. **Contact:** Horizons Unlimited, P.O. Box 2061, Salmon, ID 83467, USA; phone (208)756-3844. *(M)*

Maine

The Fall of Maine: The vivid colors and crisp smells of autumn in New England are experienced on an 8-day wilderness camping and ca-

The Infinite Odyssey offers wilderness camping trips both in Maine and Colorado; here a backpacker pauses on a ridge in the Rockies during a combination rafting and hiking trip. (The Infinite Odyssey)

noeing trip through Baxter State Park in north-central Maine. Offered to adults aged 20 and over, the journey focuses on wildlife observation prior to the onset of winter; campers may see moose, loons, beavers and other creatures as they prepare for the cold months ahead. A highlight of the trip is a hike up Mt. Katahdin, Maine's highest peak. The days are warm, the nights cool at this time of year. The group leaves and returns to the town of Millinocket. **Cost:** $390 includes transportation, food, guide. **When:** September. **Contact:** The Infinite Odyssey, 57 Grant St., Waltham, MA 02154, USA; phone (617)899-6050. ***(M)***

Montana

Backpacking the Big Sky Country: Licensed guides lead small groups of 12 or less on wilderness backpacking trips into the Montana Rockies. Generally lasting about a week, the outings take backpackers into Yellowstone National Park, the Beartooth Primitive Area, and the Great Bear and Bob Marshall wilderness areas. Five or 6 miles are covered each day, and individual pack loads run 25 to 35 pounds. Private outings on foot, skis or snowshoes can also be arranged in appropriate seasons. Families are welcome, though children must be at least 8 years old. A full range of camping equipment is provided. **Cost:** $250. **When:** Summer. **Contact:** High Country Adventures, P.O. Box 176, Helena, MT 59601, USA; phone (406)443-2842.

New Hampshire

Highland Hikes for Youth: The fundamentals of spring and winter hiking are taught to youths between the ages of 13 and 18. Two- or 3-day spring hikes are arranged in several mountain areas in the Northeast. During winter months participants snowshoe up to a campsite near a mountain summit the first day. Camping is done in tents while the outside temperature drops to far below freezing. The following day hikers climb peaks along ridge areas until the downward descent. Cross-country ski trips are also available, with general instruction provided as well. **Cost:** $35 to $55 depending on location and duration. **When:** Year-round. **Contact:** N & N Enterprises, Inc., Box 438, Allston, MA 02134, USA; phone (617)783-3568.

New Mexico

Black Range Backpack: Hikers led by a naturalist and environmental educator wander on foot for a week through the proposed Aldo Leopold Wilderness of the Black Range in southwestern New Mexico. Starting from Silver City, group members trek gradually upwards, studying the ecology of the Sonoran, Montane and Canadian life zones as they gain the higher elevations. Emphasis is placed on understanding a broad range of environmental issues connected with the region's past and future: the field ecology and natural history of the area, wilderness ethics, the role of federal agencies in public land management and the role of wilderness preservation in environmental education. Hikers are also introduced to the Indian folklore and gold rush history for which the area is famous. Backpacking equipment should be supplied by participants. **Cost:** $260 includes guide. **When:** September. **Contact:** American Wilderness Alliance, 4260 E. Evans, Denver, CO 80222, USA; phone (303)758-5018.

The Gila by Foot: Once the home of the Apache Indians, the Gila Wilderness is an area replete with both historic and prehistoric evidence of desert Indian civilization. During a 10-day journey, trip members visit the Gila Cliff Dwellings National Monument and explore habitations built 700 years ago. Hiking and camping is done in the wilderness area, part of the Mogollon Rim. The many springs and rivers help the area remain green and well watered even though surrounded by much dry country. Fresh vegetation contrasts with the colorful rocks of the canyons. There are many trails to choose from for a variety of scenic trips. **Cost:** $250 includes food, equipment. **When:** May. **Contact:** Three Eagles Expeditions, Inc., P.O. Box 2606, Jackson, WY 83001, USA; phone (307)733-4673.

Backpackers from the Yukon to the Appalachians have similar hiking chores: building a fire, setting up camp, packing gear and preparing for another day on the trail. (Gov't. of the Yukon Territory)

North Carolina

Tarheel Trips: Individuals seeking instruction in wilderness living or looking for a guided backpacking trip can schedule departures from Cullowhee, North Carolina. Participants venture into the Shining Rock Wilderness, Joyce Kilmer Memorial Forest, Slickrock Creek Wilderness and the Great Smoky Mountains National Park. Backpackers can also arrange trips into the Pisgah and Nantahala national forests. Each year 2 extended trips outside of the North Carolina area are undertaken. Instruction in rock climbing, canoeing and kayaking may also be requested. **Cost:** On request. **When:** Year-round. **Contact:** Cullowhee Wilderness Outfitter, P.O. Box V, Cullowhee, NC 28723, USA.

Oregon

Birthday Backpacking: A group of women celebrates Amelia Earhart's birthday by taking a week-long backpacking trip in the Hidden Wilderness between Mt. Hood and Mt. Jefferson. Departing from Estacada, backpackers hike 4 to 6 miles a day, taking time to swim in lakes and streams. Menus for the trip stress healthy food, and participants bake a cake for Amelia over the coals. During the trip the group leader teaches skills relating to outdoor cooking, campsite selection, map and compass reading, first aid procedures and minimum impact camping techniques. The trip is sponsored by a nonprofit group seeking to teach women outdoor skills in a supportive atmosphere. **Cost:** $250 includes food, camping equipment, leader. **When:** July. **Contact:** Keep Listening, Box 446, Sandy, OR 97055, USA; phone (503)622-3895.

Pennsylvania

Appalachian Outfitting: Campers rent equipment for 2 short hikes into the mountains of Pennsylvania and West Virginia. Outfitters provide all necessary gear and equipment for 4-person groups embarking on 1- or 2-night adventures. Food is available from the outfitters, or campers may bring their own. A 1-nighter starts between 6 and 9 a.m.; a 2-nighter starts at 4 to 7 p.m. and ends between 4 and 7 p.m. on the second day. Hikers under 16 must be accompanied by an adult. Guides are available. **Cost:** $120 for 4 people includes food, $80 for 4 people does not include food. **When:** Year-round. **Contact:** Mountain Streams and Trails Outfitters, P.O. Box 106, Ohiopyle, PA 15470, USA; phone (412)329-8810.

Allegheny Expedition: A small group of women learns to live safely and comfortably in the wilderness during a 12-day back-

Self-guided backpacking trips can be arranged by hikers who have adequate experience and trail maps. (Keith Gunnar)

packing trip in the Allegheny National Forest. Group members hike 4 to 10 miles a day, learning such skills as wilderness cooking, use of map and compass, first aid and recognition of edible plants. Expedition leaders stress conservation practices and sensitivity to the environment. Participants must be 18 years of age or older. The trip departs from Chautauqua, New York. **Cost:** $245 includes transportation, food, leaders, camping gear. **When:** June. **Contact:** Western Door Wilderness School, Box 534, 17 South Ave., Chautauqua, NY 14722, USA; phone (716)357-5561; or 172 N St., Salt Lake City, UT 84103, USA; phone (801)322-5381.

Texas

Chihuahua Desert Exploration: From a base in Texas, groups cross the Mexican border on trips lasting 2 to 4 weeks. Activities include caving, rafting, climbing and strenuous hiking through the limestone formations and canyons in the Chihuahua Desert and Rio Grande country. The "expedition for the spirit" offers participants a chance to discover something about the beautiful desert wilderness and about themselves. The groups, led by 2 guides, are limited to 5 men and 5 women. The minimum age is 22 and no experience is required. Equipment and a selection of natural foods are provided. **Cost:** $460 and $720. **When:** April to October. **Contact:** Desert Dance, Box 77, Terlingua, TX 79852, USA; phone (915)371-2211.

Utah

Kanab Canyon Hike: An 8-day trip covers a wide variety of terrain in Kanab Canyon, a part of the Grand Canyon. Participants explore narrow canyons, broad desert plateaus, steep cliffs, sand beaches and pine forests, traversing altogether between 35 and 40 miles. Beginning at Sowats Point, hikers travel down Kanab Canyon, along the Colorado River and up Deer Creek Canyon, across Surprise Canyon and finally to Monument Point. Wildlife is abundant, and some Indian ruins are seen. Relatively strenuous hiking is involved, and participants must be at least 18 years old. Trips may be arranged on a custom basis with 90 days advance notice. **Cost:** Depends on group size and includes equipment, food, guide. **When:** April, May, September, October. **Contact:** Trailhead Ventures, P.O. Box CC, Buena Vista, CO 81211, USA; phone (303)395-8001. ***(M)***

Wilderness Hiking: Groups of 5 may go on backpacking and river floating trips in the Utah wilderness. Possible routes are varied and may change with every trip. In the San Rafael Swell or Wasatch Range, backpackers may travel to Zcmi Mine, Burro Spring, No Man's Mountain, Devil's Monument, Ghost Rock and the Fathers, twin pinnacles named for priests who followed the Old Spanish Trail. Other possible trips follow a narrow slickrock trail between 2 canyons called Devil's Racetrack, or proceed to Indian Cave, high on the sheer wall of Coal Wash. The itinerary is determined by the interests and abilities of the guide and participants. Activities vary according to individual tastes and backpackers may spend time rock col-

Desert Dance offers a 2- to 4-week "expedition of the spirit" in the Texas desert to give backpackers an opportunity for self-discovery through rock climbing, caving, rafting and hiking. (Desert Dance)

lecting, photographing, sketching or searching for hidden desert springs, Indian ruins and remnants of outlaw hideouts. Charter trips for groups of 10 to 20 can also be arranged. **Cost:** $275 for 5 days, $365 for 7 days, $495 for 10 days includes guide, camping equipment, meals. **When:** May to October. **Contact:** Tu-Kay Renegades, 49 N. Main, Clawson, UT 84516, USA; phone (801)384-2608.

Vermont

Inns along the Trail: Seven country inns along a 60-mile section of Vermont's Long Trail are organized like the European hut system to accommodate backpackers making day hikes. Participants on a 6-day trip stay at a different inn each night, with a daily car shuttle available to move cars to the new trail end each night. Hikers either walk on the Long Trail, a moderately difficult trail conforming to the ridge line of the Green Mountains, or on less strenuous back country roads that parallel the inn-to-inn route. One of the more beautiful stretches of the route is along the Sherburne Pass-Appalachian Gap, where small mountain streams intersect the trail and high glacial lakes lie nearby. **Cost:** $241 includes accommodations, meals, car shuttle. **When:** By arrangement. **Contact:** Churchill House Inn, RFD #3,

Rt. 73E, Brandon, VT 05733, USA; phone (802)247-3300.

Green Mountain Montage: Travelers with a limited amount of time but a desire to experience many outdoor activities may find a special 1- to 2-week trip to be a good solution to their dilemma. Hiking, horseback riding, bicycling and canoeing are means of travel through the countryside of the Green Mountain State. The hiking sections of the first week's journey traverse trails in the Chittenden and Lincoln areas while the horseback segment in the Stowe region includes lessons as desired, picnic rides and a possible overnight campout. A bicycle trip out of Woodstock starts the second week, followed by hiking near Lincoln. Various rivers in central Vermont (the exact selection depends on water conditions) are explored by canoe. Country inns provide participants with comfortable lodging, excellent meals and swimming opportunities as preparation and reward for each day's events. **Cost:** $293 for 1 week, $526 for 2 weeks includes meals, lodging, guides. **When:** July, August. **Contact:** Hike-Skitour Vermont, RFD 1, Chester, VT 05143, USA; phone (802)875-3631 or 875-3613. ***(M)***

Washington

Hiking in Icicle Canyon: Visitors may backpack into remote areas near campsite locations in the Stuart Range of the Wenatchee National Forest. A year-round opportunity exists for visitors to explore all facets of outdoor living. Participants of all ages are encouraged to share in many of the campsite activities such as cooking or helping build a river raft from cut logs. Backpackers may also find a trail to gold-panning sites accessible only by foot. For beginners, instruction in backpacking and camping techniques is available by advance arrangement. **Cost:** $3 a day for tents to $270 a week includes heated tent lodging, meals, transportation. **When:** Year-round. **Contact:** Family Adventures, Inc., P.O. Box 312, Leavenworth, WA 98826, USA; phone (509)548-7330.

Glacier Peak Wilderness Trip: Located on the western side of Lake Chelan, the remote Glacier Peak Wilderness is dominated by massive glaciated peaks rising out of dense forests of fir, spruce, larch and whitebark pine. On an 11-day trip participants experience flowered valley floors and alpine meadows, craggy peaks and rock spires that cradle fields of blue-green ice. There are numerous lakes throughout the region, the most famous being Image Lake, mirroring Glacier Peak. Participants explore the richly foliated valley floors, climb up to the timberline and over several passes, cross snowfields, examine many of the ice formations at close range, and camp next to cascading streams and chilly alpine lakes. The hiking is fairly difficult, and trip members should be in good physical condition. **Cost:** $330 includes equipment, food, guides. **When:** August. **Contact:** The Wilderness Institute, 333 Fairfax, Denver, CO 80220, USA; phone (303)393-0400.

West Virginia

Fall Foliage Weekend: After an orientation meeting on Friday, hikers set out Saturday morning for 2 days on trails in the Allegheny Mountains of eastern West Virginia. Along the trail they receive instruction in trip planning, safety on the trail, route finding, environmental protection, food planning and preparation, and equipment use and care. Campers are given the opportunity to view some of the most colorful and varied foliage in the country, along the eastern woodlands of West Virginia. The group is led by an experienced guide. **Cost:** $60 includes equipment, food. **When:** September. **Contact:** TransMontane Outfitters Ltd., P.O. Box 325, Davis, WY 26260, USA; phone (304)259-5117 or (804)784-3615.

Cleaning to Hearts Content: During a weekend conservation trip in the Allegheny National Forest, participants sweep the Minister Creek and Hearts Content areas of all garbage and fire circles. Park Service rangers organize the clean-up and work alongside volunteers throughout the weekend. Participants should bring shovels and garbage bags and be prepared for hard work. Equipment can be provided, but group members must reserve it in advance; no food or transportation is provided. **Cost:** Free. **When:** September. **Contact:** Wilderness Trails, 728 Prospect Ave., Cleveland, OH 44115, USA; phone (216)696-5222.

Wyoming

The Backcountry of Yellowstone: The vast majority of Yellowstone National Park's 3,600 square miles is nearly pristine wilderness, and hikers have the choice of a 7- or 10-day trip designed to explore some of this area. The Yellowstone backcountry contains grazing bison and elk, grizzly bears, wolves, pelicans, swans and horned antelope. Participants may observe a variety of thermal features including geysers and hot springs, mud pots and kaleidoscopic rainbows of algae. Walks through petrified forests feature crenelated cliffs of volcanic tuff as well as mountains of volcanic

Wyoming's Gros Ventre Wilderness offers backpackers terrain ranging from wildflower-draped meadows to steep rock ridges. (Wyoming Travel Commission)

glass and basalt columns. **Cost:** $250 to $280 includes equipment. **When:** July, August. **Contact:** Three Eagles Expeditions, Inc., P.O. Box 2606, Jackson, WY 83001, USA; phone (307)733-4643.

Rocky Roads: Hikers explore the peaks, valleys, flora and fauna of Wyoming's Rocky Mountains on custom-designed backpacking trips originating in Jackson. Instructional in nature, the trips last anywhere from a day to 2 weeks or more as participants learn a wide variety of back-country skills, including low-impact camping, basic survival techniques and wilderness cooking. The region's geology and natural history are also covered. The pace is fairly moderate, and layover days are usually scheduled, but participants should be in good physical shape. **Cost:** On request. **When:** Summer. **Contact:** Wild Horizon Expeditions, Box 2348, Jackson, WY 83001, USA; phone (307)733-5343.

Exploring the Mountains of Yellowstone: The backcountry of the north-central Rockies in Montana and Wyoming is the site of 1- and 2-week backpacking adventures for teenagers between 13 and 18. While in and around Yellowstone National Park participants learn orienteering, non-technical climbing, fishing, outdoor cooking and exploration. Traveling in all weather conditions, supervised groups hike over a variety of terrain. Young explorers learn the distinction between adapting to and intruding into the wilderness. The meeting point for the trip is Billings. **Cost:** $225 to $450 includes ground transportation, equipment, food, maps. **When:** June to August. **Contact:** Yellowstone Wilderness Guides, Box 446, Red Lodge, MT 59068, USA.

RESOURCES

Clubs and Associations

American Camping Association
Bradford Woods
Martinsville, IN 46151, USA
Phone (317)342-8456

American Indian Travel Commission
10403 W. Colfax Ave., Suite 550
Lakewood, CO 80215, USA
Phone (303)234-1707

American Youth Hostel Association
National Campus
Delaplane, VA 22025, USA

Appalachian Mountain Club
5 Joy St.
Boston, MA 02108, USA
Phone (617)523-0636

Appalachian Trail Conference
Box 236
Harpers Ferry, WV 25425, USA
Phone (304)535-6331

Bruce Trail
33 Hardale Crescent
Hamilton, ON Canada L8T 1X7

Camping Club of Great Britain and Ireland
11 Lower Grosvenor Pl.
London SW1W OEY, Great Britain

Canadian Hostelling Association
75 Nicholas St.
Ottowa, ON Canada K1N 7B9
Phone (613)233-7738

The Chalet Club
P.O. Box 3849, Grand Central Sta.
New York, NY 10017, USA
Phone (212)490-0126

Florida Trail Association, Inc.
4410 NW 18th Pl.
Gainesville, FL 32605, USA
Phone (904)378-8823

Forest Campers Association
79 Hill Farm Wy.
Southwick, Sussex, Great Britain

International Backpackers Association
P.O. Box 85
Lincoln Center, ME 04558, USA
Phone (207)794-6062

Matterhorn Sports Club
3 W. 57th St., Dept. A
New York, NY 10019, USA
Phone (212)486-0505

National Campers and Hikers Assn.
7172 Transit Rd.
Buffalo, NY 14221, USA
Phone (716)634-5433

National Parks and Conservation Assn.
1701 18th St. NW
Washington, DC 20009, USA
Phone (202)265-2717

New England Trail Conference
33 Knollwood Dr.
East Longmeadow, MA 01028, USA

North American Family Campers Assn.
P.O. Box 552
Newburyport, MA 01950, USA
Phone (617)462-9541

Sierra Club
1050 Mills Tower, 220 Bush St.
San Francisco, CA 94104, USA
Phone (415)981-8634

South American Explorers Club
Casilla 3714
Lima 1, Peru

WEXAS International Office
Suite 354, Graybar Bldg.
420 Lexington Ave.
New York, NY 10017, USA
Phone (212)697-6126

Wilderness Society
1901 Pennsylvania Ave. NW
Washington, DC 20006, USA
Phone (202)293-2732

Women in the Wilderness
13 Columbus Ave.
San Francisco, CA 94111, USA
Phone (415)982-4588

Youth Hostels Association
Trevelyan House, St. Albans
Herts. AL1 2DY, Great Britain

CAVING

By going into a cave you enter a twilight zone beneath the ground. Momentarily blinded by the sudden darkness, you pause to regain your bearings. The chill from the damp rock surfaces penetrates through your clothing. All is silent except for the slow drip of water off stalactites and the gurgling of a small underwater stream.

There are an uncounted number of caves around the world, with 30,000 known caves in the United States alone. Inhabited by blind crayfish, strange salamanders and albino fish, caves are evolutionary laboratories without light. Here pigmentation has disappeared and eyestalks have degenerated as species adapted to darkness.

Although caving is definitely not a sport for everyone, opportunities exist to explore with speleologists the sinkholes, sea caves, mines, lava tubes and caverns of the world. You can take a walking tour of Carlsbad Caverns in New Mexico or squeeze through an unexplored Peruvian passageway with headlamp and ropes. You can learn basic caving techniques while exploring caves in England or be taught water navigation, surveying skills and safety procedures while descending shafts on Vancouver Island. Indiana's limestone caves are explored on 2-day trips, and a 5-week caving course is offered in Wyoming's La Caverna de Tres Charros.

Caving combines physical skill and coordination with the excitement of exploring the unknown. By wading through near-freezing streams, spelunking into black pits, diving subterranean lakes or squeezing through an 8-inch by 2-foot crawlway, you'll gain an inside look at our planet's unusual wildlife and geological formations underground. □

Long icicles frame a winter view from the entrance to a terminal ice cave at Paradise on Mt. Rainier, a short hike from the park's main lodge. (Keith Gunnar)

CAVING

CANADA

British Columbia

Canadian Caving: New caves are constantly being discovered on Vancouver Island, and most are high ceilinged, well ventilated and fairly comfortable to explore. A week-long trip beginning and ending at Campbell River investigates a number of these caves from easy horizontal systems to complex vertical shafts. Practice with a helmet and light source is followed by instruction in caving techniques including chimneying, water navigation, surveying and safety procedures. Unique dark-adapted fauna and delicate geological formations are found in the caverns. Precautions are taken to protect the fragile cave environments. **Cost:** $300 includes transportation from Campbell River, food, equipment, guides. **When:** July. **Contact:** ECOsummer, Box 191, Heriot Bay, BC Canada V0P 1N0.

EUROPE

England

Underground Instruction: A variety of courses for novice, intermediate and advanced cavers lasts from a day to a week. Those with little or no caving experience have several choices: a day trip provides a brief and general introduction with a visit to a cavern in the Dales; on weekend courses, students learn the origin, location and characteristics of caves during evening lectures and visit caves during the day; and a week-long course for those with a strong interest provides a thorough grounding in theory and techniques, as well as an introduction to a caving club. Cavers with some experience can take another week-long course based in the Northern Pennines, during which they practice new techniques and safety procedures and learn more about cave formations and characteristics. More advanced courses include a cave leadership training course, lasting a week, which prepares prospective guides for a certification examination. Arrangements can also be made for custom courses for clubs and special groups. **Cost:** $11 for day trip, $40 for weekends, $104 for week-long courses, $140 for certification assessment includes food, lodging, instruction, transportation. **When:** Year-round. **Contact:** Whernside Cave & Fell Centre, Dent, Sedbergh, Cumbria LA10 5RE, Great Britain; phone Dent (05875)213.

Miners Welcome: The Cheddar region of western England is full of underground passages, both natural caves and abandoned mines. Cavers investigate these subterranean caverns during a week-long trip based at a hostel at St. Briavel. While exploring mine shafts, participants recreate the history of the mining industry as they find abandoned equipment and other remains. The natural caverns explored provide novices with a good introduction to caving. No prior experience is required. The trip is open only to hostel association members. **Cost:** $116 includes food, accommodations, guide. **When:** August. **Contact:** YHA Adventure Holidays, Trevelyan House, St. Albans, Herts., Great Britain; phone St. Albans 55215.

SOUTH AMERICA

Peru

The Depths of Palcamayo Valley: After meeting in Lima, spelunkers journey by train to Palcamayo Valley, a region of Peru well known for its more than 60 caves and deep caverns with depths of up to 1,384 feet. On the 5- to 7-day trip, 1 day is spent in Tarma before the group sets up base camp near Huagapo's Cave at an elevation of 10,518 feet. Exploration of different caves and archaeological ruins precedes a full day spent investigating Huagapo's Cave. With a horizontal entrance, access to the cave is not difficult. Once inside spelunkers see a great number of stalactites and stalagmites, walk in large vaults and see an underground river. Participants should be prepared to walk through water, crawl in low galleries and use ropes and ladders in climbing different portions of the cave. Moving out into the light, the group visits the weaving town of San Pedro de Cajas before spending the final day on the train en route to Lima. **Cost:** $35 a day includes transportation from Lima, accommodations, meals while in camp, guides, caving equipment. **When:** May to September. **Contact:**

Caving enthusiasts sometimes have to employ the techniques of rock climbers while exploring new subterranean passages. (South Dakota Department of Tourism)

Trekking & Andes, P.O. Box 3074, Lima 100, Peru. *(M)*

UNITED STATES

Indiana

Underneath the Hoosier State: Caves in southwestern Indiana are explored on a variety of 2-day trips. Each of the limestone caves, formed by underground streams, is different in character. Some are large caverns which participants can easily walk through while viewing the stalagmites and stalactites. In other caves group members must crawl for hundreds of yards. The caves stay at a constant 55°F, and explorers should dress appropriately. Groups depart from Indianapolis by 12-passenger van, and all equipment for cave exploration is provided. The guide for the trip has 15 years of caving experience in the Indiana, Kentucky and Missouri area. Each trip explores 2 caves. **Cost:** $39 includes roundtrip transportation from Indianapolis. **When:** April, May, October, November. **Contact:** Hoosier Wilderness Expeditions, 8660 Bazaar, Indianapolis, IN 46240, USA; phone (317)846-6868.

South Dakota

Caving in Hells Canyon: A 4-hour trip introduces groups of up to 10 people to caving in the fifth largest cave in the world. Participants receive an orientation to Jewel Cave National Monument in the Hells Canyon area of the Black Hills prior to exploring about 3,000 feet of passageway. Since part of the trip is made on hands and knees or on stomachs through tight crawlways, it is limited to those in good physical condition. Each person is required to pass through an 8½-inch by 2-foot handspan squeeze before entering the cave. Participants should dress warmly and bring ankle-high boots with rubber soles. The cave is noted for its spectacular rock and crystal formations. **Cost:** $2. **When:** June to August. **Contact:** National Park Service, Jewel Cave National Monument, Custer, SD 57730, USA; phone (605)673-2288.

West Virginia

Walk, Stoop and Crawl: In one of the best natural cave areas in the eastern United States participants must walk, stoop and crawl in order to participate in spelunking lessons and trips lasting a minimum of 1 day. Instruction is thorough and takes place in caves that are basically horizontal and have not been artificially altered in any way. Spelunkers explore underground streams that cascade over rocks, learn about the special animals that have their homes underground and come to understand the processes that shaped the unique and delicate formations found below the earth's surface. Temperatures down below are around 55°F and the air is humid. Getting muddy and wet is to be expected so a change of clothing should be brought along. Vertical cave climbs are conducted for a minimum of 2 days for those who are interested in vertical caving. **Cost:** $20 for 1 day; $60 for 2 days; $30 for each additional day from Davis includes guide, meals, instruction, all caving equipment; discounts for groups and families. **When:** By arrangement. **Contact:**

Caving is more than just pure adventure, it is a lesson in geology and cave formation. (NOLS)

TransMontane Outfitters Ltd., P.O. Box 325, Davis, WV 26260, USA; phone (304)259-5117 or (804)784-3615.

Wyoming

Wilderness Survival and Speleology Course: The first 20 days of a 35-day course in caving are spent above ground learning camping, conservation and wilderness skills before participants enter the subterranean passages of La Caverna de Tres Charros in the Big Horn Range. Moving through crawlways, group members observe natural features and practice vertical and horizontal caving techniques. Participants learn about equipment selection and maintenance. Also on the itinerary is instruction in photography, biology, geology and subsurface hydrology. Responsible exploration of these remarkable underground environments requires a thorough knowledge of minimum-impact techniques. **Cost:** $815 includes equipment, meals, local transportation. **When:** July. **Contact:** National Outdoor Leadership School, Box AA, Lander, WY 82520, USA; phone (307)332-4381.

RESOURCES

Clubs and Associations

American Spelean History Association
1117 36th Ave. E.
Seattle, WA 98102, USA

British Cave Research Association
2, Broad Elms Close
Sheffield S11 9ST, Great Britain

Cave Research Foundation
206 W. 18th Ave.
Columbus, OH 43210, USA

National Caves Association
Rt. 9, Box 106
McMinnville, TN 37110, USA
Phone (615)668-3925

National Speleological Society
Cave Ave.
Huntsville, AL 35810, USA
Phone (205)852-1300

Speleo Anthro Club
P. AZ S. Pietro 6
60047 Sassoferrato, Italy

Speleo-Club de Paris
7 rue la Boetie
75008 Paris, France

Speleological Union of Ireland
c/o 1 Sweetman's Ave.
Blackrock, County Dublin, Ireland

CULTURAL EXPEDITIONS

Traveling to a distant land means leaving the security of your own culture behind. It means meeting new people, learning new customs, trying unusual foods—and reaffirming the unity of all people. Anthropologists have made a science characterizing each culture and determining how it fits into the global configuration of humanity. Jet travel now makes it possible for *you* to experience the diverse cultures of the world just a few hours after stepping from your front door.

From a Sing-Sing in New Guinea to an exorcism ceremony in Asia to a village feast in Samoa, foreign culture and ritual are no longer experienced only by anthropologists. Whether you have a week or several months, $200 or $10,000, cultural trips of every duration and cost are being offered worldwide.

You can explore the lost Inca city of Machu Picchu in Peru, climb the Great Pyramid of Khufu in Egypt or see the Taj Mahal by full moon. In Sri Lanka you can witness the *perahera,* a procession of 70 gaily decorated elephants with costumed dancers, drummers and chiefs in full regalia. Or you can join a photographic trip that circles the world in 65 days, visiting a remote Himalayan village by helicopter and the Hindu Kush by Land Rover.

Whether you are lured by the mysteries of Stonehenge, the Buddhist monasteries of Ladakh or the Mayan temples of Guatemala—the great cultures of the world, both enduring and past, have never been so accessible. Now is the time for you to discover them for yourself. □

For these descendants of the Mayans, whose culture once flourished in Guatemala, marketplace bartering is an everyday occurrence. Participants on an expedition sponsored by Forum Travel International are welcome to try their negotiating skills. (Keith Gunnar)

CULTURAL EXPEDITIONS

AFRICA

Trans-Africa Medicine Trip: Participants traverse the continent from Senegal to Kenya during a 23-day tour that includes meetings with African herbalists, priests and healers who explain and demonstrate traditional medical practices. The trip begins with a flight from New York to Dakar in Senegal, a country of mixed religious backgrounds including Muslims, Christians and animists who deal with medical problems in differing ways. From there group members fly southeast to the Ivory Coast, where 3 days are spent touring by coach through coffee and cocoa plantations, visiting a witch doctor's school and talking with a doctor about the work done in a leper hospital in Zaranou. In Togo trips are made to the lake dwellers' village of Ganvie, entirely built on stilts over the water of Lake Nocoue, and to a market where traditional doctors purchase herbs, animal skeletons and other talismans and ingredients needed for their work. Participants stop for 2 days in Ghana, then fly to Nairobi, Kenya; from Nairobi a side trip is made to the Masai Mara Game Reserve for views of black-maned lions, buffalo, elephants, zebras and blue-shanked topi. The final days of the trip are spent in Kisumu near Lake Victoria, where group members are introduced to local tribal doctors before returning to Nairobi, for flights to New York via London. **Cost:** $3,000 includes roundtrip airfare from New York, hotel accommodations, some meals, all transportation in Africa, guides. **When:** Year-round. **Contact:** East African Travel Consultants Inc., 33 Bloor St. E., Suite 206, Toronto, ON Canada M4W 3H1; phone (416)967-0067. *(M)*

Egypt

Cultural Tour in the Land of the Pharaohs: A 19-day tour studies culture along the Nile. Participants begin with 4 days in Cairo, making side trips to Memphis and the Fayyum. Travelers fly to Aswan for a 3-day stay which includes a day trip to Abu Simbel, site of the stately temples of Ramses II and Queen Nefertari. Trip members then embark on a 5-day cruise down the Nile, arriving at Luxor to see tombs in the valleys of the Kings, the Queens and the Princes. After a stop in Minya, travelers are driven back to Cairo for a final banquet. **Cost:** $2,440 includes roundtrip airfare from New York, hotels, meals, taxes. **When:** January. **Contact:** Archaeological Tours, 424 Madison Ave., New York, NY 10017, USA; phone (212)758-0500.

ASIA

Afghanistan

Bamiyan and Nuristan Exploration: A 23-day expedition to Afghanistan features visits to Bamiyan, a village famous for its enormous Buddhas carved out of the side of a cliff, and to Nuristan, a rarely visited area with a distinctive

In Kenya, participants can meet with Masai healers during a trans-Africa excursion to 5 countries offered by East African Travel Consultants. (Pan American World Airways)

culture. Participants fly from New York and stop first in the capital city of Kabul. Traveling by Land Rover, expedition members visit the bazaars and fortress of Herat and the Shrine of Ali in Mazar-i-Sharif. After flying to Bamiyan, the group takes a day trip to the lakes at Band-i-Amir. A drive through Nuristan and then over the Khyber Pass is followed by a flight to Karachi for a 3-night stay. A day trip to Mohenjodaro, site of the Indus Valley civilization, precedes a farewell dinner and a return flight to New York. Accommodations are in hotels at most stops, except for a tent camp in Nuristan and a yurt camp in Bamiyan. **Cost:** $3,346 includes transportation from New York, accommodations, meals, guides. **When:** April, May, August to October. **Contact:** Society Expeditions, P.O. Box 5088, University Sta., Seattle, WA 98105, USA; phone (206)324-9400. *(M)*

India

Srinagar and Leh Tour: Travelers investigate the differences in Hindu, Muslim and Buddhist cultures on a 22-day tour focusing on the cities of Delhi, Srinagar and Leh. Departing from London, participants fly to Delhi for 5 days of sightseeing highlighted by a side trip to the Taj Mahal at Agra. Then the group flies on to Srinagar, capital city of the Muslim province of Kashmir. Six nights are spent here staying in houseboats with central heating; meals are provided from a choice of Indian, Kashmiri or European food. Visitors tour the city in gondola-like shikaras and have opportunities for walking and riding in the nearby foothills, possibly spending a night in a village. The trip's climax is a 6-day expedition by jeep to Leh, capital city of the province of Ladakh. After visiting its Buddhist monasteries, the group returns to Srinagar and concludes the trip with flights to Delhi and London. Accommodations are a hotel in Delhi and outdoors in sleeping bags on the Ladakh trek. **Cost:** $1,670 from London includes transportation, all accommodations, most meals. **When:** June to

August. **Contact:** Exodus Expeditions, 167 Earls Court Rd., London SW5, Great Britain; phone 01-373-7895; or Adventure Center, 5540 College Ave., Oakland, CA 94618, USA; phone (415)654-1879. ***(M)***

Japan

The Heritage of Nippon: Participants visit major cities, rural villages and national parks on a 24-day expedition that studies how history, nature and tradition have influenced the development of Japanese society. Traveling by bus, boat and train, the group visits the Ginza shopping district and Imperial Palace in Tokyo; the ancient former capital city of Kyoto; the birthplace of Japanese Buddhism at Nara; Kamikochi in the Japanese Alps; and Shodo Island in the Inland Sea. Activities include a day trek to study silk-making, a visit to the Suzuki Music School, a hike to observe the rare snow monkeys of Kanbayashi and a daylong excursion to Lake Biwa, Japan's largest lake. Group members gain personal contact with the Japanese through home stays and lodgings at traditional Japanese inns. The trip begins in Tokyo and ends in Osaka. **Cost:** $1,790 includes transportation in Japan, accommodations, meals (except in Tokyo and Kyoto), guide. **When:** May, June, October. **Contact:** Nature Expeditions International, 599 College Ave., Palo Alto, CA 94306, USA; phone (415)328-6572. ***(M)***

Mongolia

Culture of Central Asia: On an unusual 22-day trip participants visit remote areas of central Asia and Mongolia, live in yurt camps (tent-type dwellings) much of the time and explore sites of cultural and archaeological interest. Participants fly to Moscow via Copenhagen, spending a day in Moscow before proceeding by air to Samarkand in Soviet Central Asia. After viewing remnants from Tamerlane's empire, the group travels by coach to the Tajik Republic and the archaeological site at Pendjiket. Participants fly to Irkutsk, in the heart of Siberia and investigate the unusual animal life at Lake Baikal. The explorers move to Mongolia for visits to a horse farm, Karakorum, the center of Ghengis Khan's empire and Ulan Bator. Three days are spent in the Gobi Desert observing wildlife, studying vegetation and watching Mongolian horsemen. Finally, a visit is made to Terelj before returning home. **Cost:** $2,640 includes airfare within Mongolia and the USSR, land transportation, accommodations, food, guide. **When:** June to August. **Contact:** Society Expeditions, P.O. Box 5088, University Sta., Seattle, WA 98105, USA; phone (206)324-9400. ***(M)***

Sri Lanka

Culture and Ceremonies: The island country of Sri Lanka has a rich cultural history dating from the fifth century B.C. Travelers investigate the remnants of this past on two 8-day trips focusing on the culture and ceremonies of the predominantly Buddhist nation. On the cultural tour participants visit a museum in the capital city of Colombo, sightsee in the sacred city of Anuradhapura, see the Dutch fortress of Galle and explore the Temple of the Sacred Tooth Relic of the

Buddha in Kandy, a cultural sanctuary where age-old customs and arts are preserved. The ceremonies and rituals tour takes travelers to observe an exorcism ceremony at Colombo, to watch firewalking and propitiation rites at the festival at Kataragama, and to see masked dancing in Hikkaduwa. A trip is made to Kandy to see the perahera, a procession of 70 gaily adorned elephants, drummers, dancers and chiefs in full regalia. Both trips begin and end at Colombo, with transportation by motorcoach on the cultural tour and by car on the ceremonies tour. Accommodations are in hotels. **Cost:** $220. **When:** Year-round. **Contact:** Walkers Tours & Travels Ltd., P.O. Box 1048, 11 York St., Colombo 1, Sri Lanka; phone 22553. ***(M)***

ATLANTIC

Greenland

Arctic Drift: During the winter of 1844-45 the explorer Gustav Holm made an expedition to an island near Angmagssalik on the east coast of Greenland and discovered the remains of a race of Eskimos living there. Participants on a 5-day trip from Reykjavik visit the island as well as other points of interest along the coast. Travel is by plane, helicopter and boat; group members cruise through drift ice to the hunting station of Quernertuarssuit and spend an entire day aboard a boat that takes them to Kungmait. Traveling amidst icebergs and seals, the boat moves to the head of the fjord where a settlement was established in 1915 and where 625 people now live. On the final day, participants explore Angmagssalik village and visit artisans who produce works of art in the Eskimo tradition. Return to Reykjavik is by air. **Cost:** $510 includes transportation from Reykjavik, accommodations, meals. **When:** January. **Contact:** Icelandic Airlines, 630 Fifth Ave., New York, NY 10020, USA; phone (212)757-8585.

North Pole

Arctic Explorations: A geographer leads an 8-day expedition that explores the geology, wildlife and culture around the Arctic. The group assembles at Resolute and makes flights totaling 1,950 miles to sites in the area of Ellesmere and Baffin islands. Visits are made to Eureka Weather Station, the Inuit settlement at Grise Fjord and a cooperative fishing camp at Koluktoo Bay. Group members learn about seal hunting, oil and gas exploration, scientific expeditions and fishing practices. On the trip's final night participants are treated to a banquet at the Arctic Circle Club Bar in Resolute. **Cost:** $1,775 from Resolute includes flights, accommodations, meals, guide. **When:** July. **Contact:** Special InteresTours, P.O. Box 37, Medina, WA 98039, USA; phone (206)455-1960.

Polar Visits: Participants fly from Resolute Bay in northern Canada to a comfortable base camp at Lake Hazen, near the tip of Ellesmere Island during a 9-day sojourn in the Arctic. Activities include dogsledding, hunting with the Eskimos, sleeping in an igloo, fishing for arctic char in the world's northernmost lake, watching polar bears

Travel by boat up the Sepik River is the only way to visit some of the more remote tribes in Papua New Guinea. (Society Expeditions)

and musk oxen, and learning about arctic ecology and Inuit culture. When a positive weather report is received, the group flies over the polar icecap to the Pole, celebrating its arrival with champagne and caviar. Champagne also accompanies a visit to the Magnetic North Pole. **Cost:** $3,700 from Resolute includes accommodations, meals, air transportation. **When:** April, May. **Contact:** Wheeler Adventures, Sea & Shore Travel, Inc., 21605 Hawthorne Blvd., Del Amo Financial Ctr./Pavillion "C", Torrance, CA 90503, USA; phone (213)540-9331.

AUSTRALASIA

Pacific Encounter: Two 36-day trips through the South Pacific emphasize contact with local residents and an appreciation of daily life in the area. Both trips depart from the west coast of the United States. The first trip makes a sweep through Tahiti, the Cook Islands, New Zealand, Australia and Fiji; the second visits only the Cook Islands, New Zealand and Australia. Participants stay at hotels, huts, guest ranches and with local families. Sites common to both journeys include Waitomo, the geysers and boiling mudpools of Whakarewarewa, Mt. Cook, a sheep station in New Zealand's Southern Alps, Lake Wakatipu and the Remarkables. In addition, the first trip visits the island of Moorea and the clear snorkeling waters off Vanua Levu. **Cost:** $2,991 to $3,891 for first trip, $3,318 to $4,219 for second trip, depending on type of lodging and airfare, includes roundtrip airfare from U.S., accommodations, some meals, guides. **When:** Year-round. **Contact:** Cook Islands Travel Service, P.O. Box 406, Berkeley, CA 94701, USA.

Entering Stone Age Villages: While traveling with an experienced natural history guide and lecturer for 18 to 23 days, participants view the great cultural contrasts within New Guinea and Australia. The trip begins with 2 days in Sydney, after which participants fly to Port Moresby where they visit the National Museum. Overland travel precedes a visit to the Haus Tamberan (Spirit Houses which are the center of village life) to see the ceremonies of various tribes including the Andagalimp dancers and the cultural re-enactments of the Chimbu and the Mud Men. Participants then travel by boat on the Sepik River to experience cultures that resemble those of the Stone Age. After 4 days on the river, adventurers fly by charter plane to the remote coastal village of Tufi, accessible only by outrigger canoe, where they stay as guests of the Yari Yari clan. After returning to Sydney, those who are staying for 23 days visit the Green Island underwater observatory, then fly to Alice Springs and Ayers Rock, the largest monolith in the world. Participants drive to the Olga Range for a day's visit before departing for Sydney. **Cost:** $2,245 for 18 days, $2,845 for 23 days includes transportation from Sydney, meals, accommodations, guides. **When:** Year-round. **Contact:** Society Expeditions, P.O. Box 5088, University Sta., Seattle, WA 98105, USA; phone (206)324-9400. *(M)*

Melanesian Photography: Photographers capture the cultural features of the primitive villages of New Guinea and the elaborate civilizations of Indonesia on a 30-day trip. Among the trip's highlights are a visit to the village of the elaborately masked "mud men"; an excursion to the Baiyer River Bird and Wildlife Sanctuary; a 3-day houseboat cruise on the Sepik River; attendance at a Simbai sing-sing performance; a 3-day exploration of the lush countryside and idyllic beaches of Bali; and a day trip to Borobudur, a large 8th-century Buddhist temple. The trip also stops in Sydney, Australia, the Indonesian capital of Jakarta and Hong Kong. A travel photographer leads the tour, and accommodations are in hotels. **Cost:** $6,147 includes transportation in New Guinea, accommodations, meals, roundtrip airfare from Los Angeles. **When:** August. **Contact:** Thru the Lens Photographic Adventures, 12501 Chandler Blvd., N. Hollywood, CA 91607, USA; phone (213)877-0181 or tollfree (800)423-2471.

Papua New Guinea

Island Culture and Traditions: Over the course of 24 days, participants explore the culture and landscape of Papua New Guinea. Study is given to the archaeological remnants scattered over the island, with special instruction in New Guinea's culture and traditions given by the expedition leaders. Participants travel through a diverse landscape which varies from rivers to coastline to highlands. Visits are made to Port Moresby, Rabaul, the Sepik River, Mt. Hagen, Goroka and the annual Sing-Sing. **Cost:** $1,890 includes meals, accommodations, land transportation, guide. **When:** May, July, September. **Contact:** Nature Expeditions International, 599 College Ave., Palo Alto, CA 94306, USA; phone (415)328-6572. *(M)*

CANADA

British Columbia

Klondike Travel: A 100-mile float plane flight over remote forest and lake wilderness begins a 7-day trip into the Alaskan frontier. On the day after the plane lands at Lake Atlin, participants may choose to take a freight canoe trip to a turn-of-the-century railroad station and sawmill and continue to an abandoned hard-rock gold rush town at Lake Tagish. During the rest of the stay, opportunities are available for hiking, fast-water canoeing and gold panning at Llewellyn Glacier. Members observe a multitude of wildflowers, visit a hidden emerald lake and investigate an abandoned trapper's cabin. Grizzly bears can sometimes be seen and photographed. **Cost:** $845. **When:** June to September. **Contact:** Special InteresTours, P.O. Box 37, Medina, WA 98039, USA; phone (206)455-1960.

Nova Scotia

Acadian Adventure: High school students join together for a month-long exploration of the rugged terrain and lifestyle of Nova Scotia. In traveling through the region participants have opportunities to speak French with residents of tiny Gaspe fishing villages and to witness the Highland Games or the Gaelic Mod. The group hikes in the mountains of Cape Breton Island, a terrain reminiscent of Scotland. Students ply the rocky coasts for lobster, tuna and haddock, then work with subsistence farmers in isolated hamlets. Some emphasis is placed on music, crafts and drama, and in Halifax students participate in native arts and crafts programs conducted at an art college. The goal of the program is to encourage each individual's growth, maturity and self-confidence, and to this end students share in the responsibilities of the trip. **Cost:** $1,325 includes camping, accommodations, equipment, transportation, guides. **When:** Summer. **Contact:** Interlocken, Hillsboro Upper Village, NH 03244, USA; phone (603)478-3202.

CARIBBEAN

Antigua

Seeking Buried Treasure: Participants on 8-day trips scan 2 long-abandoned military sites, one on Antigua and the other on Guadaloupe, with metal detectors and other equipment in the hopes of finding objects of value. On Antigua the trip is centered in the Nelson's Dockyard area, in which several forts once used by the Royal Navy still stand. Chances exist of finding buried cannonballs, buttons, bottles, old coins and other items. The Guadaloupe trip visits other abandoned forts, ruins of plantations and deserted beaches where participants can operate their metal detectors. Individuals may take home a portion of any treasure they find, but by law must give part of it to the local government. Accommodations are in cottages. **Cost:** $475 for Antigua, $695 for Guadaloupe includes transportation from Miami, accommodations, guide; food and some ground transportation extra. **When:** April to October. **Contact:** Adventurers International, 215 E. Horatio Ave., Maitland, FL 32751, USA; phone (305)645-1332. *(M)*

CENTRAL AMERICA

Belize

Rum Point Field Studies: An 8-day program of informal field studies covers social anthropology, ethnology and archaeology. While living at Rum Point at a local inn, participants learn about the 3 major cultures in the area: the Creole, the Garifuna and the Kekchi Maya. Other ethnic groups are visited on the Placencia Peninsula and visits are made to archaeological sites in the mountains of southern Belize. There are also opportunities for sport diving. **Cost:** $300. **When:** December to April, June, July. **Contact:** Oceanic Expeditions, 240 Ft. Mason, San Francisco, CA 94123, USA; phone (415)441-1106.

Guatemala

Mayan Medley: Mayan ruins are explored on a 15-day journey through the varying terrain of Guatemala. From Guatemala City, members of the trip drive through highlands to the marketplace at Chichicastenango and then proceed to Lake Atitlan and its 3 nearby volcanoes. The ruins of Kaminal Juyu, "the place of the dead," provide a brief stopover before a return to Guatemala City. Explorations are made across the country to Copan, a cultural and scientific center of the Mayas that boasts unrivaled stone sculpture, hieroglyphic stairways, altars and ball courts. The 60 acres of ruins include rare 3-dimensional carvings as well as low and high reliefs that are more typical in the Mayan culture. Stops at Quirigua, Tikal, Antigua and San Antonio Aguas Calientes give opportunities to investigate ruined cities and temples, working villages and the natural environment. The ruins at Tikal, the largest

Mayan temple yet discovered, spread over nearly 25 miles of jungle, and include as many as 10,000 structures. **Cost:** $698 from Guatemala City includes accommodations, transportation, food. **When:** February, April, July, September, November, December. **Contact:** Forum Travel International, 2437 Durant, No. 208, Berkeley, CA 94704, USA; phone (415)843-8294.

EUROPE

England

Rustic Albion: On a 17-day trip through England that avoids the usual tourist routes, participants travel by minibus and find accommodations in private homes and small inns. At the beginning of the trip, in Dorset, the group visits prehistoric Cerne Giant and 4,000-year-old Maiden Castle as well as an 11th-century swannery. Next on the route is the Slimbridge Wildfowl Trust on the Berkeley Castle estate and the Cotswolds, where participants can hike among the gently rolling hills. More hiking is planned for the High Peaks region of Derbyshire and the Suffolk countryside. The group has permission to enter the Minsmere wild bird reserve, a haven for over 100 species of birds. Also visited are Oxford University, Blenheim Palace, Norwich Cathedral and London. Participants should be prepared for considerable walking. **Cost:** $1,885 from London includes accommodations, most meals. **When:** June. **Contact:** Hanns Ebensten Travel Inc., 55 W. 42nd St., New York, NY 10036, USA; phone (212)354-6634.

Greece

Traveling to the Temples of Zeus and Artemis: Travelers on a trip of 17 days to Greece witness monuments of ancient Greek culture. After a flight to Athens, participants stay in a hotel and tour for 2 days before setting out across Greece to visit places such as the temple of Wingless Victory and the Acropolis, where the Parthenon was built. On the fourth day, after passing through the Corinth Canal and the city's ruins, participants drive along the coast roads to Epidaurus and its well-preserved theater. At Mycenae archaeological sites originally excavated during the 19th century by Heinrich Schliemann are open to the public. Group members continue to the vast triangular site on the banks of the Eurotas—reminders of ancient Sparta. Mystra contains examples of architecture from the Byzantine period and participants have a day to study them before proceeding to Olympia, site of the original Olympic Games. The following day is spent at Delphi where group members investigate the many archaeological sites. Participants also have the option of visiting Ioannina, Meteora, Pella or Cape Sounion before the return flight from Athens to Canada. **Cost:** $1,250 includes hotel accommodations, some food, transportation. **When:** May to August. **Contact:** Azalai Explorers Inc., Suite 1006, 75 The Donway W., Don Mills, ON Canada M3C 2E9; phone (416)449-8044.

MEXICO

Railing through Mexico: Travelers

view the cities and rural areas of Mexico on a 2-week train tour through the heart of the country. Starting either in Los Angeles or El Paso, passengers board the "El Fronterizo," a train that heads south from the border to Mexico City. Along the way they pass mountains, farmland and small villages. Once in Mexico City, a bus is taken to various points of interest, including the Government Palace and the Museum of Anthropology. The train passes on to Oaxaca, Monte Alban, the ruins of Mitla and the Pyramids of Teotihuacan. The trip swings through Taxco and Guadalajara before heading north toward the border. **Cost:** $795 from El Paso, $875 from Los Angeles includes transportation, accommodations on the train, guide service. **When:** July to December. **Contact:** Ralph Peck Associates, P.O. Drawer 72, Whittier, CA 90608, USA; phone (213)693-6626.

Chihuahua

South of the Border: Mexico City is the first stop on a 2-week trip designed to explore a full spectrum of cultural, archaeological and historical sites. Included on the trip are visits to Jalapa, a historic city containing large collections of Totonac and Olmec antiquities; the Mayan ruins of Palenque half hidden in jungle; and the architectural intricacies of Uxmal. In addition, participants have time to explore local villages where they may shop or visit with the inhabitants. Much leisure time is planned into the itinerary, providing members with an unhurried travel experience. The pyramids of Teotihuacan provide the archaeological highlight of the trip before the return to Mexico City. **Cost:** $965 includes roundtrip airfare from Los Angeles, accommodations, meals, guides. **When:** December to February. **Contact:** Wampler Tours, P.O. Box 45, Berkeley, CA 94701, USA; phone (415)843-6602. ***(M)***

PACIFIC

Fiji

Fiji Grassroots: Explorers on a 22-day trip departing from Los Angeles have the chance to stay in a number of Fijian villages and participate in the daily life, local economy and hospitality of the island residents. Except when in transit, accommodations are in *bures* or village huts, and the daily diet is that of the natives. After flying via Nadi and Suva, travelers board a 110-foot converted whaler and sail to Toberua Island. Several days are then spent in each of 7 small villages. Activities include attending church, joining in a seafood feast, ceremonial singing and dancing, and enjoying informal contact with villagers. Upon departure from each village the expedition makes a material gift to the residents toward whatever village fund is currently being gathered. Anyone from school age on up may participate on the trip, but good health, a tolerance for primitive conditions and a willingness to respect local customs are necessary. **Cost:** $2,390 includes transportation from Los Angeles, food, accommodations, activities, village gifts, guide. **When:** July. **Contact:** Goodtravel Tours, 5332 College Ave., Oakland, CA 94618, USA; phone (415)658-2060.

Western Samoa

Samoan Traditions: A 15-day trip enables a group of travelers to experience the traditional Polynesian culture of Samoa in a variety of situations. After flying from the west coast of the U.S. via Hawaii and Pago Pago, the group spends several days in the city of Apia exploring the market, taking an outrigger trip with local guides and touring agricultural and cultural sites. Group members then fly to Sava'i, the largest and one of the least Westernized islands of Samoa, where they stay with local families. Activities include visits to archaeological sites and a lava field, swimming, observing traditional ceremonies, instruction in Samoan crafts and outrigger excursions. Extra days can be scheduled in either Samoa or Hawaii after the trip's end. **Cost:** $569 from Samoa includes land transportation, food, accommodations, activities, guide; all airfare extra. **When:** July. **Contact:** Goodtravel Tours, 5332 College Ave., Oakland, CA 94618, USA; phone (415)658-2060.

SOUTH AMERICA

Ecuador

Photo Travel: For 21 days, 18 participants journey through Ecuador and Peru on a trip designed specifically for photographers. The group is led by a photographer and veteran South American traveler who conducts camera workshops during the trip. After catching a flight from San Francisco to Ecuador, photographers spend 4 days in the Napo River region of the Amazon Basin. A dramatic contrast in terrain is provided by the next stop on the itinerary—glacier-encrusted Mt. Cotopaxi. Visits are also made to several of South America's finest Indian markets. One week is spent exploring the Urubamba Valley region before flying to Machu Picchu. In the final 2 days of the trip photographers capture the Inca ruins on film before flying back to San Francisco. **Cost:** $1,225 from Ecuador includes transportation, guide, accommodations, meals. **When:** June. **Contact:** The Avenue Travel, 1728 Solano Ave., Berkeley, CA 94707, USA; phone (415)843-8294.

Peru

Inca Spots: Trips lasting 17 and 22 days examine Peruvian culture and history while exploring deserts, barren plateaus and isolated mountain valleys. After 2 days in Lima, participants explore the ruins of Pachacama, a ceremonial center visited by Pizarro. Behind the walls of the Santa Catalina Convent in Arequipa, which was just recently opened to the public, lies a miniature 16th-century city rich with colonial frescoes, cobblestone streets and grilled balconies. From Arequipa, the group proceeds to the ancient Inca capital of Cuzco, a blend of whitewashed adobe houses. Further explorations are made to places such as Machu Picchu, Sacsayhuaman, Chincheros, Puno and La Paz. The 22-day trip continues to Huaraz, Trujillo and Chan Chan, capital of the mighty Chimu Empire. **Cost:** $894 to $1,192 includes accommodations, transportation, food. **When:** January, March, June, August, September, November, December. **Contact:** Forum Travel International, 2437 Durant, No. 208, Berkeley, CA 94704, USA; phone (415)843-8294.

UNITED STATES

Wyoming

Rendezvous Country: The area of western Wyoming where fur trappers used to meet is known as "rendezvous country." During a 10-day expedition that begins and ends in Salt Lake City participants investigate archaeological, geological and historical sites of interest under the leadership of a scholar knowledgeable about the area. Visits are made to the Green River basin, the Absaroka Range, Yellowstone and the Grand Tetons, with the trip culminating at the modern rendezvous celebration that commemorates Wyoming's past. **Cost:** $690 from Salt Lake City includes meals, accommodations, transportation, guide. **When:** June, September. **Contact:** Nature Expeditions International, 599 College Ave., Palo Alto, CA 94306, USA; phone (415)328-6572. ***(M)***

WORLD

Around the World in 65 Days: Photographers get a chance to see and record a variety of cultures and landscapes during a 65-day worldwide trip from Los Angeles to New York. Staying in hotels and flying from place to place, the group spends 2 to 6 days in most locations. The areas visited include major Japanese cities, Hong Kong, Bali, Southeast Asian centers, Kathmandu, Delhi, Kashmir, Kabul, Isfahan, Cairo and Luxor. Side trips are frequently offered to points of particular visual interest, such as a remote Himalayan village reached by helicopter, or the Bamian Valley in the Hindu Kush visited on an overland excursion. Cultural events are often attended in the cities. **Cost:** $9,389 includes all transportation, food, accommodations, guide. **When:** September. **Contact:** Thru the Lens Photographic Adventures, 12501 Chandler Blvd., N. Hollywood, CA 91607, USA; phone (213)877-0181 or tollfree (800)423-2471.

OVERLANDING

Budget travelers eager to see the world will be pleased by the variety of overland expeditions now available. For as little as $10 a day you can join a 90-day expedition from Bombay to London that crosses the Great Sand Desert of Iran, boats through the Greek Islands and makes a detour through the French Riviera. Or you can spend 16 weeks exploring the length of Africa from Johannesburg to London for $12 a day including food, transportation, camping equipment and guide.

Overlanding is a great way to travel with a group of adventurous friends or to experience the camaraderie that evolves among strangers thrown together during a long-distance trip. Group sizes range from 6 to 30, with the average being about 20 people. While most participants are usually in their 20s and 30s, physical fitness and an ability to cope with the unexpected are more important than age. On the more rugged overland trips you will be asked to help pitch tents and prepare meals, as well as pry the vehicle out of mudholes, soft sand, rivers and bogs. Less rigorous trips offer travel by motorcoach with accommodations in cabins.

A few pioneering trip operators in the United States and Great Britain planned the first overlanding expeditions during the 1960s. Now more than 100 companies take thousands of people across the world's continents each year in Land Rovers, Bedford trucks and 4-wheel drive vehicles. You can travel by train and steamer on a 2,670-mile route along the Nile through Egypt and Sudan, journey by motorcoach on an 82-day trip from London to Kathmandu via Russia or ride elephantback through the bamboo jungles of southern India during a 4-week expedition from Bombay to Madras.

Whether you decide to circle the Australian continent in a camping coach, explore Papua New Guinea by foot, raft and plane, or travel 28,000 miles from New York to Rio de Janeiro, you will find yourself immersed in the culture of each new place visited. For those who have the time and temperament, overlanding trips combine both world exploration and self-discovery—adventure at its best. □

A local passenger ferry is often the sole means of transport for modern overlanding vehicles that must cross a remote river or lake. (Encounter Overland)

OVERLANDING

AFRICA

West African Expedition: A 14-week overland expedition beginning in either Nairobi, Kenya or Southampton, England travels by truck across West Africa, concluding with a ferry crossing to Europe and a 7-day tour of Spain and France. The route, starting in Nairobi, passes through Kenya, Sudan, Nigeria, Benin and Upper Volta, down the Niger River through Mali and Niger, and south through Upper Volta to the Atlantic Coast. Turning north, the expedition enters the Sahara and continues through Algeria and Morocco. Throughout the trip, participants share in the daily camp work and help transport the truck over difficult spots such as river crossings and desert sand. Once through Morocco, the group embarks on a ferry at Ceuta to cross the Strait of Gibraltar. On the final leg of the trip, the group motors through Spain and France to finish up in Southampton. The route from Southampton reverses the order, ending in Nairobi. **Cost:** $1,750 includes transportation from starting point, camp accommodations, equipment; $10 a day for food kitty. **When:** February, July, December from Nairobi. **Contact:** Adventure Africa, Stablings, 34b High St. Ramsbury, Marlborough, Wiltshire, Great Britain; phone (06722)569.

East African Safari: A 4-week expedition in Tanzania and Kenya begins in Dar es Salaam with a trip across the plateau of the Masai Steppe to Mt. Kilimanjaro. Porters assist with supplies on a climb of Mt. Kilimanjaro, which is a long, hard hike rather than a technical climb. Next the expedition travels to Ngorongoro, a crater 10 miles in diameter containing large concentrations of wildlife, and to the surrounding Serengeti Plains, home of great herds of wildebeest, gazelle and giraffe. Here and in the neighboring Masai Mara Game Reserve the expedition's high, open-topped trucks provide good opportunities for observation and photography. The expedition stops at the crater lake of Nakuru in the Kenyan highlands, which teems with flamingoes and other bird life. Participants also explore the foothills of Mt. Kenya before stopping in Nairobi. The route from Nairobi to Dar es Salaam passes through Tsavo National Park and Mombasa and along the Indian Ocean, stopping at the Gedi ruins. **Cost:** $590 from Dar es Salaam includes all costs. **When:** July, August, December. **Contact:** Encounter Overland, 369 Pine St., Suite 516, San Francisco, CA 94104, USA; phone (415)421-7199. ***(M)***

Desert and Rain Forest Overland: Members of a 3- to 4-month expedition cross the African continent from Morocco to Kenya through the Sahara, the equatorial rain forests of Central Africa and the veldt of East Africa. The group travels by specially equipped Bedford truck and camps out in 2-person tents. The trip begins in London, and the expedition quickly crosses Europe to the Mediterranean. After stopping at Fez and Marrakech in Morocco, members cross into the Sahara, which takes them across Algeria and into Niger. In Algeria the route passes through Ain Salah, historic restocking site for camel caravans, and Tamanrasset, ancient capital of the Tuareg. The expedition sometimes camps in abandoned villages or possibly the football field of an occupied village. The expedition crosses Zaire, until the group climbs to the equator at 7,000 feet. Participants may climb Nyiragongo, an active volcano near Lake Kivu. From Zaire the expedition enters Rwanda and crosses the Mountains of the Moon into Tanzania. In Kenya trip members visit the game reserves of East Africa, ending up in Nairobi. Expedition members should be prepared for physical discomfort and should be reasonably fit. **Cost:** $1,800 includes transportation, food, equipment. **When:** January, March, April, May. **Contact:** Exodus Expeditions, 167 Earls Court Rd., London SW5, Great Britain; phone 01-373-7895; or Adventure Center, 5540 College Ave., Oakland, CA 94618, USA; phone (415)654-1879. *(M)*

French West Africa Expedition: Travelers spend 28 days in West Africa exploring 4 countries via train, plane, river and road transportation. Flying from New York, the group spends 3 days in Dakar before heading into the interior by way of a 30-hour train trip to Mali's tree-lined capital city of Bamako. Two days later, trip members follow the Niger River as it passes through Segou and Djenné, traveling in a fully equipped truck to reach Mopti. A 4-day river cruise in a large motorized piroque familiarizes participants with the people, animals and ways of the Niger River. Members then fly back to Mopti for a road trek to Ouagadougou, the capital of Upper Volta. From there overlanders travel farther south to the cities of Tamale, Kumasi, Takoradi and Accra, from where they return to New York. The group camps under the stars in Mali and stays at hotels in Dakar, Bamako, Ouagadougou and the Ghanaian cities. **Cost:** $3,388 includes airfare from New York, meals, accommodations, local transportation. **When:** January. **Contact:** Exploration Africa, 17 Inkerman St., Toronto, ON Canada M4Y 1M5.

Desert Exploration: Specialized expeditions through the Sahara offer a variety of itineraries depending on the aims of each group. A qualified lecturer accompanies each expedition as it travels throughout the desert in areas from the Nile to the Atlantic. Two or 3 fully equipped Land Rovers provide transportation. Because groups are small, each member plays a vital role in achieving the aims of an expedition. **Cost:** On request. **When:** By arrangement. **Contact:** Exploration Sahara, 16A Soho Sq., London W1V 5FB, Great Britain; phone 01-734-1072.

London to the Cape Overlanding: An individualized approach predominates during a 4-month trip through parts of Europe, the Sahara, Central Africa and South Africa to the Cape. Traveling by 4-wheel drive Bedford trucks, using Land Rover station wagons as necessary, overlanders go to remote regions by way of sometimes rugged detours and infrequently used trails. Along the way participants have a chance to meet the diverse peoples of Africa—the Bedouins, who camp in tents woven from goat hair and grass; the Tuareg, who ride camels along age-old trade routes; and the Pygmies, who hunt in the dense rain forests of equatorial Africa. Trip members experience untamed conditions throughout the journey, and uncontrollable elements often become a challenge to overcome. While a general itinerary is planned, each individual party makes day-to-day diversions, detours and route-planning decisions depending on political climates and group needs. **Cost:** $1,300 includes transportation from London. **When:** March, September, October. **Contact:** The Great African Adventure Co. Ltd., 233 Station Rd., Leigh-on-Sea, Essex, Great Britain; phone 0702 (southend) 73122.

During the course of a 3- to 4-month Exodus Expeditions trans-Africa trip, participants cross the Oubangui River, which forms part of the northern border of Zaire. (Exodus Expeditions and Adventure Center)

Africa from the Bottom Up: A trip by expedition truck takes participants from Johannesburg to London over the course of 16 weeks. Visits are made to most of Africa's major game parks, and there are many opportunities for side trips. The first leg of the journey visits South Africa, Botswana and Zambia, with camping on the edge of the Okavango Swamps, where a dugout may be hired to track hippos and buffalo. Stops are made at Gaborone, Maun, Chobe National Park and Victoria Falls. In Tanzania and Kenya travelers visit Mikumi National Park, Dar es Salaam, Kilimanjaro, Nairobi, Mombasa, Ngorongoro Crater and Serengeti National Park. Through the dense jungles of Central Africa, participants travel in Rwanda, Zaire and the Central African Empire, with a visit included to the active volcano of Nyiragongo. Camping on the Atlantic coast of Cameroon follows during the excursion through West Africa. Finally the trip crosses the Sahara to visit Niger, Algeria and Morocco before crossing the Strait of Gibraltar to traverse Spain and France to London. Nights are spent camping (with occasional exceptions), and participants share cooking, cleaning and some road-clearing chores. **Cost:** $1,820 includes food, transportation, equipment, guide. **When:** February to November. **Contact:** Tracks, 165 Kensington High St., London W8 6SH, Great Britain; phone 01-937-3028. *(M)*

Journey up the Nile: Members of a 28-day expedition use a variety of modes of public transport on a 2,670-mile route along the Nile

During a 2-week trip through Tunisia, overlanders visit the ruins at Dougga that remain from the days when the Roman Empire extended into northern Africa. (Society Expeditions)

River through Egypt and Sudan. The trip starts in Cairo with a train trip to Aswan, stopping in Luxor to visit the temples of Karnak, the Valley of Kings and the Theban necropolis. A steamer takes participants from the Aswan Dam to Wadi Halfa in Sudan, where they take a train across the Nubian Desert to Khartoum, at the confluence of the Blue and White Niles. After a 4-day stopover in Khartoum, the expedition journeys by train to Kosti, where the *Nile Steamer* plies the Upper White Nile. On the 9-day steamer trip through southern Sudan, frequent stops are made at towns along the banks of the river, an area of swamps inhabited by crocodiles and hippos. At Juba members fly to Kenya, where the trip ends with a short drive from Mt. Kenya to Nairobi. Group members stay at inexpensive hotels along the route. **Cost:** On request. **When:** By arrangement. **Contact:** Trailfinders, 46 Earls Court Rd., London W8 6EJ, Great Britain; phone 01-937-9631.

Botswana

Bush Country Safaris: Participants view wild animals in their natural settings on a journey through the parks and riverlands of eastern Botswana. Starting in Johannesburg, travelers spend 14 days camping, hiking and driving through the southern African bush. Stops include a base camp at Okavango Swamp, where animals roam through grasslands and lagoon country; Chobe National Park, filled with elephants, antelope and a great variety of bird life; and famous Victoria Falls at the heart of the Zambezi River. Adventurers return to Johannesburg through the Transvaal high veldt. Dugout canoes are available for exploration of the river shallows, where hippos and buffalo may still be found. **Cost:** $586 from Johannesburg includes transportation, camping accommodations. **When:** April to November. **Contact:** Adventure Center, 5540 College Ave., Oakland, CA 94618, USA; phone (415)654-1879. *(M)*

Morocco

Moroccan Trek: A 17-day journey travels south past the chateaux of central France, across the Pyrenees, into Spain and across the Strait of Gibraltar to Morocco. The group makes its first Moroccan stop at Fez where the traditional bazaars offer goods made by local artisans, and one is expected to dicker furiously over prices. Marrakech, the next stopping place, lies at the foot of the High Atlas Mountains. Camels and donkeys travel through the streets of the red-walled city, while nomads from the Sahara mingle in its maze of alleys and cobbled walks. A popular place in the evening is the main square, where snake charmers, acrobats and faith healers are among the entertainers. The group travels up the coast to Tanger via Casablanca and Rabat, stopping for swims in the Atlantic. Crossing the Strait of Gibraltar, the journey proceeds to Spain, before the last night is spent in Paris. **Cost:** On request. **When:** By arrangement. **Contact:** Centaur Overland Travel Ltd., 146 Halfway St., Sidcup, Kent DA15 8DF, Great Britain; phone 01-302-5959.

Mapping the Atlas: Travelers explore Morocco, home of the Moors and Berbers, in a 3-week motorized expedition starting in Tanger, Morocco. The expedition travels to Fez, a city of many artisans, visiting along the way the ruins of Volubilis, a second-century Roman capital. From Fez the route climbs into the cedar forests of the Middle Atlas Mountains before twisting down into the Sahara. The expedition forges ahead through the desert for several days then turns toward the Atlantic Ocean. After crossing the High Atlas Mountains, trip members stop at the oasis city of Marrakech and then continue to the Atlantic at Rabat. On the way back the route passes along the coast through Asilah. Expedition members are fully involved in the operation of the trip, from pushing the Bedford trucks through soft sand to buying camping provisions. **Cost:** $370 from Tanger. **When:** June to September. **Contact:** Encounter Overland, 369 Pine St., Suite 516, San Francisco, CA 94104, USA; phone (415)421-7199. ***(M)***

Overland from Casablanca: Members of 2- and 3-week expeditions pursue an overland route from the fringes of the Sahara through the Atlas Mountains to the Atlantic Ocean, beginning and ending at Casablanca. The 2-week expedition travels east to Fez by way of Rabat, then south to Meski Oasis and through the Todra Gorge to Marrakech. After a day in Marrakech the expedition drives to Essaouira, an ancient Portuguese town on the Atlantic coast, and then follows the coast to Casablanca. The 3-week expedition follows the same route, with the exception of a 4-day detour between Marrakech and Essaouira passing through Taroudant and Tafraoute; the rest of the extra week is spent in more leisurely exploration along the way. Overlanders travel by Land Rover and desert truck and camp en route. **Cost:** $475 to $578 includes food, ground transport, equipment, roundtrip airfare from London. **When:** June through September. **Contact:** Treasure Treks Ltd., Third Floor, Panton House, 25 Haymarket, London SW1Y 4EN, Great Britain; phone 01-839-4267; or Adventure Center, 5540 College Ave., Oakland, CA 94618, USA; phone (415)654-1879. *(M)*

Sudan

Tribal Sudan Trek: Accompanied by a professional anthropologist, an overland journey of 3 weeks takes participants into the hinterlands of Darfur, Kordofan and Equatoria. As they motor across the Sudan, trip members mingle with peoples like the Dinka and Shilluk. Due to the exploratory nature of the trip, there is no set itinerary. Schedules permitting, some time is spent in the Imatong Mountains and the natural game park of Nimule, known for the variety and number of animals to be seen in a small area. **Cost:** $1,890 includes roundtrip airfare from London, all land arrangements. **When:** February, March. **Contact:** Explore Beyond Ltd., 167 Earls Court Rd., London SW5, Great Britain; or Adventure Center, 5540 College Ave., Oakland, CA 94618, USA; phone (415)654-1879. *(M)*

Tunisia

Traveling to the Land of the Lotus-Eaters: Participants camp and stay in inexpensive hotels while traveling by minibus through Tunisia for 2 weeks. From the fertile north to the Saharan south, travelers see a variety of terrain and lifestyles. After flying to Tunis from London, the group boards a minibus and journeys to the Roman ruins of Thubaro Majus, then continues south to Kairouan, El Djem amphitheater, La Lousa beach and Sfax. Participants spend 2 days on Djerba Island, the "land of the lotus eaters" of Greek legend and, after exploring Matmata's underground cave dwellings, head toward the date palms of Tozeur oasis on the edge of the great Chott el Djerid wilderness. Turning north, group members visit El Kef and explore the Roman town of Dougga, the Tell mountain region and the ancient ruins of Carthage. A day in Tunis precedes the return flight to London. **Cost:** $289 to $295 depending on departure date includes roundtrip transportation from London, guide, camping equipment; $80 kitty covers hotels, most meals. **When:** December to April. **Contact:** Penn Overland Tours Ltd., 122 Knightsbridge, London SW 1, Great Britain; phone 01-589-0016; or 330 Sutter St., San Francisco, CA 94108, USA; phone (415)391-5728.

ASIA

Bombay to London Overland: Aurangabad is the first stop after leaving Bombay on a 90-day excursion through Asia. Caves visited in the area contain early Buddhist and Hindu sculpture. Between Delhi, India and Kabul, Afghanistan, the group visits Amritsar and its Golden Temple of the Sikhs, the ancient Greco-Buddhist center of Taxila and the fort at Attock that overlooks the Indus River. While in southern Iran, a tour of the fringes of the Great Sand Desert is conducted. Two nights are spent in Esfahan before traveling to Tabriz, Istanbul and Athens. The expedition continues by boat from the coast of western Greece to Brindisi, Italy. Pompeii, Rome, Florence, Pisa, the Riviera and Paris complete the European section of the trip. A 4-wheel drive vehicle provides transportation throughout the journey. **Cost:** $820. **When:** January to March. **Contact:** Aardvark Expeditions, 14 Coleridge Rd., London N8, Great Britain; phone 01-340-7598.

East-West Overland: Participants go by bus on a 2½-month expedition across Asia and Europe. Travelers descend from Kathmandu, Nepal to the plains of northern India, stopping at the holy city of Benares. After stopping at Lahore in Pakistan, the expedition winds its way up the Kabul Gorge in Afghanistan. Travelers continue to Iran, entering the Great Sand Desert before visiting the ancient Persian cities of Bam and Persepolis. After 12 days in Iran, travelers proceed to Lake Van, 8,205-foot

On a Capers 400 Club journey through India, participants traverse Himalayan passes at elevations up to 14,000 feet and with views of peaks such as this of 26,760-foot Manaslu, near the Tibetan border. (Keith Gunnar)

Nemrut Dagi, ancient Goreme, Roman Ephesus and Istanbul in Turkey. Delphi and Athens are explored in Greece before the group moves on to Venice, Florence and Pisa in Italy.The group reaches the trip's end in London on the 80th day. **Cost:** $500 includes transportation from Kathmandu, accommodations, most meals. **When:** March, April, July, August, September. **Contact:** Asian Greyhound Ltd., 15 Kings Rd., Windsor, Berkshire, Great Britain; phone Windsor 69122.

Trans-Asian Expedition: On a flexible itinerary of 11 or 12 weeks, an expedition-equipped truck transports participants from London to Kathmandu, where they may continue to Sydney over another 5 weeks. Accommodations are at campsites in Europe and Asia. Europe is crossed at a fairly brisk pace before the first major stopovers in Istanbul and Turkey's southern coast. Explorations are made of mosques, ruins and other places of interest. These explorations continue as the trip visits Goreme, eastern Anatolia, Lake Van, the Kurdistan region of Iran, Esfahan, Shiraz, Persepolis and Meshed, with a choice between the Tehran route or the cross-desert route. Afghanistan is visited with a stopover in Kabul, and then India with stops in Amritsar, Kashmir and Corbett National Park. After following the Ganges to the pilgrim city of Benares, the trip takes one of several routes up the mountains to Kathmandu. An opportunity to trek to Helmu is offered. Those continuing to Sydney fly to Bangkok and take a 3-week trip through Thailand and Malaysia, traveling by train and bus with

A Turkish village near the ancient ruins of Knidos can be reached by jeep from Marmaris, a day's ride away, or by boat from Bodrum. (Carol Baker)

local guides. Next is a flight from Singapore to Perth and a 2-week overland journey through the remote outback to Sydney. Any or all of this trip may be made in reverse. **Cost:** $1,364 to $1,650 London to Kathmandu, $2,930 to $3,020 London to Sydney includes transportation, accommodations, camping equipment, most meals, guide. **When:** February to October. **Contact:** Exodus Expeditions, 167 Earls Court Rd., London SW5, Great Britain; phone 01-373-7895; or Adventure Center, 5540 College Ave., Oakland, CA 94618, USA; phone (415)654-1879. *(M)*

Overland Asia and the Middle East: For 87 days a group of up to 20 people travels overland via Bedford bus from London to Kathmandu. En route, accommodations are provided in 2-person tents combined with some stays in hotels in Afghanistan, Pakistan and India. Though every trip is designed to suit the interests of the group, the itinerary usually includes the Syrian Desert and Damascus, Palmyra, Jerusalem, Amman, Petra, Aqaba and Baghdad. Driving through mountain passes of Afghanistan, Kashmir and Middle Eastern deserts provides scenes of star-filled skies and nomadic camel and donkey trains moving to their winter quarters. Itineraries are subject to change depending on road conditions and the changes in political climates in the Middle East. **Cost:** $630 to $840 includes tolls, ferries, group equipment. **When:** September, March, June. **Contact:** Hann Overland, 17 Stanthorpe Rd., London SW16, Great Britain; phone 01-769-6659; or Adventure Center, 5540 College Ave., Oakland, CA, 94618, USA; phone (415)654-1879. *(M)*

London to Kathmandu via Russia: An 82-day motorcoach trip from London to Kathmandu makes a 3-week foray into eastern Europe and the Soviet Union and visits little-seen areas of Asia. After crossing the channel, the trip heads for Warsaw, stopping in Germany where the group picks up an Intourist guide for the next 3 weeks. Three nights are spent in Moscow for sightseeing and exploring before moving on to Kiev. After a visit to Odessa and Husi, participants proceed to Romania and then to Greece, visiting ancient ruins and sampling local life in small taverns and seaside towns. Another 3-night stay in Istanbul provides opportunities for exploration before the trip moves on, mostly along the Mediterranean to Gallipoli, Izmir, Ephesus, Side and Selifko. A stop is made at the cliff city of Goreme before entering the desert on the way to Esfahan. In Afghanistan travelers visit the remote capital of Kabul for 3 nights before crossing the Khyber Pass to the Swat Valley, Peshawar, Rawalpindi, Lahore and Jammu. In Srinagar members spend 3 nights on a houseboat then head on to Agra—for a visit to the Taj Mahal, and Benares—for a short raft trip down the Ganges

before arriving in Kathmandu. Nights are spent camping and in inexpensive hotels. This is a participatory trip, with travelers sharing cooking and cleaning chores. The itinerary may be traveled in reverse. **Cost:** $995 from London, $1,130 from Kathmandu includes transportation, guide; improvised kitty covers food, accommodations. **When:** March to May from Kathmandu; July, August from London. **Contact:** The Sundowners Ltd., 8 Hogarth Pl., London SW5 0QT, Great Britain; phone 01-373-5623; or Adventure Center, 5540 College Ave., Oakland, CA 94618, USA; phone (415)654-1879. ***(M)***

Afghanistan

Central Asian Camping: With its fortified towns, 12,000-foot passes and nomadic people, the Central Route through Afghanistan is difficult and occasionally dangerous. A 3-week camping trip travels a circular route beginning and ending in Kabul and making stops at Peshawar, Kandahar, Herat, Chakhcharan and Bamiyan. Much of the country is extremely remote and urban comforts are few. Visits are made to the Khyber Pass, the gun- and opium-producing town of Darrah, an ancient oasis dating back to Alexander, the Helmand River, Lashkar Gah Palace and the 12th-century Minaret of Jam. The track is rough into the Hindu Kush; all of this area is difficult mountain terrain, but it is followed in the trip by a free day at the scenic Lakes of Band-i-Amir. After visiting Bamiyan with its huge Buddhas, travelers follow the Old Silk Route through Hajigak and Unai passes (both over 10,000 feet) back to Kabul. A few hotels may be used, but camping is the norm, with participants sharing the cooking and cleaning chores. **Cost:** $1,135 includes transportation from London, camping equipment, guide; $92 food kitty. **When:** May to October. **Contact:** Penn Overland Tours Ltd., 122 Knightsbridge, London SW 1, Great Britain; phone 01-589-0016; or 330 Sutter St., San Francisco, CA 94108, USA; phone (415)391-5728. ***(M)***

India

Into India: Travelers embarking by plane from New York spend a month exploring India by jeep, plane and foot. Lodging within the country is provided in a variety of places including a houseboat on

Dal Lake in the Himalayas and a hotel that was once the Maharaja's residence. One part of the journey takes group members to Tibetan Ladakh, an area bordering China that has just been opened to foreigners. There the route traverses 14,000-foot Zojilla Pass whose rock faces are carved with Buddhas that appear through the mists on either side of the road. Trekkers also cross Rohtang Pass at 13,050 feet and descend to Lahul. Audiences with both the Dalai Lama and the Maharaja are included in the schedule of travel, and group members have opportunities to visit ancient monasteries. The home flight to New York leaves Bombay early on the 32nd day of the trip. **Cost:** $4,500 includes all transportation from New York. **When:** July, August. **Contact:** Capers 400 Club, 1010 N. Palm Ave., Los Angeles, CA 90069, USA; phone (213)657-0916.

Bamboo Jungle by Elephant: A highlight of a 4-week journey through southern India is an elephant ride through bamboo jungles near Mudamalai to view monkeys, porcupines, antelope and occasionally the elusive tiger. Members of the trip depart from Bombay and proceed northeast to the caves at Ajanta, which contain paintings dating back to 100 B.C. Participants drive by truck to the city of Goa and then to Mysore, location of magnificent gardens, sun yellow buildings and the famous palace of the Maharajas. The road leads up the Kunda Hills to Ootacamund and continues through Mudamalai to the lakes and forests in the Cardamom Hills and the Periyar Wildlife Sanctuary, where participants explore the creeks and inlets in a small boat and may see elephants, wild pigs, bison and tigers. After arriving at the state capital of Trivandrum, with its sands and gentle surf at Kovalam Beach on the Malabar Coast, trip members visit rubber plantations and the massive Shiva temple at Madurai for a final sight of the southern tip of India. Return flight is via Madras. **Cost:** From $480 includes transportation from Bombay, all-inclusive. **When:** November, December. **Contact:** Encounter Overland, 369 Pine St., Suite 516, San Francisco, CA 94104, USA; phone (415)421-7199. ***(M)***

Subcontinent Overland: India and Nepal are explored in 3-week trips that begin at Delhi and end in Kathmandu. Travelers camp out and occasionally stay in hotels while visiting the Taj Majal, Jaipur, the temples of Khajuraho, Uttar Pradesh and Benares, to name a few points of interest. In Nepal a flight around Mt. Everest may be scheduled. Another trip exploring southern India starts in Bombay and concludes in Madras, and features the Ajanta Caves, the Temples of Ellora, Belur and Halebid, Mysore, Cochin, the Lake Periyar Game Sanctuary and Mahabalipuram. The expedition camps at government rest houses and Dak bungalows, with an occasional inexpensive hotel stay. **Cost:** $999 from London; $480 from Delhi or Bombay. **When:** December, reverse direction trips in January. **Contact:** Penn Overland Tours Ltd., 122 Knightsbridge, London SW1, Great Britain; phone 01-589-0016; or 330 Sutter St., San Francisco, CA 94108, USA; phone (415)391-5728. ***(M)***

Mongolia

In the Land of Genghis Khan: A 2-week trip visits the contemporary cities and ancient desert settlements of Mongolia. Travelers begin and end the trip in London, flying first to the capital city of Ulan Bator for several days' exploration. Highlights of the city are the national museum and numerous Lamaist sites, including a museum that was once a temple, Mongolia's sole remaining lamasery and the Grand Lama's residence. On the fifth day, participants travel southwest to the Gobi Desert, where they spend 3 nights experiencing a taste of nomadic life based in a ger, or traditional nomadic tent. A full day in the desert is spent investigating its more than 300 varieties of plant life. After a return flight to Ulan Bator, overlanders take a jeep ride through spectacular scenery to the ancient capital of Karakorum, founded in 1270 during Genghis Khan's lifetime. Finally, a day trip is made from Ulan Bator by jeep to scenic Terelzh before the return flight to London. Accommodations, except in the desert, are in hotels. **Cost:** On request. **When:** July, August. **Contact:** New Explorers S.A., The Comosa Building, P.O. Box 8320, Panama City, Panama 7.

Pakistan

Exploring Pakistan by Jeep: Traveling by jeep and on foot for 19 days, participants explore the Chitral and Hunza valleys and visit the Kalash tribe. Departing from Rawalpindi, participants travel through Swat and Dir to Chitral, where 20,000-foot Tirich Mir dominates the skyline. With the aid of porters and guides, the group then treks 13,500-foot Shandur Pass to Lake Phundur where they travel by jeep to Jilgit, a rest stop once used by caravans on the Chinese Silk Road. The trip ends in the mountainous Hunza Valley. **Cost:** $1,536 to $1,598, depending on departure date, includes roundtrip airfare from London, all land arrangements. **When:** May to August. **Contact:** Explore Beyond Ltd., 167 Earls Court Rd., London SW5, Great Britain; or Adventure Center, 5540 College Ave., Oakland, CA 94618, USA; phone (415)654-1879.

(M)

Sri Lanka

Wildlife and Culture of Sri Lanka: National parks, waterfowl nesting areas and religious and historical sites highlight the itinerary of a 25-day exploration of Sri Lanka. An extensive system of reserves and sanctuaries, and the remains of numerous advanced civilizations dating back more than 3 millenia characterize the island's 25,000 square miles. Participants use buses, trains, jeeps, ferries and small boats to explore a number of designated wildlife areas hosting leopards, elephants, deer, bears and wild boars. Group members visit some of Asia's most extensive nesting areas of heron, ibis and storks, and those interested may investigate temples and archaeological sites documenting the country's long history. The party also makes a trip to the religious pilgrimage site of Katagarama to observe the rites of pain denial and trance induction. Accommodations are in hotels, remote bungalows

Participants on overlanding expeditions in Mongolia may have an opportunity to stay in a yurt, a circular tent still used by nomadic Mongol peoples. (Society Expeditions)

and homes of local residents, and throughout the trip there are opportunities for swimming, snorkeling, hiking and photography. Ten percent of the trip cost is donated to a nature preservation organization. **Cost:** $945 includes transportation from Colombo, food, accommodations, group equipment, guides. **When:** June. **Contact:** Journeys, Box 7545, Ann Arbor, MI 48107, USA; phone (313)995-4658.

Rail Adventure: Train trips of 1 to 6 days are available for travelers interested in exploring the historic and cultural fascinations of Sri Lanka. A 1-day trip that winds its way up the mountains amidst lush greenery and terraced rice fields to the hill capital of Kandy offers participants a view of the Temple of the Tooth, the Tea Garden and factory, the Botanical Gardens and Elephant Bath. On another trip, Sri Lanka's ruined cities are seen—Buddhist temples, shrines and palaces of the great Sinhala civilization which flourished between the third century B.C. and the tenth century A.D. Other trips include Wilpattu, the second largest animal reserve in the northwest area, and the ruined city of Anuradhapura. **Cost:** On request. **When:** Year-round. **Contact:** Railtours, Rail Sta., Colombo Fort, Sri Lanka; phone 35838.

ATLANTIC

Iceland

High Country Camping Expedition: Participants depart from Reykjavik on a 13-day trip designed to explore a variety of Icelandic landscapes and culture. An overland bus is used for transportation across the rugged terrain. The first overnight is spent in Thjorsardalur, an area nearly destroyed by volcanic eruptions from nearby Mt. Hekla. The group heads northward into the highlands west of Veidivotn and then to the glacier at Tungnafellsjokull where camp is set up in Jokuldalur, the valley of glaciers. Spectacular mountain scenery dots the Sprengisandur trail, which eventually descends and leads members into Bardardalur. A day's excursion to the caldera at Askja and its surrounding craters provides a view of one of Iceland's volcanic, lunarlike landscapes, and in Namaskard members witness active hot springs and sulfur pits. The principal town of the north

An overland bus fords a stream near Veidivotn, an area of many lakes, while traveling through the interior of Iceland on a trip with Arena Tours. (Kristin Tregillus)

coast, Akureyri, is visited before the journey into the highlands of Hveravellir, a thermal area between two large glaciers. On the last day, participants travel to Gullfoss (Golden Falls) and the Great Geyser area, proceeding to Thingvellir, the ancient cliff-rimmed site where the Viking parliament was founded in 930 A.D. **Cost:** $452 includes local transportation, food, tent accommodations, guides. **When:** June to August. **Contact:** Arena Tours, Hvasseleiti 26, Reykjavik, Iceland; or Adventure Center, 5540 College Ave., Oakland, CA 94618, USA; phone (415)654-1879. ***(M)***

Around Iceland: A 10-day trip beginning and ending in Reykjavik travels around the perimeter of Iceland, making stops at fjords, waterfalls, a bird sanctuary, glaciers and volcanoes. On the second day, participants make an afternoon visit to Thingvellir, the lava arena where the ancient Viking parliament, the Althing, met for centuries. Another day is spent at the lake, Myvatn, a haven for species of northern birds, and at Grjotagja where there are subterranean thermal swimming pools. Continuing south, the route extends to Skaftafell National Park, a green oasis beneath Oraefajokull, the highest peak in Iceland. The trip concludes with a drive along the southern coastline with views of the Westman Islands just offshore. Reykjavik is reached during late afternoon on the 10th day. **Cost:** $708 includes transportation, meals, accommodations, guide. **When:** June to August. **Contact:** Icelandic Airlines, 630 Fifth Ave., New York, NY 10020, USA; phone (212)757-8585.

AUSTRALASIA

Commonwealth Coaching: Overlanders on a 30-day trip visit cities and countryside along the southeastern coast of Australia and tour the length of New Zealand. Travel is primarily by motorcoach, and accommodations are in inns and hotels along the route. Departing from San Francisco, the group flies to Melbourne, where they visit the

Trek through this page for the best adventures of the year.

Start here for your sampling of our spectacular camping tours and overland expeditions.

First, our European Camping Tours. Exciting journeys by motorcoach lasting from 21 to 62 days. Featuring well-planned itineraries, guided sightseeing tours and the exhilarating experience of camping out. Examples: **Arctic Circle**—an exploration of Scandinavia's most breathtaking lands. **Western Europe**—an eight-country sweep of the historical and cultural centers of Europe…and everything in between. **Greece and Turkey**—an unusual in-depth excursion into two of Europe's most fascinating countries.

Then there's our Transcontinental Expeditions. More rugged, more challenging. Overland travel by expedition truck or motorcoach—from a 15-day mini-trek to a 3½ month journey. Including: **Africa**—an enlightening adventure into the heart of the Dark Continent. **Scandinavia, Russia & Japan**—a trek of intrigue and challenge as you travel overland by Trans-Siberian Express, Motorcoach and Steamship. **Europe, Asia and Australia**—119 days, 16,000 miles and 3 continents… a vast and incredible journey.

And there are others.

For complete details, write or call for a free brochure.

TREK ADVENTURES

A CORTELL GROUP COMPANY

3 E. 54th St., New York, N.Y. 10022 • (212) 751-3250

nearby Sir Colin Mackenzie Wildlife Sanctuary to observe kangaroos, koala bears and other unique Australian fauna. The scenery on the Australian junket ranges from the alpine terrain of the Snowy Mountains to the coastal landscape south of Sydney. Participants return to Melbourne before flying to Auckland to begin 10 days touring both North and South islands. A highlight is a day tour of the Milford Sound region, with its magnificent alpine and lakeland scenery. From Christchurch, participants fly back to Auckland, then on to the Fiji Islands; a day is spent there relaxing on Mana Island before a late evening transfer to the airport and the return flight to the West Coast. **Cost:** $1,925 includes land transportation, accommodations, meals, guides. **When:** January to May, September to November. **Contact:** Australian Travel Service, Rockefeller Ctr., 1270 Ave. of the Americas, New York, NY 10020, USA.

Around the World Down Under: Participants spend 45 days traveling from Los Angeles to New York the long way. Starting with a flight to New Zealand, they cruise and fly around this southern English outpost for a week before moving on to Australia. After a day in Sydney, travelers fly into the outback for several days of desert views, kangaroos and a visit with aboriginal tribes in the north. On day 17 adventurers leave Australia for New Guinea, where treks into the jungle familiarize them with the famous "mud men" of the Asaro Valley. After 2 days in Singapore, participants set out for Borneo and the independent state of Brunei. Here travelers have the option of staying in a local village or canoeing into the wild interior. After a few days, the group reunites to fly to Kuala Lumpur for a visit to the Malaysian jungle. Travelers pass some time on the French island of Reunion before proceeding to Madagascar. Participants continue to Rome for a final dinner before flying to New York. Accommodations are in hotels. **Cost:** $8,450 includes transportation from Los Angeles, meals, accommodations. **When:** June. **Contact:** Capers 400 Club, 1010 N. Palm Ave., Los Angeles, CA 90069, USA; phone (213)657-0916.

Australia

Great Sandy Desert Expedition: A 15-day motorized expedition out of Perth traverses the Great Sandy, Gibson and Victoria deserts, three of Australia's most arid and isolated areas. The expedition travels north during the first 3 days, through wheat settlements, gold diggings and ghost towns to join the Canning Stock Route. The going is slowed by sand ridges encountered along the route, some as high as 120 feet. The expedition follows the Gary and Gunbarrel highways to the Warburton Aboriginal Settlement, and on through the Great Victoria Desert, where stops are made at some of the rockholes and caves. The expedition passes through Laverton, Windarra, Menzies, Kalgoorlie and Merredin on the way back to Perth. Overland expeditions to other areas in Australia are also available. **Cost:** On request. **When:** April to September. **Contact:** Amesz Adventure

During a 22-day Freedom Holidays trip through New Zealand, participants visit Maori villages. At Whakarewarewa, south of Rotorua, a guide explains the construction of a model Maori building. (Air New Zealand)

Tours, P.O. Box 232, Morley 6062, Australia.

Barrier Reef and Gold Coast: A 16-day trip visits areas of scenic and cultural interest on the mainland and offshore islands of southeastern Australia. After several days of sightseeing and travel through Melbourne, Canberra, Sydney and Kempsey, participants head down the Gold Coast visiting Mt. Cootha, Hervey Bay and the resort town of Noosa Heads. Several days are then spent on Fraser, Great Keppel and the Barrier Reef islands, including a stop at Carnarvon National Park for some hiking. Trip members finally return to Melbourne via Lightning Ridge. Except for the first few nights, participants camp out. Meals are occasionally taken at local restaurants. A shorter 12-day version of the trip is also available. **Cost:** $415 for 16 days from Melbourne, $409 for 12 days from Brisbane includes transportation, some food, group equipment, guide. **When:** Year-round. **Contact:** Centralian Staff Camping Tours, 1 James St., Clayton, Melbourne, Victoria 3168, Australia; phone 544-5211.

Busing across the Continent: A 50-day trip in specially designed camping coaches circles the Australian continent, visiting capital cities of the mainland states as well as major tourist attractions such as the Great Barrier Reef, Alice Springs and Ayers Rock. The tour begins in Brisbane, but may be joined at a variety of points along the way.

Participants often camp in camping reserves throughout the trip and may join brief boat excursions at some places. Camping gear is supplied, and meals are prepared by experienced personnel. **Cost:** $705 includes land transportation, food, camp fees. **When:** October. **Contact:** Cobb and Co., 82 Wentworth Ave., Sydney, Australia; phone 212-3511.

Outback Walkabout: Travelers depart from Sydney to explore the Australian desert and coast for 27 days. Participants start up the eastern coast, driving and camping along the shore of the Great Barrier Reef, with 2 cruises out to the reef itself. After proceeding to the interior, visits to such outposts as Mt. Isa and Katherine Gorge are planned. After a stop at Darwin, travelers trek out to the west-central desert to visit Alice Springs and Ayers Rock. The group then moves south to the opal-mining town of Coober Pedy and the southern coast before returning to Sydney via Narrandera. **Cost:** $539 includes transportation from Sydney, driver, camp cook, most meals, camping equipment. **When:** April to October. **Contact:** Goway Travel Ltd., 53 Yonge St., Second Floor, Toronto, ON Canada M5E 1J3; phone (416)863-0799; or Adventure Center, 5540 College Ave., Oakland, CA 94618, USA; phone (415)654-1879. *(M)*

Coongie Lakes—Birdsville Safari: A trek of 14 days designed primarily for those interested in ornithology and wildlife photography travels cross-country over Sturts Stony Desert to the Coongie Lakes complex where a base camp is made. The Coongie Lakes area, set in rugged sandhill country, is the largest permanent inland body of water in Australia. The region gives ample opportunities for bird study, photography and general relaxation, with a variety of wildlife species to observe. After spending 2 or 3 days at the camp, participants visit other remote lakes and water holes. A rarely used private track is taken into the Mt. Serle sheep station through country not often visited. Besides wildlife observation, other interests include aboriginal rock carvings and paintings and an overnight stay in the historic Birdsville Pub. Covering a total of 3 states, the trip offers a complete outback experience. **Cost:** On request. **When:** By arrangement. **Contact:** Transcontinental Safaris, The Ravine Wildlife Reserve, Kangaroo Island, South Australia, Australia; phone The Shackle 6. *(M)*

Alice Springs Overland: Led by an experienced bushman, groups of 5 to 10 people spend 10 days exploring the outback between Alice Springs and Perth. The one-way camping trip includes Ayers Rock, the Olgas, the Petermann Ranges, Docker Creek and aboriginal settlements. Participants camp under the stars along the Gun Barrel Highway and the gold fields of Kalgoorlie. Outback conditions and climate can be harsh, so participants must be reasonably healthy and willing to tolerate primitive conditions. Special packages including airfare within Australia, and accommodations and guides in Alice and Perth are available. Expert photographic assistance is provided on the trip. **Cost:** $375 includes meals, equipment; $570 to $850 for special packages. **When:** October to December. **Contact:** Visitours Tour Service, Box 388, Alice Springs, NT 5750, Australia; phone 522350.

New Zealand

All of New Zealand: Twenty-two days of overland travel take a group of adventurers through New Zealand, from Christchurch to Auckland. Nights are spent camping, and daytime activities vary from hiking and visiting areas of scenic interest to watching Maori craftsmen at work in villages. On South Island participants travel to Mt. Cook, New Zealand's highest peak; spectacular Milford Sound; the alpine center of Queenstown; Fox and Franz Josef glaciers; and the beaches at Nelson. Then, after a ferry ride to Wellington on North Island, visits are made to Tongariro National Park, the mineral pools at Rotorua, New Zealand's northern extremity at Ninety Mile Beach and Auckland, the country's largest city, where the trip ends. Free days throughout the trip allow participants to choose their activities. **Cost:** $399 to $423, depending on season, includes transportation from Christchurch, food, camping accommodations, activities, guides. **When:** November to March. **Contact:** Freedom Holidays, P.O. Box 21097, Christchurch, New Zealand; phone 556-446.

Papua New Guinea

Coast and Highland Expedition: Participants of a 16-day trip to Papua New Guinea explore its rugged, mountainous countryside by foot, river raft and plane. Travelers are provided with a perspective into the varied cultures of the island where over 700 distinct languages are spoken. Trip members board inflatable rafts and float down the Watut River past gold-mining country and through Watut Gorge with over 100 major rapids. From the coastal town of Lae, participants fly into the highlands to Mt. Hagen. After a moderate climb to Mt. Giluwe, at 14,330 feet the second-highest peak in the country, participants descend to Baiyer River and Wildlife Sanctuary whose inhabitants include birds of paradise and the cassowary, which looks like a cross between an ostrich and a peacock and is indigenous only to New Guinea. By hiking to an overnight hut on the shores of alpine Lake Pindaunde, just over 12,000 feet, a sweeping view is gained of New Guinea and the islands beyond. The trip concludes at Port Moresby. **Cost:** $1,360 to $2,795 depending on departure location, includes meals, camping equipment, guides, flights. **When:** June to October. **Contact:** Adventure Center, 5540 College Ave., Oakland, CA 94618, USA; phone (415)654-1879. *(M)*

CANADA

Treks into the Land of the Midnight Sun: Originating in Calgary, a 6-week adventure for teenagers commences with a visit to the chuckwagon races, rock shows, exhibits, float parade and rodeo at the Calgary Stampede. From the Canadian metropolis, participants journey through Dinosaur Park to the mountain peaks of Banff National Park and Lake Louise for hikes and swims in the area. After a visit to Jasper National Park, travel is via the Alaskan Highway through northwest Canada and southwest Alaska before arrival in Fairbanks. From a base camp at the Kenai National Moose Range and Wilderness Area, trip members take daily horseback trips into the glaciated surroundings. An all-day ferry ride through the inlet of the Kenai Peninsula brings participants to Anchorage and the trip's end. **Cost:** $1,495 includes airfare from Calgary, equipment, food. **When:** July. **Contact:** American Trails West, 92 Middle Neck Rd., Great Neck, NY 11021, USA; phone (516)487-2802. *(M)*

Camping in Western Provincial Parks: A selection of 1-, 2- or 3-week camping trips in the Rocky Mountains provides trip members with a wide variety of outdoor experiences. Mt. Robson Provincial Park, Glacier National Park, and Banff and Jasper national parks highlight most of the trips, which all begin in Vancouver, British Columbia. On the Columbia Icefield, participants walk on ice before taking a dip in Lake Louise. Opportunities for fishing, horseback riding and hiking are ample throughout most of the trips. In addition to the wilderness areas visited, historic areas are also explored, such as the deserted town of Tulameen near Osoyoos Lake, a once-famous gold mining area. Another old mining town, Barkerville, provides the opportunity for visitors to try gold-panning themselves. The 21-day trip covers 2,700 miles and also includes a visit to Dawson Creek,

Participants on a 2-week Maupintour trip in Alberta take a cruise on Maligne Lake, located in Jasper National Park on the eastern slope of the Canadian Rockies. (Keith Gunnar)

the starting point of the Alaska Highway. **Cost:** $245 to $735 includes camping gear, transportation, food, gold pans. **When:** By arrangement from June to September. **Contact:** Black Tusk Touring and Guide Service Ltd., 3064 St. Kildas Ave., North Vancouver, BC Canada V7L 2A9; phone (604)985-9223.

Town and Country Overlanding: A 26-day trip through 5 Canadian provinces and 9 states provides travelers with a diverse view of a large part of the North American continent. Departing from either Vancouver or Toronto, participants experience both the urban culture of Vancouver and Chicago and the barrenness of icefields, vast prairies, and towering mountains. The Canadian portion of the itinerary brings participants into the Old West by means of a visit to the Calgary Stampede, with bucking broncos and colorful parades. At Banff, there is time for hiking, canoeing and studying wildlife. Group members also see the geysers and hot springs in Yellowstone National Park. Other activities include river rafting in Fraser Canyon, cycling in Vancouver's Stanley Park, horseback riding in Winnipeg's Portage La Prairie as well as riding cable cars in Calgary. **Cost:** From $559. **When:** June to September. **Contact:** Goway Travel Ltd., 53 Yonge St., Second Floor, Toronto,

ON Canada M5E 1J3; phone (416)863-0799; or Adventure Center, 5540 College Ave., Oakland, CA 94618, USA; phone (415)654-1879. ***(M)***

Alberta

Northwest Scenic Travel: A 2-week trip beginning in Vancouver guides participants through a region of spectacular natural beauty—the Canadian Rocky Mountains. After a visit to Vancouver's famed Stanley Park and Gastown, group members travel by ferry to the distinctly British city of Victoria. Returning to the mainland, the group travels eastward by motorcoach, crossing the Fraser River and the Cariboo Mountains along the Yellowhead Highway into the Rockies. Side trips and stops along the route give participants a chance to investigate scenic areas and historical sites. Entering Alberta near Mt. Robson, the trip descends to Jasper National Park on the eastern slope of the Rockies. After a cruise on nearby Maligne Lake, the group turns southward along the Columbia Icefield Parkway toward Lake Louise. On the way to Lake Louise, the group stops to explore the surface of Athabasca Glacier. Accommodations at Lake Louise are in the Chateau Lake Louise, situated at the foot of Victoria Glacier. Some of the other spots highlighted on the trip include Banff National Park, the Valley of Ten Peaks, Yoho National Park and Calgary, where the trip terminates. A reverse itinerary is also available. **Cost:** $1,055 includes land transportation, most meals, special events, guides. **When:** May through September. **Contact:** Maupintour, P.O. Box 807, Lawrence, KS 66044, USA; phone (913)843-1211.

CENTRAL AMERICA

Overland South of the Border: A variety of individualized overlanding trips is available to the Panama Canal Zone, Belize and Guatemala. Generally a 2-month, full-circle trip is planned from Brownsville or Laredo, Texas through all Central America via Yucatan. After reaching the Panama Canal Zone, return is via Oaxaca and Veracruz to the U.S. border. A 1-month roundtrip journey from Guatemala to the Panama Canal Zone, and a 2-week, one-way trip from Guatemala to the Panama Canal Zone are also available. Travelers interested in experiencing the rest of the southern hemisphere may take a 1-month roundtrip journey from Guatemala through El Salvador, Honduras, Belize and Yucatan. All trips use 4-wheel drive vehicles and provide participants with a great degree of freedom in determining the itinerary. **Cost:** $18 to $20 a day plus $10 a day for shared expenses. **When:** By arrangement. **Contact:** AMTREK-Overland Expeditions, P.O. Box 206, Santa Clara, CA 95052, USA.

Busing down to Panama: Dense jungles, open deserts, active volcanoes, mountain passes, Caribbean beaches and coastal plains are explored by travelers on a 7½-week overland trip from San Francisco to Panama. A small bus takes participants through the desert land of Baja California to an overnight ferry at La Paz. The journey continues to Mexico City and then to Veracruz. The thick forests of the Yucatan Peninsula contain remains of the Mayan and Aztec cultures; at Palenque overlanders find the "Temple of Inscriptions," and at Chichen Itza the remnants of a former Mayan/Toltec city of ritual and sacrifice are explored. Entering Guatemala from Belize, participants reach Tikal and the beautiful lakes and colorful markets of the Quiche Indians. On the way to Lake Atitlan, the bus ascends the steepest road in all of Latin America. In Honduras the group examines the famous stele of Copan, the oldest Mayan site. After passing through the dry, hilly countryside of Nicaragua, participants find cool rivers, highlands and greenery at the trip's end in Panama. The trip may also be taken from Panama to San Francisco. **Cost:** From $880 includes transportation, meals, accommodations, guide. **When:** September to November. **Contact:** Encounter Overland, 369 Pine St., Suite 516, San Francisco, CA 94104, USA; phone (415)421-7199. *(M)*

EUROPE

Overlanding in Search of Prehistoric Art: A 19-day journey weaves a path leading to many of Europe's outstanding examples of prehistoric art. Participants visit 14,000-year-old caves in southern France and Spain, including the caves at Altamira, known for the quality of their paleolithic murals. In addition, group members visit the famous structure of Stonehenge in England. Participants are housed in country inns, castles and chateaux throughout the journey. **Cost:** $2,708 includes all land costs; airfare extra. **When:** October. **Contact:** Adventure Tours and Travel Unlimited, Suite 414, Airport Plaza Bldg., 19415 Pacific Hwy. S., Seattle, WA 98188, USA; phone (206)824-2192.

Overlanding the Atlantic Coast: A 45-day camping trip by motorcoach takes travelers to France, Spain and Morocco. Originating in London, participants cross the English Channel and spend time sightseeing in France and Spain, stopping in Rouen, the Loire Valley, Chenonceaux, Dordogne, Perigueux, Madrid, Granada and Toledo. After crossing the Mediterranean, the group treks across the Sahara and stops at the Todra Gorge and Meski Oasis before climbing the Atlas Mountains. Descent is made through redstone passes into Marrakech and the trading city of Jemaa el Fna. The trip moves up the coast through Casablanca, crosses to Spain and returns to England via a 2-night sea crossing from Santander. **Cost:** $516 includes food kitty, transportation, camping equipment, guide. **When:** June, August, September. **Contact:** Continental Coach Tours Ltd., 139 Earls Court Rd., London SW5 9RH, Great Britain; phone 01-370-1305 or 01-370-1044.

Soviet Sojourns: A series of trips takes participants to see the major cities of eastern Europe. One 15-day trip surveys cultural centers of the Danube and Adriatic and another trip of the same length covers 6 cities, with a finale in East

Transit Travel offers a 38-day overland and camping trip by motorcoach through Scandinavia, the Soviet Union and Europe, with prices beginning at $805. (Transit Travel Ltd.)

and West Berlin. On a 22-day trip travelers visit 8 eastern European cities. A fourth journey focuses on Russia, visiting architectural treasures, icons and paintings in such cities as Yaroslavi, Vladimir and Suzdal. The cathedrals of Moscow are seen, as well as Leningrad's Hermitage and the golden-domed St. Sophia in Kiev. Accommodations are in hotels, and special dinners and entertainments are arranged. **Cost:** $822 to $1,226 plus airfare. **When:** By arrangement. **Contact:** Maupintour, P.O. Box 807, Lawrence, KS 66044, USA; phone (913)843-1211.

Western European Youth Trip: For over a month people of high school age explore the cities and countryside of Holland, France and England. In Holland participants make a 6-day biking trip through the sand dunes, along the rural bicycle roads, over dikes, and past windmills and farms that are mostly below sea level. Four days are spent in Amsterdam seeing the paintings of Rembrandt, Van Gogh and other Dutch artists. From Holland by train, through Belgium to Amboise in the chateaux country, students explore provincial France. Five days are spent in Paris among its boulevards, shops, theaters, museums and churches. A channel steamer transports the group to England, where first they explore the city of Norwich, famous for its magnificent Norman cathedral. Here each student has a chance to live for a week with an English family. From Norwich participants go by train to Windermere where they pack knapsacks and join local young people for a week of hiking from town to town along the lakes and tarns, over the fells and through the hills and villages of

Cumbria. The traveling ends in London for a week's stay. **Cost:** $2,130 includes airfare from New York, Boston or Montreal, meals, accommodations. **When:** July. **Contact:** Putney Student Travel, Inc., Putney, VT 05346, USA; phone (802)387-5885.

Trans-European Travel: In a group of 25 to 37 people, adventurers travel through 16 countries during a 9-week grand tour. Participants travel in coaches equipped with a P.A. system for informational commentary from the guide. The responsibilities of shopping and preparing meals are shared by all. From London, the group proceeds to Paris, Limoges, Barcelona, Antibes, Venice, Florence, Rome and Capri. Each stop includes visits to museums, markets, historical landmarks and cathedrals, as well as opportunities to experience the local nightlife. From Capri, adventurers take a ferry across the Adriatic Sea to the archaeological sites and secluded beaches of Corfu. Participants spend 2 weeks in Greece, including a week-long cruise off the coast of the Greek islands. Returning to the mainland at Istanbul, the group begins the return journey to London, using a different route that includes Turkey, Bulgaria, Yugoslavia and Hungary. Participants then travel through Vienna and Salzburg to Lucerne, then on to Munich, Heidelberg, Cologne, Amsterdam and Brugge. The August and September trips proceed in the opposite direction. **Cost:** $804 to $840 depending on departure date includes transportation from London, guide, camping fees; $156 for food kitty. **When:** April to November. **Contact:** Tracks, 165 Kensington High St., London W8 6SH, Great Britain; phone 01-937-3028. ***(M)***

Scandinavia and Russia: A 38-day trip takes a group of travelers aged 18 to 30 through Scandinavia, the Soviet Union and eastern and western Europe. The party travels by motorcoach and spends most nights camping out, and the trip begins and ends in London. The first major stopover is Amsterdam, followed by the crossing to Sweden and stops in Ljungskile, Oslo, Drammen, Kinsarvik, Stockholm and Helsinki; en route the expedition members visit spectacular fjords. Three nights in Leningrad and 4 in Moscow make up the bulk of the U.S.S.R. portion of the trip, as participants visit museums, cultural performances and points of historic interest. Then, after stops in Smolensk and Minsk, a leisurely swing through eastern Europe includes visits to Warsaw, Krakow, Prague and West Berlin on the way back to London. Meals are generally taken in camp, with some opportunities to sample local cuisine. **Cost:** $805 to $871, depending on season, plus a food kitty of $122, includes food, group equipment, transportation, accommodations, guides. **When:** May to August. **Contact:** Transit Travel Ltd., 43 Kensington High St., London W8 5ED, Great Britain; phone 01-937-6662; or USSTS, 801 Second Ave., New York, NY 10017, USA; phone (212)867-8770.

England

Country Walks: Striking a balance between sightseeing and hiking is the basic aim of a 23-day trip to unusual places in rural England. Led by a British author, mountaineer and explorer, participants visit prehistoric stones on Dartmoor, centuries-old Cotswold Hill villages, mountains and castles in Wales, the walled medieval city of York, and Hadrian's Wall. Traveling by microbuses, participants journey from Cornwall to Scotland. A maximum of 10 participants is allowed, and inns or guesthouses provide lodging. **Cost:** $1,470 for lodging, meals, guides, local transportation. **When:** April, September. **Contact:** Mountain Travel Inc., 1398 Solano Ave., Albany, CA 94706, USA; phone (415)527-8100. ***(M)***

Camping through the Countryside: Twenty days of camping introduce participants to English countryside, Scottish Highlands, pubs, tearooms and historical sites found in Britain. Beginning in London, a coach specially equipped for the journey sets out up the west side of the island, making its first stop in the fortified town of Chester. The route continues through the Lake District and over the Scottish border to Loch Lomond, where a boat trip is planned. Following the Road to the Isles, participants enjoy the highland views of Glencarron and the Gorge and Falls of Measach before heading eastward to Inverness. Other stops in Scotland include the Highland malt whiskey distillery in Strathspey, Royal Balmoral Castle, Forth Bridge and Edinburgh, where the Scottish Crown Jewels are on display. Crossing back into England, the trip heads southwards through the Cheviot Hills to Hadrian's Wall, which participants may walk along to reach the Roman town of Hexham. The trip ends in London. **Cost:** $389 includes transportation from London, group equipment, guides, food. **When:** June to August. **Contact:** Penn Overland Tours Ltd., 122 Knightsbridge, London SW1, Great Britain; phone 01-589-0016; or 330 Sutter St., San Francisco, CA 94108, USA; phone (415)391-5728. ***(M)***

France

Cote d'Azur Excursion: Minibuses provide transportation for groups of 16 people or less traveling for 1 week along the Cote d'Azur. A day in St. Tropez is included in the trip, where a visit to the beach or town may be arranged. The return journey normally provides a night stop in Paris or at Belleville, just north of town. Camping accommodations are at sites near centers of culture and activity, like the beaches at Napoule. Generally group members are between 18 and 28 years of age. Camping tents and cooking utensils are provided. **Cost:** Available on request. **When:** Year-round. **Contact:** Centaur Overland Travel Ltd., 146 Halfway St., Sidcup, Kent DA15 8DF, Great Britain; phone 01-302-5959.

Greece

Overlanding to Asia Minor: Travelers board an overland coach in London for a 28-day roundtrip journey to Greece and Turkey. The route to Istanbul passes through Cologne, Munich, Vienna, Budapest, Belgrade and Sofia. Those who wish may take day trips to the Black Sea or down to the Sea of Marmara. Traveling via Tekirdag through the border town of Ferral, travelers head on to the fishing town of Kavalla in Greece. After a day or so in Kavalla, the trip continues to Platamon. The more adventurous can climb Mt. Olympus before traveling via Delphi to Athens. The return route begins with a ferry ride to Corfu where travelers can spend the day on a catamaran or hire a scooter to investigate the island beaches. From Corfu, the expedition boards a ship for Bari, then drives along the Rimini coast to Venice. Over the Brenner Pass the group reaches the heart of the Austrian Tyrol at Innsbruck before passing through Cologne again en route to London. Along the way participants camp in tents and take turns preparing meals. **Cost:** $418 from London includes transportation, camping fees and equipment, guides; $66 food kitty. **When:** May to August. **Contact:** NAT Eurotours Ltd., 38 Poland St., London W1, Great Britain; phone 01-734-1087; or Trek Adventures, 3 E. 54th St., New York, NY 10022, USA; phone (212)751-3250. ***(M)***

Netherlands

Individualized Camping Trips: Seven-day camping trips starting out in Amsterdam are offered to those who wish to explore the cultural and historical features of Holland. The emphasis is on flexibility. A Volkswagen camper with unlimited mileage is supplied, as well as tents, sleeping bags, pots and pans, ice buckets, cutlery, tables and chairs. A transfer from the Amsterdam airport is provided to the campgrounds 10 miles away, where participants can pick up their camper and set off on an independent journey. **Cost:** $231 a week. **When:** Year-round. **Contact:** Continental Campers, Inc., 1194 Walnut St., P.O. Box 306, Newton, MA 02161, USA; phone (617)964-5090.

Scotland

Caledonia Overland: In 4 days travelers explore the Scottish capital city of Edinburgh and the Lake District. An English breakfast begins the first day on which participants are guided through the Edinburgh Castle and the streets of Edinburgh, lying on the Firth of Forth in the county of Lothian. After a 1-day trip to the scenic Trossachs, visitors travel south into the Lake District, where there are opportunities to photograph the lovely Scottish hillsides and beautiful lake scenery. At the end of the fourth day, participants are transported back to London. **Cost:** $118 from Edinburgh. **When:** May, July, August, September, October, December. **Contact:** Tracks, 165 Kensington High St., London W8 6SH, Great Britain; phone 01-937-3028. ***(M)***

Spain

Iberian Overland: A 2-week journey travels by minibus through Portugal and Spain. Designed for single people ages 18 to 35, the expedition stays mostly at campsites equipped with showers and laundry facilities. Participants quickly motor across France and cross the border into Spain. Passing through Spanish countryside, overlanders reach Portugal and proceed to Lisbon. Here visitors may see the old Moorish Quarter shining white in the sun by day and dance to traditional Portuguese music in taverns by night. The travelers drive on to Lagos, a typical Algarve fishing village, and then to Seville, a city of white houses covered with vines. In Seville participants may visit such buildings of classical architecture as the Moorish tower of Gralda and the Mudejar palace of Alcazar. The trip's final stop at Madrid provides an opportunity to see the works of Goya at the Prado Museum and the open-air cafes of the Plaza Mayor. **Cost:** $156 to $175 from London includes land transportation, guides. **When:** June to October. **Contact:** Tentrek Expeditions, Ltd., Tentrek House, Sta. Approach, Chislehurst, Kent BR7 5NW, Great Britain; phone 01-467-3473.

Yugoslavia

Balkan Overland: A small group of teenagers joins peasants going to market, uses sheepherders as trail guides and rides with fishermen to Aegean islands on a 33-day trip to Yugoslavia and Greece. The trip begins with family stays in and around Belgrade and includes later stays with families in Greek villages. Participants hike in the mountains of Bosnia-Herzegovina, visit bazaars in Sarajevo, swim at the beaches of Dubrovnik and conclude the trip amid the monuments of Athens. Accompanied by 2 adult leaders, the group travels by bus and train and camps out frequently; the trip's itinerary is flexible. **Cost:** $1,325 includes transportation in Yugoslavia and Greece, meals, accommodations, leaders. **When:** July. **Contact:** Crossroads International, Hillsboro, NH 03244, USA; phone (603)478-5251. *(M)*

MEXICO

Mayan Overland: Participants help plan the itinerary of a 23-day journey via minibus through Guatemala and Mexico. Overlanders rendezvous with an experienced guide in Mexico City and camp or stay in inexpensive hotels during the trip, buying food and sharing meals as a group when possible. After visiting the pyramids at Teotihuacan, the group drives to the city of Taxco, known for its silver. Participants go to a local market in Oaxaca and also visit Monte Alban, an ancient complex of pyramids, palaces and observatories. Entering Guatemala, the expedition spends several days at Lake Atitlan, surrounded by volcanoes, and travels to the Indian town of Chichicastenango. En route to Guatemala City overlanders walk to the edge of Agua Volcano and visit the ancient capital of Antigua. The journey concludes with stops at Chichen Itza, a Toltec city, the Mayan ruins at Uxmal, and Merida, the largest city in the Yucatan. **Cost:** $359 from Mexico City includes ground transportation, guide, camping equipment; $12 a day covers food, fees. **When:** December to April. **Contact:** Trekamerica, Inc., 62 Kenway Rd., Earls Court, London SW5 0RD, Great Britain; phone 01-370-4013; or Adventure Center, 5540 College Ave., Oakland, CA 94618, USA; phone (415)654-1879. *(M)*

Baja California

Overlanding Baja's Back Roads: One-way trips of 7 days in the Baja peninsula depart from Cabo San Lucas. Participants proceed at a

Overlanders on a 23-day Trekamerica expedition view the Mayan ruins at Palenque in the Yucatan jungle. (Christian Kallen)

leisurely pace in 4-wheel drive vehicles, sticking to side roads and deciding the itinerary along the way. Whether on the coast or in desert backcountry, overlanders travel whenever possible on roads that avoid the new trans-peninsular highway. Sometimes the group camps under the stars on a Pacific Ocean beach or next to the Sea of Cortez, and sometimes in the interior among the cardon cacti or the boojum trees. At certain times of the year, gray whales can be seen with their new calves surfacing close to shore. **Cost:** $450 includes meals, camping equipment, ground transportation, accommodations, guide. **When:** January to late March. **Contact:** Canyoneers, Inc., P.O. Box 2997, Flagstaff, AZ 86003, USA; phone (602)526-0924. ***(M)***

Yucatan

Mayan Cultural Overland Trip: A trip of 15 days in the Yucatan of southeast Mexico features visits to Mayan ruins. After flying from San Francisco to Merida, participants spend a day there sightseeing and visiting the nearby ruins at Dzibilchaltun. En route to Palenque where several days are spent, stops are made at Uxmal and Kabah for viewing more ruins, including the pyramid at Edzna. Participants travel next to the Caribbean coast via Xpujil, Becan and Kohunlich. Then during 2 days in Akumal they visit the 600-foot-deep well of Cenote Azul. A 2-day stay at undeveloped Isla Mujeres is followed by a stop at Valladolid. One of the last ruins visited is the famous site of Chichen Itza. **Cost:** $698 includes transportation, food, accommodations, guide. **When:** February to December. **Contact:** Forum Travel International, 2437 Durant, No. 208, Berkeley, CA 94704, USA; phone (415)843-8294.

MIDDLE EAST

Camping in the Cradle of Civilization: Participants spend 3 weeks traveling in the region of the Tigris and Euphrates rivers, visiting some of the oldest continuously inhabited towns known to man, and exploring ruins, castles and Middle Eastern suqs. The trip begins with a flight from London to Amman, followed by a drive south in a bus on the Kings highway to Madaba. Travelers spend 2 nights near Petra exploring the Rose Rock Valley, one of the world's most remarkable archaeological sites, discovered in 1812. Two additional days are spent in Aqaba where participants camp on the beach and snorkel over the coral reefs in the Gulf of Aqaba. The trip then heads east, across the black basalt Syrian desert to Baghdad and Babylon in the Tigris/Euphrates drainage system. In Aleppo, a caravan city and fortress inhabited for 7,000 years, participants visit a suq and spend 2 nights before moving inland via Apamea to Syria's fertile coastal plain. One night is spent camping in the ruins of Palmyra, after which trip members move on to Damascus. The trip returns to Jordan, spending the night at Jerash under the stars by the Roman Forum. A flight from Amman to London concludes the trip. **Cost:** $770 includes roundtrip airfare from London, all land transportation, camping and cooking equipment, guide; $90 for food kitty. **When:** June to September. **Contact:** Hann Overland, 17 Stanthorpe Rd., London SW16, Great Britain; phone 01-769-6659. *(M)*

Iraq

Mesopotamian Monuments: The Hittites, Assyrians, Egyptians, Romans and Mongols all have left traces of their cultures in Mesopotamia, the region between the rivers Tigris and Euphrates. A 22-day camping trip visits cultural remnants of this region, including monuments of the great kingdom to the south once known as Babylonia. The trip begins with a flight from London to Ankara, from where overlanders travel by Land Rover or desert truck to see the palace and fortress in Mosul. After exploring the ancient sites of Nineveh and Babylon, participants proceed to the Tigris/Euphrates delta in southern Iraq. Here they spend 2 or 3 days among the Marsh Arabs, a people who maintain their traditional lifestyle, with canoes the chief mode of transportation. The return to London is by air. **Cost:** $1,184 includes roundtrip airfare from London, ground transportation, food, guide, camping equipment. **When:** April, May, October. **Contact:** WEXAS International, 45 Brompton Rd., Knightsbridge, London SW3 1DE, Great Britain; phone 01-589-0500. *(M)*

Israel

Desert Drives: A variety of trips lasting a half-day to 3 days takes participants into the Negev and Sinai deserts. Several of the trips involve hiking, with visits to Bedouin camps for tea, the Canyon of Inscriptions where travelers have left engravings on the canyon walls, St. Catherina's Monastery, King Solomon's Pillars and numerous oases. On longer trips nights are spent in Bedouin camps. Accommodations, though scheduled, may be changed at the guide's discretion, so the charge is flexible. **Cost:** From $19 for half-day to $100 for 3 days. **When:** Year-round. **Contact:** Johnny Desert Tours, Commercial Centre, P.O. Box 261, Elat, Israel; phone 059-6777.

Dead Sea and Desert Expedition: Members of a 2-week expedition camp at recognized camping grounds and stay in hotels while exploring Israel. The trip begins in

Tel Aviv, where the expedition drives north along the Mediterranean to Haifa and then east to the Sea of Galilee, where a day is spent visiting sites of historical interest. Driving south through Old Jericho, the expedition descends to the Dead Sea region, the lowest inhabited spot on earth. En route participants can swim in the Dead Sea and visit the Bar Kochba Caves and the palace-fortress of Masada. The route south leads through Sodom to the Gulf of Aqaba, where participants can swim and snorkel in the coral grottos, and then north by way of King Solomon's Mines into the Negev Desert. Here the expedition stops at the Mitzpeh Ramon crater and the ruined caravanserai of Avdat. The route continues north through Beersheba to the Mediterranean kibbutz center of Ashqelon and east to Jerusalem. Participants spend 4 days exploring Jerusalem before returning to Tel Aviv. **Cost:** $754 includes roundtrip airfare from London, food, transportation, equipment. **When:** July, August. **Contact:** Penn Overland Tours Ltd., 122 Knightsbridge, London SW1, Great Britain; phone 01-589-0016; or 330 Sutter St., San Francisco, CA 94108, USA; phone (415)391-5728. ***(M)***

Jordan

Middle East Trip: Participants drive by minibus to the Greco-Roman ruins of Jerash to begin a 2-week trip. The sixth-century mosaic pavement map of Palestine is seen in Madaba during the journey to biblical Mt. Nebo from where Moses saw the Promised Land. An old route with spectacular mountain scenery is taken to the high fortress of El Karak, where one can see as far as the Dead Sea and the Jordan Valley. The group proceeds along a road through Tafila for a 2-day camp and exploration of the archaeological site and rock-cut city of Petra. Travelers may walk or ride through El Siq Gorge and climb high paths to the Nabatean Altars. Two days are also spent in Aqaba for swimming, snorkeling and coral diving. Participants then leave for the strange pink oasis of Wadi Rum, a Bedouin encampment where there is a chance for a brief camel trek. The party then heads north to Khan el Zebib and the eighth-century Arab desert palaces at Meshatta, Kharameh and Azraq, Lawrence of Arabia's wartime headquarters. **Cost:** $625 includes roundtrip airfare from London, transportation, equipment. **When:** June to August. **Contact:** Penn Overland Tours Ltd., 122 Knightsbridge, London SW1, Great Britain; phone 01-589-0016; or 330 Sutter St., San Francisco, CA 94108, USA; phone (415)391-5728. ***(M)***

Turkey

Turkish Circle: Travelers follow a circular route through Turkey that encompasses urban centers, the central valley of Cappadocia and the Mediterranean coast on a 3-week trip beginning and ending in Istanbul. After a few days of orientation in Istanbul, the party sets out to the southeast through Ankara to Cappadocia, where trip members visit the cities of Kaymakci and Derinkuyu and the underground hideouts of persecuted Christians. The group then drives south across the Anatolian Plateau and down through the Taurus Mountains to the coast. Beginning near Syria at Mersin, the route follows an arc all the way along the coast to the Dardanelles, in northwest Turkey. Along the way stops are made at sunny beaches, Crusaders' castles, Roman amphitheaters and modern ports. Participants spend nights camped under the stars, and share in the preparation of meals. **Cost:** $360 includes transportation from Istanbul, food, equipment, guide. **When:** On request. **Contact:** Encounter Overland, 369 Pine St., Suite 516, San Francisco, CA 94104, USA; phone (415)421-7199. *(M)*

Camping at Crossroads: Overlanders explore Turkey, for centuries the cultural crossroads between Europe and the Middle East, during a 22-day camping trip flying from London. Beginning with 2 days in Istanbul, the trip highlights both cultural and natural attractions. After crossing the Bosporus and exploring Ankara, participants head southeast to the Anatolia region, with its hundreds of subterranean churches tunneled into the bleak, lunar landscape. Group members spend several days swimming and hiking at Sikifke and Alanya. Then visits are made to the hot springs and amphitheater at Pamukkale, the site of ancient Ephesus, Troy and Mt. Uludag. Two more days in Istanbul precede the return to London. Overland travel is by truck. **Cost:** $582 includes transportation from London, equipment, guide; meals and camping accommodations extra. **When:** June to September. **Contact:** WEXAS International, 45 Brompton Rd., Knightsbridge, London SW3 1DE, Great Britain; phone 01-589-0500. *(M)*

Yemen

Traversing Plateaus of the Middle East: An Arabic-speaking guide leads groups of 8 to 12 adventurers through the mountainous Republic of Yemen. For 10 days participants travel by overland vehicle and by foot to altitudes of 11,500 feet on this 2-week adventure. Flying from Paris, the group boards overland vehicles in Taez, then stops for the night in Djibla. Damat and the extinct volcano of Hammam are reached by a rutted road. From the village at the base of the crater, participants hike to a small lake in the crater, relax in the nearby hot springs and the next day traverse valleys and volcanic mountains to reach the citadel town of Reda. Small villages in this richly cultivated region offer traditional teahouses as respite for the travelers. Before passing through the high outer walls and towers of the only surviving example of Babylonian architecture, overlanders can see the domes and minarets of the 48 mosques in San'a. From a gigantic crag covered with castles and gilded stone houses, participants walk through fields to Shibam, then climb up a narrow path while mules transport their baggage. A Turkish citadel at the top of the escarpment gives access to Kwakaban, a town bordered on 3 sides by sheer rock. **Cost:** $1,480 from Paris includes transportation, meals, accommodations, guide, equipment. **When:** July to September. **Contact:** Explorator, 16, place de la Madeleine, 75008 Paris, France; phone 226-66-24.

Fijian dancers can be observed on a 23-day Goodtravel Tours expedition in the South Pacific. (Richard A. Goodman)

PACIFIC

Island Hopping in the South Pacific: A flexible 23-day trip takes travelers to American Samoa, Western Samoa, Fiji and Tahiti by air and local buses. Three different accommodation plans are offered for differing budgets. The trip begins with a flight from Los Angeles to Pago Pago for a night, and then continues at Lalomalava on the relatively unwesternized island of Savaii. Three nights' accommodation in the midst of a functioning, traditional Samoan village provide time for exploration and sightseeing plus side trips to plantations and the massive, truncated pyramid of Pulemelei. Next is a flight to Lefaga for 2 nights, with opportunities for fishing, snorkeling and outrigger exploring. The next 2 nights are spent at Apia, one of Samoa's more cosmopolitan towns, before a flight to Suva, Fiji, for a stay of 6 nights. Besides sightseeing and exploring the town, participants take a trip to Orchid Island with its rare Fijian parrots, sea turtles and mongooses. Then 3 nights of sightseeing in Nadi precede a flight to Papeete, Tahiti, the final stop on the trip; most of the 5 days here are spent exploring the area at leisure. The return to Los Angeles is by air. **Cost:** $1,099 to $1,404, depending on type of accommodations and date, includes transportation from Los Angeles, food, accommodations, excursions, guide. **When:** May to December. **Contact:** Goodtravel Tours, 5332 College Ave., Oakland, CA 94618, USA; phone (415)658-2060.

SOUTH AMERICA

South America Overland: Traveling in a Mercedes schoolbus, participants on a 15-week expedition travel around the South American continent. The trip begins and ends in Bogota and features visits to the ruins of Machu Picchu, Lake Titicaca, the Amazon by local riverboat, the Atoari Indian Reserve, and cities including Quito, Lima, Rio de Janeiro, Brasilia and Caracas. Participants may also choose from a number of optional activities during the trip: horseback riding in the Colombian Andes; a trip to the Galapagos archipelago; hiking the Inca Trail; and flights over the Nazca lines, to Tierra del Fuego and over Angel Falls in Roraima, Venezuela. Group members stay in hotels in the cities, and pitch camp while traveling through the countryside. It is possible to join the trip for just 1 or 2 months for reduced prices. **Cost:** $610 for 1 month, $1,220 for 2 months, $1,420 for 15 weeks; airfare to Bogota is extra. **When:** January, April, July, October, December. **Contact:** Aardvark Expeditions, 14 Coleridge Rd., London N8, Great Britain; phone 3407598.

Pan-American Overland: A 6-month trip covers 28,000 miles from New York to Rio de Janeiro by way of Alaska. Overlanders travel in two 4-wheel drive vehicles, each with 3 or 4 passengers and a guide. The trip begins by crossing the United States and Canada to reach Fairbanks, where participants take a boat trip south through Alaska's Inside Passage. Highlighting the trip's South American section is a week-long sailing trip in the Galapagos Islands off Ecuador. The itinerary is very flexible, and river rafting, canoeing and mountaineering may all be undertaken. The expedition usually camps, but hotels are also used about once a week. The guides speak Spanish and Portuguese and are familiar with archaeology, anthropology and various outdoor activities. **Cost:** $5,600 covers all costs, including airfare from Rio de Janeiro to New York. **When:** October. **Contact:** Americas Expedition, 40 Sturgis Rd., Bronxville, NY 10708, USA.

South America from Top to Bottom: An expedition ranges across tropical jungle to coastal desert on the way from Barranquilla, Colombia, to Rio de Janeiro. The 15-week trip, which travels 13,000 miles and passes through 8 countries, may be taken in reverse direction and also offers a 2,000-mile side trip to Tierra del Fuego for an additional week. Leaving Colombia in specially designed trucks, the group motors to Peru to visit the remains of the Chimu capital Chan Chan and Machu Picchu, "Lost City of the Incas." The expedition continues past Lake Titicaca, through Bolivia and south to Chile. Here the 16-week option continues south along the length of Chile, camping along the way near Moreno Glacier, a glacier that is still growing. The trip turns north through Argentina, passing through the Pampas, and after crossing Paraguay reaches the Brazilian border, where the Iguazu River crashes over a huge horseshoe rim to form the 250-foot Iguazu Falls. Participants may also choose one of several possible river explorations by motorized canoe along the way. Travelers should be in good health and willing to put up with some hardships. The expedition camps most of the way, and extremes of weather can be expected. **Cost:** $2,360 for 15 weeks, $2,480 for 16 weeks includes all costs from Barranquilla to Rio or vice versa. **When:** Southbound in June, September, October; northbound in February, May, November. **Contact:** Encounter Overland, 369 Pine St., Suite 516, San Francisco, CA 94104, USA; phone (415)421-7199. *(M)*

Spanish-American Sojourn: An 82-day voyage through Brazil and up the spine of the Andes begins at Rio de Janeiro and travels to Sao Paulo—two modern cities bordering the vast Brazilian hinterland. A passage across the great Iguazu Falls takes sojourners to the city of Buenos Aires. After passing through Mar del Plata, travelers move into the Argentine heartland, where they may explore the Andean foothills of San Martin. Bariloche, the next stop, is a ski resort known for its alpine vistas and Santiago is the Chilean stopover before the mountains of Bolivia. It is here that travelers reach La Paz, at 12,500 feet the highest capital in the world. Crossing the mountains again, participants arrive in Cuzco and visit native villages on Lake Titicaca. Several more days are spent in Peru before heading north to Quito. In Bogota participants may view the Spanish architecture or attend a bullfight, still a national sport. Conditions vary throughout the trip, facilities may be crude and the voyaging rough. **Cost:** $1,280 to $1,595 depending on departure date includes transportation, guides, excursions. **When:** May to October. **Contact:** Goway Travel Ltd., 53 Yonge St., Second Floor, Toronto, ON Canada M5E 1J3; phone (416)863-0799; or Adventure Center, 5540 College Ave., Oakland, CA 94618, USA; phone (415)654-1879. *(M)*

Venezuela

Angel Falls Expedition: Eighteen trekkers are accompanied by a guide on a 25-day expedition up 9,044-foot Mt. Roraima and then to a point overlooking Angel Falls. Group members fly from London to

Goway sponsors an 82-day expedition through South America from Rio de Janeiro to Bogota. Here, participants camp on the Peruvian Alti Plano. (Goway Travel Ltd.)

Caracas, then on to Ciudad Bolivar and finally over the Gran Sabana's highland savanna to Santa Elena. From here participants walk through rolling savanna for 2 days to the Roraima base camp on the banks of the Kikenaam River. After climbing 2,800 feet to the Rondon camp at the savanna's top, members make a steep climb through forest and up a ledge of ascent to the summit, camping there amid its unusual rock shapes. After retracing the trail to Santa Elena, participants fly to Canaima, where they journey up the Carrao River over 2 sets of rapids to Orchid Island. Passing over the Churun River and riding into the gorge of Auyantepui, the group sets up base camp for Angel Falls, the world's largest waterfall. After climbing to a rocky promontory overlooking the falls, participants return downriver and fly to Caracas for a 2- or 3-day visit. The return to London concludes the trip. Group members buy and prepare food and help pack supplies during the trip. **Cost:** $1,700 includes roundtrip transportation from London, leader, porters, most meals, accommodations. **When:** November. **Contact:** Thomas Cook Ltd., P.O. Box 36, Thorpe Wood, Peterborough PE3 6SB, Great Britain; phone Peterborough (0733) 632000.

UNITED STATES

Exploring the Southwest: A 28-day camping trip through the Southwest begins in San Francisco and ends in Albuquerque, New Mexico. The expedition travels in 4-wheel drive minibuses. Among the many natural attractions along the route are Yosemite National Park, Death Valley National Monument, the Grand Canyon and Utah's Monument Valley and Zion National Park. Participants spend a day rafting on the Stanislaus River in California and descend by mule and on foot to the floor of the Grand Canyon. The expedition also visits archaeological sites such as the prehistoric cliff dwelling ruins of the Anasazi people. Here group members take an overnight trek, learning about the Anasazi way of life. The modern Navajo, Hopi and Pueblo cultures are also explored. **Cost:** $935 includes meals and equipment while camping, some hotel accommodations, roundtrip transportation from San Francisco. **When:** May, June, July, September, October. **Contact:** American Safari, 386 60th St., Oakland, CA 94618, USA; phone (415)652-7825. ***(M)***

Exploring the Western United States: Teenagers explore several western and central states on a 4-week motorcoach expedition. Frontier towns of the Old West and national parks such as Arches, Mt. Rushmore, Grand Teton, Yellowstone, Zion and others are featured on the activity-packed trip. Participants spend an evening on the Colorado River, camping on a sandbar in the midst of canyon walls, hike or cycle among the Tetons, hike the ancient cliff dwellings at Mesa Verde and crawl through the myriad passageways and tunnels of Jewel Cave. Ten-speed bikes are provided for the trip, and swimming, horseback riding and many outdoor sports are available to participants. **Cost:** $895 includes transportation from Denver, equipment, guides, meals, entertainment. **When:** June, July. **Contact:** American Trails West, 92 Middle Neck Rd., Great Neck, NY 11021, USA; phone (516)487-2802. *(M)*

Hiking and Hosteling in the Southwest: Youth (14-17) and adult (18 and over) groups travel by van and on foot for a month through Colorado, Arizona, Utah and Wyoming. Participants climb Pike's Peak; hike in the Grand Canyon, Zion and Bryce canyons and the Petrified Forest; visit cave dwellings at Mesa Verde; swim in the Great Salt Lake; and raft the Snake River. Travelers camp out in the Rockies as well as stay in hostels. The trip begins and ends in Boulder, Colorado. **Cost:** $570 covers food, accommodations, transportation, leader, group activities. **When:** July. **Contact:** American Youth Hostels, National Campus, Delaplane, VA 22025, USA; phone (703)592-3271 or toll free (800)336-6019.

Cultural Experience in the Southwest: Beginning in Boston and ending in Albuquerque, 8 to 12 high school-age participants drive across the United States to spend a month in the Southwest, living with Navajo families and hiking and traveling through grasslands and desert to points of interest. The final week's itinerary is open, to be determined by the group. While living with the Navajos, students share in their daily life and chores. Local residents take the group on hikes and drives to caves, waterfalls, and ruins to learn of the region's diverse history, influenced by Navajo, Comanche, French, Mexican, Spanish and English cultures. Late in the month at least 1 longer hike is planned. The trip may also be taken in reverse order. Some scholarship help is available. **Cost:** $975 covers food, accommodations, group equipment, leaders, transportation. **When:** July, August. **Contact:** Crossroads International, Hillsboro, NH 03244, USA; phone (603)478-5251. *(M)*

Minibus Trip in the West: A month-long journey departs from Paris by plane for a camping trip through parts of Nevada, California, Utah, Arizona and Colorado. The trip enables participants to live in and explore areas of the western United States that interest them. Visitors may view the Grand Canyon and the Sierra Nevadas and camp in national parks. Though the itinerary is flexible and dependent on the wishes of the participants, outings to the Navajo and Hopi Indian tribal lands are usually scheduled. Some meals are provided, but attempts are made to use local foods whenever possible; the French-speaking guides provide all camping equipment. **Cost:** $800 includes roundtrip airfare from Paris, camping equipment, some meals. **When:** June to September. **Contact:** Jerrycan Expedition, Ave. Legrand 86, 1050 Brussels, Belgium; phone (02)648-22-69.

Overland from Sea to Shining Sea: The United States is explored coast to coast on a 6-week overland trip with camping at night and visits to a wide variety of scenic and cultural sites by day. Transportation is in small minibuses. Highlights en route from New York to Los Angeles include visits to the Carlsbad Caverns, a New Mexican Indian pueblo, Mesa Verde National Park, Lake Powell, the Grand Canyon, Lake Tahoe and Yosemite National Park. Urban and cultural sights include Washington, DC, New Orleans, Houston's space center, Las Vegas, San Francisco and Los Angeles. The itinerary is open to group improvisation, and a leisurely pace allows time for individual exploring. The trip may also be made from west to east. **Cost:** $685 to $715, depending on date, plus $15 a week food kitty includes transportation, equipment, sightseeing, guide. **When:** May to October. **Contact:** Trekamerica, Inc., 62 Kenway Rd., Earls Court, London SW5 0RD, Great Britain; phone 01-370-4013; or Adventure Center, 5540 College Ave., Oakland, CA 94618, USA; phone (415)654-1879. *(M)*

Southwestern Sights: A 13-day trip by van through the Southwest includes stops at points of scenic and historic interest and time out for moderate hikes. Beginning and ending in El Paso, the trip visits the Grand Canyon, Petrified Forest National Park, Lake Powell, Natural Bridges National Monument, the Anasazi Indian dwellings at Mesa Verde National Park and historic Santa Fe. Participants ride the narrow-gauge steam railway from Durango to Silverton, then continue by jeep to the top of Engineer Mountain. A tour of the hydroelectric works at Hoover Dam and visits to a show and the casinos in Las Vegas conclude the trip. Participants spend nights in campgrounds with convenient modern facilities. **Cost:** $545 includes food, transportation, equipment, activities, guide. **When:** July. **Contact:** Western Safaris, Inc., 3379 Wedgewood Dr., El Paso, TX 79925, USA; phone (915)592-5984. *(M)*

California

High Desert Camping: Traveling in 4-wheel drive vehicles for 8 days, participants leave the heat of the desert valley for the springtime conditions found at 6,000 to 12,000 feet above sea level. Groups of 10 to 15 camp either in tents or under the stars in the remote backcountry between the Nevada desert and the Sierra Nevadas. Travelers spend 2 days on the crest of the White Mountains among the oldest living things on earth: the bristlecone pines, some more than 4,000 years old. Overlanders explore Bodie, a ghost town that as a California State Historical Park has been preserved in an arrested state of decay. In addition to stores, homes, churches and school buildings, group members investigate an extensive collection of freight wagons and mining machinery collected in the mining town. Participants journey over stagecoach roads and mining trails to several abandoned mining communities before returning to the desert floor for a ride back to Palm Desert. **Cost:** $395 from Palm Desert includes transportation, camping equipment, most meals, guides. **When:** June, August, September. **Contact:** Desert Expeditions, Inc., P.O. Box 1404, Palm Desert, CA 92260, USA; phone (714)346-6927. ***(M)***

Colorado

Across the Great Divide: Participants embark on journeys of a half day or longer from Denver into the mountains of the Continental Divide. Traveling by 4-wheel drive vehicles driven by experienced guides, groups wander over old pioneer trails. Activities along the way include fishing, hiking, cross-country skiing, panning for gold and visits to ghost towns and old mining camps. Camping and fishing equipment is provided. Rates for groups are also available. **Cost:** $25 to $199. **When:** Year-round. **Contact:** The Mountain Men, 11100 E. Dartmouth, No. 219, Aurora, CO 80014, USA; phone (303)750-0090.

Scenic Jeep Trips: Experienced guides explain the history and lore of the Vail Valley in Colorado on morning or afternoon jeep trips. The trips range in length from 2 to 4 hours and include visits to ghost towns, abandoned mines, and game viewing areas. One of the popular trips is the Moniger excursion, which takes participants along the edge of the Eagles Nest Wilderness for 2 hours to view the alpine meadows. Included on the trip are 2 homesteads of the Piney River and the scenic country of the White River National Forest. A 3-hour trip winds through high meadows of Red and White Mountains for views into the Gore Range. Game is usually seen on this trip. On a 45-mile circular trip, participants visit the Gilman Mine on the way to Ptarmigan Mountain. The route descends along Wearyman

Creek to Turkey Creek before another climb to Shrine Pass. **Cost:** $6 to $16 includes transportation. **When:** June to August. **Contact:** Vail Guides, Inc., P.O. Box 1474, Vail, CO 81657, USA; phone (303)476-5387. *(M)*

Nevada

Desert Meanderings: The Great Basin and Mojave Desert are explored in safari vehicles on overland excursions of varying length departing from Reno. Routes are chosen according to participants' interests and desire for challenge; activities include driving rugged jeep trails, racing across salt flats, following emigrant trails, exploring ghost towns, hiking in forested desert ranges and kayaking on rivers and lakes. Small groups are led by guides who share their knowledge and skills in biology, botany, wilderness survival, photography, history and related subjects. Quality camping equipment is provided, and tasty meals are cooked over open fires. **Cost:** $95 for weekend trips to $700 for longer expeditions. **When:** Year-round. **Contact:** High Desert Expeditions, P.O. Box 18346, Steamboat, NV 89511, USA.

Utah

Canyonlands by Jeep: Participants can explore Canyonlands National Park on journeys of 2 to 13 days. Travel by 4-wheel drive vehicles and on foot provides choices among several different trips within the park. Visits are made to the old Gold Queen Mine, Hammond Canyon and Abajo Peak on the Blue Mountain trip, or Mexican Cry Mesa, Carrizo Mountains and Lukakachuka Mountains on the Four Corners journey. On one trip the group follows the route the Mormons used in the 1880s on their way to Bluff, Utah. Participants who take the Golden Circle trip start in Monticello and travel to the Valley of the Gods, the Navajo Reservation, the Grand Canyon, Standing Rocks and several other points of interest. Combination jeep, hiking, river float and packstock trips are available on request. One-day trips can be taken year-round with a minimum of 2 participants. **Cost:** $50 for 1 day; $65 a day for 6 to 10 days includes all camping equipment, transportation, meals, guides. **When:** April to November. **Contact:** Canyonland Tours, Inc., 180 S. Second E., Monticello, UT 84535, USA; phone (801)587-2929.

Southwest Camping Trips: Six-day camping trips through Arizona and southern Utah begin in Las Vegas, where participants are picked up and bused to remote campsites. The camps are located at or near such scenic sites as Zion National Park, Bryce Canyon, Lake Powell, the Grand Canyon, the Hopi and Navajo Indian reservations and Petrified Forest National Park. Campsites are normally chosen in remote areas, away from normal tourist haunts. Expedition personnel make camp and cook meals. The group usually stays at each campsite for 2 days to allow time for some exploration of the area. Longer trips of up to 12 days can be arranged. **Cost:** $275 from Las Vegas. **When:** April, May. **Contact:** L.D. Frome, Outfitter, RFD, Afton, WY 831110, USA; phone (307)886-5240.

RESOURCES

Clubs and Associations

American Adventurers Association
444 NE Ravenna Blvd., Suite 301
Seattle, WA 98115, USA
Phone (206)523-2980

Calgary Explorers' Club
c/o Dept. of Geography
University of Calgary
2920 24th Ave. NW
Calgary, AB Canada T2N 1N4

The Explorers Club
46 E. 70th St.
New York, NY 10021, USA
Phone (212)628-8383

Globetrotter's Club
BCM, Roving
London WC1 6XX, Great Britain

Guide Europeenne du Raid
15 quai de Conti
75006, Paris, France

Guildford Travel Club
MS. J.J. Tubbs
"Cliffe End," 9 Ridgemont
Guildford, Surrey, Great Britain

National 4-Wheel Drive Association
P.O. Box 386
Rosemead, CA 91770, USA

Overland Club
Third Floor, Queens Arcade
Auckland 1, New Zealand

Royal Automobile Club
RAC Touring Services
P.O. Box 92, RAC House
Lansdown Rd.
Croydon CR9 9DH, Great Britain

Special Travel
c/o Christopher Portway
Jasan, White Ash Green
Halstead, Essex, Great Britain

Trail Finders
48 Earls Court Rd.
London W8, Great Britain

Travel Wise Club
444 Robson St.
Vancouver, BC Canada V6B 2B5

WEXAS
International Office
45 Brompton Rd.
Knightsbridge, London SW3
Great Britain

Expedition Consultants

Quest 4 Ltd.
Ashton Wold
Peterborough PE8 5LZ, Great Britain
Phone Oundle 2614

Vehicle Rental

Four by Four Ltd.
Twickenham Rd.
Feltham, Middlesex, Great Britain

Fram Expeditions Ltd.
c/o John Hamilton
69 Ledi Dr.
Bearsden, Glasgow G61 4JN
Great Britain

Guerba Expeditions Ltd.
Stokehill Farm, Erhlestoke
Devizes SN10 SUB, Great Britain

Land-Roving Ltd.
30 Sidbury
Worcester, Great Britain

Vantage Motor Co.
88 the Avenue
Highams Park
London E4, Great Britain

RESEARCH EXPEDITIONS

Once the domain of academic institutions, museums and private foundations, scientific research is now an activity also available to the general public. As a paying participant, you not only help fund the research, but you assist in all the day-to-day activities required to meet the research goals. In return for your physical and financial support, you benefit by working side-by-side with specialists—learning and living every aspect of the field project—for a week or several weeks.

If you are a biologist but always wished you had been an anthropologist, you can join a 3-week trip to Hokkaido Island in Japan to study the Ainus, a Caucasoid people thought to have inhabited Japan before the Japanese. Students in a quandary over what career to pursue can apply for scholarships to join any number of research projects that just might make the decision easier. Academic credit is available on most expeditions, so you can pursue your personal and educational goals at the same time you're having an unusual vacation.

Everyone's skills are needed to make an expedition a success, from cooking meals, recording data and photographing specimens to excavating pot sherds. Research trips tap dormant talents and teach new skills, provide entry into cultural and wilderness areas inaccessible to most tourists, and create a stimulating atmosphere in which to learn. Physicians are often given discounts to participate as expedition doctors.

You can study megalithic monuments in Scotland, be an apprentice archaeologist on a dig in Majorca, or study spadefoot toads in Arizona or rhesus monkeys in Nepal. A 3-week expedition to the land of fire and ice investigates the geology and glaciology of Iceland. On a 700-mile journey through Australia you can help name new species of sand wasps. Each expedition is a unique blend of personalities and talents mixing people of all ages. The group dynamics on a research trip are often as interesting as the project itself. Whether you study avian ectoparasites in Trinidad, volcanoes in Guatemala or the pygmy octopus of Florida, you will learn as much about yourself as you will about the subject you are investigating. □

Participants on a University Research Expeditions trip in Africa receive a practical lesson in the construction of a desert dwelling used by nomads. (University Research Expeditions Program)

RESEARCH EXPEDITIONS

AFRICA

Egypt

Akhnaten Excavation: Joining a team of Egyptologists and archaeologists, participants act as site supervisors, planners and surveyors in the excavation of a temple built 30 centuries ago on the banks of the Nile in the city of Thebes. For 3 weeks team members stay in a small villa a short walk from the temple built in honor of the sun god, Aten, by command of Akhnaten. In addition to supervisory duties, volunteers sketch and photograph artifacts, mend pots, test soil samples and spend 1 day each week on field trips to nearby sites. Operating under a concession granted by the Egyptian government's Department of Antiquities, the project aims to unearth information on everyday life in ancient Thebes and Akhnaten's revolutionary art style and religion. Field conditions are rigorous and participants should be prepared for an abundance of insects and temperatures ranging from 105° to 125°F. **Cost:** $890 from Luxor includes transportation, accommodations, meals, instruction; scholarships are available. **When:** June, July. **Contact:** Earthwatch, P.O. Box 127 AG, Belmont, MA 02178, USA; phone (617)489-3030. *(M)*

Kenya

Bushbabies' Habits: A 22-day expedition studies the feeding habits of the bushbaby, or galago, a primitive primate closely related to the ancestors of the entire primate order. Living in the Gedi Forest on the coast, participants use red lights to observe the nocturnal foraging and feeding activities of the primates. Some animals are trapped and marked in an attempt to correlate their feeding habits with their social organization. The area is humid and hot with occasional rain, and researchers sleep in tents or huts. Academic credit is available. **Cost:** $1,075 includes food, accommodations, equipment, leader. **When:** June to October. **Contact:** Earthwatch, P.O. Box 127 AG, Belmont, MA 02178, USA; phone (617)489-3030. *(M)*

ASIA

Japan

Into Hokkaido's Past: The human and natural history of Hokkaido Island, in northern Japan, is the subject of 3 weeks of study in classrooms and in the field. Participants meet in Sapporo, Hokkaido's capital, for 2 days of orientation lectures on the island's geography, natural history and early culture. Then they proceed to one of the region's mountain ranges for field work, which involves mountaineering, studies of the Ainu culture at various sites and bio-ecological studies of the region's natural habitats. Students may have the chance to interview Ainus, a Caucasoid people thought to have inhabited Japan before the Japanese. Field trips are made throughout the expedition to areas of special interest, such as the hot springs at

During a 3-week research trip on Hokkaido Island in Japan, participants visit members of the Ainu culture, seen here drinking saké as part of a housewarming ceremony. (American Institute for Exploration)

Noboribetsu, Akan Lake and the Ainu communities at Nibutani. Accommodations in the field are in tents. **Cost:** $420 includes transportation from Sapporo, food, accommodations, group equipment, instruction, activities. **When:** June. **Contact:** American Institute for Exploration, 1809 Nichols Rd., Kalamazoo, MI 49007, USA; phone (616)381-8237. ***(M)***

Nepal

Rhesus Research: Because of its similarity to humans, the rhesus monkey is an important aid in scientific research. Participants on a 15-day trip in Kathmandu study troops of monkeys that inhabit 2 ancient temples to determine what their dietary requirements are and how youngsters acquire eating habits. Living at a comfortable house where they share chores, researchers bicycle daily to the site, where deer and peacocks mingle with the monkeys. Field research with monkeys is fairly new, so chances exist for original work. Temperatures are in the 70s under generally clear skies, and the research area is fringed by the spectacular Himalayas. Academic credit is available. **Cost:** $1,075 includes food, accommodations, equipment, leader. **When:** October. **Contact:** Earthwatch, P.O. Box 127 AG, Belmont, MA 02178, USA; phone (617)489-3030.

ATLANTIC

Iceland

The Land of Ice and Fire: The glaciers, volcanoes, geysers and ice caps of Iceland are studied during a 3-week expedition to learn more about the glaciology, botany, ornithology and geophysical characteristics of the island. Team members meet in Reykjavik and proceed to the Oraefi area of Skaftafell National Park, where a great ice cap and its effect on the surrounding landscape are studied. Several other regions are then investigated as well, including the remote and little-explored area east of Jokulsarlon, where future expeditions are planned. Instruction is provided to participants in glacial mapping, observing and recording birds and the classification of other data. In addition, there is an emphasis on cooperative and productive teamwork. Academic credit is available, as is some financial aid. **Cost:** $500 includes transportation from Reykjavik, food, accommodations, equipment, instruction. **When:** July. **Contact:** Expedition Training Institute, Inc., P.O. Box 171, Prudential Ctr. Sta., Boston, MA 02199, USA; phone (617)922-0577. *(M)*

AUSTRALASIA

Australia

Studying Sand Wasps in the Outback: On a 700-mile study near Perth, photographers, naturalists and observers join a University of Georgia professor in the discovery and naming of new sand wasp species. In the test area, which includes the dune areas, warm, breezy Rottnest Island and the desert country of Kalgoorlie, as many as 10 different species have been found in a single sand dune. Teams work in the field between 9 to 4, when wasps are awake, and work in intervals of 2-week stints. In searching for new species, team members locate and excavate nests, observe and record behavior, examine parasites and nest architecture, prepare Maila Malaise traps and mount voucher specimens. Participants camp out and take side trips into the Yanchep Game Preserve for a look at Australia's animals, including kangaroos, koalas and kookaburras. Much recording is done photographically, through slides and movies. **Cost:** $875 includes food, shelter. **When:** January, February. **Contact:** Earthwatch, P.O. Box 127 AG, Belmont, MA 02178, USA; phone (617)489-3030.

CANADA

British Columbia

Monashee Mapping: The largely unexplored Monashee Mountains are investigated on foot and by canoe on a 26-day expedition departing from Revelstoke. In the near future the Monashees will likely become park or recreational land, so an inventory of the re-

On the islands off the Labrador coast, participants on a 3-week University Research expedition excavate a site where members of the Thule culture lived as early as 900 A.D. (University Research Expeditions Program)

gion's flora, fauna and physical geography are needed for land management planning; this is the goal of the trip. The first part of the expedition is spent making a biophysical inventory of the Kirby Lakes area, in the central Monashees, using a wide variety of surveying and collecting techniques. Then a canoe trip is made down the Columbia River from Mica Dam to Revelstoke, through a valley soon to be dammed and flooded. A detailed photographic record of the region is made for historical purposes. Other activities available throughout the trip are hiking, climbing, caving, swimming and photography. Academic credit is available, as is some financial aid. **Cost:** $475 includes transportation from Revelstoke, food, equipment, guide. **When:** August. **Contact:** Expedition Training Institute, Inc., P.O. Box 171, Prudential Ctr. Sta., Boston, MA 02199, USA; phone (617)922-0577. *(M)*

Newfoundland

Eskimo Archaeology: Archaeologists believe that the Inuit Eskimos who now inhabit the central Labrador coast descend from the Thule culture which spread from Alaska into the eastern Arctic between 900 and 1200 A.D. For 3 weeks interested persons may join a research team investigating sites on the small islands off the coast of Labrador near Nain, a small Eskimo village. The team is looking at the nature and time of Eskimo entry, the changes in subsistence and settlement patterns and the nature of Eskimo/European/American contact. The team surveys, maps and describes the environmental features of the sites, makes test excavations of some and keeps detailed records of any cultural material unearthed. Participants should be in good shape and be prepared to hike and camp. College credit is available. **Cost:** $950 from Nain includes food, equipment, transportation. **When:** June to August. **Contact:** University Research Expeditions Program, M19 Wheeler Hall, University of California, Berkeley, CA 94720, USA; phone (415)642-6586. *(M)*

CARIBBEAN

Trinidad and Tobago

Watching Birds of the West Indies: The forests of the northern mountain range of Trinidad are the habitat of cuckoos, hummingbirds, flycatchers, tanagers and honeycreepers. Here team members may assist an entomologist in the study of these birds and their ectoparasites for 21 days. Walking hilly trails from dawn to midmorning, participants capture birds trapped in nylon collecting nets, releasing them after their insect colonies have been removed. The ectoparasites are then sorted and prepared for further research. Apart from guidance in field and laboratory procedures, participants work independently. Lodging is provided at the Simla Biological Station, an hour from coastal beaches. The team moves to the island of Tobago for the final 3 days of the study. Academic credit is available. **Cost:** $800 from Port of Spain includes meals, accommodations, transportation, equipment; scholarships are available. **When:** March. **Contact:**

Two participants on an International Zoological expedition tag a snake for range and population studies in the jungle of Belize. (International Zoological Expeditions)

Earthwatch, P.O. Box 127 AG, Belmont, MA 02178, USA; phone (617)489-3030.

CENTRAL AMERICA

Belize

Natural Science Research: Relatively little research has been conducted in Belize, a country that still offers diverse opportunities for study: untouched forest, deep jungle, abundant limestone caves, unpolluted water, unknown species. Two-week expeditions under the supervision of experienced instructors are offered to high school or college students interested in archaeology, zoology, botany, marine biology, entomology, ornithology or limnology. There are 3 field stations for the project: one is in the extreme south of Belize, in the mountains of the primary rain forest; another in the central foothills, within reach of the principal limestone caverns and a tropical cenote; the third a marine biological station 14 miles off the coast and directly on the barrier reef. **Cost:** From $500 a person includes roundtrip airfare from the U.S., food, accommodations, equipment, instruction, transportation. **When:** Year-round. **Contact:** International Zoological Expeditions, 210 Washington St., Sherborn, MA 01770, USA; phone (617)655-1461.

Costa Rica

Tropical Forest Ecology: The delicate harmony between most elements of the tropical forest ecosystem is revealed to participants on a 2-week study of the complex vegetation system of Costa Rica's coast. A biology professor heads a fast-moving research unit that travels from one collecting point to another by 4-wheel drive vehicles. Participants gather specimens of insects, flowers, fruits and seeds and then assist in their identification, preparation and packing. The teams stop in different villages to eat supper and sleep. Academic credit is available. **Cost:** $825 from San Jose includes meals, accommodations, instruction, equipment, transportation; scholarships are available. **When:** June and July. **Contact:** Earthwatch, P.O. Box 127 AG, Belmont, MA 02178, USA; phone (617)489-3030.

Saving Tapezco's Rain Forest: The incredible diversity of animal and plant life in Costa Rica's tropical rain forests is threatened as the lands are cleared for cattle grazing and agriculture. A 3-week trip investigates the area around the Tapezco River, in the northeastern part of the country, to collect, catalog and save specimens of threatened flora and fauna. Last year this expedition collected over 54,000 plants and insects, many of them rare or recently discovered, including 289 orchid bees in brilliant shades of blue, green and copper. Research duties include tending traps, preparing material for preservation, keeping records and caring for live specimens. Participants live in screened bunkhouses during the hot, humid weather. Academic credit is available. **Cost:** $900 includes food, accommodations, equipment, leader. **When:** August. **Contact:** Earthwatch, P.O. Box 127 AG, Belmont, MA 02178, USA; phone (617)489-3030.

Guatemala

Volcano Research Expedition: During a 4-week visit to several volcanoes in the Sierra Madre participants aid in geological research. At a small lake near the Pacoza Volcano participants make bathymetric maps and take temperature readings while learning research techniques. After climbing to the summit of Augo Volcano, which destroyed Antigua, the capital of Guatemala, in 1541, team members collect sediment samples from the remnants of the crater lake which may contain information concerning prehistoric eruptions from nearby volcanoes. The expedition ends with a rafting trip down the Dulce River. Some knowledge of the Spanish language is helpful. **Cost:** $575 plus airfare. **When:** June. **Contact:** Expedition Training Institute, Inc., P.O. Box 171, Prudential Ctr. Sta., Boston, MA 02199, USA; phone (617)922-0577. *(M)*

Panama

The Birds of Change: Contrary to previous scientific belief, recent research has indicated that the composition of various bird species in a stable mainland area like Panama's forests changes over time. The object of a 17-day research trip is to help determine what factors cause these changes and if patterns of extinction can be predicted. Mornings are spent tending mist nets, and afternoons are taken up identifying, weighing, banding and releasing the captured birds. Instruction is offered in these techniques. Participants stay in a communal lodge 5 miles northwest of Gamboa, in the Canal Zone, and share cooking and camp chores. Academic credit is available. **Cost:** $725 includes food, accommodations, instruction, leader. **When:** March, July. **Contact:** Earthwatch, P.O. Box 127 AG, Belmont, MA 02178, USA; phone (617)489-3030. *(M)*

EUROPE

England

Studying the British Coast: Two 25-day expeditions make a close examination of a portion of Great Britain's coastline, one in the Welsh Devon area and the other in Scotland. While no previous experience is necessary, participants should have a strong interest in ocean ecology. Living in various marine stations and some local villages, the expedition members receive on-site training in relevant skills, such as nature illustration, photography, collection of algal specimens and intertidal field study. The expedition results are combined into a natural history report for possible publication. Non-research activities include exploring the regions on foot, sailing, canoeing and studying local cultures. Academic credit is available as well as some financial aid. **Cost:** $750 from London includes transportation, food, accommodations, equipment, instruction. **When:** July. **Contact:** Expedition Training Institute, Inc., P.O. Box 171, Prudential Ctr. Sta., Boston, MA 02199, USA; phone (617)922-0577. *(M)*

Italy

Neolithic Italy: The Tavalier Plains of southern Italy, about half an hour from the Adriatic coast, contain remnants from a settlement dating back 9,000 years. A 22-day research program enables participants to help investigate various aspects of the early culture. Housed nearby in a converted farmhouse, trip members collect pottery sherds from the area, help identify sites from aerial photos, excavate the main site, and prepare and catalog recovered material. The climate is hot and dry. Previous archaeological research experience is not necessary. **Cost:** $990 includes food, accommodations, instruction, equipment. **When:** July, August. **Contact:** University Research Expeditions Program, University of California, M19 Wheeler Hall, Berkeley, CA 94720, USA; phone (415)642-6586. *(M)*

Scotland

Sea Bird Study: Participants may spend 20 days studying birds on the island of Foula, about 20 miles west of mainland Shetland. The purpose of the expedition is to continue long-term studies of the great skua and other native sea birds. Team members assemble at Brathay for a coach drive to Aberdeen, then travel by ferry and fishing boat to Foula. Although the group has a craft and a laboratory that provide shelter on the island, some nights are spent camping. The expedition is limited to 20 members with interest or experience in ornithology. **Cost:** $281 from Ambleside includes transportation, accommodations, meals, equipment. **When:** July. **Contact:** Brathay Exploration Group, Brathay Hall, Ambleside, Cumbria, Great Britain; phone Ambleside (09663)2531.

Rebuilding a Stone Circle: A 17-day research trip in Scotland studies the original location and orientation of a megalithic monument. The recumbent stone circle stood at Strichen since prehistoric times, but in 1812 a tenant farmer pulled it down; the landlord ordered the circle rebuilt but it was done carelessly and in the wrong location. In 1965 the stones were moved again to make room for planting, and this time were dumped unceremoniously at the bottom of the field. Participants on the expedition examine ceramics, charcoal, cremation remains and hand tools, look at other nearby monuments and their astronomical orientation, visit local museums and talk to area farmers and residents to locate other remnants in the vicinity. Accommodations and meals are at a comfortable inn nearby. While the only requirement is that participants be between 17 and 55 years of age, skills in excavating techniques, surveying, photography and drawing are particularly welcome. **Cost:** $725 includes transportation from Aberdeen, food, accommodations, activities. **When:** April. **Contact:** Earthwatch, P.O. Box 127 AG, Belmont, MA 02178, USA; phone (617)489-3030.

Spain

Archaeological Find in the Balearic Islands: A tiny village in the western corner of the Mediterranean is the setting for 16 to 20 days of archaeological research. Classic excavation techniques are employed, and, in addition to field work, participants assist in the museum and laboratory identifying finds or doing ceramic reconstruction, bone classification, illustration and microphotography. The fossils and artifacts from the rock shelter of Son Matge and the cave of Son Muleta have origins in Europe and Mesopotamia, and have proven the presence of human life in Majorca as early as 6,000 years ago. The historical significance of the research is enhanced for participants by lectures and briefings from the staff. Apprentice archaeologists live in dormitories and have some free time to roam the countryside and beaches. **Cost:** $775 includes meals, accommodations, instruction, transportation, equipment; scholarships are available. **When:** June, August, September, December. **Contact:** Earthwatch, P.O. Box 127 AG, Belmont, MA 02178, USA; phone (617)489-3030.

MEXICO

Yucatan

Yesterday's Yucatan: Only in the past few years has the tiny village of Tinum, on the Yucatan peninsula, developed any contact with the outside world; there is now one telephone, and a dirt road links the town with Valladolid. A team of researchers under the direction of an archaeologist familiar with the town spends 3 weeks studying the inhabitants, the physical geography of the area and social relationships in and around Tinum. The tools used are tape recorders, still and movie cameras, notebooks and sketch pads. After meeting in Merida the team travels to Tinum and becomes submerged in daily life there; besides living with residents of the town, researchers visit Merida, Isla Mujeres and several nearby archaeological sites for close examination of pre-Columbian ruins. Academic credit is available, as is some financial aid. **Cost:** $575 includes transportation from Merida, food, accommodations, equipment, guide. **When:** June, July. **Contact:** Expedition Training Institute, Inc., P.O. Box 171, Prudential Ctr. Sta., Boston, MA 02199, USA; phone (617)922-0577. ***(M)***

MIDDLE EAST

Israel

Judean Archaeology: The Natufians were the first nomadic group to settle in the Judean Hills of Israel, about 12,000 years ago, and a 3-week expedition studies one of their settlements at Hayonim Cave. Recent excavations have shown that the Natufian society underwent drastic changes and that burial practices reflect the more hierarchical structure brought on by economic and social gains. Participants on the trip work side by side with Israeli researchers directed by a Hebrew University archaeologist, uncovering new graves and habitations and learning more about Natufian burial practices. The work involves recording, digging, plotting, removing and screening artifacts. Lectures are presented by the dig leaders on a variety of topics relevant to Natufian and neolithic prehistory, and field trips are made to Mt. Carmel and the Jordan Valley. There are opportunities to work in the labs, to learn to identify microfauna and to clean and label artifacts. Accommodations are in a school, with shared cooking facilities and hot showers. While no special skills are required, photography, drafting or drawing is useful. **Cost:** $550 includes food, accommodations, activities, transportation from Tel Aviv. **When:** July. **Contact:** Earthwatch, P.O. Box 127 AG, Belmont, MA 02178, USA; phone (617)489-3030.

Holy Land Digging: Five major archaeological digs in the Holy Land welcome either skilled or unskilled assistants on 2-week trips departing from London. Most of the labor involved is manual, such as shoveling, hauling and cleaning, but those with skills in photography, surveying or other relevant areas may find use for them. The 5 sites are Giloh, an Iron Age excavation in a southern suburb of Jerusalem; Tel Anafa, one of Palestine's richest Hellenic finds; an occupational history project at Yogneam, northwest of Megiddo, where researchers have already established a continuous sequence from Islamic to Israelite times; the Byzantine level of Shikmona, in the city of Haifa, which also has Persian and Babylonian levels; and the City of David, also known as Silwan, which features the remarkable Hezekiah's Tunnel, hewn 1,600 feet through solid rock around 7,000 B.C. **Cost:** On request. **When:** May to August. **Contact:** Project Expeditions Ltd., 36 Russell St., London WC1B 3PP, Great Britain.

PACIFIC

Hawaii

Studying Endangered Birds: Under the leadership of a zoologist, participants seek to find out why the number of Hawaiian bird species is diminishing and what can be done to save them. The ongoing research project, which accommodates different groups in three 2-week periods, is especially aimed at determining to what extent blood diseases introduced from the mainland affect bird survival. Stationed within the lush tree fern forests of Hawaii Volcanoes National Park, research teams set mist nets each day before sunrise at elevations from sea level to around 5,000 feet; members band and measure the captured birds, then release them after taking blood smears for lab analysis. Participants also learn to

Researchers taking part in a 2-week Earthwatch study of endangered Hawaiian bird species gather data to determine possible conservation methods. (Bob Citron)

identify and study some of Hawaii's 51 remaining bird species. Transportation to observation sites is by 4-wheel drive vehicles, though participants do some hiking as well. Group members lodge in a dormitory and share in the preparation of meals. **Cost:** $625 to $650 includes meals, lodging, ground transportation, scientific equipment, leaders. **When:** December, February, April. **Contact:** Earthwatch, P.O. Box 127 AG, Belmont, MA 02178, USA; phone (617)489-3030.

SOUTH AMERICA

Chile

Observing the Guanaco of Patagonia: Where the Andean chain splinters into waterfalls and glacial lakes adventurers join a wildlife ecologist for 2 weeks to study the relationship between the camel-like guanaco and its environment and social behavior. All-day treks over hilly shrubland alternate with days to rest and review data. Participants camp in the Paine Towers National Park just north of the Strait of Magellan where one of the few remaining herds of guanaco lives. Observation teams map the movements of the small, gentle animals, collecting and recording data on group size, habitat use, territorial defense, birth rate and newborn survival. Over-hunting and deterioration of their environment have endangered the animal, and participants are part of an effort to improve the guanaco's chance of survival. Academic credit is available. **Cost:** $925 from Punta Arenas includes food, accommodations, transportation, equipment, field gear, guide; scholarships are available. **When:** December. **Contact:** Earthwatch, P.O. Box 127 AG, Belmont, MA 02178, USA; phone (617)489-3030.

Ecuador

Folk Medicine Research: For thousands of years preliterate societies have used indigenous plants as medicines, developing a high degree of skill in their cultivation and application. A 16-day trip investigates the little-known botanical medicine of Ecuador's Saraguro Indians; the project is made urgent by the increasing destruction of native plants and the acculturation of indigenous peoples. Living in a pension in Saraguro, researchers collect, describe and illustrate plant specimens, assisted by Saraguro Indian families. Medicine men are interviewed for insights into plant domestication and folk medicine. Fairly rigorous high-altitude hiking is rewarded by spectacular views and a comfortable climate. Academic credit is available. **Cost:** $750 includes food, accommodations, equipment, leader. **When:** July. **Contact:** Earthwatch, P.O. Box 127 AG, Belmont, MA 02178, USA; phone (617)489-3030.

UNITED STATES

Alaska

Bering Sea Research Institute: A 2-month interdisciplinary program of summer field courses and research projects is based in Dutch Harbor on Unalaska Island. It is open to faculty and students of various universities and others with a special interest in the Aleutian-Bering Sea region. The academic program includes courses in marine and terrestrial biology, ecology, geography, geology and meteorology, along with opportunities to conduct guided research projects in Russian-American history, education, undersea exploration and resource management. Fifteen-foot inflatable boats are used for transport between the islands. Some possible field studies include photographing archaeological sites of caves, graves and Aleut villages, studying flora and fauna of the islands, tracing the migration of sea birds and diving and exploring shipwrecks. An objective of the program is to develop new arctic and subarctic specialists to help plan the proper utilization of the resources of northern areas. **Cost:** $400 includes food, lodging, transportation at site, foul-weather gear. **When:** July, August. **Contact:** American Institute for Exploration, 1809 Nichols Rd., Kalamazoo, MI 49007, USA; phone (616)381-8237. *(M)*

Arizona

Spadefoot Census: The spadefoot toad burrows in the desert soil for 9 months, emerging at the first summer's rain to breed. For 3 weeks participants assist a professor in gathering data on spadefoot toads on the lower elevations of the Chiricahua Mountains. The research work consists of identifying species, counting and sampling populations, recording observations of nighttime breeding and activities and measuring how far the toads have traveled. The team is based in cabins at the Southwestern Research Station. The chief requirement for participants is a lot of patience. **Cost:** $785 includes meals, accommodations, transport at research station. **When:** June, July. **Contact:** University Research Expeditions, University of California, M19 Wheeler Hall, Berkeley, CA 94720, USA; phone (415)642-6586. *(M)*

California

Bigfoot Expedition: Bigfoot, or Sasquatch, is one of the 93 mammalian species reported in southwestern Oregon and northwestern California, and it is in this region that expedition members search for this elusive being. Each team learns the basics of tracking and collects data such as hair samples and fecal matter, and also learns about the local flora and fauna. The expeditions are led by scientists, naturalists or trackers. Members should have some backpacking experience and select the expedition that matches their level of experience. **Cost:** On request. **When:** Year-round. **Contact:** Beamer Expeditions, P.O. Box 285, Canoga Park, CA 91305, USA; phone (213)883-3522. *(M)*

Florida

The Elusive Octopus: The pygmy octopus is small enough to fit in a cupped hand and lives on the sandy bottoms of shallow bays, hiding in empty mollusk shells. A research team led by an animal psychologist spends 18 days investigating octopi at St. Joseph Bay. The team studies the creature's behavior patterns by collecting and examining live specimens, charting distribution, conducting night observations and doing lab work. Accommodations are in 2-person tents with cots in a nearby park. Participants should be good swimmers with skin diving or snorkeling experience. **Cost:** $575 includes food, accommodations, equipment, leader. **When:** October. **Contact:** Earthwatch, P.O. Box 127 AG, Belmont, MA 02178, USA; phone (617)489-3030.

Marine Research at Crystal River: Participants study large bird rookeries, Indian mounds and tidal pools during an 8-day stay at the confluence of the Crystal and Salt rivers. The intensive program involves studies in both gulf and freshwater environments. Based at the Marine Science Station, students travel by boat to river headwaters to observe and collect specimens, then utilize well-equipped laboratories and holding tanks for the study and preservation of the specimens. All work is done in conjunction with a biologist/naturalist who coordinates the program. Program members have access to library, dormitory and dining hall facilities. An interest in marine sciences and membership in the Oceanic Society are requirements for participation. **Cost:** $210 from Crystal River includes accommodations, meals, equipment, transportation. **When:** July. **Contact:** Oceanic Expeditions, 240 Ft. Mason, San Francisco, CA 94123, USA; phone (415)441-1106.

Georgia

Feasting Raccoons: Each spring raccoons eat large numbers of eggs laid by loggerhead sea turtles. Teams of researchers on 19-day expeditions to St. Catherine's Island study how the seasonal predation affects raccoon foraging, turtle nesting, and the populations of both species. Team members learn to track raccoons by fitting them with radio transmitters and monitoring their activities by signal. Night patrols are conducted on the beach to search nesting sites for signs of foraging. Lodging is provided in furnished cabins. Participants should be prepared to work irregular hours. **Cost:** $450 to $475 includes food, accommodations, equipment, leader. **When:** April, June, July. **Contact:** Earthwatch, P.O. Box 127 AG, Belmont, MA 02178, USA; phone (617)489-3030.

Sea Turtle Research: The Savannah Science Museum offers participants a chance to spend a week working on a research project at the Wassaw Island National Wildlife Refuge near Savannah. The object of the project is to learn more about the habits of the Atlantic loggerhead sea turtle *(Caretta caretta),* an endangered species. The female loggerhead comes ashore during the summer to lay eggs in a nest buried in the sand, and participants spend the night patrolling the beaches in search of turtles to tag and measure. In addition to learning about the habits of the sea turtles and field research techniques, project members can explore the island and help with National Wildlife Refuge Management projects. Participants should be in good health and be prepared to endure some discomfort. **Cost:** $120 a week includes transportation to and from the island, food, housing. **When:** May to July. **Contact:** Wilderness Southeast, Rt. 3, Box 619 AA, Savannah, GA 31406, USA; phone (912)355-8008. ***(M)***

Idaho

Devonian Idaho: During the Devonian period 400 million years ago, Idaho was covered by a great sea that extended from Alaska to Mexico, and it was during this period that creatures first crawled out of the sea and onto land. To better understand this crucial evolutionary step and the physical environment of the time, researchers on a 12-day trip investigate the area's fossils. A good deal of walking is involved as participants note changes in rock and fossil composition, scout for fossils, record the thickness of geological strata, and identify, mark and transport fossils. Accommodations are in tents at a nearby national park, with shared cooking and camp chores. Academic credit is available. **Cost:** $600 includes food, accommodations, equipment, leader. **When:** July. **Contact:** Earthwatch, P.O. Box 127 AG, Belmont, MA 02178, USA; phone (617)489-3030.

Nevada

Field Biology in the Great Basin: As part of a 2-week research team making a comprehensive study of the fauna and flora of an isolated and little-known area, participants learn how to observe and analyze the ecological aspects of the mountain ranges, plateaus and desert regions of the Great Basin. Team members travel to collecting sites over primitive roads and open terrain, sleeping in tents, abandoned mining settlements and ghost towns in a physically challenging exercise in "learning how to see." Field briefings and instructions in basic biology are part of the daily program in this ancient lake bed area. Participants prepare live traps and help collect, measure and release small mammals; collect and preserve plant specimens, and learn how to perform soil sampling, and determine pH, temperature and rainfall measurements. Extremes in weather and temperature are to be expected since the expedition moves from the desert floor to the alpine regions. **Cost:** $725 from Reno includes meals, accommodations, instruction, equipment, transportation; scholarships are available. **When:** July, August. **Contact:** Earthwatch, P.O. Box 127 AG, Belmont, MA 02178, USA; phone (617)489-3030.

Southwestern Archaeology Study: A weekend trip examines the 10,000-year-old relationship between humans and the environment in the Lake Tahoe and Carson Sink areas. Led by a professor of archaeology, participants are given a picture of daily life through the centuries by studying how environmental factors affect settlement location, social organization and mythology. While camping in the area trip members learn about rock art, petroglyphs and aboriginal technology. College credit is available. **Cost:** $90 includes food, instruction, activities. **When:** April, May. **Contact:** University Extension, University of California, Davis, CA 95616, USA; phone (916)752-0880.

Oregon

Northwest Rockhounds: Fossil hunters, gem collectors and photographers join scientists on trips lasting 1, 2 and 3 weeks to explore remote areas. The focus of the expeditions is to locate new gem sites and fossil beds in Oregon. Expeditions begin at The Dalles, where orientation sessions, lectures and seminars are conducted by regional experts. From there participants travel by overland vehicles to investigate gem and fossil sites in various localities where field camps have been established. The trips involve a great deal of climbing (mountaineering skills are not required), horseback riding and some boating. Nights feature camp cooking and scientific and cultural talks. **Cost:** $400 a week from The Dalles.

When: Summer. **Contact:** American Institute for Exploration, 1809 Nichols Rd., Kalamazoo, MI 49007, USA; phone (616)381-8237. *(M)*

Natural Science Field Study: A wide variety of trips is available to those interested in doing field studies of various kinds. Several projects are based at Camp Hancock Field Station, an outdoor learning center located in the John Day River Valley. Originally established as a paleontology camp, it now hosts programs in natural history, astronomy, lapidary work, and various related subjects such as photography, lab work, survival skills and archaeological techniques. Other trips take place in the field. A 9-day alpine field camp in the Mt. Jefferson Wilderness examines alpine life systems and geology while a 6-day course in ecology and natural science takes place at Long Lake near Warrenton. Summer research teams investigate an archaeological site at Indian Canyon, the ecology of Crooked River National Grassland, and the paleontology and paleobiology of remains at the Nut Beds deposit of the Eocene Clarno formation. Most of the trips have age limits, usually between 11 and 18 years, though some are open to entire families. **Cost:** $40 to $175 includes food, accommodations if applicable, instruction, equipment. **When:** May to September. **Contact:** Oregon Museum of Science and Industry, 4015 SW Canyon Rd., Portland, OR 97221, USA; phone (503)248-5938.

South Dakota

A Mammoth Undertaking: In 1975 a bulldozer clearing land for a housing development in the Black Hills uncovered several massive bones; these were the first animal remains from a site which has since yielded 22 mammoths as well as the remains of numerous smaller creatures. Researchers on a 16-day expedition use a wide variety of techniques to examine, date and preserve the remains and to investigate other factors such as pollen, sedimentation and micro-fauna, which indicate prehistoric climatic and ecological conditions. Tasks include searching for artifacts, surveying and leveling, establishing a metric grid, making radiocarbon tests and helping establish a permanent field exhibit. Expedition members are housed in tents, with kitchen and shower facilities nearby. Academic credit is available. **Cost:** $675 includes food, accommodations, equipment, leader. **When:** July. **Contact:** Earthwatch, P.O. Box 127 AG, Belmont, MA 02178, USA; phone (617)489-3030.

Virginia

Archaeological Study in Front Royal: Secondary and college students spend 2, 4, or 8 weeks on 3 dig sites of the paleo-early archaic periods. Field study involves excavating Indian habitations, hunting and butchering stations, and pottery areas; a staff of geologists, pedologists and paleo-ecologists assists the group as they inspect the 12,000-year-old sites. Students spend their days in the field and evenings at lectures or in labs; weekends are free. College credit is available on the 4-week program. **Cost:** $150 to $800 depending on length of dig and credit requested; $50 a week for food and lodging.

When: June to August. **Contact:** The Catholic University of America, Dept. of Anthropology, Washington, DC 20064, USA; phone (202)635-5080.

Washington

The Glacier Chase: The movement and condition of glaciers is thought to interact extensively with climate changes, but little research on this relationship has been done. A team of participants assists in the study of glaciers in the Olympic Mountains on a rugged 27-day trip departing from Seattle. Participants should have some previous training in strenuous outdoor living and be prepared for a difficult and challenging experience. After meeting and organizing in the Olympic rain forest, the party hikes into the mountains to live on a glacier for 3 weeks. There they measure depth, movement and surface features in collaboration with a University of Washington team. The project concludes with a dramatic high alpine traverse of several Olympic peaks. Academic credit is available as well as some financial aid. **Cost:** $545 includes transportation from Seattle, food, equipment, instruction. **When:** August. **Contact:** Expedition Training Institute, Inc., P.O. Box 171, Prudential Ctr. Sta., Boston, MA 02199, USA; phone (617)922-0577. *(M)*

RESOURCES

Clubs and Associations

Archaeological Institute of America
260 W. Broadway, Dept. EX
New York, NY 10013, USA
Phone (212)925-7333

Archaeology Abroad Service
31/34 Gordon Sq.
London WC1, Great Britain

Egypt Exploration Society
2-3 Doughty Mews
London WC1, Great Britain

Expedition Research, Inc.
P.O. Box 467
Annapolis, MD 21404, USA
Phone (301)268-3222

Explorers Club
46 E. 70th St.
New York, NY 10021, USA
Phone (212)628-8383

Field Studies Council
9 Devereux Ct., Strand
London WC2, Great Britain

Iceland Information Unit
Losehill Hall
Peak National Study Ctr.
Castleton via Sheffield S30 2WB,
Great Britain

International Oceanographic
Foundation
3979 Rickenbacker Causeway
Virginia Key
Miami, FL 33149, USA

Scientific Exploration and
Archaeological Society
P.O. Box 39
Merrifield, VA 22030, USA

Scott Polar Research Institute
Cambridge CB2 1ER, Great Britain

Society for American Archaeology
c/o Culbert, Dept. of Anthropology
University of Arizona
Tucson, AZ 85721, USA

Society for the Preservation
of Archaeological Monuments
P.O. Box 5564, University Sta.
Seattle, WA 98105, USA
Phone (206)324-9406

BICYCLE TOURING

Velocipedes, or "boneshakers," were first developed in Europe during the nineteenth century. Since then they have evolved from contraptions with wooden frames and metal-rim wheels to pedal machines with sleek chassis and a 10-speed gear range. England pioneered the sport of bike touring, followed closely by Germany and France. Now it is popular worldwide as more people have taken to two wheels for health and economic reasons—and because biking is just plain fun.

Kids and grandparents alike are up on spokes. You can join a 20-day bike trip through scenic Greece and Bulgaria, try a 2-week pedaling jaunt around the island of Hawaii, or shift gears from Oregon to Virginia over the 4,450-mile TransAmerica Trail inaugurated in 1976. Weekend bike trips tour the flatland and back-country roads of Florida, and self-guided tours cover 200 miles of Vermont farmlands, with participants staying overnight in country inns. Most trips are accompanied by a sagwagon to pick up tired pedalers.

Whether you have a day or several months, a few dollars or several hundred, there are trips of varying duration and cost. If you don't mind an uphill effort, you can cycle over the Cascade Mountains of Washington, puff through the foothills of the Peruvian Andes, pedal the Swiss Alps or cross 7 passes from 9,000 to 12,000 feet in the Rockies. If coasting and flatland cruising are more your speed, you can bike downhill through Death Valley for a weekend, coast over covered bridges in Indiana or meander through the wine country of New York.

Bicycling is not only the most efficient means of conveying muscle power into propulsion, it's also the best way to experience the environment. Sitting atop your 2-wheeler, you can feel the rain, hear birds call, smell spring flowers, see roadside wildlife and chat with the townspeople. Whatever your frame of mind, bicycling is a great way to see your neighborhood—or explore the world. □

Cyclists often see back roads and rural landscapes missed by auto travelers. Here, a bike cruises past a historic covered bridge in the scenic back country of Vermont. (John Freidin/Vermont Bicycle Touring)

BICYCLE TOURING

CANADA

Northwest Passage: A 28-day bike trip for strong riders takes a circuitous route covering 1,300 miles from Missoula, Montana to Seattle, Washington via the Trans-Canadian Highway. The route has not been biked before, so the daily itinerary is flexible to enable participants time to establish a route for future use. From Missoula the party heads north to Jasper, crosses the Rockies near some of the highest peaks and then drops southwest at the Thompson Ice Field to join the Trans-Canadian Highway at Kamloops. This is followed through British Columbia to Vancouver, where bikers head south to Seattle. Nights are spent camping. **Cost:** $297 includes food, group equipment, maps, guide. **When:** June, July. **Contact:** Bikecentennial, P.O. Box 8308, Missoula, MT 59807, USA; phone (406)721-1776. *(M)*

Bicycling the Pacific Northwest: Participants on a 35-day bicycle and hiking trip through the Northwest meet in Vancouver, British Columbia, before boarding a ferry to the San Juan Islands for a few days of island hopping, clamming and swimming. Then, after a return visit to Vancouver, travelers continue by train through British Columbia's glaciers, streams, forests and icefields to the mountain city of Jasper. On hikes in Jasper and Banff national parks, outdoor enthusiasts explore Bow Glacier Falls, Sundance Canyon, Sentinel Pass and Banff Hot Springs as well as Lake Louise. Biking involves gradual climbs on wide-shouldered roads. Participants camp and stay in hostels along the way. The trip ends in Calgary. **Cost:** $920 from Vancouver includes accommodations, gear. **When:** July, August. **Contact:** The Biking Expedition Inc., P.O. Box 547, Hall Ave., Henniker, NH 03242, USA; phone (603)428-7500.

Maritime Biking: A 33-day cycling trip allows a group of high school students to explore Montreal and camp in the scenic Maritime Provinces. After meeting in Montreal and spending several days there, the group takes a train to Amherst, Nova Scotia, where they begin biking and camping. The route, rarely more than a few miles from the sea, takes them to uncrowded beaches with good swimming, small fishing villages, inland lakes and rivers, and remote towns on Cape Breton where Gaelic is spoken. Clambakes, theater performances and hikes highlight the trip, which ends with a train ride from Cape Breton back to Montreal with a 2-day stopover in Quebec. **Cost:** $1,155 includes transportation from Montreal, food, equipment except bicycles, guides. **When:** July. **Contact:** Putney Student Travel, Inc., Putney, VT 05346, USA; phone (802)387-5885.

Alberta

Across the Prairies: A variety of outdoor activities awaits participants on a 35-day trip to the Canadian Rockies. Departing from New

York City by air to Edmonton, group members travel by train across the prairies before unloading the bikes and embarking on a 400-mile ride along the Jasper-Banff Highway. Bikers make day hikes in Jasper National Park and across the Columbia Icefield. Extended wilderness hikes make good hiking boots a necessity. Scheduled on the itinerary are visits to Bow Glacier Falls, Banff Hot Springs, Sundance Canyon, Mt. Edith Cavell, Sentinel Pass and Emerald Lake. Pedallers wend their way through forests of spruce, pine and aspen and often spot bears, elk, bighorn sheep, golden eagles and mountain goats living in remote areas of the park. Accommodations are in hostels. **Cost:** $892 includes meals, guide, accommodations; $30 emergency fund. **When:** July. **Contact:** American Youth Hostels, National Campus, Delaplane, VA 22025, USA; phone (703)592-3271 or toll free (800)336-6019.

Banff, Yoho and Jasper Cycling: Cyclists wishing to explore the spectacular scenery of the Canadian Rockies can choose between two 5-day camping tours or a 6-day mountain lodge package. On the lodge trip, bikers ride west from Banff to Lake Louise and into Yoho National Park, where they stay in a lodge at Emerald Lake for 2 nights before returning to Banff; the total distance covered is about 130 miles. The 5-day biking and camping trip to Jasper involves more strenuous riding. The route follows the Icefields Parkway to Bow Summit and Peyto Lake, passing the massive Columbia Icefield, the largest body of ice south of the Arctic. Waterfalls, mountain lakes and wildlife including moose and bear highlight the trip. Also available is another biking/camping trip along the Golden-Radium loop, a spectacular 235-mile ride through Kicking Horse Pass and along the Columbia River. **Cost:** $385 for lodge tour, $200 for either camping tour, includes food, accommodations (lodge or tenting), support vehicle, guides. Bicycles available for $40. **When:** May to October. **Contact:** Rocky Mountain Cycle Tours, Box 895, Banff, AB Canada T0L 0C0; phone (403)762-3477.

British Columbia

Gulf Islands Biking: A group of women cycles the quiet roads and camps out on the beaches of the Gulf Islands, located in the Georgia Strait off the east coast of Vancouver Island. Cyclists on the week-long trips meet in Anacortes, Washington, take a ferry through the San Juan Islands and then bike on Vancouver Island to a ferry that takes them to the Gulf Islands. The spring trip is slower paced, using a base camp and allowing time for walking up the bigger hills; the faster paced fall trip features long days of riding to arrive at beachside campsites for dinner. The trips are sponsored by a nonprofit group that stresses teaching wilderness skills to women in a supportive environment. Food is purchased each day along the way; all participants share in meal planning. **Cost:** $250 includes food, ferry fees, camping equipment, group leader. **When:** May, October. **Contact:** Keep Listening, Box 446, Sandy, OR 97055, USA; phone (503)622-3895.

Nova Scotia

Biking through the Maritimes: The rolling hills of Nova Scotia and the flat farmlands of Prince Edward Island are explored during a 31-day bicycle trip to the Maritime provinces. Departing from Portland, Maine by ferry, participants land in Yarmouth, Nova Scotia and start a journey that leads to uncrowded ocean beaches, inland lakes, salmon rivers and famous Fundy National Park. From Yarmouth bicyclists pedal past forests and lakes, through the fertile apple-growing Annapolis Valley. Taking a ferry to Prince Edward Island, they meet with rust-colored sands and ocean beach parks. Bikers carry all their own gear, including camping equipment, since accommodations are in the provinces' abundant parks. The terrain of Nova Scotia is more rugged than Prince Edward Island, though both are challenging to cyclists. **Cost:** $819 from Portland includes transportation, guide, accommodations, meals. **When:** June to August. **Contact:** The Biking Expedition Inc., P.O. Box 547, Hall Ave., Henniker, NH 03242, USA; phone (603)428-7500.

Biking along Canada's Atlantic Coast: A month-long trip for high school students from many different countries begins in Halifax and explores the east coast of Canada. Group members learn about the culture of the area by meeting farmers in the Northumberland Strait region, stopping at fishing villages on Prince Edward Island and participating in the Highland Games held annually at Antigonish. As the trip winds along the rocky Atlantic coast, many traditional town festivals are encountered. Group members can choose various destinations such as the huge inland lake of Bras d'Or, or the coal-mining town of Sydney on Cape Breton. Participants share responsibilities such as cooking, and should bring their own bicycles and be in good physical shape. **Cost:** $695 from Halifax includes meals, accommodations. **When:** July. **Contact:** Crossroads International, Hillsboro, NH 03244, USA; phone (603) 478-5251. ***(M)***

Coastal Bicycling: Beginning cyclists are welcome on a 12-day trip which explores Nova Scotia. After meeting in Bar Harbor, participants are transported by ferry to Yarmouth, where the biking begins. The terrain consists of mildly rolling hills and long flat stretches of coastline. Emphasis is placed on meeting the people of the area, among them Acadian farmers and fishermen who familiarize cyclists with stories of Nova Scotia's history and culture. A visit is planned to the Bay of Fundy to see the highest tides in the world, and time is provided for informal explorations of deserted islands and rural fields. Included in the course is instruction in first aid, bicycle mechanics and minimum-impact camping. **Cost:** $375 from Bar Harbor includes transportation, meals, accommodations, guide. **When:** May. **Contact:** The Infinite Odyssey, 57 Grant St., Waltham, MA 02154, USA; phone (617)899-6050. ***(M)***

Cycling the Maritimes: Most of a month-long bicycle trip for people ages 13 to 17 is spent cycling near the ocean in the Maritime provinces. Participants gather in Rochester, Vermont for an overnight train ride to Nova Scotia, where they cycle along back roads past coves and inlets exploring tidal pools, digging clams and visiting small towns. Then a ferry ride takes cyclists to Prince Edward Island. Here the route winds past farms, fields of wildflowers and small fishing villages. A ferry is then taken to the Magdalen Islands where only French is spoken, and cyclists explore miles of sand dunes, high cliffs and rolling countryside. The entire trip is highly flexible as far as each day's activities are concerned, and plenty of time is allotted for learning about the local culture. Possible activities include helping farmers work their fields, assisting on fishing wharves, making day hikes and visiting with residents in their homes. Nights are spent camping. The trip ends at Halifax, where participants catch a plane home. **Cost:** $835, plus a $25 refundable emergency fund includes transportation from Rochester, camping equipment, food, activities, guide. **When:** June to August. **Contact:** Student Hosteling Program of New England, Inc., Maple Hill, Rochester, VT 05767, USA; phone (802)767-3297.

Quebec

Aux Bicyclettes: High school-age youths on a 28-day trip cycle through 4 areas of the French-speaking province of Quebec: the Laurentian Mountains above Montreal, the shores of the St. Lawrence River, the Gaspe Peninsula and the Magdalen Islands in the Atlantic. The cycling averages 3 to 5 hours a day, leaving plenty of time for swimming in blue lakes, sampling the fare of French bakeries and exploring fishing villages. Two leaders accompany each trip, but trip members as a group decide on activities for frequent layover days. Cyclists camp out along the way, with everyone sharing in food buying, cooking and camp chores. The trip begins in Boston and ends at Halifax Airport in Nova Scotia. Participants can provide their own 10-speed bikes or rent them. **Cost:** $920 includes food, leaders, biking and camping equipment, activities, insurance. **When:** June, July. **Contact:** Student Hosteling Program of New England, Inc., Maple Hill, Rochester, VT 05767, USA; phone (802)767-3297.

EUROPE

Cycling the Rhine Valley: Youth and adult bikers on a 30-day journey through the Rhine Valley depart from Luxembourg. Following the vineyard-banked Moselle to the Rhine, cyclists pedal south along the river amid mountaintop castles to Heidelberg, then Strasbourg, with its magnificent cathedral, and over the Swiss border to Lucerne. Time is available for hikes into the Alps before cycling to Bern, Switzerland's capital. Bikers finish the journey in Luxembourg. The cycling is easy and trains are used on occasion. **Cost:** $1,020 from Baltimore/Washington includes airfare, land transportation, hostels, meals, guide; $50 emergency fund. **When:** June. **Contact:** American Youth Hostels, National Campus, Delaplane, VA 22025, USA; phone (703)592-3271 or toll free (800)336-6019.

Bulgaria

Balkan Biking: Cyclists can see scenic areas of Greece and Bulgaria up close on a 20-day trip. Visits are made to Corinth, Patras, Missolonghi, Meteora and Thessaloniki in Greece before crossing two 5,000-foot passes into Bulgaria, where a visit is made to the spectacular Rila monastery. The trip concludes in the capital city of Sofia. Food, lodging and sagwagon expenses are handled out of pocket on a daily basis. The biking is of medium difficulty, and participants must be 21 or older. **Cost:** $50 registration fee; about $40 a day includes food, accommodations, transportation. **When:** September. **Contact:** International Bicycle Touring Society, 2115 Paseo Dorado, La Jolla, CA 92037, USA; phone (714)454-2441.

England

Cycling Country Lanes: The gently rolling terrain of the East Anglian countryside provides relaxed cycling holidays for individuals and small groups of no more than 6. Bicycle rentals are available by the week with a variety of touring options. A package trip with prearranged itinerary and accommodations is offered, and travelers may also preselect their own route and accommodations or simply rent cycles and find accommodations on their own. All trips begin and end in the village of Yoxford and pass over the peaceful rural byways of Suffolk County. Meals may be taken at inns and restaurants, or bikers may prepare their own picnic fare. **Cost:** $100 to $112 a week includes rental bicycles, maps, accommodations with bed and breakfast; $30 to $36 a week for bicycle rental only. **When:** Year-round. **Contact:** East Anglia Cycling Holidays, The Bookshop, Yoxford, Suffolk, Great Britain; phone (01)720-5648.

Bicycling through British History: Cyclists pedal around England on 15- and 17-day trips that originate in London. The Cotswold Hills challenge some cyclists, though riders may move at their own pace. The cyclists wind their way through the Colne River Valley, Shedworth and its Roman villa, Oxford and Bath before arriving at Stonehenge. Cycling along the Wylye Valley provides side trips to

Bicyclists on an International Bicycle Touring Society outing walk their bikes down a rocky path in a sparsely vegetated and remote Cornish valley. (International Bicycle Touring Society)

Steeple Landford, Great Wishford and Westbury. At Winchester travelers view Winchester College and the remains of Wolvesey castle and cathedral. Begun in 1079, the cathedral itself blends several styles of architectural design and contains 7 elaborately carved chantry chapels, tombs with the remains of ancient kings and medieval wall paintings. The Winchester monks share bread and ale with cyclists, keeping alive the 800-year-old tradition of giving aid to the traveler. **Cost:** $929 from London includes meals, accommodations, guide. **When:** July to August. **Contact:** Euro-Bike Tours, P.O. Box 40, DeKalb, IL 60115, USA; phone (815)758-8851.

Cornish Cycling: A 9-day trip is based in the coastal town of St. Ives, Cornwall. An artist's colony at the tip of the Cornwall peninsula, St. Ives is less than a day's ride from Land's End. Each day a new tour is undertaken, including visits to the Scilly Isles, to Penzance and along the rocky and stormy coast. **Cost:** About $20 a day from St. Ives includes lodging, food. **When:** April. **Contact:** International Bicycle Touring Society, 2115 Paseo Dorado, La Jolla, CA 92037, USA; phone (714)454-2441.

France

Bicycling Le Paysage: The French countryside provides the backdrop for two 3-week cycling trips along 600 miles of rolling, winding roads. The ride is geared to any cyclist; fast riders may race while slower riders may enjoy the scenery at a more leisurely pace. The journey is scheduled to cover about 46 miles each day. Bicycling on lightly traveled roads through fields, forests, farms and vineyards, participants visit several of France's museums and cathedrals. The route passes through Chartres, Chateaudun, Blois, Tours, Azay-le-Rideau and Vendome before a return to Versailles. **Cost:** $1,637 and $1,368 from New York includes transportation, hotel accommodations, most meals. **When:** June, September. **Contact:** Bike Tour France, P.O. Box 32814, Charlotte, NC 28232, USA; phone (704)332-8265.

The cycling tradition is much stronger in Europe than in the United States, and bikers generally find good roads and hospitable reception there. Here, two cyclists make a triumphant entry into a Bavarian village. (Gerhard's Bicycle Odysseys)

Germany

Bavarian Cycling: The back roads of Germany and Austria provide relatively easy biking on a 2-week trip. From Frankfurt, trip members are bused to Heidelberg where the bike ride to Salzburg, Austria begins. Participants are accompanied by a van which carries all equipment and tired cyclists when necessary. Cyclists pedal past vineyards, magnificent castles and the Neckar River. No more than 35 miles separate rest stops along the route, and participants find accommodation at local hotels in Heidelberg, Rothenburg, Munich and Krautheim. Entering through one of Rothenburg's 30 gates, participants bounce along the cobblestoned streets of the medieval town. From Munich, cyclists head through miles of silent forest and visit baroque churches that line parts of the path. The trip ends at Salzburg after participants cross into Austria. **Cost:** $765 includes bus transportation, hotels, breakfasts and most dinners. **When:** June to September. **Contact:** Gerhard's Bicycle Odysseys, 1137 SW Yamhill, Portland, OR 97205, USA; phone (503)223-5190. ***(M)***

Netherlands

Going Dutch: Across the uniformly flat terrain of Holland, the Dutch have created a network of bicycle paths and roads not accessible to cars. During a 23-day trip, a group of teenagers aged 14 to 17 travels along these routes and visits small fishing villages, canals, museums, castles and cities. The group departs from New York and flies to Amsterdam where they meet with Dutch guides. Once on bikes, participants travel through the countryside with frequent stops for rest and refreshment; the trip has been designed so that no stretch of bicycling is too strenuous even for novices, and a van carries luggage from point to point. One side trip is a visit to Terschelling, an island created centuries ago when the North Sea invaded the land; it is a 2-hour ferry ride from the mainland, and participants stay at a hostel set in the island's sand dunes. Other stops include the the province of Friesland, the weaving center of Almelo in central Holland and the cherry orchards at Tiel. Accommodations are in youth hostels along the way. **Cost:** $990 includes roundtrip airfare from New York, meals, accommodations, guides, van, activities. **When:** Summer. **Contact:** International Bicycle Tours, 12 Mid Pl., Chappaqua, NY 10514, USA; phone (914)238-4576.

Dutch Cycle and Sail: A 2-week trip for 16- to 21-year-olds spends the first week exploring Holland by bicycle and the second sailing the Waddenzee. Departing from London, the group of about 10 meets a similar group of Netherlanders for the cycling exploration. The flexible itinerary includes visits to Amersfoort, Apeldoorn and Arnhem. There is time for stops at points of interest and numerous side trips along the way; nights are spent camping or at hostels. Participants then take a bus to Amsterdam and Enkhuizen, where they board a sailing clipper for a week's investigation of the Dutch islands and coast. While living onboard participants learn about sailing and the history of the area, finally returning to London by train. **Cost:** $320 includes transportation, food, accommodations, equipment, guides. **When:** July. **Contact:** YMCA National Centre, Lakeside, Ulverston, Cumbria LA12 8BD, Great Britain; phone Newby Bridge (04483) 758.

Switzerland

Countryside Cycling: A 2-week bicycling trip through the market towns and historic villages of Switzerland and France begins on the Swiss side in Lausanne. After a brief orientation session, the cyclists head for France via Nyons and Geneva, passing through vineyards, orchards and forests. Despite the mountainous terrain, flat routes are followed wherever possible and the group never travels more than 31 miles a day. There is plenty of time for taking unplanned excursions and meeting the local people. Upon returning to Switzerland, the group spends a few days exploring the towns of Interlaken and Lucerne by bike and bus. Nights are spent in hotels. **Cost:** $495. **When:** May through October. **Contact:** Directions Unlimited, 344 Main St., Mt. Kisco, NY 10549, USA; phone (914)241-1700.

Bicycling through Wine Country: Equipped with bicycles, participants pedal along country lanes through several vineyards, including Le Cote and Chablis, during a 5-day trip originating in Lausanne. Bikers round Lake Geneva, following a varied route visiting both Swiss and French cities including Geneva, Lausanne, Montreux and Evian-les-Bains. Participants cycle a grand total of 118 miles averaging about 20 miles each day. Visits are made to the Roman and medieval town of Nyons, Hermance, the medieval village of Yvoire where fresh lake fish is the specialty, Thonon-les-Bains, the fishing villages of Tourronde and Meillerie and St. Gingolph on the Swiss border. The final day of the trip covers 22 miles and includes a steep climb shortly after leaving Vevey. Accommodations are in hotels. **Cost:** $292 from Lausanne includes accommodations, bike rentals, guide, breakfast. **When:** May to October. **Contact:** Welcome Swiss Tours, 7 Ave. Benjamin-Constant, 1003 Lausanne, Switzerland; phone (021) 20 68 21.

Yugoslavia

Slavic Cycling: Cyclists become acquainted with the diverse terrain and peoples of Serbia, Bosnia, Croatia and Slovenia on a 25-day trip through Yugoslavia. Departing from Belgrade, bikers ride southwest to Dubrovnik, along the coast to Trieste and east to Zagreb where the trip ends. Trip members should be experienced cyclists, as the cycling averages 50 miles a day and is somewhat difficult. Accommodations are at moderately priced hotels and inns, with baggage transported by a sagwagon. Participants must be at least 21 years old. **Cost:** On request. **When:** May. **Contact:** International Bicycle Touring Society, 2115 Paseo Dorado, La Jolla, CA 92037, USA; phone (714)454-2441.

PACIFIC

Hawaii

Cycling around the Big Island: Bicyclists travel about 400 miles around the Big Island during a 2-week trip that includes visits to black sand beaches and colorful orchid fields. The route provides a variety of terrain, ranging from flat areas to moderate grades. Participants visit active volcanoes, Akaka Falls, Puna Lava Flows and Puukohola Heiau (Temple of Old Hawaii). Cyclists learn about the history of the island people and find time for visits with local residents. Accompanied by a sagwagon, participants carry minimal loads during the ride. Adequate repair parts, tools and mechanics are available throughout the trip. Seven nights are spent camping, with another 6 nights spent in hotels and cabins. Participants should supply their own bicycles and helmets, but bike rentals are available. **Cost:** $375 from Hilo includes accommodations, meals. **When:** Year-round. **Contact:** Bicycle Tours—Hawaii, c/o Pacific Sports Products, 110 Alae St., Hilo, HI 96720, USA; phone (808)961-6936. ***(M)***

Maui by Bike: The tropical jungle and coast of Maui are the setting for a 12-day tour by bicycle. The exploration of the island's natural environment includes visiting the underwater grottoes at Wainapanapa

Caves, snorkeling on reefs, swimming at Seven Pools National Park, hiking on Haleakala Volcano and picnicking at Waimoku Falls. Nights are spent in campgrounds, except for a final hotel night in town. The group covers no more than 25 to 30 miles by bike on any single day, so no previous bicycle touring experience is necessary. **Cost:** $425 includes transportation on Maui, meals, tents, accommodations. **When:** August, December. **Contact:** Pacific Adventures, P.O. Box 5041, Riverside, CA 92517, USA; phone (714)684-1227.

SOUTH AMERICA

Peru

Pedaling Peru: While bicycling on paved mountain roads around Cajamarca and Huaraz, participants visit local villagers and Peruvian bikers. The 21-day trip begins with a flight to Peru from Miami or Los Angeles then continues with some cruising on the Peruvian coast to view pre-Incan ruins such as Chan Chan. Biking on quiet roads through the foothills of the Andes, participants climb to mountain villages by one of 2 routes. One loop reaches Cajamarca at approximately 9,000 feet before returning to the coast by another road. Another route passes through the Cordillera Blanca and reaches Huaraz at 10,140 feet. Along the route participants sleep in moderately priced hotels, private homes or school houses, or camp out. **Cost:** $890 from Peru includes guide, accommodations, food, camping equipment. **When:** July, August. **Contact:** Andean Outfitters, P.O. Box 7007, Angels Camp, CA 95222, USA; phone (209)736-4830. *(M)*

UNITED STATES

Atlantic Cycling: A youth trip of 30 days along the Atlantic coast begins in the historic city of Philadelphia. Cyclists head east to the New Jersey Pine Barrens, then to the Atlantic Ocean. There are opportunities to swim, surf, water ski, fish and beachcomb along the coast from New Jersey to Virginia. Cycling is moderate. The Mason-Dixon Line is crossed to Cape May, city of Victorian "gingerbread" mansions. The group then ferries across the Delaware Bay on the way to Assateague Island to explore the Wildlife Nature Trail. Wild pony herds can be seen roaming the marshes at Chincoteague, and at Williamsburg participants see a fully restored colonial village. The trip ends with a visit to Washington, DC. Groups consist of 9 members, who camp during most of the

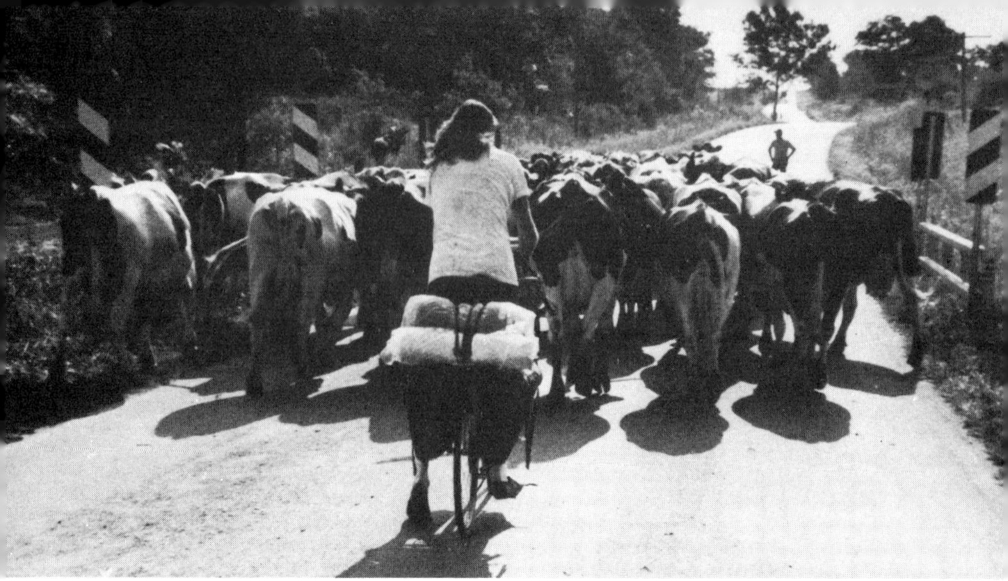

Near Ash Grove, Missouri, a cyclist on the 4,450-mile TransAmerica Bicycle Trail becomes ensnarled in commuter traffic. (Bill Wagner/Bikecentennial)

trip. **Cost:** $415 includes food, accommodations, accident and health insurance, group leaders; $30 for emergency fund. **When:** July. **Contact:** American Youth Hostels, National Campus, Delaplane, VA 22025, USA; phone (703)592-3271 or toll free (800)336-6019.

Country Biking: A trip combining the sites of early American history with long stretches of fine country cycling lasts 34 days. Beginning in Philadelphia, young people ages 14 and over cycle west through Pennsylvania Dutch towns and farmland. A broad spectrum of American history provides the atmosphere for much of the journey, which includes a visit to John Brown's fortress at Harpers Ferry and a raft trip down the Shenandoah River. Virginia's 100-mile Skyline Drive is cycled in the Shenandoah Mountains. After a hiking expedition along Appalachian trails, the group proceeds southeast to Jefferson's Monticello, Jamestown and Williamsburg, the colonial capital of Virginia. The trip ends with a visit to Washington, DC. **Cost:** $450 includes food, accommodations, health and accident insurance, group leaders. **When:** July. **Contact:** American Youth Hostels, National Campus, Delaplane, VA 22025, USA; phone (703)592-3271 or toll free (800)336-6019.

TransAmerica Bicycle Trail: Travelers ready for an epic journey can join 7 to 10 other cyclists for a ride across the United States from Astoria, Oregon to Yorktown, Virginia. A total of 4,450 miles are covered in 90 days, with camping along the way. From the rocky Oregon coast, cyclists climb over the volcanic Cascade Mountains, follow the Salmon, Clearwater and Lochsa rivers, then puff over the Bitterroot Mountains into Montana. As the challenge of the Rockies begins, participants ride through Yellowstone and Grand Teton national parks. Cyclists welcome the level terrain of Kansas, then move on to the rolling hills of the Missouri Ozarks. The group glides through the lowlands of Illinois and Kentucky before challenging the Appalachians. Cyclists end the trip at the historic triangle of Jamestown, Yorktown and Williamsburg in Virginia. During the trip at least 14 days are set aside to allow participants time to explore and rest. **Cost:** $975 includes food, leader, camping fees. **When:** May to August. **Contact:** Bikecentennial, P.O. Box 8308, Missoula, MT 59807, USA; phone (406)721-1776. *(M)*

Western Wheeling: After a few short practice runs in Wisconsin and South Dakota bikers embark on a 40-day tour of parks in the western United States. Yellowstone and Grand Teton national parks mark the beginning of the challenge as group members bike and camp their way west. Lake Tahoe or Yosemite Valley are next on the agenda—2 difficult areas which test a biker's skill and endurance. The trip is rounded off by sightseeing in San Francisco, Los Angeles and spots in Mexico, with bike tours into remote areas. The Grand Canyon, the Navajo Indian Reservation, Zion and Bryce Canyon national parks and the foothills of the Rockies complete the excursion. **Cost:** $1,347 includes use of bikes, camping equipment. **When:** July. **Contact:** North American Tour-a-Camp, Rockland County YMCA, P.O. Box 581, Nyack, NY 10960, USA; phone (914)358-0919.

California

Russian Weekend: A 2-day bicycle trip follows the Russian River through scenic California countryside. Accompanied by an equipment van, participants begin cycling at the Sonoma Coast Beach recreation area and head inland along the river. The group covers about 25 miles each day, riding through an area of rolling hills, meadows and redwood forests, and stops for the night beneath the towering Armstrong Redwoods. Some time is allotted for swimming and individual exploration, and cyclists must provide their own lunches. **Cost:** $33 includes 2 meals a day, group equipment, van, guide. **When:** May. **Contact:** Adventure Unique Inc., 19 Washington St., Santa Clara, CA 95050, USA; phone (403)446-2347. *(M)*

Biking to Death: A weekend trip in Death Valley features spectacular desert scenery and a route that is almost all downhill. From the Friday afternoon meeting in Riverside to the Sunday drive back out of the valley, the itinerary covers about 100 miles and passes landmarks such as Scotty's Castle, Furnace Creek, Devil's Golf Course and Dante's View, where one can see Badwater at 282 feet below sea level and Mt. Whitney at 14,495 feet, the lowest and highest points in the contiguous United States. Accommodations are in hotels and at campgrounds. **Cost:** $100 includes roundtrip transportation from Riverside, accommodations, food, guides. **When:** April. **Contact:** Pacific Adventures, P.O. Box 5041, Riverside, CA 92517, USA; phone (714)684-1227.

Colorado

Cycling through the Mountains: A trip beginning and ending in Durango wanders for 7 days through mountainous terrain, stopping overnight in various mining towns and resort areas. Before the cycling gets underway, participants begin the excursion with a ride on the narrow-gauge train from Durango to Silverton. From there the route leads over alpine trails through the Uncompahgre and San Juan national forests, into Montezuma Valley and finally to Mesa Verde National Park where group members can explore the area's prehistoric cliff dwellings. Cyclists cover 25 to 30 miles a day, with 2 days of 50-mile rides; if the pace proves too much for some cyclists, a sag-wagon is available for rest periods. Participants must provide their own 10-speed bikes. **Cost:** $250 includes accommodations, most meals, map book, guides. **When:** July. **Contact:** Bike Dream Tours, Inc., P.O. Box 20653, Houston, TX 77025, USA; phone (713)771-1172.

Rocky Going: An exploratory bike trip traverses a number of high passes in the Rockies, setting up a route for use in future years. Cyclists cover 605 miles in 16 days from Winter Park to Durango. Two national parks are visited, Rocky Mountain and Mesa Verde, as are several areas of historical interest, including Crested Butte, Telluride and the restored mining town of Central City. Nights are spent in campgrounds. Participants cross at least 7 mountain passes, ranging from 9,000 to 12,000 feet in elevation, so cyclists need to be in excellent shape and have good biking skills. There is no fixed itinerary; instead, bikers work from a map and a general schedule. The route they follow will become part of the Great Parks Bicycle Route, to stretch from Jasper, Alberta to southern Colorado. Those living near sea level should spend several days acclimatizing before the trip. **Cost:** $173 includes meals, group equipment, maps, leader. **When:** July, August. **Contact:** Bikecentennial, P.O. Box 8308, Missoula, MT 59807, USA; phone (406)721-1776. *(M)*

Delaware

Between the Bays: The area between Chesapeake Bay and Delaware Bay is explored by bike on an

Long climbs and fine views characterize the Great Parks Bicycle Route, traversing the Rockies from Jasper to Missoula. (Bikecentennial)

8-day tour. Starting and finishing in Wilmington, bikers meander through unspoiled Delaware and Maryland countryside on small back roads with few hills. The area is rich in history, and many small towns and points of interest are investigated at a leisurely pace. Food, accommodations and sagwagon expenses are handled out of pocket on a daily basis. The cycling is easy, and participants must be 21 or older. **Cost:** $35 registration fee; around $35 a day includes food, accommodations, sagwagon, guide. **When:** September. **Contact:** International Bicycle Touring Society, 2115 Paseo Dorado, La Jolla, CA 92037, USA; phone (714)454-2441.

Florida

Suwannee Byways: Four weekend cycling trips travel over flatlands and gentle hills on rural back roads near the Suwannee River, in northern Florida. Beginning and ending in White Springs, the trips cover from 23 to 55 miles a day, with extra miles for experienced cyclists and less demanding routes for beginners. All tours feature picnic lunches and swimming in springs, lakes or the Suwannee River. Participants may take time to look at antiques and curios and to learn of regional lore in the Stephen Foster Center in White Springs. Accommodations are in small hotels or motels on 3 of the trips and at a springside campsite on the other. Special 3-day trips are offered on holiday weekends. **Cost:** $80 includes meals, accommodations, baggage transport. **When:** Year-round. **Contact:** Suwannee River Bicycle Tours, P.O. Box 319, White Springs, FL 32096, USA; phone (904)397-2757.

Indiana

Covered Bridge Bike Tours: Parke County offers maps and descriptions of bicycle routes through its covered bridge area. Routes are mapped out in 5-mile, 18-mile and 32-mile segments. Bikers may see many of the 36 covered bridges remaining in the area, as well as the restored turn-of-the-century town, old coal mining towns, chapels, old mills and the Little Raccoon and Wabash valleys. The bridges are built with Burr arches, and many have windows through which 19th-century travelers saw oncoming traffic. **Cost:** Free. **When:** Year-round. **Contact:** Parke County, Inc., P.O. Box 165, Rockville, IN 47872, USA; phone (317)569-5226.

Maine

Sail and Cycle: Group members depart from Camden harbor early Monday morning aboard a sailboat equipped with gear, food and bicycles. The next week is spent in the Penobscot Bay area, where participants arrange their own relaxed itineraries; bikes can be taken ashore on either the islands or the coast for exploring excursions along the roadways of the Blue Hill Peninsula, Vinalhaven Island and Isle au Haut. All of the islands provide excellent hiking trails and participants can swim either from the islands or the sailboat. Camp is pitched ashore on some nights, with a special lobster bake arranged during one of the island layovers. Cyclists of all abilities may participate and groups are limited to no more than 10. **Cost:** $275 from Camden includes boat, crew, guide, accommodations on board, meals. **When:** On request. **Contact:** Overland Rolls, 1 Center St., Brunswick, ME 04011, USA; phone (207)725-5119. ***(M)***

Seacoast Cycling: From Boothbay Harbor, Maine, high school students cycle along the Atlantic seacoast to Canada in 29 days. Meeting in Rochester, Vermont, students bring bicycles and receive other touring equipment which is theirs to keep. In addition to cycling over rolling terrain, participants spend time in fishing villages, boat on inland lakes and take day hikes through seaside fields and up mountains overlooking the ocean. Tents provide shelter for the group which camps in state and national parks. Cyclists spend 1 week exploring the islands, seaside mountains and shoreline of Acadia National Park. Base camp is on Isle au Haut and participants walk the island trails to beachcomb on Boom Beach, Squeaker Cove and Thunder Gulch. Bikers wheel onto many ferries including one that crosses the border into Canada and deposits the group on Campobello Island and nearby Deer Island for a few days of exploring lighthouses, fishing weirs, bogs and fog forests. The trip ends at Bangor International Airport where participants make connecting flights home. **Cost:** $805 from Rochester includes guides, food, insurance, all equipment except bicycles. **When:** June to August. **Contact:** Student Hosteling Program of New England, Inc., Maple Hill, Rochester, VT 05767, USA; phone (802)767-3297.

Michigan

Meandering through Michigan: Cyclists peddle over back roads in the vicinity of Lake Michigan on weekend and 3-day trips. Novice routes cover 10 to 15 miles a day; experts travel as much as 60 miles. The trips visit such places as apple and cherry orchards, maple forests, sandy beaches, the Betsie River, and the area's lakes, including Lake Michigan. A number of alternate routes are available on all trips so that cyclists of differing abilities can be accommodated. Participants may supply their own bikes or rent them. Lodging is in country inns. **Cost:** $80 to $125 for a weekend, $102 to $123 for 3 days includes accommodations, food, activities, guide. **When:** May to October. **Contact:** Michigan Bicycle Touring, 511 Second St., Jackson, MI 49203, USA; phone (517)784-2029 or 592-8620.

New Hampshire

Exploring Backroads on a Bike: Cyclists explore New England by bicycle, canoe and on foot during a 31-day trip. Starting in New Hampshire, cyclists pedal many of the lightly traveled back roads that cut through the green valleys, quaint villages and small towns of the state. A visit to Lake Sunapee provides travelers with the opportunity to take a side trip to Vermont on the way to Hanover and Dartmouth colleges. Heading into the White Mountain National Forest, participants take a break from cycling and hike mountain trails to the top of Mt. Washington, the highest peak

Two cyclists catch their breath, confer and enjoy the sunshine by a stone wall in rural New Hampshire. (The Biking Expedition)

in the northeast. Group members also visit the White Mountain Festival of Arts as part of the trip. Bikers then continue to North Conway and take a 3-day canoe trip on the Saco River into Maine en route to Lake Winnipesaukee. Aboard the Mt. Washington ferry, cyclists cross the lake and continue the journey through rolling woods and farmlands of central New Hampshire. Bikers carry full-load packs and camp along the way. The trip terminates in Boston. **Cost:** $737. **When:** June to August. **Contact:** The Biking Expedition Inc., P.O. Box 547, Hall Ave., Henniker, NH 03242, USA; phone (603)428-7500.

Learning by Cycling: Bicycles provide the primary means of travel for participants in a 3-week outdoor course beginning and ending in Hanover, New Hampshire. Course activities include cycle maintenance and repair, physical conditioning, rock climbing, emergency care and rescue, outdoor living, natural history exploration and a final expedition planned and carried out by students. After leaving Hanover, New Hampshire, the group travels across the Green Mountains of Vermont to the Adirondack Mountains of New York and back. Participants are expected to supply their own 10-speed bicycles and cycling helmets. **Cost:** $650 includes accommodations, meals; financial aid is available. **When:** July, August. **Contact:** Dartmouth Outward Bound Center, Box 50, Hanover, NH 03755, USA.

New York

Wheeling through Wine Country: A group of 10 to 12 cyclists travels around several of the Finger Lakes on a 6-day tour through New York's wine region beginning and

Far removed from the mainstream of twentieth-century life, the back roads of New England offer cyclists a world of farmhouses, one-lane roads and rolling pasturelands. (The Biking Expedition)

ending in Watkins Glen. The basic routes average 25 to 40 miles a day but those wishing a more challenging ride can take longer routes of up to 55 miles a day. Shorter rides can be arranged with the sagwagon driver. Though terrain is relatively level along the lakeshore, the land between the lakes is very hilly and offers some real challenges. Accommodations and meals are found in lake resorts and wine producing towns. Additional time may be spent visiting points of interest such as the Glass Center in Corning where workers fashion Steuben crystal by hand, the wineries in Hammondsport and, at the beginning or end of the trip, the group visits underground grottos and 18 waterfalls in Watkins Glen. Sagwagon transfers are available to and from Elmira airport and the Watkins Glen bus station. Scouting of the routes has shown traffic to be minimal. **Cost:** $250 from Watkins Glen or Elmira includes transportation, accommodations, meals, guides, sagwagon. **When:** September. **Contact:** Bike Dream Tours, P.O. Box 20653, Houston, TX 77025, USA; phone (713)771-1172.

Pennsylvania

Amish Biking: Cyclists on weekend trips travel through the Pennsylvania countryside in June. Lodging and meals are in economical college dormitories, with access to their recreational facilities. One trip takes place in the rolling farmlands of the Lehigh Valley near Allentown, an area that features a local game preserve, various historical sites and a bike racing center. A second trip, based in Millersville, near Lancaster, penetrates the heart of Pennsylvania Dutch country, known for its distinctive architecture, farmers' markets and Amish homesteads. On both trips cyclists need to be in fairly good physical condition and supply their own bikes. **Cost:** $59 includes food, accommodations, activities, guide, mechanic. **When:** June. **Contact:** Scenic Cycling, P.O. Box 15461K, Philadelphia, PA 19149, USA; phone (215)331-2607.

Tennessee

Tennessee Two-Wheeler: A week-long autumn tour through the backcountry of Tennessee offers cyclists the opportunity to see many rural handicrafts and arts close-up. Participants meet at Montgomery Bell State Park about 50 miles south of Nashville on a Saturday afternoon and return on Sunday a week later. The route follows back roads and trails resplendent with fall colors. Generally 45 to 65 miles a day are covered through hilly terrain; a transport vehicle accompanies the group for those wishing shorter rides. Visits are made to numerous small towns to watch quiltmakers, listen to local stories and sample the area's famous pies. There is little traffic in the area and accommodations are in small inns and hotels along the way. **Cost:** $250 from Montgomery Bell includes accommodations, most meals, map book, guide. **When:** October. **Contact:** Bike Dream Tours, Inc., P.O. Box 20653, Houston, TX 77025, USA; phone (713)771-1172.

Texas

Two Texas Trips: Two bicycling trips through the hill country of

Texas are offered: one through the wildflower area of central Texas and the other from San Antonio to the Mexican border. The first trip, lasting 4 days, originates and ends in La Grange, 85 miles west of Houston. Spring brings as many as 40 different wildflowers to this area dotted with Czech and German villages, historic sites and local fairs such as the Winedale Festival. Riders travel 40 to 45 miles a day for 3½ days, with optional routes ranging up to 60 miles over relatively easy terrain. The second trip is a week's tour through Alamo country, beginning and ending in San Antonio. The countryside has dramatic canyonlands laced with rivers, followed by the hilly Pecos region near the Mexican border. Flowering cactus, wildflowers and a wide variety of bird life are evident on the trip. Between 45 and 65 miles are covered each day through moderate to challenging terrain. Participants cross the Mexican border at Ciudad Acuna, then return to San Antonio and the United States by bus. Both trips are accompanied by a sagwagon to provide shorter riding days if desired. **Cost:** $150 for central Texas trip; $250 for southern trip includes accommodations, breakfasts and dinners, maps, sagwagon, guide. **When:** March for central Texas, May for southern trip. **Contact:** Bike Dream Tours, Inc., P.O. Box 20653, Houston, TX 77025, USA; phone (713)771-1172.

Vermont

Biking in Vermont: Weekend and midweek cycling trips are offered to explore the Vermont countryside. Bicycling is easy to moderate, with flexibility of both time and itinerary; the pace is up to the individual. Several New England inns are used along the way for overnight spots and during the day riders explore a variety of swimming stops, classic New England villages and natural resting places. Side trips are available, depending on skill, energy and enthusiasm. The weekend trip is based on a 15- to 20-mile loop, with suggestions for further travel. The midweek tours are 20 to 45 miles a day and are suitable for strong beginners, intermediate or advanced cyclists. A van accompanies each trip to carry luggage and offer assistance if necessary. Groups are limited to 20 participants. **Cost:** $85 for weekend tour, $210 for midweek trip includes lodging, meals, leader. **When:** May to October. **Contact:** Bike Vermont, Inc., P.O. Box 75, Grafton, VT 05146, USA; phone (802)843-2259.

Country Inns by Bicycle: Cyclists tour through Vermont's farmlands and gentle mountain country on self-guided trips of 2 days to 2 weeks and longer, spending nights in a number of the area's historic inns. The most popular trip covers 200 miles in 7 days, beginning at the Churchill House Inn on the western face of the Green Mountains, then following a route which circumscribes the southern half of Vermont. Stopping places include the Kedron Valley Inn in Woodstock, the 1811 House in Manchester and the Tulip Tree Inn, an early 19th-century country home in Chittenden. Cyclists can also tackle shorter tours, such as a weekend 100-miler that takes in Fort Ticon-

For between $85 and $126, Vermont Bicycle Touring offers 2- and 3-day self-guided trips in the summer and fall. The flexible itinerary allows participants to cycle 10 to 75 miles a day, depending on how far their legs will carry them. (John Freiden/Vermont Bicycle Touring)

deroga and the Hubarton Battlefield, or a shorter run up through the Champlain Valley. Longer trips of 2 weeks or more can also be organized along variations of the 200-mile route, using the network of country inns for stop-over points along the way. Ten-speed bikes with bags and panniers can be rented for any of the tours. **Cost:** $160 for 7 days includes lodging, breakfast and dinner. **When:** Summer. **Contact:** Churchill House Inn, RFD #3, Rt. 73E, Brandon, VT 05733, USA; phone (802)247-3300.

Short New England Bike Trips: The countryside and small villages of Vermont are visited on 2- and 3-day bicycle tours, designed for adults and families. Each rider is provided with a map and directions and rides at his or her own pace. Evenings are spent at informal country inns. Trips for every level of ability—from 10 to 75 miles a day—visit Woodstock and Middlebury, travel along the Ottuaquechee and Black rivers, pass through Chester, Grafton and Dorset, and cruise the shores of Echo, Morey, and Willoughby lakes. Tours are available to all areas of the state. **Cost:** $85 for 2-day trips, $126 for 3-day trips includes breakfast and dinner, accommodations, guide. **When:** May to November. **Contact:** Vermont Bicycle Touring, RR 2, Bristol, VT 05443, USA; phone (802)388-4263. ***(M)***

Bike trips of 1 to 9 days are offered by Northwest Bicycle Touring Society from British Columbia to Oregon. Here, two cyclists travel the Cape Meares Loop north of Tillamook, Oregon. (Lloyd Jones/Northwest Bicycle Touring Society)

Washington

Pacific Northwest Cycling: Ferry rides, island explorations, fishing villages, mountain views and winding roads are featured on a moderately paced cycle trip lasting 5 days and beginning in Anacortes. After a day and night in the San Juan Islands, cyclists return to the mainland and the fishing town of La Conner. The route continues across Deception Pass Bridge and south on Whidbey Island. Cyclists then take the ferry to Port Townsend across Puget Sound for a day exploring the once-major port and the area around Discovery Bay before returning to Whidbey Island. The final day offers continuous views of the Olympic Mountains and Canada as the group follows the shoreline back to Anacortes. Accommodations are in inns along the way. Bicycles may be rented with advance notice. **Cost:** $300 includes lodging, breakfasts and dinners, ferries, guides. **When:** July to September. **Contact:** Bicycle Tours Northwest, 535 Cass St., Port Townsend, WA 98368, USA; phone (206)385-4425.

Northwest Passage: Bike enthusiasts are invited to spend 1 to 9 days traveling the back roads and main routes of northwestern Washington. The single-day trip is a 50-mile loop in the Skagit and Samish flats area west and north of Mt. Vernon. Those who elect to take a 2-day excursion have a choice: either the 117-mile loop tour from Seattle to Port Townsend and Fort Worden, passing Winslow, Bainbridge Island, Agate Pass and the Olympic Peninsula; or the Mt. Rainier tour, passing from Enumclaw to Paradise, Stevens Canyon and Cayuse Pass. A 3-day excursion takes place on Orcas Island in the San Juan Islands. Participants who elect the 9-day trip bike 450 miles through Washington and British Columbia and visit such points as the Olympic Peninsula, Victoria, the San Juan Islands, Point Roberts, the Fraser River Valley, Whatcom County and Whidbey Island. Accommodations and meals vary for each trip. **Cost:** Upon request. **When:** May to September. **Contact:** Northwest Bicycle Touring Society, P.O. Box 724, Mercer Island, WA 98040, USA; phone (206)243-1880.

Wisconsin

River Falls Loop: On a leisurely 4-day bike trip, a group of women cruises through the Wisconsin countryside on a loop beginning and ending in River Falls. Following the contours of gently rolling hills cyclists explore back roads, try out swimming holes, stop at country parks and dine in local restaurants. Camp is pitched in a new spot each night. The trip accommodates beginners and experienced cyclists, as more and less ambitious riders can split up onto routes varying from 25 to 45 miles a day. The outfitter offers other bike trips for women, with routes available in southeast Minnesota, in the Northfield area and along the St. Croix River. **Cost:** $72 includes food, maps, guide. **When:** May. **Contact:** Woodswomen, 3716 Fourth Ave. S., Minneapolis, MN 55409, USA.

RESOURCES

Clubs and Associations

Amateur Bicycle League of America
Box 669, Wall St. Sta.
New York, NY 10005, USA

American Youth Hostels
National Campus
Delaplane, VA 22025, USA
Phone (703)592-3271

The Association of Cycle
and Lightweight Campers
30 Napier Wy.
Wembley, Middlesex HA0 4UA
Great Britain

Bicycle Manufacturers Association
1101 15th St. NW
Washington, DC 20005, USA
Phone (202)452-1166

Bikecentennial
P.O. Box 8308
Missoula, MT 59807, USA
Phone (406)721-1776

Canadian Cycling Association
333 River Rd.
Vanier City, ON Canada K1L 8B9
Phone (613)746-5753

The Cyclists Touring Club
69 Meadrow
Godalming, Surrey GU7 3HS
Great Britain

Feder. Francaise de Cyclotourisme
8 rue Jean Marie Tego
75013 Paris, France

Friends of Bikeology
1035 E. De La Guerra St.
Santa Barbara, CA 93103, USA

League of American Wheelmen
19 S. Bothwell
Palatine, IL 60067, USA
Phone (312)991-1200

U.S. Cycling Federation
P.O. Box 669, Wall St. Sta.
New York, NY 10005, USA
Phone (212)344-2808

WILDERNESS SURVIVAL

Our ancestors of long ago feared the unknown, coped with predators and harsh climates, and banded together in groups to survive. For most of us, modern technology and urban environments have all but eliminated such daily struggles for survival. But what *would* you do if you broke a leg on a hiking trip; got trapped in your car during a blizzard; or ran out of food miles from anywhere?

Wilderness survival courses are offered across the United States and abroad to teach people how to survive in every type of environment and climate. The programs, which last from a few days to a month and cost between $60 and $1,000, are also available to special interest groups. Young people can learn about wildlife ecology and conservation while backpacking and camping through the Blue Ridge Mountains in North Carolina. Women are taught orienteering, first aid and leadership skills by women during hiking trips in central Oregon. Physicians can sign up for seminars on mountaineering medicine in the Sierras. Other programs concentrate on group behavior, leadership training and decision-making for businessmen and outdoor educators.

The courses include opportunities to participate in all types of adventurous activities. You can cross-country ski in Colorado while learning winter survival techniques, shelter construction and avalanche detection. In Alberta, Canada, you can hike and ride on horseback while learning tepee construction, leatherwork and identification of edible and medicinal plants. You can even try rock climbing, whitewater paddling and caving while learning emergency first aid in the mountains of North Carolina.

Most programs teach minimum-impact camping and emphasize ecological awareness. They also build self-reliance and confidence. So whether you learn rescue techniques and solo survival in the Sawtooth Mountains of Idaho, forage for edible fruits, roots and leaves in the Great Smoky Mountains of North Carolina or build an igloo in the Wind River Range of Wyoming, you will find a tough, but memorable experience. And you'll be better prepared to cope with the unexpected both at home and in the wilderness. □

Experienced snow campers are never without a shelter; this combination igloo and snow cave will house four people comfortably. (Keith Gunnar)

WILDERNESS SURVIVAL

CANADA

Alberta

Indian Wilderness Experience: Young people spend 12 days on the Stoney Indian Reserve located between Calgary and Banff. Here they learn traditional crafts including tepee construction and leather work. Horsemanship is emphasized, as well as self-reliance and wilderness survival techniques. Backpacking and horsepacking trips are made into the surrounding area, penetrating rugged terrain where participants may observe moose, deer, bighorn sheep, buffalo and wild horses. Special guides have been selected to instruct participants on Indian ways of coping with the wilderness, with an emphasis on minimum environmental impact. Campers learn how to identify edible and medicinal plants and how to recognize animal trails and weather indicators. **Cost:** $275 includes meals, accommodations, equipment, transportation to and from Calgary. **When:** June to September. **Contact:** Stoney Wilderness Center, Box 204, Exshaw, AB Canada T0L 0C0; phone (403)881-3049.

Yukon Territory

St. Elias Wilderness Exploration: Kluane National Park is the base for 2 weeks of backpacking and mountaineering in the Canadian wilderness. Following a bus trip from Whitehorse in the Yukon Territory to Kluane Lake, participants set up base camp. No specific itinerary is followed for the remainder of the trip so that participants may take advantage of terrain and weather conditions to plan their own expeditions. Possible day and overnight outings for mountaineers include ascents of nearby Mt. Wallace, Outpost Mountain and Mt. Cairns. Backpackers may hike around Vulcan Mountain by following a route along the Slims River Valley to the foot of the Kaskawulsh Glacier, continuing east along the Kaskawulsh River, north to the Jarvis River and back. During the excursions, there are opportunities to observe and photograph wildlife which inhabit the park, such as moose, Dall sheep and lynx. **Cost:** $530 includes guides, food, accommodations, transportation. **When:** August. **Contact:** Canatrek Mountain Expeditions, P.O. Box 1138, Banff, AB Canada T0L 0C0; phone (403)762-3143.

EUROPE

England

Drakes Island Adventures: Drakes Island, a 6-acre craggy outcrop in Plymouth Sound, is the setting for a week of varied outdoor activities for young people. Two instructional sessions are offered: a live-in week for those aged 12 to 17 and a non-residential one for those aged 8 to 17. Participants explore the island's rich history reflected in its fortress walls, gun sites and a network of tunnels once used for ammunition hauling. Primary activities include sailing small boats, rock climbing on a steep buttress that slopes out of the sea, canoeing off a tapered shoreline and learning marine biology through skin and scuba diving. As students' skills develop, they take short expeditions via sailboat and canoe to the many bays and coves in the sound. **When:** July, August. **Contact:** Drakes Island, Mayflower Centre, Central Park, Plymouth PL2 3DG, Great Britain; phone (0752)54112.

Lake District Adventure: Young men between the ages of 16 and 21 can take a 21- to 26-day course that covers a wide array of wilderness skills. The course, offered in the Lake District, teaches expedition planning, mountaineering, camping, lake and river canoeing, skiing and caving as well as mountain rescue and first aid. In addition, the winter courses include instruction in ice ax use, building snow caves and skiing. Individual responsibility is emphasized, and some attention is given to public speaking, group interaction, public service and artistic skills. The course culminates with a 3-day unaccompanied expedition in a group of 4, through the Lake District's high fells. **Cost:** $376 to $436, depending on length, includes food, equipment, instruction, transportation. **When:** Year-round. **Contact:** Outward Bound Ullswater, Ullswater, Cumbria, Great Britain; phone 08536.

Sweden

Wilderness Training: During a 3-week wilderness training seminar, participants prepare for a survival test in which groups of 4 set out on a pre-planned route using their survival skills and eating only what nature provides. The rations during the training period, consisting of fish, plants and berries, are gradually cut back in preparation for the test. Equipment is provided for the test, and instructors wait on call in Kvikkjokk. At the high mountain camp instruction addresses the more difficult tasks of emergency bivouacking, first aid and self-reliance. Training is adapted to each participant's needs. **Cost:** On request. **When:** August. **Contact:** IWT Survival, Fjallstation Kvikkjokk, 96045 Kvikkjokk, Sweden.

Switzerland

Alpine Educational Expedition: A comprehensive educational program in the Swiss Alps is designed for high school students. The 22-day backpacking expedition begins in the village of Lauterbrunnen with several days of preparation and orientation. Conditioning sessions and the use and care of equipment are taught, as well as first aid, trail safety, and map reading. En route hikers sleep in tents and study the geology and biology of the Alps. Each day's study may vary from how to choose a campsite to how to identify local flora and fauna to when and how to build a snow cave. Alpine farming, ecology, wilderness ethics and the history of mountain climbing are also discussed. Toward the end of the trek, there is intensive training in knot and rope handling, mountain safety and rescue, rock climbing, belaying, rappelling and the use of ice ax and crampons. After returning to Lauterbrunnen Valley, students attempt a climb of the Breithorn, a 12,000-foot peak. Though the climb is not hazardous, it chal-

A 2-day seminar in wilderness medical aid is offered in the southern Appalachians by Wolfcreek Wilderness; here students practice an emergency evacuation. (Wolfcreek Wilderness)

lenges the alpine skills learned during the trek. **Cost:** $1,095. **When:** July, August. **Contact:** Earth Journeys, 3400 Peachtree Rd., Atlanta, GA 30326, USA; phone (404)231-0073.

Wales

Staying Alive: A number of wilderness skills are taught over the course of 3 weeks on an Outward Bound program. Intended for ages 16 to 20, the course takes place in the Welsh countryside on land and water, culminating in a solo survival trip in the Dovey Forest. The course is based at a converted country house; from there, participants travel to the sea for experience with dinghies, cutters and canoes. On land, students learn about rescue and first aid, food planning, environmental awareness, wilderness travel, wild edibles and other aspects of outdoor life. The solo trip is planned and executed with a minimum of instructor supervision. Throughout the course discussions and debate help the students interpret and apply what they learn. Above average physical ability is not required. **Cost:** On request. **When:** On request. **Contact:** Outward Bound Wales, Rhowniar Centre, Tywyn Gwynedd LL36 9HT, Great Britain; phone 0654-710-521.

UNITED STATES

Alaska

Camping on Alaskan Peaks: Participants spend 2 weeks in the Arrigetch Peaks of Alaska's Brooks Range. Campers fly in to an established base camp, with an open itinerary allowing for day hikes or extended trips into the surrounding area. Much of the Brooks Range is still unexplored and untouched, and wildlife abounds, including wolves, lemmings, grizzly bears, caribou and bird life. Fall colors are already out, and opportunities for photography are ample. Participants fly out at trip's end. **Cost:** $620 includes transportation, meals, equipment, guide. **When:** August. **Contact:** Aurora Borealis Expeditions, 132 Eileen Circle, Burnsville, MN 55337, USA.

Alaska Traveler: A 4-week wilderness trek is offered in the Wrangell Mountains near the Alaska-Yukon border. Starting from the town of McCarthy, participants fly into a very remote area and set up their first camp among the high peaks and massive glaciers of the region. The purpose of the trek is to train participants in wilderness skills, including general mountaineering, advanced camping adaptations, logistics and expedition planning. The Wrangell area itself is also studied—group members learn about the region's history, flora and fauna. Conservation techniques and minimal-impact camping are also taught as the group treks through alpine forests, crosses mountain ranges and fords rivers. **Cost:** $975 includes food, instruction, group equipment, climbing gear. **When:** July. **Contact:** Hondo Rast & Co., P.O. Box 231, Hamilton, MT 59840, USA; phone (406)363-3440. *(M)*

Arctic Wildlife Camps: Wilderness youth camps are located on the southeastern slope of the Brooks Range, near the Arctic National Wildlife Range. This area is without human-made structures, roads, trails or vehicles. A base camp and 8 permanent outlying camps ranging in distance from 2 to 18 miles from the base are open to youths 9 years old and up for 10 days or more. Camp staff and leaders train and assist campers in wilderness travel and living, which may include plant and animal identification, pack dog handling, mountain navigation, arctic ecosystems and guiding techniques. An 85-mile canoe trip on an Alaskan river is available for more experienced campers. The region, which has never been permanently inhabited by people, is rich in wildlife. **Cost:** $70 a day includes all expenses upon arrival at base camp. **When:** June to September. **Contact:** Wilderness Wildlife Camps, Frontier Lodge, Star Rt., Box 60177, Fairbanks, AK 99701, USA. *(M)*

Arkansas

Ozark Wilderness Leadership Seminar: A 10-day course is designed for people interested in developing skills in outdoor education. Participants learn such things as group problem solving, wilderness camping, environmental ethics, rock craft, river canoeing and first aid. Discussions are held on a wide variety of topics, including experiential philosophy. The course is taught in the remote hills and streams of the Arkansas and Missouri Ozarks. No previous experience is necessary for participation, and enrollment is limited to 16. **Cost:** $150 plus equipment. **When:** June. **Contact:** Touch of

Nature Environmental Center, Southern Illinois University, Carbondale, IL 62901, USA.

California

Tahoe Wilderness Course: An intensive 14-day course in wilderness leadership is offered to small groups in the Tahoe National Forest, part of the Sierra Nevada Range. An experienced climber and guide provides instruction in outdoor skills and arranges special situations for testing participants' abilities. Activities include climbing high peaks, finding routes and leading the group through the wilderness. Emphasis is placed on low environmental impact. The minimum age is 13. **Cost:** $280 includes equipment, transportation, food, instruction. **When:** July, August. **Contact:** Mountain People School, 157 Oak Spring Dr., San Anselmo, CA 94960, USA; phone (415)457-3664.

Mountain Medicine Seminar: A 3-day course in the Sierras is presented specifically for mountaineering physicians and leaders of expeditions and climbing groups. Instruction is intense and progressive with emphasis on technique and theory. The course structure includes lectures, discussions and demonstrations with time reserved for bouldering, climbing and enjoying the nearby hot springs. Participants who wish to spend more time actively climbing may combine the mountain medicine seminar with a 5-day basic or advanced rock climbing course. The seminar is limited to 35 participants. A syllabus is available upon request. **Cost:** $185 includes equipment and some meals. **When:** May. **Contact:** Palisade School of Mountaineering, P.O. Box 694, Bishop, CA 93514, USA; phone (714)935-4330.

Colorado

Tennessee Pass Winter Survival: Eighty hours of instruction are offered during an 8-day cross-country skiing and winter survival camp in central Colorado. Skiing techniques are taught as trip members traverse the Collegiate Range near Leadville, and a base camp is established in Tennessee Pass; special cold-weather tents and equipment are used for camping at the 10,500-foot site. Under the supervision of 4 experienced instructors, participants learn winter survival techniques such as shelter construction, detection of avalanche hazards, route finding and medical treatment of frostbite and hypothermia. Clothing, equipment, pacing and rhythmic breathing are also discussed as part of the winter back-country travel course. A certificate of training is issued to each person completing the course. University credit is available. **Cost:** $178 includes instructors, special equipment. **When:** January. **Contact:** Iowa Mountaineers, 30 Prospect Pl., P.O. Box 163, Iowa City, IA 52240, USA; phone (319)337-7163.

Outdoor Adventure Courses: Seven-day courses provide an intensive introduction to the techniques and practice of technical rock climbing, whitewater river rafting and high alpine mountaineering. Instruction in rock climbing encompasses all aspects from basic knot tying and belaying to steep face climbing and rappelling. Two-day rafting trips on the Arkansas River offer a rigorous introduction to paddling through fast, narrow rapids. The mountaineering expedition attempts to scale a 14,000-foot peak in the Crestone area of the Sangre de Cristo Mountains. Each course is based out of a primitive 800-acre working ranch located at 9,000 feet. Participants stay in tents or large tepees and are expected to share cooking and camping responsibilities. Offered weekly throughout the summer, each course is limited to 12 participants to maintain a staff-to-student ratio of 1 to 4. Each member is asked to specify personal expectations and goals for the course; progress in meeting these goals is monitored by the instructors and shared with other participants. Whenever possible, responsibility for the planning and organization of activities is handled by a mutual decision-making process. **Cost:** $250 includes instruction, food, equipment. **When:** June to August. **Contact:** Outdoor Leadership Training Seminars, 2220 Birch St., Denver, CO 80207, USA; phone (303)333-7831. *(M)*

Wilderness Photography: Travelers develop skills in nature photography on trips of 5, 10 or 23 days in primitive areas. The journeys are designed to combine studies of the environment with backpacking, survival training and photography. Other possible experiences include whitewater rafting, caving, mountaineering and rock climbing. The 10-day expedition includes 2 days of organization and training at the beginning, then a few days of processing and printing at the end. All courses are geared to each participant's level of experience. All group equipment, including a darkroom setup, is provided; participants must supply their own photographic equipment and basic clothing. **Cost:** $150 for 5 days, $325 for 10 days, $625 for 23 days. **When:** By arrangement. **Contact:** Wilderness Encounter, 720 Grand Ave., Glenwood Springs, CO 81601, USA; phone (303)945-8365. *(M)*

Idaho

Mountain Survival Course: All aspects of mountaineering and outdoor survival are covered in a 21-day course in the Sawtooth Mountains. Skills included are snow and rock climbing, conservation, compass and map reading and search and rescue techniques. Stu-

On an Outward Bound course in Idaho's Sawtooth Range, a student has a dual confrontation: with a steep rock face, and with his own limitations. (Northwest Outward Bound)

dents travel in remote, primitive country without their instructor, sometimes eating only what they can forage from the wilderness. Average strength is required, but participants should be in good health. **Cost:** $600 includes transportation from Sun Valley, food, some equipment. **When:** June, July, August. **Contact:** EE-DA-HOW Mountaineering, P.O. Box 207, Ucon, ID 83454, USA; phone (208)523-9276.

Wilderness Skills Courses in the Rockies: Ten- to 24-day mountaineering, backpacking and rock climbing courses are conducted within the Big Horn Crags portion of the Idaho Primitive Area, a region of high alpine lakes rimmed by precipitous cliffs, crags and spires. Based at a camp on Panther Creek, students in the 10-day course become familiar with techniques of food preparation, equipment organization, mountain hiking, navigation, basic rock climbing and cross-country travel among the 9,000-foot summits of the primitive area. During the 18-day course students become familiar with the use of chocks, nuts and natural runners as a means of increasing their ability to use natural features in climbing situations. Participants who enroll in the 24-day course study every aspect of backpacking and mountaineering. In the final phase of the course, students split up into small groups which plan and execute their own expeditions. **Cost:** $350 for 10 days, $550 for 18 days, $700 for 24 days includes most wilderness gear, food, course tuition, transportation from Salmon to base camp. **When:** June to August. **Con-**

tact: Horizons Unlimited, P.O. Box 2061, Salmon, ID 83467, USA; phone (208)756-3844. ***(M)***

Minnesota

Lake Minnetonka Winter Camping: A weekend adventure, designed to familiarize participants with the basics of winter camping and travel, offers novices a chance to learn cross-country skiing and to drive a dog team. The group departs from the Twin Cities to camp on a wilderness island in Lake Minnetonka, Minnesota. Members are taught wilderness survival, the basics of ski touring, how to use snowshoes and dogsledding techniques. Instruction is given by experienced guides. Camp meals are shared in tepees, and evenings can be spent discussing winter lore or skiing by moonlight. Families are welcome if the children are over 13. Groups are limited to 14 people. **Cost:** $56 plus transportation includes meals, instruction, all major equipment except skis. **When:** January, February. **Contact:** Lynx Track Winter Travel, 5375 Eureka Rd., Excelsior, MN 55331, USA; phone (612)474-5190.

New Hampshire

Presidential Hiking: A variety of terrain ranging from high treeless tundra to forested mountains provides young hikers with a 27-day outdoor experience in the area of the Presidential and the Franconias ranges. Hikers are exposed to remote wilderness areas including Mahoosuc and Kilkenny and receive instruction in campcraft, orienteering, natural history, outdoor cooking and low-impact camping methods. Sensitivity to the fragile mountain ecosystem is emphasized, as well as acceptance of physical challenge and group cooperation. **Cost:** On request. **When:** July, August. **Contact:** Interlocken, Hillsboro Upper Village, NH 03244, USA; phone (603)478-3202.

New York

Art and Adventure: An unusual program offers reading and study of wilderness-related literature followed by 5, 10 or 21 days of actual field experience in wilderness living and survival. The course begins with substantial independent reading of American classics bearing on the wilderness, followed by group discussion and review. Students then gather in small groups under a naturalist/instructor to learn techniques in wilderness orientation, survival, river fording, rock climbing, mountaineering and other skills. The course takes place either in the Adirondacks or the Colorado Rockies; a Canadian version is also offered, involving Canadian reading material and field experience in northern Ontario. College credit is available. **Cost:** $185 to $625, depending on length and location of trip, includes tuition, equipment, transportation, food, instruction. **When:** June to October. **Contact:** Adirondack Institute, 8 Dana Hall, Skidmore College, Saratoga Springs, NY 12866, USA.

North Carolina

Blue Ridge Backpacking: Young people ages 13 to 16 learn about wildlife ecology and conservation and gain backpacking and camping skills as they hike through the Blue Ridge Mountains near Hendersonville. The 12-day program begins with an orientation meeting at a conference center in Hendersonville; participants can make arrangements to be met at the Asheville Airport or Hendersonville bus station. The 40- to 45-mile backpacking trip includes travel on trails and back roads as well as cross-country hiking. Three leaders accompany each trip, with a maximum of 18 participants. **Cost:** $275 includes food, guides; backpacks and ground pads may be rented. **When:** June to August. **Contact:** Environmental Adventures, National Wildlife Federation, 1412 16th St. NW, Washington, DC 20036, USA; phone (703)790-4363.

Encountering the Wilderness: Twelve participants work as a team to integrate mind and body through the medium of the wilderness during backcountry experiences of 2 to 6 days. Learning by doing, participants receive instruction in backpacking, use and care of equipment, sanitation, map and compass reading, food planning and preparation, dressing for the environment, first aid and natural history. On 4-day courses students learn rappelling and expedition planning as well. The 6-day course includes all of the above plus instruction in rock climbing. Participants experience personal growth through graduated physical challenges, group discussions, problem solving, deep relaxation, sensory awareness exercises, journal keeping, new games, initiative training and a solo experience in the wilderness. Certain courses are designed exclusively for teenagers. **Cost:** $64 to $155 includes instruction, transportation, food, equipment. **When:** June to August. **Contact:** Jesse Brown's Expeditions, 2843 Eastway Dr., Charlotte, NC 28205, USA; phone (704)568-2152.

Adventure Education: A wide variety of wilderness courses ranging from 5 to 23 days are offered for those interested in personal growth. Winter courses are conducted in the Florida Everglades. Sessions are also offered 9 months a year in the North Carolina mountains, which contain the highest peaks in the East. Activities include backpacking, rock climbing, orienteering, solo physical training, service projects, whitewater paddling, caving and emergency first aid. **Cost:** $680 for 23 days; some scholarship aid is available. **When:** Year-round. **Contact:** North Carolina Outward Bound School, P.O. Box 817, Morganton, NC 28655, USA; phone (704)437-6112.

Edible Plants Training: Based in the Cataloochee Cove area of the Smoky Mountains, a 4-day program of leisurely day hikes concentrates on the edible fruits, roots, flowers, leaves and mushrooms of the area. Instruction is provided in recognizing, gathering, preparing and using the foods and medications which grow wild. The ideal time for hunting nature's foods coincides with the end of the nesting season, so the time is good for bird watching as well. Moving from lower elevation forests to a high ridge top with Canadian zone forests of spruce and fir, participants may observe variations in flora and fauna. **Cost:** $60 includes meals, tents, camping fees. **When:** August. **Contact:** Wilderness Southeast, Rt. 3, Box 619 AA, Savannah, GA 31406, USA; phone (912)355-8008. *(M)*

Oregon

Northwest Mountain Trips: Guided ascents of Mt. Washington, Three Fingered Jack, the Three Sisters, Mt. Hood, Mt. St. Helens and Mt. Adams are among the alpine outings offered for both beginning and experienced climbers. Winter survival classes on Mt. Hood cover snowshoeing, igloo and snow cave construction and mountain rescue techniques. Backpacking trips featuring glacial travel and exploration are available into any of the region's wilderness areas. **Cost:** $30 a day for climbs; other costs on request. **When:** Year-round. **Contact:** Johann Mountain Guides, P.O. Box 2334, Lincoln City, OR 97367, USA; phone (503)996-3232. *(M)*

Off the Map: Women backpackers explore a remote, arid mountain region of central Oregon on a week-long trip. Participants rely on their compasses and observation skills, as detailed maps of the area do not yet exist. The trip is strenuous, with 8 to 12 miles of hiking daily, so previous backpacking experience is required. A nonprofit group seeking to teach women outdoor skills in a non-competitive atmosphere sponsors the trip, and the group leader teaches participants wilderness survival skills. Dinners during the trip are 1-pot meals featuring whole grains and complementary proteins. The trip departs from Zigzag, Oregon. **Cost:** $200 includes food, camping equipment, group leader. **When:** August. **Contact:** Keep Listening, Box 446, Sandy, OR 97055, USA; phone (503)622-3895.

Winter Mountaineering in the Wallowas: Cross-country skiing and winter mountainteering are taught in a 20-day survival course in northeastern Oregon. The course begins at Catherine Creek in the Wallowa Mountains with instruction in cross-country skiing and snow camping. Students build igloos and snow caves and learn to use maps and compasses. Then using the skills they have acquired, group members climb one of the peaks in the range. Other features of the course are a solo— where the student is left alone with minimal food and basic shelter— and a day

In Oregon's Three Sisters Wilderness, a group of hikers sets out on an Outward Bound survival course. (Northwest Outward Bound)

of local community service. The course concludes with a 3-day cross-country ski expedition with minimal instructor supervision. No experience is required. **Cost:** $610 from Pendleton, Oregon. **When:** January, February, March. **Contact:** The Northwest Outward Bound School, 0110 SW Bancroft, Portland, OR 97201, USA; phone (503)243-1993. ***(M)***

Utah

Survival Training: One phase of a 24-day seminar emphasizes survival in the wilderness. Participants are taken to an area where they are taught survival techniques. Basic skills acquired during the training include first aid, goal setting, meal planning and solo backpacking. Another phase of the program emphasizes personal success experiences: opening interpersonal communication, building self-esteem and decision making. **Cost:** On request. **When:** By arrangement. **Contact:** Outdoor Seminar Retreats, Box 1301, Salt Lake City, UT 84101, USA; phone (801)355-0110.

Vermont

Multi-Mountain Backpacking: A variety of backpacking programs is available for young people ages 11 to 18 in the Green Mountains of Vermont, the White Mountains of New Hampshire and the Adirondack Mountains of New York. The trips, lasting from 1 to 3 weeks, concentrate on how to live and travel comfortably out of doors. A 2-week program begins with a 4-day training session on Killington Mountain, then continues with 9 days of climbing the rocky summits of the Adirondack and Green mountains or exploring low-lying bogs and swamps. Hikers study nature and mountaineering techniques on a 19-day trip which includes wild food days, mountaintop bivouacs and a solo hike. Adults and families are invited to participate in a 1-week program which includes a 5-day expedition into a selected mountain area after 2 days of training. It is designed to introduce beginning hikers to the mountains and to provide them with enough experience to continue backpacking on their own. **Cost:** $260 for 2 weeks, $345 for 3 weeks includes meals, guides; equipment included only on the 2-week trip; $170 for adults, $135 for children on family outings includes meals, leaders; $35 for equipment package. **When:** June to August. **Contact:** Killington Adventure, Killington, VT 05751, USA; phone (802)422-3333.

Washington

Mountaineering Leadership Course: Based at a high camp in the North Cascades, students learn skills which enable them to introduce others to the mountain environment. The 5-day course includes instruction in minimum impact backpacking, climbing ethics, leadership responsibilities, first aid and basic mountaineering skills which make for safe mountain travel. Rock and snow climbing as well as an overnight hike are also included. All the activities are designed to show how to bring a group into the wilderness with as little environmental damage as possible. Groups meet in Mazama on the North Cascades Highway before heading into the mountains. **Cost:** $200 includes group equipment, meals, transportation from Mazama, instructors. **When:** June, July, September. **Contact:** Liberty Bell Alpine Tours, Mazama, WA 98833, USA; phone (509)996-2250.

(M)

North Cascades Mountain Course: An 8-day course teaches mountaineering in the area around Silver Star Mountain in the North Cascades. Designed for people over 21 who lack the time to take the longer "standard" course, the program is rigorous but physically less demanding than the standard course; lighter packs are used and less hiking is done. The course covers campcraft, backpacking, map and compass navigation, rock climbing, rappelling and snow travel. Participants make use of these skills on a 24-hour solo with minimal supplies and an ascent of a North Cascade peak. **Cost:** $300. **When:** June to August. **Contact:** The Northwest Outward Bound School, 0110 SW Bancroft, Portland, OR 97201, USA; phone (503)243-1993. ***(M)***

West Virginia

Survival Study in the Dolly Sods: A wilderness school taking place in the Dolly Sods Wilderness, part of the Monongahela National Forest, teaches a group of 12 people ages 14 and up a wide variety of camping and mountaineering skills. The course lasts 10 days and originates in Cleveland, Ohio. Rigorous and comprehensive, the course curriculum includes climbing techniques, map and compass use, leadership and "followership," wilderness cooking, conservation, survival, trip planning, weather forecasting and first aid; strenuous hiking is involved. Temperatures can range from 80°F in daytime to 20°F at night as participants travel through an unspoiled area inhabited by deer, beavers, squirrels and numerous other animals, as well as a wide variety of birds. Students have the option of bringing their own food and gear or having them supplied by the outfitter. No previous experience is needed. **Cost:** $125 includes instruction, technical equipment, transportation from Cleveland; $20 for gear, $55 for food. **When:** July. **Contact:** Wilderness Trails, 728 Prospect Ave., Cleveland, OH 44115, USA; phone (216)696-5222.

Wyoming

Snow Studies: Participants are offered 2 different courses in avalanche research and winter mountain conditions. The first is a 4-day backcountry course for ski touring enthusiasts which takes place both in the field and in the classroom. Topics discussed include mountain snowpack, avalanche dynamics and characteristics, terrain analysis, mountain weather, wet snow, rescue and forecasting. Field work consists of slab recognition, identification of weak layers and route finding. The second course is offered at Jackson Hole and lasts 5 days. It emphasizes ski area forecasting and stability evaluation. Time is divided equally between classroom and field activities. **Cost:** $140 and $190 includes course tuition and some technical equipment. **When:** January, February. **Contact:** American Avalanche Institute, Box 308, Wilson, WY 83014, USA; phone (307)733-3315.

Ski Touring and Winter Mountaineering Course: Fifteen-day courses are offered in the Wind River, Teton, Absaroka and Snake River ranges. During a typical course participants spend a week moving up to the timberline while learning equipment care and handling. During this period there is instruction in snow camping, ski technique, ski waxing, avalanche safety, snow theory, cold-weather physiology and winter ecology. At higher elevations members learn shelter con-

A hiker studies a map of Wyoming's high country, under the supervision of a National Outdoor Leadership School instructor. (NOLS)

struction including building igloos and communal snow caves. Weather permitting, the course attempts a nontechnical peak ascent. An extended 21-day course is also offered for the serious student. Minimum age requirements for all courses are 16. **Cost:** On request. **When:** Seasonal. **Contact:** National Outdoor Leadership School, Box AA, Lander, WY 82520, USA; phone (307)332-4381.

Yellowstone Survival Course: Passing silently through forests shrouded in rising steam from underground fumaroles, cross-country skiers can well understand why Yellowstone was holy ground to the Indians. For 15 days participants in a winter travel and survival course explore the region and its natural features, which range from Rocky Mountain peaks to lowland geysers and thermal mud springs. Emphasizing long-distance cross-country skiing, the course provides instruction in technique, waxing, snow physics, cold-weather physiology and avalanche safety. Course topics also include igloo and snow cave construction, expedition planning and emergency procedures. All instruction stresses ecological awareness and minimal impact camping techniques. For the exceptionally hardy there is an extended 21-day version of the course. **Cost:** $425 includes instruction, guides, food, group equipment. **When:** December to March. **Contact:** National Outdoor Leadership School, Box AA, Lander, WY 82520, USA; phone (307)332-4381.

Wind River Winter Trip: A course primarily designed for experienced warm-weather campers who wish to extend their experience to winter camping and travel makes a 1- to 2-week expedition into the Wind

River Range. The mountains present remote regions of frozen lakes, unbroken powder and abundant wildlife. Instruction is offered in shelters, including igloos, tents and snow caves; snowshoes, skis and high alpine touring; food, stoves and cooking; first aid; and navigation and expedition planning. Participants should be in good physical shape. **Cost:** $185 to $365, depending on length of trip includes food, all equipment, transportation, instructor/guide. **When:** January to March. **Contact:** Skinner Brothers Mountaineering, Box B, Pinedale, WY 82941, USA; phone (307)367-2270. *(M)*

Wilderness School: A month in the Wyoming wilderness provides extensive instruction and experience for children 10 years and older in survival, horsemanship, backpacking, rock climbing and water travel. Survival skills covered include sanitation, conservation, fire building, emergency shelter construction, fishing, trapping, cooking and identifying edible plants, with these skills tested in a controlled survival situation. All students have their own horse for the month and are instructed in the basics of horse handling and care. Backpacking equipment and techniques are covered as well as map reading, first aid, and search and rescue. Beginning rock climbing is offered to acquaint students with the basics of mountaineering, with an emphasis on safety measures. Finally, a water travel session is held at Green River Camp, with instruction in personal flotation, raft building, river crossing and related skills. Students reside in tepees during the sessions. **Cost:** $850 includes food, all equipment, instruction, transportation. **When:** June, July. **Contact:** Skinner Brothers Mountaineering, Box B, Pinedale, WY 82941, USA; phone (307)367-2270. *(M)*

RESOURCES

Clubs and Associations

Canadian Orienteering Foundation
P.O. Box 6206, Terminal
Toronto 1, ON Canada M5W 1P6

Larry Dean Olsen Survival Assn.
Box 1301
Salt Lake City, UT 84101, USA

New England Orienteering Club
c/o Bengtsson
Garrison House Ln.
Sudbury, MA 01776, USA

Orienteering Services USA
Box 547
La Porte, IN 46350, USA
Phone (219)326-7462

Rainbow Camp and
Wilderness Survival School
Anaconda, MT 59711, USA

Survival International
36 Craven St.
London WC2N 5NG, Great Britain

United States Orienteering Assn.
933 N. Kenmore St., Suite 317
Arlington, VA 22201, USA

United States Orienteering Federation
P.O. Box 500
Athens, OH 45701, USA

Air Adventures

AIR ADVENTURES

From the days of pedal planes with flapping wings to the Wright brothers and the daredevil barnstormers, man has dreamed of flight. The twentieth century spawned every type of flying machine imaginable, from blimps and hang gliders to flying wings and rockets. Charles Lindbergh flew solo across the Atlantic, Neil Armstrong left his footprints on the moon. Now it is possible for *you* to share in the joy of flight, whether strapped beneath the nylon wing of a hang glider, suspended from a colorful hot air balloon or diving in free-fall at 120 miles an hour.

The best thing about air adventures is that you needn't travel far or spend a great deal of money to participate. Small craft airports across the country offer introductory sailplane flights that put you in the cockpit for as little as $20 to $30. A few hours of instruction for $50 to $80 enable you to hurl yourself out of a plane at 2,700 feet to experience the thrills of parachuting. Hour-long hot air balloon flights range from $45 to $90; a first flight hang glider course costs as little as $49. You can even ride in the Goodyear blimp for $8 and parasail over the beaches of Acapulco for $7.

Inexpensive power plane flights are also available worldwide. Get a bird's-eye view of Diamond Head, the Haleakala Volcano and the barren wastelands of Kahoolawe during a day-long flight to 8 Hawaiian islands. See Mt. McKinley the easy way—by plane—on 1- and 2-hour flights over Mt. McKinley National Park. Swoop through 130 miles of the Grand Canyon on hour-long scenic flights. Hover over the beaches and jungles of Sri Lanka in a 4-seater helicopter or flightsee over the ice fields of Mt. Cook National Park in New Zealand.

If you are hooked on hot air ballooning, you can join a 2-week trip through France during the grape harvest, float over wildlife in Kenya or earn an aeronaut's license in a combination ground and flight school in California. Soaring courses in the French Alps and throughout the United States offer instruction in competition and aerobatic techniques. From your first static line parachute jump you can advance to barrel rolls, back loops and group free-fall formations.

These opportunities and hundreds more offer people of all ages and professions a chance to fly, glide, float and spin through the air in ways only dreamed about 100 years ago. And who knows? In another decade or two it might be possible to board a space shuttle for the moon or live in a space station. □

Shortly after dawn a group of balloonists hangs poised over the California countryside ready for takeoff. At a signal the tethering lines will be released allowing the craft to float free. (Val Hawes)

BALLOONING

AFRICA

Kenya

Ballooning above Masai Mara: A panorama of the plains in southwest Kenya is afforded during an hour-long balloon flight above the Masai Mara Game Reserve just to the east of the Tanzanian border. Often unaware of the balloon's presence, herds of giraffe, zebra, and wildebeeste can be seen grazing throughout the early morning flight. There are no modern obstructions such as buildings or telephone wires, which makes for a breathtaking view and wonderful photography. The two 5-passenger balloons are followed by a ground crew in 2 vehicles. Participants can stay at the Keekorok Lodge in the Masai Mara Reserve. Following the flight, a champagne breakfast is served to the passengers. **Cost:** $125 a person. **When:** July to March. **Contact:** Balloon Safaris Ltd., Box 47557, Nairobi, Kenya; phone 22860.

EUROPE

France

Ballooning over the Wine Country:

In the Loire Valley, a balloon is prepared for launch at the Domaine de Selliac. One-hour flights over the chateau country of France are offered by the Bombard Society. (Buddy Bombard)

Participants travel by motorcoach and hot air balloon through the regions of Champagne, Burgundy and the Loire Valley for 2 weeks during the grape harvest. Balloons are launched from town centers, medieval castles and historic chateaux for 1-hour flights covering 2 to 15 miles. Group members alternate riding in 2-person, professionally piloted balloons with riding in chase vehicles to meet balloonists with champagne as they land; participants may choose to remain on the ground throughout the trip. Members stay at hotels along the way. **Cost:** $2,689 includes round-trip transportation from New York, meals, accommodations. **When:** September, October. **Contact:** The Bombard Society, Suite 1823, 30 E. 42nd St., New York, NY 10017, USA; phone (212)697-6230 or toll-free (800)223-7733.

UNITED STATES

California

Ballooning above the Vineyards: Unobstructed panoramas of the vineyards in California's Napa Valley are offered during balloon flights lasting an hour or more. Starting in the early morning, the balloon bags are filled with hot air and readied for lift-off by 3 commercial instructors. Piloted by an FAA-certified instructor, the balloon skims the vines and climbs to the clouds. Landings are attended by a waiting crew which follows the balloon's path. Longer flights are concluded with a picnic brunch. Each of the 3 balloons can carry 4 passengers. **Cost:** $50 to $70. **When:** Year-round. **Contact:** Adventures Aloft, P.O. Box 2500, Yountville, CA 94599, USA; phone (707)255-8688.

Napa Valley Champagne Flight: Beginning at sunrise, participants help launch a hot air balloon for an hour flight over California's wine country. The aeronaut guides the balloon over vineyards and farmland using "wind sense" and adjusting altitude by changing the air temperature inside the balloon. After a gentle descent to a field or pasture, balloonists are joined by the ground crew for a champagne breakfast. Certified instruction is also offered. **Cost:** On request. **When:** Year-round. **Contact:** Aerostat Renaissance, P.O. Box 3536, Napa, CA 94558, USA; phone (707)255-6356. ***(M)***

San Francisco Ballooning: Demonstration flights take participants over the countryside surrounding the San Francisco Bay area. The balloon lifts off shortly after dawn and floats for an hour or so to the landing site, where the touchdown is celebrated with a champagne toast. The cost of the ride may be credited toward the purchase of a balloon or a course of flight instruction. Flight instruction emphasizing ecological aeronautics is available for an FAA commercial or private pilot certificate. Nearly every month balloon rallies and activities are held to promote the sport. **Cost:** $150 for 2 for the demonstration ride includes breakfast; $650 to $1,500 and up for flight instruction. **When:** Year-round. **Contact:** Balloon Excelsior, Inc., 1241 High St., Oakland, CA 94601, USA; phone (415)261-4222.

Colorado

Wilderness by Land and Air: Travelers spend 6 days hiking and ballooning through the La Garita Wilderness of south-central Colorado. After 1 night at a balloon resort in Del Norte, participants journey deep into the wilderness by jeep and then by foot. Then 3 days are spent wandering through the wilderness area at a leisurely pace. The guides instruct hikers on various aspects of survival training as progress is made along the trail. The group is met on the fourth day by balloonists who take members out of the mountains and high over the San Luis Valley some 10 miles downwind. A chase team meets the balloons as they touch down, and the group drives back to Del Norte for a final afternoon and evening of relaxation at the resort. The ballooning takes place only in good weather, which occurs most of the season. **Cost:** $410 to $430 includes lodging, meals, gear, guides. **When:** June, September. **Contact:** American Wilderness Experience, P.O. Box 1486A, Boulder, CO 80306, USA; phone (303)444-2632. ***(M)***

San Luis Valley Balloon Ranch: A 140-acre ranch in southern Colorado combines hot air balloon trips and lessons with more conventional activities. Located 200 miles from Denver, the ranch is surrounded by the Rio Grande National Forest and

Spectacular early morning or sunset balloon flights over Wisconsin's Green Lake can be taken from the Heidel House Resort. (The Heidel House)

the Great Sand Dunes in the Rocky Mountains. Participants may enjoy excellent ballooning in the open spaces, and the dependable weather conditions of the area are well-suited for observation, chase and easy recovery. The ranch features a launch area, balloon school, training site and radio-equipped chase vehicles to facilitate hour-long flights. In summer, guests may also river raft, hike, ride horses, fish and play tennis; in winter, guests may ice skate, snowmobile and downhill and cross-country ski. The ranch also offers accommodations and meals. **Cost:** $45 for 1-hour flights, $85 for introductory course, $800 for complete certification course with 10 hours of flight time. **When:** May to February. **Contact:** The Balloon Ranch, Star Rt., Box 41, Del Norte, CO 81132, USA; phone (303)754-2533. ***(M)***

Florida

Blimp Ride over Miami: A unique opportunity is available for a half-hour ascent in the 160-foot-long *Mayflower*, popularly known as the Goodyear Blimp. Ascents are available on a day-to-day basis from its winter home in Miami. Passengers ride in the small gondola, viewing the world from altitudes of 1,000 to 3,000 feet and cruising at 35 miles an hour. A maximum of 6 persons a flight is taken aloft, with reservations made the day of the flight. Trips may be temporarily suspended when the airship is required for special network television or other engagements. **Cost:** $8 adults, $5 children under 12. **When:** November to April. **Contact:** Goodyear Airship Operator, 950 MacArthur Causeway, Watson Island, Miami, FL 33123, USA; phone (305)358-7644.

Michigan

The Buoyant Arts: Charter flights and instruction in the art of ballooning are available from a balloon center in eastern Michigan. Two-passenger flights that cover about 8 miles can be arranged for departure at either sunrise or sunset. Ten-week ground school classes in ballooning techniques and the theory of aerostation are offered in conjunction with Oakland University's Division of Continuing Education. Aeronauts can obtain a Ballooning Certificate by taking 10 hours of flight training and 15 hours of pre-flight and post-flight instruction. The center also sponsors a balloon club for pilots and ground crews. **Cost:** $95 for flight; $1,250 for certification instruction. **When:** By arrangement. **Contact:** Highamerica,

P.O. Box 87, Rochester, MI 48063, USA; phone (313)852-0666.

North Carolina

Ballooning over the Smokies: The forested wilderness of the Great Smoky Mountains on the border of Tennessee and North Carolina is viewed from a balloon during a 2-hour flight. Passengers are picked up at their motel or chalet and transported to the take-off site near historic Gatlinburg, Tennessee. After a briefing on inflation, take-off, flight and landing procedures, a maximum of 4 riders is taken aloft in the large gondola. During the flight, if conditions permit, each passenger is permitted to fly the balloon. The view of the countryside is beautiful and photography is encouraged. **Cost:** $260 for 4 persons. **When:** June to September. **Contact:** Balloon Safaris, Rt. 6, English Mountain, Sevierville, TN 37862, USA.

Certified instruction as well as scenic flights over California's wine country are offered by Aerostat Renaissance. (Aerostat Renaissance)

Oregon

Northwest Hot Air: Participants learn the art of ballooning from experienced instructors, both on the ground and in the air. Three basic types of courses are offered. The first is a series of earthbound classes held at Portland State University and an inn at Beaverton. The second option is in-the-air training done in either privately supplied or rented aircraft. The final course offering is in pre- and postflight instruction and involves practical instruction covering the material from both the ground school classes and in-the-air training classes. Participants may also serve as the ground crew for the flights of others. **Cost:** From $5 an hour to $150 an hour. **When:** April to July. **Contact:** Northwest Aviation, P.O. Box 468, Portland, OR 97207, USA; phone (503)228-0089.

Virginia

Ballooning over Farmlands: Demonstration balloon flights are available near historic Manassas, Virginia. Rides depart in early morning or early evening for 1 to 2 hours over scenic Virginia farmlands, ending with a champagne celebration. Flight training is also offered and consists of complete ground school and 10 hours of flight time. **Cost:** $200 for a demonstration ride, $1,500 for training (2 people).

One- to 2-hour balloon flights take off near Manassas, Virginia, and float over rolling countryside and historic estates and mansions. (Blue Ridge Balloon Port)

When: By arrangement. **Contact:** Blue Ridge Balloon Port, 11010 Bristow Rd., Bristow, VA 22013, USA; phone (703)361-1690.

Washington

Aloft in the Northwest: Hot air balloons fly 1 or 2 persons over the verdant landscape of the Skagit Valley. Lasting 1 to 1½ hours, flights take place near Mt. Vernon and are followed by a champagne picnic beside the Skagit River. Flight training is also available, and the cost of an introductory flight may be applied toward ballooning course tuition. **Cost:** $150 per flight. **When:** By arrangement. **Contact:** Aloft Ltd., P.O. Box 15628, Seattle, WA 98115, USA; phone (206)362-5040.

Wisconsin

Hot Air over Water: Participants may view the sunset while aloft in a 70-foot hot air balloon. One- and 2-hour flights glide along over Green Lake, Lake Puckaway, Little and Big Twin lakes, Puchyan River and Fox River. Flights of varying duration are also offered, including a morning champagne flight. Piloted by licensed commercial aeronauts, the flights include a guaranteed pickup at the point of landing. Lodging is provided in a Swiss-style chalet in the town of Green Lake. **Cost:** $85 includes return vehicle after balloon transportation. **When:** On request. **Contact:** Heidel House, P.O. Box 537, Green Valley, WI 54941, USA; phone (414)294-3344.

RESOURCES

Clubs and Associations

Balloon Club of America
P.O. Box 114
Swarthmore, PA 19081, USA

Balloon Federation of America
2516 Hiawatha Dr. NE
Albuquerque, NM 87112, USA
Phone (505)298-5284

Federation Aeronautique International
Siege Social a Paris
6, rue Galilee
Paris, France

International Society
of Balloonpost Specialists
Statenlaan 2a
The Hague, Netherlands

Les Femmes de l'Air
535 S. Crane
Independence, MO 63124, USA

SOARING

EUROPE

England

Catching the Updraft: A 6-day gliding course is offered to both youths and adults at the Lakes Gliding Club airfield. Flying is done in T49 Capstan 2-seaters, with launches made by aerotow or, in the event of high winds, by winches on the ground. Flights afford views of the countryside around Barrow in Furness, on the coast of the Irish Sea. Courses begin on Sunday evenings and end the following Saturday, allowing make-up time on Saturday for flying time lost due to bad weather during the week. **Cost:** $170 includes dormitory accommodations, meals, instructor, equipment. **When:** July, August. **Contact:** YHA Adventure Holidays, Trevelyan House, St. Albans, Herts., Great Britain; phone St. Albans 55215.

France

Soaring over the Alps: Chamonix in Upper Savoy marks the starting point of a 2-week training course in glider flying. Take-offs are from slopes such as Tignes, Meribel, La Plagne, La Clusaz and Alpes d'Huez. Flights range from Plan Praz to Plaine des Praz in 7 to 10 minutes, and from Grands Montets to Les Chosalets in 13 to 20 minutes. Half-day beginners' courses take place at Chamonix every afternoon, and complete training courses are also available. **Cost:** $24 for half-day course; $200 for complete training course; $495 for 2-week package includes room, board. **When:** Summer. **Contact:** Hobby Voyage, 8 rue de Milan, 75009 Paris, France.

PACIFIC

Hawaii

Soaring over Oahu's North Shore: The prevailing tradewinds on the northwest shore of Oahu create favorable soaring conditions for experienced and neophyte enthusiasts alike. A variety of instructional programs is available providing students use of 1- to 3-person gliders. A program geared toward earning a private pilot license includes: 7 hours of solo flight plus 20 solo flights using aerotow; instruction on FAA written exam; and oral and flight test preparation for FAA flight examination. An average of 6 to 10 hours (20- to 30-minute lessons) is available for solo flight preparation. **Cost:** $10 an hour for instructional fee; $150 to $500 for license fees. **When:** Year-round. **Contact:** Honolulu Soaring Club, Inc., Box 626, Waialua, HI 96791, USA; phone (808)623-6711.

UNITED STATES

Arizona

Sierra Estrella Gliding: Scenic glider and sailplane flights and instruction are available in an area exceptionally suited to soaring. During spring and summer, thermal lifts rise from the desert daily, and during fall and winter, ridge and wave soaring are excellent due to the nearness of the Sierra Estrella. Passengers may enjoy scenic flights over the mountains as well as aerobatic glider flights which include loops, rolls and inverted flight. Soaring and flying instruction, glider competition and glider aerobatic techniques are also organized by the gliderport. All models of Schweizer sailplanes are available for instruction, rental or sale. **Cost:** $18 for trainer flights, $50 for high performance flights, $30 for aerobatic flights. **When:** Daily year-round. **Contact:** Arizona Soaring, Inc., P.O. Box 27427, Tempe, AZ 85282, USA; phone (602)568-2318. *(M)*

California

Sailplane Instruction: A complete sailplane training program is offered near the town of Hemet. An introductory ride in which participants may momentarily fly the plane is given to those who are curious about the sport. Then they may sign up for a course intended to procure FAA certification. Thermals and sheer lines in the valley around Hemet allow pilots to climb above Mt. San Jacinto and move eastward across the desert. The gentle soaring days encourage good cross-country flights in the 100-mile range. Student learning certificates allow solo flights and can be issued to anyone 14 years of age or older. **Cost:** On request. **When:** Year-round. **Contact:** Sailplane Enterprises, P.O. Box 1650, Hemet, CA 92343, USA; phone (714)658-6577.

Colorado

Rocky Mountain Soaring Instruction: A gliderport in Colorado's

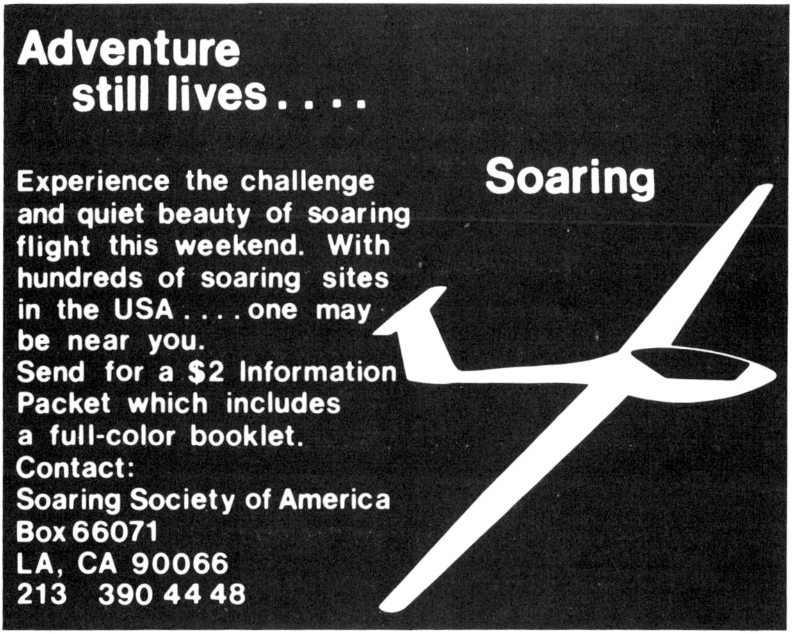

high plateau country surrounding Colorado Springs offers soaring instruction and sailplane rentals. Courses are flexible and students are given private instruction. Half-hour introductory flights are available, as is a mini-course; their fees may be credited toward a complete course if desired. Other courses cover preparation for solo which involves 25 flights of practice take-offs, landings and flight maneuvers. A solo license course requires 28 flights and 7 hours of solo time. A power pilot soaring course prepares the student to solo in 6 to 8 flights. **Cost:** $25 for introductory flight, $65 for mini-course, $420 to $580 for other courses. **When:** Daily year-round. **Contact:** Black Forest Gliderport, 9990 Gliderport Rd., Colorado Springs, CO 80908, USA; phone (303)495-4144. ***(M)***

Colorado Springs Youth Soaring Camp: Youths 14 to 18 may combine custom-designed soaring instruction in the front range of the Rocky Mountains with backpacking training at a camp near Pikes Peak. All soaring instructors are FAA licensed, and training is given in Schweizer sailplanes. Experienced pilots may receive advanced soaring instruction, and solo flying is available. Group members learn backpacking skills on a trip into the Sangre de Cristo Mountains in the San Isabel National Forest and in the Lost Creek area of the Pike National Forest. Skills taught include high altitude hiking, first aid, compass reading, ropes and knots, and wilderness survival. **Cost:** $950 includes equipment, meals, accommodations. **When:** June to August. **Contact:** Black Forest Gliderport, 9990 Gliderport Rd., Colorado Springs, CO 80908, USA; phone (303)495-4144. ***(M)***

Georgia

Georgia Gliders: A gliderport 40 miles south of Atlanta offers instruction and equipment rental for novices and sailplane pilots alike. The port's facilities include 2 tow planes and 10 Schweizer gliders, including 2 competition-class 1-35s. Roughly 25 flights are needed before a beginner may solo, although pilots with a power license have qualified to solo in as few as 10 flights. Club membership and block rates are also available and novices can take introductory flights. **Cost:** About $325 for a beginner to qualify for solo; $14 to $20 for hourly rental, $18 for introductory flight. **When:** Year-round. **Contact:** Peach State Gliderport, P.O. Box 52, Williamson, GA 30292, USA; phone (404)688-8222.

Minnesota

Soaring over Minneapolis: A number of instructional courses, rental arrangements and other services are available to soaring pilots. Although no flight training package is available, instruction is offered with charges based on the pilot's ability and progress. Generally, students require about 25 lessons to become competent at solo flight. Each lesson lasts about 20 to 30 minutes, though schedules are flexible. Requirements for a private glider pilot's license necessitate solo competence, 7 hours of solo flight including 20 solo glider flights launched by aerotow, and passage of the FAA flight test. Tows and rentals are available. **Cost:** $5 to

$475 depending on course, rental or training. **When:** Year-round, weather permitting. **Contact:** White Bear Gliding, Benson's Airport, White Bear Lake, MN 55110, USA; phone (612)871-8036.

Montana

Soaring at Teton and Yellowstone: The mountains at the base of the Teton Range on the Idaho-Wyoming border at Driggs are the setting for a variety of year-round soaring opportunities for beginning and licensed pilots alike. Beginners may enroll in an introductory mini-course which includes 2 flights, one 4,000-foot tow and one 1,000-foot tow, instructional book and logbook. Students may also enroll in a license course, solo course, or a more advanced power pilot transition course. Glider rentals, tows and rides are available as well. Winter ridge and wave soaring provide enthusiasts with ample opportunity in the sport or in sailplaning. While soaring in the brisk, silent sky, pilots often view the irregular patterns of skiers mak-

Sierra Nevada Soaring offers rides to sailplane enthusiasts on the air currents and thermals over the Sierra Nevada. An introductory ride is available for only $16. (Sierra Nevada Soaring)

ing their way down the powdery slopes below. In summer, soaring buffs may also partake in a variety of whitewater sports available in the national parks in addition to riding the air waves. **Cost:** $12 an hour to $1,052 depending on type of instruction includes equipment, instruction. **When:** Year-round. **Contact:** Red Baron Soaring, Box 247, Teton Peaks Airport, Driggs, ID 83422, USA; phone (208)354-8131.

Nevada

Sailing the Mountain Waves: The thrill of flying on waves and thermal lifts generated by the Sierra Nevada range is a treat to soaring enthusiasts near Reno. Sailplane rides offer the inexperienced an opportunity to soar over the arid countryside, and rentals, tows and other facilities for aircraft are available for more experienced fliers. **Cost:** $16 for introductory ride; $14 to $20 for glider rental; $8 for tow; $12 an hour for instruction. **When:** Wednesday through Sunday year-round. **Contact:** Sierra Nevada Soaring, P.O. Box 60036, 4895 Texas Ave., Stead Airport, Reno, NV 89506, USA; phone (702)972-7757.

New Jersey

Center for Soarers: The Blairstown Airport, just an hour's drive west of New York City, offers a variety of soaring services. Those interested in motorless flight can take a demonstration ride or sign up for a series of lessons. Instruction is offered for beginners, experienced pilots wishing more advanced knowledge, or power pilots who want to make the transition to soaring. Sailplanes, supplies and instruction materials are available for sale or rent. Hiking, swimming and camping facilities, and various hotel accommodations are conveniently located near the airport. **Cost:** On request. **When:** Daily, year-round. **Contact:** Tocks Island Soaring Inc., 361 Walnut St., Nutley, NJ 07110, USA; phone (201)667-9234.

New York

Soaring Instruction: Complete soaring courses are available near the famous Harris Hill in western New York. A division of a major sailplane manufacturer, the school has facilities for several types of training. An introductory program includes 3 dual soaring flights and a soaring manual. A complete soaring course leads students from initial instruction to a private glider certificate. Fifty flights are involved, one of which is a cross-country dual flight, and 12 hours of flying time are scheduled. Other services and courses offered are a commercial soaring course, an instructor's course, auto or winch tows, and cross-country retrieve. Flights for 1 or 2 passengers are also available. **Cost:** $60 for introductory program to $875 for complete private course; $15 to $25 for passenger flights. **When:** May to September. **Contact:** Schweizer Aircraft Corp., P.O. Box 147, Elmira, NY 14902, USA; phone (607)739-3821.

(M)

Catskill Soaring: Established in 1927, Wurtsboro Airport in the Catskill Mountains is the nation's oldest gliderport. Soaring services offered include demonstration

rides, equipment rental, and instruction of all types: beginner's lessons, intermediate and advanced instruction, commercial and instructor ratings and power pilot transition courses. Flights are made over the scenic Catskills. Ample camping, recreational and hotel facilities are available in the area. **Cost:** On request. **When:** Year-round. **Contact:** Wurtsboro Airport, Rt. 209, Wurtsboro, NY 12790, USA; phone (914)888-2791.

Pennsylvania

Upcurrents in the Lehigh: The Lehigh Valley is the site for soaring flights and introductory lessons in the sport. The flights last 15 to 30 minutes and give the passenger an overhead perspective of the valley while riding the thermal lifts and ridge upcurrents. A 20-minute introductory lesson briefs the rider on the techniques involved and offers a chance to actually fly the dually controlled sailplane. The airport also serves rated pilots who wish to add a sailplane rating to their certificate. **Cost:** $15 to $20 for 10 to 15 minutes, $25 for a 25-minute introductory lesson. **When:** Year-round. **Contact:** Kutztown Aviation Service Inc., Kutztown Airport, Kutztown, PA 19530, USA; phone (215)683-3821.

Texas

Southern Soaring: At an airfield near Austin, Texas, gliding enthusiasts at all levels of ability can take courses to improve their pilot ratings. The beginning course leads to pilots being able to fly solo, and once a solo pilot demonstrates the ability to stay in the air for at least 5 hours, cross-country flights can be taken away from the immediate airport area. The first cross-country flight is 30 miles long, and subsequent flights increase in distance. Courses are also designed for experienced power airplane pilots who want to gain experience in soaring. **Cost:** $75 to $450 includes instruction and aircraft. **When:** On request. **Contact:** Windermere Soaring School, Rt. 2, Box 491, Spicewood, TX 78669, USA; phone (512)693-4663.

Utah

Western Mountain Soaring: Good soaring conditions prevail year-round in a valley of the Wasatch Range. Both novice and experienced gliding enthusiasts can increase their soaring skills in courses that lead to a private glider rating after 70 flights or a total of 7 hours solo time, plus the completion of a written exam. Courses are also offered to private power pilots who wish to add a sailplane rating to their existing license. On the beginner's first flight basic soaring techniques are explained, and the student may take the controls under the instructor's supervision for a short glide above Heber Valley. Skiing, hiking and camping are also available in the area, which is adjacent to Wasatch Mountain State Park and Deer Creek Reservoir. Accommodations can be arranged in nearby motels or at campgrounds. **Cost:** On request. **When:** Year-round. **Contact:** Heber Valley Flying Service, Inc., RR 1, Box 443-A, Heber City, UT 94032, USA.

Virginia

Gliding over Virginia: In a series of hourly lessons, participants learn to soar on the rising air currents above the Blue Ridge Mountains. Under the guidance of an instructor, students are taught how to take off and land, make gentle turns and find thermals. When the techniques of gliding have been mastered, students begin solo flights. After flight time requirements and a written test have been completed, students are checked out by an FAA examiner before receiving a private pilot's certificate. The gliders are late-model Schweizers—a 2-seat 2-33A for instruction flights and a single-seat 1-26 for advanced solo work. Rentals and tow service are available for certified pilots. **Cost:** $25 an hour plus tow includes rental, instruction. **When:** April to November. **Contact:** Warrenton Soaring Center, P.O. Box 185, Warrenton, VA 22186, USA; phone (703)347-0054.

Washington

Certified Soaring: Beginners' instruction in sailplane piloting, or soaring, is offered near Issaquah. The course results in certification through an FAA Private Pilot's License with a Glider rating. Other soaring services are offered at the skyport, including equipment rentals and single flights. Instructional programs available include a "transition course," which qualifies a currently licensed private pilot to obtain Glider certification; basic ground school; advanced soaring instruction, tailored to each student's needs; and instruction toward commercial and instructor ratings. **Cost:** $875 for certification course, $400 for transition course, $25 for single, 2,500-foot tow; other rates on request. **When:** By arrangement year-round. **Contact:** Soaring Unlimited, 12422 68th Ave. NE, Kirkland, WA 98033, USA; phone (206)454-2514.

RESOURCES

Clubs and Associations

Denver Soaring Council
1145 Cook
Denver, CO 80210, USA

Honolulu Soaring Club
Box 626
Wailua, HI 96791, USA
Phone (808)623-6711

Mid-Atlantic Soaring Association
Frederick Municipal Airport
Frederick, MD 21701, USA
Phone (301)663-9753

Midwestern Soaring Association
6120 W. Cleveland
Gladstone, MO 64119, USA
Phone (816)537-6074

National Aeronautic Association
821 15th St. NW
Washington, DC 20005, USA

New England Soaring Association
Airport Dr.
Southbridge, MA 01550, USA

Northern Pacific Sports and Recreation
P.O. Box 2317
Renton, WA 98055, USA

Soaring Society of America
P.O. Box 66071
Los Angeles, CA 90066, USA

Soaring Symposia
408 Washington St.
Cumberland, MD 21502, USA

Southern California
Soaring Association
28612 Parthena St.
Canoga Park, CA 91306, USA

FLYING

AFRICA

Kenya

Sky Safari: In special planes, 10 participants at a time are taken aloft for a unique view of wildlife herds. After meeting in Nairobi, the group heads for Aberdare National Park in Nyeri for a full-day drive in the rain forest. Later during the 16-day safari, trip members visit Meru and Samburu game parks to see elephants, giraffes, leopards, lions and rhinos. Other stopovers include Colcheccio with its zebras and greater kudu, and the Masai Mara Game Reserve where 2 days are spent at a tented camp viewing lions, wildebeests, baboons and bushbucks. Planes take participants over each of the parks and reserves to observe the wildlife. At Masai Mara a hot air balloon flight is available to view the herds soundlessly from above. **Cost:** $1,700 a person includes meals, accommodations, charter aircraft flights. **When:** June to November. **Contact:** Lindblad Travel, Inc., 8 Wright St., Westport, CT 06880, USA; phone (203)226-8531 or tollfree (800)243-5657. ***(M)***

ANTARCTICA

South Pole Flights: Leaving Auckland, New Zealand for a 13-hour flight over Antarctica, passengers view the surrounding area and 12,450-foot Mt. Erebus before flying west over the Magnetic South Pole. In good weather alternate routes include Cape Hallet and McMurdo Sound in Ross Sea. The flight is available only in conjunction with a roundtrip Air New Zealand flight from North America. **Cost:** $350. **When:** November. **Contact:** Air New Zealand, Suite 1000, 510 W. Sixth St., Los Angeles, CA 90014, USA; phone (213)629-5454.

ASIA

Sri Lanka

Hovering over Beaches and Jungles: Flying in 4-seat helicopters from hotel bases, adventurers take short trips over a variety of the natural sights of Sri Lanka. The island has many wildlife sanctuaries with elephants, bears, leopards, deer and jungle fowl, as well as numerous beaches for surfing, boating, water-skiing and swimming. The native Buddhist and Hindu peoples have a rich history, and several temples and festivals can be explored first-hand. **Cost:** On request. **When:** By arrangement. **Contact:** Helitours, Box 594, Colombo 2, Sri Lanka; phone 31584 or 33184.

AUSTRALASIA

Excursions to the South Pacific: A 17-, 22- or 29-day trip to the South Pacific provides travelers the opportunity to visit Australia, New Zealand, Fiji and Tahiti. All trips depart from Los Angeles and include overland trips to 3 of Australia's major cities: Sydney, Canberra and Melbourne. In New Zealand trip members climb Evans Pass to the Summit Road to view Lyttleton Harbor with its many bays and inlets. In addition, a 40-minute ski plane ride to the upper snowfields of the Tasman Glacier is scheduled. A flight to Rotorua brings visitors to the Whakarewarewa Maori Village, the heavily forested Mamaku Hills and Waitomo Caves. Also scheduled is a trip along the underground river into the Glow Worm Grotto. Visitors leave New Zealand after driving through rich farmlands to the city of Hamilton. The Tahiti portion of the trip includes a cruise across the Sea of Moon for a day on the fabled island of Moorea. **Cost:** $2,220 to $3,646 includes roundtrip airfare from Los Angeles, meals, accommodations. **When:** Monthly. **Contact:** Air New Zealand, Suite 1000, 510 W. Sixth St., Los Angeles, CA 90014, USA; phone (213)629-5454.

Australia

Flights to the Olgas: Small aircraft flights are available to visit Ayers Rock and the Olgas in central Australia. Half-day and day trips depart from Alice Springs in the early morning for Ayers Rock, stop for a tour around its base, then continue 15 miles west to explore Mt. Olga before a return flight in the early afternoon or evening. Overnight, 2-day and 3-day trips spend more time in the vicinity of Ayers Rock and allow time for a climb of Mt. Olga. A flight to the aboriginal settlements of Docker River or Ernabella is added to the 3-day trip. Accommodations are at a motel near Ayers Rock. Other trips include weekly mail flights to remote cattle stations and flights over aboriginal settlements and geographical features. **Cost:** $25 to $140. **When:** Year-round. **Contact:** Connair, 51 Todd St., Alice Springs, NT 5750, Australia; phone 52-1755.

New Zealand

Glacier Flights: Glacier areas and rain forests may be viewed on a variety of 1-day flying trips departing from Lake Tekapo. Participants may choose flights over the ice fields of the Franz Joseph and Fox glaciers, Mt. Cook National Park and South Island, with opportunities to stop and sightsee at midday. Much of the country seen by air is completely inaccessible by road. On the South Island route passengers arrive at Milford Sound for lunch, then set off again to view Sutherland Falls and Lake Te Anau. The route takes participants through glacier-carved valleys to Queenstown for a short stop, then north to Wanaka, Hawea, Lake Benmore and the Mackenzie country to Tekapo. **Cost:** $5 to $45. **When:** Year-round. **Contact:** Air Safaris, Box 21, Lake Tekapo, New Zealand; phone 880.

Helicopter Ski Lift Adventure: Plane or helicopter transport is offered to and from areas selected in the Tapapa, Wharetoto and Kaimanawa regions. The service begins with a flight to Taupo, where individuals can choose destinations into the backcountry. Activities into remote areas include horse trekking, whitewater rafting and fishing. The Tapapa area contains 18,000 acres of beech forests and tussock grassland. The Wharetoto region covers 5,800 acres and is bounded by the Repia, Otupua and

Mohaka rivers. The Kaimanawa region consists of 18,000 acres situated near the headwaters of the Ngaroro River. Large areas of tussock land reach upward to the beech forests with sika and red deer among the trees. The rivers adjacent to this area have a large number of trout, and eels can be found downstream. Either hut or tent shelter is available in all the traveled areas. Guide service is also available. **Cost:** $50 from Taupo to airstrips, $130 a day for field guide service; helicopter transport prices on request. **When:** By arrangement. **Contact:** Lakeland Aviation Ltd., P.O. Box 858, Taupo, New Zealand; phone 2364.

Papua New Guinea

Stone Age Air Safari: A 17-day expedition explores Papua New Guinea by twin-engine aircraft, focusing on its primitive native tribes. Members observe peoples who have retained much of their Stone Age culture due to their inaccessible location. The expedition visits the Biami people on the Nomad River and the people of the remote Oksapmin area. The group also spends several days exploring the culture of the Sepik River area and the Kuka Kuka of the Marawaka Valley. Participants also travel up the Bensbach River to see the area's wildlife, which includes wallabies and crocodiles as well as numerous species of birds. The expedition is composed of 7 members plus an experienced guide and pilot. **Cost:** $4,435 from Los Angeles includes transportation, accommodations, meals. **When:** March, May, July, October, November. **Contact:** Society Expeditions, P.O. Box 5088, University Sta., Seattle, WA 98105, USA; phone (206)324-9400. ***(M)***

PACIFIC

Hawaii

Eight Island Plane Trip: The Hawaiian Islands are seen by air during a 1-day trip. Participants board twin-engine aircraft from which they see Hanalei Valley on Kauai, the 2,000-foot waterfalls of Molokai, the huge crater of Diamond Head on Oahu, the Haleakala Volcano of Maui and the barren wastelands of Kahoolawe. During several landings along the route, passengers are able to take side trips to nearby points of interest, dine on native food and see cultural and historic sites. **Cost:** $110 includes air and land transportation, meals, guides. **When:** Year-round. **Contact:** Hawaiian Air Tour Service, 2371 Kalakuau Ave., Honolulu, HI 96815, USA; phone (808)923-6577.

Helicopter to Milolii: Visitors to Kauai have the opportunity to get an overview of the island's spectacular scenery via helicopter. Flights vary in duration and provide access to remote areas of the island, including Milolii which is known for its rare shells; Nualolo Aina and Nualolo Kai, location of abandoned taro patch terraces and homesites; and other sites in the "Valley of the Lost Tribe," where traces of an early civilization still exist. The flight to Milolii begins with a trip to the Waimea Canyon where the variations of canyon coloration and frequent waterfalls are observed from 4,000 feet up. From this altitude, the waterfalls and archaeological sites along the Na Pali coast are also viewed. **Cost:** $80. **When:** Year-round. **Contact:** Papillon Helicopters, Princeville Airport, P.O. Box 608, Hanalei, Kauai, HI 96714, USA; phone (808)826-9180.

UNITED STATES

Southwest Nature Studies: From Santa Fe participants embark on a day-long air/land trip into New Mexico, Colorado, Utah and Arizona exploring famous landmarks, geological formations and Indian ruins. Adventurers fly over the rainbow-striped canyons and wind-carved buttes of the Painted Desert, the gorges of the Rio Grande, Bandelier National Park, Puye Cliff Dwellings and numerous prehistoric Pueblo villages and ruins. Participants proceed through the inaccessible canyons of the Chama River, landing in Monument Valley. The trip continues by jeep through a labyrinth of buttes, spires and natural arches to Navajo dwellings. Participants return to the plane for more aerial viewing before touching down in Santa Fe by sunset. On another trip, participants concentrate on learning how to read the landscape as the group flies to the Chaco, Salmon and Aztec ruins that are now archaeological sites. Ancient road patterns, unexcavated pueblos, kivas and ancient reservoirs can be seen from the air. On the ground, adventurers explore ceremonial chambers and study the ecology of past environments. **Cost:** $100 to $200 for 1-day trips includes transportation from Santa Fe airport, guide, lunch. **When:** Year-round. **Contact:** Southwest Safaris, P.O. Box 945, Santa Fe, NM 87501, USA; phone (505)988-4246.

Southwest Natural History Trip: A trip focusing on the natural history of the American Southwest—New Mexico, Colorado, Utah and Arizona—uses a 6-passenger bush plane for transportation. This allows wide topological overviews, "classroom" time while in flight and the ability to cover large distances within a 6-day trip. The trip

Float planes are used to carry passengers into Alaska's wilderness areas for backpacking, fishing, skiing or photography expeditions. (Pete Karp)

begins and ends in Santa Fe and visits numerous Indian ruins including Anasazi dwellings in Aztec, Salmon and Chaco canyons; Pueblo Bonito; the Mesa Verde cliff dwellings; Canyonlands in Utah; Navajo dwellings in Monument Valley; and Marble Canyon. The trip's fifth day is spent rafting the San Juan River, with its rapids and ruins, while studying first-hand the geological formations of the area. Most stops include jeep transportation to nearby points of interest, including one with a visit to and lunch at a traditional Navajo Indian hogan. Horseback riding can sometimes be incorporated, with advance notice. The pilot serves as instructor and guide. **Cost:** $699 includes food, camping accommodations, transportation, guide; discounts for larger groups available. **When:** April to October. **Contact:** Southwest Safaris, P.O. Box 945, Santa Fe, NM 87501, USA; phone (505)988-4246.

Alaska

Flights over Fort Yukon: On the banks of the Yukon River just north of the Arctic Circle, Fort Yukon has operated as a fur-trading center since 1847. On a 5-hour trip participants fly from Metro Field in Fairbanks to a guided tour of the reconstructed Hudson's Bay Company Fort and other points of interest in the village, including fish wheels for drying salmon. After spending 2 hours on the ground, passengers take a return flight following the route of the trans-Alaska oil pipeline. **Cost:** $74. **When:** Daily year-round. **Contact:** Air North, P.O. Box 60054, Fairbanks, AK 99706, USA; phone (907)456-5555.

Alaska by Bush Plane: A charter bush aircraft service flies adventurers to remote areas of Alaska for photography, skiing, climbing, camping or hiking expeditions. The outfitter is headquartered at Snowshoe Lake, set amidst the Alaska, Talkeetna, Wrangell and Chugach mountain ranges; passengers may begin their flights in Anchorage if they prefer. Several remote cabins are available for rent, some including motorboats. All trips are arranged on an individual basis. The planes can carry 2 or 3 passengers plus gear, and transport rates are based on flying time. **Cost:** $60 to $100 per hour of flying time; $20 to $40 a day per cabin. **When:** Summer. **Contact:** Alaskan Airventures, Snowshoe Lake, Star Rt. C, Box 8762, via Palmer, AK 99645, USA.

Flying above Mt. McKinley: Several flights, lasting between 1 and 2 hours, are available above Mt. McKinley National Park. Sights include the Denali earthquake fault, which runs 110 miles between Mt. McKinley and Mt. Deborah. These

2 peaks were once adjacent, and from the air it can easily be seen how they have moved apart. Dall sheep are visible along the higher ridges, and hundreds of caribou can be spotted during their summer migration. Moose are plentiful among the willow browse in the eastern part of the park. Glaciers streaked with lines of volcanic ash can also be seen from the plane. **Cost:** $30 to $40 a person. **When:** By arrangement. **Contact:** Denali Flying Service, P.O. Box 82, McKinley Park, AK 99755, USA; phone (907)683-2261.

Three Thousand Six Hundred Pontoon Miles: A charter air trek leaves from Juneau for a 2-week survey of Alaska's wilderness, parks and cities. By 6-seat pontoon plane, trip members cover a circuit that includes stops at Seward, Prince William Sound, Mt. McKinley National Park, Fairbanks, Fort Yukon, Nome, and Katmai National Monument as well as McNeil River Bear Sanctuary for the final touch-down in Anchorage. About 20 hours of flying time are logged on this trip, with many of the panoramic views being provided at altitudes as low as 100 feet above the mountainous landscape. Camps and lodges provide accommodations. **Cost:** $1,800; $2,046 includes roundtrip airfare from Seattle. **When:** June. **Contact:** Mountain Travel Inc., 1398 Solano Ave., Albany, CA 94706, USA; phone (415)527-8100. ***(M)***

Arctic Bush Flying: Opportunities are available to accompany working bush pilots on flights from Nome to remote areas on the tundra and the Bering Sea. Travelers can join mail carriers on a variety of flights and journey to secluded arctic settlements such as Little Diomede Island and the villages of Wales and Gambell. On lengthy mail runs during the summer passengers can disembark at an intermediate point and be picked up on the plane's return trip. From Little Diomede located in the Bering Sea on the International Date Line, it is possible to see the Siberian coast just 22 miles away. At Wales and Shishmaref hunting and fishing continue to be the major livelihood for the Eskimo population. A reindeer station established at Golovin in 1896 offers a good view of the large herd. Gambell, on St. Lawrence Island, is of particular interest to bird watchers, naturalists and archaeologists. **Cost:** $55 to $95 depending on the chosen destination. **When:** Year-round. **Contact:** Munz Northern Airlines, Nome Airport, Nome, AK 99762, USA; phone (907)443-2215.

Arctic Adventures: Wilderness explorers, river runners, photographers and backpackers can determine their own expedition lengths and pick specific areas of exploration within Alaska's remote regions of the Noatak and Kobuk rivers. Bush plane service into the wilderness departs from Kotzebue, just north of the Arctic Circle. The inhabitants of the region are mainly Eskimos who live in small bush communities. The terrain varies from vast areas of tundra lakes to the Brooks and Baird mountain ranges. Expedition services offered to adventurers include reprovisioning, base site relocation, progress monitoring and planning consultation. The northern season is short and the rugged, remote terrain requires that participants be self-reliant and experienced outdoorspeople. Air transportation to Kotzebue can be arranged from the lower states through Seattle and Anchorage. **Cost:** $325 to $975 depending on the expedition base site, includes bush plane transportation, site relocation and reprovisioning. **When:** June to September. **Contact:** Northwest Arctic Alaska, P.O. Box 733, Seattle, WA 98111, USA; phone (206)324-4437.

Mt. McKinley Overview: For travelers who want to see McKinley without making a rugged overland trek, flights of slightly over 2 hours are offered for a minimum of 4 passengers which explore the mountain's major features and give members a view of the surrounding country. The flight leaves from Anchorage and travels north, up the Susitna River past the old railroad settlement of Talkeetna and into the Alaskan Range. Approaching the mountain, the plane climbs to 10,000 feet, then after a close look glides down over the sheer faces of the Ruth and Kahiltna glaciers. At the lower elevations, participants are likely to see moose, black bears or grizzly bears. The flight then returns to Anchorage. **Cost:** $95. **When:** By arrangement. **Contact:** Rust's Flying Service, Box 6325, Anchorage, AK 99502, USA; phone (907)243-1595.

Southern Air Tour: One of Alaska's more scenic regions, Prince William Sound, is only a short distance from Anchorage. Travelers can fly over the varied land and seascapes of the sound on a flight that leaves from Anchorage and lasts slightly over 2 hours. The plane flies up Turnagain Arm after leaving the city, circles the Alyeska ski resort, rises above the crest of Portage Glacier and finally descends toward Prince William Sound, an area of fjords, heavily timbered islands and glaciers. Participants get a good closeup view of the Columbia Glacier, and on the return trip over the Chugach Range have a chance to spot mountain sheep and goats

At Juneau, backpackers load their gear into a float plane which will fly them to a remote Alaskan lake. (Craig Sternagel)

and black bears. The plane flies over Lake George, the Knik Glacier and Matanuska Valley farmlands before setting down in Anchorage. **Cost:** $95 (minimum of 4 persons). **When:** By arrangement. **Contact:** Rust's Flying Service, Box 6325, Anchorage, AK 99502, USA; phone (907)243-1595.

Arizona

Grand Canyon Flying: A variety of narrated scenic air trips over the Grand Canyon provides visitors with the opportunity to view the expanse of the national park in a few hours. One- and 2-hour flights are available, and both originate on the South Rim of the park. Flights are available between the North and South rims of the canyon for access to meals, overnight accommodations and mule trips on the North Rim. Three-hour air explorations include views of Glen Canyon Dam, Lake Powell, Painted Desert, Marble Canyon and the Havasupai Indian village. The 3-hour trips cover about 350 miles of terrain. The 1-hour trip covers 130 miles and includes views of Snoopy Rock, Phantom Ranch, Mooney Falls and the Havasupai Indian village. **Cost:** $24 to $68; less for children. **When:** Year-round. **Contact:** Grand Canyon Airlines, P.O. Box 186, Grand Canyon, AZ 86023, USA; phone (602)638-2407.

Grand Overflight: Participants spend 1 day and a night visiting the Grand Canyon, from both the ground and the air. The trip begins with a flight from the South Rim that winds its way through the canyon, flying under the rim at certain intervals. The plane passes river rapids, waterfalls, extinct volcanoes and ancient Indian villages. At one point it soars through the narrow pass between Powell Plateau and the North Rim. Once the group arrives back at the airport, arrangements are made for participants to travel to the South Rim for a ground view of the region just viewed from the air. **Cost:** $142 includes 2 meals, accommodations. **When:** May to September. **Contact:** Scenic Airlines, 241 E. Reno Ave., Las Vegas, NV 89119, USA; phone (702)739-1900.

Florida

Exploring the Everglades: On a 4-day journey through the Everglades by plane and boat, trip members examine the many biological zones in the area. After meeting in Miami, group members spend the first day flying in a private plane above the "River of Grass" to gain an overall picture of the swampy land and to survey routes. Stops are made for meals, photography and a closer look at the ecology of the area. During the next 3 days, participants travel through the Everglades by airboat learning about the various ecosystems, hammocks and heads while camping in remote parts of the interior. The sloughs and grass-filled prairies are explored, and participants have a chance to see many varieties of birds, native orchids and rare tree snails. Side trips to other Florida wilderness areas are also available. **Cost:** $345 includes transportation, meals, accommodations. **When:** Year-round. **Contact:** Wilderness Experiences, Rt. 1, Box 554, Thonotosassa, FL 33592, USA; phone (813)986-2963. ***(M)***

HANG GLIDING

CANADA

British Columbia

Teachers of Flight: A hang gliding school in Invermere offers both summer and winter hang gliding courses, ranging from introductory flights to complete, 12-day HGAC certification instruction; custom lessons at any level of expertise are offered as well. The course in winter is taught at a ski area, making a combination of the 2 sports possible. One package is a weekend lesson beginning Friday evening with orientation and flight simulation and finishing with flights on the training hill Sunday. The school also makes house calls: instructors can travel 1,000 miles in any direction to teach a group of at least 12 people. **Cost:** $95 for weekend course includes equipment, instruction; other rates on request. **When:** July to August, December to March. **Contact:** Eagle's Nest School of Hang Flight Ltd., Swansea Hang Glider Corp., Box 897, Invermere, BC Canada VOA 1KO; phone (604)342-9378.

CENTRAL AMERICA

Guatemala

Hang Gliding School: One-month courses cover the theory and practice of hang gliding. Classes in theory are held at night in Guatemala City and include films and a flight simulator; the practical aspects are taught in the field on Saturdays. Private lessons are also available on a daily or hourly basis. **Cost:** $100 includes equipment. **When:** Four times a year. **Contact:** Vuelo Libre, 20 Calle 3-50 Zona 10, Guatemala City, Guatemala; phone 32 42 52.

EUROPE

Norway

Scandinavian Sky Sailing: The steep mountains and narrow valleys of Norway are ideal for hang gliding, and instruction in the sport is offered at several sites. The Norwegian Hang Gliding School, based in Oslo, arranges courses throughout the country. A school at Vikersund offers special courses for beginners in an area that includes the giant "ski flying" hill which was the site for the 1977 world championship. Hang gliding is also available in northern Norway through clubs at Narvik and at Bodo, situated just above the Arctic Circle and reached by air or rail from Oslo. Numerous hang gliding clubs are located throughout Norway. **Cost:** On request. **When:** On request. **Contact:** Norwegian and Swedish National Tourist Offices, 75 Rockefeller Plaza, New York, NY 10019, USA; phone (212)582-2802.

UNITED STATES

California

Fly Right: Beginning and advanced hang gliding techiques are taught at a school in Sylmar. A first flight course includes an evening of preparatory ground school and one day of flying. All levels of expertise are taught on an individualized

High above Gunnison National Forest near Crested Butte, Colorado, a hang glider maneuvers his "wing" above a gentle slope.

basis; experienced pilots can learn how to locate thermals, find the center of lift, attain greater height and use a variometer. Instructor/observers issue USHGA Hang Ratings at no charge. The school also offers equipment sales and rentals. **Cost:** $49 for first flight course; other rates on request. **When:** Year-round. **Contact:** Windhaven Hang Gliding Schools Inc., 12437 San Fernando Rd., Sylmar, CA 91342, USA; phone (213)367-1819.

Colorado

Hanging above Aspen: Hang gliding provides spectacular views of the Rocky Mountains. Enthusiasts may take a half-day beginning course in the sport, using the best equipment available. The courses take place near Aspen, with Mt. Aspen the jump-off point. **Cost:** $20 includes equipment. **When:** April to August. **Contact:** Aspen Reservations, Inc., P.O. Box 4546, Aspen, CO 81611, USA; phone (303)925-4000.

Hang Gliding from Mt. Zion: Double surface airfoil hang gliders provide participants interested in instructional and recreational free flight with the means of achieving powerless, silent locomotion. Basic instruction commences with a ground school lecture and the use of a flight simulator before students learn the body positions used in flight. Instruction includes a total of 20 hours (4 hours each lesson) of actual practice in preflight techniques, ground handling, take-off and landing procedures, and directional and air speed control. Participants are encouraged to thoroughly understand the theory of flight, basic airfoil design and meteorology. The 20 hours of outdoor flight instruction are solid preparation for later flights of 10, 30 and even 75 miles. All equipment is available on a rental-for-purchase basis. **Cost:** $30 for single lesson of 4 hours; $90 for 5-lesson package. **When:** By arrangement. **Contact:** Golden Eagle Gliders, 501 Lookout Mt. Rd., Golden, CO 80401, USA; phone (303)277-1300.

Kentucky

Introductory Lessons: People interested in experiencing the excitement of hang gliding can take inexpensive introductory lessons near Louisville. Students receive ground instruction covering preflight, postflight and assembly procedures, then proceed to actual flight training from one of the operator's smaller slopes. Special group rates are available. **Cost:** $30. **When:** By arrangement. **Contact:** Derby City Kite Sales, 8400 Blue Lick Rd., Louisville, KY 40219, USA; phone (502)969-6295.

Michigan

Riding the Midwest Wind: Daylong individual instruction in windsurfing and hang gliding takes place in the classroom and outdoors in New Buffalo. Aspects of aerodynamics, weight shift control, safety and construction of the glider are covered in blackboard instruction, illustrated by the use of a model. Students begin with flat-area runs to get the feel of the glider before harnessing in and taking off for short flights from a gentle hill. Warren Dunes State Park or 135-foot Mt. Baldy are used for repeated flights in which the student works on turning and banking. Certification programs up to the Hang 3 level are all tailored to the stamina and ability of the individual, though participants can expect to obtain their Hang 1 classification in one day. Windsurfing is also taught on an individualized basis using the windsurfer turntable, a simulator that allows the student to go through the same corrective motions that are required on the 12-foot windsurfing board. After an hour on the simulator, and blackboard instruction for the non-sailor, the day is spent on either Lake Michigan or on the calmer waters of Lake Pine. Certified individuals may rent equipment without instruction. **Cost:** $45 for 5 to 8 hours includes instruction, equipment. **When:** Year-round. **Contact:** AA Flightsystems, Inc., 10 N. Barton St., New Buffalo, MI 49117, USA; phone (616)469-1643.

Montana

Western Sky Gliding: Beginning hang gliding instruction is offered during 1-day courses near Billings. Most courses take place on Sunday, while weekday lessons can also be arranged for groups of 6 or more at locations up to 200 miles from Billings. During the lessons the *Guide to Rogallo Flight Basic* is used, and students are given various articles on hang gliding to read before their flight. Hang gliders can also be purchased at the school. **Cost:** $15 a lesson includes basic instruction. **When:** By arrangement. **Contact:** Beartooth Hang Gliders, 3010 Rimrock Rd., Billings, MT 59102, USA; phone (406)656-5409.

New Hampshire

New England Hang Gliding: Schools located at Attitash, Cranmore and Pleasant in the Mt. Washington Valley provide instruction to beginners wishing to experience the feeling of flight. A beginning plan is available to students and includes 3 hours of intensive instruction and introduction to the sport, with emphasis on safety and understanding of flight theory. All levels of instruction may be arranged on a group or individual basis as well. Following the ground instruction, neophytes practice glider handling and begin an instructor-assisted first take-off run on a gentle slope. After a few practice runs, students take to the air and land softly in the grassy tuft below. The Attitash school provides students with hills as high as 2,300 feet with a vertical drop of 1,525 feet and northern exposure. Cranmore, elevation 2,000 feet, provides a vertical drop of 1,500 feet and western exposure, while Pleasant, at Bridgton, Maine, provides a vertical drop of 1,400 feet. **Cost:** $10 to $25 depending on type of instruction. **When:** June to October. **Contact:** Sky People Hang Gliding School, Box 898, North Conway, NH 03860, USA; phone (603)356-5872.

North Carolina

Gliding at Nag's Head: Novice and intermediate hang gliding courses are taught along the soft sand dunes on the Atlantic coast within view of the site of the Wright brothers' historic flight. Individual lessons as well as 3- and 6-lesson packages are offered. During the first lesson the student takes 5 flights in addition to the novice ground school. Participants should wear long pants and tennis shoes. **Cost:** $19 to $39 for individual classes, $65 to $145 for packages. **When:** Year-round. **Contact:** Kitty Hawk Kites, P.O. Box 386, Nag's Head, NC 27959, USA; phone (919)441-6247.

Pennsylvania

Hang Gliding: A basic course in hang gliding is offered at locations in Pennsylvania, New Jersey and New York. The course includes a 2-hour indoor class designed to familiarize students with the history of hang gliding, the theory of hang gliding flight, and the common sense safety rules that must be observed. Control movements are practiced in the flight simulator. A 2-hour ground running session is next, in which students practice controlling the glider while on flat ground and learn preflight inspection. Then there is a 4-hour flying period in which participants practice take-offs, smooth flights and safe landings. After completion of the basic course, everyone is invited for a following day of instruction for 6 hours. **Cost:** $45 for basic course, $20 for follow-up. **When:** Year-round. **Contact:** Up-It, 1103 Cottman Ave., Philadelphia, PA 19111, USA; phone (215)722-8212.

A hang glider pilot over farmland zeroes in on a landing spot in the field below. (Judy Frostega)

RESOURCES

Clubs and Associations

Aeroklub Polskiej
Rzeczypospolltej Ludowej
ul. Krakowskie Przedmelscle 55
00-71 Warsaw, Poland

Alberta Hang Glider Association
Box 4063, Postal Sta. C.
Calgary, AB Canada T2T 5M9

Ambil Ltd.
P.O. Box 551
Tel Aviv, Israel

The Australian Hang Gliding Assoc.
G.P.O. Box 1706
Adelaide 5001, South Australia

Canadian West Coast
Hang Gliding Association
P.O. Box 77123, Sta. S
Vancouver, BC Canada V7L 1N3

Canterbury Hang Gliding Club
P.O. Box 22-481
Christchurch, New Zealand

CIDCAVA
Bulevar Artigas 1913
Montevideo, Uruguay

Dansk Dregeflyver Union
Bremensgade 11, 1 tv
2300 Copenhagen S., Denmark

Deutscher Hangeglieterclub
Hauptstrasse 16
881 Burghagel, Germany

Federation Belge de Vol Libre
249, rue Royale
1030 Brussels, Belgium

International Hang Gliding Secretariat
WOK
6435 Kossen, Austria

Irish Hang Gliding Association
12-P Home Farm Park
Dublin 9, Ireland

Japan Hang Glider Association
5-12-18 Yafumo Meguru-ku
Tokyo 152, Japan

Konstantin K. Kobozev
CCCP-141141 Moscow District
Udelnaya, Dzerjinskovo 14
Soviet Union

New Zealand Hang Gliding Assn.
P.O. Box 6680
Te Aro, Wellington, New Zealand

Scottish Sailwing Association
c/o W. Cowell, The Castle
Edinburgh, Great Britain

Swiss Hang Gliding Association
Badener Strasse 109 CH8004
Zurich, Switzerland

U.S. Hang Gliding Association
Box 66036
Los Angeles, CA 90066, USA
Phone (213)390-3065

PARACHUTING— PARASAILING

EUROPE

Parasailers' Overland Trip: An overland trip of 8 weeks through Europe and North Africa focuses on parasailing, as well as sailing and hang gliding. The trip originates and ends in England and visits France, Spain, Morocco, Algeria, Tunisia, Sicily, Italy and Switzerland. The party of about 18 stops at prime parasailing sites en route, including a mountain base north of Madrid for private parasailing, ballooning, hang gliding and parachuting. In North Africa a series of semipermanent base camps is established for side trips and activities, including bicycling, sand sailing and parasailing. The European portion of the flexible itinerary is primarily a travel tour; most leisure time is spent in Africa. **Cost:** $1,722 includes food, transportation, accommodations, equipment, guide. **When:** May, July, September. **Contact:** Skytrek Overland Expeditions, Hill End Farm, Tyttenhanger Green, Barley Mow Ln., St. Albans, Herts., Great Britain; phone St. Albans 56193.

England

The Peterborough Jump: A 2-day introductory course in the sport of parachuting is offered at Peterborough's Sibson Aerodrome, Great Britain's largest civilian parachuting center. Students who make satisfactory progress can make their first jump at the end of the 2 days of training; additional jumps at reduced rates can be made on a per-jump basis. Courses begin most Thursdays and Saturdays. Graduates qualify for an expedition still in the discussion stage which would involve jumping into a remote area and hiking back out. **Cost:** $80 includes instruction, equipment, 1 jump; $7 each for additional jumps. **When:** Year-round. **Contact:** Thomas Cook Ltd., P.O. Box 36, Thorpe Wood, Peterborough PE3 6SB, Great Britain; phone Peterborough (0733)632000.

PACIFIC

Hawaii

Parasailing on the Kona Coast: Participants may sail for 10 minutes over Kailua Bay on a kite-like parachute towed behind a jetboat. Passengers are secured by a harness, which frees the hands for photography. A waterproof camera or camera casing is recommended. **Cost:** $20. **When:** Daily year-round. **Contact:** Big Island Adventures, P.O. Box 2639, Kailua-Kona, HI 96740, USA; phone (808)329-2676.

(M)

UNITED STATES

California

The First Jump: A course in parachuting, lasting 3 to 5 hours, enables neophytes to make their first jump the same day. At an airport in Pope Valley, just over the mountains from the Napa Valley, participants receive ground instruction in the basics—exiting from the

In a number of skydiving courses, students make their first jump on the same day that they receive initial ground training. (U.S. Parachuting Association)

aircraft, steering the parachute, landing techniques and emergency procedures. Then, weather permitting, students make a static line jump, in which the ripcord is attached to the aircraft and trips itself automatically. Subsequent jumps are available at a reduced rate; they include individual instruction where required. Parachutists must be 16 or older, and those 16 and 17 need parental approval. First jump courses are given every Saturday, and on other days by arrangement.

Cost: $75 for first jump includes instruction, equipment, log book, jump; subsequent jumps are $15. **When:** Year-round. **Contact:** Pope Valley Parachute Center, 1996 Pope Canyon Rd., Pope Valley, CA 94567, USA; phone (707)965-3400.

Michigan

Leaps and Landings: Beginning parachutists are offered a complete first jump course on weekends at a drop zone near Tecumseh, Michigan. Classes begin at 10 a.m. on

Saturday and Sunday, and participants who are anxious to jump may receive their ground instruction and make the first jump on the same day. Once the student has made the initial leap, 4 subsequent static line jumps are required before progressing into free-fall. Training in more advanced jumping techniques is also offered. Participants must be at least 16. **Cost:** $45 for first jump course includes all equipment, jumpmaster, aircraft. **When:** On request. **Contact:** Tecumseh Parachuting Service, Tecumseh, MI 49286, USA; phone (517)423-7720.

New Jersey

Sky Diving Course: Beginners can learn to parachute in a day during a course at the Burlington County Air Park near Lumberton, New Jersey. The course is held on Saturdays and Sundays. Automatic opening systems are installed on the main and reserve chutes, and ground-to-air radio systems are provided to help guide the student to the landing area. **Cost:** $70. **When:** Year-round. **Contact:** Ripcord Paracenter Inc., Burlington County Airport, Medford RD, NJ 08055, USA; phone (609)267-9897.

Ohio

Sport Parachuting over Cleveland: Participants progress from a minimum of 5 static line jumps, in which the parachute is opened from the aircraft, to 30 or more supervised free-fall jumps. Starting at an altitude of 2,700 feet and working up to as much as 12,500 feet, jumpers practice turns, figure eights, back loops, barrel rolls and relative work. Relative work involves 2 or more parachutists who work together in the air to form stars or circles, pass batons and perform other exercises. Indoor training is also offered. Ages 16 to 18 must have a parent present or notarized release. Equipment is available for rent. **Cost:** $55 for first static line jump, decreasing to $15 for last (fifth) static line jump; $12 for free-fall jumps. **When:** February to November. **Contact:** Cleveland Sport Parachuting School, RR 2, Box 215, Garrettsville, OH 44231, USA; phone (216)548-4511.

Texas

Sky Diving over Dallas, Austin and Houston: Sky diving lessons, including 5 jumps, are available for beginners and experienced jumpers during classes held near each of the three Texan cities. Beginners enroll in 5½-hour ground courses which include instruction in equipment handling and parachute theory. After the classroom session, which also includes a training film and lectures, students practice procedures at a drop zone while reviewing classroom discussions prior to making the actual jumps. For enthusiasts with more background in the sport, additional advanced training is available in parachute packing, free-fall maneuvers and competitive sky diving. **Cost:** $18 to $85. **When:** Weekends year-round. **Contact:** Texas Skydiving Centers Inc., 5301 Parkland Ave., Dallas, TX 75235, USA; phone (214)824-3540.

Washington

Parachuting in Issaquah: Persons wishing to experience free-fall parachuting participate in day-long training sessions originating from an airfield in Issaquah. The training includes classroom film and slide presentations introducing beginners to the basics of parachuting and equipment. This is followed by training on aircraft exit, canopy steering, emergency procedures and landings. Participants take a lunch break before boarding the airplane. Then, from an altitude of 2,800 feet and accompanied by a jumpmaster, individuals make their first jump. For trained jumpers, a variety of altitude drops is available. **Cost:** $12 to $50 includes equipment, training, aircraft. **When:** Year-round. **Contact:** Issaquah Parachute Center, Skyport Airfield, P.O. Box 765, Issaquah, WA 98027, USA; phone (206)392-2121.

Wisconsin

The Sky's the Limit: Interested persons learn the art of parachute jumping from experienced professionals. On the ground and up in the skies over southern Wisconsin, participants develop skills in safe parachuting. Upon successful completion of the ground training classes, potential jumpers are sent up for their first static line (or automatic parachute opening) jump; as the student advances, higher jumps are made until the free-fall jump. Training includes basic orientation, observation of all phases of sport jumping, instruction in stable-fall procedures and familiarization with equipment. Opportunities are available for competitive jumping as well. Participants need to be 18 or over and in good health. **Cost:** $65 for first jump training, $120 for 6-jump package. **When:** May to October. **Contact:** Southern Wisconsin Skyhawks, Inc., Rt. 1, Box 453, Bristol, WI 53104, USA; phone (414)857-2007.

RESOURCES

Clubs and Associations

Aero Club
Lidorstrasse 5
6006 Lucerne, Switzerland

Aeroklub
Prinz Egen Strasse 12
Vienna, Austria

Australian Parachute Federation
P.O. Box 21
Doveton, Victoria 3177, Australia

Canadian Sport Parachuting Association
P.O. Box 848
Burlington, ON Canada L7R 3Y7

Deutscher AeroClub
Lyoner Strasse 16
6000 Frankfurt/Main 71, West Germany

Federation Argentina de Paracaidismo
Anchorena 275
Buenos Aires, Argentina

Federation Francaise Parachutiste
35 rue St. Georges
Paris 9-E, France

Irish Parachute Association
15, Upper Pembroke St.
Dublin 2, Ireland

National Collegiate Parachute League
P.O. Box 104
Monterey, CA 93940, USA

Norges Luftsportforbund
Nedre Slottsgate 17
1, Oslo, Norway

Para Club Caracas
Apartado 80016
Caracas 108, Venezuela

U.S. Parachute Association
806 15th St. NW, Suite 444
Washington, DC 20005, USA

Water Adventures

RIVER RAFTING

Each year over a million people climb into pontoon rafts, paddle boats, dories, sportyaks and motorized rafts to float the whitewater of the world. Screaming and cheering they hang on through cataracts, drop into boat-length holes, lurch over gigantic standing waves and even fall out as they paddle the more popular rivers and challenge the new. Rapids named Meatgrinder, Boulder Drop, Widow Maker and Death Rock attract hundreds of people to the excitement, camaraderie and challenge of river rafting.

Thoreau once wrote that "rivers are a constant lure to the adventurous instinct of mankind." Today you can raft near crocodiles on the Omo River in Ethiopia, rush through 300 sets of rapids on a 4-day trip in Australia, paddle the Reventazon ("Bursting") River of Costa Rica, or float through the French Alps. Real thrill-seekers can raft the wild water of the Bio-Bio in Chile, paddle over ledges and falls on the Chattooga River of *Deliverance* fame, or ride the rapids on the "River of No Return" in Idaho.

You can join a rafting trip for a half-day or a couple of weeks, let the guide handle the oars, or do the paddling yourself as part of a team. To learn the paddling commands and successfully maneuver through your first set of rapids is an experience never to be forgotten. Competitions between boats, waterfights with bailing buckets, riverside cook-outs and camps pitched upstream from roaring rapids are all a part of river trips. Guides take pride in their abilities to "read the river" and to cook gourmet meals.

Rafting workshops and guide schools are offered in California, all-women rafting trips are available in Oregon, and special river trips for the family, a group of friends or an out-of-doors business conference can also be arranged. Most raft trips are offered from March to September, but in Tennessee you can raft the Ocoee River year-round, paddle into November on the Youghiogheny in Pennsylvania or float the Rio Grande from November to January in Texas.

Rafting trips take you through some of the most remote wilderness areas of the world. They teach new skills, build self-confidence and expose you to some of the best swimming, hiking, fishing and wildlife viewing places. Whether you are eager to explore archaeological sites, pan for gold, pursue nature photography or camp under the stars, a rafting trip can combine all of these activities with the thrill of whitewater. □

For $40 a day, rafters on 1- or 2-day Wildwater Expeditions trips on the New River in West Virginia experience some of the most exciting whitewater in the East. (Thomas R. Dragon/Wildwater Expeditions Unlimited Inc.)

RIVER RAFTING

AFRICA

Ethiopia

Rapid Running on the Omo: Travelers in river rafts join about 1,600 hippos and 200 crocodiles on the remote Omo River in Ethiopia. Members work together during the expedition and should be in excellent physical condition to run a river that tumbles and spumes over scores of cataracts and rapids. As the Omo winds through dense jungle, dramatic savannas and 4,000-foot forested gorges, participants see a variety of African wildlife on shore as well as 400 species of tropical birds. Participants may also observe Nile perch which often weigh 200 pounds or more. On the lower shores of the river, rafters have the opportunity to interact with the Bodi tribe, a people who adorn themselves with decorative scars, ear or nose rings, and clay lip plates. The rafters pass through or around countless waterfalls including the 1,000-foot Royal Falls. Waterslides, tributary swimming holes and hot springs are also encountered. **Cost:** $1,950 for 28 days, $2,040 for 32 days includes guide, ground transportation, meals, rafting equipment. **When:** September, October. **Contact:** Sobek Expeditions, P.O. Box 761, Angels Camp, CA 95222, USA; phone (209)736-2924. *(M)*

ASIA

India

Floating the Zaskar: Rafters on a month-long trip float the entire length of the Zaskar River, from its headwaters below the glaciers of the Punjab Himalaya to its confluence with the Indus near Ladakh's ancient capital of Leh. Participants drive from Srinagar across the Zoji-La Pass at 11,500 feet and up the Suru Valley to a remote trailhead; here they begin the week-long hike to the river, visiting Ringdom Gompa on the way. At Phe they launch pontoon rafts in the river. The Zaskar cuts a fairly swift course through deep gorges resembling parts of the Grand Canyon, reaching otherwise inaccessible hamlets and monasteries rich in Tantric Buddhist art. Camping on beaches some of which have been literally untouched by humans, the expedition travels in the shadow of 20,000-foot peaks. At Nimu jeeps meet the party, and 3 days are spent exploring the Indus Valley, center of Ladakhi culture, before the return to Srinagar. **Cost:** $1,650 from Srinagar includes food, transportation, group equipment, guide. **When:** August, September. **Contact:** Himalaya, 3023 Franklin St., San Francisco, CA 94123, USA; phone (415)441-2933. *(M)*

Trisuli and Upper Ganges Rafting Trips: Participants can combine river rafting, cultural explorations, wildlife viewing and trekking on 17- to 24-day trips in the northern Indian district of Garhwal. On the first trip, group members travel to the upper Ganges where a week is spent rafting through a remote gorge between Tehri and Deoprayag. Another trip begins with a 9-day trek above Dehra Dun, starting at 6,000 feet; participants walk through densely forested foothills to the Bandarpunch Glacier, set beneath 20,000-foot peaks. From Yamnotri Pass, group members follow a Hindu pilgrimage trail to the Ganges, then set out in rafts toward Rishikesh and Delhi to conclude the 24-day journey. The third trip starts with a 4-day float trip on Nepal's Trisuli River and concludes with a week-long run on the upper Ganges. Participants need no previous whitewater experience. **Cost:** $1,875 to $2,195 includes hotel accommodations in cities, meals, guides, rafting equipment, camping gear, all transportation during the trip; airfare from New York extra. **When:** October, November, December. **Contact:** Lute Jerstad Adventures, P.O. Box 19527, Portland, OR 97219, USA; phone (503)244-4364. ***(M)***

AUSTRALASIA

Australia

River Running in New South Wales: Up to 300 sets of rapids, depending on rainfall, are negotiated on a 5-day float trip down the Nymboida River. Beginning in Coff's Harbour, participants are shuttled to the put-in point near Dorrigo. Once on the river, rafters encounter perils ranging from staircase drops to 90-foot chutes while passing through dense rain forest. Trip members spend approximately 5 hours a day on the river and may be asked to assist in "roping" the rafts through shallows encountered in the early part of the trip. The wildness of the Nymboida River makes protective helmets and life jackets mandatory. Guides set up camp along the riverbank at night, and precautions are taken to avoid degrading the natural environment. Return transportation to Coff's Harbour is provided from the take-out point at Nymboida. **Cost:** $211 to $247 includes guide, food, equipment. **When:** November to May. **Contact:** Australian Whitewater Expeditions, P.O. Box 3077, Sydney, N.S.W. 2001, Australia; phone 969-1457.

New Zealand

Alpine River Rafting: New Zealand's backcountry is explored on 1-day river rafting trips. Passengers and craft are transported 16 miles upstream from Woodstock into the high country reaches of the Waimakariri River. At this point, accompanied by an experienced guide, the raft sets off downstream in the alpine river waters. Along the way a number of stops are made including one for a picnic lunch. All raft parties should take clothing which can get wet, and a pair of soft shoes. Passengers should be in good physical condition. **Cost:** $17 for the trip only, $6 for road transportation. **When:** October to March. **Contact:** Canterbury and Alpine Travel Ltd., P.O. Box 8107, Christchurch, New Zealand; phone 65-022.

North Island Rafting: Groups of 5 or more fly from Taupo into the surrounding hills for raft trips through remote, untouched terrain, highly recommended for photographers and naturalists. Paddling inflatable rafts, participants spend 1 to 5 days or more rafting wild rivers and viewing sheer cliffs, waterfalls and virgin bush. The area is populated with a variety of wildlife including sika, goats, wild sheep and wild cattle. Discounts for large groups are available. **Cost:** $50 a day. **When:** Year-round (except in winter). **Contact:** Kaimanawa Tours & Treks, P.O. Box 321, Taupo, New Zealand; phone 87902.

Papua New Guinea

New Guinea in Old Bottles: A 27-day trip to Papua New Guinea begins and ends in San Francisco and encompasses a variety of environments and experiences. After a float down the fairly calm upper waters of the Watut River through gold-mining country, the party enters Watut Gorge, where over 100 major rapids are encountered during 3 days of rafting. Participants then travel to an active volcano off the north coast for hiking, and scale the country's highest peak, 14,760-foot Mt. Wilhelm. The trip finishes with a walking traverse of the Kokoda Trail, site of fierce fighting in World War II. The area's diverse wildlife, including many spectacularly plumaged birds, highlights the trip. **Cost:** $3,205 includes roundtrip airfare from San Francisco, food, camping accommodations, equipment, transportation, guides. **When:** May, June, September, October. **Contact:** Sobek Expeditions, Inc., P.O. Box 761, Angels Camp, CA 95222, USA; phone (209)736-2924. ***(M)***

CANADA

British Columbia

Chilcotin-Fraser Whitewater: Members of a 10-day expedition through the Chilcotin-Fraser river area make their way using a variety of transportation. The trip commences in Vancouver and includes the Surge Narrows with its 9-knot tidal current; tidal rapids in Okisollo Channel; a 45-minute flight over the Homatko Icefields; and a campsite located at Chilko Lake. Whitewater experiences include runs in the Chilko River, the Chilcotin River, Moran Canyon, and the Bridge River Rapids. Expedition members are then transported to Lillooet where they board a train that travels back through the Coast Range. **Cost:** $835 includes meals, transportation. **When:** June to September. **Contact:** Canadian River Expeditions Ltd., 1005 Highland

Canterbury and Alpine Travel Ltd. offers day-trips into the high country reaches of the Waimakariri River in New Zealand for as little as $17. (Canterbury and Alpine Travel Ltd.)

Dr., West Vancouver, BC Canada V7S 2G7; phone (604)926-4436. ***(M)***

Hell's Gate Run: Participants have the opportunity to raft on both the Fraser and Thompson rivers in southwestern British Columbia during a 3-day trip. Departure by bus is made from Yale to Spences Bridge where the rafts are put into the river; the 85-mile river journey takes group members back to Yale through all the major rapids on the Thompson and Fraser including Hell's Gate. Camp is pitched on the river bank for the 2 nights spent on the river. **Cost:** $140 for adults, $115 for children includes bus transportation, meals, T-shirt, guides. **When:** May, June, September. **Contact:** Cascade River Holidays, P.O. Box 65, Yale, BC Canada V0K 2S0; phone (604)863-2332. ***(M)***

Thompson and Fraser Rafting: A variety of whitewater experiences on the Thompson and Fraser rivers lasts from 2 to 7 days and covers various stretches of water. Trips begin in Lytton, where the Thompson and the Fraser converge, and run the rivers between Savona, Boston Bar, Ashcroft, Yale and Lytton. Wildlife is abundant in the area, including beavers, deer, bears, salmon, eagles, ospreys, hawks, kestrels, falcons and kingfishers. The rafts are 22 feet long and are powered by outboard motors. Whitewater instruction is available in the spring. **Cost:** $99 to $258, depending on duration and location, includes transportation to and from Lytton, food, equipment, guide. **When:** May to September. **Contact:** Kumsheen Raft Adventures, Suite 116, 525 Seymour St., Vancouver, BC Canada V6B 3H7; phone (604)669-0415. ***(M)***

Whitewater Challenge: Dropping from the alpine country of the Coast Range to the desert canyons of the Fraser Plateau, the Chilko and Chilcotin river system has some of the most challenging whitewater in North America. A 7-day trip begins at Chilko

Lake and continues on the Chilko River through deep forest to Lava Canyon for a 20-mile canyon run consisting of gigantic waves, boat-length holes and heavy whitewater. The river emerges into open country, past broad, sandhill arroyos (or "hondoos"), an old homestead and a bighorn sheep reserve before the conclusion of the trip. **Cost:** $550 includes meals, guides, rafting equipment. **When:** August. **Contact:** Outdoor Adventures, 3109 Fillmore St., San Francisco, CA 94123, USA; phone (415)346-8700. ***(M)***

Northwest Country River Rafting: Whitewater rapids on the Fraser River give rafters some spectacular runs on a 6-day trip through western Canada. Traveling between Soda Creek and Yale for a total of 225 miles, rafters maneuver through French Bar, Moran Canyon, Hells Gate, Saddle Rock and other rapids along the Fraser's deep canyons. With 4 to 6 hours a day spent on the river, participants have plenty of time to explore early Indian dwellings, abandoned gold mines, log cabins and Indian rock carvings. Campsites on sandy beaches near historic sites are the base for swimming and hiking in many places along the river. Sharp-sighted participants may spot Rocky Mountain sheep, herons and other wildlife. Watching salmon leap the rapids is an additional feature of late summer trips. **Cost:** $360 for 6 days includes food. **When:** July to September. **Contact:** Whitewater Adventures Ltd., P.O. Box 46536, Vancouver, BC Canada V6R 4G8; phone (604)736-2135. ***(M)***

Northwest Territories

Through a Distant Park: A raft trip lasting about 14 days runs the South Nahanni River through the entire length of Nahanni National Park. Rafters meet in Watson Lake and travel by float plane north over some spectacular geological formations to the put-in point, near the South Nahanni's confluence with Glacier Creek. The party moves downstream for the next week, hiking to nearby hot springs, portaging past high waterfalls, taking photographs and watching for wildlife, which includes moose, caribou, Dall sheep, wolves, bears, beavers, eagles and swans. Late in the trip, participants hike into Caverne Valerie, the largest cave yet discovered in the Northwest Territories, to see its ancient animal remains and dramatic geological formations. The return to Watson Lake is by float plane. **Cost:** $1,650. **When:** July. **Contact:** North-West Expeditions Ltd., P.O. Box 46596, Vancouver, BC Canada V6R 4G8; phone (604)736-2135. ***(M)***

Ontario

Excursions on the Ottawa: One- and 2-day trips are offered on the Ottawa River, about 1½ hours west of Canada's capital. Participants run the river in 38-foot motorized rafts at flood stage during the late spring and early summer, or use paddle rafts from July to September. Challenging whitewater and warm temperatures characterize trip conditions. Group rates are available. **Cost:** $45 for 1 day, $115 for 2 days includes all river equipment; participants provide their own tents and sleeping bags.

When: May to September. **Contact:** Wilderness Tours, Box 661, Pembroke, ON Canada K8A 6X9; phone (613)238-2361.

CENTRAL AMERICA

Costa Rica

Bursting River: The Reventazon River is little known to rafters but offers some fine whitewater; the name translates as "bursting," which describes some of its rapids. Participants on a day trip travel by bus from San Jose to Pejibaye, the put-in point, where those who wish to help navigate are issued paddles. The first 2 hours are fairly gentle, with only a few rapids encountered before the lunch stop at a riverside meadow. After lunch the pace picks up steadily until arrival at Angostura, where the party takes out and returns to San Jose. Orchids and other wildflowers, butterflies, and tropical birds including toucans, parrots, cormorants and martins can be observed all along the river. **Cost:** $55 includes bus transportation from San Jose. **When:** On request. **Contact:** Costa Rica Expeditions, Apartado 43, Turrialba, Costa Rica; phone 56-03-95; or P.O. Box 4112, Woodside, CA 94062, USA.

Guatemala

Rafting through the Jungle: A 23-day rafting expedition in the Lacandon jungle of Guatemala and Mexico focuses on Mayan ruins. The itinerary includes Bonampak, Laguna Miramar and its island ruins, Tecolote, Yaxchilan, Piedras Negras, Palenque and many smaller ruins. Participants learn basic whitewater, safety and wilderness camping skills, and see a variety of exotic birds and other wildlife. There are also opportunities for hiking, swimming and fishing. **Cost:** $880 from San Cristobal de las Casas, Mexico. **When:** March. **Contact:** Sacred Monkey Expeditions, Box 363, Jerome, AZ 86331, USA; phone (602)634-5711. *(M)*

Rafting the Pathway of the Gods: Once known as the "pathway of the gods," the Usumacinta River may be explored along with the Mayan ruins on its shores on a 13-day rafting trip. Departing from Villahermosa, Mexico, participants help row on the calm stretches and moderate rapids of the Usumacinta as it passes through the jungle.

Rafters stop to swim and explore the deep green pools at the waterfalls of Budsilja River. Participants also investigate the stone sculptures, carved stelae and polychrome ceramics at the Mayan sites of Yaxchilan and Piedras Negras. The take-out point is near Palenque in Mexico, site of another Mayan ruin. **Cost:** $765 includes equipment, meals. **When:** March. **Contact:** Wilderness World, 1342 Jewell Ave., Pacific Grove, CA 93950, USA; phone (408)373-5882. ***(M)***

EUROPE

France

Alpine Exploration: Rafters explore whitewater rivers in the French Alps and Pyrenees on a 2-week trip originating and ending in Lyon. Several dozen rivers are under consideration for the trip, most known only to European kayakers and never before rafted. The exploratory nature of the trip requires flexibility and cooperation among the participants. Definitely on the itinerary is the Grand Canyon of the Verdon River, where the river dives underground for several hundred yards through a formation called the Emerald Vault. Most of the river stretches rafted are between 10 and 30 miles long and drop 30 to 50 feet a mile, offering challenging rapids. Time is provided to sample local culture and cuisine. The trip is limited to about 6 members. **Cost:** $1,400 includes transportation from Lyon, food, accommodations, equipment, guide. **When:** June. **Contact:** Whitewater Voyages/River Exploration Ltd., 1225 Liberty St., El Cerrito, CA 94530, USA; phone (415)236-7219.

Norway

Norwegian Woods: A variety of Norwegian rivers and forests are explored on a 12-day trip combining rafting with some hiking. After meeting in Oslo, participants take a train to the Flam Valley, ride a steamer through several fjords and drive into the high country for oar and paddle rafting on 4 rivers—the Tisleia, the Begna, the Hallingdal and the Etna. Several days are spent hiking around a lodge in the wilderness area of Jotunheimen, with its highlands, glaciers, waterfalls and mountain peaks. The group then travels north for another series of 1- and 2-day river trips down the Bovra, Sjoa and Lagen rivers. The trip ends in Oslo. **Cost:** $1,522 from Oslo includes transportation, food while camping, group equipment, accommodations, guide. **When:** June. **Contact:** American River Touring Association, 1307 Harrison St., Oakland, CA 94612, USA; phone (415)465-9355.

Yugoslavia

Slavic River Run: Flowing through the spectacular Dinara Range, the waters of the River Tara are traveled by raft during a 10-day journey. Starting from the medieval town of Dubrovnik, travelers set out on traditional handcrafted log rafts to float past rugged mountains with steep cliffs rising from the riverbed to form a 3,400-foot canyon. The water is clear and clean with rushing rapids and stretches of whitewater. Rafters may go ashore to explore limestone caves and hike meandering trails to villages along the route. Guided by local woodsmen, participants have the opportunity to learn the region's history, folklore, ecology and culture. Pitching tents in the meadowlands along the shore and sharing campfire meals round out each day's activities. Upon returning to Dubrovnik, the old-world towns of Zabljak and Foca are visited during the International Music and Folk Dance Festivals in progress throughout the summer. **Cost:** $860 includes camping equipment, meals, lodging, guides. **When:** June to August. **Contact:** American River Touring Association, 1307 Harrison St., Oakland, CA 94612, USA; phone (415)465-9355.

MEXICO

Mexican Wilderness Whitewater: Some of the finest whitewater in Mexico and Central America is featured on a 15-day journey down remote sections of the Rio Grande de Santiago. Hundreds of rapids highlight the 200-mile trip through the canyons of Mexico's plateau. During the last part of the trip group members reach a small hot spring that shoots out of a rock wall into the river. Rafters who can communicate in Spanish have plenty of opportunity to talk with the local people along the river. **Cost:** $535 includes transportation from Guadalajara. **When:** March. **Contact:** Expeditions by Wayne Hussing, 11120 Raphel Rd., Upper Falls, MD 21156, USA; phone (301)592-7247.

Agua Mexicana: A number of whitewater rivers in Mexico's interior can be run by either kayak or pontoon raft on trips ranging in length from 3 to 7 days. The rivers, located near Taxco and Tampico, flow through jungle-covered valleys and run the gamut from clear green waters to muddy, silty rapids similar to the Colorado. All trips depart from Mexico City and float through areas where people live as they have for hundreds of years. Three-day trips are offered on the Balsas and Amacuzac, 5-day outings on the Amacuzac and Moctezuma, and week-long trips on the Moctezuma, the wildest and most remote. Some trips may also be run on the highly challenging Santiago River. **Cost:** About $45 a day includes transportation from Mexico City, food, equipment, guide. **When:** Year-round. **Contact:** Texas Canoe Trails, Star Rt. 2, Box 866B,

New Braunfels, TX 78130, USA; phone (512)964-3760. *(M)*

MIDDLE EAST

Turkey

Turkish Tandem: A 20-day expedition includes 6 days rafting the Euphrates and Coruh rivers. Flying in from New York, travelers tour Istanbul before flying on to the old Roman town of Malatya. From here participants take a bus to the Euphrates to spend 3 days rafting through a series of large cataracts. When the river slows down upon breaking from the Adiyaman Plateau, rafters take out and travel by plane and bus to Isper. Here group members put in for a 3-day float on the challenging Coruh River, called "the Crazy River" by those living on its shores. The take-out point is Artvin near the Russian border, from where participants fly back to Ankara before the return flight to New York. During the trip visits are made to small Turkish villages, the Mausoleum of Antiochus I on Mt. Nemrut and an abandoned monastery on the shores of the Euphrates. Travelers stay in hotels while in cities and camp out in tents on the rafting portions of the trip. **Cost:** $1,495 from Istanbul includes land and air transportation, meals, hotels, rafting equipment, guides. **When:** May to July. **Contact:** Sobek Expeditions, Inc., P.O. Box 761, Angels Camp, CA 95222, USA; phone (209)736-2924. *(M)*

SOUTH AMERICA

Chile

The Bio-Bio by Raft: Rafters travel through heavy whitewater for 15

days on the Bio-Bio, the largest river in Chile, named by the Mapuche Indians after the song of a native bird. Participants follow the river down the steep western slope of the Andes, camping on the banks and stopping at hot springs along the way. The absence of snakes and mosquitoes in this region is a feature that many participants may appreciate. When not challenged by the river's powerful rapids, adventurers observe and photograph the scenery including a 9,700-foot-high smoking volcano. The Andes present snow-capped panoramic views and participants pass by alpine lakes, glaciers and many tributary waterfalls including one plunging 230 feet directly into the main river. **Cost:** $1,065 includes ground transportation, guides, rafting equipment, meals. **When:** January to March. **Contact:** Sobek Expeditions, Inc., P.O. Box 761, Angels Camp, CA 95222, USA; phone (209)736-2924. *(M)*

Peru

Rafting in the Andes: The remote and untouched Apurimac River is rafted on a 22-day trip that also involves considerable hiking in the Cordillera Vilcabamba. After a day in Lima, participants fly to Cuzco, spend a day there, then take a train to Machu Picchu. Following a day at the ruins, the party travels by train and truck into the mountains for a 6-day hike. The trail passes through the heart of the Andes and leads to Apurimac Canyon, where the group puts in and begins rafting. For 8 days they paddle through the Peruvian wilderness, camping on the river bank each night. Takeout point is at a remote inn and return to Lima is by truck and plane. **Cost:** $1,795 from Lima includes transportation, food, equipment, guides. **When:** July, August. **Contact:** Andean Odyssey Tours, 2141 14th St., Suite 1, Boulder, CO 80302, USA. *(M)*

Urubamba Expedition: A 16-day trip down the Urubamba River is divided into 2 sections, on the upper and lower portions of the river. Participants fly from Miami to Lima, then to Cuzco at 11,000 feet in the Andes. The pre-river activities include exploration of the Inca fortresses of Sacsahuaman, Pisac and Ollantaytambo. The group then descends from the highlands via a narrow-gauge railroad through cactus country to the lush cloud forest of the upper Urubamba River. At Pongo Mainique the Urubamba breaks out of the Andes between vertical walls of granite overhung with dense jungle and enters the Amazon Basin. The trip ends with a flight above the unexplored mountains of the northern Cordillera Vilcabamba and an aerial view of the remote falls of Cutibireni, followed by an overland trip to the coast across the Andes. **Cost:** On request. **When:** October, November. **Contact:** Andes Whitewater & Amazon Expeditions, 310 W. Grandview Blvd., Erie, PA 16508, USA; phone (814)866-0701; summer: Box 4845, Stateline, NV 89449, USA; phone (702)588-3002. *(M)*

Peruvian Adventure: The Chimu ruins at Chan Chan and the Andean cities of Cuzco and Machu Picchu, once the hub of the Inca Empire, make Peru an interesting country for archaeologists and travelers alike. Beginning at Cuzco, 5- to 8-day trips provide participants with opportunities to explore a variety of ancient landmarks and artifacts. Routes used are the Urubamba River run and the Inca Trail to Machu Picchu. Cuzco itself provides stone streets and colorful shops. Knowledgeable guides provide an introduction to Peruvian culture, both ancient and modern. **Cost:** $297 for 5 days, $250 for 6 days, $460 for 8 days. **When:** May to September. **Contact:** Explorandes, Nicolas de Pierola 662, 238933. 205, Lima, Peru; phone 23-6992. *(M)*

Peruvian River Trips: River runners may choose inflatable rafts, Indian balsa rafts or canoes to navigate either calm waters or whitewater on Peruvian rivers. For those seeking tranquil travel, a balsa raft trip is offered down the Pachitea River; participants visit gold panners working the banks of the Black River. Rafters desiring the challenge of whitewater may try a trip by inflatable raft on the turbulent waters of the Maranon River. A tamer whitewater experience is offered by Indian balsa raft or canoe down the Huallaga River; the trip departs from Tingo Maria or Tocache and travels downriver to Juanjui or Shapaja. **Cost:** On request. **When:** On request. **Contact:** Transcontinental S.A., Adventure Travel Dept., Jr. Ocona 180, Of. 406, Lima, Peru; phone 273901.

UNITED STATES

Alaska

Rafting above the Arctic Circle: A combination hiking and river rafting trip of 14 to 16 days traverses tundra and forests on the southern edge of the Brooks Range. Participants fly from Bettles, just above the Arctic Circle, to the small Eskimo village of Anaktuvuk, where they begin a 75-mile hike to remote Mt. Doonerak. Fresh food is flown into the campsite, and participants explore the remains of mining and trapping settlements in the surrounding country. After passing through the Gates of the Arctic National Monument, participants spend the rest of the trip rafting the Koyukuk River's main channel to Bettles, the trip's final destination. Participants may fly from Bettles to Mt. Doonerak by bush plane and complete only the river portion of the trip in 8 days. Family rates are available. **Cost:** $950 to $1,250 for hiking and rafting, $850 for rafting trip only includes rafts, food, flight from Bettles to Anaktuvuk, bush pilot surveillance for emergency use, guide. **When:** June to September. **Contact:** Alaska Fish and Trails Unlimited, Star Rt., Box 20154, Fairbanks, AK 99701, USA. *(M)*

North Country River Rafting: The ever-changing Chilikadrotna River provides the setting for an 11-day rafting experience. A group of 10 people or less negotiates the Chilikadrotna with water conditions ranging from still and subdued to raging whitewater. From Dillingham a float plane delivers participants to Twin Lakes, the starting point for the 106-mile run. Moose, bears, wolves and spawning salmon may be sighted along the way. **Cost:** $1,000. **When:** July. **Contact:** Alaska Raft Adventures,

Box 73264, Fairbanks, AK 99707, USA; phone (907)452-1465. *(M)*

Kobuk River Raft Adventure: The initial 8-mile stretch of whitewater introduces an exciting and challenging river voyage. Nestled on the south slope of the Brooks Range, Walter Lake is the starting point of a 12-day raft trip into the wilderness of Alaska. Wolves, bears and moose may be visible as rafters navigate the river for 150 miles. The group takes out at the Eskimo village of Kobuk and flies from there to Kotzebue. Free time is available to explore this northwest coast village where mainland and native cultures meet. **Cost:** $1,200 includes equipment, food, transportation to and from the starting point. **When:** July. **Contact:** Alaska Raft Adventures, Box 73264, Fairbanks, AK 99707, USA; phone (907)452-1465. *(M)*

Tatshenshini River Trip: A trip down the Tatshenshini and Alsek rivers provides visitors with a taste of moderate whitewater wilderness experience. During a week-long trip that puts in near Dalton Post the journey goes into the Yukon Territory and back into British Columbia where the Tatshenshini joins the Alsek. Trip members drift past the faces of numerous glaciers and view the area's geologic forces at work. Lowlands are forested and contain an abundance of wildlife, and the rivers teem with salmon during the fall. The trip's take-out point is near the American-Canadian border above Dry Bay on the Gulf of Alaska. The return flight to Juneau adds to the wilderness experience with views of Mt. Fairweather, the highest point in British Columbia, as well as the scarred Lituya Bay which still shows signs of the recent avalanche and tidal wave disaster. In addition, the return flight passes over the many peaks at Glacier Bay. **Cost:** On request. **When:** July. **Contact:** Alaska Wilderness Expeditions, Inc., P.O. Box 7814, Ketchikan, AK 99901, USA.

Arctic Adventures: Participants on 8- to 15-day expeditions experience the arctic wilderness of northern Alaska. Starting deep in the Gates of the Arctic country, group members raft their way down the Noatak, Kobuk or Alatna rivers. Along the way, campers view the unspoiled Brooks Range, home of caribou, grizzly bears and mountain goats. The voyages are exploratory in nature, and participants should be prepared for some frontier hardships and to assist in loading, rigging and other expedition work. Trips are also offered on the Tatshenshini and Copper rivers. **Cost:** $750 to $1,500. **When:** August. **Contact:** Colorado River and Trail Expeditions, Inc., 5058 S. 300 W., Salt Lake City, UT 84107, USA; phone (801)261-1789 or 485-8572.

Rafting in the Brooks Range: Beginning in the proposed Gates of the Arctic National Park, the Noatak River bisects 12,000 square miles of untouched wilderness. Participants on 11- to 22-day trips can raft either the upper or lower portions of the river, or combine the two itineraries. The upper Noatak weaves through a vast basin of tundra, rimmed by the DeLong and Baird mountains. Group members fly to the river's headwaters, follow it for 135 miles and finally rendezvous with the plane near the confluence of the Noatak and Cutler rivers. Those who choose to travel the lower Noatak set out from Cutler River and travel 195 miles downstream to the Eskimo village of Noatak. The lower Noatak is a major transportation route for Eskimos, and small groups are encountered during their fall hunting and fishing trips. The combined itineraries make for a 22-day, 330-mile expedition. **Cost:** $1,045 to $1,881 includes air charter, food, equipment, guide. **When:** August, September. **Contact:** ECHO: The Wilderness Company, Inc., 6505 Telegraph Ave., Oakland, CA 94609, USA; phone (415)658-5075. ***(M)***

Rafting the Yukon Headwaters: Lakes Bennett, Tagish and Atlin, located in the northwest corner of British Columbia, form the headwaters of the Yukon and are the setting for a week-long trip. Participants gather in Skagway, Alaska for sightseeing and an overnight stay, and then travel by rail to Carcross, British Columbia. Here the rafting begins through the lake system and onto the Yukon with visits to ghost towns and points of interest along the way. The final 2 days are spent in Atlin sightseeing and making a day trip to a hot mineral spring. **Cost:** $550 includes food, accommodations, equipment, sightseeing, guide. **When:** July, September. **Contact:** Klondike Safaris, P.O. Box 1898, Skagway, AK 99840, USA.

Floating the Kobuk: A small group of rafters accompanied by an experienced wilderness guide floats down the Kobuk River on 11- and 14-day trips. The trips begin with a flight by float plane from the town of Kobuk to the river's headwaters at Walker Lake. After fishing and exploring here for a day or two, participants put in for a 145-mile river journey past towering mountains to Kobuk. Along the way rafters learn how to handle the boat and become familiar with local flora and fauna. Nights are spent camping along the river banks. **Cost:** $1,035 for 11 days, $1,097 for 14 days includes roundtrip transportation from Bettles, meals, rafting and camping equipment, guide. **When:** August, September. **Contact:** The Northern Wilderness Company, P.O. Box 25795, Seattle, WA 98125, USA; phone (206)633-3946. *(M)*

Mountain and Glacier Rafting: The rugged St. Elias Mountains, several active glaciers and a plethora of rare wildlife surround rafters on a 10-day trip down the Tatshenshini River. The party gathers in Haines and drives about 3 hours to Dalton Post, an abandoned hunting station at the confluence of the Tatshenshini and Klukshu rivers, where the rafting trip begins. The river courses beneath countless 8,000-foot peaks and through setaceous forest where bald eagles, grizzlies, moose, mountain goats, beavers, muskrats, wolverines and foxes may be seen. Edible plants found along the river are part of the daily diet. Participants may hike along the surface of one of the region's unnamed glaciers to listen to the creak of the moving mass of ice. The northern lights illuminate the night sky. **Cost:** $1,020 includes transportation from Haines, food, group equipment, guides. **When:**

June to August. **Contact:** Sobek Expeditions, Inc., P.O. Box 761, Angels Camp, CA 95222, USA; phone (209)736-2924. *(M)*

Float Trips in the Brooks Range: Rafters float through hundreds of miles of uninhabited wilderness near the Continental Divide on 10- or 21-day float trips down the Noatak, one of the most remote river systems in Alaska. The Kobuk River is the site of another 10-day float trip in which participants fly to Walter Lake and use whitewater rafts and kayaks. The rich Kobuk fishery supports an abundance of birdlife, and rafters see bald and golden eagles, osprey, kingfishers, ravens, arctic terns and gulls as well as wildlife such as wolves, foxes, moose and bears. Travelers take out at the Eskimo village of Kobuk. **Cost:** $650 for Kobuk trip, $695 for 10-day Noatak trip, $995 for 21-day Noatak trip includes guides, food, outfitting, transportation. **When:** July for Noatak, August for Kobuk. **Contact:** Sourdough Outfitters, Bettles, AK 99726, USA; phone (907)692-5252. *(M)*

Arizona

Trips on Foot and by Raft: A series of 4- to 6-day combination hiking and river rafting trips in the Grand Canyon commence at Lees Ferry, Tanner Trail and Havasu Canyon. The trips involve hikes of 8 to 26 miles and river runs as long as 125 miles. Travelers carry necessary gear while negotiating the lively waters of the Colorado River as it makes its way through Marble Canyon. During the hiking portion of each trip, participants arrive at Havasu Falls, visit an Indian village and travel along footpaths. Camps are located along the river bank wherever possible, though some sites are located in commercial campgrounds. Surrounded by rust-colored rock along the river, rafters shoot through whirlpools and drift along stretches of quiet water. All transportation is provided from the departure point at Flagstaff. **Cost:** $160 to $240 includes equipment, meals, transportation, guides. **When:** September. **Contact:** Canyoneers, Inc., P.O. Box 2997, Flagstaff, AZ 86003, USA; phone (602)526-0924. *(M)*

Grand Canyon River Rafting: The muddy, swirling waters of the Colorado River provide an exciting river rafting trip through the jagged rock walls of the Grand Canyon. A bus transports passengers from Las Vegas to the staging area at Lees Ferry for a 9-day float to Pierce Ferry. A shorter trip lasting 6 days ends at Whitmore, 188 miles downstream from Lees Ferry. Passengers may also board at Whitmore for a 4-day trip. Participants should bring sleeping bags weighing not more than 5 pounds. Rain gear is essential, as participants often get wet and the water is quite cold. The trip ends with a banquet in Las Vegas. **Cost:** $375 from Lees Ferry to Pierce Ferry, $275 for 6 days, $125 for 4 days. **When:** May to September. **Contact:** Georgie's Royal River Rats, Box 12489, Las Vegas, NV 89112, USA; phone (702)451-5588. *(M)*

California

River Rafting on the Tuolumne: Led by highly experienced guides, these 2- to 4-day trips down the wild Tuolumne River are not for everybody. Only those with white-water experience should consider taking this roller-coaster ride on some of the most thrilling rapids that California has to offer. Less demanding trips are available on other rivers but this is the one with the explosive excitement that veteran river-riders demand. Children under 12 will not be accepted and only the guides will be allowed to handle the oars. **Cost:** $125 for 2 days, $155 for 3 days, $185 for 4 days includes food, gear, transportation back to point of origin. **When:** April to October. **Contact:** Adventours—Wet & Wild, Inc., Box B, Woodland, CA 95695, USA; phone (916)662-6824. *(M)*

Tuolumne Canyon Cruising: River runners set rafts into the water at Lumsden and spend the next 17 miles on a stretch of the Tuolumne River that boasts over 60 rapids. Trips are run most of the spring and summer, but autumn trips are especially beautiful as the canyon's colors change. **Cost:** $125 to $170 includes meals, all essential river equipment, guides. **When:** April to September. **Contact:** American River Touring Association, 1307 Harrison St., Oakland, CA 94612, USA; phone (415)465-9355.

Western Whitewater: In a fleet of 4 to 5 boats, rafters can join up to 30 other people in 2- to 4-day trips down the Klamath, Merced, Stanislaus, American and Tuolumne rivers. During the journey, participants choose between joining a paddle crew to navigate a course down the river, paddling inflatable kayaks (on the Klamath only), or sitting back while guides handle the oars. The Klamath flows through the heavily forested coastal range and provides warm waters with plenty of rapids and swimming holes. Camp is pitched on sandbars or along shore. Tumbling out of Yosemite National Park, the Merced during spring run-off presents a 20-mile run highlighted by ⅜-mile-long rapids and a 20-foot (portaged) waterfall. Rafters who want excitement can run the Tuolumne as it plunges down 585 feet over 17 miles. **Cost:** $97 to $230 depending on the river, partici-

Participants can take an intensive instructors course from Whitewater Voyages; the 7-day workshop on the American and Stanislaus rivers in California costs $315. (Whitewater Voyages/River Exploration Ltd.)

pant's age, day of the week, number of days out; includes equipment, meals, instruction, guides. **When:** April to October. **Contact:** ECHO: The Wilderness Company, Inc., 6505 Telegraph Ave., Oakland, CA 94609, USA; phone (415)658-5075 or 658-5080. ***(M)***

Whitewater Workshops: California's second-largest river, the Klamath, serves as a whitewater classroom for 5 rafting workshops. The workshops vary in length from 3 to 6 days and include both oar and paddle instruction. A 67-mile run takes rafters from Horse Creek to Ti Bar on the upper Klamath, and those unable to attend the full workshop may join the 40-mile rarely run section of the river from Horse Creek to Happy Camp. A more challenging run is from Happy Camp to Ti Bar—30 river miles. The emphasis of the trips is on the theory and technique of whitewater boating, canoe strokes in paddle rafts, equipment purchase, maintenance, first aid, rescue activities and wilderness ecology. **Cost:** $115 to $200 includes meals, accommodations, instruction. **When:** April, July. **Contact:** James Henry River Journeys, 1078 Keith, Berkeley, CA 94708, USA; phone (415)527-4649.

A Week's Whitewater Course: A week-long course taught on the American River provides intensive instruction in whitewater rafting. The course focuses on reading rapids and raft guiding, and the instructors use either oars or paddles, depending on student interest. Other skills covered include boat patching and repair, safety techniques and camping. Rafters spend nights on the riverside, at primitive and developed campsites. In addition to the prescheduled sessions, the course can be run by special arrangement for groups of 3 or more students. **Cost:** $175 to $210, depending on number of students, includes food, equipment, instruction. **When:** June, August and by arrangement. **Contact:** Mother Lode Outdoor School, 581 Continental Dr., San Jose, CA 95111, USA; phone (408)578-5434. *(M)*

California Rafting: River rafters can run any or all of 7 whitewater rivers in California, be it a short 1-day float down the popular Stanislaus or a longer 4-day excursion deep into the Siskiyous on northern California's Klamath River. The rivers each offer a different challenge and mood. The Tuolumne is the wildest run, pouring from Yosemite in one of the steepest navigable river gradients in the world. Another run, the east fork of the Carson, takes rafters down the eastern slopes of the Sierras, starting in California and ending in Nevada with landscapes from Sierra meadows to desert canyons along the way. Runs down the American River are also available. Participants camp at night along the rivers. **Cost:** $35 to $180, depending on the trip, includes river equipment, meals, guides. **When:** March to September. **Contact:** OARS Inc., P.O. Box 67, Angels Camp, CA 95222, USA; phone (209)736-2924 or 736-2661. *(M)*

Rapid Rafting: Two-day trips are offered on the American and Stanislaus rivers. The American River trip begins with a few rapids widely spaced by gentle current. Further downstream, the canyon constricts into a gorge, the river gathers speed, and rafters race through several miles of continuous whitewater. The Stanislaus River offers the fastest water at the beginning of the trip, starting one minute after the put-in point and continuing for 5 miles. The canyon through which the river flows has high limestone cliffs and river-scoured rocks. New Melones Dam is nearing completion, and while it is not clear when the canyon will be flooded, there is not much time left to see the canyon unchanged. **Cost:** $55 for 1 day, $110 for 2 days. **When:** April to August for American River, April to September for Stanislaus River. **Contact:** Outdoor Adventures, 3109 Fillmore St., San Francisco, CA 94123, USA; phone (415)567-9938. *(M)*

Whitewater Women: Three 5-day whitewater trips for women explore different aspects of river life. The Klamath River in northern California is the setting for an unusual trip which uses dream recording and guided fantasies to focus the participants' experience of challenge, adaptability and courage. A similar trip, also on the Klamath, combines self-awareness and confidence exercises with more specific instruction in whitewater skills. A third course on Oregon's Rogue

River teaches women to become whitewater guides. Intensive instruction is offered in all aspects of river travel, with special emphasis on safety techniques and emergency procedures. All 3 trips include both oar and paddle work, with opportunities for kayaking as well. **Cost:** $230 for each trip includes food, group equipment, instruction, transportation, guide. **When:** June to September. **Contact:** Outdoor Education Association, 11468 Redwood Hwy., Wilderville, OR 97543, USA; phone (503)479-4215.

Klamath River Run: The Klamath River snakes through the Siskiyou Mountains of northern California to flow into the ocean in the heart of the redwood country. Participants travel 40 miles down the river on a 6-day raft trip beginning near the Scott River. The first half of the trip traverses a relatively easy section of the river, allowing individuals to run rapids in inflatable kayaks if they wish. The rest of the trip is a more standard river run and passes through forested mountains and past rocky outcroppings. As a highlight of the downstream portion of the trip rafters may wade in the waist-deep water of Ukonom Creek to a miniature amphitheater hidden in the forest. The take-out is at Happy Point. **Cost:** $215 for adults, $160 for children under 12. **When:** June to August. **Contact:** Outdoors Unlimited, 2500 Fifth Ave., Sacramento, CA 95818, USA; phone (916)452-1081. ***(M)***

Whitewater Guide School: For 7 days participants in an intensive instructors workshop learn fundamental and advanced skills in maneuvering oar and paddle rafts, reading whitewater, surviving in the wilderness and handling emergency situations. Four days are spent on the Stanislaus River and 3 days on the American. Participants specialize in either rowing or paddling during the program (wet suits are necessary), and it is recommended that students have experience in Red Cross first-aid techniques before embarking on the course. The guide school also provides instruction in the operation of wilderness stoves and basic wilderness cooking. **Cost:** $315 includes equipment, instruction, transportation. **When:** March to May, September. **Contact:** Whitewater Voyages/River Exploration Ltd., 1225 Liberty St., El Cerrito, CA 94530, USA; phone (415)236-7219.

Floating Western Rivers: Several California rivers are used for a variety of whitewater river experiences lasting from 1 to 4 days. The Stanislaus River, originating in the High Sierras, combines whitewater with lush side canyons and explorable creeks, as well as numerous abandoned gold-mining sites. Indian petroglyphs and pestle holes, evidence of the Miwok Indian culture, are also visible. The American River provides a challenging 18-mile whitewater run where trip members negotiate such rapids as the Meatgrinder and Troublemaker. The Eel River is a spring river, permitting a brief running season with 2- to 5-day trips. Other trip locations available to rafting enthusiasts are the Kern, Merced, Klamath, King and East Carson rivers. **Cost:** $45 to $180 depending on trip includes equipment, food. **When:** March to October. **Contact:** Zephyr River Expeditions, P.O. Box 2607, Sonora, CA 95370, USA; phone (209)532-6249. *(M)*

Colorado

Colorado River Float: Participants board rafts midway between Steamboat Springs and Vail to begin a 4- to 5-hour float down the upper Colorado River. Rafters have a choice of paddling a guided raft or photographing the alpine scenery while experienced boat handlers do the rowing. The trip is especially designed for those who want a taste of rafting and do not have the time to enjoy a longer expedition. Occasional stretches of whitewater and a hearty picnic lunch along the shore are guaranteed. The entire journey, including a bus trip to the river, takes approximately 10 hours. **Cost:** $25 for adults, $18 for children under 18 includes equipment, lunch, guides, roundtrip transportation from Steamboat Springs. **When:** June to September. **Contact:** Adventure Bound, Inc., 6179 S. Adams Dr., Littleton, CO 80121, USA; phone (303)771-3752. *(M)*

Canyon River Runs: The desert canyon country of southern Utah and southwestern Colorado is outstanding in its archaeologic and geologic interest; the rivers that run through this country enable rafters to combine whitewater adventure with exploration of the region. In Utah, participants may take trips of 2 to 6 days on the San Juan River which is often compared to the Colorado River in the Grand Canyon, although it lacks the awesome rapids of the Colorado. The Dolores River in Colorado is accessible in the early summer, and provides challenging rafting opportunities for veterans of other river experiences on 3- and 6-day trips. Rafts are piloted by experienced boatmen/guides, and a shuttle return to the departure point is included on all trips. **Cost:** On request. **When:** May, June. **Contact:** Colorado Rivers-Tours, P.O. Box 1386, Durango, CO 81301, USA; phone (303)259-0708.

Three Canyons of the Dolores River: Oar-powered, inflatable boats designed specifically for the area transport rafters down the Dolores River on trips lasting 2, 3 and 4 days. Camping on beaches and banks, rafters travel in small groups guided by veteran river runners. Participants can choose to run any of 3 canyons on the Dolores. On the 4-day trip beginning at 6,000 feet, rafters descend through the canyon at a drop rate of nearly 80 feet a mile through forests of evergreens and ponderosa pines. Another trip lasts 3 days and travels through Slick Rock Canyon, offering 36 miles of pink, red and white sandstone cliffs studded with pinion and juniper forests. Participants on the 2-day trip run The Narrows, one of the longest rapids in the Colorado system and part of Gateway Canyon. In the lower portion of the run participants may spot deer, geese, herons and beavers. Rafters bus back to Cortez from Slick Rock and Dolores canyons while those on the Gateway Canyon trip bus back to Grand Junction at the end of the run. **Cost:** From $135 for 2 days to $295 for 4 days includes transportation, equipment, meals, guides. **When:** April, May. **Contact:** Outlaw Trails Inc., P.O. Box 336, Green River, UT 84525, USA; phone (801)564-3477. *(M)*

Roaring Fork River Trips: Day trips leaving from Glenwood Springs are offered on the Roaring Fork and Colorado rivers. For those wishing a half-day trip, a route begins on the Roaring Fork and terminates at Riverside Park; those out for the day stay on the boat and continue through the confluence of the Roaring Fork and the Colorado floating down that river to take-out at South Canyon. The area is rich in striking geological formations, and fairly rugged rapids are encountered, including Shoshone, Horseshoe Bend and Cemetery. Lunch is served, but a "brown bag" arrangement can also be made. Rafters not desiring a guide can rent rafts and equipment for their own trips. **Cost:** $18 for half-day, $22 for full day ($14 and $18 without lunch) includes food, rafts, equipment, guide; $23 a day for raft rental. **When:** On request. **Contact:** Wilderness Encounter, 720 Grand Ave., Glenwood Springs, CO 81601, USA; phone (303)945-8365. *(M)*

Georgia

Rafting the Chattooga: A guide accompanies each raft on a day-long journey down the Chattooga River, famous for both its whitewater rapids and as the location of the film *Deliverance*. Rafters meet for the Chattooga trips in the morning at the Chattooga Outpost in Sumter National Forest. Participants have the opportunity to paddle the rafts on wild and scenic whitewater characterized by frequent ledges and falls of up to 6 feet. Paddlers find that the river drops a total of 275 feet in the final 6 miles. Lunch is provided on the trip and participants are transported back to the Outpost sometime around 5 p.m. Waterproof bags are supplied for cameras. Raft trips are also run on the Nantahala River in North Carolina and the Ocoee River in Tennessee. **Cost:** $30 includes lunch, guides, transportation, equipment. **When:** Year-round. **Contact:** Nantahala Outdoor Center, Star Rt., Box 68, Bryson City, NC 28713, USA; phone (704)488-2175. ***(M)***

Southeastern Rapids Trips: Rafters spend 1 or 2 days exploring the Chattooga River along the Georgia-South Carolina border. A full-day float down the Chattooga includes over 40 sets of rapids, waterfalls and wild southern scenery. A calmer section, with a dozen rapids and large mountain vistas, is also available. Adventurers may also spend 2 days on the river, with wilderness camping and a steak dinner at night; if participants wish, the second day may be given to hiking through mountain areas such as Chauga Gorge, Raubun Bald and the Bartram Trail. Participants must be good swimmers. Smorgasbord lunches are available on all trips, and camping is allowed in the surrounding Sumter National Forest. **Cost:** $35 and $100. Canoe and kayak instruction is also offered. **When:** April to October. **Contact:** Southeastern Expeditions, Inc., Suite 220, 1955 Cliff Valley Wy. NE, Atlanta, GA 30329, USA; phone (404)329-0433.

Idaho

Running the "River of No Return": Participants can choose to battle the whitewater of either the Salmon River or the Middle Fork of the Salmon River on 5-day raft trips. The rivers traverse a wild and scenic gorge in the Idaho Primitive Area, transporting rafters through country of granite and pine that abounds in bighorn sheep, deer, otters, hawk eagles and other wildlife. Participants see old mining camps, deserted homesteads, hermits and hotsprings on the shoreline and in the canyons while floating through clear water and numerous large rapids. Salmon River trips meet at the Salmon City Airport and Middle Fork trips at the Bear Valley Air Strip. Group size is between 10 and 20 persons. **Cost:** $260 for Salmon River trip, $360 for Middle Fork trip includes meals, guides, rafting equipment. **When:** July to September. **Contact:** Adventure River Expeditions, 4211 Mars Wy., Salt Lake City, UT 84117, USA; phone (801)278-1867. *(M)*

Rafting Hells Canyon on the Snake: Adventurers can journey for 6 days through the deepest river gorge in North America. The Hells Canyon stretch of the Snake River is over a fifth of a mile deeper than the Grand Canyon and has more than enough whitewater for an exciting journey. Guided by veteran rafters, the trip begins with a discussion on wildlife and conservation so participants will have minimal impact on the river ecosystem. Rafters camp on beaches along the shore and have plenty of time for swimming and exploring side canyons. The journey is made in 9- and 16-foot neoprene boats that are completely equipped for safety. **Cost:** $325 from Boise includes equipment, meals, guides, instruction. **When:** September. **Contact:** American Wilderness Experience, Box 1486A, Boulder, CO 80306, USA; phone (303)499-0056. *(M)*

Whitewater on the Middle Fork: Numerous challenging rapids highlight a 6-day trip by oar-powered raft down the Middle Fork of the Salmon River. After meeting in Salmon, rafters travel by van or small plane to the put-in point at the river's headwaters. For 3 days, they encounter some whitewater and stop at a hot springs amid high alpine scenery before the river enters a steep-walled canyon where Indian pictographs and a greater concentration of wildlife are seen. As the river picks up volume from many side streams, the rapids grow in intensity; a long stretch of whitewater precedes arrival at the takeout point, where the Middle Fork flows into the Main Salmon. Transportation is provided back to Salmon or Missoula, Montana. **Cost:** $425 to $445, depending on number in party, includes transportation

from Salmon, food, equipment, guides. **When:** June to August. **Contact:** Frontier Expeditions, Inc., P.O. Box 839, North Fork, ID 83466, USA; phone (208)865-2200; winter: 3921 S. Helena St., Aurora, CO 80013, USA; phone (303)693-0349.

Main Salmon Float Trip: Rafters journey on the Main Salmon for 4 days during a 5-day trip on the "River of No Return." A maximum of 24 participants meet in Boise for a charter flight to the town of Salmon, then the group boards a bus and rides to the put-in point at Corn Creek. In each whitewater raft 4 participants and 1 guide run the river to Mackay Bar Lodge, where participants spend 2 nights and 1 day kayaking, backpacking, horseback riding or exploring Indian caves. While on the river participants camp on sandy beaches and have time for exploring, swimming and photography. Depending on river conditions, participants may have the opportunity to handle the oars on trips with more than 16 participants. On the morning of the sixth day, river runners conclude the trip with a flight back to Boise. **Cost:** $485 from Boise includes transportation, river equipment, meals, guides, accommodations. **When:** June to September. **Contact:** Mackay Bar, 3190 Airport Wy., Boise, ID 83705, USA; phone (208)344-1881. ***(M)***

To Hells Canyon and Back: Adventurers descend 1½ miles into a gorge separating the Wallowa Mountains and the Seven Devils to spend 6 days on a river running expedition. In the course of 85 miles participants plummet over furious rapids and float across the gentle straits of the Snake River in Hells Canyon. During the first 2 days rafters encounter a precipitous drop which has created some of the best cataracts in the deepest gorge in North America. The imprint of past inhabitants can be seen in Stone Age shelters, petroglyphs, weathered homesteads and worn corrals. As a natural sanctuary, the canyon gives rafters the opportunity to observe abundant mammals, birds and fish while hiking or rafting. Participants have ample time for exploring and photographing and are returned to Boise when the trip comes to a close. **Cost:** $370 for adults, $295 for youths includes accommodations, food, guides, roundtrip transportation from Boise. **When:** June, July. **Contact:**

OARS Inc., P.O. Box 67, Angels Camp, CA 95222, USA; phone (209)736-2924 or 736-2661. *(M)*

Oar-Powered Rafting on the Salmon: For 6 days participants journey in oar-powered rafts through one of the last wilderness areas in the United States. The group meets in the town of Salmon then buses to the river put-in. River runners with an extensive background in natural history guide participants past high mountain peaks to campsites on sandy beaches. Meals are prepared by the guides, but participants set up their own tents. A Salmon River trip is well suited to families with children as the river is fairly tame. Rafters may see black bears, deer, elk, bighorn sheep, mountain goats and other wildlife. July and August provide warm water for swimming. From the take-out point near Riggins, participants are transported to McCall Airport where individuals make their own arrangements for returning to Salmon or Boise; those who wish may have their cars driven to the take-out point. **Cost:** $385 for adults, $289 for children includes transportation from Salmon to McCall, guides, meals, rafting equipment. **When:** June to September. **Contact:** Western Rivers of Idaho, P.O. Box 7129, University Sta., Provo, UT 84602, USA; phone (801)377-9750 or tollfree (800)453-1482. *(M)*

Highwater Rafting: A variety of river trips is available to participants in 3-, 6- and 10-day durations. The 3-day journey is a 36-

mile float through Hells Canyon on the Snake River, with transportation from Boise included. Six-day excursions include: a journey down the Main Salmon River, which contains excellent rapids and borders the largest contiguous wildlife region in the country; an 85-mile trip through Hells Canyon; a 110-mile journey along the Salmon Middle Fork, including Impassable Canyon and a series of rapids; a spring float down the Owyhee River, little known but quite lively; and a 77-mile trip down the Main Salmon combined with a horseback ride through the Upper Crooked Creek region. The 10-day journey mixes 4 days on the Salmon with a horsepacking expedition through the Nez Perce National Forest. **Cost:** $245 to $695 includes all equipment except sleeping bags, food, transportation to Boise, Lewiston or Salmon. **When:** April to September. **Contact:** Wilderness Encounters, Inc., P.O. Box 3417, Boise, ID 83703, USA; phone (208)343-7728.

Maine

A Day on the River: Day-long rafting trips travel over stretches of whitewater on the Kennebec and Penobscot rivers. Offered on weekdays, the Kennebec trip begins at Moosehead Lake, proceeds on the river's headwaters and plunges through steep-walled canyons to The Forks. The Penobscot trip takes place on weekends, beginning at Chesuncook Lake and following the river along the foot of Mt. Katahdin. Both trips are preceded by a continental breakfast at a base camp in Greenville and include a lunch cookout. Return is made to Greenville by 6 p.m. **Cost:** $43. **When:** On request. **Contact:** Eastern River Expeditions Inc., 824 Petem Rd., Kingsville, MD 21087, USA; phone (301)879-8555. ***(M)***

Minnesota

Family Rafting: A 5-day trip is offered in inflatable "Huck Finn" rafts down the St. Croix and Namekagon rivers, national wild and scenic rivers punctuated by occasional rapids and whitewater. Canoes and kayaks are also provided for those interested in running rapids in smaller boats. During a moonlight float planned for 1 night of the trip, participants see deer, raccoons and great blue herons. The trip starts near Trego and ends at Snake River Ferry, 50 miles downriver. Families are easily accommodated. **Cost:** $180 (20 percent off for children under 17). **When:** June. **Contact:** Spirit Waters, 5375 Eureka Rd., Excelsior, MN 55331, USA; phone (612)474-5190. ***(M)***

Montana

Flathead Floating: Half- and full-day trips float past the white sandstone cliffs and high rock walls of a canyon on the Lower Flathead River. The trips leave from West Glacier or Polson, and float down a portion of the river below Kerr Dam. High and sustained whitewater is encountered, and bird life and waterfowl are plentiful along the route. **Cost:** $15, $30 and $150 includes transportation from Polson, equipment, guides; reduced rates for children. **When:** Daily April to September. **Contact:** Glacier Raft Company, Box 264, West Glacier, MT 59936, USA; phone (406)888-5541.

New Mexico

Rio Grande Rapids: The Rio Grande Gorge is the home of the wildest whitewater on the 1,900-mile Rio Grande, and an overnight rafting trip runs this stretch for 17 miles. Rafters meet at Taos Junction Bridge, arriving early if they wish to walk to a spectacular view of the gorge. Then, putting in at Dunn's Bridge they float through calm, flat areas and sheetsided, blackrock gorges. Travel is by either oar- or paddle-powered rafts, and the night is spent camping out near a hot spring. The guides provide instruction in the area's natural features and history en route. The take-out point is in Rio Grande State Park. **Cost:** $80 includes food, transportation, equipment, guides. **When:** May, June. **Contact:** Far Flung Adventures, Box 31, Terlingua, TX 79852, USA; phone (915)371-2489.

North Carolina

French Broad Whitewater: Rafters float through the mountain country of western North Carolina on a 1-day excursion down 7½ miles of the French Broad River. During the 6-hour trip, which departs daily from the town of Hot Springs near the Appalachian Trail, participants float by huge boulders and wooded mountains rising high above the whitewater. Lunch and all necessary whitewater equipment are provided. **Cost:** $20 includes transportation between Hot Springs and the river. **When:** April to November. **Contact:** Smoky Mountain River Expeditions, Inc., P.O. Box 398, Hot Springs, NC 287433, USA; phone (704)622-7260.

Oregon

Rafting the Rogue River: Rafters travel for 5 days from Galice to Foster Bar through the pine-forested areas of the Northwest. In addition to whitewater, the Rogue also offers excellent swimming pools. One day is set aside for exploration on foot during which rafters may spot elk and bears. Paddleboats are available as well as the standard rafts equipped with oars. **Cost:** $258 adult, $233 youth; vehicle shuttle $30 additional. **When:** July to September. **Contact:** ECHO: The Wilderness Company, Inc., 6505 Telegraph Ave., Oakland, CA 94609, USA; phone (415)658-5075. ***(M)***

Owyhee River Boating: Six-day dory trips down the Owyhee are scheduled during the best water flow, offering lively rapids interspersed with unruffled calms. The rims of the canyon are unspoiled, and here participants may see antelope and eagles. Other wildlife observed along the route may be deer, mink, bobcats, bighorn sheep and wild horses. Of geologic interest are the glistening black bluffs of basalt from which issue pure springs and waterfalls. Erosion has exposed fossils and brought agates and other gemstones down to the beaches, creating interest for the rockhound who would otherwise be unable to explore these remote areas. Boats enter the river at Rome, a 2-hour drive from Boise. The trip is limited to 16 persons.

Cost: $296 includes food, equipment, guide. **When:** May. **Contact:** Grand Canyon Dories, P.O. Box 3029, Stanford, CA 94305, USA; phone (415)851-0411.

Hells Canyon Float Trips: Hells Canyon, bounded by the Payette and Nez Perce national forests on the Idaho side and by the Wallowa-Whitman National Forest on the Oregon side, is the site of an 85-mile adventure by raft. From Hells Canyon Dam to the confluence of the Snake and Grande Ronde rivers, trip members spend 6 days riding through thundering rapids, fishing, swimming and hiking in a relaxed camp atmosphere. Participants float the river in oar-powered rafts. As the rafts pass through the deepest canyon in the United States, all the life zones of North America come into view, from alpine tundra to desert environment. Participants may have their cars shuttled to the take-out point or fly back to Oxbow at the end of the trip. **Cost:** $355, plus $45 for flight, $80 for car shuttle. **When:** May to September. **Contact:** Hells Canyon Navigation Co., P.O. Box 145, Oxbow, OR 97840, USA; phone (503)785-3352. ***(M)***

Hells Canyon Float Trip: A 6-day trip by oar-powered raft runs the Snake River through Hells Canyon, the deepest gorge in the United States. The float begins at Hells Canyon Dam and continues past the Imnaha and Salmon rivers to the confluence with the Grande Ronde River, a total of 85 miles. Along the way participants can visit old homesteads, explore abandoned mines and view Indian pic-

On Oregon's Rogue River, guides handle the oars while participants hang on through a boulder-strewn drop. Wilderness World's 5-day Rogue trips are offered from June to September. (Wilderness World)

tographs. On autumn trips the Snake also provides good fishing for smallmouth bass, rainbow trout and crappie. The trip begins and ends at Boise. **Cost:** $435 includes air shuttle from Lewiston, food, guide, gear. **When:** May to October. **Contact:** Idaho Adventures, P.O. Box 834 AD, Salmon, ID 83467, USA; phone (208)756-2986. ***(M)***

Rafting through the Desert: A 5-day rafting trip down the Owyhee River combines whitewater with desert canyon scenery. Putting in at Rome, participants cover a 64-mile stretch of the remote river in southeastern Oregon before taking out at Leslie Gulch. Camp is set up along the river's shores, from where rafters hike up side canyons, possibly encountering desert sheep, wild mustangs, mink and bobcats. The river itself provides good fishing for bass, rainbow trout and catfish, and caves and petroglyphs of Indians pre-dating any known tribe are found along its banks. Travel is in 12- to 17-foot inflatable rafts in groups of 20 or fewer people. **Cost:** $425 includes rafting equipment, meals, guides, tents. **When:** April to June. **Contact:** Lute Jerstad Adventures, P.O. Box 19527, Portland, OR 97219, USA; phone (503)244-4364. *(M)*

Shooting Deschutes: In groups of 10 with 2 instructors, participants learn the skills necessary for running rivers in all types of watercraft: how to manage paddle rafts, "read" water, pick routes through the rapids and load and unload boats. Situated in north-central Oregon, the Deschutes flows north into the Columbia through a deep sandstone and basalt canyon, offering challenging whitewater during the 8-day course. Participants begin the expedition with instruction in the basic skills of food preparation, shelter construction and minimum impact travel. Students also stop along the banks of the river, journey to side canyons and engage in rock climbing, rappelling, hiking and exploring. In all courses participants spend 24 hours on a solo, a time spent camping alone with minimal but adequate food, gear and shelter. **Cost:** $300 includes equipment, meals, instruction, guides. College credit/scholarships available. **When:** June to August. **Contact:** The Northwest Outward Bound School, 0110 SW Bancroft, Portland, OR 97201, USA; phone (503)243-1993. *(M)*

Deschutes and John Day Floats: The Deschutes River runs for 100 miles through a deep and spectacular canyon where spirited rapids are interspersed with quick flowing riffles before it joins the Columbia River near The Dalles. Five-day trips cover the entire 97 miles from Warm Springs to the Columbia. Floating about 20 miles a day, participants stop on the third day to resupply and portage around Sherars Falls. Float trips are also offered on 2 sections of the John Day River. For 3 days, rafters travel 45 miles from Service Creek to Clarno, a briskly flowing stretch with varied scenery and fossil formations along the banks. A 4-day trip from Clarno to Cottonwood features an immense canyon dominated by basalt cliffs and occasionally challenging whitewater. For those interested, instruction in whitewater rafting techniques and an opportunity to row are also available. **Cost:** From $180 for 3 days to $300 for 5 days. **When:** April to September. **Contact:** Northwest River Trips, Rt. 1, Box 11B, Tygh Valley, OR 97063, USA; phone (503)544-2317. *(M)*

Guidance for Guides: Students in an intensive 3-day workshop gain necessary skills to become professional guides or simply learn advanced techniques for independent river running. Safety precautions and emergency procedures are stressed as a framework for developing technical skills, with special emphasis on mental skills—overcoming self-doubt, increasing concentration abilities, dispelling illusory dangers and handling fear. Reading and class time complement the actual river experience. The course operates at several locations: Portland State University and either the Deschutes or Rogue River; California State at Sacramento and the Klamath River; or California State at Chico and the Klamath. Academic credit is available. **Cost:** $250. **When:** June to Septem-

ber. **Contact:** Osprey River Trips, Inc., 11468 Redwood Hwy., Wilderville, OR 97543, USA; phone (503)479-4215. ***(M)***

Rogue River Float: Four-day float trips are offered down one of the first rivers to be classified "Wild and Scenic." Each afternoon, participants set up camp along the banks, with plenty of free time left for swimming, fishing and exploring the surrounding area which features creeks and waterfalls, blooming rhododendrons, ferns and a number of creatures including bears, deer, beavers, ospreys and elk. Rafters are accompanied by experienced whitewater guides who are excellent camp cooks and knowledgeable about natural history. Most participants opt to ride in oar-powered rafts rowed by the guides, but those who wish may join a crew of 6 to 8 who paddle their own boat under guided supervision. Inflatable canoes are available on some trips and inflatable kayaks are well-suited to the lively rapids of the Rogue. **Cost:** $190 includes guide, meals, rafting equipment, transportation back to put-in. **When:** July, August. **Contact:** Outdoor Adventures, 3109 Fillmore St., San Francisco, CA 94123, USA; phone (415)346-8700. ***(M)***

Running the Owyhee: Participants take 5 days to float through the remote desert canyon of the Owyhee River in southeastern Oregon. The journey can be made in inflatable canoes, kayaks, sportyaks, U-paddle rafts or guide-operated, oar-powered rafts. At night, participants camp by the river on sandy beaches and gather around an open fire for meals. During the day as well as in the evening rafters have time for fishing, hiking, photography, swimming and relaxing. Members embark near Rome and in the course of the journey observe Indian artifacts, hot springs and a variety of desert animals and birds. Whitewater occurs with increasing frequency during the 60-mile trip. After take-out, the group returns to Boise. **Cost:** $325 includes all rafting and camping equipment, guides, meals, transportation from Boise. **When:** April, May. **Contact:** Primitive Area Float Trips, Inc., P.O. Box 585, Salmon, ID 83467, USA; phone (208)756-2319.

Rogue Wild River Expeditions: Boats are put in the Rogue River near the town of Almeda and are taken out 4 days later near Agness after taking river voyagers through some of Oregon's most scenic country. Floating in either rubber rafts or wooden drift boats, group members may fish and swim in quiet spots as they drift through the whitewater of the renowned Rogue River. One of the most exciting stretches of water is Devil's Staircase, where the river drops 20 feet in 300 yards. In the evenings participants may watch for deer and black bears near the riverside lodges which provide accommodation. Shorter trips, including fishing expeditions, are offered during the fall and winter. **Cost:** $160 to $350, depending on length of trip, includes equipment, food, accommodations, guide. **When:** May to March. **Contact:** River Trips Unlimited, 900 Murphy Rd. W., Medford,

OR 97501, USA; phone (503)779-3798. *(M)*

Rafting the Grande Ronde: Ninety miles of the Grande Ronde River are covered in a conservation-oriented 5-day trip through lush canyons carved from basalt. One of Oregon's most remote rivers, the Grande Ronde offers whitewater action down its length until it joins the Snake River. The Whitman National Forest, which borders the river, is famous for its herds of deer and elk. The final leg of the trip, from the Washington-Oregon border to Hellers Bar, may be taken as a separate 2-day trip. **Cost:** $100 for 2 days, $270 for 5 days includes all meals, rafting equipment, transportation to and from river. **When:** May to July. **Contact:** Rivers Northwest, 141 Eagle St. NE, Winslow, WA 98110, USA; phone (206)842-5144. *(M)*

River Outfitting: During 1- to 5-day trips on several of Oregon's rivers, participants may choose to paddle 1-person inflatable kayaks or ride in large rafts that are piloted by experienced river runners. For those wishing to use inflatable kayaks, outfitters provide trip itineraries as well as instruction. A support raft carries all personal gear and camping equipment. Groups may choose from the Rogue, Klamath, Umpqua and Deschutes rivers. The Rogue and Klamath offer steep black-walled canyons, abundant wildlife and waters that are safe even for the beginner. More skill in paddling and maneuvering is required on the Umpqua and Deschutes trips. The Umpqua is the less traveled of the 2 rivers and has a number of campsites among the evergreens and deep foliage that border the river. On all trips stops are made for exploring trails along the river, photography, swimming and relaxing. **Cost:** $30 to $240 depending on location and length of trip includes transportation to the put-in point, guides, meals, camping and rafting equipment, instruction. **When:** May to September. **Contact:** Sunrise Scenic Tours, P.O. Box 447, Klamath Falls, OR 97601, USA; phone (503)882-0033. *(M)*

Roguish Rafting: Rafters travel past banks green with fir, pine and oak trees on a 5-day trip down 50 miles of the Rogue River in southwestern Oregon. Participants put in at Galice, pass through rapids at

During half-day trips offered by Nantahala Outdoor Center, paddlers negotiate 4 miles of uninterrupted rapids on Tennessee's Ocoee River. (Nantahala Outdoor Center)

Blossom Bar and Devil's Backbone, proceed through the narrow, shadowed gorge at Mule Creek and take out at Agness. Frequent stops are made to allow time for photography, hiking, swimming and fishing. Guides steer the rafts and prepare all meals, and rafters camp out overnight. The trip is suitable for all ages. **Cost:** $245 includes raft, guide, meals. **When:** June to September. **Contact:** Wilderness World, 1342 Jewell Ave., Pacific Grove, CA 93950, USA; phone (408)373-5882. *(M)*

Pennsylvania

The Great Gorge of the Youghiogheny: Ohiopyle is the meeting place for rafters embarking on a 1-day trip down the Youghiogheny. From Park Headquarters participants take a shuttle bus to the put-in near the falls. Trips run rain or shine, and rafters should be prepared for any turn of the weather. Before the float trip begins, guides give a brief lesson in the basics of safety and river rafting. Midway on the river, rafters stop for lunch and some land exploration. Photographers should take a trip that begins early in the day in order to have the sun shining into the valley for the entire day. Guides provide interesting information on the history of the area from precolonial to modern times. At the end of the trip, having safely run several rapids, rafters are transported back to Park Headquarters in Ohiopyle. **Cost:** $20 on weekdays, $25 on weekends and holidays includes transportation from Ohiopyle, guides, rafting equipment, lunch. **When:** May to November. **Contact:** Mountain Streams and Trail Outfitters, P.O. Box 106, Ohiopyle, PA 15470, USA; phone (412)329-8810.

South Carolina

Chattooga and Nolichucky Trips: Day trips are offered for both beginning and experienced rafters on the Chattooga and Nolichucky rivers. Participants run the Chattooga in groups of 4, paddling 12-foot rafts. The 7-hour trip is relatively easy and is open to people ages 12 and older. No previous rafting experience is necessary as guides provide instruction in proper techniques for running rapids. Rapids are larger and more frequent on the Nolichucky trip, as the river drops into a canyon 11 miles long. Larger rafts are used on the Nolichucky, and rafters must be at least 13 years old; previous river running experience is recommended. **Cost:** $20 to $30 includes equipment, food, guide. **When:** March to November. **Contact:** Wildwater Ltd., Long Creek, SC 29658, USA; phone (803)647-5336; winter, 400 West Rd., Portsmouth, VA 23707, USA; phone (804)397-6658.

Tennessee

Out on the Ocoee: Half-day raft trips run Tennessee's Ocoee River, along a 4½-mile stretch of almost continuous rapids. Because the river is controlled by a TVA dam, the water flow is usually good, even in dry summer months. Participants meet near the town of Ocoee and, after a brief orientation, proceed to the river and put in. Photography is possible but awkward, due to the uninterrupted rapids. Scheduled trips run twice daily from May through September, and off-season trips can be made by arrangement. **Cost:** $15 includes transportation to and from the river, equipment, guide. **When:** Year-round. **Contact:** Nantahala Outdoor Center, Star Rt., Box 68, Bryson City, NC 28713, USA; phone (704)488-2175. *(M)*

Running the Nolichucky: Day trips are offered down 8½ miles of the Nolichucky, an uncrowded river offering moderately challenging whitewater. Class III and IV rapids alternate with quiet sections where rafters can observe the alpine scenery and wildlife, take photographs and relax. An optional outdoor dinner follows the trip. **Cost:** $25 includes transportation back to put-in point, lunch, equipment, guide. **When:** May to October. **Contact:** Nolichucky Expeditions, Inc., Box 484, Erwin, TN 37650, USA; phone (615)743-3221.

Texas

Rio Grande in Winter: The quiet, isolated reaches of the Rio Grande's lower canyons set the stage for a week-long rafting trip. In midwinter the weather is comfortably warm, and there is a great deal of quiet water for peaceful floating or paddling kayaks and canoes. Rafters cover about 100 miles traveling through some of America's most isolated countryside, passing caves, hot springs, spires, arches and natural bridges. Time is allowed for hiking up side canyons and relaxing by the riverside and informal instruction is offered in rafting, kayaking, canoeing and wilderness skills. **Cost:** $275 includes food, equipment, guide. **When:** November to January, March. **Contact:** Outdoor Leadership Training Seminars, 2220 Birch St., Denver, CO 80207, USA; phone (303)333-7831. *(M)*

A Grande Vacation: Winter trips on the mighty Rio Grande, which forms the border between Texas and Mexico, last from 4 to 8 days and travel through Big Bend National Park. Rafters pass through a number of canyons as deep as 1,500 feet, the longest being 25-mile Boquillas Canyon in the Sierra del Carmen. Participants may see artifacts from the Apache and Comanche people who used to inhabit the region. Daytime temperatures range from 65° to 70°F, dropping to around 40° at night; almost every sunset is spectacular. Details concerning location are available on request. **Cost:** On request. **When:** December, January. **Contact:** Zephyr River Expeditions, P.O. Box 2607, Sonora, CA 95370, USA; phone (209)532-6249. *(M)*

Utah

Rafting in Dinosaur National Monument: For 3 days adventurers follow part of the route taken by Major John Wesley Powell on his epic 1869 exploration. The 44-mile oar-powered trip on the Green River takes participants through "Hell's Half Mile" and Disaster Falls. While seeing wildlife such as deer, water fowl, beaver and big horned sheep, rafters can speculate about the giants of the reptile age that used to inhabit the swamps and humid plateaus above Lodore Canyon. Unsinkable neoprene pontoons and experienced guides make this whitewater journey a safe one. **Cost:** $150 to $170 includes meals, rafting equipment, guides, transportation from Steamboat Springs; $12 for rental of camping equipment. **When:** May to September. **Contact:** Adventure Bound, Inc., 6179 S. Adams Dr., Littleton, CO 80121, USA; phone (303)771-3752. *(M)*

Charter Floats: Groups of 20 or more may arrange for rafting trips on the Green or Colorado river. A day-long trip travels down either river, and a 2-day float on the Green provides opportunities for hiking and viewing petroglyphs. Also available on either a scheduled or chartered basis is a 2-day trip on the Colorado near Arches National Park. Travel on all trips is by neoprene rafts powered by oars. **Cost:** $20 for 1 day, $60 for 2 days includes meals, guides, equipment. **When:** April to September. **Contact:** Adventure River Expeditions, 4211 Mars Wy., Salt Lake City, UT 84117, USA; phone (801)278-1867. *(M)*

Through the Eye of Cataract Canyon: A 6-day rafting-camping trip is available along the last free-flowing section of the Colorado River. Participants begin and end the trip in calm waters but navigate rapids such as Brown Betty, Rapid Transit and Big Drop in between. Sandstone canyons along the river have been eroded by the wind into unusual natural formations. Hikes can be made to tributary waterfalls and landmarks, with opportunities to swim there and along the river. At the end of the trip rafters relax on Lake Powell, named after the explorer who first floated the Colorado over a century ago. **Cost:** $285 includes roundtrip transportation from Moab, meals, rafting equipment, guides, accommodations the night before launching. **When:** May to September. **Contact:** OARS Inc., P.O. Box 67, Angels Camp, CA 95222, USA; phone (209)736-2924 or 736-2661. *(M)*

Paddling the Green: Putting in at Sand Wash, participants float the Green River on a 7-day self-piloted river trip or a 5-day guided journey. Rafters handle the oars of a 7-foot Sportyak through 95 miles of the river on the 7-day venture. A seasoned rafter instructs participants all along the trip, and a support raft carries food and supplies; if participants wish, they can ride out the larger rapids in the support raft instead of their Sportyaks. Those who prefer a more leisurely trip, yet still wish to experience the challenges of whitewater can join the 5-day trip through Desolation and Grey canyons. Wildlife abounds and participants have the time to explore side canyons, investigate abandoned ranches or lie on white-sand beaches. On both trips rafters camp on the banks of the Green and the guides prepare all meals. **Cost:** $465 for Sportyak trip,

$345 for raft trip includes transportation from Grand Junction, meals, instruction, guides. **When:** Sundays from May to September. **Contact:** Outlaw Trails Inc., P.O. Box 336, Green River, UT 84525, USA; phone (801)564-3477. *(M)*

Desolation Row: Four-day rowing expeditions float participants through the Green River Wilderness in the Desolation Canyon and Grey Canyon regions. Professional guides lead groups along 97 miles of rushing water including such rapids as Coal Creek, Rattlesnake, Three Fords and more than 50 others. The itinerary begins in Grand Junction, where participants are met and bused to the airport for a charter flight into Sand Wash; here the journey downstream begins. It continues until the middle of the fourth day, when the group leaves the river for a bus ride back to Grand Junction. All meals and accommodations on the river are provided. **Cost:** $190 individual, $171 group or family. **When:** May to September. **Contact:** Western Adventure Safaris, Inc., P.O. Box 1732, Grand Junction, CO 81501, USA; phone (303)242-6621. *(M)*

Monument Valley Run: Starting in Bluff, participants row unsinkable Sportyaks for 6 days on the San Juan River in southeastern Utah. Each member of the group is given a fully equipped Sportyak to row through red rock gorges 2,000 feet in depth, seeing ruins of ancient Indian civilizations and experiencing small but exciting rapids along the way. Plenty of time for off-river exploration is available; the group may hike along the Honaker Trail, Slickhorn Canyon and Grand Gulch. The minimum age for the trip is 14. **Cost:** $400 for 6 days includes meals, equipment, guides. **When:** April to October. **Contact:** Wild & Scenic Inc., P.O. Box 2123A, Marble Canyon, AZ 86036, USA; phone (602)355-2222. *(M)*

Virginia

In the James: Day trips down the James River offer an unusual combination of challenging rapids and urban scenery. The trips run about 10 river miles, from Pony Pasture to Dock Street, with whitewater that sometimes reaches Class IV. Part of the trip runs through James River Park, a 350-acre wild area that hosts a variety of animal and bird life including rabbits, possums, raccoons, turtles and over 160 species of birds. But the route also passes under 12 bridges and past landmarks such as a huge Confederate cemetery, the Civil War camp Belle Isle, numerous gabled colonial mansions, and the downtown industrial district of Richmond. Lunch is served on the banks en route. **Cost:** $17 to $20 includes equipment, transportation, food, guides. **When** April to October. **Contact:** James River Experiences Ltd., P.O. Box 25015, Richmond, VA 23260, USA; phone (804)794-3493.

Washington

Floating the Skykomish: Rafters float forested reaches of the Skykomish River on day trips. The river flows from the western slopes of the Cascade Range near Stevens Pass along the north side of Mt. Index and then enters a deep canyon, offering participants a series of alternating pools and Class IV rapids; in the pools steelhead, chinook and pink salmon are visible swimming upstream. The put-in point for the trip is about 45 minutes from Seattle. Moonlight trips on the river are also offered, as are trips down the Toutle, Queets and Wenatchee rivers. Special youth and group rates are available. **Cost:** $28 for day trips, $35 for night trips includes food, equipment, guide. **Contact:** The Northern Wilderness Company, P.O. Box 25795, Seattle, WA 98125, USA; phone (206)633-3946. ***(M)***

Rafting in the Cascades: Float trips ranging from 1 to 5 days take participants down isolated rivers in Washington's Cascade Range. On the west slopes of the Cascades trips are scheduled down the Sauk and Suiattle rivers, the Skagit River, the Nooksack River and the Skykomish River. The Sauk and Suiattle rivers, in the Glacier Peak Wilderness, are run on day and overnight trips which negotiate over 30 major rapids; the Skagit River is run in a 3-day trip through the North Cascades National Park, where participants can see one of the nation's largest concentrations of bald eagles. The Skykomish River is especially demanding, owing to harsh rapids which increase in difficulty yearly because of rock erosion. On the east slope of the Cascades a 5-day trip runs the Methow, from Mazama through apple-growing country and Black Canyon to the Columbia River; and 1- to 3-day trips take participants down the Wenatchee River, where the whitewater is especially exciting in the summer months. **Cost:** $40 to $150 for adults includes transportation back to the starting point; youth fares 15 to 25 percent less. **When:** Year-round. **Contact:** Pacific Northwest Float Trips, 829 Waldron St., Sedro Woolley, WA 98284, USA; phone (206)855-0535 or 855-0417. *(M)*

Olympic Peninsula Rafting: The lush Olympic rain forest can be experienced on float trips down rivers fed by the snow-capped peaks of the Olympic Mountains. With 5 passengers to a boat, daily trips are offered on the Queets, Hoh and Quinault rivers in Olympic National Park. Groups are encouraged to participate in all aspects of the river trip, keeping in mind the environmental ethics of rafting. The trips depart from Lake Quinault Lodge at 9 a.m. and return at 5 p.m. **Cost:** $25 for adults, $20 for children includes lunch, transportation to and from the river. **When:** June to September; winter weekends by reservation. **Contact:** Rivers Northwest, 141 Eagle St. NE, Winslow, WA 98110, USA; phone (206)842-5144. *(M)*

Weekend River Trips: Rafting the rivers of the Pacific Northwest offers a profusion of trip possibilites, all of which can be explored on weekend trips throughout the year. Whitewater day trips running from April to October explore the Wenatchee, Sauk and Toutle rivers which flow westward from the flanks of the Cascade Mountains. From September through November, special interest trips concentrate on the abundance of mushroom species which flourish in the rainy climate of Puget Sound. The rest of the year, winter trips visit lonely, frost-laden rivers where osprey, eagles, deer and other wildlife wait out the winter months along the still-flowing rivers. **Cost:** $35 for day trips. **When:** Year-round. **Contact:** Zig Zag River Runners, REI Adventure Travel, 1525 11th Ave., Seattle, WA 98122, USA; phone (206)322-7800.

West Virginia

Blue Ridge Rafting: River-running novices make half-day guided runs down West Virginia's Shenandoah River, near the town of Harpers Ferry. Rubber rafts are used on the trip, and all the necessary safety equipment is provided. A briefing on river skills precedes the run. **Cost:** $15 to $20 includes lunch, equipment, guide. **When:** By arrangement. **Contact:** Blue Ridge

Outfitters, Rt. 340, Harpers Ferry, WV 25425, USA; phone (304)725-3444.

Something New: The New River is one eastern river that compares with the Colorado for whitewater. Day trips cover 17 of its most exciting miles where the river drops about 240 feet. The ride offers spectacular views of the river canyon and its environs along with 17 Class IV and V rapids. Weekday trips are recommended for less crowded conditions. **Cost:** $38 to $42, depending on size of party, includes transportation from Lansing, equipment, lunch, guides. **When:** April to November. **Contact:** Class VI River Runners, Inc., P.O. Box 78, Lansing, WV 25862, USA; phone (304)574-0704. *(M)*

New River Rafting: Paddling along in a large rubber raft, passengers enjoy the beauty of the Appalachian Mountains along the New River, which has carved a magnificent gorge. River experts guide the raft through quiet waters, until the current picks up and suddenly the raft is charging through the froth and turbulence of rapids. In midday, rafters pause to share lunch on the riverbank. The New River is one of the earth's oldest rivers and has been called the "Grand Canyon of the East." One- and 2-day trips leave Hico every day in the summer and every weekend in off-season to give guests the opportunity to experience this wild water. Transportation is provided to the put-in point and a tram takes rafters out of the canyon at Hawk's Nest State Park. **Cost:** $32 for day trips, $85 for 2 days includes equipment, meals, transportation to and from the river. **When:** April to October. **Contact:** Mountain River Tours Inc., Box 88, Sunday Rd., Hico, WV 24854, USA; phone (304)658-5817. *(M)*

West Virginian Variety: Day trips on the Cheat, Gauley and New rivers reveal the variety of environments in West Virginia's wilderness. The Cheat River combines rapids and calm stretches as rafters experience the river's growth to-

Rafting trips of 1 to 5 days are available for as little as $18 on Wyoming's Snake River, which winds through Grand Teton National Park. (Grand Teton Lodge Co.)

wards Cheat Lake; the trip concludes with a motor tow into the lake, providing a spectacular view of Cheat Canyon. The Gauley trips are for experienced rafters only, as a constant series of boiling rapids confronts participants on their way downstream from Summersville Dam. The New River meanders quietly through the grandeur of the Appalachian Mountains and then begins a series of steep drops and large rapids before flattening out again, where rafters are towed to Hawk's Nest Park and take a tram up out of the canyon. **Cost:** $23 to $30 for Cheat trip, $25 to $40 for New trip includes lunch, transportation, equipment, guides; Gauley trip rates on request. **When:** April to October. **Contact:** North American River Runners, P.O. Box 193, Sylvania, OH 43560, USA; phone (419)882-8654.

Wildwater from Thurmond: Participants on a 1- and 2-day river trip experience the New River Canyon, sometimes called the Grand Canyon of the East. Nestled in the foothills of the Appalachian Mountains, the canyon provides turbulent whitewater passing beneath towering hills and rock formations. Participants camp overnight along the riverbanks on the 30-mile route. The year-round float trips include hot meals. Three trips are also made yearly down the Gauley River. **Cost:** $40 per day includes equipment, guide. **When:** Year-round. **Contact:** Wildwater Expeditions Unlimited Inc., P.O. Box 55, Thurmond, WV 25936, USA; phone (304)469-2551. *(M)*

Wyoming

Snaking through the Mountains: Three trips provide whitewater excitement on Wyoming's Snake River. Two of the outings are day trips built around an elaborate riverside meal, and the third is an overnight trip; all 3 begin and end in Jackson, with transportation provided to and from the river. A midday trip plies a turbulent stretch of the Snake and stops for lunch at a traditional spot, called "Lunch Counter Rapid," which provides views and photographic opportunities of other boaters negotiating the stretch. Another trip takes place in the afternoon and evening and stops for a steak fry at a scenic spot. The overnight trip provides a more extensive look at the Snake River Canyon and its wildlife, with participants pitching camp at the mouth of Bailey Canyon. Again, the meals are a featured highlight. All equipment except personal items is supplied, and the guides on all trips provide informal instruction in the human and natural history of the region. **Cost:** $18 to $50 for adults, $13 to $40 for children, depending on trip. **When:** Summer. **Contact:** Mad River Boat Trips, P.O. Box 525, Wilson, WY 83014, USA; phone (307)733-6203.

Grand Teton Float Trip: A 5-day wilderness river trip provides participants with the opportunity to see the Grand Teton and Jackson Hole region from a rubber raft or canoe. For the first 3 days, rafters float the upper Snake River and Jackson Lake, with time allotted for hiking into high alpine canyons, swimming, fishing in mountain streams and observing moose, elk, otter, eagles and Canada geese. Then they take on the lower Snake River to raft through Grand Teton National Park and back to Jackson Hole. **Cost:** $385 includes meals, equipment, guide. **When:** May to September. **Contact:** Parklands Expeditions, Inc., P.O. Box 371, Jackson Hole, WY 83001, USA; phone (307)733-3379.

RESOURCES

Clubs and Associations

American Rivers Conservation Council
317 Pennsylvania Ave. SE
Washington, DC 20003, USA
Phone (202)547-6900

American Whitewater Affiliation
P.O. Box 1584
San Bruno, CA 94066, USA

Eastern Professional River
Outfitters Association
P.O. Box 252
Hot Springs, NC 28743, USA

Outdoor Education Association
11468 Redwood Hwy.
Wilderville, OR 97543, USA

Western River Guides Association
994 Denver St.
Salt Lake City, UT 84101, USA

CANOEING

Dugout canoes are still widely used by tribes throughout the Amazon Basin for hunting, transportation and communication between remote river villages. Once used by North American Indians and peoples of the South Pacific, dugout canoes were constructed by chopping and burning out the interiors of logs. The Maoris of New Zealand fashioned war canoes over 60 feet long in this manner. In time, log canoes in North America evolved into light frames of wood covered with skins and bark. Curved bows maximized the ratio of strength to weight and streamlined the boats' passage through the water.

Today canoes are used worldwide for whitewater sport, fishing, racing and wilderness exploration. Modern canoes are made of aluminum, magnesium, plastic and glass fibers, molded plywood or canvas over wood frames. Some canoes are built with square sterns for outboard motor attachments, others are designed for sailing and paddling with single-blade paddles. A pastime both relaxing and at times rugged, canoeing can be enjoyed by people of all ages wherever there is a stretch of water.

If you don't know how to canoe but would like to learn, there are courses offered in Canada, Wales and throughout the United States that teach the basic strokes, maneuvers and paddling postures. Some even teach wilderness survival skills and whitewater techniques. There are canoeing seminars for high school students, weekend trips for the whole family, and special canoeing, camping and hiking trips offered to senior citizens.

Once you've mastered some of the basic skills, you can join any number of organized canoeing trips to wilderness areas otherwise inaccessible. You can paddle by dugout canoe down the Usumacinta River to visit Mayan ruins on a 2-week expedition in Guatemala, or you can follow old Indian routes through northern Ontario on a trip that glides quietly past minks, beavers, muskrats and otters. In Maine you can paddle the Allagash Wilderness Waterway and in South Carolina the Chattooga River, or you can explore the 15,000 square miles of lakes and streams in the Boundary Waters Canoe Area between Minnesota and Ontario.

If you have an afternoon—or a whole month—to spare, you can travel the routes of the French voyageurs, view wildlife on river banks, feel the excitement of whitewater or just drift into the American past—all by climbing into a canoe. □

Canoeing combines the peace of paddling quiet pools with adrenaline-charged entries into churning rapids. Here two canoeists put technical skills to use in whitewater. (Wolfcreek Wilderness)

CANOEING

CANADA

Trans-Canadian Paddling: Canoe trips lasting up to 25 days are offered on 11 rivers in Quebec, Ontario, Saskatchewan and the Northwest Territories. Canoeists at any skill level can be accommodated: a trip which is designed for whitewater novices is offered on the Dumoine River in Quebec; the Coppermine and Keele rivers in the Northwest Territories provide more challenging stretches of water suitable for experienced paddlers. Participants take charter flights to the put-in points on less accessible rivers such as the Attawapiskat in Ontario. Instructional whitewater trips are offered each weekend during the summer. **Cost:** $325 to $1,050 includes canoes, meals, air charters where necessary, guides; $60 to $150 for weekend instructional outings. **When:** May to September. **Contact:** Trail Head, 1341 Wellington, Ottawa, ON Canada K1Y 3B8.

British Columbia

Provincial Paddling: A week-long canoeing trip in Tweedsmuir Provincial Park explores the Sigutlat Lakes region at a leisurely pace. Participants fly from Vancouver to Bella Coola and continue by float plane into Tweedsmuir Provincial Park. Covering a total of 30 miles, paddlers experience a variety of canoeing conditions, ranging from fast-moving streams over gravel bottoms to log-jammed slow waters and sections meandering through shallow ponds and marshlands. Plenty of time is allowed for trout fishing and viewing wildlife such as moose, deer, grizzly bears, mountain goats and coyotes. The trip ends with return flights to Bella Coola and Vancouver. Participants must be experienced canoeists. **Cost:** $720 includes roundtrip airfare from Vancouver, meals, guide, most camping equipment. **When:** August. **Contact:** Canadian Wilderness Experiences, Box 46304, Sta. G, Vancouver, BC Canada V6R 4G6; phone (604)325-9118. ***(M)***

Canoeing the Sea Islands: Canoe trips among the islands off the coast of British Columbia are offered in 2-week sessions. Trips depart from Gold River on a coastal freighter for passage up Nootka Sound to Esperanza. Then travelers paddle through the inlets in double cockpit canoes, camping on uninhabited islands and cooking their meals over driftwood fires. The area has lost very little of its primitive character, and canoeists have the chance to experience the life lived there for centuries by its native peoples. Ample time is allotted for beachcombing, canoe exploration and hikes in the forests. **Cost:** $185 includes canoe, equipment, guide; $18 for freighter passage. **When:** June to September. **Contact:** Northwest Waters, P.O. Box 212, Portland, OR 97207, USA.

Canoeing Survival: A cooperative rural retreat located on a 30-mile-long mountain lake on Vancouver Island offers a 6-day instruction and survival skills program for high school-age people. A day is spent at the center learning basic canoeing skills, working a rope course and becoming acquainted with fellow students. Late that day participants canoe out to a nearby point to improvise shelters, build fires and search out useful wild plants. Then, over the next 4 days, the party paddles south on Buttle Lake to the mouth of the Wolf River for exploring, fishing and learning survival skills in the remote rain forest. No previous experience is necessary, and a solo survival test is not part of the trip. This trip may be preceded or followed by a stay at the lodge, which offers a variety of outdoor opportunities. **Cost:** $225 includes equipment, food, instruction. **When:** July. **Contact:** Strathcona Park Lodge, Outdoor Education Society, Box 2160, Campbell River, BC Canada V9W 5C9; phone Campbell River radiophone operator.

Vancouver Bay Voyages: Freedom to explore is the keynote of partially guided 7-day canoe trips on Jervis Inlet in Vancouver Bay. A float plane brings participants from Vancouver Harbor across Howe Sound and up the coast to base camp on Vancouver Bay. During the first 3 days trip members become acquainted with the area, practice canoeing techniques and get the feel of the daily wind and tidal patterns. While paddling through the 50-mile-long inlet past 8,000-foot mountains with cascading waterfalls, participants have the opportunity to explore the interti-

Hundreds of remote lakes in British Columbia await exploration by canoe. Two canoeists enjoy the serenity of Tabour Lake, near Prince George. (Canadian Travel Bureau)

Clear, calm and silent, a wilderness lake welcomes the quiet passage of canoes, which offer paddlers unique opportunities to view wildlife and explore remote areas. (Keith Gunnar)

dal zones and hike in the surrounding forests along abandoned logging roads. Group members decide how far to canoe each day. The only scheduled stop is a rendezvous with a supply boat to replenish food stocks. At the end of the trip participants are flown by float plane back to Vancouver Harbor. Trip members should provide their own camping equipment. An extended trip to Porpoise Bay in Sechelt Inlet is also available. **Cost:** $150 includes equipped canoes, instruction, guide at base camp, food, cooking equipment; $75 for float plane fare. **When:** July to September. **Contact:** Western Outdoor Adventures Ltd., 16115 32nd Ave., White Rock, BC Canada V4B 4Z5; phone (604)531-3969.

Northwest Territories

Canoeing through Taiga and Tundra: Almost completely uninhabited, the 1,300,000 square miles of the Northwest Territories provide numerous wilderness canoeing opportunities. Parties of 6 are assembled for trips lasting a minimum of 12 days on a variety of rivers through a terrain of tundra and taiga. Guided by a biologist/ecologist, participants explore a land green with lichens, grasses, mosses, sedges and dwarf shrubbery, a land where water covers about 38 percent of the ground. Traveling in almost continuous daylight, all voyagers paddle and help set up camp along sandy beaches. Headnets are provided for the occasional times when insects are overwhelming. Wildlife including herds of caribou, musk oxen, arctic wolves, moose and grizzlies may easily be photographed. Birdlife is teeming and ornithologists can request canoe trips designed to maximize viewing of waterfowl, falcons and eagles. There are routes to challenge the most avid whitewater canoeist as well as routes suitable for those with no previous canoeing experience. **Cost:** $805 to $1,565 from Yellowknife or Fort Smith includes guide, group equipment, food, air charters. **When:** June to September. **Contact:** Canoe Arctic Inc., 9 John Beck Cresc., Brampton, ON Canada L6W 2T2; phone (416)451-0290.

Ontario

Wild Winisk: Two canoe trips down Winiskisis Channel and the Winisk River can be taken either separately or together. On the first trip, lasting 11 days, participants paddle down 125 miles of whitewater in Winiskisis Channel to its confluence with the Winisk River, through countryside that gradually changes to tundra. Herds of caribou frequent the area, and the channel is full of speckled trout. Where the 2 waterways meet, canoeists can either take a 261-mile float plane flight back to Armstrong or continue for another 10 days and canoe 162 miles down the fast-flowing Winisk River to Hudson Bay. In this remote tundra region, inhabited by caribou, Canadian geese, polar bears, Arctic foxes and beluga whales, 300-year-old trees grow to only 4 feet in height. After arriving in Hudson Bay, the party returns to Armstrong via float plane. **Cost:** $777 for either trip, $1,540 for both includes transportation from Armstrong, food, group equipment, guide. **When:** August. **Contact:** Canoes North/Canoes South, Box 5656, Armstrong, ON Canada P0T 1A0; phone (807)583-2055. *(M)*

Algonquin Wilderness by Canoe: An 8-day voyage departs from Toronto and travels by canoe and on foot through the lakes and rivers of Algonquin Provincial Park. The park covers nearly 3,000 square miles and provides opportunities to observe a variety of plants and animals, including deer, moose, wolves, beavers and black bears. Trip members portage equipment overland and must be able to swim. Food is packed, and group members share in the cooking and other camp chores. **Cost:** $165 includes food kitty, camping gear, park permits, transportation from Toronto. **When:** June to August. **Contact:** Goway Travel Ltd., 53 Yonge St., Second Floor, Toronto, ON Canada M5E 1J3; phone (416)863-0799; or Adventure Center, 5540 College Ave., Oakland, CA 94618, USA; phone (415)654-1879. *(M)*

Timagami and Dumoine River Trips: Canoeists with some experience can spend 3 weeks on the main river systems in the Timagami area or 2 weeks on the Dumoine River. Two different trips are offered in the Timagami region, one for youths 14 to 16 and one for those 17 and older. On the latter trip canoeists travel north into the Lady Evelyn watershed, then work upstream for 4 or 5 days encountering numerous rapids and falls. Younger participants spend 1 or 2 days at the base camp on Lake Timagami planning their expedition, selecting the menus and assisting in the general organization before leaving on a canoe trip of 16 to 18 days. Depending on the interests and skill level of the group, the trip may travel on the upper Lady Evelyn River or the Makobe River. **Cost:** $625 for Dumoine, $750 for Timagami includes transportation from Kipawa and Timagami, guides, instruction, food, all equipment. **When:** July, August. **Contact:** Headwaters, P.O. Box 288, Timagami, ON Canada P0H 2H0.

Northern Canoeing: A 28-day trip offers canoeists with basic skills an opportunity to sharpen their skills by canoeing on the Missinaibi River in northern Ontario. The group meets in Sudbury and puts in at nearby Missinaibi Lake. In this area once traveled by Indians, traders and explorers, participants may spot otters, beavers, minks and muskrats. Canoeing is on both calm water and whitewater, and guides teach canoeing techniques such as portaging, lining and whitewater strokes. The take-out point is the town of Moosonee on James Bay, from where participants are transported back to Sudbury. **Cost:** $975 includes transportation from Sudbury, camping equipment, meals. **When:** June. **Contact:** The Infinite Odyssey, 57 Grant St., Waltham, MA 02154, USA; phone (617)899-6050. *(M)*

Timagami Canoeing: An 8-week summer program offers canoeing opportunities for youths 8 to 18. Eight-year-olds may expect short canoe trips of 2 or 4 days; more challenging trips of up to 3 weeks are planned for older campers. The trip routes explore the remote reaches of the Timagami Provincial Forest and are chosen to match the skills and strengths of the canoeists. Some of the routes for novices include the Lady Evelyn water system, Obabika Lake and the Matabitchewan River; the Sturgeon or Grassy rivers are a couple of the routes for intermediates. Other trips planned are on James Bay and the Dumoine, Winisk and Spanish rivers. **Cost:** $600 for 4 weeks, $1,080 for 8 weeks includes accommodations, meals, equipment, instruction. **When:** June through August. **Contact:** Wanapitei, 7 Engleburn Pl., Peterborough, ON Canada K9H 1C4; phone (705)743-3774; summer, Lake Timagami, ON Canada P0H 2H0; phone Timagami Island 1-R-13 (New Liskeard). *(M)*

Yukon Territory

Yukon Canoe: Below the Yukon's rugged high peaks, boreal spruce forests and quiet rivers offer canoeists fairly easy routes through remote areas full of wildlife. An 11-day trip, beginning and ending in Whitehorse, explores this terrain. Canoeists drive 130 miles to put in at Quiet Lake in the Big Salmon range, then paddle 155 miles down the Big Salmon River to join the Yukon River. From there another 80 miles brings them to Carmacks, the take-out point. Moose, grizzly bear, lynx, fox, wolves, wolverines, weasels, beavers, ducks, Canadian geese and bald eagles are among the region's wildlife; the flora includes a profusion of summer wildflowers. Some still-productive gold fields are passed along the way. **Cost:** $553 from Whitehorse includes food, equipment, transportation, guides. **When:** July. **Contact:** REI Adventure Travel, Inc., 1525 11th Ave., Seattle, WA 98122, USA; phone (206)322-7800. *(M)*

CENTRAL AMERICA

Guatemala

Guatemalan River Expedition: The first part of a 2-week trip in the jungles of Guatemala is spent using dugout canoes to reach Mayan ruins in the area near the Usumacinta and La Pasion rivers. Tropical wildlife, such as turtles, alligators and water birds, are seen after leaving the border town of Sayaxche. Stopping at the Mayan river city of Yaxchilan, excavated only a few years ago, participants view hieroglyphic stairways and bas-relief stelae surrounded by virgin rain forest. A 6-hour hike over jungle trails takes expedition members to Dos Pilas, only recently discovered and as yet unexcavated. Returning to Lake Peten Itza, the group drives over rough roads to the well-known ceremonial center of Tikal. Two days are reserved for exploration of this extensive pre-Columbian site before flying back to Guatemala City. **Cost:** $2,125 includes roundtrip airfare from London, all land arrangements. **When:** March, November. **Contact:** Explore Beyond Ltd., 167 Earls Court Rd., London SW5, Great Britain; or Adventure Center, 5540 College Ave., Oakland, CA 94618, USA; phone (415)654-1879. *(M)*

Ruins by River: Ten days of travel on the remote Usumacinta River and a week of land sightseeing explore Latin culture old and new. Traveling in small dugouts, participants investigate a number of archaeological sites along the river, including Tikal, Palenque, Dos Pilas, Aguateca, Altar de Sacrificios, Yaxchilan and a recently discovered site near Playa del Caribe. Nights are spent at encampments and lodges along the river. The river portion of the trip ends at San Cristobal de las Casas as travelers shift to the Mexican countryside, nearby Indian villages, markets and museums, with nights spent in hotels. **Cost:** $998 includes accommodations, most food, equipment, transportation, sightseeing costs, guide. **When:** January to March. **Contact:** Forum Travel International, 2437 Durant, No. 208, Berkeley, CA 94704, USA; phone (415)843-8294.

EUROPE

France

Descending the Ardeche: A descent by canoe of the Ardeche

Canoeists paddle down the Fraser River near Mission, BC, as the voyageurs once did in the nineteenth century. (Canadian Gov't Travel Bureau)

When explorer John C. Fremont tried to float Fremont Canyon in 1842 he was stopped by the raging waters of the North Platte River; now the Alcova Reservoir provides canoeists a safer route through this canyon. (Wyoming Travel Commission)

River, which has cut a 600-foot-deep canyon through the edge of the Massif Central, is part of a 15-day trip in France. Paddlers spend the first 2 days learning to canoe near the town of Vallon-Pont-d'Arc, then spend 3 days canoeing the Ardeche. Rapids alternate with calm stretches during the descent as the canoeists pass under a 200-foot-high natural bridge and by the medieval walls of Aigueze. Participants stop to swim on quiet sections of the river and camp overnight on its banks. After the canoeing portion of the trip, the group spends the second week camping near St. Tropez on the Cote d'Azur, where trip members may sail, snorkel, scuba, water-ski, wind-surf and go horseback riding. Though no canoeing experience is necessary, participants must be able to swim 50 yards and be at least 18 years old. One of the trips is reserved for families and people over 30. **Cost:** $360 to $440, depending on departure date, includes roundtrip airfare from London to Montpellier, meals, tent accommodations, canoeing equipment. **When:** June to September. **Contact:** WEXAS International, 45 Brompton Rd., Knightsbridge, London SW3 1DE, Great Britain; phone 01-589-0500. ***(M)***

Norway

Scandinavian Paddling: Just over 200 miles north of Oslo lies Lake Femund, set in the midst of a rich wildlife area where canoeists can paddle either in organized groups or on their own. Accompanied by an English-speaking guide, paddlers circumnavigate the lake, make frequent hikes to nearby mountains and camp on shore during a week-long trip. Alternatively, groups wishing to guide themselves can rent canoes, camping equipment, maps, compasses and various tools on a daily or weekly basis. The area, which is dotted with numerous lakes and waterways, contains eagles, bears, reindeer and other wildlife. **Cost:** $126 for 1-week trips, $15 to $17 a day for outfitting. **When:** Summer. **Contact:** Femund Canoe Camp, N-2445 Femundsenden, Norway; phone Engerdal 119.

Wales

Complete Canoeing: A week-long beginners' course in all aspects of canoeing is based at an outdoor activities school in northern Wales. Skills covered include basic strokes, rolls and some kayak techniques; attention is also given to areas such as equipment maintenance and repair, expedition planning and proper clothing. The course takes place in the school's pool and on nearby lakes, whitewater rivers and the sea, where surf canoeing is taught. Weather permitting, the course culminates with an overnight canoe/camping trip. The school also offers more advanced and specialized canoe instruction for those especially interested in whitewater or surf canoeing. **Cost:** $132 includes food, accommodations, equipment, instruction; other rates on request. **When:** April to September. **Contact:** Plas Y Brenin, Capel Curig, Betws y Coed, Great Britain; phone (06904)280.

SOUTH AMERICA

Peru

Dugout Canoes on the Amazon: While exploring Peru for 15 days, adventurers travel 2 headwater rivers of the Amazon, investigate the cities of Lima and Cuzco and visit several of the major Inca ruins. Participants fly from Vancouver to Lima, then spend time exploring the city and bartering at the markets before heading out to the jungle. Accompanied by experienced guides, group members paddle in dugout canoes through the Amazon jungle and travel to the Andean highlands for a journey in paddle rafts. Participants explore and photograph many ruins, the highlight being Machu Picchu, the "Lost City of the Incas," before concluding the journey with the return flight to Vancouver. **Cost:** $1,195 includes airfare, ground transportation, meals, accommodations, guide. **When:** May, June, August to October. **Contact:** Whitewater Adventures Ltd., P.O. Box 46536, Vancouver, BC Canada V6R 4G8; phone (604)736-2135. ***(M)***

Venezuela

Deep in the Jungle: Canoe expeditions lasting 17 days are offered to several very remote rivers, deep in the Venezuelan jungle. Participants fly from Miami to Caracas and then to Canaima, where a plane is chartered to the river's headwaters. Trips are run on the Caura, the Aro, the Paragua and the Orinoco rivers, all located in virtually unexplored areas. Participants need to be seasoned canoeists or have skills in other fields such as botany, gemology or Spanish. Half of the area's 14,000 species of plants are unclassified; over 1,500 species of birds also inhabit the region. A film of the expedition is made available to members after the trip. **Cost:**

$1,832 includes roundtrip airfare from Miami, transportation, equipment, food, guide. **When:** January to March. **Contact:** Canoes North/ Canoes South, Box 5656, Armstrong, ON Canada P0T 1A0; phone (807)583-2055. *(M)*

UNITED STATES

Alaska

Seymour and More: A group of 8 canoeists and 2 guides travels by float plane from Juneau to Seymour Canal for a week of paddling around Admiralty Island. The island, located on the Alexander Archipelago, is under consideration as a national wilderness area, and the trip enables participants to investigate its flora, fauna and topography. The highest concentration of nesting bald eagles in America is found there; participants also find many wild edibles, and practical instruction is offered in wilderness survival en route. Other area wildlife includes porpoises, humpback whales, brown bears, Sitka blacktail deer, ravens, migrating salmon and a wide variety of waterfowl. The return to Juneau is by float plane. **Cost:** $550 includes transportation from Juneau, food, equipment, guides. **When:** July. **Contact:** Alaska Discovery Enterprises, P.O. Box 26, Gustavus, AK, USA; phone (907)697-3431.

Canoeing Misty Fjords: Canoeists explore the boundary between southeast Alaska and Canada in Misty Fjords Wilderness, marked by glaciated mountains, mineral springs and mountain lakes. From Ketchikan, participants are transported by plane and boat to Misty Fjords for a 4-day exploration of the waterways and surrounding wilderness, abundant with wildlife such as bears, deer, wolves, eagles, falcons and songbirds. A guide is provided for every 4 participants. The weather is often wet and cold, and trip members should dress appropriately. **Cost:** $400 includes roundtrip transportation from Ketchikan, most camping equipment, meals, equipped canoes, guides. **When:** Summer, by arrangement. **Contact:** Alaska Wilderness Expeditions, Inc., P.O. Box 7814, Ketchikan, AK 99906, USA.

Wild River Canoeing: Completely outfitted canoeing trips of 6 to 8 days are offered to adventurers wanting to explore the central Brooks Range, former home of the Nunamiut Eskimos and Athabascan Indians. The trip is designed for people willing to take an active part in the wilderness; everyone helps with chores at the camps that are established along the river. Five-mile-long Wild Lake is the starting point of an 8-day voyage up meandering Wild River. Swift and shallow for part of the way, the river also has calm stretches where participants may see beavers swimming in the river or near their dams, eagles, molting Canada geese and bull moose. The North Fork of the Koyukuk River is relatively easy to canoe except for a 2-mile stretch of Class II rapids. For 6 days, canoeists pass moose, black and grizzly bears, waterfowl, wolves and old mining cabins. As on the other canoe trip, there is ample time to hike and photograph. **Cost:** $450 for the Wild, $400 for the Koyukuk includes transportation to and from Bettles, food, equipment, guide. **When:** June for Wild River, August for Koyukuk. **Contact:** Sourdough Outfitters, Bettles, AK 99726, USA; phone (907)692-5252. *(M)*

California

Gorging: Canoeists can take a weekend trip on the Colorado River through Topock Gorge and Havasu Wildlife Refuge, with instruction supplied as needed. After meeting in Riverside and camping Friday night in Park Moabi, participants begin paddling early Saturday. Basic canoeing techniques are demonstrated, then 2 days are spent exploring the river at a leisurely pace, with stops for hikes, swimming, wildlife observation and photography. A visit is made to Picture Rock, a major Indian petroglyph site, shortly before pitching camp Saturday night. Take-out the next afternoon is at Castle Rock, followed by a drive back to Riverside. **Cost:** $68 includes transportation from Riverside, food, equipment, instruction. **When:** March to June. **Contact:** Pacific Adventures, P.O. Box 5041, Riverside, CA 92517, USA; phone (714)684-1227.

Canoe through Havasu: A 3-day trip takes canoeists from Park Moabi through Havasu Wildlife Refuge and spectacular volcanic terrain to Lake Havasu. The group receives instruction in basic canoe strokes, maneuvering, river safety and etiquette before moving out into the main current of the Colorado. The volcanic spires of Topock Gorge, jagged pinnacles, cliffs and sand washes highlight the first day on the river. The second day is used as a layover for short canoe excursions, hikes or swimming; Indian petroglyphs, bighorn sheep, burros, coyotes, and migrating waterfowl can be seen in the area. Canoeists reach Lake Havasu on the third day, where transportation back to Park Moabi awaits. The weather is hot and dry in summer, temperate in winter. **Cost:** On request. **When:** Year-round. **Contact:** Sandstone Outfitters, P.O. Box 137, Cardiff, CA 92007, USA; phone (714)436-1955.

Colorado

Canoes on the Colorado: On a quiet stretch of the Colorado River between Loma, Colorado and Westwater, Utah participants and guides canoe for a weekend. The river passes through a wilderness protected by 1,000-foot sheer canyon walls that make the area accessible only from the river. The trip's leisurely pace allows time for hiking into remote side canyons and discovering spectacular sandstone formations. Participants should have some canoeing experience. **Cost:** $75 includes equipment, food, guides. **When:** June to September. **Contact:** North Woods Canoe Trips, 2659E S. Xanadu Wy., Aurora, CO 80014, USA; phone (303)750-8438.

Florida

Everglades the Old Way: Canoe trips of 2 and 3 days are available in the 10,000 Islands area of the northern Everglades. Guides lead groups through brackish water passages and around the hundreds of dry islands in the region. The area was once the home of the Calusa Indians, and their artifacts may be found along with shells, wildlife and plantlife native to the region. Fishing is good in most areas; no license is needed for saltwater fishing in the Everglades. Family weekend trips of the same length and program are also available for those with children over 9 years of age. The trips are limited to 12 people including a guide. **Cost:** $75 for 2 days, $95 for 3 days; $40 to $50 for children. **When:** November to April. **Contact:** Tropical Camper, P.O. Box 970891, Miami, FL 33197, USA; phone (305)253-3984.

Georgia

Up the Suwannee: Canoeists on a 6-day trip paddle from the edge of the Okefenokee Swamp through the cypress and sweetgum forests of the Suwannee River's broad upper flood plain. After canoeing the river from its source to the Gulf trip leaders know the best spots on the upper stretches of the river. Groups find magnificent scenery as they wind around bends beneath sandstone cliffs where moss-draped live oaks and pines hang over clear water and sunflecked sandbars. Along the banks, deer, otters and alligators may be seen; very few signs of humans intrude upon the natural setting. The trip is a good one for photographers. No canoeing experience is required of participants. **Cost:** $325 includes food, canoes, paddles, life vests, community camping gear, guides. **When:** April, December. **Contact:** University of the Wilderness, P.O. Box 1687, Evergreen, CO 80439, USA; phone (303)674-9724. *(M)*

Indiana

Canoeing Sugar Creek: Putting in at Crawfordsville, canoeists can navigate downstream for up to 29 miles on Sugar Creek in western Indiana. Rental canoes are available either by the day or by the week, with put-in and pickup service to various points along the river. Between Crawfordsville and Cox Covered Bridge, the final take-out point, there are 8 places where the river intersects highway bridges which can be used as take-out points. Reservations for rental canoes are required. **Cost:** $8 a day or $35 a week for canoe rental; cushions, extra paddles, cartop canoe carriers and canoe trailers available at extra cost. **When:** April to November. **Contact:** Bob Clements Canoe Rentals and Sales, 911 Wayne Ave., Crawfordsville, IN 47933, USA; phone (317)362-6272, weekends 362-9864.

Maine

North Country Expeditions: The Allagash River and its 8 connecting lakes comprise the 85-mile-long Allagash Wilderness Waterway. A variety of trips 3 to 10 days long combines canoeing and camping throughout this area. The most popular trip begins at Telos Lake and requires 7 days to complete the route to Allagash Village, offering lake canoeing along with the excitement of moderate rapids. Other trips take canoeists on the upper West Branch of the Penobscot River with a side trip to Lobster Lake, and on Telos, Eagle, Churchill and Chesuncook lakes. Allagash Lake itself may be reached by wading up Allagash Stream from Chamberlain

Sunrise County Canoe Expeditions offers trips lasting a day to a month through the forests and meadows of New England, on rivers such as St. John in Maine. (Sunrise County Canoe Expeditions)

Lake. Whitewater is encountered on the St. John River and East Branch of the Penobscot River, and should be attempted by experienced canoeists only. **Cost:** $19 a day includes canoe, camping equipment, food; $6 to $130 for transportation. **When:** May to September. **Contact:** Allagash Wilderness Outfitters, Frost Pond, Star Rt. 76, Greenville, ME 04441, USA; December to April, 36 Minuteman Dr., Millinocket, ME 04462, USA; phone (207)723-6622. ***(M)***

Sunrise County Canoe Voyages: Small groups canoe from a day to a month in the northeastern United States through terrain ranging from rugged forested country to vast natural meadowlands. Canoeists can find smooth water, falls, portaging, easy rips, and highly technical whitewater on the St. Croix, Machias, East Machias and Dennys rivers and the Grand Lake chain. The guides tailor difficulty and pace to individual preferences. Participants receive instruction in all facets of canoeing and experience comfortable living in the north woods while either helping with cooking and camp chores or leaving it all to the guides. The group is on the water early each morning before the mist rises. Camp is set up early enough in the afternoon for swimming, hiking and relaxing. Wildlife in the area includes loons, moose, bald eagles and black bears. **Cost:** $45 to $75 a day, depending on size of party includes canoes and equipment, meals, instruction, guide. **When:** May to October. **Contact:** Sunrise County Canoe Expeditions, Inc., Cathance Lake, Grove Post Office, ME 04638, USA; phone (207)454-7708.

Minnesota

Portaging and Paddling: Experienced guides join participants in Ely, Minnesota to begin 7- and 10-day canoe trips through the Boundary Waters Canoe Area or through Quetico Provincial Park. Traveling with 9 other companions including the guides, participants are grouped according to interests and ability, with some trips de-

Not all canoeing is part of an organized trip; enthusiasts can rent or buy gear and head out on their own, like these people on Washington's Lake Kachess. (Keith Gunnar)

signed for families, some for photographers and some for canoeists who want a challenge. Instruction in paddling, campcraft and portaging is given to beginners. Evening campfires with songs, stories and discussions of the human and natural history of the region are a part of the voyage. Paddling and portaging alternate with days at camp where participants may take side trips, hike, fish or relax. **Cost:** $350 for 7 days, $425 for 10 days from Ely includes guides, all equipment, food, transportation. **When:** June to August. **Contact:** North Woods Canoe Trips, 2659E S. Xanadu Wy., Aurora, CO 80014, USA; phone (303)750-8438. *(M)*

Pays d'en Haut Wilderness Trips: The high country of the Canadian wilderness is the site of canoe expeditions lasting 3 and 4 weeks. Participants from 13 to 17 years of age are divided into compatible age groups of no more than 8 members. The proper use of camp tools and canoeing skills are taught with an emphasis on safety. Canoeists can expect to carry heavy packs and canoes over both long and short portages, and to help in all camp duties such as gathering firewood, pitching tents, cooking and washing dishes. Learning about the wildlife and voyageur history is included as part of the experience. Transportation to and from St. Paul is provided. **Cost:** $300 for 3 weeks, $400 for 4 weeks includes transportation, meals, canoeing and camping equipment, instruction, guide. **When:** June to August. **Contact:** Pays d'en Haut, 1932 Ashland, St. Paul, MN 55104, USA; phone (612)647-9939.

Whitewater Women: A group of experienced women canoeists spends 3 days running moderate whitewater on a Minnesota river. After meeting in Minneapolis, the party heads out to either the Brule,

Kettle or Flambeau River, depending on the water levels. Instruction and practical experience enable participants to sharpen their canoeing skills, with 2 instructors present to provide individual attention. Several other canoe trips are offered, including a family or beginners' cruise on Minnehaha Creek, a 4-day outing on the Totogatic and Namekagon rivers and an autumn outing combining hiking and canoeing in the Boundary Waters Canoe Area. **Cost:** $75 includes food, equipment, instruction. **When:** May. **Contact:** Woodswomen, 3716 4th Ave. S., Minneapolis, MN 55409, USA.

Montana

Canoeing Historic Waters: The Missouri River, once frequented by keelboats and steamboats when it was the principal pioneer route to the Northwest, is the waterway for guided and self-guided canoe trips of varying lengths. Canoeists put in at Ft. Benton, Montana, the beginning of the Mullan Trail, and can paddle as far as Kipp State Park, a 160-mile stretch of river which was once a major gold rush route. Along the banks, monuments and landmarks document the river's rich history. Pick-up service from Kipp State Park or upriver is available. **Cost:** $54 to $75 depending on trip length includes canoe, gear, pick-up. **When:** May to September. **Contact:** Missouri River Cruises, Inc., Box 1212, Ft. Benton, MT 59442, USA; phone (406)622-3295. *(M)*

New Jersey

River School: A 3-day trip is an opportunity for the beginner to learn all the basics of river canoeing. Experienced instructors teach participants such primary skills as the 8 basic strokes, the 4 most useful maneuvers in canoeing, proper leaning postures and how to "read" different formations of water. For more advanced canoeists, an intermediate course lasting 3 days is offered; it involves international Class III and IV whitewater regions, where greater skill is needed and teamwork is essential. A special 8-day combination of the 2 courses is also offered. **Cost:** $58 for 3 consecutive Saturdays, $80 for 3 days, $183 for 8 days. **When:** April to August. **Contact:** South Branch Canoe Cruises, P.O. Box 173, Lebanon, NJ 08833, USA; phone (201)782-9700.

New York

Floating in the Adirondacks: Two rivers in the Adirondack Mountains, the St. Regis and the Raquette, are explored on a canoe trip that lasts either 12 or 24 days. Most of the water is Class I and II, but occasional stretches of rapids enable the novice canoeist to sample some whitewater. In addition, nontechnical climbs are made on Blue and St. Regis mountains, affording broad views of the area. Local wildlife likely to be seen includes herons, ducks, loons and beavers; the flora in and out of the water is also examined. On both trips and particularly during the 24-day version, an open schedule permits time for side trips, layovers and individual activities. Participants meet in Chautauqua. **Cost:** $245 for 12 days, $475 for 24 days includes transportation, food, equipment, guides. **When:** July.

Contact: Western Door Wilderness School, Box 534, 17 South Ave., Chautauqua, NY 14722, USA; phone (716)357-5561; or 172 N St., Salt Lake City, UT 84103, USA; phone (801)322-5381.

North Carolina

Whitewater Instruction Program: The rivers of North Carolina are the site of whitewater canoe clinics and week-long camping trips for canoeists of all levels of ability. Weekend clinics begin with an orientation session on equipment and safety followed by 2 days on the Little Tennessee, the Nantahala or other rivers. A 5-day trip takes beginning canoeists on a gentle section of the French Broad River with the goal of becoming intermediate paddlers by the time they take out at Hot Springs 75 miles downstream. Class III and IV water is encountered as the river breaks through the Appalachian Mountains. For intermediates, a 5-day program provides instruction while running a variety of rivers in the Smoky Mountain area, such as the Oconaluftee, Tuckaseigee and Nolichucky. Advanced canoeists may learn decked boat racing or follow an instruction certification program. All courses may be taken on decked boats or open canoes. Private instruction and women's clinics are also available. **Cost:** $100 for weekend clinics, $250 for 5 to 6 days includes instruction, equipment, transportation, all meals and, depending on the trip, lodging. **When:** April to November. **Contact:** Nantahala Outdoor Center, Star Rt., Box 68, Bryson City, NC 28713, USA; phone (704)488-6407. *(M)*

Blue Ridge in the Spring: From a base camp at 2 cabins in the Sherwood Forest near Brevard, North Carolina, participants make day trips to high peaks, rushing waterfalls and deep forests. One day is spent on the Tuckaseigee River in canoes or kayaks for those with kayak experience. Those who do not wish to stay with the group may take a room in Brevard or rent a cabin in Sherwood Forest and join the group for day trips. **Cost:** $20 a day includes food, all gear and trained guides; $5 a year for membership. **When:** March. **Contact:** Polivalues, Inc., 101 Maplewood Ave., Clearwater, FL 33515, USA; summer, Audubon Colony, Rt. 1, Brevard, NC 28712, USA.

South Carolina

Long Creek Canoeing: On the Chattooga and other area rivers, instruction in canoe and kayak technique is offered during classes lasting from 1 to 3 days. Operating out of Long Creek, the courses teach basic strokes, equipment use, safety techniques and other skills. Custom canoe and kayak trips can be arranged as well. **Cost:** $35 for 1 day, $75 for 2 days, $100 for 3 days includes food, equipment, instruction. **When:** Summer. **Contact:** Wildwater Ltd., Long Creek, SC 29658, USA; phone (803)647-5336; winter, 400 West Rd., Portsmouth, VA 23707, USA; phone (804)397-6658.

Texas

Lone Star River Trips: Canoeists can take trips lasting 2 days down several rivers in the central Texas hill country. A typical river is the Guadalupe, originating in the

Edwards Plateau above Kerrville and flowing over 100 miles through high limestone bluffs and grassy banks lined with cypress and pecan trees. A number of rapids are encountered, and paddlers can expect to see deer, wild turkeys, foxes and other animals along the way. Similar trips are run on the Frio, Medina, Pedernales and San Marcos rivers. Instruction is offered as needed on the outings; guides prepare campsites and meals. **Cost:** $75 includes food, equipment, instruction, guide. **When:** March to November. **Contact:** Texas Canoe Trails, Star Rt. 2, Box 866B, New Braunfels, TX 78130, USA; phone (512)964-3760. *(M)*

Utah

Canyon Canoeing: Participants are offered a package of equipment for 4- to 10-day expeditions through the canyonlands of the Green River. Starting in Moab, canoeists are transported to their launching point in the town of Green River. They are equipped with canoes, paddles and life jackets, and given instructions for their float through Canyonlands National Park. Participants may then travel to pickup points 70, 80, 90 or 120 miles downstream, the 120-mile point being the confluence of the Green and Colorado rivers. Rates are contingent upon the placement of the customer's car in a company yard at Moab and include 2 persons to a canoe, and haul-out of 2 persons plus gear. **Cost:** $100 to $115; minimum $150 for any group package. **When:** Year-round. **Contact:** Tex's

River Expeditions, P.O. Box 67, Moab, UT 84532, USA; phone (801)259-5101.

Vermont

On the Otter: Participants paddle canoes through scenic farmlands and woods and past quaint villages on 50 navigable miles of Otter Creek between Emerald Lake and Lake Champlain. On a 3-day voyage beginning in Wallingford, paddlers travel through the countryside at a leisurely pace, stopping each night at an old New England inn. The first day canoeists snake through the village of Clarendon on a 16-mile run to Rutland. During the second day, the group paddles under covered bridges and gets a good view of the surrounding Green and Taconic mountains. A 17-mile run on the final day takes participants to Middlebury, where they have a choice of lodgings at 2 inns dating from the 1800s. The creek is mostly flat water, and the route is planned to avoid portages. **Cost:** $300 includes food, lodging, canoes, car shuttle. **When:** June to September. **Contact:** Churchill House Inn, RFD #3, Rt. 73E, Brandon, VT 05733, USA; phone (802)247-3300

New England Whitewater: Teenaged river runners spend 2 days floating down tame to moderately challenging whitewater in Vermont, New Hampshire and western Massachusetts. On each trip the basics of the sport are treated: river reading, portaging, loading and paddling skills. Although it is recommended that all participants have at least 2 days of camping experience, it is not imperative for the late-season journeys. All group members must be strong swimmers. Trips are run down the White and Battenkill rivers in Vermont, the Green River in Massachusetts, and the Saco and Androscoggin rivers in New Hampshire. All group equipment is provided. **Cost:** $45 to $50. **When:** April to June. **Contact:** N & N Enterprises, Inc., Box 438, Allston, MA 02134, USA; phone (617)783-3568.

Paddle into Spring: Two weekend workshops, one for experienced canoeists and one for beginners, explore the rivers of Vermont and New Hampshire during the spring runoff. The early spring runoff generates Class II to IV whitewater, and a group of experienced paddlers runs several rivers, using wet suits in the cold water. The beginners' course starts on a Friday evening with classroom instruction, but takes place later in the spring when the water is not so high; flat water canoeing is included with whitewater stretches. Both trips camp overnight by the river. **Cost:** $85 for advanced course, $75 for beginners' course includes food, transportation from Boston, equipment, instruction. **When:** April, May. **Contact:** Treeline Associates, 56 Boston St., Middleton, MA 01949, USA; phone (617)774-6536.

Virginia

Old Dominion State Canoeing: Basic and advanced canoeing courses are offered on the rivers of Virginia and surrounding states. Led by an experienced canoeist who has published several canoeing guidebooks, participants learn the sport the best way possible—on the water, with instructors nearby. Calm river and whitewater canoeing are taught with a ratio of 1 instructor for every 2 students. Students may spend 1 or 2 days on overnighting weekends canoeing on such rivers as the Potomac, Shenandoah, Youghiogheny and Rappahannock. Weekend overnights are spent camping in local parks. The exact choice of river depends upon the time of year and the water conditions of each river. In addition to canoeing, participants may try kayaking or rafting alongside the canoeing class. Academic credit is available from some local colleges. Included in the cost are canoe rentals and instruction. **Cost:** $16 for 1 day canoeing instruction; $28 for 2 days of canoeing or rafting. **When:** April to September. **Contact:** Louis J. Matacia, 2700 Gallows Rd., Vienna, VA 22180, USA; phone (703)560-8993.

Shenandoah River Canoe Trips: Commissioned guides knowledgeable about local wildlife lead canoeists down the legendary Shenandoah River on trips of variable lengths. Rugged cliffs rising from the banks of the river contain caves and caverns that participants may explore along the way, and white-tailed deer, raccoons, and great blue herons populate the area. Canoeists glide through Class I and Class II rapids between Shenandoah National Park on the Blue Ridge and the George Washington National Forest on Massanutten Mountain. The water of the Shenandoah is clean and participants can swim in it as well as camp along its banks. If canoeists decide to

Nantahala Outdoor Center offers a variety of canoe trips and whitewater instruction on North Carolina's rivers, from beginners' classes to Class IV runs through the Appalachian Mountains. (Henry Wallace/Nantahala Outdoor Center)

Many canoeing guides also function as outfitters, supplying equipment, instruction, directions and moral support. (Keith Gunnar)

make the journey without a guide, route planners give advice and help in matching the trip, route and equipment to individual abilities and interests. **Cost:** $80 for 3 days; $60 for 2 days includes guide, meals, canoeing and rafting equipment. **When:** Year-round. **Contact:** Shenandoah River Outfitters, Inc., RFD 3, Luray, VA 22835, USA; phone (703)743-4159.

Wisconsin

Unguided Wisconsin Trips: Canoe trips begin just past the last dam on the Wisconsin River near Sauk City, and take passengers past sandbars, islands and marshlands towards the confluence of the Wisconsin and Mississippi rivers. Trips last anywhere from 1 to several days and provide opportunities for both beginning and experienced canoeists to explore the uninhabited Midwest. This section of the Wisconsin River is scheduled for inclusion in the Wild Rivers Act, a ruling which will protect it from future land development. Tent sites and pickup shuttle service for rental or privately owned canoes are available all along the river. **Cost:** $15 for 1 day includes canoe, paddles, preservers, drinking water, maps, transportation back to canoe base; for longer trips, $7 for 1st day, $6 for each additional day includes canoe. **When:** June to September. **Contact:** Blackhawk Ridge, P.O. Box 92, Sauk City, WI 53583, USA; phone (608)643-3775.

Canoe Flambeau River: Flambeau River State Forest provides the setting for a 4-day river run. The trip commences in Oxbow, and after 45 river miles ends at Flambeau Lodge. Whitewater techniques are taught to those with interest in tackling some fast water by kayak or canoe. For those of a less energetic bent, large "Huck Finn" rafts are available for relaxed river floats. Short hikes are planned as well as swims, camp meals and evening bonfires. A moonlight float is possible. Early summer provides ideal high water for ease of navigation and opportunities to view wildlife along the river banks. **Cost:** $158 includes guides, full instruction, meals. **When:** June. **Contact:** Spirit Waters, 5375 Eureka Rd., Excelsior, MN 55331, USA; phone (612)474-5190.

Wyoming

Paddling in the Park: Canoe trips in several areas of Yellowstone National Park are offered on a custom basis, generally lasting between 3 and 8 days. Shoshone and Lewis lakes can be explored by using the short channel between them, or paddlers can investigate the southeast arm of Yellowstone Lake. On these trips a guide leads the party and prepares food and campsites. Outfitting is also offered for self-guided trips, with camping and canoeing equipment, food, and transportation supplied. **Cost:** $35 a day for guided trips, $15 to $20 a day for outfitting. **When:** Summer. **Contact:** Savage Outfitters, General Delivery, Macks Inn, ID 83433, USA; phone (406)646-7687; winter, 116 W. 24th St., Sioux Falls, SD 57105, USA; phone (605)338-7608.

RESOURCES

Clubs and Associations

Alaska Pioneers Canoers Association
Box 931
Soldotna, AK 99669, USA

American Canoe Association
Box 9137
Chicago, IL 60690, USA

American Indian Center Canoe Club
115 N. Walnut
Boise, ID 83702, USA

American Rivers Conservation Council
317 Pennsylvania Ave. SE
Washington, DC 20003, USA

Canadian Canoe Association
33 River Rd., Place Vanier
Vanier City, ON Canada K1L 8B9

Eastern Professional River
Outfitters Association
P.O. Box 2997
Flagstaff, AZ 86003, USA

Everglades Canoe Club
239 NE 20th St.
Delray Beach, FL 33440, USA

Indooroopilly Club
P.O. Box 36
Indooroopilly, Queensland, Australia

International Canoe Federation
905 6th St. SW
Washington, DC 20024, USA

Irish Canoe Union
91, Kilfenora Rd., Kimmage
Dublin 12, Ireland

Metropolitan Canoe and Kayak Club
c/o American Red Cross
150 Amsterdam Ave.
New York, NY 10023, USA

United States Canoe Association
1818 Kensington Blvd.
Ft. Wayne, IN 46805, USA

Wilderness Canoe Association
Box 901, Sta. A
Scarborough, ON Canada M1K 5E4

Rentals

Rent-A-Canoe Directory
Grumman Boats
Marathon, NY 13803, USA

National Association of
Canoe Liveries and Outfitters
P.O. Box 515
Big Rapids, MI 49307, USA
Phone (616)796-3907

KAYAKING

Eskimos were the first to build kayaks by shrinking seal or other animal skins over a wooden frame. Masterpieces of primitive engineering, kayaks enabled hunters to approach wildlife noiselessly and paddle through turbulent, ice-filled seas. Even today Eskimos draw the bottom of a parka over the cockpit rim, fastening it tightly with a drawstring. Then if the boat capsizes in rough water, they can roll upright without taking in any water. Propelled by a double-bladed paddle, kayaks are essential to the harsh life from the Bering Sea to the east coast of Greenland.

Kayaking as a sport developed in southern Germany around the turn of the century. Since the mid-1950s kayaks have been made from plastic and fiberglass and used for whitewater slalom and calm-water racing. Kayaks can be rented, constructed from kits or purchased right off the rack. From small children who are just big enough to see over the cockpit to folks decades older, people of all ages enjoy kayaking.

You might start with a weekend kayaking course on the American River in California to learn safety procedures, use of equipment, the Eskimo roll, and basic paddling techniques, or you might join a kayaking clinic in Colorado that teaches slalom and whitewater skills. Once you've mastered the art of kayaking, you can sign up for a 23-day expedition to New Zealand that takes on the country's best whitewater rivers, you can try kayak surfing and explore Loch Ness in Scotland, or you can paddle among whales, sea lions and dolphins along the coast of Baja California.

Kayaking trips combine the best of wilderness camping and the discovery of new places with the building of self-reliance and muscular coordination. In addition, paddling trips enable you to enjoy other activities such as hiking, fishing, photography and visits to historical sites. By inflating a kayak on a river bank, picking up a paddle and squeezing into the cockpit, you can enjoy the eddies and rapids of the world. □

Kayaks are light and narrow enough that they can move in almost any direction relative to the current—even vertically. (Keith Gunnar)

KAYAKING

AUSTRALASIA

New Zealand

New Zealand Frontier: A group of 10 experienced kayakers runs a number of remote New Zealand rivers on a 23-day trip departing from Seattle. After flying to Auckland participants drive to Wairakei, their base for a trial run down the Aratiatia River; over the next few days they run the Mohaka, Tongariro and Whangachu (all Class III), and the Upper Tongariro (Class IV). After a ferry ride to South Island, kayakers run the Buller River and take a helicopter to the Landsborough River. Traveling to Arrowtown, they paddle the Kawarau (Class IV and V) and Shotover (Class IV) before a visit to Milford Sound. The final runs are on the Hollyford River, with fairly easy water but spectacular scenery, and on the moderately difficult Pukaki before the return to Seattle via Christchurch and Auckland. Weather and water levels may alter the itinerary. Most nights are spent camping, and participants must submit a resume of their boating skills when applying for the trip. **Cost:** $2,595 includes transportation from Seattle, most meals, accommodations, most equipment, guides. **When:** February. **Contact:** Kayak New Zealand, P.O. Box 1772, Bellevue, WA 98009, USA.

CANADA

British Columbia

West Coast Kayaks: The west coast of Vancouver Island is explored on a week-long kayak trip. Participants begin with a pool session in Vancouver to master necessary kayaking skills and then proceed north to the coast. An area of inlets and small islands, the coastline offers plenty of opportunities for the kayaker and is rich in wildlife, tidal communities and virgin cedar

Kayaking instruction usually takes place in small classes which begin in a pool and then progress to shallow open water. Here a group of students prepares for their first offshore session. (Canadian Hostelling Association)

forests. Participants enjoy such activities as jigging for fish, swimming and relaxing on remote beaches. Some instruction is given en route on the area's flora, fauna and ecology. **Cost:** $199 includes food, equipment, transportation, instruction. **When:** July. **Contact:** Alpine Crafts Ltd., 1286 Kingsway, Vancouver, BC Canada V5V 3E1; phone (604)873-4915.

Haida Way: Twelve days in the Queen Charlotte Islands, home of the Haida Indians, allow a small group of participants to explore a variety of terrains and coastlines aboard sailing kayaks. After flying from Vancouver, the party spends a few days in the sheltered inlets around Louise Island to become familiar with the boats. Kayakers then move to the more exposed coastline, following it as far south toward Lyall Island as weather allows. The emphasis is on observing the flora and fauna of the area, with the chance of seeing orcas and sea lions. Haida art is also investigated. About half the food eaten on the trip is foraged, mainly from the sea. **Cost:** $550 includes transportation from Vancouver, food, equipment, guides. **When:** July. **Contact:** ECOsummer Canada, Box 191, Heriot Bay, BC Canada V0P 1N0.

EUROPE

Scotland

Pick of the Lochs: Kayaking instruction and week-long kayak trips are offered on Scotland's lochs. A kayaking center on the shores of Loch Lomond provides instruction in kayaking techniques, safety and rescue procedures; visits are made to islands on the loch, and lunches are taken on the beach. Week-long trips by kayak explore Loch Lochy, Loch Oich and Loch Ness as well as sections of the Caledonian Canal. Weather permitting, kayak surfing is included. Participants must be at least 14 years old. **Cost:** $86 a week for instruction, $58 a week for trips includes equipment, instruction, meals, accommodations. **When:** June to August. **Contact:** Scottish Youth Hostels Association, 7 Glebe Cresc., Stirling FK8 2JA, Great Britain; phone Stirling 2821.

MEXICO

Baja California

Bahia de Conception Kayaking: Along the most rugged and isolated part of the Baja coast, participants journey by kayak and folbot from Mulege to San Sebastian or Laredo. The San Sebastian trip takes 12 days and covers 35 miles while the Laredo trip takes 18 days and covers 85 miles. Kayaking, snorkeling and food gathering skills including pole and spear fishing are taught in Bahia de Conception. Food is carried on the journey but there is also a heavy reliance on catching red snapper and other fish along the way. During the exploration, paddlers see whales, sea lions, dolphins and extensive bird life. The trip is strenuous and requires good health and endurance. **Cost:** $350 for 12 days, $480 for 18 days includes transportation from Mulege, guides, instruction, food, equipment. **When:** October, November.

The kayaking tradition is at least as strong in Europe as it is in the United States. There the waterways available include canals as well as rivers. (Office National du Tourisme, Luxembourg)

Contact: James Henry River Journeys, 1078 Keith, Berkeley, CA 94708, USA; phone (415)525-6578.

PACIFIC

Hawaii

Water Sports around Maui: Trip members spend 5 days kayaking, snorkeling and sailing around the remote islands near Maui. After meeting in Kahului, participants are transported by sailboat to a base on one of the islands where camp is set up. From here, group members can snorkel among the coral reefs, ride the surf in 2-person kayaks or pilot one of the sailboats. Rafts provide participants with the opportunity to investigate ancient Hawaiian villages, petroglyphs, shipwrecks and hidden caves, accessible only from the sea. Local foodstuffs are used in meals. The group size is limited to 20, and the minimum age is 8. **Cost:** $345 includes most camping equipment, transportation, meals. **When:** Year-round. **Contact:** International Aquatic Adventures, Inc., 2047 Broadway, Boulder, CO 80302, USA; phone (303)444-5829 or toll-free (800)525-2545.

UNITED STATES

Alaska

Alaskan Glacier Kayaking: A 7-day kayak trip for experienced and inexperienced kayakers alike commences with a charter flight from Yakutat to Russell Fjord. Klepper kayaks are provided, and 2-person crews are chosen. Ample practice time is provided for beginners. The trip includes kayaking the Russell Fjord and spending 2 nights on Oster Island, some 200 yards from the face of Hubbard Glacier. The glacier itself adds excitement by calving almost constantly. Each party member is responsible for her/his own tent, boat and cooking while on the trip. The trip ends at a pickup point on the opposite side of Russell Fjord with a charter flight back to Yakutat. **Cost:** $750 includes kayak, food, transportation. **When:** June to August. **Contact:** Alaska Discovery Enterprises, P.O. Box 26, Gustavus, AK 99826, USA; phone (907)697-3431.

Princely Kayaking: Kayak trips are offered in and around Prince William Sound, lasting either 5 or 12 days. Participants on both trips are transported from Anchorage by float plane or power boat. The shorter trips take place out of a base camp on the Sound, where kayakers sleep in tents and make forays to surrounding coves and points of interest. Time is allotted for hiking, photography and relaxation. Participants on the 12-day trips leave base camp and paddle along the shoreline, pitching camp each night. A stop is made at Nellie Juan Glacier. Some hiking is done along the steep fjords on the sound, and waterfowl can be seen in abundance. On both trips, participants are returned to Whittier by power boat and take a train back to Anchorage. Custom trips can be arranged. **Cost:** $550 for 5 days, $990 for 12 days includes transportation from Anchorage, food, accommodations, equipment, guide. **When:** May to August. **Contact:** Bear Bros., Star Rt. A, Box 18B, Anchorage, AK 99507, USA; phone (907)344-5760.

Glacier Bay Kayaking: The Glacier Bay Wilderness is the setting for an 18-day kayaking trip. After taking a ferry from Juneau, participants board 2-person Klepper kayaks for explorations of the glacier-rimmed inlets of the bay. Paddlers may spot seals, porpoises and whales as well as puffins, terns and eagles. Some hiking on glaciers is also featured, giving kayakers a chance to investigate remnants of the mining era, snowfields, moraines, hidden caves and the rocky coast of Glacier Bay. A similar trip is available for students 16 or older who would like to acquire mountaineering skills in addition to kayaking techniques; the 35-day trip takes them to Glacier Bay and Haines. In Kluane National Park, instruction is available in first aid and basic mountaineering skills, which are put to use on climbs on nearby peaks. **Cost:** $960 for kayaking trip, $1,570 for student course includes transportation from Juneau, camping accommodations, meals. **When:** August for kayaking, June for mountaineering. **Contact:** The Infinite Odyssey, 57 Grant St., Waltham, MA 02154, USA; phone (617)899-6050.

(M)

Northern Lights Semester: Students spend 75 days studying on land and sea, beginning with a month of folboting in Prince William Sound, where they observe whales and icebergs. While camping along the conifer-lined shore, the group reviews a basic curriculum of outdoor living skills and environmental awareness. The second phase of the trip involves a full-scale, 3-week glacier expedition. Instruction covers route finding, crevasse rescue, snow and ice climbing, geology and glaciology. A major peak is scaled once the group has developed sufficient skill. The final weeks of the course are spent in Mt. McKinley National

Park, studying the biology and ecology of the tundra. **Cost:** $2,100 includes supplies, meals, instruction. **When:** June to August. **Contact:** National Outdoor Leadership School, Box AA, Lander, WY 82520, USA; phone (307)332-4381.

Arctic Kayaking: Participants travel for a minimum of 14 days via paddle- and sail-powered kayaks along the south-central Brooks Range. Each trip is planned with the interests and resources of group members in mind. Activities while on or near the Kobuk River can vary from prospecting to studying archaeology. The trip is guided by experienced mountaineers who are familiar with plant, bird and wildlife identification. Photographers have the opportunity to capture varied terrain and flora and fauna in an isolated wilderness environment. **Cost:** $80 a day includes meals, equipment, guides. **When:** June to August. **Contact:** Otis B. Driftwood Adventures Unlimited, 8701 Kathleen, Anchorage, AK 99502, USA.

Kayaking Glacial Tidewater: For 1 week individuals maneuver kayaks in the upper reaches of Russell Fjord and Hubbard Glacier, surrounded by the sounds of birds and calving glaciers. The trip begins at Juneau with a flight to the Russell Fjord where time is allowed for leisurely exploration into Nunatak Fjord, another wilderness area. Further on, participants camp at Oster Island, which lies about 650 feet from the face of Hubbard Glacier. Though the glacier calves almost constantly, moments of silence are filled with the cries of hundreds of birds from nearby rookeries. No previous kayaking experience is necessary as no rapids are encountered along the trip. **Cost:** $570 includes roundtrip transportation from Juneau, equipment. **When:** July, August. **Contact:** Sobek Expeditions, Inc., P.O. Box 761, Angels Camp, CA 95222, USA; phone (209)736-2924. ***(M)***

California

Kayaking from the Ground Up: Students spend 3 weeks building and then using their own kayaks for a circumnavigation of Santa Catalina Island. The program is divided into 3 basic parts: construction of the kayaks, water work and instruction on basic kayaking skills, and a series of lectures and field trips designed to introduce students to the environment of the island. During the trip, camping sites include Silver Canyon, Ben Weston Beach, Parson's Landing and Goat Harbor. Each day enough time is given to hiking and observation of the native flora and fauna so that students may have a practical nature experience. **Cost:** On request. **When:** Summer. **Contact:** Catalina Island School, Toyon Bay, P.O. Box 796, Avalon, CA 90704, USA; phone 611 (operator assistance required).

Kayaking for Novices: The Coloma Run, on the south fork of the American River, is the site of a weekend kayaking course for beginners. On this well-known novice's run, students gain confidence through practicing safety procedures, equipment use and basic paddling techniques. A limit of 4 students per instructor guarantees individual attention, with some time spent in the water on both days. Overnight accommodations are at a nearby campsite. All equipment is supplied, but students must dress warmly (wet suits can be rented). **Cost:** $50 to $60, depending on number in party, includes food, camping accommodations, instruction, equipment. **When:** June to September. **Contact:** Mother Lode Outdoor School, 581 Continental Dr., San Jose, CA 95111, USA; phone (408)578-5434. *(M)*

Klamath Caper: At a designated campground on the Klamath River Highway, participants and guides meet for an orientation session before starting on a 3-day trip down the Klamath River. The trip is an appropriate one for beginners since everyone is instructed in boat handling techniques and water safety procedures. Each participant is provided with a kayak as guides lead small groups in follow-the-leader style through bouncy chutes and riffles. Steady, easy paddling and gliding are typical; faster downstream progress depends upon the current. Nights are spent at campgrounds along the shore. On the second and third days, more challenging whitewater is experienced. Thirty miles downstream, the group concludes the trip by boarding vans and riding back to the launching point. **Cost:** $185 from Klamath River Highway includes transportation, guides, meals, equipment. **When:** June to September. **Contact:** Orange Torpedo Trips, P.O. Box 1111, Grants Pass, OR 97526, USA; phone (503)479-5016. *(M)*

Colorado

Paddling Instruction: A kayak expert instructs students privately or during 2-, 4- and 6-day clinics. The kayaking school is located near the Colorado River at the junction of the Roaring Fork and Crystal rivers. For paddling techniques and slalom instruction, participants practice on a school pond. Individuals then navigate their craft on the Roaring Fork, Crystal and Colorado rivers

Several California rivers contain stretches well-suited for novices learning kayaking techniques and safety procedures. Here a kayaker paddles through some moderate riffles on the Stanislaus. (Christian Kallen)

during practice sessions relating to currents and slalom technique. Groups are also introduced to various grades of river running on the Arkansas River. A 2-day clinic for candidate instructors and an exam for certification are also available. Various accommodations are possible during the 6-day program and may include dormitory lodging or camping. All students are asked to have a physical exam before attending any course and should be in good physical condition. **Cost:** $10 to $220, depending on duration of trip and accommodations, includes instruction. **When:** June, July. **Contact:** Roger Paris Kayak School, Rt. 1, Box 9, Carbondale, CO 81623, USA; phone (303)963-2433.

Idaho

Salmon and Snake Special: Using inflatable kayaks, 15 river runners paddle through the narrow volcanic canyons of the Lower Salmon and Snake rivers for 4 days. Numerous rapids, huge waves and swells make this Class III voyage better suited to those with previous kayaking experience. Guides and paddlers in a ratio of 1 to 3 or 4 meet in Lewiston, then drive to Skookumchuck Park for orientation, instruction and drills in boat handling techniques and water safety procedures. Traveling in individual kayaks, participants average 18 miles a day and camp on beaches along the way. The course winds through Green and Blue canyons to a convergence with the Snake River and a final 22-mile run to the take-out point at Grande Ronde. From there the group travels by van to a celebration dinner at Lewiston. **Cost:** $275 from Lewiston includes transportation, guides, food, equipment. **When:** July, August. **Contact:** Orange Torpedo Trips, P.O. Box 1111, Grants Pass, OR 97526, USA; phone (503)479-5061. ***(M)***

Maine

Learning Whitewater Kayaking: A 2-week program for boys 14 and older stresses instructional skills in fundamental whitewater kayaking. Students learn basic skills such as rolling, river reading and kayak paddling, while experiencing the water of Maine's Pleasant Lake and the faster currents of the St. Croix River. The Mattawamkeag River provides challenging whitewater near the end of the course. Students are required to display excellent swimming ability to join the program. The campsite is a short trip from Maine's highest peak, Mt. Katahdin in Baxter State Park. **Cost:** $310. **When:** Summer. **Contact:** Maine Wilderness Canoe Basin, 246 Neptune Dr., Groton, CT 06340, USA; phone (203)536-7980.

Oregon

Northwest Kayaking: One- and 3-day trips paddling inflatable kayaks on the Rogue River offer an introduction to kayak handling. On the 3-day trip, kayaks pass through small and intermediate rapids, progressing to more difficult whitewater. By the third day, paddlers take on Mule Creek Canyon, Devil's Staircase and Clay Hill rapids before arriving at Illahee in the late afternoon. Overnight stops at lodges along the river allow time for hiking into the forested canyon country, photography and a visit to Zane Grey's cabin at Winkle Bar. **Cost:** $35 for day trips, $200 for 3 days includes all costs from start of the trip to return to headquarters. **When:** June to September. **Contact:**

Orange Torpedo Trips, P.O. Box 1111, Grants Pass, OR 97526, USA; phone (503)479-5061. *(M)*

Kayak School: The first 5 days of a 9-day kayaking course consist of day-long outings on different sections of the Rogue River, increasing in difficulty as the days pass. Skills taught include dry and wet exits, basic strokes, the Eskimo roll, surfing, safety and rescue techniques and kayak etiquette. In evening sessions, the group discusses the day's events, reviewing wilderness skills, first aid and expedition preparation, with supplemental slides and movies. Skills are then put to the test on a 4-day trip down the lower Rogue. Traveling in traditional touring formation, kayakers encounter 40 miles of challenging whitewater and rapids. Crafts beach at Foster Bar on the last day and students are transported back to the riverhouse. The course may also be taken in 5-day segments. **Cost:** $540 for 9 days, $300 for each 5-day session includes meals, lodging, instruction. **When:** June to September. **Contact:** Sundance Expeditions, 14894 Galice Rd., Merlin, OR 97532, USA; phone (503)479-8508.

Utah

Sportyak Workshops: Instruction in Sportyak use, including pivoting, pulling and pushing, ferrying and righting, is given along quiet stretches of the Green River's Desolation Canyon. Groups test their skills on rapids like Steer Ridge, Wire Fence and Rattlesnake. The trip lasts 8 days and includes time spent drifting quietly, studying canyon geology and rock formations, observing wildlife such as eagles, herons and hawks, and hiking up side canyons to visit cliff dwellings, petroglyph sites and old horse trails leading to abandoned ranches. **Cost:** $525 includes equipment, meals, flight to put-in, post-trip return transportation. **When:** June to September. **Contact:** Wild and Scenic, Inc., P.O. Box 2123A, Marble Canyon, AZ 86036, USA; phone (602)355-2222.

Washington

Cascades Paddling: Instruction is offered in 7-day segments for prospective or experienced kayakers. Taking place on Lake Wenatchee in the Cascade Mountain foothills, the course is designed for students of all ages and abilities, allowing participants to work and develop at an individual pace. The instructor-to-student ratio is 1 to 5, and all equipment is provided. In addition to activity on the lake, instruction and practice take place on the White, Chiwawa, Nason and Wenatchee rivers. All participants must be able to swim 100 yards. Safety and rescue techniques, river reading, trip planning and flat water skills are also studied. Meals and lodging are provided at the Cougar Inn; bedding is included and the rooms are dormitory-style. **Cost:** $250 includes food, lodging, instruction and equipment. **When:**

June, July. **Contact:** White Water Sports, 307 NE 71st St., Seattle, WA 98115, USA; phone (206)523-5150.

RESOURCES

Clubs and Associations

American Whitewater Affiliation
P.O. Box 1584
San Bruno, CA 94066, USA

Citrus County Kayak Club
c/o Rademaker, Rt. 1, Box 415
Floral City, FL 32636, USA

Hawaii Kayak Club
407-D Keariani St.
Kailea, HI 96734, USA

Metropolitan Canoe and Kayak Club
c/o American Red Cross
150 Amsterdam Ave.
New York, NY 10023, USA

Montana Kayak Club
c/o Abelin, Box 2
Brady, MT 59416, USA

Ocean Kayak and Touring Club
c/o Canadian Hostelling Assoc.
3425 W. Broadway
Vancouver, BC Canada V6R 2B4

Oregon Kayak and Canoe Club
c/o Kiel, P.O. Box 692
Portland, OR 97207, USA

Vancouver Kayak and Canoe Club
4022 W. 27th
Vancouver, BC Canada V6S 1R7

Washington Kayak Club
c/o Aaker, Box 24264
Seattle, WA 98124, USA

Western Wyoming Kayak Club
Donald L. Hahn, Gen Del.
Wilson, WY 83014, USA

Whitewater-Northeast Kayak Club
Box 1081
Spokane, WA 99201, USA

39854

SAILING

The bright red and green-striped spinnaker snaps taut in a downwind rush of warm air as you sail through the British Virgin Islands. On a 5-day trip off the coast of Santa Barbara you learn celestial navigation, sharpen sailing skills and explore secluded coves. An 88-foot schooner carries you and your bicycle to picturesque ports along the coast of New England. Now it is possible to sail the same waters that brought Europeans to America, floated pirates through the Caribbean and transported the pharaohs up the Nile.

Sailing trips are offered on nearly all the waters of the world for any length of time. You can sail a 46-foot brigantine off Cape Breton in the northeast Atlantic, crew on a gaff-rigged schooner along the French coast and among the islands of Great Britain or snorkel from a 48-foot yawl on the Sea of Cortez. A 50-foot ketch sails through the South Pacific islands on 2- and 3-week trips, and a 52-foot Frisian sailing scow plies the waters off Holland. If you are willing to work you can even join a 21-month circumnavigation of the world on a 55-foot yacht.

Three basic types of trips are available to people of all ages. You can "bareboat" on a rental boat that comes complete with all equipment and cooking gear; you can join a "cruise-and-learn" trip with an instructor who teaches sailing and navigation skills as you go; or you can just sit back and relax as a skipper and crew take care of the sailing.

Whether you want to hoist sails, plot the course with a sextant and make a spinnaker run through a Scottish sound, or read a book on the deck of an 82-foot gaff-rigged yawl as you sail through the Balearic Islands off Spain, you can enjoy a high seas adventure that most people only dream about. □

A single-masted sailboat makes full use of the prevailing winds during a summer cruise in the waters around Washington's San Juan Islands. (Elizabeth Watson)

SAILING

AFRICA

Egypt

Nile Sail Trek: Participants fly from London to Cairo to begin a 15-day exploration of Egypt, including sailing down the Nile River in feluccas. The felucca is a swift, low-riding sailboat with no motor, and sleeps 6 persons on deck under a canvas canopy. Sites visited include the Temple of Luxor, built in the age of Amenhotep III and famous for its lotus bud columns, and the temple of Karnak, largest of all Egyptian temples. If passengers desire, a side trip by donkey may be taken from the west bank of the river to the Necropolis and the Valley of Kings. From Luxor it takes 7 days to reach Aswan by boat, which gives everyone a chance to experience a bit of Egyptian culture during village stops where food is bought at local markets. Participants help sail the boat, cook the food, and plan each day's itinerary. **Cost:** $720 to $780 depending on departure date includes roundtrip airfare from London, local transportation, guide, food. **When:** Year-round. **Contact:** WEXAS International, 45 Brompton Rd., Knightsbridge, London SW3 1DE, Great Britain; phone 01-589-0500. *(M)*

ASIA

Thailand

Yachting in the Tropics: A well-equipped yacht is home to sailors on a 2-week voyage in the Andaman Sea from Phuket, Thailand to Penang, Malaysia. Living aboard a 38-foot sloop sleeping 9, participants sail past coral islands, white sand beaches, deserted coves and jungle shores alive with monkeys and colorful birds. Trip members learn the ropes of ocean sailing as they help the skipper and 1-person crew with shipboard duties. The trip also provides chances for snorkeling, scuba diving and swimming. The weather is generally warm and sunny, and the water is clear to 60 feet. Most nights are spent at anchor, though some night sailing may be undertaken. Participants spend a night in a hotel before and after the sail. **Cost:** $355 includes food, accommodations, equipment, skipper, crew. **When:** On request. **Contact:** Encounter Overland, 369 Pine St., Suite 516, San Francisco, CA 94104, USA; phone (415)421-7199. *(M)*

AUSTRALASIA

New Zealand

Tequila Float: A small group of boaters sails the 42-foot sloop *Tequila* through New Zealand's waters on trips ranging in length from 10 days to 3 weeks. Although an exact itinerary is not set, each trip has a different emphasis, and novices as well as experienced sailors are welcome. All trips originate in Auckland and are limited to 5 participants. A 10-day voyage plies the waters within easy reach of Auckland. Two 14-day expeditions are run; one joins the 120-mile Whangaroa Race, while the other moves at a more leisurely pace. A 3-week trip travels to the Three Kings Islands, where participants observe and learn about the archipelago's unusual bird and sea life. Nights are mainly spent on board while moored in scenic small bays and coves. **Cost:** $450 for 10 days, $630 for 14 days, $945 for 21 days includes food, accommodations, instruction, guide. **When:** November to January. **Contact:** Ocean Voyages, 1709 Bridgeway, Sausalito, CA 94965, USA; phone (415)332-4681.

CANADA

Sailing Maritime Coastlines: Aboard a 46-foot brigantine, group members embark from Baddeck, Cape Breton, on an individualized cruise of the waters northeast of New England. The specific location and duration of the voyage depends solely on the desires of the participants. Locations visited on former trips include the Newfoundland fjords, the French Islands of St. Pierre and Miquelon, the Bras d'Or Lakes, the St. Lawrence Islands and, farther north, the straits of Belle Isle and Southern Labrador. The trips may last from 6 days to 1 month. Possible itineraries also include explorations along the coast of Labrador and parts of Greenland or a trip from Nova Scotia to Maine at the season's end. Accommodations onboard provide facilities for charter groups of up to 4. Showers with hot and cold freshwater are available. **Cost:** $150 to $170 a day includes meals, crew, accommodations on board. **When:** Summer, by arrangement. **Contact:**

Participants on Glad Tidings voyages off the eastern coast of Canada can create their own itineraries for trips lasting a week to a month. Prices begin at $170 a day. (Glad Tidings)

Glad Tidings, Box 394, Oakland, ME 04963, USA.

British Columbia

Strait Sailing: Group members spend 6 days sailing among the islands and fjords of the Georgia Strait on the coast of British Columbia. In skippered and outfitted boats 26 to 46 feet long, participants study sailing skills, navigation, weather, tide and currents, anchoring and marine ecology. The group also has a chance to learn about the preparation of fresh seafood. Small coves and estuaries are explored with canoes, and group members also travel inland to visit historical sites, wilderness lakes and waterfalls. The journeys begin at Heriot Bay, about 100 miles north of Vancouver. No previous sailing experience is necessary. **Cost:** $200 for 6 days includes food, boat, skipper. **When:** July to August. **Contact:** Sailing Explorations, Box 91436, West Vancouver, BC Canada V7V 3P1; phone (604)929-6364.

CARIBBEAN

Antilles Cruising: Individualized yacht cruises of varying durations are available to the U.S. Virgin Islands, the Grenadines and Martinique. Cruises are geared toward group desires and can include fishing and diving in the Caribbean. Snorkeling gear, water-skiing equipment and sailing dinghies are available onboard for group members. Cruising guests may share the onboard duties or simply relax as they choose. Meals are often prepared from seafood caught during the day's run. **Cost:** $50 to $70 a day includes meals, equipment. **When:** Year-round. **Contact:** Blue Water Cruises, Box 758-AX, St. Thomas, VI 00801, USA; phone (809)774-0650. *(M)*

One by Land, One by Sea: Water sport enthusiasts combine a week ashore and a week afloat in the Caribbean. The trip's first 7 days are spent at a resort on St. Lucia's Marigot Bay offering facilities for a wide array of outdoor activities; these include scuba diving, snorkeling, small boat sailing, windsurfing and water-skiing. The second week is spent aboard one of several available charter ships, including a 42-foot twin screw cruiser which can cover long distances quickly, a 65-foot ketch, a 90-foot brigantine and a 115-foot, gaff-rigged ketch. Participants can visit small ports, prime scuba spots and remote coves during the week at sea; depending on the boat used, from 4 to 8 people can participate. Another option is to spend the full 2 weeks at sea, beginning and ending the trip in Marigot Bay. **Cost:** $752 to $1,193 for shore/sea trip, $2,100 to $3,968 for 2-week sail includes food, accommodations, activities. **When:** Year-round. **Contact:** Russell Yacht Charters, 126 Davis Ave., Bridgeport, CT 06605, USA; phone (203)366-4561. *(M)*

British Virgin Islands

Sailing Instruction in Caribbean Waters: A variety of sailing instruction aboard trainer boats is available in the Bahamas and British Virgin Islands to novice and experienced sailors alike. A beginning course enables students to live onboard a 30-foot sailboat and to learn the basics of sailing, anchoring, piloting, safety and docking through both mock situations and onboard practical experience. The intermediate course is conducted in Tortola, British Virgin Islands where students concern themselves with the finer points of sailing including coastal piloting, heavy-weather sailing, basic mechanics and reefing before spending 8 days in the protected waters of the islands. A finishing course of 2 weeks for more advanced sailors is launched from St. Vincent and allows students to live onboard and cruise north to St. Lucia and Martinique experiencing the whims and ways of deep-water sailing. The course is intensive though unstructured; the goal is personal practice of skills and theory learned in previous sailing courses. **Cost:** $29 to $112, depending on the number of students. **When:** Year-round. **Contact:** Caribbean Sailing Yachts, Ltd., Roadtown, Tortola, British Virgin Islands; or Box 491, Tenafly, NJ 07670, USA; phone tollfree (800)631-1593.

Caribbean Sail: Travelers spend 7 days sailing the waters of the British Virgin Islands. Starting from Virgin Gorda, participants aboard a 90-foot barquentine cruise through Sir Francis Drake Channel and visit Tortola, Jost Van Dyke, Cooper Island, Salt, Wreck and Peter islands and Norman Island, thought to be the setting of Stevenson's *Treasure Island*. Activities include helping to steer the boat, swimming, snorkeling, scuba diving and trimming the sails. Ample time is provided for such onshore activities as beachcombing and exploring. **Cost:** $350 to $420 includes meals, accommodations, diving and fishing equipment. **When:** November to May. **Contact:** *The Pride*, Inc., P.O. Box 22069, Ft. Lauderdale, FL 33335, USA; phone (305)523-7090.

U.S. Virgin Islands

Sailing Instruction in the Virgin Islands: Group members can take sailing lessons for 2 or 5 days while visiting St. Thomas in the Virgin Islands. During the 2-day course, participants receive morning lectures on basic techniques, then board 24-foot Rainbows for sailing in the afternoons. The 5-day course follows a similar itinerary for the first 2 days, after which participants combine sailing practice with land exploration. Arrangements for 1-day sails on a larger vessel to St. John's can be made. The longer course is designed for either begin-

ners or more experienced sailors. In all courses group members sail fiberglass keel sloops. **Cost:** $110 to $395 for 2 days, $195 to $495 for 5 days, depending on the number of persons includes instruction, use of sailboats. **When:** Year-round. **Contact:** Annapolis Sailing School Headquarters, 601 Sixth St., P.O. Box 3334, Annapolis, MD 21403, USA; phone (301)267-7205 or toll-free (800)638-9192.

EUROPE

Sailing Britain and Brittany: Group members with previous sailing experience embark on 8- or 15-day journeys along the islands of Great Britain and the French coast. As active members of the crew, participants take a hand in all sailing duties aboard the gaff-rigged schooner *Hoshi*. The regions visited include Ireland, Scotland, the Hebrides, the Channel Islands and southwest Brittany. A highlight of the season is the "Old Gaffer's" race in the Solent, held each year in September. **Cost:** $375 for 8 days, $750 for 15 days includes accommodations onboard. **When:** May to September. **Contact:** Oceanic Expeditions, 240 Ft. Mason, San Francisco, CA 94123, USA; phone (415)441-1106.

England

Small Boat Sailing Course: A 5-day course in sailing small boats is offered at an outdoor activities camp near Tunbridge Wells, in southeast England. Twelve-foot boats accommodate 2 students and 1 instructor, so the teaching is individually paced; most students are sailing solo by the third day. Bewl Bridge reservoir, where the instruction takes place, is one of the region's largest inland lakes, and the sea is nearby for those who wish to try their skills there. Accommodations are dormitory style, with lunches taken at the course site. Instruction is offered at the beginner or intermediate level for either young people ages 10 to 16 or adults, and the course results in Royal Yachting Association certification. Films and lectures in the evening supplement daytime experience. **Cost:** $136 includes food,

Running through one of the sounds on the west coast of Scotland, an experienced group of young sailors navigate their boat. (Sailboat Vacations Scotland)

accommodations, instruction, transportation, equipment. **When:** July, August. **Contact:** Bowles Outdoor Pursuits Centre, Eridge Green, Tunbridge Wells TN3 9LW, Great Britain.

Italy

Tyrrhenian Sailing: The Tyrrhenian Sea is surrounded by the Tuscan Archipelago to the north, the Italian mainland to the east, Corsica and Sardinia to the west and Sicily to the south. Sailors explore the sea for 15 days in 27-foot boats with 4 berths. The itinerary is flexible, depending on the winds; participants usually visit such places as Giglio, a small mountainous island with a medieval village perched above its harbor, and Elba, the island to which Napoleon was exiled. Breakfast and lunch are taken at sea, and the sailors go ashore to sample the highly regarded Tuscan cuisine for dinner. A skipper leads the trip, though anyone with experience sailing a dinghy should be able to handle the boats. **Cost:** $480 to $620, depending on date of departure, includes roundtrip airfare from London to Rome, use of boat, fuel, skipper. **When:** June to September. **Contact:** WEXAS International, 45 Brompton Rd., Knightsbridge, London SW3 1DE, Great Britain; phone 01-589-0500. *(M)*

Netherlands

Low Country Sailing: Participants 10 years and older study the art of sailing in the Netherlands. Courses in both beginning and advanced sailing are given on a 1- and 2-week basis aboard 52-foot Frisian sailing scows. Other activities include rowing, fishing, swimming and small-ship sailing. Accommodations are in 1- to 4-person dormitory rooms. Groups are separated by age: 10 to 14, 15 to 22 and 22 to 60. Private and group lessons are available. **Cost:** $125 to $230 includes instruction, equipment, accommodations, meals. **When:** May to September. **Contact:** Zeilinstituut "De Bird," Egon B.P. Brenninkmeijer, Heeg (Friesland), Holland.

Scotland

School for Sailors: A school located on Loch Earn offers complete sailing courses on the loch and along the coast. Courses include basic instruction, intermediate helmsmanship, racing courses, and advanced seamanship, with each session remaining flexible to meet the individual needs and desires of students. Cruising courses are taught among the coastal islands of the West Highlands. All courses culminate in qualification for a Certificate of Competency. The bulk of instruction is on board, rather than in classrooms. Some non-certificate sailing and cruising holidays are also offered. **Cost:** $260 a week includes instruction at any level, accommodations, meals, equipment. **When:** April to September; 15 percent discount in May and June. **Contact:** Loch Earn & Coastal Sailing School, Aberturret House, by Crieff, Perthshire PH7 4HA, Great Britain; phone Crieff 2292.

Sailing in the Hebrides: A maximum of 6 crew members sail for 14 days on the 35-foot sloop *Sickle Moon*. Sailing through the Hebrides Islands, members visit the fishing port of Tobermory and the islands of Mull, Canna, Skye, Uist, Harris and Lewis. Crew members hike on shore, meeting people and visiting local marketplaces. On the Isle of Canna, 3 days are spent examining the Viking ruins and the colonies of sea birds. On Skye, participants hike for 2 days in the wild and uninhabited Black Cullin Mountains—an excellent rock climbing country. The longest sail is an overnight sojourn to Loch Eil. The trip ends with a 3-day visit to Edinburgh. **Cost:** $950. **When:** May and July. **Contact:** Mountain Travel Inc., 1398 Solano Ave., Albany, CA 94706, USA; phone (415)527-8100. ***(M)***

Bonnie Boating: Warmed by the Gulf Stream, the west coast and offshore islands of Scotland offer over a thousand miles of rugged coastline, mountains, glens, rivers and lochs. Sailing enthusiasts may charter a variety of yachts for trips of any length along this region stretching from the Mull of Kintyre to the Isle of Sky. Departing from the fleet's base at Clynder, sailors may explore historic coastal sites on a leisurely cruise or they may attempt a more challenging spinnaker run through a sound; yachts suitable for racing are also available. Skippered cruises, on which the crew does all navigation and planning, are offered for newcomers, as well as bareboat and crewed charters for experienced sailors. **Cost:** $1,105 to $1,180 a week for boat plus $150 per person for skippered cruise includes provisions, skipper, first and last night's accommodations ashore; other rates on request. **When:** April to October. **Contact:** Sailboat Vacations Scotland, Stroul Bay, Clynder, Dunbartonshire, Great Britain; phone Clynder 430.

MEXICO

Mexican Sail: A small group of 2 to 5 participants plies the waters off western Mexico in a 48-foot yawl. Each 8-day outing has a different itinerary; currently scheduled are a trip to the Sea of Cortez, La Paz, the east coast of the Baja peninsula and offshore islands; and one to a number of destinations along the mainland from Mazatlan to Manzanillo, including San Blas, Puerta Vallarta, Yelapa, Tenacatita and other ports of call. The participants can be novice sailors or experienced, adults or children, and informal instruction is offered along the way. Itineraries can be individually planned to suit each group's desires. Snorkeling, land exploration and fishing augment the sailing activities. **Cost:** $450 includes food, accommodations, instruction, activities, guide. **When:** June to December. **Contact:** Ocean Voyages, 1709 Bridgeway, Sausalito, CA 94965, USA; phone (415)332-4681.

MIDDLE EAST

Turkey

Cruising the Aegean Coast: One- and 2-week sailing trips on an 82-foot gaff-rigged yawl, the *Eblis,* visit many of the remote islands and coastal regions of the Aegean Sea off Turkey. Departing from Samos, the *Eblis* follows a flexible route between the Greek islands of Samos and Rhodes. Stops are made at the islands of Patmos, Lipso and

Leros and the uninhabited Gulf of Kos on the Turkish coast, though each trip's route and daily schedule are determined by the weather and passengers' wishes. The area is rich in myths and history, and a number of archaeological sites are visited. **Cost:** $655 and $1,225 includes food, accommodations, activities, transportation. **When:** May to September. **Contact:** Oceanic Expeditions, 240 Ft. Mason, San Francisco, CA 94123, USA; phone (415)441-1106.

PACIFIC

Northern Pacific Passage: Students with all degrees of experience in seamanship take part in a voyage between Seattle and Hawaii. Sailing for 2½ to 3 weeks from Seattle to the islands or taking slightly longer to return, participants live aboard 36- to 50-foot yachts rigged for cruising in the open ocean. Because the voyage is designed to give students experience in deep water sailing, all members serve as crew and take part in standing watch, steering, handling sails and preparing meals. Students should provide wet weather gear and sleeping bags. **Cost:** $875 to Hawaii or return includes meals, instruction. **When:** June, September. **Contact:** Rawhide Harris Ocean Sailing School, 2401 N. Northlake Wy., Seattle, WA 98103, USA; phone (206)633-5135.

Hawaii

Sandwich Island Sailing and Hiking: Travelers spend 10 days sailing

Visitors to islands in the Pacific find that catamarans provide a fast and simple means of travel. (Guam Visitors Bureau)

around and trekking over the island of Hawaii. The journey begins with 6 days of sailing fast, nimble Hobie Cats along the island's coast; no prior experience in sailing is needed. As the group sails down the coast, anchorages are made at various spots where the snorkeling, spear fishing and surfing are good and where coastal parks and villages may be visited. The next part of the trip brings participants inland to hike through terrain first explored by Captain Cook. Group members pass through rain forest, savanna and volcanic desert before reaching the rugged seacoast once again. Highlights along the route include a descent into Kilauea Volcano and a visit to the ruins of Wahaula Heian, the oldest temple in Hawaii. The journey ends in Hilo. **Cost:** $650 includes meals, guide, catamarans. **When:** April to October. **Contact:** Sobek Expeditions, Inc., P.O. Box 761, Angels Camp, CA 95222, USA; phone (209)736-2924. ***(M)***

UNITED STATES

Handling Reality: Women can charter the 32-foot sloop *Reality* for trips of virtually any length and destination off the New England coast. The skipper and first mate/registered nurse who make up the crew offer passengers an opportunity to participate actively in the sailing of the craft or to relax and enjoy the ride. Parties of 1 to 4 can be accommodated, either for direct sails, seaborne business meetings or aimless meanders. **Cost:** $75 to $100 a day, depending on size of group, includes boat, services of crew; food extra. **When:** Summer months. **Contact:** Reality Adventures, Inc., P.O. Box 4, Bennett Rd., Northwood, NH 03261, USA; phone (617)846-7481.

Alaska

Cruising Prince William Sound: In a coastal wilderness region explored by Captains Cook and Vancouver nearly 200 years ago, participants may cruise for a week or 13 days aboard sailboats that leave from Whittier, 40 miles southeast of Anchorage. Trip members rent a 22-foot Tanzer sailboat which follows a larger guide boat through the sound and along scenic coastline offering secluded coves, tidewater glaciers and sculptured fjords. Guides provide sailing lessons until participants have acquired enough seamanship experience to skipper the boat on their own. Week-long cruises either sail north up to Port Wells and around

Esther Island or go south down Culross Passage to Port Nellie Juan. Longer trips sail to Columbia Glacier or further south through the Nellie Juan Wilderness Study Area to Icy Bay. For participants who wish to enjoy a skippered cruise, berths are available aboard the guide boat. In May, cross-country skiing can be combined with sailing, while hiking is best after mid-July when the snow disappears from the upper elevations. To reach Whittier, participants must travel by train either from Anchorage or Portage. **Cost:** $750 to $1,400 includes fully equipped sailboat, navigation equipment, charts, raft for trips ashore. **When:** May to September. **Contact:** Alaska Wilderness Sailing Safaris, P.O. Box 4-275, Anchorage, AK 99509, USA; phone (907)277-0160.

California

Educational Channel Cruise: A learning cruise to the Channel Islands offers a scenic and educational experience to those with some, little or no sailing experience. Sailing or pursuing a variety of other outdoor activities by day and camping by night, participants sail for either 3 days through the southern islands or 5 days through the northern islands. On the 3-day trip visits are made to Catalina Island, where a nature hike and a visit to the remains of the Canalino Indians can be made, and to San Clemente Island, where a night sail is made to the island's northwest harbor. The 5-day cruises stop at Santa Barbara Island, with its abundant wildlife including large seal and sea lion colonies; Anacapa Island, featuring a pelican nesting ground and a museum; and Santa Cruz Island, an excellent spot for diving. Hiking, snorkeling and informal instruction in ecological and historical aspects of the region fill out the trips. **Cost:** $195 for 3 days,$315 for 5 days includes food, accommodations, equipment, guides. **When:** May to October. **Contact:** Aventura Sailing Association, 35102 Del Obispo St., Dana Point, CA 92629, USA; phone (714)493-9493.

Coastal Cruising: A 3- or 5-day jaunt 25 miles off the coast of Santa Barbara provides sailors with the chance to sharpen skills in day sailing or weekend gunkholing. Instruction in areas such as sail trimming and adjustment, helmsmanship, celestial navigation and use of a sextant are available for both the novice and seasoned sailor. Sailing conditions in the Santa Barbara Channel cover the range from mild to exhilarating. Summer in the channel is warm and delightful, while the fresh breezes of winter provide some of the year's best aquatic conditions. **Cost:** $230 to $335 includes boat equipment, instructors, meals, accommodations. **When:** Year-round except December. **Contact:** Coast Navigation School, 22 N. Milpas, Santa Barbara, CA 93102, USA; phone (805)963-7837.

Channel Islands Sail: Sailors take the helm, raise and trim the sails, and ponder nautical charts on 2-day sailing trips to the Channel Islands off the coast of southern California. Both novice and experienced sailors are welcome to crew the 42-foot ketch *Le Dauphin Amical* as the skipper teaches sailing and navigation techniques during the cruises. The trips go to either Anacapa or Santa Cruz islands and include time to beachcomb, fish, dive and explore. Also offered is a day sail to watch whales. A marina at Ventura is the departure point for all trips. **Cost:** $100 for Anacapa Island, $105 for Santa Cruz includes meals; $50 for day sail. **When:** February to November. **Contact:** Pacific Adventures, P.O. Box 5041, Riverside, CA 92517, USA; phone (714)684-1227.

Seaworthy Women: Women can learn to handle a boat or just enjoy the cruise on a sailboat skippered by a 2-woman crew. Day sails are offered, as well as weekend or 3-day sails to Catalina or Paradise Cove. On 5-day trips to Catalina and 7-day trips to Santa Cruz Island, sailors have time to swim, dive and explore coves at secluded anchorages. The boat provides full accommodations for 5 passengers. Beginning, intermediate and ad-

Seaworthy Women offers 1- to 7-day skippered cruises for women to islands off the coast of southern California; prices begin at $15 for a day sail. (Weezy Wold/Seaworthy Women)

vanced sailing classes are also offered. **Cost:** $15 for day sail; $60 to $280 depending on length of trip includes meals, accommodations; $55 for class. **When:** Year-round. **Contact:** Seaworthy Women, 2210 Wilshire Blvd., Suite 254, Santa Monica, CA 90403, USA; phone (213)397-7728.

Florida

Sailing Biscayne Bay: Aboard a sailing yacht group members may travel for a few hours, a day or an evening on Biscayne Bay, visiting the Seaquarium, Viscaya, Cape Florida State Park or Islandia. In addition, charters of a longer duration are available, including trips through the Florida Keys and along offshore coral reefs. The 39-foot fiberglass diesel-powered yacht can be chartered by groups of up to 6, either by the hour, day or week. Participants may also choose to sail to the Bahamas. **Cost:** On request. **When:** Year-round. **Contact:** Florida—Bahamas Sailing Charters, 505 Majorca Ave., Coral Gables, FL 33134, USA; phone (305)858-3218.

Sailing in Florida Keys and Everglades: Students snorkel among coral reefs, explore the Everglades and sail in the Gulf of Mexico near the Florida Keys during a 2-week program. Climbing aboard a pulling boat at Big Pine Key, students sail south of the Keys into the crystal waters of the Florida reefs reaching into the Gulf Stream. Group members navigate north and east across the Florida Bay, penetrating the dense forests of mangroves in the Everglades National Park. The outdoor experience includes a 3-day solo outing within the park boundaries. During this period students identify and study the lowland birds such as roseate spoonbills, pelicans, ibises and the flamingos which are indigenous to the area. Following an exploration of the shallow creeks and bays of the Everglades, participants travel along the windward passage offshore, through the Gulf of Mexico and back to the Keys for the conclusion of the program. **Cost:** $525 includes meals, accommodations, equipment. **When:** November to April. **Contact:** Hurricane Island Outward Bound School, Box 429, Rockland, ME 04841, USA; phone (207)594-5548.

Maine

Sailing Penobscot Bay: Sailing in Penobscot Bay is one of several outdoor activities available to participants during a 5-week New England trip. Aboard an 88-foot schooner, the group learns from a naturalist what lives and grows in Maine's waters, as well as the intracacies of sailing, knot tying and navigation. Other activities of the trip, which departs from Portland, include bicycling on backcountry roads and canoeing the length of the Allagash Wilderness Waterway. Two special projects of the trip are working with local farmers and climbing Maine's highest peak, Mt. Katahdin. The responsibilities of daily chores, bicycle maintenance, and first aid are shared by members of the group. **Cost:** $1,025 includes food, accommodations, transportation from Portland. **When:** June, July. **Contact:** The Infinite Odyssey, 57 Grant St., Waltham, MA 02154, USA; phone (617)899-6050. ***(M)***

A large, triangular spinnaker can be used to harness as much of the wind's energy as possible. (Keith Gunnar)

Maryland

Sailing from Scratch: Three beginners' sailing courses at Annapolis in Maryland offer students basic classroom and on-the-water instruction on Chesapeake Bay. In a single-weekend course, participants receive an intensive dose of training; 4 hours are spent in the classroom and 8 hours in fiberglass sailboats. Basically the same instruction is offered on another schedule which lasts 4 weeks. Meeting 1 day a weekend, the course is designed for students with limited weekend free time. A longer 5-day course repeats the weekend program for the first 2 days, then allows 3 practice days for participants to solidify their new skills. Students may take family and friends sailing during the practice sessions. **Cost:** $98 to $195 depending on length of course. **When:** April to October. **Contact:** Annapolis Sailing School Headquarters, 601 Sixth St., P.O. Box 3334, Annapolis, MD 21403, USA; phone (301)267-7205 or tollfree (800)638-9192.

New York

Spring Sailing: Novices and those already trained in the basics of sailing take advanced courses during the month of April. Three days at 4 hours a day are spent in introductory and refresher courses on 27-foot Solings. Class size is between 3 and 4 students. Four courses are offered—a learn-to-cruise package; an advanced/refresher spinnaker class; a basic racing course which covers regular sailing as well; and a spinnaker workshop designed to teach students how to make a working sail out of the spinnaker. Half-season and full-season rates are available.

All courses last 3 days with the exception of the spinnaker workshop, which runs for 4 half-day sessions. **Cost:** $109 to $139 includes tuition, gear. **When:** April. **Contact:** The New York Sailing School, 340 Riverside Dr., New York, NY 10025, USA; phone (212)864-4472.

South Carolina

Sailing Instruction at Palmetto Dunes: Students can learn sailing skills during 6- and 7-day courses based at Sea Pines Plantation on Hilton Head Island, which is bordered by the protected waters of Port Royal Sound on one side and by the Atlantic Ocean on the other. Aboard 27-foot sailboats, group members study the basics of boat handling, navigation and reading of the water and weather. Instruction is also given in rigging, heeling, wind shift adjustment, emergency procedures, docking and knot and spinnaker techniques. By the end of the course, students are able to sail the boat without instructors aboard. **Cost:** $219 includes instruction. **When:** May to October. **Contact:** Offshore Sailing School, Ltd., 820 Second Ave., New York, NY 10017, USA; phone (212)986-4570 or tollfree (800)221-4326.

Washington

Sailing the Sound: The San Juan Islands and Cascade and Olympic mountains provide the backdrop for a 5-day instructional, live-aboard cruising expedition on Puget Sound. Instruction on all aspects of sailing is covered, from docking and anchoring to setting sails and using spinnaker gear. Both optical and electronic methods of navigation are demonstrated and used. Ports of call include Roche and Rosario harbors, where hotels converted from turn-of-the-century mansions provide swimming pools, saunas and showers. Weekend trips devoted to roaming the waters and visiting Puget Sound ports are also available out of Seattle. **Cost:** $300 for 5-day cruise includes sailing gear, instructors, breakfast, lunch; $69 for weekend cruise includes sailing gear, meals. **When:** On request. **Contact:** Cascade Sailing School, 2300 W. Ninth #35, Olympia, WA 98502, USA; phone (206)943-8085.

San Juan Sailing: A 5-day trip takes passengers among the San Juan Islands of the Pacific Northwest. While meandering from Anacortes to Fidalgo Island to San Juan and Orcas islands, group members may receive sailing instruction and help navigate the boat. Sail trim and reefing, helmsmanship, docking and anchoring, spinnaker handling and sailing safety are among the topics covered. When the boat docks at Friday Harbor, Roche Harbor and Rosario, passengers may disembark for horseback riding, hiking, tennis and swimming. One night is kept open for guests to pick the anchoring spot, which could be a town already visited or a deserted beach on one of the outer islands. The 50-foot boat sleeps up to 8 people and is equipped with private staterooms and 2 heads with hot showers. **Cost:** $300 includes lunch, snacks, instruction. **When:** May to October. **Contact:** Seawind

Seawind Sailing School offers a 5-day instructional cruise among the San Juan Islands during the summer months, with opportunities for hiking, riding and other activities ashore. (Elizabeth Watson)

Sailing School, 6535 Seaview Ave. NW, Seattle, WA 98117, USA; phone (206)246-7245.

Sailing the Strait of Juan de Fuca: Departing from the fishing village of LaConner, a new 60-foot staysail ketch cruises the San Juan Islands, the Strait of Juan de Fuca and the Pacific coast of British Columbia. The trips, which last 5 days or longer, are determined by the interests of the passengers and are limited only by the dictates of good seamanship. Sailing in Canadian waters is possible with a private party; parties of 6 or less can reserve the boat for cruises of varying length. Six-day cruises are available for individuals and couples if a minimum group of 5 can be formed. Information about other local cruise vessels can also be provided. **Cost:** Private parties: 6 for $1,800; 5 for $1,650; 4 or less $1,500 for 6 days; includes meals, accommodations onboard, captain and crew. **When:** May to September. **Contact:** Sindbad Cruises & Charters, 7010 31st St. NE, Seattle, WA 98115, USA; phone (206)329-3360.

WORLD

Around-the-World Cruise: A 21-month circumnavigation of the world is offered to sailing enthusiasts familiar with shipboard routine or to novices who are willing to learn and work. Participants travel and live aboard a well-equipped 55-foot sailing yacht with a professional crew that includes a captain, first mate and chef. The itinerary provides for visits to remote ports and reefs in areas such as the South Sea Islands, the Indian Ocean and the Mediterranean and Black seas. Optional instruction onboard includes big-boat seamanship, celestial navigation and scuba diving; a compressor is available on the boat. A marine science and diving expert accompanies the expedition. **Cost:** $1,000 a month includes all living provisions; 3-month minimum preferred. **When:** Departs in February or March. **Contact:** Voyage, 1009 Susan Rd., Philadelphia, PA 19115, USA.

RESOURCES

Clubs and Associations

American Sailing Council
666 Third Ave.
New York, NY 10017, USA

International Oceanographic Foundation
3979 Rickenbacker Causeway
Virginia Key, Miami, FL 33149, USA

National Association of Engine
and Boat Manufacturers
P.O. Box 5555, Grand Central Sta.
New York, NY 10017, USA
Phone (212)697-1100

Oceanic Society
Bldg. 240, Ft. Mason
San Francisco, CA 94123, USA
Phone (415)441-5970

Ocean Youth Club
2 Stoke Gardens, Gosport
Hampshire, Great Britain

Sail Training Association
Bosham, Chichester
Sussex, Great Britain

Yacht Cruising Association
Old Stone House, Judges Terrace
Ship St., E. Grinstead
Sussex RH19 1A6, Great Britain
Phone (0342)311366

WINDJAMMING

Nothing stirs one's yearning for a carefree life at sea more than the wind blowing hard in the sails of a 4-masted schooner. From primitive dugout-style rafts with rectangular sails to the fifteenth-century Spanish galleons that sailed the seas as both warships and traders, wind-propelled ships have been the most important means of ocean travel.

The first revolution in ship design came when the stem, stern, keel and molded hull replaced the simple structure of the raft and dugout. The invention of the lateen sail—a triangular sail trimmed so as to take wind on either side—and the addition of the sternpost rudder made it possible to sail closer to the wind. The use of the magnetic compass and astrolabe for angle measurements made navigation more accurate, sailing safer. These inventions heralded the era of open-ocean sailing, when new sea routes were being developed to link the continents of the world. Beginning with Prince Henry of Portugal, Columbus and Magellan, a succession of captains probed the far reaches of the seven seas.

The spirit of ocean exploration still lives aboard numerous sailing ships that ply the oceans of the world. You can climb onto a 90-foot brigantine for a trip through the British Virgin Islands, sail a gaff-rigged windjammer along the southern coast of New England, or explore Lake Champlain on a 78-year-old, 80-foot schooner. On each trip you are welcome to help hoist the sails, take the helm, stand watch, learn to navigate and help weigh anchor—or you can just sit back and relax.

The trips take you to historic whaling ports in New England, to picturesque Penobscot Bay in Maine and through the privateering waters of the Caribbean. Shore excursions for lobster feeds and beachcombing, swimming, snorkeling and scuba diving on shipwrecks are some of the other pastimes available to passengers. Trips range in price from $109 for 2 days of sailing along New England's coast to $350 for 7 days of sailing in the Caribbean. You can even join a 10-month circumnavigation of the globe on the windjammer *Yankee Trader* for $7,350.

Windjammer cruises enable passengers to enjoy the open-seas experience of sailing without having to take full responsibility for handling the boat. Captains right out of historical sailing novels and capable crews add a personal touch to each voyage. Cruises are a great way to throw your cares to the wind as you relive the days of the buccaneers, merchants and explorers who sailed the great seas. □

Participants sailing on the 90-foot brigantine Romance *in the British Virgin Islands experience sea travel from another era. Kimberly Cruises offers the 8-day trip, relying on the prevailing trades to determine exact itinerary.* (Kimberly Cruises)

WINDJAMMING

CARIBBEAN

British Virgin Islands

Virgin Island Sailing: Sixteen passengers share the facilities of the 90-foot brigantine *Romance* on an 8-day trip. The ship has no set itinerary, but makes use of the trade winds to visit the largest number of islands, anchoring in a different island cove each afternoon. Passengers explore coral gardens, view colorful tropical fish and make shore excursions. Onboard ship, cabins have double berths, large skylights, wash stands and ample luggage space. Fresh water showers are also available. The vessel is the world's only brigantine in regular passenger service, and was designed under the supervision of the Royal Danish Government for Greenland trade. **Cost:** On request. **When:** Year-round. **Contact:** Kimberly Cruises, Box 5086, St. Thomas, VI 00801, USA; phone (809)774-9003.

Caribbean Sail: Travelers spend 7 days sailing the waters of the British Virgin Islands. Starting from Virgin Gorda, participants aboard *The Pride,* a 90-foot barquentine, cruise through Sir Francis Drake Channel and visit Tortola, Jost Van Dyke, Cooper Island, Salt, Wreck and Peter islands and Norman Island, thought to be the setting of Stevenson's *Treasure Island.* Activities include helping to steer the boat, swimming, snorkeling, scuba diving and trimming the sails. Ample time is provided for such onshore activities as beachcombing and exploring. **Cost:** $350 to $420 includes meals, accommodations, diving and fishing equipment. **When:** November to May. **Contact:** *The Pride,* P.O. Box 22069, Ft. Lauderdale, FL 33335, USA; phone (305)523-7090.

U.S. Virgin Islands

Virgin Islands Cruise: Participants spend 8 days sailing in the Virgin Islands aboard a skippered windjammer. Embarking from St. Thomas in the west and sailing to Virgin Gorda in the east, group members stop each night in a different secluded bay. Activities include snorkeling, exploring various islands and shipwrecks and visiting native villages; participants also have ample opportunity to assist in sailing the boat and to learn such skills as knot tying, rope splicing and sail maintenance. **Cost:** $275 to $315 includes meals, accommodations on board, guide. **When:** Year-round. **Contact:** Westindiaman Cruises, Home Port, St. Thomas, VI 00801, USA; phone (809)774-5630.

EUROPE

England

Schooner Sojourns: Aboard schooners embarking from England and sailing along the European coast, participants on 2-week training cruises serve as crew. Trips use the schooners *Winston Churchill* and *Malcolm Miller*. The 2-week trip is designed for young people ages 16 to 24 and involves students in most of the normal shipboard activities: cleaning and maintenance of the

Two-week training cruises offered by STA Schooners off the coast of northern Europe give young sailors a chance to develop sailing skills. (A. Bromley-Martin/STA Schooners)

ship, rigging, steering, galley work and standing watch. No previous experience is required. Ports visited range from Bergen to Brest, and trainees must provide their own transportation to and from the various ports in Great Britain where the trips begin and end. Most of the time is spent sailing, although ample time is allowed in port for onshore activities. **Cost:** $560 includes insurance, berth, meals. **When:** March to December. **Contact:** The STA Schooners, Bosham, Chichester, Sussex, PO18 8HR, Great Britain.

UNITED STATES

Semester at Sea: Students participate in a fully accredited educational experience for 8 weeks aboard the 100-foot schooner *Harvey Gamage.* The campus extends from Maine to the Bahamas, and 15 college credits are earned through courses in coastal oceanography, icthyology, navigation, seamanship and maritime history. Ports of call to educational institutions, research laboratories, museums and historical sites complement the curriculum. Students are responsible for operating and crewing the gaff-rigged schooner that carries 4,200 square feet of sail. Snorkeling gear, small boats and a mini-sailboat are available for instructional or recreational use. A maximum of 24 students participate each semester. **Cost:** $3,200 includes tuition, room, board, laboratory fees. **When:** September, March. **Contact:** Dirigo

On a Dirigo Cruises windjamming excursion off the coast of Maine, participants help sail and navigate the schooner Harvey Gamage. *The week-long trip costs $295.* (Maine Dept. of Commerce and Industry)

Cruises, Schooner *Harvey Gamage,* 39 Waterside Ln., Clinton, CT 06413, USA; phone (203)669-7068. ***(M)***

Into the Mystic: Aboard a classic gaff-rigged windjammer, travelers can sail the historic coast of southern New England for either 2 or 5 days. The trips begin at Mystic, Connecticut, and follow an itinerary set by wind, weather and the discretion of the captain. Possible ports of call include Narragansett Bay, Block Island, Montauk, Greenport and the famous whaling port of Sag Harbour. Occasional trips are made up the Connecticut River to Essex. The vessel, *Mystic Whaler,* is a 2-masted, 100-foot schooner similar in design to many whalers of a century ago, but it is equipped with modern accommodations and equipment. It carries up to 44 passengers, who can participate in the handling of the boat if they wish. **Cost:** $109 to $145 for 2 days, $265 to $349 for 5 days, depending on season and type of accommodations, includes food, transportation from Mystic, accommodations, activities. **When:** May to October. **Contact:** *Mystic Whaler,* 7 Holmes St., Mystic, CT 06355, USA; phone (203)536-4218.

Maine

Down East Windjamming: Penobscot Bay is explored during a 6-day cruise out of Rockland on board the two-masted schooner, *J. & E. Riggin*. Participants explore deserted islands and quiet fishing villages. While under sail they may choose to lend a hand with steering or trimming, assist in the galley or simply relax on deck. Penobscot Bay provides some of New England's best sailing conditions as well as spectacular scenery. Many varieties of marine life and wildlife can be observed along the coast including seals and whales. **Cost:** $245 to $285 includes accommodations, meals. **When:** June to September. **Contact:** Capt. Dave Allen, Schooner *J. & E. Riggin,* Box 571, Rockland, ME 04841, USA; phone (207)594-2923.

Windjamming New England: A week-long trip on board the 83-foot schooner *Mary Day* leaves each Monday during the summer months for visits to the coastal islands and towns of Isle au Haut, Matinicus and Frenchboro. The windjammer, built in 1962, carries 4,500 square feet of sail hoisted on masts made of west coast Douglas fir. Departing from Camden, trip members often join in the work on board, including hoisting sails and keeping decks clear. Participants have the full experience of wind sailing since the ship has no engine except for the auxiliary power of the yawl. The schooner anchors each night in a picturesque harbor, allowing time for passengers to row ashore to explore remote island villages. **Cost:** $250 includes meals, accommodations. **When:** June to September. **Contact:** Coastal Cruises, P.O. Box 798, Camden, ME 04843, USA; phone (207)236-2750.

Summer Coastal Cruises: Cruises along the New England coast aboard the schooner *Harvey Gamage* leave from the city dock in Rockland at 10:00 a.m. on Mondays during the summer. A week of sailing follows, past pine-edged seascapes and rocky coastlines, stopping each evening at a different island. Wind and tide determine the exact itinerary, but passengers can expect to visit such ports as Camden, Stonington, Monhegan, Boothbay and Christmas Cove. The atmosphere is informal and trip members are welcome to participate in the operation of the ship. Swimming equipment, fins, masks and snorkels are provided for those hardy enough to brave the 60° New England waters. A sailboat is also carried aboard for those who wish to learn to sail or just sharpen their sailing skills. Passengers occupy staterooms with 2, 3 or 4 berths. The small sacrifices of limited electricity and hot water are more than compensated for by the coastal scenery, fresh air and relaxation aboard ship. **Cost:** $295 includes meals. **When:** Mondays from June to September. **Contact:** Dirigo Cruises, Schooner *Harvey Gamage*, 39 Waterside Ln., Clinton, CT 06413, USA; phone (203)669-7068.

(M)

Sailing Down East: The 19th-century sailing schooner *Isaac H. Evans* sails from Rockland on Monday morning and returns about noon the following Saturday. Visits are made to places like Stonington, Frenchboro, Vinalhaven and Swans Island, along with places untouched by modern civilization. The coastline offers a variety of natural features to explore with its many islands, bays and passages. The boat anchors each night in a protected harbor, and the yawlboat becomes a ferry to and from shore. A small rowing boat is available for individual trips. Cabins are equipped with ample standing headroom, electric lighting, running water and outside windows. Passengers are welcome to board Sunday night before the trip begins. The vessel accommodates 22 guests at a time, with a minimum age limit of 16. **Cost:** $265 June and September; $285 July, August. **Contact:** Capt. Douglas K. Lee, Schooner *Isaac H. Evans*, Box 482, Rockland, ME 04841, USA; phone (207)594-8007.

Windjamming Northeastern Waters: The craggy coastline of Maine's Penobscot Bay and environs is the setting for a 6-day windjamming cruise departing from Rockland. Though the destination of each day's journey is determined by fluctuations in wind, weather and tide, participants usually sail to several of the spruce- and fir-covered islands from Cape Elizabeth to Bar Harbor. The vintage 132-foot vessel anchors in a different harbor each night, and passengers may go ashore to explore historic locations such as Swans Island and Isle au Haut. Nights are usually cool and days clear and warm, with steady strong winds suitable for extensive cruising. Passengers care for individual staterooms and are welcome to share in the onboard chores of sailing the windjammer, such as helping to hoist sails. Food is prepared fresh and often includes lobsters right out of the water. Weather permitting, passengers eat meals on deck in the fresh sea air. **Cost:** $295 a week includes room, meals, blankets. **When:** June to September. **Contact:** Maine Coast Cruises, Windjammer Wharf, Rockland, ME 04841, USA; phone (207)596-6060; winter 326-8856.

Sailing Penobscot Bay: Five-day windjammer cruises in the Penobscot Bay area enable passengers to enjoy the experience of being at sea without having the responsibility of handling a boat. Participants cruise aboard the *Mattie* or *Mercantile,* both old-time Yankee merchant vessels. Trips depart Monday mornings from Camden, and itineraries vary with wind and weather conditions. The ships are anchored at different harbors each night, with time allowed to swim or to go ashore to visit coastal towns. Passengers stay onboard in comfortable cabins, and New England family-style meals are cooked on the galley's wood stove. **Cost:** $205 to $225. **When:** June to September. **Contact:** Maine Windjammer Cruises, Inc., P.O. Box 617, Camden, ME 04843, USA; phone (207)236-2938.

Down East Cruise: The islands and the coast of Maine are the setting for a 7-day trip aboard the *Nathaniel Bowditch.* The 81-foot schooner sails the waters between Boothbay Harbor and Bar Harbor, stopping frequently for beachcombing and sightseeing. Passengers are welcome to assist in the daily routines of sailing, which may include hoisting sails or navigating along the rocky shorelines. When the ship is moored, participants may fish for mackerel, pollack, bluefish and other species. Accommodations on the ship are small, but cozy, and meals are served onboard. In the evening participants may go ashore or provide their own entertainment on deck. **Cost:** $225. **When:** June to September. **Contact:** Capt. Gilbert E. Philbrick, Schooner *Nathaniel Bowditch,* Harborside, ME 04642, USA; phone (207)326-4496; summer, 326-4440.

New England Sailing Voyage: Passengers on a 1-week cruise sail the Maine coast on the windjammer *Angelique.* The boat departs from Camden, Maine and sails between Boothbay Harbor and Northeast Harbor, an area dotted with hun-

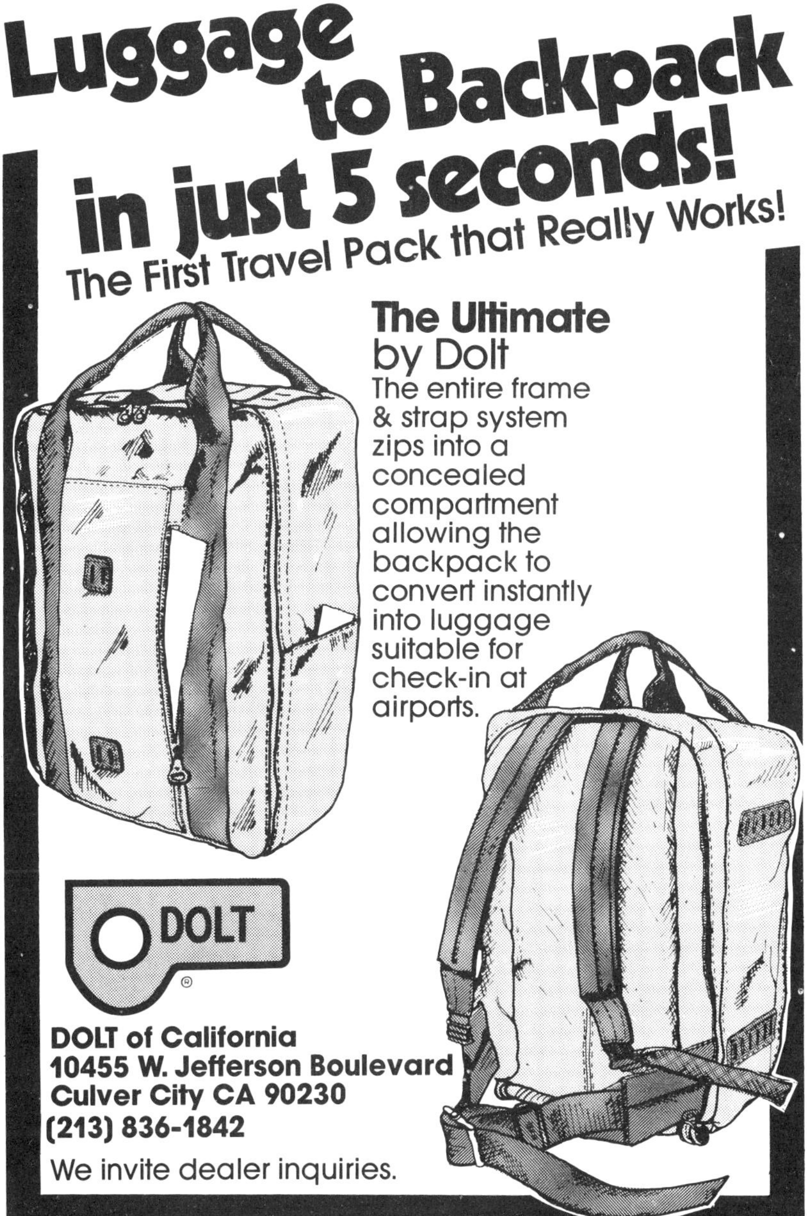
Luggage to Backpack in just 5 seconds!
The First Travel Pack that Really Works!
The Ultimate
by Dolt
The entire frame & strap system zips into a concealed compartment allowing the backpack to convert instantly into luggage suitable for check-in at airports.
DOLT
DOLT of California
10455 W. Jefferson Boulevard
Culver City CA 90230
(213) 836-1842
We invite dealer inquiries.

dreds of spruce-fringed islands. The crew does the sailing and galley work, but passengers who are so inclined can help sail the ketch as well as learn how to chart a course, tie knots, and other seafaring skills. **Cost:** From $260 to $285 depending on departure date includes meals, accommodations onboard. **When:** June to September. **Contact:** Yankee Packet Company, Box 736, Camden, ME 04843, USA; phone (207)236-8873.

Maine Sail: With the first morning tide, participants set sail from Camden to travel along the coast of Maine on a course determined by the weather. During 6 days aboard the 112-foot *Rosemary* or the 121-foot *Adventure,* sailors take the helm, learn to navigate, help weigh anchor or haul up the sails if they wish. The schooner may sail in the shadow of the hills of Mt. Desert or cross Blue Hill Bay for an anchorage among the hundreds of rockbound islands in Penobscot Bay. Evenings are spent ashore exploring small fishing villages or singing sea chanties around the fireplace and pump organ in the main cabin. There are opportunities to row ashore for hikes, and once each trip the whole group has a Down East lobster cookout on the beach. **Cost:** $225 from Camden includes transportation, accommodations, meals, instruction; reduced rates in June and September. **When:** June to September. **Contact:** Yankee Schooner Cruises, Box 696, Camden, ME 04843, USA; phone (207)236-4449.

Maryland

Sailing Chesapeake Bay: Travelers spend either 2 or 5 days sailing historic Chesapeake Bay aboard a 100-foot gaff-rigged schooner. The voyages begin and end at Annapolis and ply the bay's eastern shore, stopping at St. Michaels, site of the Chesapeake Bay Maritime Museum, Oxford, Cambridge and other ports of call. The extensive, intricate system of coves and inlets on the estuary provides numerous scenic moorages for overnight stops; days are spent under sail as much as possible. Participants have the opportunity to hoist sails and steer the boat, which is built along the lines of the classic whalers of the nineteenth century but is outfitted with modern equipment and accommodations. Each trip's exact itinerary is determined by wind, weather and the discretion of the captain. **Cost:** $109 to $155 for 2 days, $265 to $349 for 5 days, depending on season and type of accommodations, includes food, transportation, accommodations, activities. **When:** May to October. **Contact:** *Mystic Whaler,* 7 Holmes St., Mystic, CT 06355, USA; phone (203)536-4218.

Rhode Island

Jamming from Newport: Sailing enthusiasts spend 2, 3 or 7 days aboard the schooner *Bill of Rights.* Departing from Newport, the ship sails for New England harbors such as Mystic, Stonington, Point Judith and Block Island. Other possible ports of call include the Elizabeth Islands, Martha's Vineyard, Padanarum, Edgartown and Nantucket, once the world's greatest whaling port. Some voyages may reach as far as the Chesapeake Bay and Annapolis. The *Bill of Rights* is a 124-foot vessel with sails totaling

6,300 square feet. Participants choose from 16 private staterooms, each well-ventilated and roomy. Meals onboard occasionally include a starlight buffet. **Cost:** $100 for 2 days, $150 for 3 days, $305 for 7 days. **When:** May to October. **Contact:** Davis, Capt. Joseph M., Jr., Schooner *Bill of Rights*, Box 447, Newport, RI 02840, USA; phone (401)724-7612.

Vermont

A Case of Champlain: Lake Champlain, which is surrounded by Vermont, New York and Canada, is explored for a relatively unplanned week aboard a 78-year-old, 80-foot, gaff-rigged schooner. The *Richard Robbins* sets sail from Burlington every Monday morning and returns there every Saturday. During the week participants can help sail the boat or assist with other chores as the wind and weather determine each day's itinerary. Anchor is normally dropped in late afternoon to allow time for swimming and exploration. Picturesque villages, an old fort and numerous islands provide land-lubber diversions. The trip offers views of the Adirondack and Green mountains. **Cost:** $295 includes food, accommodations, activities. **When:** May through October. **Contact:** Champlain Windjammer Co., Box 722, Ridgewood, NJ 07450, USA; phone (201)445-6957; summer, Box 195, Vergennes, VT 05491, USA; phone (802)759-2411.

Washington

Puget Sound Sailing School: A 101-foot schooner is the classroom for 10-day sailing lessons offered to high school-age youths. The course begins at Shilshole Bay Marina in Seattle with some orientation and preliminary sailing. Then the schooner leaves to spend the following days in Puget Sound and the San Juan Islands, with the trainees serving as crew. Students have galley and watch duties, and sail the schooner when the wind is favorable. There is free time for small boat sailing, rowing and exploring. **Cost:** On request. **When:** On request. **Contact:** Youth Adventure, Inc., P.O. Box 23, Mercer Island, WA 98040, USA; phone (206)232-4025.

WORLD

Yankee Circumnavigation: Participants explore the world on a 10-month southern cruise. Starting from Miami, the windjammer *Yankee Trader* sails through the Panama Canal before reaching Pitcairn Island, Easter Island and Tahiti. Many other islands are visited as the group sails through the South Pacific and Indonesian Isles. After Singapore sail is made for Madagascar and Zanzibar as well as the rest of the southeast African coast. The group crosses the Atlantic to reach the mouth of the Amazon before taking an island-hopping cruise through the Caribbean and back to Miami. Passengers may serve as crew members if they wish. Those interested are advised to enclose a recent photograph in their application. **Cost:** $7,350 includes room and board, expenses onboard. **When:** February. **Contact:** Windjammer "Barefoot" Cruises, P.O. Box 120, Miami Beach, FL 33139, USA; phone (303)373-2466.

CRUISING

Boats have long been used to explore new places or link civilizations. Columbus sailed across the Atlantic to discover new waterways, Darwin explored the Galapagos Islands on the H.M.S. *Beagle,* Humboldt traveled the Amazon Basin by raft and canoe, and Speake and Burton navigated the White Nile. For centuries boats have been the only means of transportation into remote areas—in many parts of the world they still are.

Today it is possible to retrace the routes of the early explorers and chart your own course on commercial cruises around the world. The trips range from luxurious to primitive, lasting a day, a month or even a year. You can join the m.s. *Lindblad Explorer* as it stops at rarely visited ports throughout the South Pacific, sign onto the 285-foot m.s. *World Discoverer* to explore the Falkland Islands and Antarctica, or join any number of cruise ships and freighters circumnavigating the world—for any portion of the trip.

If larger vessels aren't your style, you can travel by motorized canoe 236 miles up the Maroni River in French Guiana, camping in village huts along the way. Felucca trips up the Nile, sailing trips in Botswana and canal cruises in the Netherlands are also available. You can even charter your own boat to explore the lochs of Scotland or sail through the Caribbean.

Not all cruises are so far from home. In the United States you can explore the rivers and swamps of southwest Florida by shanty boat and swamp buggy for 5 days or travel the canal systems of New York on 3-day voyages. The 50-foot yacht *Chaik* cruises Alaska's Glacier Bay on 6-day trips. Jetboats carry passengers on 1- and 2-day jaunts up Oregon's Rogue River.

Whether you are looking for a way to float your cares away or learn about the wildlife, peoples and history of the world; whether you have 2 days or a year—there are cruise trips available of every duration and cost. The next time you feel a yearning to see the birthplace of Lenin, live among the Jivaro Indians in Peru or explore the coast of New Zealand, why not do it by boat? □

The icy waters of the Bering Sea can be cruised aboard Zodiac rafts powered by outboards. This group is exploring the area near Akutan Island in the Aleutian archipelago. (American Institute for Exploration)

CRUISING

AFRICA

Botswana

Picnic on Lake Gaborone: A day cruise on Lake Gaborone combines some wildlife viewing with a picnic and recreational stop on a scenic piece of shoreline. The trip departs from Gaborone, and several hours of sailing, depending on the wind, take the 4-berth sailboat to a base camp on the lake's far shore. En route the party can stop at Goat Island, where vervet monkeys and pythons are among the inhabitants. All along the lakeshore numerous birds can be seen, including herons, cormorants, egrets, fisheagles and kingfishers. During the basecamp stop, participants can hike, paddle a small boat in the lake, fish or simply relax; the boat returns in the afternoon, arriving in Gaborone at about 5 p.m. **Cost:** $13 includes transportation, food, guide; small boat and fishing gear rental extra. **When:** On request. **Contact:** Holiday Safaris (Pty) Ltd., Private Bag 16, Gaborone, Botswana; phone 2015.

Egypt

One Thousand Miles up the Nile: A trip to study Egypt's past uses London's British Museum for orientation and then a cruise ship and airplane to go up 956 miles of the Nile River. The expedition, which lasts 16 days in all, begins with a flight to London where a day's stopover allows time for a museum visit under the guidance of an expert. Participants then fly to Cairo and spend 4 nights there, sightseeing and making excursions to nearby monuments including the Pyramids and Sphinx. A flight to Luxor follows, and after a visit to the Valley of the Kings, Karnak and Esna, participants board a cruise ship for a trip upriver to Edfu, Kom Ombo and Aswan's old and new dams. Travelers then proceed by felucca to the botanical gardens and the Mausoleum of Aga. A short visit to Abu Simbel and another 2 nights in Cairo complete the trip before the flight home. **Cost:** $1,950 to $2,430, depending on type of accommodations, includes transportation from Cairo, meals, guide. **When:** September to May. **Contact:** Lindblad Travel, Inc., 8 Wright St., Westport, CT 06880, USA; phone (203)226-8531 or tollfree (800)293-5657. ***(M)***

ANTARCTICA

Cruising Antarctica: For 25 to 30 days travelers can cruise the Antarctic and journey overland through Argentina. After a flight from Miami, participants spend several free days exploring Buenos Aires at leisure. A morning flight to Rio Grande precedes an overland journey to Ushuaia where the group boards the m.s. *World Discoverer,* a 285-foot cruising liner. Travelers may observe the navigation of the vessel from the semibridge. The itinerary of the shorter trip includes a 2-day stop at the Falkland Islands while the cruise of longer duration continues past Cape Horn through the Drake Passage to the Antarctic Peninsula. Along the peninsula, penguin rookeries, seals, albatrosses, icebergs, ice floes and scientific stations can be seen. Many aspects of natural history are observed and photographed along the coast of the 5½-million-square-mile landmass. Those on the shorter journey cruise to Puerto Natales, Chile for a brief stay, dock at Ushuaia, then retrace the route back to Miami. The other trip proceeds to the Falkland Islands for 2 days followed by 2 days at sea. En route to Buenos Aires, the last port of call, travelers stop at Mar del Plata. After a day of exploration in Buenos Aires, participants board a plane for the return flight to Miami. **Cost:** $2,575 to $4,075 from Miami includes transportation, guide, accommodations, meals on ship, breakfast on shore. **When:** January. **Contact:** W. David Campbell Travel Ltd., 527 Madison Ave., Suite 1207, New York, NY 10022, USA; phone (212)752-8908.

AUSTRALASIA

New Zealand

Doubtful Sound Cruises: The vessel *M. V. Waverley* affords participants the opportunity to sail deep into Doubtful Sound on the west coast of New Zealand. Two- and 3-day voyages start at Deep Cove and proceed to the head of Hall's Arm and Crooked Arm before anchoring for a night at First Cove. The cruise continues up Crooked Arm for a day of fishing, exploration onshore and off-vessel sailing. Evening finds the group moored at Blanket Bay. The final day of the voyage opens with a jaunt to Goal Passage for lobstering before the return to Blanket Bay and Deep Cove. Evenings are spent in entertainment or fishing; possible catches include grouper, blue cod and tuna. **Cost:** $95 on weekends, $162 on weekdays includes meals, accommodations. **When:** On request. **Contact:** Fiordland Cruises Ltd., P.O. Box Manapouri, New Zealand; phone Manapouri 609.

EUROPE

England

The Changing Thames: Aboard a 72-foot hotel barge, a group of 6 passengers cruises through the back country and towns of England on the Thames River. Traveling from Windsor to Oxford or vice versa, the party sees the evidence of 2,000 years of English history during the 6-day trip. Participants visit Runnymede, site of the Magna Carta's signing in 1215; Windsor, where the boat cruises beneath the world's largest inhabited castle; the college at Eton; Wargrave, where the evening is spent with local residents; Henley-on-Thames, home of the royal rowing regatta; Dorchester, with its famous abbey; the university town of Oxford; and many other rural spots. Some meals are taken at local restaurants, and a minibus accompanies the cruise for shoreside sightseeing. **Cost:** $550 to $700, depending on season and type of accommodations, includes food, accommodations, transportation, activities, guide. **When:** April to October. **Contact:** Floating Through Europe, 501 Madison Ave., New York, NY 10022, USA; phone (212)832-6700. ***(M)***

France

Barge Trip in France: The delicious food of France's most famous culinary region can be sampled en route through the Burgundy countryside aboard the *Palinurus*. The food, wine and history of the area are experienced for 3 weeks along the Burgundy and Nivernais canals between Dijon and Baye, Montbard and Auxerre, or Auxerre and Baye depending on itinerary. Burgundy's past is evident from the barge as it floats past chateaux, medieval towns, churches and ancient forests. Each of the 3 trips visits different attractions, among them the Pouilly tunnel, the 12th-century castle of Chateauneuf and the battlefield of Alesia, where the Gauls fought Julius Caesar's troops in 52 B.C. Visits can be made to the medieval villages of Flavigny and Semur or to the fortified town of Beaune, the center of the wine trade where auctions are held in famous 15th-century hospices. **Cost:** $390 to $510 depending on occupancy and season. **When:** April to October. **Contact:** Continental Waterways Ltd., 22 Hans Pl., London SW1, Great Britain; phone 01-584-6773.

Netherlands

The Mild West: Boaters cruise western Holland's placid waterways aboard a 62-foot hotel barge during a week-long trip. Canal cruising is a strong tradition in the Netherlands, and local residents are hospitable to participants who take the circular route beginning and ending in Amsterdam. Highlights of the itinerary include Delft, with its celebrated marketplace; Gouda, famous for cheese; the busy port of Rotterdam; Utrecht, full of Roman influence and boasting a striking Gothic cathedral; Haarlem, with its art museum; and the scenic countryside between these towns. A few meals are taken at local restaurants. Other onshore activities include bicycling, guided sightseeing and walks. Some trips emphasize a particular feature, such as tulip fields or the heritage of the Dutch Masters. **Cost:** $555 to $745, depending on season and type of accommodations, includes food, accommodations, activities, transportation. **When:** May to October. **Contact:** Floating Through Europe, 501 Madison Ave., New York, NY 10022, USA; phone (212)832-6700. ***(M)***

Scotland

Scotch and Water: Several areas of Scotland offer protected coastal waters and scenic inland waterways ideal for extensive boat travel. Those without much prior experience can travel 60 miles along the Great Glen from Inverness through Loch Ness and through the Caledonian Canal to Loch Lochy and Ft. William. Experienced cruisers can explore the tidal waters below Ft. William to Loch Linnhe, the Isle of

Aboard rental cruisers that cost $100 a day, groups can explore Scotland's extensive inland waterways and sheltered coastal waters. (Canals Europe)

Mull and the Firth of Lorn. Also accessible to experienced boaters is the Firth of Clyde, an area featuring spectacular granite peaks on the Isle of Arran; nearby are the city of Dunoon, the Kyles of Butte and the Crinian Canal, all in sheltered water where one is never more than 12 miles from land. Since a number of rental packages are available, arrangements are made individually. **Cost:** Approximately $100 a week. **When:** Year-round. **Contact:** Canals Europe, 220 Redwood Hwy., Mill Valley, CA 94941, USA; phone (415)388-7908.

Soviet Union

Volga Boat Trip: A 10-day cruise down the Volga River on a 216-passenger Soviet cruise ship explores several ports between Kazan and Rostov-on-Don. The ship is boarded in Kazan, capital of the Tatar Republic and rich in historical relics and art, and after 2 days of sailing reaches its first port of call, Ulianovsk, the birthplace of Lenin. After some sightseeing, the trip proceeds to Zhiguli, one of the Volga's best-known recreation spots. After a stop at Maiden's Island for swimming and sunbathing, passengers arrive at Volgograd, where a sightseeing tour is taken. A stop at Green Port-on-Don precedes the trip's conclusion at Rostov-on-Don, where a Cossack museum is among the attractions. The cruise may be taken in conjunction with a roundtrip package from San Francisco which includes sightseeing in and around Moscow as well. **Cost:** $595 includes transportation from Kazan to Rostov-on-Don, food, double-occupancy accommodations, shore excursions. **When:** June. **Contact:** Siemer & Hand, Ltd., 465 California St., San Francisco, CA 94104, USA; phone (415)397-6737.

INDIAN OCEAN

Seychelles

Cruising Forgotten Islands: Aboard the yacht *Dwyn Wen* 10 guests cruise for 10 days among the Seychelles located in the Indian Ocean. Trip members make shore excursions and snorkeling trips during the course that passes Praslin, LaDigue, Cousin and Bird islands. Shore excursions made in landing craft are planned for all of these islands and atolls. The return trip is via Mahe. **Cost:** $775 to $1,075 includes food, cruise transportation. **When:** Year-round. **Contact:** Lindblad Travel, Inc., 8 Wright St., Westport, CT 06880, USA; phone (203)226-8531 or tollfree (800)243-5657. ***(M)***

PACIFIC

Isles of the South Pacific: Participants make stops at rarely visited ports in the South Pacific aboard a large, well-equipped cruise ship. A 28-day trip begins with a flight from Los Angeles to Auckland. After a day's sightseeing there, travelers fly on to Christchurch to board the m.s. *Lindblad Explorer*. The ship cruises from island to island, visiting New Caledonia, New Hebrides, the Santa Cruz and Banks islands, Fiji and Western Samoa. A flight from Pago Pago to Los Angeles completes the journey. Another 36-day trip continues northwest from Pago Pago, visiting the Phoenix, Gilbert, Marshall and Caroline islands on the way to the Philippines. Participants return by air from Manila to Los Angeles. Accommodations are on board ship and in hotels on shore. **Cost:** $4,840 to $7,540 for 28-day trip, $6,500 to $10,200 for 36-day trip, depending on type of accommodations, all-inclusive from Christchurch; airfare from Los Angeles extra. **When:** March, April. **Contact:** Lindblad Travel, Inc., 8 Wright St., Westport, CT 06880, USA; phone (203)226-8531 or tollfree (800)243-5657. ***(M)***

SOUTH AMERICA

Ecuador

Galapagos Trip: The tri-hull yacht *Delfin* is used to transport passengers through the Galapagos Islands to study the area's natural history for 5 to 8 days. After flying from Quito or Guayaquil to Baltra, participants board the boat and cruise to Academy Bay, at Santa Cruz island, to visit the Charles Darwin Research Station. Multilingual, trained naturalist guides give a tour of the facility where the participants receive a lecture on Galapagos wildlife and visit a breeding ground for tortoises. For onshore visits, tough outdoor wear and solid hiking boots with rubber soles for walking on lava are recom-

A pamacri, a wooden boat with a thatched palm roof, docks after a 90-minute cruise from Iquitos on Peru's Yanayacu River. (Amazon Lodge & Safaris)

mended. Normal summer weight clothing is used aboard ship. The itinerary includes stops at Sullivan Bay, James Island, Barrington, Puerto Baquerizo and Tagus Cove, among others. **Cost:** $365 to $695. **When:** Year-round. **Contact:** Metropolitan Touring, P.O. Box 2542, Quito, Ecuador; phone 524-400; or Adventures Associates, Suite 116, 5925 Maple St., Dallas, TX 75235, USA; phone (214)357-6187 or tollfree (800)527-2500.

French Guiana

Up the Maroni: Four days of motorized canoeing up the Maroni River highlight an 8-day trip through French Guiana. Participants begin the expedition with a flight from Pointe-a-Pitre, Guadeloupe, via Fort-de-France to Cayenne, where they drive to Cabet-Comte for a night by the river. They spend the next day on a boat trip to the Salut Islands, visiting the penal colony, and make a stop at St. Laurent of Maroni. On the trip's third day they begin their 236-mile journey up the Maroni, a remote and primitive waterway lined with small, hospitable villages; nights are spent in the huts of local residents. On the seventh day the party visits the Roucouyenne Indians and arrives at Maripasoula, where they catch a flight to Cayenne. After a brief stop and a meal participants fly on to Paris. **Cost:** On request. **When:** On request. **Contact:** Club Med, Inc., 40 W. 57th St., New York, NY 10019, USA; phone tollfree (800)528-3131.

Peru

Amazon River Trip: Departing from Iquitos, Peru, participants may experience the Amazon jungle on 2 different trips. The first trip escorts visitors by motorboat for a 90-minute ride on the Amazon River to the Amazon Lodge, which stands 100 yards from the shore on the Yanayacu River. After crossing a beautiful lagoon by canoe, travelers meet Jivaro Indians who demonstrate such age-old practices as the use of blowguns. The second trip is an extension of the first, providing participants with the experience of spending a night in the jungle. The itinerary for both trips is flexible, allowing trip members the opportunity to become acquainted with as much of the area and its people as possible. **Cost:** $36 to $58 for day tour, $54 to $85 for overnight, $78 to $109 for 2 nights, includes meals, boat transportation. Price depends on group size. **When:** Year-round. **Contact:** Amazon Lodge and Safaris, P.O. Box 10251, Lima, Peru; phone 239940.

UNITED STATES

Alaska

Glacier Bay Cruise: Voyagers board the *Chaik,* a fully equipped 50-foot yacht, and journey into Alaska's Glacier Bay National Monument or Tracy Arm Glacier Wilderness. The tidewater glaciers of these wilderness areas can be seen in their full splendor from the sea. The group explores areas abounding with seals, whales, eagles, mountain goats, sea bird rookeries and many other unique flora and fauna. Certified for up to 30 passengers, the *Chaik* sleeps 10 in semi-private accommodations, and trip routes and duration vary. Glacier Guides also offers 6-day wilderness backpacking and glacier exploring trips via the *Chaik.* **Cost:** From $600 a day for chartering boat, $595 for backpacking trip. **When:** June to August. **Contact:** Glacier Guides, Inc., 205 S. 300 W., St. George, UT 84770, USA; phone (801)673-3697.

Florida

Shanty Boat Sojourn: Participants cruise for 5 days along the rivers and swamps of southwestern Florida. Starting from Ft. Myers on the coast, the shanty boat (a combination houseboat and touring craft) winds its way along the Caloosahatchee River until it reaches Lake Okeechobee. Participants find the area good for fishing, as well as bird watching, sunning and sightseeing. Accommodations are in double-occupancy cabins below deck; meals are served in a central galley. Included in the trip is an air-boat ride on Lake Hicpochee and a swamp-buggy cruise through the waterlands. Throughout the trip passengers take time to inspect the area's flora and fauna. **Cost:** $260. **When:** November to May. **Contact:** Cap'n Stan, Rt. 14, Box 434AT, Ft. Myers, FL 33905, USA; phone (813)694-3401.

New York

Route Canals: The various canal systems in New York state provide scenic and historic routes for 2- and 3-day cruises. Traveling aboard the motor cruiser *Emita II,* passengers stop at points of interest, learn local history from the crew and see rural New York from an unusual perspective. Three-day cruises on the Erie Canal travel one-way between Syracuse and either Lockport or Albany. They can be taken in either direction, as transportation is provided back to the point of departure. Another 3-day voyage travels the Champlain Canal from Albany to Whitehall and back again. Those with less time can take a 2-day trip on the Cayuga-Seneca Canal, which connects the Erie Canal to Cayuga and Seneca lakes, making the cruise from Syracuse to Geneva and back again. On some trips overnight accommodations are in shoreside hotels, while in most cases nights are spent on the boat. **Cost:** $110 to $130 for 2 days, $200 to $220 for 3 days includes transportation back to departure point, food, accommodations, guides. **When:** June to October. **Contact:** Mid-Lakes Navigation Co., Ltd., P.O. Box 61, Skaneateles, NY 13152, USA; phone (315)685-8500.

Oregon

Whitewater Jetboat: Oregon's Rogue River is the scene of a 104-mile jetboat trip through pools, riffles, rapids and hidden channels. All roads cease above the town of Agness where the whitewater begins. The trip passes the 1,500-foot vertical rock walls known as Paradise Canyon. Boat pilots tailor each trip to the interests of those aboard, and the number of people per trip is kept to a minimum. There are opportunities to observe deer, otters, eagles, wildflowers and a variety of geological features. The full trip takes 2 days, beginning in coastal fog and coming into the sunshine a few miles upstream. Casual clothing is recommended. **Cost:** $62 for adults, $40 for children on the 2-day trip; $25 for adults, $15 for children on the 1-day trip. **When:** April to November. **Contact:** Court's White Water Trips, Box 1045, Gold Beach, OR 97444, USA; phone (503)247-6504.

RESOURCES

Clubs and Associations

Boat Owners Association of the U.S.
880 S. Pickett
Alexandria, VA 22304, USA
Phone (703)823-9550

Club Washington
411 N. Washington St., Suite 302
Alexandria, VA 23314, USA
Phone (703)836-2000

Cruising Club of America
100 William St.
New York, NY 10038, USA
Phone (212)285-2850

Freighter Travel Association
40-21 Bell Blvd.
Bayside, NY 11361, USA

Seven Seas Cruising Association
P.O. Box 38
Placida, FL 33946, USA

Rentals

Worldwide Yacht Charter Guide
456 Shelbourne
Grosse Point Farms, MI 48236, USA
Phone (313)881-5095

HOUSEBOATING

If you've ever dreamed about living on a houseboat, opportunities now exist to fulfill your fantasies in some of the most beautiful areas of the world. Houseboats can be chartered for relaxing on Dal Lake among the majestic Himalayas, exploring the coastline of Chesapeake Bay, cruising the scenic shore of Shuswap Lake in British Columbia or floating down Mark Twain's Mississippi.

Safe and easy to operate, houseboats can be crewed by beginners after just 30 minutes of instruction. Most come equipped with navigational charts, fuel, water, cooking utensils, full galley and heads. Some even have water skis and tow-along dinghies. They range in length from 26 to 55 feet and comfortably sleep 6 to 14 people in bunks and staterooms. Rented for a day, a weekend or the entire summer, houseboats are an ideal way to travel with the whole family for as little as $4 a day to $775 a week.

In addition to leisure and relaxation, houseboats also provide access. From a floating base camp on Kashmir's Dal or Negin lakes, you can trek in the Himalayas, join nearby river trips, tour Ladakh by jeep and shop in the area's colorful bazaars. A houseboat is one of the best ways to experience the swamps and wildlife of the Everglades or to explore historical sites from Vermont to New York along eastern waterways, including the Erie Canal.

So the next time you are trying to figure out how to spend your family vacation or where to plan a reunion with old friends, consider renting a houseboat. Whether you end up fishing in a secluded cove on Rainy Lake in Ontario or cruising along the Appalachian foothills on Kentucky's Lake Cumberland, you'll enjoy a leisurely trip where you can chart your own course and set your own pace. □

A group of houseboaters explores the shoreline of Lake Powell. The spectacular lake was formed by the Glen Canyon Dam in 1963 and stretches 180 miles from northern Arizona into southeastern Utah. A number of marinas there offer houseboats for rent year-round. (Del E. Webb Corp.)

HOUSEBOATING

ASIA

India

Srinagar Houseboating: Stays of any length can be booked aboard a variety of houseboats on Dal Lake, ranging from deluxe to simple, and priced accordingly. The boats may be rented for a relaxing stay in the lush surroundings of Kashmir or tied in with various activities, including camping on Himalayan peaks, jeep tours of Ladakh, shopping in the area's bazaars, sightseeing and fishing. Advance reservations are necessary and arrangements can be made for airport pickup in Srinagar. **Cost:** $4 to $26 a night includes food, accommodations, some services. **When:** Year-round. **Contact:** M.S. Baktoo & Sons, P.O. Box 32, Srinagar, Kashmir, India; phone 8698.

Dal Lake Floating: Houseboats situated on Kashmir's Dal and Negin lakes may be rented for almost any length of stay. With a spectacular view of the Himalayas, the floating houses offer access to a wide range of recreational activities including area sightseeing, hiking, photography, skiing, swimming, boating, trekking and river trips. The Dal Lake area was once the retreat of kings, when its lush foliage and striking alpine surroundings first earned it the name "earthly paradise." Some of the houseboats are large and deluxe and can accommodate large groups; others are smaller and more economical. **Cost:** On request. **When:** Year-round. **Contact:** Shabina Travel, Shabina No. 328, Dal Lake, Srinagar-190001, Kashmir, India.

CANADA

British Columbia

At Home on the Water: Participants wake to the sounds of loons and other waterfowl while staying on houseboats in the Shuswap Lake area of eastern British Columbia. Houseboaters may cruise along 1,000 miles of shoreline and moor at sandy beaches, sleepy settlements or modern marinas. Sleeping 6 adults comfortably, the 36-foot boats have dinghies for trips to shore, and privately owned boats can be towed along behind. Participants may swim or fish from the boat or may hike ashore to search for wildflowers and Indian artifacts. Boats are rented on a weekly basis in summer and on a daily, 3-day or weekly basis in the off season. Complete boat operating instructions are given before departure. **Cost:** $535 a week from June to September; from $95 for 1 day to $395 a week during off season. **When:** Year-round. **Contact:** Explorer Houseboat Rentals Ltd., Captain's Village (Scotch Creek), R.R. 1, Chase, BC Canada V0E 1M0; phone (604)955-2235.

Ontario

Living on Rainy Lake: The half-million acres of Rainy Lake, on the U.S.-Canadian border 275 miles north of Minneapolis-St. Paul, can be explored for anywhere from a day to a week aboard rental houseboats. The crafts range in length from 36 to 50 feet and sleep from 4

Houseboats on Srinagar's Dal Lake provide a relaxing way to explore Kashmir and enjoy spectacular views of the Himalayas. (Shabina Travel)

to 14 people. The lakeshore on both sides of the border is accessible only by water, providing a protected wilderness area for large concentrations of wildlife there and on the lake's 1,500 islands. Small outboards and canoes are also available to supplement boaters' mobility. Houseboaters who want to find the most secluded coves or the best fishing spots can hire a guide to accompany them for all or part of the trip. **Cost:** $70 to $200 a day, $315 to $895 a week, depending on boat. **When:** May to first freeze. **Contact:** Northernaire Floating Lodges, Box 510, Island View Rt., International Falls, MN 56649, USA; phone (218)286-5221.

UNITED STATES

Arizona

Wahweap Rentals: Houseboats and powerboats are available for rental on the shores of Lake Powell in southern Utah and Arizona. Houseboat sizes range from 36 to 50 feet, with sleeping facilities for 6 to 12 people. Houseboats are all of the very stable and seaworthy pontoon style. Powerboats come in sizes from 14 to 18 feet. Possible areas to visit include Wahweap Bay, Glen Canyon Dam and Bridge, Rainbow Bridge and Antelope Island. The powerboats are rented hourly, daily or weekly. The houseboats are fully equipped with fuel, water, utensils, range and oven, icebox and toilets. Water skis, dinghies, grills and bedding are also available for rental. **Cost:** $330 to $850 depending on length of trip and houseboat size, $4 to $400 for powerboat. **When:** Year-round. **Contact:** Wahweap Lodge and Marina, P.O. Box 29040, Phoenix, AZ 85038, USA; phone tollfree (800) 528-6154.

California

Cruising on Lake Havasu: Participants ply the waters of the Colorado River around Lake Havasu and of the lake itself aboard rented houseboats. About 50 river miles from Park Moabi to Parker Dam are available for cruising, and the lake is 30 miles long and about 3 wide, providing a large area for the boater to explore. Private coves and secluded beaches can be found along the way. Attractions include unusual rock formations, rare birds and wildlife, and the bizarre sight of London Bridge land-bound in the desert. Detailed instructions on operation of the craft are delivered upon pickup, which is at Park Moabi. **Cost:** On request. **When:** Year-round. **Contact:** Colorado River Houseboats, P.O. Box 915, Needles, CA 92363, USA; phone (714)326-4777.

Florida

Through the Everglades: Participants explore the backwaters of Everglades National Park on weeklong sojourns by houseboat. Boats depart from Flamingo, the southernmost point on the U.S. mainland, and cruise the placid waters of Coot, Whitewater and Tarpon bays. Fishing from the boats is excellent, and participants may tow their own or rented skiffs for excursions. The park's mangrove swamps and exotic birdlife provide endless photographic opportunities. Available for rent are 36-foot boats that sleep 8, 34-foot boats that sleep 6 and a 28-foot boat sleeping 4. **Cost:** $545 to $600 a week, depending on size of boat, during winter; $485 to $550 a week during summer includes fuel, all cooking ware and utensils, linen. **When:** Year-round. **Contact:** Flamingo Houseboat Corp., Everglades National Park, Flamingo, FL 33030, USA; phone (305)358-3945.

Indiana

On the Brookville: Cruising the waters of Indiana's Brookville Reservoir may be done aboard rental houseboats ranging in length from 32 to 45 feet. The reservoir, 15 miles long, is rimmed by 62 miles of shoreline dotted with inlets and bays, all open to houseboats. The area offers opportunities for hiking, small boating, botanical study, fishing and relaxing. Beaches around the reservoir provide bases for swimming. The houseboats may be rented for a weekend, a 5-day week or a full week; the smallest boats can handle 6 persons, the larger ones 8. **Cost:** $200 to $350 for weekends, $400 to $575 for 7 days includes houseboat, equipment, maps. **When:** Year-round. **Contact:** Horn's Houseboats of Indiana Inc., Box 265, Columbus, IN 47201, USA; phone (812)342-4966.

Iowa

Houseboating Big Muddy: Fully equipped and inspected houseboats from 30 to 42 feet can be rented for use on the Mississippi River in the Iowa region. The houseboats include all bedding, dishes, cooking utensils, furniture and fuel for stoves. Sleeping facilities aboard the craft accommodate 6 to 10 people. Reservations are recommended to assure a houseboat during the summer months, as the area is a popular Midwestern recreation center. **Cost:** $333 to $666, depending on size of houseboat and season. **When:** April to September. **Contact:** A-1 Rental Center, Ninth St. and White Hwy. 52-3, Dubuque, IA 52001, USA; phone (319)583-2112.

Kentucky

Cumberland Cruise: Thirty-four- to 46-foot houseboats are available for rent along the shores of Lake Cumberland. Renters choose between 1 day, 4 days or a week to cruise along the 1,255 miles of shoreline, bays and deep, clear lakewater. The region around Lake Cumberland is

Under the sheer canyon walls of Lake Powell, which display vivid geological strata, these houseboaters moor at a sandy beach. (Del E. Webb Corp.)

made up of the foothills of the Appalachians and is forested with various hardwood trees as well as being carpeted with Kentucky bluegrass. **Cost:** $55 to $500. **When:** Year-round. **Contact:** Grider Hill Dock, Albany, KY 42602, USA; phone (606)387-5501.

Missouri

Huck Finn Houseboating: Floating homes are available for 2 days to 1 week of rental along the Mississippi River just north of St. Louis. Starting from Piasa Harbor renters may take houseboats up and down the region made famous as the boyhood home of Mark Twain. Each boat features a complete galley, marine lavatory and toilet, sundeck, and all Coast Guard required safety equipment. Linen, cookware and navigational charts are also included. No experience in houseboating is required; a demonstration run is given to each new customer. **Cost:** $140 to $450. **When:** April to November. **Contact:** House of Martin Sales Enterprises, P.O. Box 9111, St. Louis, MO 63117, USA; phone (314)725-6320.

New York

Erie Area: Out of a marina on Vermont's Lake Champlain, houseboats may be rented to travel the lake, the Richelieu River, the St. Lawrence River, Lake Ontario and the Erie Canal. This area, dotted with historical remains of an era when the Erie was a major commercial waterway, offers scenic natural areas, too. Using either a 34-foot or 40-foot houseboat, renters may choose from a wide variety of routes: to the 1,000 Islands area via the Richelieu; to Niagara and Taughannock Falls; into Lake Ontario to Rochester and Toronto; down the Champlain Canal from Troy to Whitehall; up the Richelieu to Montreal and Quebec; and others. Provided with each houseboat is a dinghy for more detailed explorations, docking and excursions. **Cost:** $430 to $475 for weekends, $640 to $770 for 7 days, depending on season and type of boat, includes houseboat, equipment, maps. **When:** May to October. **Contact:** Houseboat Vacations, Inc., 1 James St., Lake George, NY 12845, USA; phone (518)668-4644.

Tennessee

Dale Hollow Houseboating: On the border between Kentucky and Tennessee lies Dale Hollow Reservoir, a 60-mile-long lake offering over 30,000 acres of water to the houseboater. The boats are available from a marina located in a deep bay of the man-made basin, and they range in length from 34 to 55 feet, sleeping from 6 to 14. Miles of wooded shoreline, numerous isolated inlets and clear water are among Dale Hollow Reservoir's attractions, offering renters activities such as swimming, water skiing, shoreline hiking and fishing. Rental packages are offered for a full 7 days, a midweek 4 days or a 3-day weekend; shorter periods can be arranged. **Cost:** $30 to $105 a day, depending on season, length of rental and size of boat. **When:** Year-round. **Contact:** Hendrick's Creek Resort, Box 2107-7, North Canton, OH 44720, USA; phone (216)854-4151 or (502)433-5353.

Utah

Living on Lake Powell: Houseboats from 32 to 50 feet in length are available to those who want to cruise Lake Powell in the southeast corner of Utah. After a short but thorough shakedown cruise, participants can operate any of the houseboats. Every season has its special attractions at Lake Powell. Winters are relatively mild with sunny days and a placid surface on the lake. Swimming and water skiing are especially popular in the summer. Spring months bring winds and the best fishing season, and even when the winds are extreme, boaters can explore in one of the numerous narrow canyons that edge the lake. Photographers find the best conditions in the fall when the sun's southward position creates rays that bathe the region in pinks and lavenders, producing extraordinary sunsets. The canyon forests are changing color at this time, too. Boats 16 feet or under can be towed behind the houseboats. Houseboats must be rented a minimum of 3 days. **Cost:** $105 to $170 a day for rental. **When:** Year-round. **Contact:** Aqua-Cruz, Halls Crossing, Blanding, UT 84511, USA; phone (801)684-2264 or 684-2265.

RESOURCES

Rentals

Camp-a-Float
101 S. 30th St.
Phoenix, AZ 85034, USA

At 6 locations in the United States, outboard powered flat boats with water and sewage hookups can be rented to accommodate motorhomes.

RESEARCH EXPEDITIONS

A trip to the Caribbean on a 50-foot wooden sloop becomes a journey to another world as you listen to the melodious songs of the humpback whale through underwater microphones. While sailing in the Galapagos, you wake at dawn to see a hundred porpoises leap across the glass-smooth Pacific less than 25 yards away. As you scuba dive in 60 feet of water off Oahu, you discover a mollusk new to science.

Whether you are 10 or 70, schooled or just plain curious, opportunities now exist for you to make a meaningful contribution to science as a participant on marine research projects around the world. You can work side-by-side with field specialists as they study coral reef ecology, explore newly discovered shipwrecks or plot the migration routes of whales. On a month-long cruise from Miami to Panama City, you can search for the Caribbean Monk seal, last seen in 1952 off Jamaica. Or you can learn to scuba dive in the British Virgin Islands as part of a 3-week expedition that teaches sailing and navigational skills while exploring the marine environment.

Lasting a week to 4 weeks and ranging in cost from $389 to $3,000, the trips offer "hands-on" experience with the toils and successes of field research. Not only might you be asked to hoist the sails, navigate and stand watch, but you may be taught how to take a census of porpoise pods, rescue beached cetaceans and tag marine turtles. Even children can study anemone feeding behavior, help deliver baby dogfish and learn survival techniques on an uninhabited island off Maine.

Covering almost three-fourths of the earth's surface, the oceans have inspired myth and tantalized people with their power and mystery. Now it is possible to participate at the frontier of discovery with scientists who are furthering our understanding of the sea. Whether you help study kelp beds off the coast of California, collect plankton in Puget Sound or decode whale songs in the Caribbean, you'll share in an experience both memorable and meaningful. □

Many seagoing research projects need both divers and non-divers; here, two participants cooperate in lowering a pressure chamber into the water. (Andrew Martinez/Expedition Training Institute)

RESEARCH EXPEDITIONS

CARIBBEAN

Search for the Caribbean Monk Seal: The Caribbean Monk seal, abundant in the West Indies when Columbus came to America, was decimated by hunters who found it unafraid of man and an easy prey; it was last sighted in 1952 off Jamaica and is now probably extinct. A month-long research cruise under the sponsorship of a Harvard University commission sails the western Caribbean Sea in an effort to locate any survivors of the species. Beginning in Miami, Florida and finishing in Panama City, the expedition visits Pedro Bank, Serranilla Bank (scene of the 1952 sighting), Serrana Bank and other reefs and islets in the area. Shipboard time not spent in observation is used for recreation and study of the species. Academic credit is available, and the expedition cost is a tax-deductible contribution. **Cost:** $2,000 includes food, accommodations, instruction, activities. **When:** June. **Contact:** The Ocean Research and Education Society, Inc., 51 Commercial Wharf 6, Boston, MA 02110, USA; phone (617)523-3455.

Antigua

Desert, Jungle and Sea: The Caribbean islands of Antigua and Barbuda present a variety of life zones as well as historical sites to investigate during a 3-week trip. Antigua has a rare combination of desert and tropical biological communities, and Barbuda is ringed with shipwrecks reflecting the region's history. Headquartered at a restored English Navy depot, trip members pursue areas of individual interest, such as diving, marine biology, natural history or human history from the Arawak Indians up through European colonization. Divers can explore the area's luxuriant coral reefs. Academic credit is available. **Cost:** $1,650 includes transportation on the islands, food, accommodations, equipment, guides. **When:** July. **Contact:** Jean-Michel Cousteau Institute, P.O. Drawer CC, Harbour Town, Hilton Head Island, SC 29928, USA; phone (803)785-3333, ext. 123.

British Virgin Islands

Leeward Research: The Leeward Islands of the Caribbean, widely considered one of the world's best cruising areas, are the setting for a 3-week sailing and marine research trip for those ages 16 to 29. After meeting in the British Virgin Islands, participants board a research vessel and cruise the region; all necessary skills are taught en route. The mission may be bird banding in the outer islands, mapping underwater terrain, or making population counts of turtles on the island of Avis. Specific subjects taught include sailing, navigation, sailing theory, botanical identification and scuba diving (a certification course). Academic credit is available as well as some financial aid. **Cost:** $775 includes food, accommodations, equipment, instruction. **When:** June, July. **Contact:** Expedition Training Institute, Inc., P.O. Box 171, Prudential Ctr. Sta., Boston, MA 02199, USA; phone (617)922-0577. ***(M)***

Learning by doing, these participants on a research trip prepare marine invertebrates for study in the lab. (International Zoological Expeditions)

Dominican Republic

Listening to the Humpbacks: The song of the humpback whale, performed by lone males on the calving grounds in the winter months, lasts 30 minutes and is continually repeated in a precise and complicated format. A 14-day sailing program studies humpback singing and its relation to whale behavior in the Caribbean. The expedition sets sail in two 50-foot wooden sloops, *Snowshoe* and *Caribe*, for the winter breeding grounds of 800 whales, the largest known assembly of humpbacks. Its mission is to record songs and correlate them with photographs of the whales and their identifying characteristics. Whale behavior is observed with special attention to interactions between single animals, calling animals, pairs and trios. Everyone pitches in with the sailing and upkeep of the boats, and takes turn standing daylight watch. Experience with photographic or recording equipment, as well as sailing experience, is helpful. Patience, powers of observation and the ability to co-exist cheerfully in cramped quarters are most important. Two expeditions are planned, one out of South Caicos Island and the other out of Puerto Plata, Dominican Republic. **Cost:** $1,175 includes all costs while at sea. **When:** March, April. **Contact:** Earthwatch, P.O. Box 127 AG, Belmont, MA 02178, USA; phone (617)489-3030.

Surveying the Humpback Whale: Under the sponsorship of a Harvard University commission, participants on a month-long expedition help study the migration of the humpback whale. Joining the ship in Puerto Plata, participants conduct an ongoing count of whale traffic, monitoring it until it reaches zero and the whales have departed for their summer feeding grounds. The ship then cruises through the windward Bahama Islands, beachcombing and searching for evidence of whales that have dropped out of the usual migration. The expedition's goal is to contribute to the understanding of the seasonality, group composition and abundance of humpback whales in the area; it terminates in Miami, Florida. Academic credit is available and the expedition cost is a tax-deductible contribution. **Cost:** $1,400 includes food, accommodations, instruction, activities. **When:** April. **Contact:** The Ocean Research and Education Society, Inc., 51 Commercial Wharf 6, Boston, MA 02110, USA; phone (617)523-3455.

Grenadines

West Indies Marine Field Research: An intensive 3-week program provides practical experience in marine field research for members of the selected crews. Participants work with professional biologists on either a specific investigation or ongoing ecology projects on the island of Carriacou in the Grenadine Islands, West Indies. Participants are trained in relevant skills: data handling and statistics, sampling designs, navigation and seamanship, scientific photography, identification of marine organisms, collection and processing of biological specimens, study of communities and populations and estimation of physical factors. Seminars and lectures are held on topics in chemistry, research planning, marine ecology, physiology and oceanography. Participants with a valid scuba certificate have opportunities to dive during the program. **Cost:** $600 to $800 depending on program includes room, board, instructional materials, use of all facilities. **When:** March to October. **Contact:** Environmental Research Projects, 105 Davenport Rd., Toronto, ON Canada M5R 1H6; phone (416)727-8108.

MEXICO

Baja California

Baja Pacific: Two trips are offered in which participants may view whales in their natural habitat. One lasting 7 days originates in San Diego and proceeds to Laguna San Ignacio midway between Scammon's Lagoon and Magdalena Bay on Baja California's southern coast. Here in the heart of the whale breeding grounds, participants may study and photograph whales and porpoises at close range from inflatable boats. Residing in tents at the base camp, trip members have ample opportunity to study marine life in the lagoon, experience the beauty of the desert and visit Mexican families at the nearby fishing village. On an alternate 8-day trip, a group drives for the first 3 days through the Central Desert, which offers a variety of plant and animal life. There is also time to explore old mines and missions en route. The remainder of the trip is spent at an island base camp in the Sea of Cortez where there are thousands of nesting sea birds, pods of finback whales, playful porpoises and innumerable sea lions. Inflatable boats are used for exploring the half-dozen small uninhabited islands of the area, as well as lagoons, waterline caves and tidepools. Participants return to San Diego by charter flight. **Cost:** $389 for each trip. **When:** January to March for 7-day trip, April for 8-day trip. **Contact:** Oceanic Expeditions, 240 Ft. Mason, San Francisco, CA 94123, USA; phone (415)441-1106.

PACIFIC

Marine Research in the Galapagos: A 3-part study of tuna and porpoise behavior is being carried out to help solve the problem of porpoises drowning in the nets during fishing operations. For 8 days, the *Regina Maris* sails along the southwestern boundary of the fishing area near the Galapagos, to conduct a census on porpoise pods, define the limits of distribution of the species encountered and study the oceanographic conditions of their habitat. On a 6-week trip, continuing studies focus on the natural behavior of the porpoise pods in unfished populations. Operating in the Galapagos, the cruise allows for stopovers in Ecuador and studies of land-based marine animals and sea birds. The third trip, sailing from Costa Rica to western central Mexico in 20 days, estimates the number of porpoises observed near shore and the other species sighted. Selected island and mainland shorelines of the region are beachcombed to rescue stranded cetacean specimens which inhabit the eastern tropical Pacific Ocean. Academic credit is available through the Harvard University Commission on Extension Courses. **Cost:** $2,000 for Part III, $3,000 for Parts I and II includes tuition, meals from staging area for each trip in South America. **When:** July, August, October. **Contact:** Ocean Research and

A Galapagos tortoise on Santa Cruz Island ("Galapagos" means giant tortoise) greets a visitor to the Charles Darwin Research Station. (Ocean Voyages)

Education Society, Inc., 51 Commercial Wharf 6, Boston, MA 02110, USA; phone (617)523-3455.

Hawaii

Identifying Marine Animals: Members of the general public may help identify new species of marine animals on a 3-week research project off Oahu's coast. Both certified divers and non-divers are needed as the team gathers specimens in 3 to 60 feet of water, seeking to confirm an apparent find last year of 2 new species of marine mollusk. Learning to identify animals and their ecological roles through the leadership of a scientific team, group members explore different sites all around the coast of Oahu. Participants spend their nights in dormitory-style accommodations in Honolulu, overlooking Diamond Head. Snorkeling ability and good physical condition are required; the weather is mild and sunny with occasional showers. **Cost:** $975 includes food, transportation, accommodations, instruction, equipment. **When:** June. **Contact:** Earthwatch, P.O. Box 127 AG, Belmont, MA 02178, USA; phone (617)489-3030.

UNITED STATES

California

Catalina Coastal Ecology: Participants spend 10 days investigating the ecology of Catalina Island on a research trip departing from San Pedro Harbor. Suitable either for scientists wishing to pursue their studies or amateurs with a strong interest in the region, the trip focuses on the interrelationships of plants and animals along the California coastline through observation and study of kelp beds, fish, invertebrates and marine mammals. Some lab work is involved. While no particular experience is required, those with diving, research or other relevant skills can utilize them. The expedition is headquartered in Toyon Bay, near good diving and hiking areas. Academic credit is available. **Cost:** $650 includes transportation from San Pedro Harbor, food, accommodations, equipment, guides. **When:** June. **Contact:** The Jean-Michel Cousteau Institute, P.O. Drawer CC, Harbour Town, Hilton Head Island, SC 29928, USA; phone (803)785-3333, ext. 123.

Maine

Studying the Ocean and its Animals: A 4-week summer program for boys 10 to 17 interested in marine biology and oceanography meets at Echo Lake. Facilities available to students include a wet and dry lab for experiments and projects, holding tanks for specimens, microscopes and scientific collecting instruments and a library, along with a fleet of water craft. At the Atlantic coast location, students study the feeding behavior of anemones as they stretch their tentacles out to passing fish, help deliver baby dogfish and induce fertilization of sea urchin eggs to observe their development. Advanced students may devise individual projects such as depth sounding the island's fjords. Guest scientists conduct field trips and present slide shows. In addition, students experience a day-trip to Little Cranberry Island to visit a typical Maine fishing village. Survival techniques are also taught on an uninhabited island. **Cost:** $675 includes food, transportation, lodging. **When:** July, August. **Contact:** Camp Beech Cliff, P.O. Box 536, Concord, MA 01742, USA; phone (617)369-4095.

Massachusetts

Educational Expeditions: Several large boats are used for sailing expeditions up and down the eastern seaboard of the United States and in the Caribbean. While the focus of the expeditions is on training in seamanship and skills in large boat handling, students ages 14 to 17 also learn about marine life and ocean ecology. A typical expedition travels from Rhode Island to Block Island and Cape Cod to join researchers investigating coastal ecology. Sailors then head to the Boston Harbor Islands for more research before concluding the trip at Gloucester, Massachusetts with a study of laboratory aquaculture. Details of planned trips are available on request. **Cost:** $25 to $30 a day. **When:** Year-round. **Contact:** Expedition Training Institute, Inc., P.O. Box 171, Prudential Ctr. Sta., Boston, MA 02199, USA; phone (617)922-0577. *(M)*

South Carolina

Elbow of the Devil: A 10-day research trip investigates the intricate salt marsh ecology of Devil's Elbow Island and the effect of increased human activity on the island. Originating and ending in Savannah, Georgia, the trip is headquartered at a research station on the coastal island off South Carolina. Participants assist with biological research projects on land and in the marshes, a marine population study on a recently sunk, 442-foot artificial reef and visit Indian sites dating from 2000 B.C. No experience is required, and academic credit is available. **Cost:** $650 includes transportation from Savannah, food, accommodations, equipment, guides. **When:** July. **Contact:** The Jean-Michel Cousteau Institute, P.O. Drawer CC, Harbour Town, Hilton Head Island, SC 29928, USA; phone (803)785-3333, ext. 123.

Washington

Puget Sound Marine Biology Cruise: A comprehensive 1-day oceanographic expedition on Puget Sound provides participants with an opportunity to observe undersea life. Plankton is easily examined by use of a plankton trawl and the many varieties brought up are viewed and identified through the microscope. Bottom dredging is demonstrated with many of the strange creatures found in the scoop being placed in the shipboard aquarium, allowing observation of the animals in a water environment. Students learn what a secchi disc is used for, how to perform a plankton tow as well as other technical testing procedures. Instruction and practical experience in navigation, weather observation and boat handling are also available. The trip offers a unique opportunity for studying many types of marine organisms not otherwise available for observation. **Cost:** On request. **When:** On request. **Contact:** Pacific Marine Institute, Inc., 11065 SE Lake Rd., Bellevue, WA 98004, USA; phone (206)454-8311.

NATURE TRIPS

A 6-foot alligator sinks quietly into the murk of an Everglades swamp just a few feet from your canoe, leaving a thin trail of bubbles to mark the spot. Gray whales cavort in a jubilant display of flukes and flippers during their breeding season in Baja's Magdalena Bay. As you snorkel in the Galapagos, a large bull sea lion glides within a few feet of your faceplate before swimming away, convinced that you aren't a threat to his harem on the shore. These and many other wildlife experiences await you on nature trips that are offered by universities, research organizations and private outfitters around the world.

You don't have to be a trained biologist to appreciate the plant and animal life of our oceans, rivers and swamplands. With the guidance of naturalists you can hike the *wad* along the Dutch coast for a day or observe puffin and petrel colonies during a week-long sailing trip off Scotland. You can share the world of sea lions and bulbous-nosed elephant seals during a 7-day cruise around the Falkland Islands. Or watch sei, minke and fin whales on a 10-day trip led by an expert from the Fauna Preservation Society of London.

Longer trips are also available, including a 3-week journey down the Amazon River from Iquitos to Leticia to study tropical rain forest ecology. During a 20-day expedition to the Galapagos Islands, you can rediscover the origin of Darwin's theory of natural selection as you visit the diverse island habitats to see marine and land iguanas, tortoises, flightless cormorants, penguins and 13 species of finches.

Most nature trips welcome people of all ages. Some cater specifically to families, providing a special experience through which parents and children can share in the excitement of discovery; others are geared to students or senior citizens. From $3.50 for a day to $1,500 for 3 weeks, from Maryland to Maui, nature trips offer one of the best ways to break away from an urban life style to make contact with the wilderness. □

In Everglades National Park, a group of walkers led by a National Park Service Guide examines the flora and fauna of the swamplands. The Everglades, third largest national park in the United States, is the nation's only remaining subtropical wilderness and hosts a huge array of wildlife, including many rare birds. (National Park Service)

NATURE TRIPS

ATLANTIC

Falkland Islands

Cruising the Islas Malvinas: The Falkland Islands archipelago, a British colony northeast of Cape Horn with less than 2,000 inhabitants, provides visitors with an interesting mixture of wilderness and civilization. Participants on weekly circumnavigation cruises of the archipelago have the chance to see large colonies of seabirds including black-browed albatrosses, petrels, shearwaters, prions, skuas and 5 species of penguins. The islands are also well known for their colonies of sea lions, elephant seals and fur seals. Longer cruises and a wider variety of activities such as hiking, scuba diving and trout fishing are also available. Between 32 and 36 passengers are included on each cruise, and are accommodated in double and quadruple cabins aboard the boat. **Cost:** About $800. **When:** On request. **Contact:** Falkland Wildlife, Drifts, Chinnor Hill, Oxford OX9 4BS, Great Britain. *(M)*

CANADA

Ontario

Whale Watching: A 10-day trip provides a chance to view dozens of whales on the lower St. Lawrence River. Participants fly from London to Montreal and travel by motorcoach to Riviere du Loup. Here 3 days are spent watching whales first from a boat, then from cliffs on shore. Species that may be seen include fin, sei, minke and even blue whales. The trip then continues to Montreal, Algonquin Park and Niagara before the return flight to London. An expert from the Fauna Preservation Society escorts travelers to provide an introduction to the birds, trees and wildflowers of eastern North America. Accommodations throughout the journey are in hotels. **Cost:** $1,500 includes round-trip airfare from London. **When:** August. **Contact:** Twickenham Travel Ltd., 2 Chester Row, London SW1W 9JH, Great Britain; phone 01-730-2297.

EUROPE

Netherlands

Walking the *Wad:* The *wad* (tideflats) off the Dutch coast can be traversed on foot at low tide, providing a close-up view of the indigenous plant and animal life. A 5- to 10-mile *wadlopen* or hike is taken along the tideflats daily from Pieterburen, with others departing from Uithuisen and Friesland. Six different walks are provided for hikers with varying abilities and desires, from 5-milers near Pieterburen to walks to the islands of Simonszand and Schiermonnikoog, Ameland, Engelsmanplaat and Rottumeroog, with a return trip by boat. Guides steer participants across sandbars and away from drop-offs. In the morning the ground is mostly exposed, but by the hike's end the water may reach as high as waist level. Flora and fauna observed include sea lettuce, oyster-catchers, curlews, plovers,

Five- to ten-mile guided hikes are offered along Holland's wad, *or coastal tideflats, during low tide.* (Paulina C. Van Spronsen)

mussels, jellyfish and seals. Participants must wear ankle-high tennis shoes and knee socks for protection from shells, and take along dry clothes in a rucksack. **Cost:** $4.00 to $10 includes transportation, guide and certificate. **When:** On request. **Contact:** Wadloop Centrum, Postbox 1, Pieterburen (GR), Netherlands; phone 05952-300.

Scotland

The Rarities of Rona: The island of Rona, 45 miles northwest of Cape Wrath, offers a combination of unusual animal life and interesting human history that is rarely experienced by travelers. A week-long trip visits Rona as well as 2 neighboring islands. Participants meet at Loch Eriboll, just east of Cape Wrath, to board the vessel and sail to Rona. Two or 3 days are spent there observing a rare fork-tailed petrel colony, watching a large population of puffins, kittiwakes, guillemots and razorbills, and investigating the remains of the island's inhabitants, who perished 3 centuries ago when oceangoing rats consumed all their food. Stops are also made at Sula Sgeir and Sule Skerry before the return sail to Loch Eriboll. Accommodations are onboard ship, with an optional campout on Rona. **Cost:** $320 includes food, transportation, accommodations, guide. **When:** July. **Contact:** Caledonian Wildlife Services, 2 Kingsmill Gardens, Inverness IV2 3LU, Great Britain; phone (0463)38257 or 33130.

MEXICO

Baja California

Whale Watching in Magdalena Bay: A week-long trip is available for viewing the California gray whale during its annual migration and breeding. Starting in San Diego, group members fly to La Paz on the Mexican coast. Traveling in small skiffs through the lagoons, participants observe and photograph the whales at close range. Some time is allowed for beachcombing and snorkeling. The bird watching opportunities are excellent, and local varieties include white ibises, snowy egrets, great blue herons, marbled godwits, black-belted kingfishers and frigate birds. Nights are spent camping on the beaches and all meals are prepared by the crew. At the end the party is flown back to San Diego. **Cost:** $530 includes food, transportation, camping equipment, guide. **When:** January, February. **Contact:** Adventures International, 4421 Albert St., Oakland, CA 94619, USA; phone (415)531-6564. *(M)*

Baja Whale Watching: An 8-day camping trip features observation of whales in the Magdalena Bay area. Departing from San Diego, participants fly to La Paz and set up base camp among the sand dunes. Participants observe California gray whales from small skiffs and explore mangrove areas and lagoons where they may view a wide variety of sea and shore birds as well as tidal marine life. There are also opportunities for hiking along sand dunes to isolated villages, exploring shell-filled beaches and fishing in the saltwater. The return bus trip to La Paz takes campers through Baja's desert, with time allotted for touring the town before the return trip to San Diego. Other trips offered in Baja include explorations by fishing boat of the Loreto and Puerta Vallarta areas and an expedition by mule to see cave paintings. **Cost:** $545 includes roundtrip transportation from San Diego, meals, camping equipment, guides. **When:** January, February. **Contact:** Baja Expeditions, Inc., Box 3725, San Diego, CA 92103, USA; phone (714)297-0506.

San Ignacio Whale Watching: Members travel by sea along the Pacific coast of Baja California to San Ignacio Lagoon, winter quarters of the California gray whale. Embarking from San Diego, on the 7½-day trip, participants make stops en route at Todos Santos Island and at San Martin Island, where harbor seals can be seen. Visits are also made to the island of San Benitos, home of California sea lions and sea elephants, and to the abandoned silver mine on Cedros Island before arriving at San Ignacio. In the lagoon group members alternate whale watching from skiffs with beachcombing, dune and marsh exploration, and a paddle down mangrove channels inhabited by several species of birds. A professional naturalist and authority on the ecology and wildlife of Baja and the California gray whale accompanies the trip. **Cost:** $550 includes meals, trip passage. **When:** December to April. **Contact:** H & M Landing, 2803 Emerson St., San Diego, CA 92108, USA; phone (714)222-1144. *(M)*

Tamaulipas

Coastal Bird Watching by Canoe: Wintertime birding is excellent in the island-studded region of Laguna Madre, a large bay almost totally enclosed by land just south of the Texas-Mexican border. Participants on a 7-day trip to the area explore the northern end of the 125-mile-long sand reef which separates Laguna Madre from the Gulf of Mexico, keeping an eye out for a large variety of mainland and shore birds unknown or uncommon in much of the U.S. Species including the caracara ("Mexican eagle"), chachalaca, American oyster catcher, roseate spoonbill and royal tern may be seen. Group members encounter few other people while exploring the area; the reef and lagoon are frequented only by transient native fishermen and an occasional Mexican Marine patrol. Canoeing experience is not required. **Cost:** $390 includes canoes and canoeing equipment, food, community gear, guides. **When:** December. **Contact:** University of the Wilderness, P.O. Box 1687, Evergreen, CO 80439, USA; phone (303)674-9724. *(M)*

PACIFIC

Hawaii

Maui Humpbacks: During a 9-day trip to Maui, participants explore the island's volcanoes and surrounding ocean. The seas off Maui are frequented by humpback whales, and trip members have the opportunity to observe, study and photograph the 50-foot sea mammals in their Hawaiian calving grounds. Participants arrive at Maui by air and use a hotel in Lahaina as a base of operations. On the second day, the group visits Haleakala, "The House of the Sun," the world's largest dormant volcano; its slopes abound with wildlife and rare birds as well as a variety of flora. Travelers spend 3 days aboard a motor/sailing vessel observing whales before casting off for the little-visited island of Lanai. The trip ends with a flight back to the mainland via Honolulu. **Cost:** $495 includes lunches aboard the

On a Nature Expeditions International trip, participants stop for a closer look at tidepool life on Guardian Angel Island, in the Sea of Cortez. (David Roderick/Nature Expeditions International)

boat, guides. **When:** April. **Contact:** Adventures International, 4421 Albert St., Oakland, CA 94619, USA; phone (415)531-6564. *(M)*

SOUTH AMERICA

Amazon Ecology: Travelers learn about the natural history and ecology of tropical rain forests on a 3-week trip down the Amazon. Participants travel from Iquitos in Peru to Leticia in Colombia in a specially chartered double-deck riverboat, stopping at simple lodges along the river. Explorations are made by small boats and canoes as well as on foot. The tropical rain forest, with its rich variety of trees and epiphytes, houses exotic birds such as macaws and toucans in addition to many species of insects and amphibians. The instructors are University of California professors of botany and zoology. There are no prerequisites for the course which is open to all interested adults. Trip members should be prepared for some discomforts, as the climate is hot and humid and there is a lot of rain and mud. **Cost:** $2,000 includes roundtrip airfare from Los Angeles, food, accommodations, river transportation. **When:** June. **Contact:** Biological Sciences, UCLA Extension, P.O. Box 24902, Los Angeles, CA 90024, USA; phone (213)825-7093.

Ecuador

Galapagos and Amazon Life Study: An extensive 20-day trip examines the flora and fauna of the Galapagos Islands and the lowland tropical rain forest of the Amazon Basin. Flying from Miami to Ecuador, trip members spend 11 days cruising the volcanic islands made famous by Darwin. Two special outings are offered: an optional 3-day side trip for the hardy to the summit of Alcedo Volcano, camping out and observing the huge population of land tortoises in the crater; and a full day at Tower

Island, rarely visited by tourists, to observe over 750,000 pairs of storm petrels and 140,000 nesting pairs of red-footed boobies. Flying from Baltra back to Guayaquil and Quito on the mainland of Ecuador, participants fly to Coca to board a floating hotel for a cruise down the Amazon. Two days of sightseeing around Quito complete the trip. Extensions to Machu Picchu are also offered. **Cost:** $1,787 to $1,897, depending on type of accommodations, includes transportation from Miami, food, accommodations, instruction, guide. **When:** June. **Contact:** Holbrook Travel, Inc., 3520 NW 13th St., Gainesville, FL 32601, USA; phone (904)377-7111.

Galapagos Adventure: Participants spend 20 days hiking, snorkeling, swimming, observing and photographing wildlife in the Galapagos Islands. Based on a sailing vessel, a small group travels with a naturalist guide from island to island, riding in small skiffs to shore for daily nature walks of 2 to 8 miles. On one such stop at James Bay, trip members walk inland to a salt crater to see Galapagos hawks and finches and then swim and snorkel with sea lions and fur seals. In the evenings the small group gathers for slide lectures, informal discussions about the natural history of the area, and a preview of the next day's activities. The trip begins and ends in Quito where a few days are allowed to explore the 9,000-foot-high capital and take field trips to nearby places of interest. College credit is available. **Cost:** $1,690 from Quito includes transportation, accommodations, meals on board ship, guides. **When:** December, January, April, June, August. **Contact:** Nature Expeditions International, 599 College Ave., Palo Alto, CA 94306, USA; phone (415)328-6572. *(M)*

Cruising the Galapagos: A 15-day cruise through the Galapagos Islands visits points of interest to study the area's natural history, archaeology and history. The initial 4 days in Ecuador are spent in the Quito area traveling through the countryside and visiting the Archaeological Museum. Then the group flies to Baltra in the Galapagos, to board a yacht. A full week is spent cruising through the islands in the company of a naturalist guide, with stops at the Darwin Research Station and nearby bays and islands. Lectures and briefings are presented each evening to enhance the day's activities. At the end of the week participants fly back to Guayaquil and visit Cuenca and the Ingapirca fortress. A 6-day excursion to the Amazon jungle may be added to the trip. The extension proceeds down the Napo River to Primavera aboard a 180-ton floating hotel. A trip by motor canoe and a hike in the jungle highlight activities. **Cost:** $1,595 for Galapagos only, $1,995 with Amazon extension includes accommodations, food, water transportation, guide. **When:** Year-round. **Contact:** Society Expeditions, P.O. Box 5088, University Sta., Seattle, WA 98105, USA; phone (206)324-9400. *(M)*

UNITED STATES

Alaska

Boreal Biology Expedition: A professional wildlife biologist leads an 18-day expedition exploring Glacier Bay and Katmai and Mt. McKinley parks. Participants study natural history and wildlife, including brown bears, birds, marine mammals, glaciers and physical geography. A special boat charter at Glacier Bay is included, and travelers have the option to extend the expedition to the Pribilof Islands. **Cost:** $1,490. **When:** June to August. **Contact:** Nature Expeditions International, 599 College Ave., Palo Alto, CA 94306, USA; phone (415)328-6572. *(M)*

California

Channel Islands Cruise: Participants on a 6½-day journey cruise among the Channel Islands off the coast of southern California, exploring free-form grottos, ancient Indian sites and weather-beaten shores. Accommodations are onboard a cruise boat, from which participants embark on excursions to the islands. Trip members may view sea lions, brown pelicans, gray whales and island foxes. A naturalist accompanies the trip. **Cost:** $470 includes accommodations, meals, guidance. **When:** December, May. **Contact:** H & M Landing, 2803 Emerson St., San Diego, CA 92108, USA; phone (714)222-1144. *(M)*

Florida

Everglades Outfitting: Camping and canoeing trips into Florida's Everglades National Park or the 10,000 Islands area may either be outfitted or fully guided. In the Everglades National Park itself there are numerous restrictions on camping (for instance, freshwater must be carried in and no driftwood may be burned), while the 10,000 Islands area is less restricted. Both offer abundant wildlife, including raccoons, possums, bobcats, bears and birds such as the rare roseate spoonbill and Everglades kite. Campers should be prepared for the area's rapid changes of weather. **Cost:** $15 per person includes canoes, tents, water jugs, cook kit, stove and lantern; $50 a party per day includes guide service, outfitting. **When:** Year-round. **Contact:** Tropical Camper, P.O. Box 970891, Miami, FL 33197, USA; phone (305)253-3984.

Photographing the Everglades: A photography seminar is the core of

During trips of up to 10 days in the Everglades or the 10,000 Islands area in southern Florida, participants refine their techniques in nature photography. (Wilderness Southeast/Dick Murlless)

a 10-day canoeing and backpacking expedition in the swamplands of the Florida Everglades. The leaders of the course instruct students on the basic concepts of outdoor photography through lectures and field trips. Participants learn advanced techniques of shooting and processing color slides. While canoeing and hiking in the surrounding subtropical wilderness students photograph the varied flora and fauna which include many endangered species. Emphasis is also placed on wilderness skills and the ecology of the Everglades. College credit is available. **Cost:** $375 includes accommodations, meals, canoes, instruction. **When:** December, January. **Contact:** Wilderness Encounter, 720 Grand Ave., Glenwood Springs, CO 81601, USA; phone (303)945-8365. ***(M)***

Massachusetts

Maritiming Minors: A 3-week, Monday through Friday day camp teaches numerous maritime skills to a group of young people ages 11 to 14. Based in Gloucester with its rich maritime history, the program uses small boats to explore the Cape Ann seashore's terrain and marine life, makes visits to factories, coast guard stations, boatbuilders' shops and other maritime sites, and does some overnight camping on offshore islands. The main emphasis is on the skills of seamanship; several voyages on which students do the sailing are scheduled, possibly to watch migrating whales as they pass through the area. An active, experimental approach is used throughout the course. Some financial assistance is available. **Cost:** $285 includes lunches, activities, equipment, transportation, instruction. **When:** July, August. **Contact:** Expedition Training Institute, Inc., P.O. Box 171, Prudential Ctr. Sta., Boston, MA 02199, USA; phone (617)922-0577. ***(M)***

HIGH
ADVENTURE
AT HALF PRICE

Underwater
Adventures

Guide

UNDERWATER ADVENTURES

The urge to explore has led humans to climb the earth's highest peaks, to cross its vast continents, to brave the jungles and deserts— and to descend into the depths of the sea. Far from being a recent sport, diving has a history almost as old as civilization itself. Over 6,000 years ago treasure hunters dove as deep as 100 feet on a lungful of air to search for mother-of-pearl and precious corals. Legends tell us that Alexander the Great was submerged in history's first diving bell in 332 B.C., and among Leonardo da Vinci's imaginative inventions was a diving outfit complete with fins. Today scuba equipment has made diving a safe activity enjoyed by millions all over the world—an adventure as close to you as the nearest lake, swimming pool or ocean.

Most dive trip operators and schools own their own equipment, so all you need bring is your swimming skill and a bathing suit. You can learn the basics of snorkeling or scuba diving in a pool at dive schools from upstate New York to landlocked Colorado, but not until you submerge yourself in the waters of the Florida Keys, the Bahamas, the Red Sea or the South Pacific can you really appreciate what diving is all about. You can search for wreckage in the waters around Hong Kong, hand-feed fish in the Red Sea off Port Sudan, swim among coral towers in Australia's Coral Sea or search for sunken warships in Truk Lagoon in Micronesia. You can even learn hard-hat diving, commercial dive techniques or underwater medicine at special schools for the advanced diver.

Diving is unlike any other form of adventure. Down in the depths, your body responds differently than it does on land. You are in another element, and the buoyancy of it lifts the burden of gravity from your movements. Sounds are distorted—some are muffled, others uncommonly clear. The quality of light is different, too, since the filtering effect of water cuts out first the red colors, then the oranges and yellows until you are swimming in an alien world of shadows. Whether you are making a brief snorkel dive on a single breath of air or exploring convoluted coral reefs for half an hour with compressed air, diving is a visit to the world beneath the surface, a world all its own. □

Sea Life Discovery offers a tropical reef biology course on Grand Cayman in the British West Indies. Professional instruction at some of the best spots in the world makes diving a safe and enjoyable adventure. (Kent Schellenger)

DIVING

AFRICA

Kenya

Scuba Divers' Safari: An 11-day safari in eastern Kenya combines wildlife viewing with diving in the Indian Ocean. Beginning in Nairobi, trip members proceed to the Masai Amboseli Game Reserve and Tsavo National Park near Mt. Kilimanjaro to view rhinos, elephants, buffalo, zebras, giraffes and cheetahs. On the fourth day, participants arrive at a rustic beach resort near the coastal city of Malindi for 5 days of diving. The site provides easy access to coral gardens, subterranean caves and barracuda groves. For the novice diver, a diploma course is available that includes a 2-day pool and 3-day open sea instruction program. **Cost:** $367 to $770 depending on group size and diving supplement includes meals, accommodations, guide, land transportation. **When:** On request. **Contact:** Bestway Tours and Safaris Ltd., Woolworth Bldg., Box 44325, Nairobi, Kenya; phone 331261, 331262, 22297.

Sudan

Red Sea Diving: The Red Sea off Port Sudan is the site of dive trips lasting 2 or 3 weeks. The waters in this area are warm and clear. Throughout the trips, dive masters and marine biologists guide participants to Sanganeb Reef, Wingate Reef, Towartit Reef, Barrier Reef and the Umbria Wreck. Large quantities of tropical fish inhabit these areas, along with barracuda, sharks, dolphins, large turtles and mantas. An average of 2 dives a day is made in groups of 6 to 20. Divers can on occasion hand-feed the fish. **Cost:** $1,298 for 2 weeks, $1,615 for 23 days includes roundtrip airfare from London, all land arrangements. **When:** July to December. **Contact:** Explore Beyond Ltd., 167

During an 11-day African safari offered by Bestway Tours and Safaris, participants can combine diving in the Indian Ocean with land activities in Kenya. (Bestway Tours and Safaris Ltd.)

Earls Court Rd., London SW5, Great Britain; or Adventure Center, 5540 College Ave., Oakland, CA 94618, USA; phone (415)654-1879.

ASIA

Hong Kong

Underwater in Hong Kong: Three or 4 of Hong Kong's best diving areas are visited during daytime trips. One site per day is visited for 3 or 4 days, with transportation from and to Hong Kong provided each day. Exact destinations depend on the weather conditions, but likely dive spots include the Nine Pins Islands, Dark Rocks, Tai Long Wan and Basalt Island. Centuries of commerce in the harbor and its environs have left a large amount of merchandise and wreckage on the bottom ideal for underwater exploration. Divers are returned to Hong Kong each evening. Participants must be certified divers. **Cost:** $111 to $125 for 3 days, $148 to $168 for 4 days, depending on size of party, includes transportation, lunch, group equipment. **When:** Year-round. **Contact:** Bunn's Diving Equipment Corp., Ltd., G.P.O. Box 5145, Hong Kong.

Philippines

Diving the Philippines: Fifteen-day dive trips enable participants to explore some of the 7,100 islands of the Philippines and make a stop in Hong Kong. Flying from the west coast of the United States, the party spends a few days sightseeing in Manila before proceeding to either Cebu or Mindoro for 8 days of diving. Both areas are relatively unspoiled and offer excellent diving conditions, from shallow reefs to enormous walls, filled with plant and animal life. A 57-foot dive boat accommodates participants during this period. Two days in Hong Kong en route back to the United States provide an opportunity to sightsee and experience the Crown Colony's night life. **Cost:** $1,580 to $1,675 for either trip, depending on season, includes transportation from the U.S., food, accommodations, equipment, guides. **When:** Year-round. **Contact:** Orientex Travel, Inc., Suite 701, 447 Sutter St., San Francisco, CA 94108, USA; phone (415)391-7370.

Remote Reef and Island Diving: Aboard a 102-foot dive boat, scuba enthusiasts accompanied by a dive master and a local guide cruise the more than 7,000 islands of the Philippines for 16 days. After sightseeing in and around Manila, the party flies to San Jose, on Mindoro Island, and sets sail. The itinerary is flexible, depending on current conditions. Among the stops are the Calaman Islands, off the north coast of Busuanga, where visits are made to Indian villages. The area's waters boast a variety of marine life including 200-pound napoleon wrasse and brightly colored angelfish. Other likely stops include Demipoc, Colocotoc Rocks, Lubutglubut and, in the final 5 days, the colorful and diverse Apo Reef, of special interest to photographers. Most of the diving sites visited are remote and unspoiled. Accommodations are onboard the boat. **Cost:** $1,800 from Manila includes food, accommodations, transportation, equipment, guides. **When:** March to June. **Contact:** See and Sea Travel Service, Inc., 680 Beach St., Suite 340, Wharfside, San Francisco, CA 94109, USA; phone (415)771-0077.

Thailand

Hotel Dives: A 7-day diving vacation in Pattaya is offered year-round by a resort hotel. The dive package includes 5 days of diving at coral reefs, tropical fish feeding grounds and shipwrecks. American dive instructors accompany each trip. Modern diving equipment and dive boats are provided. Arrangements include 6 nights, accommodations, breakfasts and lunches, diving equipment, guides and transportation to and from dive sites. **Cost:** $199 a person for double occupancy, $249 single accommodations. **When:** Year-round. **Contact:** Holiday Inn Sands Hotel Sales Office, Eighth Floor, Kongboonma Bldg., Silom Rd., Bangkok, Thailand; phone 2330802; or Holiday Inn Sands, Pattaya, Thailand; phone 418755.

ATLANTIC

Bermuda

Mid-Atlantic Plunge: Beginning and new divers take half-day journeys out along the reefs of Bermuda. Starting with snorkels, divers learn the basics of diving and diving safety before graduating to scuba gear and more advanced diving techniques. The classes start in shallow water and work their way down, eventually moving on to inspect old shipwrecks. The reefs are full of living and dead coral as well as sea fans and many different types of tropical fish. A highlight of the journey is a visit to the Arcade Walk, a coral formation that resembles an underwater mall. Two dive boats are available, each glass-bottomed and fully equipped. **Cost:** On request. **When:** Year-round. **Contact:** Dave McLeod's Skin Diving Adventures, The Gables Guest House, Paget, Bermuda; phone 1-6207.

AUSTRALASIA

Australia

Keppel Islands: Divers explore the Great Barrier Reef from Great Keppel Island, 30 miles east of Rockhampton. Dive spots are varied throughout the island group, featuring corals, bommies, caves and drop-offs. Large inflatable sports boats are used as platforms during the dives and a pickup boat with a propeller guard is in attendance. Divers must be of certified competency and hold a current diver's medical certificate. Equipment is available for rental. **Cost:** $739 a week, depending on accommodations and time of year includes airfare from Brisbane. **When:** May to January. **Contact:** Safari Diving Services, P.O. Box 29, Clayfield, Brisbane, Queensland, Australia, phone 07-574321.

Exploring the Coral Sea: Divers travel the waters around Australia, particularly the Coral Sea, aboard the fully equipped 79-foot dive boat *Coralita*. After a day's exploration in Sydney, divers fly to Rockhampton on the north Queensland coast and

Dave McLeod's Skin Diving Adventures helps beginning divers gain the skills they need to explore beds of unusual, dome-shaped brain coral in Bermuda's underwater seascape. (Bermuda News Bureau)

drive to the *Coralita's* berth. An overnight cruise takes the party to the outer edge of the Great Barrier Reef, where the fairly shallow water hosts a great variety of marine life including the clownfish, which lives in the tentacles of the sea anemone. The next 2 weeks are spent about 200 miles away in the Coral Sea, with its 150-foot-deep waters surrounded by 40 miles of reef, making for calm, clear water. Divers swim among coral towers that rise to within a few feet of the surface, viewing giant nudibranchs, mollusks, eels, butterfly fish, giant clams and countless other marine creatures. Some night diving is done before the return to Yeppoon and then Sydney. **Cost:** $2,300 from Sydney includes food, accommodations, transportation, equipment, guides. **When:** October. **Contact:** See and Sea Travel Service, Inc., 680 Beach St., Suite 340, Wharfside, San Francisco, CA 94109, USA; phone (415)771-0077.

Papua New Guinea

Bootless Diving: A wide array of diving services is offered in and around Bootless Bay, at the Papuan Barrier Reef. Prearranged day trips are available, as well as certification courses and custom outings by charter boat. Spectacular coral formations, high visibility and an abundance of colorful, sometimes tame marine life make the area attractive to divers. Those with no experience can take a short introductory course culminating in a supervised dive; those wishing to be certified can take a standard course; and experienced divers can make night dives and sign up for exploratory trips. Equipment is available for rent. **Cost:** $22 for short snorkeling trip, $53 for scuba trip to Coral Sea area, from $105 for certification course; other rates on request. **When:** Year-round. **Contact:** Tropical Diving Adventures, P.O. Box 1644, Boroko, Papua New Guinea.

CANADA

Alberta

Edmonton Plunges: A dive center in Edmonton offers services ranging from basic certification or custom advanced instruction to charter and organized dive trips. The basic certification course takes 6 weeks with a total of 38 hours of instruction in both pool and open water. Advanced instruction is arranged on a custom, individually paced basis. Charter diving trips vary from day and weekend excursions to lakes near Edmonton to week-long outings to British Columbia's best dive sites. A 2-week trip is made twice yearly to a tropical site in the West Indies, the South Pacific, the Red Sea or the Caribbean. **Cost:** On request. **When:** Year-round. **Contact:** Mount Ocean Sports, 10133 82nd Ave., Edmonton, AB Canada T6E 1Z5; phone (403)433-0096.

Nova Scotia

Maritime Dive: Underwater enthusiasts spend 1 to 7 days exploring the wreck-filled reaches off Louis-

Day-long trips for both scuba divers and snorkelers can be taken at tropical sites from Fiji to the Bahamas for as little as $10 to $25. (William Sleeper)

bourg, Nova Scotia. Since 1733 ships have foundered and sunk under the difficult tides and treacherous currents of the Cape Breton shelf; now participants may inspect such wrecks as the *Evelyn*, the *Montara*, the *Afgan Prince* and the *Langley Range*. The 1-day package allows divers 2 dives to the various wrecks; 2-, 3- and 5-day trips travel to between 4 and 10 wreck areas. The 7-day excursions, which require 10 to 24 dives, allow divers to either camp or stay at a motel in Sydney. Diving guides, lunch and a lobster dinner are included in each tour. Diver certification is required. **Cost:** $35 to $515. **When:** June to October. **Contact:** Dive Cape Breton Ltd., P.O. Box 130, Louisbourg, NS Canada B0A 1M0; phone (902)733-2877 or 733-2840.

Ontario

Georgian Diving: Georgian Bay, a large inlet off Lake Huron and one of North America's richest shipwreck areas, is the setting for a 5-day dive trip leaving from Reynolds, Ohio. Accommodations are at an inn in Tobermory, at the tip of Bruce Peninsula. The first 2 days of the trip are spent diving the numerous wrecks which lie near shore and thus are accessible from the beach. Then 2 more days are spent aboard a charter dive boat, exploring some of the wrecks which lie in deeper waters further offshore. Opportunities for underwater photography are excellent. **Cost:** $185 includes transportation from Reynolds, food, accommodations, boat, guide. **When:** September. **Contact:** Sub-Aquatics, Inc., 8855 E. Broad St., Reynolds, OH 43068, USA; phone (614)864-1235.

CARIBBEAN

Bahamas

Bahamas Treasure Diving: Two different trips allow qualified divers to assist in a licensed salvage operation, looking for treasure on ancient shipwrecks. The first trip, based in Nassau, is for certified divers who can live either at guest houses or on a dive boat; the second trip is based in the Abacos, or Bahamas Out-Islands, and involves searches in areas containing known wrecks. Certified divers are preferred, but the trip is also open to non-certified divers. On both trips there is some time for shell collecting, underwater photography and individual exploration of the area. **Cost:** About $350, varying with time of year, includes roundtrip airfare from Florida, accommodations, salvage license, guide. **When:** Nassau trip year-round, Abacos trip May to August. **Contact:** Adventurers International, 215 E. Horatio Ave., Maitland, FL 32751, USA; phone (305)645-1332. ***(M)***

Underwater Medicine: Techniques for diving-related medicine and cardiac support are taught in a week-long session held in Freeport. Participants may finish the week by achieving Provider Level certification in Advanced Cardiac Life Support. Intended for physicians, nurses, dentists and paramedics who may be called upon to deliver emergency medical treatment to divers, the course requires a month of fairly intensive prior study at home. The week's program combines didactic and practical sessions covering decompression sickness, recompression procedures, physical examination of divers, airway management, dysrhythmia recognition, defibrillation, useful drugs and other topics. There is free time every day for recreational diving, including some night dives, with scheduled trips to nearby reefs. The Freeport area also offers opportunities for beachcombing, hiking and duty-free shopping. **Cost:** On request. **When:** May. **Contact:** Atlantis Safaris, P.O. Box 530303, Miami Shore, FL 33153, USA; phone (305)754-7480.

San Salvador and Roatan: Two trips are offered to prime dive sites in the Caribbean: one travels to Roatan, off Honduras, and the other to San Salvador, an out-island of the Bahamas. The Roatan trip is based at a resort on the north side of the island, in cottage accommodations that provide easy access to the beach and dive boats. On San Salvador participants stay in the island's only resort and dive the protected reef area. Both trips visit high-visibility areas that contain numerous tame fish and an abundance of coral and other marine life. The Roatan trip features 2 dives a day while the San Salvador trip involves 3. **Cost:** $369 plus airfare for Roatan trip, $495 including airfare from Ft. Lauderdale for San Salvador trip; both include food, accommodations, diving. **When:** March for Roatan trip, May for San Salvador. **Contact:** Elmer's Watersports, 2508 Gross Point Rd., Evanston, IL 60201, USA; phone (312)866-8775.

Diving in Andros: A week on Small Hope Bay, on the scenic island of Andros, enables experienced or novice divers to explore the world's largest coral reef. The reef is protected and still teems with marine life; within 15 minutes of shore are shallow gardens, caves, high pillars, tame fish and a 185-foot drop-off. Accommodations are in small cabins made of coral rock and Andros pine situated in a beachfront grove. Other features of the trip are comfortable temperatures (between 72°F and 85°F), high-visibility waters, instruction and rentals. The trip can include either 1 or 2 dives a day. **Cost:** $315 to $547, depending on type of accommodations, includes lodging, most meals, diving and equipment, guide; other rates on request. **When:** Year-round. **Contact:** Small Hope Bay Lodge, P.O. Box N 1131, Nassau, Bahamas; phone (809)328-2014.

Barbados

Caribbean Wreck Diving: Scuba divers spend 7 days exploring old wrecks off the coast of Barbados. Each day divers head out from their onshore accommodations to search for sunken French, English, Spanish and Dutch vessels, using an underwater metal locator. Experienced guides accompany each group; daily itineraries include dives in the mornings and afternoons. Evenings are unscheduled so that participants may explore the island's forts, old plantations, extinct settlements and interior treasure sites. **Cost:** $750 includes room, dinners, airfare from Florida. **When:** June to December. **Contact:** Adventurers International, 215 E. Horatio Ave., Maitland, FL 32751, USA; phone (305)645-1332. ***(M)***

Diving in Barbados: A wide variety of diving activities is available through a dive center in Barbados. Beginning to advanced level instruction is offered. The trips available range from 1-hour snorkeling trips at a shipwreck and 1-tank dives at nearby reefs to glass-bottom boat rides. Sailing and water-skiing outings are also available. Most equipment can be rented on location and group rates can be arranged. **Cost:** $2 an hour for snorkeling; $20 for 1-tank dive trips; $5 for glass-bottom boat trip. **When:** Year-round. **Contact:** Scuba Safari, Hilton Dr., St. Michael, Barbados, West Indies; phone 60621.

British Virgin Islands

Virgin Islands Diving: Introductory scuba courses and underwater diving trips in the British Virgin Islands are arranged according to the desires of the divers. The introductory course consists of training on land followed by a shallow-water dive to practice skills. Students dive at over 50 dive sites, including the wreck of the *Rhone,* sunk in 1867. Both underwater photography and marine biology instruction are available by arrangement. In the interest of conservation no spearfishing, lobstering or taking of live coral is permitted. **Cost:** $50 for diving course, $25 to $40 for dive trips includes equipment, boat, guide. **When:** Year-round. **Contact:** Kilbrides Underwater Tours, Box 40, Virgin Gorda, British Virgin Islands; phone 42746. ***(M)***

Custom Dives: The British Virgin Islands are the setting for scuba tours, instruction and photography. Time spent underwater and dive sites visited depend on the experience and preferences of divers involved. Depths can vary from 10 to 140 feet in over 60 diving locations, with all activity based on Tortola. Full equipment rentals are available, along with 3-hour instruction periods and underwater photography sessions. For all activities equipment is included in the package prices. Group rates are available on request. Dive trips generally last a half day and leave from Road Harbor twice daily. **Cost:** $24 to $40 for scuba tours and instruction; $40 to $475 for photography-oriented trip. **When:** Year-round. **Contact:** Marler Industries Ltd., P.O. Box 108, Road Town, Tortola, British Virgin Islands; phone 42839.

Cayman Islands

Photography for Divers: A 7-day course for scuba divers interested in underwater photography is offered in the waters of Grand Cayman. A typical day begins around 7 a.m. with a review of the previous day's photography. Then participants travel to Spanish Bay Reef for an underwater session. After lunch another session is held, then 2 to 3 hours of lecture and discussion follow on various aspects of underwater picture-taking followed by a session on night photography. Topics include composition, photo-biology, strobe work and maintenance of underwater equipment. **Cost:** $689 includes accommodations, meals, tank, backpack, weights, instruction. **When:** February, March. **Contact:** Jim and Cathy Church, P.O. Box 80, Gilroy, CA 95020, USA; phone (408)842-9682.

The wreck of the Balboa *is one of the most popular dive sites off Grand Cayman. Divers can choose from a number of trips that explore the reefs and wrecks around the island.* (Sea Life Discovery)

Biology Course for Divers: A marine biology course on tropical reef ecology is being offered to divers at Grand Cayman in the British West Indies. This is a chance for divers with little or no science background to learn about the varied marine life of the reefs. The college-level course, taught by professional marine biologists, combines informal classroom discussions illustrated with slides and guided underwater field trips to Cayman's prolific reefs. The 10-day trip provides ample time for diving and photography. **Cost:** $950 includes accommodations, meals, diving, instruction. **When:** June. Later dates to be announced. **Contact:** Sea Life Discovery, 19915-A Oakmont Dr., Los Gatos, CA 95030, USA; phone (408)353-1766.

Above and Below Water: A variety of diving and sailing experiences is offered in Grand Cayman, part of the British West Indies. Basic training is available in both of these sports, as well as expedition equipment for those interested in exploring the surrounding waters. Scuba diving classes last 6 days and include full certification. Day and half-day trips are available in which divers observe the tropical fish and coral. A 40-foot motor sailboat can also be chartered for a moonlight cruise with dinner served onboard, or for inter-island trips of 3 days or longer. Small sailboats can be used for individual itineraries. **Cost:** $187 for 6-day scuba course, $8 an hour for sailing instruction; other prices on request. **When:** Year-round. **Contact:** Surfside Watersports, P.O. Box 26, Grand Cayman, British West Indies; phone 9-2724.

Dominican Republic

Caribbean Scuba Diving: Six full days of diving are offered along the coastal waters of Santo Domingo. Setting out by boat from beachfront accommodations, a maximum of 20 participants dive the warm Caribbean waters in a variety of marine settings. Divers make close observations of colorful tropical fish and underwater scenery. The city of Santo Domingo itself was founded in 1496 and is the oldest settlement by Europeans in the Western Hemisphere. Both divers and non-divers may explore the city, including its ancient cathedral where the ashes of Columbus are reputedly buried. **Cost:** $385 for divers includes boats, tanks, weights, guides, lunches, accommodations; $299 for non-divers. **When:** Year-round. **Contact:** Aquaventures, P.O. Box 1816, Max Henriquez Urena No. 89, Santo Domingo, Dominican Republic; phone 566-7608.

Haiti

Arcadin Diving: Upon arrival in Port au Prince, participants commence an 8-day diving journey to the Arcadin Islands. Individuals board dive boats which transport them to the Arcadin Islands where they explore the 40-foot stands of brightly colored coral rising off the white sand bottoms. Shuttling to and from the hotel and dive spots, divers explore the outer fringes of the coral cays, often inhabited by huge manta rays and other varieties of tropical fish. Night dives are optional. Divers visit the islands of La Gonave to view the huge underwater escarpment abounding in sea life. Participants witness voodoo ceremonies after a full day of snorkeling and skin diving off the village shore. Since no strong currents occur in the Arcadin Cays, divers may leisurely explore the brilliantly lit crystal coral caves. Participants head back to the 45-mile-long wall of La Gonave where they may drift through natural aqueducts worn through the living coral. Participants return by air to Miami. **Cost:** $389 from Port au Prince includes accommodations. **When:** On request. **Contact:** Poseidon Ventures Tours, 359 San Miguel Dr., Newport Beach, CA 92660, USA; phone (714)644-5373.

Jamaica

Ocho Rios Diving: The town of Ocho Rios is the setting for an 8-day diving and recreational trip. Beginners can take an introductory course and those with some experience can dive right in, using a dive boat to reach some of the area's richest spots. Other activities available include tennis, sailing, glass-bottom boat trips, viewing exhibits of native dances and ceremonies, tours through local plantations, golf, cruising and individual exploring. Divers can also take an NASDS scuba certification course involving 6 pool sessions and 6 supervised open water dives. Participants stay in a hotel. **Cost:** $292

Divers can spend 8 days in the clear waters of the Netherlands Antilles for $715. Sea Life Discovery's experienced leaders guide participants through the colorful marine environment. (Bonaire Tourist Information Office)

to $499, depending on type of accommodations and meal plan; $175 for certification course. **When:** Year-round. **Contact:** Caribbean Holidays, Inc., 711 Third Ave., New York, NY 10017, USA.

Netherlands Antilles

Underwater in the Netherlands Antilles: A marine biologist and NAUI scuba instructor accompany participants to Bonaire for diving and snorkeling. Group members meet in Miami, then set up home base in a hotel overlooking the southern Caribbean. For the next 8 days the group dives by day and night amid coral, sponges and schools of friendly fish. Snorkelers are welcome, too, with plenty of time allowed for swimming at white sand beaches, island excursions and photography. On the final day participants have the option of making excursions to Aruba, Curacao and South America or returning to Miami. All trips take a naturalistic approach to diving and offer informal study of marine life with knowledgeable and experienced leaders. **Cost:** $715 for divers, $630 for snorkelers includes all meals, double-occupancy accommodations, guided reef trips, unlimited diving, land tours. **When:** July. **Contact:** Sea Life Discovery, Inc., 19915-A Oakmont Dr., Los Gatos, CA 95030, USA; phone (408)353-1766.

Puerto Rico

Submerging in Vieques: Charter diving trips can be arranged with a dive center located on the Caribbean coast of Vieques Island. Groups of no more than 6 divers set up a home base in the small fishing village of Esperanza, then venture out among growing coral reefs in a 36-foot dive boat. Chances are that the group is the sole scuba expedition on the island. Participants and instructor/guides determine an itinerary based on the group members' desires and skills. Diving courses are offered year-round for the total beginner and for those at more advanced levels as well. Accommodations are available at 3 guest houses near the beach. **Cost:** $25 for a 2-tank dive, $15 for a single; $10 to $30 a night for accommodations. **When:** Year-round. **Contact:** Vieques Divers, Duffy's Esperanza, Isla Vieques, PR 00765, USA.

St. Kitts

St. Kitts Diving: Eight days on the island of St. Kitts, the first English settlement in the Caribbean, allow time for 4 dives in the region's waters and some exploration of the island. The area was the site of many naval battles in the 16th and 17th centuries, and divers still find battle remnants. The reef life is rich and largely untouched, with many areas even unexplored; searches are currently underway for the remains of James Town, a city alleged to have sunk during an earthquake in the 16th century. Diving instruction can also be arranged. Another dive package, lasting 4 days, also features 4 dives. **Cost:** $295 for 8 days, $160 for 4 days includes 2 meals a day, accommodations, equipment, 4 dives, guide. **When:** Year-round. **Contact:** Ocean Terrace Inn, P.O. Box 65, Fortlands, St. Kitts, West Indies; phone 2754.

St. Vincent

Diving off St. Vincent: A week-long package provides complete accommodations and daily diving in the Caribbean. The area features clear water and abundant marine life. Non-diving activities available include hiking and visiting the recently active volcano, Soufriere. Diving instruction and certification, from level 1 to level 4, are also offered. All diving equipment may be rented. Trips may also be arranged to nearby islands. **Cost:** From $217 to $243 depending on accommodations and meal plan. **When:** Year-round. **Contact:** Dive St. Vincent Ltd., Box 864, St. Vincent, West Indies.

Trinidad & Tobago

Private Dives: A small resort on Tobago offers a private beach, landscaped grounds, diving boats and equipment and other facilities on a week-long diving trip leaving from Toronto. Every day is spent diving the reef just offshore, with all equipment supplied. Photographers, naturalists, recreational divers and even non-divers can enjoy the high-visibility water and abundant marine life. Other activities include tennis, glass-bottom boat rides, exploratory hikes and swimming. A non-diver package is also offered that includes glass-bottom boat trips or scuba diving instruction. **Cost:** $599 for divers, $519 for non-divers includes transportation from Toronto, most meals, accommodations, activities, equipment. **When:** Year-round. **Contact:** Scuba Consultants Travel, 1370 Clyde Ave., Ottawa, ON Canada K2G 3H8; phone (613)226-1207.

U.S. Virgin Islands

From Beachside to the Deep: Exploration of countless reefs around St. Thomas is offered during a variety of instructional and open water dives with the oldest certified diving school on the island. Available are reef dives by day and night from various beaches as well as shallow water training which includes comprehensive pre-dive orientation and instruction. **Cost:** $22 to $35 includes dives or instruction, transportation, equipment; discounts are available for those with their own gear. **When:** Year-round. **Contact:** Joe Vogel Diving Co., Box 7322, St. Thomas, VI 00801; phone (809)774-2321.

Scuba Courses in the Caribbean: Beginning and experienced divers visiting the Virgin Islands can upgrade their scuba techniques and certification levels in courses that cover basic instruction and work up to skills at the divemaster's level. The basic scuba certification course involves 24 hours of instruction spread out over 6 days, with time divided between classroom sessions and actual diving experience near Coki Point. From there, students go on to open water and night diving courses, or they can choose from a variety of guided scuba tours through the coral forests of the reef off St. Thomas or to shipwrecks along the coast. **Cost:** $75 to $300 for courses includes all transportation to dive sites, all equipment. **When:** On request. **Contact:** Virgin Islands Diving School, P.O. Box 9707, St. Thomas, VI 00801, USA; phone (809)774-8687.

CENTRAL AMERICA

Belize

Private Island Diving: Located approximately 15 miles off the coast of Belize, a 1,200-acre island is available exclusively to divers. An 8-day stay allows for thorough exploration of the nearby waters which

The coastline and offshore reefs of the U.S. Virgin Islands await divers year-round. Joe Vogel Diving Co. offers beach, reef and wreck diving, as well as instruction. (Carol Baker)

include a 176-mile-long reef a mile off shore. The water temperature is 85°F, the visibility is 200 feet and the diving accommodations are directly at the water's edge. Tropical fish observation, lobster hunting, sightseeing and photography may be enjoyed. **Cost:** $670 from Little Rock includes transportation, meals, accommodations, tanks, weights, boats, all diving. **When:** Year-round. **Contact:** Cap'n Frogs of Arkansas, Inc., 11401 Rodhey Parham, Little Rock, AR 72212, USA; phone (501)227-9005.

Caribbean Barrier Reef Diving: The world's longest, "living" barrier reef is only a half-mile off Ambergris Caye, a 26-mile-long island in the Caribbean. Here divers can create their own customized diving experience with the assistance of experienced local divers. Adventurers reach the island by small plane or boat from Belize and stay at a comfortable rustic hotel. Certified divers have access to waters with visibility up to 250 feet, reef canyons, holes and special "blue holes" reached by float plane. Participants need only bring lightweight gear since tanks, belts, packs, weights, fins, snorkels and even boats can be rented. Protected snorkeling inside the great barrier reef, underwater photography, beachcombing, deep sea fishing for tarpon, marlin and barracuda and bird watching are other activities which trip members may enjoy. Local guides are available for interests ranging from coastal exploration and jungle trekking to high sea adventures. **Cost:** $35 to $45 for single room, $50 to $70 for double, depending on season, includes meals. **When:** Year-round. **Contact:** Casa Solana, Rt. 1, Box 40, Palacios, TX 77465, USA; phone (512)972-3314.

Gulf of Honduras Scuba: The second longest barrier reef in the world can be explored off the coast of Belize on a series of dives in the Gulf of Honduras. Diving trips for a minimum of 8 divers are offered including a 4-dive trip in local waters and a 2-day trip to the famous Belizean blue hole for 2 compression dives. Caves, drop-offs and wrecks are explored, and an abundance of native Caribbean marine life can be seen and photographed. Opportunities are also available to dive at Turneffe Island and its 250-fathom coral drop-offs. **Cost:** $50 to $65 a day includes 3 meals, tanks, air, backpacks, weights. **Contact:** Club 99 Scuba-Belize, P.O. Box 164, Belize City, Belize.

Ambergris Caye Underwater Caving: Northeast of Belize City, the small island of Ambergris Caye is the launching point for sailing, snorkeling and scuba diving in warm Caribbean waters. The second largest barrier reef in the world lies a quarter mile off the white sand beaches that extend from the hotel/dive center where travelers stay. Inexperienced divers can snorkel and free dive in shallow, protected waters alive with tropical fish. Visibility is seldom less than 50 feet and caves, cuts, drop-offs and coral forests are all accessible. The fish are easy to approach, and divers equipped with underwater cameras can get close-ups without special lenses. With almost 500 species of birds in Belize, bird watchers have a chance to see some unique forms such as the great curassow, the keel-billed toucan and jabiru stork. Special trips can be arranged for ornithologists. **Cost:** $18 to $35 for accommodations, meals; $55 for full day, $35 for half-day includes boat rental for 4 persons. **When:** Year-round. **Contact:** Paradise House Hotel, P.O. Box 888, Belize City, Belize; phone 2403.

Honduras

Diving the Gulf Stream: Clear-water diving enthusiasts stay at a resort on the island of Roatan off the coast of Honduras and make dives on either side of a barrier reef whose outer edge is washed by Gulf Stream waters. Visitors discover a variety of caves, ledges, fish and coral species on their scuba explorations, with guides suggesting spots likely to be of interest. The island, largest of the Honduran Bay Islands, was once a hide-out for pirates, and divers are encouraged to watch for signs of undiscovered shipwrecks. Since the barrier reef is still an unspoiled undersea environment, divers are prohibited from coral picking, live shelling or using spear guns when they explore it. Land-based activities on the 33-mile-long island include room, meals, boats, guides, snorkeling equipment, small sailboats, transportation to and from Roatan Airport. **When:** Year-round. **Contact:** Anthony's Key Resort, P.O. Box 18412, Dallas, TX 75218, USA; phone (214)328-4244. *(M)*

Roatan Roaming: Three different resorts in Roatan accommodate divers for week-long stays. One resort faces directly onto a reef containing every type of formation found in the Caribbean. Open-air beachfront bungalows house divers at another resort, where the diving is done by boat. The third resort is set in the middle of a 35-mile barrier reef, on a 30-acre botanical garden. **Cost:** $210 to $359 plus airfare includes 7 days' diving, accommodations, most meals. **When:** Year-round. **Contact:** Bay Travel Diving Adventures, 2435 E. Coast Hwy., Corona del Mar, CA 92625, USA; phone (714)675-4321. *(M)*

Coral Reef Diving: The exploration of a spectacular variety of coral, sponge and fish life is readily available off the shore of Roatan in the Caribbean. Anthony's Key Resort, where accommodations are arranged for 7 nights, is midway between 20 miles of coral reef. There are at least 30 distinct diving areas within 15 minutes of the resort. Among these is West End Point where there is an abundance of colorful sponges, groupers and angel fish. At Bear's Den, an opening in about 30 feet of water leads to a 200-foot complex of caves and caverns. Each morning, divers and

guides meet to pick that day's dive spots. The package also includes a night dive, sailing and horseback riding. Airfare is not included and participants must provide mask, fins, and regulator. **Cost:** $359 for divers, $269 for non-divers. **When:** March. **Contact:** Go Diving, Inc., 715 Florida Ave. S., Minneapolis, MN 55426, USA; phone (612)544-7168. *(M)*

Remote Island Adventure: A resort village on Roatan Island, largest of the 3 Islas de la Bahia (Bay Islands) off the coast of Honduras, becomes the living quarters for those wishing to explore the island environment for any period of time. More than 700 varieties of colorful tropical fish and 8 or 9 kinds of parrotfish alone can be observed in the clear waters of the Caribbean. Sunken vessels plundered by Henry Morgan, a notorious pirate of the 17th century, await diver exploration. Picnic or hiking trips can be arranged to the nearby ruins of 1,000-year-old Mayan villages. The climate in Roatan is pleasant year-round due to the trade winds, ocean currents and proximity of the 9,000-foot coastal mountain ranges. **Cost:** $35 to $45 a day depending on accommodations; 1-week scuba packages available. **When:** Year-round. **Contact:** Reef House Resort, Oakridge Harbor, Roatan Island, Honduras.

Islas de la Bahia Diving: A resort on the Roatan Bay Islands, off the north coast of Honduras, offers scuba and skin diving, snorkeling and swimming opportunities. Divers and non-divers alike may enjoy other activities such as boating, hiking, horseback riding and the study of Mayan archaeology. A 32-mile-long reef protects the area, and the islands are virtually free of insects. The average temperature varies between 81°F in the day and 69°F in the night, with the water temperature at 80°F. **Cost:** $30 to $55 a day depending on accommodations and time of year includes meals, equipment. **When:** Year-round. **Contact:** Spyglass Hill, c/o Roseo Affiliates, 630 N. Western Ave., Lake Forest, IL 60045, USA; phone (312)234-2222.

Panama

Panamanian Plunge: Scuba divers explore the waters off the isthmus for 10 days. Starting from Baltimore, the group flies to Panama City for a 2-day stay at the El Panama Hotel. Then 7 days are spent on Isla Grande exploring its coral-filled waters. Starting from around 40 feet below the surface, the reefs run mainly to black coral areas that teem with tropical fish. Fishing is included, as is a New Year's Eve party and a tour of the Miraflores Locks. Two tank dives a day are scheduled; air refills are unlimited. The group returns to Baltimore on the tenth day. **Cost:** $749 includes airfare, meals on Isla Grande, accommodations. **When:** December. **Contact:** Divers Den, Inc., 8105 Harford Rd., Baltimore, MD 21234, USA; phone (301)668-6866 or 668-6869.

EUROPE

Malta

The Maltese Aquan: Divers explore Mediterranean marine life on short trips offered by a dive center on the northeast Maltese coast near Valletta. Novices in a hurry can take a 2-hour course that enables them to dive in shallow waters; a 6-hour course covers more specific diving and safety techniques. Day and half-day trips from shore or by inflatable boat and longer day trips to the neighboring islands of Comino and Gozo aboard a 40-foot dive boat are available. Other services include diving equipment sales and rentals, small sailboat rentals, and instruction and equipment for windsurfing. **Cost:** $9 for guided shore dives, $25 for Comino trips, $12 for basic instruction; other rates on request. **When:** Year-round. **Contact:** Divewise Services Ltd., Charles House, New St., Birzebbugia, Malta; phone 871353.

INDIAN OCEAN

Maldive Islands

Spice Islands Diving: Living aboard a 74-foot motor sailboat with a crew of 10, divers have the opportunity to experience the rich diving region of the Maldive Islands off the southwest coast of India. Diving sites include the steep outer slopes where big pelagic fish drift by, shallow coral gardens resplendent with a myriad of tropical fish, and passes where sharks gather. Land exploration takes place on Sri Lanka, with visits to tea plantations in the mountains, the Sigirya fortress and Polommaruwa, site of a sophisticated civilization 800 years ago. **Cost:** $1,450 plus airfare includes all expenses aboard the boat. **When:** August. **Contact:** See and Sea Travel Service, Inc., 680 Beach St., Suite 340, ,Wharfside, San Francisco, CA 94109, USA; phone (415)771-0077.

MEXICO

Baja California

Underwater Photo Course: A week aboard a fully equipped dive boat in the Sea of Cortez provides the opportunity for divers to take a complete course in the art of underwater photography. Participants meet in San Diego, California and spend a night there before flying to La Paz and boarding the boat. They then cruise the scenic, clear waters of the area with a professional marine photographer while learning underwater camera techniques. A variety of equipment and film processing facilities are onboard, so students can inspect their own work soon after shooting. At the end of 6 days the boat docks in La Paz and the party returns to San Diego. **Cost:** $995 includes transportation from San Diego, food, accommodations, equipment, instruction. **When:** March. **Contact:** Silent World Divers, Inc., 14444 SE Eastgate Wy., Bellevue, WA 98007, USA; phone (206)747-8842.

Guerrero

Las Gatas Sea Camp: At a beach club accessible only by boat from the town of Zihuatanejo across the bay, participants study the marine environment and take part in a variety of sea-related activities. Zihuatanejo can be reached by road from Acapulco 120 miles to the south, or via a 35-minute flight from Mexico City. Group members can stay from 1 to 6 weeks, living on the beach in palm thatched bungalows. Everyone is expected to pitch in and help with camp maintenance, shopping and logistics in addition to taking part in educational and recreational activities. These include gathering information on local marine life, practicing life saving and first aid, learning to sail and going on scuba and skin diving excursions off Las Gatas Beach. Overnight cruises and campouts are also part of the curriculum. A scuba certification program is available, but in order to take part group members must stay a minimum of 3 weeks. **Cost:** $200 per week, $1,000 for 6 weeks, includes meals, sailboat and scuba gear, biology and marine ecology courses, accommodations, instructors; $140 for scuba certification. **When:** July, August. **Contact:** Travel Plans International, 1301 W. 22nd St., Oak Brook, IL 60521, USA; phone (312)986-0330.

Quintana Roo

Yucatan Scuba Trips: Cozumel, on the Caribbean edge of the Yucatan Peninsula, is the setting for 4- to 9-day diving excursions that combine scuba lessons with guided dives along the coastal reefs. Arriving from Houston, enthusiasts dive areas such as Palancar Reef or Santa Rosa Reef, a spectacular wall dive down a steep ocean slope. Water temperatures remain around 75°F, with a 200-foot visibility that provides good conditions for underwater photographers. Novices may take a complete scuba course in Cozumel during trips of 7 days or longer; skills are practiced in Chancanab Lagoon, followed by classroom sessions and beach dives. The last 2 days of the course involve check-out dives off the boat. Divers should bring all their own equipment except for tanks and weights, which are provided. **Cost:** $239 to $325 includes roundtrip airfare from Houston, tanks, weights, lunch on diving days, guide, boat. **When:** April to December. **Contact:** Blue Water Diving School, 910 Westheimer, Houston, TX 77006, USA; phone (713)528-0634.

Diving Inn: Excellent visibility, year-round warm water, spectacular reefs and abundant sea life make the island of Cozumel a top-rated diving area. A beach-front inn provides 4- and 8-day packages for scuba divers and snorkelers wishing to explore the area. Divers take boat trips with bilingual guides to such nearby spots as Palancar with its coral reefs, Maracaibo with its groupers and game fish, and Paradise with its king crabs. Novices can dive the easier shallow reefs, while experienced divers explore labyrinthine drop-offs, caves and tunnels. **Cost:** $105 for snorkelers, $125 for scuba divers for 4 days; $249 for snorkelers, $299 for scuba divers for 8 days includes dives, boat, diving equipment, all meals, accommodations. **When:** Year-round. **Contact:** Galapago Inn Dive Resort, Apartado Postal 289, Cozumel, Quintana Roo, Mexico; phone (987)2-06-63.

Diving Palancar: Spectacular Palancar Reef, off Cozumel, is explored daily on a week-long dive trip. Staying in a beach-front hotel and taking meals there or in town, participants depart from the dock each morning at about 9:30 and travel out to the reef, which offers a wide variety of diving spots within a short distance. Palancar is a huge reef with giant pinnacles, 100-foot walls covered by sponges and gorgonians and numerous caves and arches; one area of the reef off Santa Rosa Beach is famous for its large schools of rays. Divers can either explore the reef's interior or "drift dive" along its outer edge, being carried gently along by the current. In addition, a few minutes' walk from the hotel is shallow Little Paradise Reef, where wade-in diving reveals a fascinating closed ecological system. **Cost:** On request. **When:** On request. **Contact:** Go Diving, Inc., 715 Florida Ave. S., Minneapolis, MN 55426, USA; phone (612)644-7168. ***(M)***

MIDDLE EAST

Israel

Red Sea Diving: Two dive centers, one in Elat and the other in Sharm el Sheikh, provide divers with access to the waters of the Red Sea. Complete services are offered, including certification instruction to YMCA, PADI and CMAS standards; guided dive outings for experienced divers; night dives; introductory dive trips for beginners; and a full line of rental equipment. Day and overnight camping excursions are available to a number of sites on the Red Sea. Also, a 6-day trip departing from Elat and finishing in Ras Muhammed provides opportunities for daily dives from a fully equipped dive boat. Camel rides and desert tours can be arranged in addition to the underwater activities. **Cost:** $25 for guided dive, $126 for certification course; other rates on request. **When:** Year-round. **Contact:** Lucky Divers, Elat Scuba Center, Ltd., Moriah-Elat Hotel, Gulf of the Red Sea, Israel; phone (059)5749.

Gulf of Aqaba Diving: Participants explore coral reefs in the Gulf of Aqaba, north of the Red Sea in either of two 7-day diving trips. These reefs are distinguished by the abundance of large umbrella corals and lavishly colored soft corals, and lionfish are present in large numbers. Both trips start with 2 days diving in the Neviot area, using the facilities of the Neviot Diving Center. From here members of the Ras Abu Galum trip proceed to the reefs of Hibiek, Suchoon, Ras Mamlach and Ras Abu Galum; on the Ras Muhammed trip members dive at Dhabab Oasis, Nabec Oasis, Sharm el Sheikh and Ras Muhammed. **Cost:** $300 for Ras Abu Galum, $330 for Ras Muhammed includes transportation from Elat, accommodations, guides, equipment, most meals. **When:** Year-round. **Contact:** Neviot Diving Center, Neviot Holiday Village, Neviot Post Elat, Israel; phone 059-3667; or La Mer Diving Seafaris, Inc., 823 UN Plaza, Suite 810, New York, NY 10017 USA; phone (212)599-0886.

United Arab Emirates

Persian Gulf Plunges: Divers on 7- and 9-day trips ply the waters of the Persian Gulf and the Gulf of Oman. The week-long trip begins in Dubai with a wreck dive in the Persian Gulf before proceeding to Fujairah for day and night dives in the Gulf of Oman. Some sightseeing is done between dives including Fahal Island before the trip finishes in Muscat. The longer trip is identical to the above but also spends a night on Seeb Island, famous for its blue falcons but also boasting a virgin reef where giant turtles, sting rays and other marine creatures live. **Cost:** On request. **When:** On request. **Contact:** Kanoo Travel Agency, P.O. Box 153, Sharjah, United Arab Emirates.

During a 17-day See & Sea Travel Service trip to the Fiji Islands, participants have an opportunity to dive both charted and unexplored reefs, caverns, and sandy bottoms inhabited by a variety of sea life. (Carl Roessler/See & Sea Travel Service, Inc.)

PACIFIC

Fiji

Exploring Fiji: For 2 weeks divers explore various locations in the Fiji archipelago, staying in local hotels and traveling aboard a fully equipped dive boat. The first major stop after a flight from the U.S. via Tahiti is Suva, where a large coral wall is located. Here divers can explore black coral trees and stands of gorgonia surrounded by colorful fish that can be hand-fed. After 5 days the trip proceeds to Gega Island, where a nearby dive site features 200-foot visibility. Other stops on the itinerary are Herald Pass, with its interesting underwater archway on the north side and dramatic 100-foot drop-off on the south; Osborne Pass, which hosts an unusual diversity of marine life including Spanish mackerel, sharks and barracudas; and finally Toberua Island, reached by a launch trip down the Wainibokasi River. Experienced guides accompany the trip and provide instruction where necessary. **Cost:** $1,600 includes airfare from the west coast of the U.S., accommodations, transportation, equipment, guides. **When:** Year-round. **Contact:** Poseidon Ventures Tours, 359 San Miguel Dr., Newport Beach, CA 92660, USA; phone (714)644-5373.

Scuba Diving off Fiji: Diving is available on a day-to-day or extended basis in the wide variety of reefs and holes around Fiji. Frequent

Custom scuba trips with Scubahire take divers to a variety of reefs around Fiji for as little as $4 a day. (Scubahire)

trips are made to the water surrounding the Beqa Barrier Reef and the Lau Group, renowned for its high visibility, abundance of marine life and uncrowded conditions. Diving may also be done from the beach. All equipment is available for hire, from tanks and regulators to charter boats and a decompression chamber. **Cost:** $4 a day, $15 a week for tanks. **When:** Year-round. **Contact:** Scubahire Ltd., GPO Box 777, Suva, Fiji; phone 361-241. ***(M)***

Diving in the Fiji Islands: For 17 days divers explore the waters around Mana and Taveuni islands, which only recently acquired diving facilities. Participants spend full diving days at Rainbow Reef on Taveuni Island, whose 19-mile-long coral structure remains largely unexplored. The reef face is a precipitous drop-off interlaced with crevices, caverns and large overhangs. Sea life is bountiful, and over the drop-off are found jacks, turtles, groupers and a few sharks. After a crossing to Mana Island, divers lunch in the afternoon and snorkel in the waters offshore. The next 4 days offer opportunities to dive to a dozen or more local reefs that rise to within 15 to 20 feet of the surface and drop to a sandy bottom at about 100 to 150 feet. **Cost:** $1,500 plus airfare. **When:** On request. **Contact:** See and Sea Travel Service, Inc., 680 Beach St., Suite 340, Wharfside, San Francisco, CA 94109, USA; phone (415)771-0077.

French Polynesia

Moorea Plunge: Divers travel to the Tahitian islands on a 7- to 10-day excursion. Starting from Papeete, participants catch a flight to the island of Moorea, where divers explore the deep coves and coral barrier reefs surrounding the island. Above water, activities include hiking to native villages, snorkeling, fishing, sailing and taking glass-bottomed boat tours. Divers should bring a lightweight wet suit, regulator, fins, mask, snorkel, depth gauge and buoyancy compensator. **Cost:** $420 to $595 includes meals, accommodations, 1 dive a day. **When:** May to September. **Contact:** Bay Travel Diving Adventures, 2435 E. Coast Hwy., Corona del Mar, CA 92625, USA; phone (714)675-4321. ***(M)***

Hawaii

Islands Diving Cruise: Divers visit up to 5 of the Hawaiian Islands on diving trips lasting 2 to 7 days. The islands, including Hawaii, Molokai, Maui and Lanai, are famous for their underwater cathedrals. Molokini, a small uninhabited island, features an extinct volcano suitable for swimming and diving. From an equipped dive boat, participants swim in 15 to 75 feet of water. Experienced divers can take deeper and more technical dives which include exploration of a sunken submarine at 130 feet and underwater caves. **Cost:** $209 to $595 all-inclusive. **When:** Year-round. **Contact:** Pacific Sportdiving Co., Inc., 4104 E. Anaheim St., Long Beach, CA 90804, USA; phone (213)433-7485.

Micronesia

Micronesia Underseas: Fifteen-day journeys to the diving areas of Palau and Truk islands bring scuba enthusiasts to waters featuring tropical coral reefs, graveyards of sunken Japanese warships, caves and giant clams that weigh nearly a half ton. At Palau, an atoll measuring about 62 miles long and 12 miles wide, participants explore a lagoon filled with 350 tiny islands that form a pattern of waterways, canals and secluded beaches. At Truk divers enter artificial reefs containing more than 40 ships of the Imperial Japanese fleet, including the *Fijikawa Maru*, a 436-foot aircraft ferry. **Cost:** $750 to $900 includes accommodations; airfare extra. **When:** June to September. **Contact:** Poseidon Venture Tours, 359 San Miguel Dr., Newport Beach, CA 92660, USA; phone (714)644-5373.

Truk Divers: Two of Micronesia's best diving spots are visited on a 3-week trip from Los Angeles. Flying via Hawaii, divers spend 8 days diving Truk Lagoon where more than 60 Japanese warships sunk during World War II wait to be explored. Protected by a great reef encircling the lagoon, the wrecks provide habitats for a diversity of sea life. Then, after a day's diving in Guam, the trip moves to Palau. After 6 days here travelers return to Los Angeles via Guam and Hawaii. Nights are spent in hotels. **Cost:** $2,912 includes transportation from Los Angeles, food, accommodations, guide. **When:** June. **Contact:** Sea Life Discovery, Inc., 19915-A Oakmont Dr., Los Gatos, CA 95030, USA; phone (408)353-1766.

New Hebrides

Port Vila Diving: Well-preserved wrecks, extensive coral formations and colorful marine life are within reach on dive trips out of Port Vila Harbor. A dive shop there offers a complete range of underwater services, including sale and rental of equipment, boat charters and regularly scheduled trips. Among the dive spots normally visited are Paradise Cove, Hat Island and Eratap Lagoon, where tunnels and blue holes await the scuba enthusiast. Divers can explore 2 wrecks lying intact in Port Vila Harbor, one a 2,000-ton 3-masted bark with a steel hull and the other a 4-engine flying boat. Trips are tailored to fit both novice and advanced divers. Snorkelers can also take full- and half-day trips to shallow water areas. **Cost:** $27 for half-day dive, $37 for full-day includes air, transportation from hotel, refreshments; other rates on request. **When:** Year-round. **Contact:** Nautilus Dive Shop, B.P. 78, Port Vila, New Hebrides.

SOUTH AMERICA

Colombia

Windward Diving: The windward side of Isla de San Andres is the setting for a resort-based diving trip that lasts a week. Two daily dives are made for 4 days, with the remaining time spent either touring the island by bicycle or car, or snorkeling and swimming in the sea or pool. Diving spots include one of the world's largest walls, a long coastline of shallow water dotted with numerous small inlets, black coral caves, and the waters around Isla de Providencia. An identical non-diver package is also offered, as is scuba certification instruction. **Cost:** $215 to $345 for divers, $110 to $235 for non-divers, depending on meal plan, includes accommodations, diving equipment. **When:** Year-round. **Contact:** Scuba Consultants Travel, 1370 Clyde Ave., Ottawa, ON Canada K2G 3H8; phone (613)226-1207.

Ecuador

Underwater Archipelago Wandering: Undersea life is as spectacular and unusual as terrestrial creatures seen by divers spending 18 days exploring the Galapagos Islands. After a day in Quito, participants fly to Baltra Island and board the 70-foot staysail schooner, *Encantada*. The diving ranges from shallow reefs to sheer pinnacles rising from the sea floor. Accompanied by a professional dive master and local naturalist, participants have the chance to investigate it all in 1 to 3 daily dives; they make 1 or 2 shore excursions every day and maximize time ashore and underwater by frequent night sailings. Near Punta Vicente Roca on Isabela Island, divers spot whales and ocean sunfish and explore a large cave filled with brilliantly colored gorgonia, sea anemone, coral and a bright yellow species of black coral. Participants spend 1 night ashore and make frequent day trips to hike and visit places such as the Charles Darwin Research Station at Academy Bay which houses the large land tortoises. An overnight stay in Quito concludes the trip. **Cost:** $2,300 from Quito includes transportation, meals, accommodations, guides, tanks, backpacks, weights. **When:** March to July. **Contact:** See and Sea Travel Service Inc., 680

Beach St., Suite 340, Wharfside, San Francisco, CA 94109, USA; phone (415)771-0077.

UNITED STATES

Alaska

Sub-Arctic Scuba: Diving courses at the University of Alaska and weekend trips to coastal diving locations provide the hardy undersea enthusiast with opportunities to explore Alaska's offshore regions. The best diving is around Seward, but other areas considered good for scuba activities include portions of the coastline around Homer, Juneau, Ketchikan and Whittier. Outfitting for most trips must be arranged through either Anchorage or Fairbanks, where diving shops have been set up to provide essential undersea gear. **Cost:** On request. **When:** On request. **Contact:** Alaska Sub-Arctic Dive Club, SR 3, Box 31136, Fairbanks, AK 99701, USA.

Arizona

Diver's Education: Scuba diving classes and organized diving trips are offered to underwater enthusiasts in Arizona. Classes are limited to 10 people and consist of 7 sessions equally divided between classroom and pool. In addition, there are 7 extra pool sessions where students work on building skills and confidence. Included in the course are 2 separate diving trips: a 1-day freshwater dive and a 2-day dive near Guaymas or Sonora, Mexico, or San Diego, California. After graduating from the basic course, divers may take underwater photography courses and advanced diving courses and participate in the school's recreation and dive travel club. Trips are sponsored to places such as Catalina Island, San Pedro Island, San Carlos in Mexico and Belize. **Cost:** On request. **When:** Year-round. **Contact:** Tucson School of Scuba Diving, Scuba Cove, 3575 E. Speedway, Tucson, AZ 85716, USA; phone (602)795-1140.

California

Ocean Diving near Monterey: In a series of 5 classes, divers with basic skills receive formal instruction in diving the open waters of the Pacific. On a 2-day trip to Monterey, students take a maximum of 4 classes, all beach dives, followed by a boat dive in the fifth lesson. Each class focuses on a skill which must be mastered before moving onto the next level. Divers learn safe ocean diving techniques, how to handle currents, and what to do in emergency situations. Underwater photography classes and basic courses taught in pools are also available. **Cost:** $60 for 5 classes. **When:** Weekends. **Contact:** Ed Brawley's Skin Diving School, 598 Foam St., Monterey, CA 93940, USA; phone (408)373-1377.

San Clemente Dive: Participants take a basic NAUI course as an introduction to scuba diving, studying equipment, safety, medical aspects, buddy systems and diving techniques. The course work occurs over a 4- to 6-week period and includes 6 classroom, 6 pool and 4 ocean sessions. Students must provide their own mask, fins, snorkel and booties. All other equipment is provided for the pool dives; students must rent tanks and other deep-sea equipment for the ocean dives. Once certified, divers qualify for half-day and 2-day expeditions offered on weekends. **Cost:** $50 for basic instruction; $8 for half-day, $44 for 2-day expeditions. **When:** On request. **Contact:** San Clemente Diving Center Inc., 129 Calle de los Molinos, San Clemente, CA 92672, USA; phone (714)496-2444.

Colorado

Rocky Mountain Diving: A wide variety of scuba courses involving both pool and open water work caters to the divergent needs of diving students. A private comprehensive course includes 6 lectures, 6 pool sessions and unlimited practice at the student's convenience. A similar session is also available for groups. Open water lake diving and advanced scuba diving, ice diving and a basic underwater photography course are other options. Overseas trips are planned from June to November to such locations as San Salvador, the Channel Islands, the Red Sea and the South Caicos. **Cost:** $75 to $300 for courses; $340 to $1,950 for overseas trips. **When:** Year-round. **Contact:** Rocky Mountain Diving Center Ltd., 1920 Wadsworth Blvd., Lakewood, CO 80215, USA; phone (303)232-2400.

Florida

Key Scuba Adventures: From a resort at Windley Key, divers enjoy waters with temperatures of 70°F in winter and visibility of 60 to 110 feet. Stretching 220 miles, the reef has depths ranging from 12 to 80 feet and is home to more than 600 species of tropical fish and 50 varieties of coral. Groups of 4 to 10 can take 4-day diving trips that include accommodations, 3 half-day dives, tank, weightbelts and air. In addition to various package trips, guided dives with licensed captains, drive-it-yourself dive boats and complete equipment rental and sales are available. Divers may investigate the area's many sunken Spanish galleons and World War II wrecks; more than half of all the gold lost in maritime disasters is estimated to be lying on the ocean floor off of the coast of Florida. Though services are geared toward certified divers, lessons in a freshwater pool are also offered. **Cost:** $16 to $25 a day depending on size of group, duration of stay, type of equipment provided; meals extra. **When:** Year-round excluding holidays. **Contact:** Coral Reef Resort, Box 575, Islamorada, FL 33036, USA; phone (305)664-4955.

Diving School: Three-week courses begin each month in open water scuba certification, tropical fish collecting, underwater photography and snorkeling techniques. Participants have the choice of taking the 32-hour course in Deerfield Beach or in Pompano Beach. Certified

Reader Service

Free Information on Request

ADVENTURE TRAVELGUIDE has made it easier for you to obtain information at no cost.Simply circle the number(s) on the adjoining postage-paid card which correspond to the number(s) below for the information you wish to receive.

We also would appreciate your answers to a few questions about yourself and your travel interests on the Reader Service Card.

1. **ADVENTURE BOUND**—River expeditions, Colorado.
2. **ADVENTURE CENTER**—Specialists featuring trekking, overland expeditions, safaris, camping tours and more, throughout the world.
3. **ADVENTURERS INTERNATIONAL**–Treasure hunting expeditions to Caribbean islands, plus Central and South America.
4. **ADVENTURES INTERNATIONAL**—Wildlife and nature safaris throughout Africa; whale watching in Baja and Hawaii.
5. **AFRICAN TRAVEL SUPERVISORS**—U.S. general agents for travel to southern Africa; safaris to the heart of the wildlife continent.
6. **ALPENLITE**—Maker of venturelite soft luggage, kangaroo bicycle and day packs, and Alpenlite backpacking equipment.
7. **AMERICAN WILDERNESS EXPERIENCE**—Horsepack and backpack treks into remote wilderness areas of the West. Colorful native guides and small groups learn to live in harmony with the wilderness.
8. **ANNAPOLIS SAILING SCHOOL**—Free color brochures on sailing, adventure, instruction.
9. **ANTHONY'S KEY RESORT**—Unlimited adventure on an exotic island off of Honduras.
10. **AUSTRALIA TOURIST COMMISSION**—Get the lowdown on Down/Under with a free "Destination Australia" booklet.
11. **AVENTURA SAILING ACADEMY**—Sailing instruction and navigational courses year-round, plus cruises, club membership and more.
12. **AVON-SEAGULL**—High-quality Avon inflatable boats.
13. **BALLOON RANCH**—Ballooning resort featuring rides and instruction, plus a wide assortment of resort activities.
14. **BICYCLE TOURS HAWAII**—Bicycle tours on the island of Hawaii.
15. **BIKECENTENNIAL**—Nonprofit service organization offers bicycle trips, trails and publications.
16. **BRADT ENTERPRISES**—Guidebooks and maps for adventurers; includes backpacking, overlanding, trekking.
17. **CANYONEERS**—River trips down the Colorado, Green, San Juan and Skagit rivers; hiking and backpacking trips through the Grand Canyon and Baja coast.
18. **CASA SOLANA**—Isolated island paradise off the coast of Belize, Central America.
19. **CONLIN-DODDS TRAVEL**—33-mile walk in New Zealand from Te Anau to Milford Sound; stopover in the Fiji islands.
20. **CROSSROADS INTERNATIONAL**—Small-group summer camping, climbing, cycling in the U.S., England, France, Scandinavia, Yugoslavia.
21. **EAST AFRICAN TRAVEL CONSULTANTS**—Natural history and wildlife camera safaris in Kenya, Zambia and Tanzania.
22. **EASTERN RIVER EXPEDITIONS**—Whitewater rafting on Maine's Kennebec and Penobscot rivers, and West Virginia's Gauley River.
23. **ECHO: THE WILDERNESS COMPANY**—Whitewater rafting: experience the excitement of the earth's remaining wild rivers.
24. **ENCOUNTER OVERLAND**—4-wheel drive camping expeditions in Africa, Asia and South America.
25. **EXODUS**—Overland expeditions in Asia and Africa; Himalayan treks and other adventure holidays by 4-wheel drive and on foot.
26. **EXPLORANDES**—Expeditions along the Inca Trail through tropical forests, over mountain passes and into archaeological ruins in Peru.
27. **EXPLORE BEYOND**—Cultural and exploratory expeditions to the Middle East, northern Thailand, East Africa and the Himalayas.
28. **FALKLAND WILDLIFE**—Weekly nature cruises to the Falkland Islands to view the unique wildlife habitats of the penguin.
29. **FRONTIER EXPEDITIONS**—Rafting trips on the Middle Fork and Main Salmon rivers in Idaho.
30. **GEORGIE'S ROYAL RIVER RATS**—Grand Canyon river trips in large or small pontoon rafts.
31. **GERHARD'S BICYCLE ODYSSEYS**—Cycling experiences with sagwagon in Ireland, Holland and Germany, or in Germany and Austria.
32. **GOODTRAVEL TOURS**—Explore the Lau Islands and experience traditional island feasts, Yaqona ceremonies and Fijian dancing.
33. **GOWAY TRAVEL**—Toronto-based trip wholesaler specializing in overland camping expeditions.
34. **H & M LANDING**—Naturalist-led voyages to the Pacific Coast and offshore islands of Baja.
35. **HAPPY TRAILS**—Backpacking trips to Guatemala, Hawaii and the Canadian Rockies.
36. **HIGH HORIZONS**—Mountain programs and camps for juniors, teenagers and adults in the Canadian Rockies; includes hiking, mountaineering, backpacking and leadership training.

37. HIGH MOUNTAIN HELI-SKIING—Ski untracked powder slopes in the Tetons; helicopters supply transportation.
38. HIMALAYA—Trekking and wilderness expeditions to Kashmir, Ladakh, Nepal, Pakistan and China.
39. HIMALAYAN TREKKING SERVICE—Treks to Nepal: Manaslu Range, Mt. Everest and Annapurna.
40. HONDO RAST & COMPANY—Full-scale expeditions into remote regions of Alaska.
41. INTERNATIONAL SCHOOL OF MOUNTAINEERING—Introductory and intermediate alpine mountaineering courses in Leysin, Switzerland.
42. JACKSON HOLE MOUNTAIN GUIDES—Educational institution and international guide service specializing in alpine climbing, mountaineering and trekking.
43. JOURNEYS—Individual or small-group treks and climbs to the Himalayas—explore Nepal's remotest areas.
44. KEN SMITH'S MIDDLE FORK RIVER TRIPS—Custom wilderness float expeditions down Idaho's Middle Fork River.
45. KITTY HAWK KITES—Fly an ultralight hang glider over North Carolina's beaches.
46. KLINEBURGER TRAVEL—Trips to every continent, across every type of terrain, and to all climates.
47. LIBERTY BELL ALPINE TOURS—Climbing school, backpacking tours, rafting trips and guide service in the heart of the North Cascades.
48. LONE MOUNTAIN RANCH—Horsepacking into the Yellowstone and Spanish Peaks wilderness under Montana's Big Sky.
49. MACKAY BAR—Float Idaho's Salmon River—"the president did."
50. MOUNTAIN MEN—Gold-panning jeep tour from Denver; fish, camp, hike, ski.
51. MOUNTAIN PEOPLE SCHOOL—Adventure-oriented courses offered in rock climbing, wilderness skills and snowshoeing.
52. MOUNTAIN RIVER TOURS—Whitewater rafting on the New and Gauley rivers cover 15 miles and 21 major rapids.
53. MOUNTAIN TRAVEL—Expeditions and outings to the remote wilderness areas of the world.
54. NANTAHALA OUTDOOR CENTER—Whitewater rafting, canoe and kayak instruction, skiing, climbing, backpacking; U.S. and foreign trips year-round.
55. NATURE EXPEDITIONS INTERNATIONAL—Nature, cultural and photography expeditions to unique environments.
56. NECKSAVER—Easily interchangeable harness and straps for carrying cameras and other instruments; dealer inquiries welcome.
57. NOAH WHITEWATER—Racing, cruising and expedition kayaks and canoes, including kits; also whitewater shirts and accessories.
58. NORTH CASCADES ALPINE SCHOOL—Climbing instruction in Washington and British Columbia, plus treks and climbs conducted worldwide.
59. NORTHWEST OUTWARD BOUND—Pacific Northwest wilderness experience courses in mountaineering, river running, backpacking.
60. OCEANIC SOCIETY EXPEDITIONS—Explore the oceans of the world on a sailing ship; trips from the North Atlantic to the South Pacific.
61. OLYMPIC ADVENTURES—Olympic Mountains, rain forests and 50 miles of wilderness beach explored on backpacking trips, snow and ice seminars, canoe and rafting trips.
62. OPEN DOOR ALASKAN WATER ADVENTURES—River trips and birding tours in south-central Alaska.
63. OREGON TRAVEL—Comprehensive vacation-planning guide, free and in color.
64. OUTDOOR ADVENTURES—Whitewater rafting on wild and scenic rivers throughout the West.
65. OUTDOOR LEADERSHIP TRAINING SEMINARS—Courses in rafting, rock climbing, mountaineering and outdoor leadership.
66. OVERSEAS ADVENTURE TRAVEL—Expeditions to Africa, Asia and South America, plus European camping.
67. PALISADE SCHOOL OF MOUNTAINEERING—Avalanche seminars, mountain medicine, ski mountaineering, basic and advanced rock climbing.
68. PETER BYRNE EXPEDITIONS—River adventures through the wilderness mountains of the kingdom of Nepal.
69. REI ADVENTURE TRAVEL—Treks in Nepal, India and South America; backpacking in Alaska, Canada and the Pacific Northwest; climbing in Russia, South America, Alaska, Canada and Mexico; river rafting in South America, Canada and Alaska.
70. ROBBINS MOUNTAIN PARAPHERNALIA—Mountaincraft Telluride is based in the most alpine village in the U.S.; rockcraft, icecraft, snowcraft.
71. ROGUE RIVER OUTFITTERS—Specializing in outfitting whitewater paddlers and cross-country skiers in southern Oregon.
72. ROLLEI OF AMERICA—Owning a Rolleiflex SL35E says something about you.
73. RUSSELL YACHT CHARTERS—Crewed yachts or bareboats along the East Coast, Caribbean and Bahamas.
74. SCHWEIZER SOARING DIRECTORY—Contact the soaring center nearest you and experience the quiet beauty of soaring flight.
75. SEA LIFE DISCOVERY—Scuba and snorkel vacations to the Caribbean, Hawaii, Micronesia and the Red Sea.
76. SEE & SEA TRAVEL SERVICE—Worldwide diving adventures offered through this long-established diver's travel agency.
77. SOUTH AMERICAN REPRESENTATIVES—Cruises down the Amazon River from Iquitos, Peru to Leticia, Colombia.

78. SOUTH AMERICAN WILDERNESS ADVENTURES—Trekking expeditions, wildlife and natural history tours, anthropology and archaeology tours, and jungle explorations.

79. SOUTHWEST SAFARIS—Natural history expeditions by raft, jeep, bush plane and foot in the southwestern U.S.

80. SPYGLASS HILL—Honduras. Diving adventures on Roatan's barrier reef.

81. STRATHCONA LODGE—Vancouver Island winter snow travel techniques program.

82. SUNDOWNERS—16 years' experience in Asia overland camping and Trans-Siberian railway camping tours.

83. SUNRISE SCENIC TOURS—Scenic and whitewater trips; specializing in inflatable kayaks, rafts and hardshell kayak instruction.

84. TEXAS CANOE TRAILS—Explore scenic rivers throughout Texas and Mexico by raft and canoe.

85. TRACKS TRAVEL—European camping tours, and overlanding from London to Johannesburg or Nairobi.

86. TRAVEL EXPLORATIONS—Trekking adventures to the Annapurna sanctuary of Nepal and the High Atlas Mountains of Morocco.

87. TRAVLTIPS FREIGHTERS—Low-cost luxury trips by freighter; free travel opportunity report.

88. TREASURE TREKS—Trek the High Atlas Mountains on a 15-day excursion including a climb to North Africa's highest peak, Mt. Toubkal.

89. TREKKING & ANDES, S.A.—Guided hikes and treks through the Peruvian Andes; desert treks and river trips also available.

90. UNITREX—Unique travel experiences; archaeology, anthropology, art, architecture, history, culture, natural history, ecology, bird watching and more.

91. WAGONS HO—Horseback, stagecoach, covered wagons, campfire programs; excellent food, everything furnished.

92. WESTERN SAFARIS—Adventure camping through the West; hiking, rafting, ghost towns and more, all in one trip.

93. WHITE PASS & YUKON ROUTE—Railtravel service between Bennett, Skagway, Fraser, Carcross and Whitehorse.

94. WHITE WATER VOYAGES—Rafting adventures in the French Alps and Spanish Pyrenees, a majestic fjord in Norway, and a twisting Himalayan gorge in Nepal.

95. WHITEWATER ADVENTURES—Sailing and rafting expeditions in Canada.

96. WILD WATER WEST—Whitewater wilderness adventures down the Colorado and Green rivers, plus trips on the Bio Bio in Chile.

97. WILDERLAND—Whitewater river adventures in the Sierras and Pacific Northwest; rafts and inflatable kayaks.

98. WILDERNESS ENCOUNTER—Wilderness rafting on the Snake River; sightseeing, whitewater excursions, beach camping and dining.

99. WILDERNESS EXPERIENCES—Russian wilderness explorations include transportation from New York City, all equipment, food and a Russian guide.

100. WILDERNESS WORLD—Free color brochure available on whitewater trips and Baja overland trips.

101. WONDER BIRD TOURS—Tours for birders and naturalists, plus Guianan rain forest birding.

102. ZODIAC OF AMERICA—The inflatable boats used by professional expedition leaders worldwide.

divers may utilize a 30-foot diving boat which is used for daily trips. Divers explore several local reefs and drop-offs, with depths ranging from 30 to 100 feet. Visibility is high throughout the diving range, and the water contains much tropical sea life including lobsters, snappers and groupers. A complete line of diving gear is available for purchase or rental. **Cost:** $130 for basic scuba course; includes equipment. **When:** Year-round. **Contact:** Professional Diving Schools of Florida, 210 N. Federal Hwy., Deerfield Beach, FL 33441, USA; phone (305)428-0560.

Illinois

Landlocked Diving: Divers explore the lakes of the Midwest through a Glendale Heights dive center which also provides instruction, from introductory and basic certification classes to courses resulting in NAUI, PADI or YMCA advanced certification. Basic courses are taught frequently at various area facilities, usually involving weekly sessions totaling around 30 hours. Holders of basic certification can take a series of 10 to 15 open water dives to achieve advanced ratings, either nearby in Wisconsin or on a special Florida trip. And those holding advanced ratings can participate in diving under ice on area lakes during the winter. Other offerings include equipment sales and rental, dive film festivals and foreign trips. **Cost:** On request. **When:** Year-round. **Contact:** Illinois Institute of Diving, P.O. Box 1096, Glendale Heights, IL 60137, USA; phone (312)858-8884.

New York

Big Apple Dive: Closed charters and weekend dives in search of shipwrecks along the New York coast bring participants to the remains of the ships *San Diego, Oregon* and *Coimbra Lightburne.* A vessel specially equipped for scientific research provides the transportation to reefs that range from 20 to 175 feet in depth. Instruction in underwater photography, instructor training, seamanship and navigation are also available. **Cost:** $10 to $500 depending on the type of dive includes guide, accommodations aboard the research vessel *Black Coral.* **When:** Year-round. **Contact:** Coastal Diving Academy, 106 Main St., Bay Shore, NY 11706, USA; phone (516)666-2127.

Diving a Great Lake: Scuba diving instruction for beginners is offered at a diving center in Rochester. The course includes 5 open-water dives in Lake Ontario and results in basic scuba certification. Equipment can be rented or purchased at the center, which also offers occasional outings to special diving spots on the lake. **Cost:** $145 includes instruction, material, certification. **When:** Year-round. **Contact:** Diving Center of Rochester, 1889 E. Main St., Rochester, NY 14609, USA; phone (716)654-9384.

Ohio

Diving a Hole in the Ground: Portage Quarry, near Bowling Green, consists of about 25 acres of water averaging 55 feet in depth, with submerged machinery (trucks, scales, etc.) available for exploration. Dive facilities are set up, and the site can be investigated at a diver's leisure. Camping is available nearby, and an air compressor

The Florida Keys offer a number of highly accessible diving areas. Courses as well as trips from a half day to a week are available from a number of operators. (Florida News Bureau)

at the quarry allows repeated dives. The dive center also runs trips to Micronesia, Lake Erie, the Florida Keys, Bermuda and other spots. **Cost:** $2 a day. **When:** Summer. **Contact:** Sub-Aquatics, Inc., 8855 E. Broad St., Reynolds, OH 43068, USA; phone (614)864-1235.

Pennsylvania

Erie Diving: By boat or from the shore divers can reach several shipwrecks in the fairly shallow waters of Lake Erie. Visibility is unpredictable when exploring the old wooden lake freighters, barges and tugs because in Lake Erie a small breeze can cloud things up quickly. An alternative diving spot is the Niagara River. The waters there are no place for a beginner, but experienced divers may find antique bottles, anchors, coins and weaponry. Canadian quarries just across the border usually provide divers with clear water, fish and sometimes old mining equipment to investigate. During the summer longer trips are scheduled to places such as Manitoulin Island in Georgian Bay, Canada. **Cost:** On request. **When:** Year-round. **Contact:** Lake Erie Skin Diving School Inc., 330 Holland St., Erie, PA 16502, USA; phone (814)454-0285.

Texas

Degrees in Diving: An extensive program of instruction for scuba divers is offered out of a dive center in Galveston. Classes for beginners are oriented towards PADI Open

Water certification, although basic certification is also offered. A course for serious divers who have obtained their Open Water ratings teaches advanced skills such as navigation, search and recovery, first aid and life saving. Once a Divemaster rating is obtained, divers may achieve such specialty ratings as Cave, Ice, Wreck, Deep, Research, and Search and Recovery Diver or can work towards becoming educators. **Cost:** On request. **When:** Year-round. **Contact:** Aqua-Trek, 804 University Blvd., Galveston, TX 77550, USA; phone (713)763-0456.

Washington

Diving Instruction: Students from ages 18 to 40 receive comprehensive training to become professional deep sea divers. Meeting 5 days a week for 6 months at the Lake Washington Ship Canal in Seattle, the course familiarizes students with all aspects of commercial diving, with special emphasis on safety. Included in the course are such topics as communications, underwater physics and physiology, decompression, equipment, underwater work, cutting and welding, salvage, demolition, rigging and boat handling. Students are provided with information regarding employment in deep sea diving. Underwater photography and television, mixed gas diving, scuba, saturation, hot water systems and first aid are further subjects covered. After 25 weeks of instruction at 30 hours a week divers receive professional certification. Financial assistance is available, and the program is veteran-approved. **Cost:** $3,950 tuition, $25 application fee; scuba gear extra. **When:** Year-round. **Contact:** Diver's Institute of Technology Inc., P.O. Box 70312, 1133 NW 45th St., Seattle, WA 98107, USA; phone (206)783-5542.

RESOURCES

Clubs and Associations

British Sub-Aqua Club
70 Brompton Rd.
London SW3, Great Britain

Council for National Cooperation
in Aquatics
51 Clifford Ave.
Pelham, NY 10803, USA

Council for Underwater Resources
and Oceans
P.O. Box 530173
Miami, FL 33153, USA

International Divers Association
P.O. Box 6657
Tamuning, GU 96911, USA

National Association
of Skin Diving Schools
1757 Long Beach Blvd.
Long Beach, CA 90813, USA

National Association
of Underwater Instructors (NAUI)
Box 630
Colton, CA 92334, USA
Phone (714)824-5540

Professional Association
of Diving Instructors (PADI)
2064 N. Bush
Santa Ana, CA 92706, USA
Phone (714)547-6696

Underwater Adventurers Association
5915½ W. Irving Park Rd.
Chicago, IL 60634, USA

World Underwater Federation
34 rue de Colisse
75008 Paris, France

RESEARCH EXPEDITIONS

By donning a scuba tank and regulator, you can plunge into the world of underwater research. Coral formations, schools of glistening fish, kelp beds and shipwrecks are a short swim away. Marine scientists have pushed back our frontiers of knowledge about life in the sea during the past century, yet much remains to be learned. On trips offered from Bermuda to French Polynesia, you can work side-by-side with specialists as they strive to save dying reefs, excavate marine archaeological sites and study sargassum seabeds.

Whether you've perfected your scuba diving skills or are a landlubber, there's a place for you on a research team. Your talents are needed to assist in all aspects of field work, from lab analysis and sediment coring to sample collecting and navigation.

You can join a 2-week archaeological trip to the Gulf of Mexico and help excavate sunken ships, recover artifacts and search for new wreck sites in an area once frequented by the Spanish Navy, or help preserve historic galleons, schooners and Yankee traders on a 3-week research trip off the Florida Keys. On both trips participants are taught underwater photography and use of map grids, plane tables and marine archaeological gear. Other expeditions investigate coral reef ecology, marine algae and underwater geological formations.

Several organizations offer scholarships and academic credit for participation on projects. Others provide training and an opportunity to try out career interests while working with experts in a number of marine fields. Whatever the motivation or rewards, an underwater marine research trip will let you experience the excitement and hard work involved in charting the depths of the sea. □

Research expeditions encompass activities from studying marine pollution near Bermuda to excavating wrecks off the coast of New Zealand. Participants are encouraged to contribute their skills and knowledge to ongoing research projects. (Scubahire)

RESEARCH EXPEDITIONS

ATLANTIC

Bermuda

Research Diving Course: A 4-week course in marine research using scuba equipment is offered out of a Bermuda biological research center located on the east end of St. George's Island well away from the main tourist areas. The course is taught by research divers and covers search procedures, underwater navigation, acoustic telemetry, marine biology and underwater archaeology. Actual diving experience is emphasized, with accompanying lectures and classroom work. Students must have basic scuba certification; academic credit is available. **Cost:** $1,200 includes food, accommodations, instruction, equipment. **When:** June. **Contact:** Bermuda Biological Station, St. George's West, 1-15, Bermuda.

Toward Cleaner Seas: A group of scientists studying marine pollution teaches a 3-week course covering the problem, its analysis and possible solutions. Located at a biological research center on St. George's Island, the course covers such areas as the effects of petroleum discharge on the intertidal community, waste water discharge and its effect on inshore waters, pelagic tar in the sargassum fields, and other topics. Techniques including extraction and chromatographic analysis are used. Both field work and lab work are involved, and academic credit is available. **Cost:** $600 includes food, accommodations, instruction, equipment. **When:** July. **Contact:** Bermuda Biological Station, St. George's West, 1-15, Bermuda.

CARIBBEAN

Grenada

Lessons of Grenada's Reef: The coral reef system off Grenada, unpolluted and healthy until recently, was discovered to contain some dead and dying reefs in 1977. For 2 weeks, a team of researchers continues the work of previous teams in surveying Grenada's reefs and attempting to document their development. Both certified divers and non-diving participants are needed, though no previous research experience is necessary. Daylight hours are spent working aboard a 33-foot dive boat; while divers learn and practice the techniques of coral survey, sediment coring and flow study, the nondivers onboard assist the divers, record data and do lab work. Lodging is in a motel at Carriacou, where the trip begins and ends. Participants must be willing to put in long working hours. Academic credit is available. **Cost:** $900 includes training, equipment, food, accommodations, leader. **When:** September, October. **Contact:** Earthwatch, P.O. Box 127 AG, Belmont, MA 02178, USA; phone (617)489-3030.

Jamaica

Reef Interlude: Divers spend 3 weeks assisting a research project studying the symbiotic relationship between marine algae and coral reefs in Jamaica's Discovery Bay. Participants serve as dive buddies to aid in underwater collection of algae samples and specimens of the corals and reef-dwelling invertebrates on which algae are found. The team is accommodated in dormitory space at the Discovery Bay Marine Lab, on the island's north coast. Participants must be scuba divers, with preference given to those experienced in handling small boats. The assembly point is Montega Bay. **Cost:** $975 includes accommodations, meals. **When:** June to August. **Contact:** University Research Expeditions, University of California, M19 Wheeler Hall, Berkeley, CA 94720, USA; phone (415)642-6586. *(M)*

Netherlands Antilles

Cavity Research: Certified scuba divers can participate on a 16-day trip investigating one of the last major frontiers of coral reef research: the geology and biology of reef cavities. The recent discovery of cavity-dwelling organisms 550 million years old has highlighted unsolved puzzles about the evolution of fragile reef systems. Living in a private ocean-front house near Bonaire's capital of Kralendijk, participants dive in 80° water with over 120-foot visibility as they photograph and collect samples, record activity in the cavities, and study geological remains. Experienced photographers are welcomed. Academic credit is available. **Cost:** $950 includes food, accommodations, equipment, leader. **When:** July. **Contact:** Earthwatch, P.O. Box 127 AG, Belmont, MA 02178, USA; phone (617)489-3030.

CENTRAL AMERICA

Belize

Learning in the Field: Participants on summer research trips have the opportunity to learn about the flora, fauna, archaeology and offshore marine environments of Belize and Guatemala. Expedition members, who are housed at the Belize Biological Station and in the homes of local residents, pursue a variety of activities depending on the trip's particular emphasis: field biology of coastal regions, archaeological reconnaissance into unexplored areas, marine biological research, scuba exploration of offshore reefs, and boat and aerial trips to other regions of interest. Academic credit can be arranged. Details are available from the operator. **Cost:** On request. **When:** Summer. **Contact:** American Institute for Exploration, 1809 Nichols Rd., Kalamazoo, MI 49007, USA; phone (616)381-8237. *(M)*

Honduras

Studying Sunlight in Coral Reefs: Members of a research team study the relationship of transmitted sunlight at various reef depths with the photosynthetic rates of several marine algae along the island of Utila, one of 3 inhabited bay islands off the Caribbean coast of Honduras. Participants 16 to 24 years old study tropical marine life for 2 weeks while diving or snorkeling. The research has been in progress for the past 3 years. Expedition members become familiar with the life of the coral reef ecosystem through observation and discussion. **Cost:** $645. **When:** July, August. **Contact:** Expedition Training Institute, Inc.,

P.O. Box 171, Prudential Ctr. Sta., Boston, MA 02199, USA; phone (617)922-0577. *(M)*

MEXICO

Quintana Roo

Sunken Ship Exploration: There are an estimated 200 wrecks in the Mexican territorial waters of the Gulf of Mexico and the Caribbean Sea. Based on records found in the archives of the Spanish Navy, about 20 wrecks have been found, most of which are located on the Chinchorra Bank Reef. An expedition to further the archaeological work in this area lasts 2 weeks. The expedition visits known wreck sites and engages in excavation, recovery operations and exploration of new sites. The Chinchorra Bank Reef lies just below the surface 25 miles east of Xoalak, a fishing village located at the southernmost tip of Quintana Roo, by the border which separates Mexico from Belize. The easterly rim consists of some of the most beautifully formed coral reefs in the world. Caverns, tunnels and cul-de-sacs created by centuries of coral growths give the reef an unearthly beauty. Headquarters for the expedition is a modern scientific complex at Akumal, Mexico. **Cost:** On request. **When:** December. **Contact:** CEDAM Int'l.,Dallas, TX 75224, USA.

PACIFIC

French Polynesia

Investigating New Life Systems: A coral atoll in the Society Islands, near Tahiti, is the setting for a 3-week investigation of South Seas ecology. Trip members assist researchers looking into both marine and terrestrial life systems in a virgin area. The expedition provides outstanding opportunities for snorkeling and diving. Extensive logistical planning is required for this still-tentative trip, so interested persons should contact the operator as soon as possible. **Cost:** On request. **When:** December. **Contact:** Jean-Michel Cousteau Institute, P.O. Drawer CC, Harbour Town, Hilton Head Island, SC 29928, USA; phone (803)785-3333, ext. 123.

UNITED STATES

Florida

An Inventory of Wrecks: A graveyard of ships along the Outer Reef Tract, 7 miles off the Florida Keys, is the setting for a 3-week archaeological inventory to help preserve historic wrecks before they are plundered for sport. Called Looe Key, the site was named for a 44-gun British frigate that sank in 1744. Now the *H.M.S. Looe* lies among galleons, schooners and Yankee traders, and the expedition's object is to identify, map and inventory them. Participants need to be certified divers capable of working in 25 to 40 feet of water, but some non-divers are needed with skills in draftsmanship or small boat handling or an interest in archaeology. Lodging is in a sea camp at Big Pine Key with complete diving facilities; researchers use a 26-foot oceanographic vessel, and divers learn to use photograph towers, mapping grids, plane tables and other marine archaeological gear. Academic credit is available. **Cost:** $975 includes food, accommodations, instruction, transportation, equipment, leader. **When:** May, August. **Contact:** Earthwatch, P.O. Box 127 AG, Belmont, MA 02178, USA; phone (617)489-3030.

Marine Science Summer Camp: A laboratory-equipped camp on Big Pine Key, just off the only living coral reef in America, allows young people ages 12 to 17 to investigate marine life firsthand. With a camper-staff ratio of 3 to 1, the school can tailor its programs closely to a student's interests and skills, with the possible activities including scuba instruction, marine archaeology, sailing, small boat handling, snorkeling, camping and arts and crafts. The core of the program is focused on marine science and includes a broad overview of invertebrates, marine botany, geology, man and the sea, and various advanced studies. Field experience is mixed with lab work. Other details, including the program's duration, are available by mail or phone. **Cost:** On request. **When:** Summer. **Contact:** Seacamp Association, Inc., Rt. 3, Box 170, Big Pine Key, FL 33043, USA; phone (305)872-2331.

Researchers on a 16-day investigation of coral reef geology and biology in the Netherlands Antilles study organisms that have remained unchanged for 550 million years. (Sea Life Discovery)

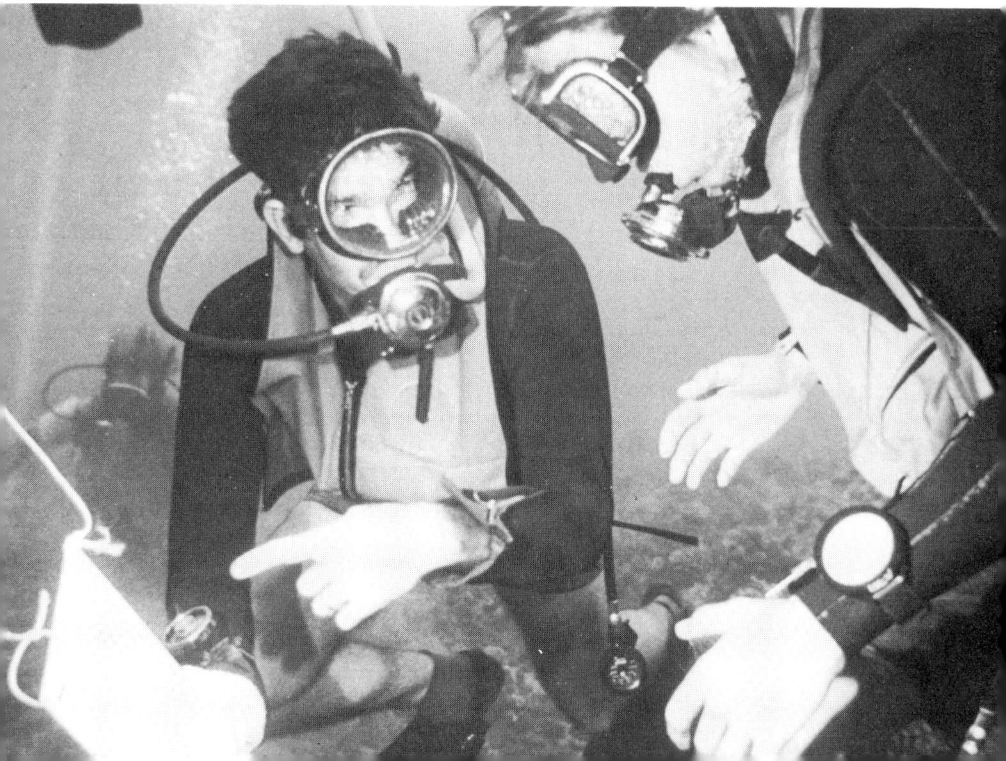

APPENDIX

ORGANIZATIONAL MEMBERS

The following is a list of the American Adventurers Association's organizational members as of July 1979—those organizations, trip operators and businesses directly involved in the adventure travel field. Many operate the trips described in this guide, and all are excellent sources of adventure travel information.

ABC Adventure Tours, 549 Howe St., Vancouver, BC Canada V6C 2C6; phone (604) 687-1614

Adventours—Wet and Wild, Inc., Box B, Woodland, CA 95695, USA; phone (916)662-6824

Adventure Bound, Inc., 6179 S. Adams Dr., Littleton, CO 80121, USA; phone (303)771-3752

Adventure Center, 5540 College Ave., Oakland, CA 94618, USA; phone (415)654-1879

Adventure River Expeditions, 4211 Mars Wy., Salt Lake City, UT 84117, USA; phone (801) 278-1867

Adventure Tours, Hotel Shaheen, 4-Gupkar Rd., Srinagar 190001, Kashmir, India; phone 5248

Adventure Unique Inc., 19 Washington St., Santa Clara, CA 95050, USA; phone (408)446-2347

Adventurers International, 215 E. Horatio Ave., Maitland, FL 32751, USA; phone (305) 645-1332

Adventures International, 4421 Albert St., Oakland, CA 94619, USA; phone (415)531-6564

Aerostat Renaissance, P.O. Box 3536, Napa, CA 94558, USA; phone (707)255-6356

Afro Ventures, P.O. Box 10848, Johannesburg 2000, South Africa

Alaska Fish and Trails Unlimited, Star Rt., Box 20154, Fairbanks, AK 99701, USA; phone (907)479-4012

Alaska Raft Adventures, Box 73264, Fairbanks, AK 99707, USA; phone (907)452-1465

Alaskan Adventure, P.O. Box 18, Hope, AK 99605, USA

Allagash Wilderness Outfitters, 36 Minuteman Dr., Millinocket, ME 04462, USA; phone (207)723-6622; May to November: Frost Pond, Star Rt. 76, Greenville, ME 04441, USA

American Institute of Exploration, 1809 Nichols Rd., Kalamazoo, MI 49007, USA; phone (616)381-8237

American Safari, 386 60th St., Oakland, CA 94618, USA

American Trails West, 92 Middle Neck Rd., Great Neck, NY 11021, USA; phone (516)487-2802

American Wilderness Experience, P.O. Box 1486A, Boulder, CO 80306, USA; phone (303)449-0056

Andean Odyssey Tours, 2141 14th St., Suite 1, Boulder, CO 80302, USA

Andean Outfitters, P.O. Box 7007, Angels Camp, CA 95222, USA; phone (209)736-4830

Andes Whitewater and Amazon Expeditions, 310 W. Grandview Blvd., Erie, PA 16508, USA; phone (814)866-0701; July to September: Box 4845, Stateline, NV 89449, USA; phone (702)588-3002

Anthony's Key Resort, 3803 Wagonwheel Ct., Plano, TX 75023, USA; phone (214)422-4300

Arena Tours, Hvasseleiti 26, Reykjavik, Iceland

Frank Arensburg, 110 Newport Ctr. Dr., #200, Newport, CA 92660, USA

Arizona Soaring, Inc., P.O. Box 27427, Tempe, AZ 85282, USA; phone (602)568-2318

Australian Himalayan Expeditions, 28-34 O'Connell St., Third Floor, Sydney, NSW 2000, Australia; phone 231-6050

Aventura Sailing Association, 35102 Del Obispo St., Dana Pt., CA 92629, USA; phone (714)493-9493

Back Country International, 1804 Magnolia Pl.,

Davis, CA 95616, USA

The Balloon Ranch, Star Rt., Box 41, Del Norte, CO 81132, USA; phone (303)754-2533

Bathurst Inlet Lodge, P.O. Box 820, Yellowknife, NT Canada X0E 1H0; phone (403) 873-2595

Bay Travel Diving Adventures, 2435 E. Coast Hwy., Corona del Mar, CA 92625, USA; phone (714)675-4321

Beamer Expeditions, P.O. Box 285, Canoga Park, CA 91305, USA; phone (213)883-3522

Bicycle Tours—Hawaii, c/o Pacific Sports Products, P.O. Box 5112, Hilo, HI 96720, USA; phone (808)961-6936

Big Island Adventures, P.O. Box 2639, Kailua-Kona, HI 96740, USA; phone (808) 329-2676

Bikecentennial, P.O. Box 8308, Missoula, MT 59807, USA; phone (406)721-1776

Black Forest Gliderport, 9990 Gliderport Rd., Colorado Springs, CO 80908, USA; phone (303)495-4144

Bob Crick High Country Outfitters, Rt. 1, Box 99A, Victor, MT 59875, USA; phone (406) 642-3233

Daniel Bonnier, 31 Rt. de Versailles, 78560 Port Marly, France

Bradt Enterprises, 409 Beacon St., Boston, MA 02115, USA

CAF Industries Inc., 101 S. 30th St., Phoenix, AZ 85034, USA

California Mountaineering and Technical Rock Climbing School, 6121 Prescott Ave., Yucca Valley, CA 92284, USA; phone (714)365-1152

Canadian Mountain Holidays Ltd., P.O. Box 1660, Banff, AB Canada T0L 0C0; phone (403)762-4531

Canadian River Expeditions Ltd., Suite 401, 845 Chilko St., Vancouver, BC Canada V8G 2R2; phone (604)926-4436

Canadian Wilderness Experiences Ltd., Box 46304, Sta. G., Vancouver, BC Canada V6R 4G6; phone (604)325-9118

Canoes North/Canoes South, Box 5656, Armstrong, ON Canada P0T 1A0; phone (807) 583-2055

Canyoneers, Inc., P.O. Box 2997, Flagstaff, AZ 86003, USA; phone (602)526-0924

Casa Solana, Rt. 1, Box 40, Palacios, TX 77465, USA; phone (512)972-3314

Cascade Corrals, Stehekin, WA 98852, USA; phone (509)663-1822

Cascade River Holidays, P.O. Box 65, Yale, BC Canada V0K 2S0; phone (604)863-2332

Class VI River Runners, Inc., P.O. Box 78, Lansing, WV 25862, USA; phone (304)574-0704

Club Andino Peruano, Los Begonias 630, #11, Lima 27, Peru

Club Tamure, 14613 Whittier Blvd., Whittier, CA 90605, USA; phone (714)523-3414

Colorado Rocky Mountain Hiking, Box 376, North Conway, NH 03860, USA; phone (603)356-3594

Coltour, Iron Camana 868, Apartado 652, Lima, Peru

Conlin-Dodds Travel Ltd., P.O. Box 2760, Sta. A, Champaign, IL 61820, USA

Consolidated Tours Ltd., 550 Sherbrooke St. W., #480, Montreal, PQ Canada H3A 1B9; phone (514)849-1259

Crooked Creek Ski Touring, Box 3142, Vail, CO 81657, USA

Crossroads International, Hillsboro, NH 03244, USA; phone (603)478-5251

Dirigo Cruises, Schooner *Harvey Gamage,* 39 Waterside Ln., Clinton, CT 06413, USA; phone (203)669-7068

Discovery Tours International, 628 NW Sixth Ave., Portland, OR 97209, USA

Dolt of California, 11920 W. Olympic Blvd., Los Angeles, CA 90064

ECHO: The Wilderness Company, Inc., 6505 Telegraph Ave., Oakland, CA 94609, USA; phone (415)658-5075

EE-DA-HOW Mountaineering, P.O. Box 207, Ucon, ID 83454, USA; phone (208)523-9276

Early Winters Ltd., 110 Prefontaine St., Seattle, WA 98104, USA

Earthtrek Expeditions & Travel, 1540 E. Edinger, Suite D, Santa Ana, CA 92705, USA; phone (714)547-5864

East African Travel Consultants Inc., 33 Bloor St. E., Suite 206, Toronto, ON Canada M4W 3H1; phone (416)967-0067

Eastern River Expeditions Inc., 824 Petem Rd., Kingsville, MD 21087, USA; phone (301) 879-8555

Eddie Bauer, 15010 NE 36th St., Redmond, WA 98052, USA

El Dorado Lodge, 806-B Fairview Rd., Columbia, MO 65201, USA; phone (314)445-1193

Encounter Overland, 369 Pine St., Suite 516, San Francisco, CA 94104, USA; phone (415)421-7199

Exodus Expeditions, 167 Earls Court Rd., London SW5, Great Britain; phone 01-373-7895

Expedition Research, Inc., P.O. Box 467, Annapolis, MD 21401, USA; phone (301)268-3222

Expedition Training Institute, Inc., P.O. Box 171, Prudential Ctr. Sta., Boston, MA 02199, USA; phone (617)922-0577

Explorandes, Nicolas de Pierola 622, Lima, Peru; phone 238933

Explore Beyond Ltd., 167 Earls Court Rd., London SW5, Great Britain; phone 01-248-9082 or 01-236-4395

Falkland Wildlife, Drifts, Chinnor Hill, Oxford 0X9 4BS, Great Britain

Floating Through Europe, Inc., 501 Madison Ave., New York, NY 10022, USA; phone (212)832-6700

Geneva Spur Ltd., 1109 Lakewood Dr., Vienna, VA 22180, USA; phone (703)281-3316

Georgie's Royal River Rats, Box 12489, Las Vegas, NV 89112, USA; phone (702)451-5588

Gerhard's Bicycle Odysseys, 1137 SW Yamhill, Portland, OR 97205, USA; phone (503)223-5190

Go Diving, Inc., 715 Florida Ave. S., Minneapolis, MN 55426, USA; phone (612)544-7168

Government of Yukon Territory, Dept. of Tourism, Box 2703, Whitehorse, YT Canada Y1A 2C6

Goway Travel Ltd., 53 Yonge St., Second Floor, Toronto, ON Canada M5E 1J3; phone (416)863-0799

Deane B. Gray, 164 Middle St., Old Town, ME 04468, USA

Guerba Expeditions Ltd., Stokehill Farm, Erlestoke, Devizes, Wiltshire SN10 5UB, Great Britain; phone Bratton 476

H & M Landing, 2803 Emerson St., San Diego, CA 92108, USA; phone (714)222-1144

Hann Overland, 17 Stanthorpe Rd., London SW 16, Great Britain; phone 01-769-6659

Happy Trails, 518 W. Arlington Rd., Erie, PA 16509, USA

Hells Canyon Navigation Co., P.O. Box 145, Oxbow, OR 97840, USA; phone (503)785-3352

High Adventure, Alan Seeger Ltd., 1 Salterns Wy., Lilliput, Poole, Dorset BH12 8JR, Great Britain; phone 0202 708471

High Mountain Helicopter Skiing, Box 2217, Jackson, WY 83001, USA; phone (307)733-3274

Hike-Skitour Vermont, RFD 1, Chester, VT 05143, USA; phone (413)584-9086 or (802) 875-3631

Himalaya, 3023 Franklin St., San Francisco, CA 94123, USA; phone (415)441-2933

Himalayan Travel Ltd., P.O. Box 481, Greenwich, CT 06830, USA

Hondo Rast and Co., P.O. Box 231, Hamilton, MT 59840, USA; phone (406)363-3440

Horizon Tours Pvt. Ltd., Post Bag 29, Srinagar 19001, Kashmir, India

Horizons Unlimited, P.O. Box 2061, Salmon, ID 83467, USA; phone (208)756-3844

Huser-Karp Outfitting Services, Inc., The Northern Wilderness Company, 23020 SE Sixth Pl., Redmond, WA 98052, USA; phone (206)392-4703 or 633-3946

In the Tracks of Fremont, Inc., P.O. Box 18346, Steamboat, NV 89511, USA; phone (702)849-1399

The Infinite Odyssey, 57 Grant St., Waltham, MA 02154, USA; phone (617)899-6050

International Aquatic Adventures, Inc., 2047 Broadway, Boulder, CO 80302, USA; phone (303)444-5829 or tollfree (800)525-2545

International School of Mountaineering, Club Vagabond, 1854 Leysin, Switzerland, phone (025)6-23-21; or 308 E. 18th St., New York, NY 10003, USA; phone (212)982-2198

Iron Pony Manufacturing, Rt. 4, Canton, GA 30114, USA

Johann Mountain Guides, P.O. Box 2334, Lincoln City, OR 97367, USA; phone (503)996-3232

Klineburger Worldwide Travel, 1519 12th Ave., Seattle, WA 98122, USA; phone (206)329-1600

Kokopeli Adventures in Learning, Inc., P.O. Box 1557, Flagstaff, AZ 86002, USA; phone (602)774-3778

Kumsheen Raft Adventures Ltd., Suite 116,

525 Seymour St., Vancouver, BC Canada V6B 3H7; phone (604)669-0415

LaMer Diving Seafaris, Inc., 823 UN Plaza, Suite 810, New York, NY 10002, USA; phone (212)599-0886

Baron F. Levin, Antig. Carret. A, Cuernavaca 5320, Tlalpao 22, DF, Mexico

Liberty Bell Alpine Tours, Mazama, WA 98833, USA; phone (509)996-2250

Lima Tours S.A., P.O. Box 4340, Lima, Peru

Lindblad Travel, Inc., 8 Wright St., Westport, CT 06880, USA; phone (203)226-8531 or tollfree (800)243-5657

Lute Jerstad Adventures, P.O. Box 19527, Portland, OR 97219, USA; phone (503)244-4364

Mackay Bar, 3190 Airport Wy., Boise, ID 83705, USA; phone (208)344-1881

Morgan Tours, 35 E. Wacker, #1746, Chicago, IL 60601, USA

Mother Lode Outdoor School, 581 Continental Dr., San Jose, CA 95111, USA; phone (408) 578-5434

Mt. Adams Wilderness Institute, Flying L Ranch, Glenwood, WA 98619, USA; phone (509)364-3511 or 364-3488

Mountain River Tours Inc., Box 88, Sunday Rd., Hico, WV 24854, USA; phone (304)658-5817

Mountain Travel Inc., 1398 Solano Ave., Albany, CA 94706, USA; phone (415)527-8100

Museum of Comparative Zoology, The Agassiz Museum, Harvard University, Cambridge, MA 02138, USA; phone (617)495-2463

Naggar Travel Agency, 667 Madison Ave., New York, NY 10021, USA; phone (212)751-0152

Nantahala Outdoor Center, Star Rt., Box 68, Bryson City, NC 28713, USA; phone (704) 488-2175

Nature Expeditions International, 599 College Ave., Palo Alto, CA 94306, USA; phone (415)328-6572

New England Divers, Inc., Tozer Rd., Beverly, MA 01915, USA

Noah Whitewater, 62 Central St., Somerville, MA 02143, USA

North American River Runners, P.O. Box 193, Sylvania, OH 43560, USA; phone (419)882-8654

North Cascades Alpine School, 1212 24th G, Bellingham, WA 98225, USA; phone (206) 671-1505

North Country Mountaineering, Inc., P.O. Box 951, Hanover, NH 03755, USA; phone (603) 643-3299

The Northwest Outward Bound School, 0110 SW Bancroft, Portland, OR 97201, USA; phone (503)243-1993

Northwest River Trips, Rt. 1, Box 11B, Tygh Valley, OR 97063, USA; phone (503)544-2317

OARS Inc., P.O. Box 67, Angels Camp, CA 95222, USA; phone (209)736-2924 or 736-2661

Open Door Alaskan Water Adventures, Box 1185, Cordova, AK 99574, USA; phone (907) 424-7466

Orange Torpedo Trips, P.O. Box 1111, Grants Pass, OR 97526, USA; phone (503)479-5061

Osprey River Trips, Inc., 11468 Redwood Hwy., Wilderville, OR 97543, USA; phone (503)479-4215

Outdoor Adventures, 3109 Fillmore St., San Francisco, CA 94123, USA; phone (415)346-8700

Outdoor Leadership Training Seminars, 2220 Birch St., Denver, CO 80207, USA; phone (303)333-7831

Outdoors Unlimited, Dept. A, 2500 Fifth Ave., Sacramento, CA 95818, USA; phone (916)452-1081

Outlaw Trails Inc., P.O. Box 336, Green River, UT 84525, USA; phone (801)564-3477

Overland Rolls, 1 Center St., Brunswick, ME 04011, USA; phone (207)725-5119

Overseas Adventure Tours, 1430 Massachusetts Ave., Cambridge, MA 02138, USA; phone (617)876-0533

Pacific Sportdiving, 4104 E. Anaheim St., Long Beach, CA 90804, USA; phone (213)433-7485

Palisade School of Mountaineering, P.O. Box 694, Bishop, CA 93514, USA; phone (714)935-4330

Panorama Viajes/Turismo S.A., P.O. Box 10065, Lima, Peru

Peaks & Fjords, P.O. Box 9575, Egertorget, Oslo 1, Norway; phone 02-22 61 60

Penn Overland Tours Ltd., 330 Sutter St., San Francisco, CA 94108, USA; phone (415)391-5728; or 122 Knightsbridge, London SW 1, Great Britain; phone 01-589-0016

Peter Byrne Expeditions, P.O. Box 777, Hood

River, OR 97031, USA; phone (503)352-7392

Proko International, 12511 Beatrice St., Los Angeles, CA 90066, USA

REI Adventure Travel, Inc., 1525 11th Ave., Seattle, WA 98122, USA; phone (206)322-7800

Rainbow Travel, 71A Trapelo Rd., Belmont, MA 02178, USA

River Trips Unlimited, 900 Murphy Rd. W., Medford, OR 97501, USA; phone (503)779-3798

Rivers Northwest, 141 Eagle St. NE, Winslow, WA 98110, USA; phone (206)842-5144

Robbins Mountain Paraphernalia, Box 4536, Modesto, CA 95352, USA

Rocky Mountain River Tours, P.O. Box 693, Pocatello, ID 83201, USA

Rogue River Outfitters, 8890 Rogue River Hwy., Grants Pass, OR 97526, USA; phone (503)582-1672

Russell Yacht Charters, 126 Davis Ave., Bridgeport, CT 06605, USA; phone (203)366-4561

Sacred Monkey Expeditions, Box 363, Jerome, AZ 86331, USA; phone (602)634-5711

Safari, P.O. Box 19972, Houston, TX 77024, USA

Safaris Equatorianos, Casilla A-122, Quito, Ecuador; phone 529-963

Schooner *Isaac H. Evans,* Capt. Douglas K. Lee, Box 482, Rockland, ME 04841, USA; phone (207)594-8007

Schweizer Soaring School, P.O. Box 147, Elmira, NY 14902, USA; phone (607)739-3821

Scubahire Ltd., GPO Box 777, Suva, Fiji; phone 361-241

Seagull Marine, 1851 McGaw Ave., Irvine, CA 92714, USA

Semjon Lass Associates, Action Tours, Box 1000, Lowell, MA 01854, USA; phone (617)459-2104; or Talisman Travel Service, 3440 Geary Blvd., San Francisco, CA 94118, USA; phone (415)668-2956

Sherpa Expeditions, 3 Bedford Rd., Chiswick, London W4, Great Britain; phone 01-994-7668; or Durbar Marg, P.O. Box 1519, Kathmandu, Nepal; phone 12422

Sierra Club Outing Dept., 530 Bush St., San Francisco, CA 94108, USA; phone (415)981-8634

Skinner Brothers Mountaineering, Box B, Pinedale, WY 82941, USA; phone (307)367-2270

Sobek Expeditions, Inc., P.O. Box 761, Angels Camp, CA 95222, USA; phone (209)736-2924

Society Expeditions, P.O. Box 5088, University Sta., Seattle, WA 98105, USA; phone (206) 324-9400

Sourdough Outfitters, Bettles, AK 99726, USA; phone (907)692-5252

South America Representatives, P.O. Box 39583, Los Angeles, CA 90039, USA

South American Wilderness Adventures, 1760 Solano Ave., Berkeley, CA 94707, USA; phone (415)524-5111

Superior Whitewater Association, P.O. Box 6264, Grand Rapids, MI 49506, USA

Swiftsure Tours Ltd., 119-645 Fort St., Victoria, BC Canada V8W 1G2; phone (604)388-4227

TX Ranch, P.O. Box 453, Lovell, WY 82431, USA; phone (406)484-2583

Taku Outfitters, Ltd., Box 30, Klahanie Dr., RR 2, Powell River, BC Canada V8A 4Z3; phone (604)483-9238

Telluride Mountaineering School, Box 67, Telluride, CO 81435, USA; phone (303)925-3603

Texas Canoe Trails, Star Rt. 2, Box 866B, New Braunfels, TX 78130, USA; phone (512)964-3760

Tracks, 165 Kensington High St., London W8 6SH, Great Britain; phone 01-937-5964

Trailhead Ventures, P.O. Box CC, Buena Vista, CO 81211, USA; phone (303)395-8001

Transcontinental Safaris, The Ravin Wildlife Reserve, P.M.B. 251 Kingscote, Kangaroo Island, South Australia 5223, Australia; phone The Shackle 6

Travel Company, P.O. Box 3128, Bellevue, WA 98009, USA

Travel Exploration, P.O. Box 17641, Denver, CO 80217, USA

Trekking & Andes, S.A., P.O. Box 3074, Lima 100, Peru; phone 462775

United Touring Co., P.O. Box 42196, Nairobi, Kenya; phone 331960, ext. 266

Universal Travel & Allied Services, Janpath Hotel, 142, New Delhi 1, India

University of the Wilderness, P.O. Box 1687,

Evergreen, CO 80439, USA; phone (303)674-9724

VIP Travel, P.O. Box 157, Sierra Madre, CA 91024, USA; phone (213)355-1438

Venturetreks Ltd., P.O. Box 3839, Auckland, New Zealand; phone 799 855

Vermont Bicycle Touring, RR 2, Bristol, VT 05443, USA; phone (802)388-4263

Victor Emanuel Nature Tours, Inc., P.O. Box 4429, Austin, TX 78765, USA; phone (512) 454-0576

WEXAS International, 45 Brompton Rd., Knightsbridge, London SW3 1DE, Great Britain; phone 01-589-0500

Virian J. Wadford, P.O. Box 173, Elk Grove Village, IL 60007, USA

Wagons Ho, P.O. Box 1879, Quinter, KS 67752, USA; phone (913)754-3347

Walkers Tours & Travels, Ltd., P.O. Box 1048, Colombo 1, Sri Lanka; phone 22553

Wampler Tours, P.O. Box 45, Berkeley, CA 94701, USA; phone (415)843-6602

Wanapitei, 7 Engleburn Pl., Peterborough ON Canada K9H 1C4; phone (705)743-3774; summer: Camp Wanapitei, Timagami, ON Canada P0H 2H0; phone Timagami Island 1-R-13 (New Liskeard)

West Ridge Manufacturing, 11920 W. Olympic Blvd., Los Angeles, CA 90064, USA

Western Adventure Safaris, Inc., P.O. Box 1732, Grand Junction, CO 81501, USA; phone (303)242-6621

Western Rivers of Idaho, P.O. Box 7129, University Sta., Provo, UT 84602, USA; phone (801)377-9750 or tollfree (800)453-1482

Western Safaris, Inc., 3379 Wedgewood Dr., El Paso, TX 79925, USA; phone (915)592-5984

Whitewater Adventures Ltd., P.O. Box 46536, Vancouver, BC Canada V6R 4G8; phone (604) 736-2135

Wilderness Encounter, 720 Grand Ave., Glenwood Springs, CO 81601, USA; phone (303) 945-8365

Wilderness Encounters, Inc., c/o Russell Adventures, 693 W. Grand River, Okemos, MI 48864, USA; phone (517)349-1182

Wilderness Experience, Inc., 20120 Plummer St., Chatsworth, CA 91311, USA; phone (213) 993-1191

Wilderness Experiences, Rt. 1, Box 554, Thonotosassa, FL 33592, USA; phone (813) 986-2963

Wilderness Experiences Inc., 356 E. 89th St., New York, NY 10028, USA; phone (212)534-7889

Wilderness Southeast, Rt. 3, Box 619 AA, Savannah, GA 31406, USA; phone (912)355-8008

Wilderness World, 1342 Jewell Ave., Pacific Grove, CA 93950, USA; phone (408)373-5882

Wildlife Outfitters, Rt. 1, Box 99B, Victor, MT 59875, USA; phone (406)642-3262

Wildwater Expeditions Unlimited Inc., P.O. Box 55, Thurmond, WV 25936, USA; phone (304)469-2551

Wrangell Mt. St. Elias Outfitters, Dan Creek, via Glenallen, AK 99588, USA

Yak Works, 10706 12th Ave. NW, Seattle, WA 98177, USA

Zambia Airways, 1 Rockefeller Plaza, New York, NY 10020, USA; phone (212)582-6637

Zephyr River Expeditions, P.O. Box 2607, Sonora, CA 95370, USA; phone (209)532-6249

INDEX I—GEOGRAPHY

A

B

C

D

E

F

K

L

M

N

O

P

INDEX II—TRIP OPERATORS

A

B

C

D

E

F

G

H

I

J

K

L

M

N

O

T

U

V

W

Y

Z